Perspectives on Classrooms and Schools

Louis Cohen
Loughborough University of Technology

Lawrence Manion
Formerly at Manchester Polytechnic

Cassell Educational Limited
Villiers House
41–47 Strand
London WC2N 5JE

British Library Cataloguing in Publication Data
Cohen, Louis
  Perspectives on classrooms and schools.
  1. Education, Secondary—England
  2. Educational sociology—England
  I. Title   II. Manion, Lawrence
  301.5'6   LC191.8.G7
ISBN 0 304 31450 1

Printed and bound in Great Britain by Mackays of Chatham PLC, Chatham, Kent

Last digit is print number: 9 8 7 6 5 4

Contents

Acknowledgements

Our special thanks go to Reader One and Reader Two, anonymous reviewers whose cogent criticisms damaged our self-concepts somewhat but considerably improved the final script.

We would also like to thank colleagues at Loughborough University of Technology and at Manchester Polytechnic, Didsbury School of Education, for their comments on the initial drafts of several chapters.

We are grateful too for the way in which Dora Durbidge located sources of crucial information that otherwise would have escaped our notice.

Finally, we are indebted to Marjorie Salsbury of the Department of Education, Loughborough University of Technology, for her help in preparing the final draft of the manuscript for publication.

Preface

Perspectives on Classrooms and Schools focuses on current educational issues that are of immediate concern to intending teachers and to those already in primary and secondary posts. The word *perspectives* in the title is purposely chosen. To the best of our knowledge, no other book on the current market addresses itself directly to the *complementarity* of what are commonly thought of as two competing social science perspectives – the *normative* with its emphasis on objective, quantitative data, and the *interpretive* with its concern for the subjective and the qualitative.

Our approach is to use both normative and interpretive studies as they are able to throw light on particular educational issues. In this respect we hold the view that although it is not possible to look down both ends of a telescope at the same time, one is not forever condemned to look down only one!

The issues upon which normative and interpretive perspectives are brought to bear are centrally concerned with classrooms and schools. They include pupils' achievement, their attitudes and behaviour in school, their judgements about teachers and their reactions to the ways they are taught. We look at how teachers view pupils and how they behave towards them. The problems of mixed ability teaching are dealt with; so, too, is the vital topic of communication in the classroom. We look at the school as an organization and the place of norms and conformity in the day-to-day lives of its members. Finally, we discuss the wider issues of multicultural education and the purposes that schools serve in contemporary society.

Our intention is to provide a general text that will meet the needs of student teachers following introductory courses in Education. At the same time we are conscious of the growing demand for a book that will serve to familiarize experienced teachers on in-service courses with current educational issues.

The book has been specifically designed with the needs of both students and tutors in mind. The selected topics are focused on classrooms and schools and deal with issues that are directly relevant to the needs of teachers. The format of the chapters, the 'box' summaries of research findings, the Enquiry/Discussion exercises, and the Selected

Reading sections are intended to meet the requirements of students and tutors in seminars, discussions, and in practical activities.

We believe that there is both a need and a demand for a general Education text that reflects a pragmatic, eclectic approach to the central issues that we include in *Perspectives on Classrooms and Schools*.

List of Boxes

1

Education and the Social Sciences

Our purpose in writing this book is to present you, the reader, with a series of perspectives on classrooms and schools. In using the term *perspective* we simply mean a point of view, a way of looking at things. As a starting point this definition is fine, but let us not rest here: there are other veins of meaning well worth exploring. Imagine a situation in which Country A is wholly dependent on Country B for its supplies of an essential commodity. Suddenly, without warning or explanation, Country B stops its shipments of the commodity: Country A quickly becomes commodity-less. A journalist in Country A, a regular contributor to its national newspaper, is anxious to account for this deprivation to his readers. In doing so, he may adopt any one of a number of possible perspectives – social, economic, environmental, political, and so on. The perspective he selects will be the one he considers most useful in explaining the position to his readers. More than this, however, his selection will imply certain assumptions, beliefs and values on his part – about Country A's needs, or Country B's obligations, for instance – and these assumptions, beliefs and values will be determined to some extent at least by the culture in which he lives. Alternatively, knowing that one perspective offers only a limited viewpoint, a partial explanation, he may choose to analyse the situation from more than one perspective if by so doing he is able to arrive at a fuller assessment of the predicament. We need not pursue the example further for we have now identified the principal characteristics of the term *perspective* in the sense we are using it, namely, it is a point of view; it naturally imposes limits on what we can see; it implies a particular set of assumptions, beliefs and values on the part of the person holding the perspective which in turn will be influenced by the culture in which he lives; there may be more than one perspective on a particular issue; and the criterion of usefulness will determine which perspectives are preferable to others in a given set of circumstances.

Now the perspective we shall be adopting in our study of classrooms and schools we may designate loosely as a *social science* one. We say 'loosely' for two reasons: first, social science itself subsumes a number of distinctive disciplines each of which has its own set of characteristic perspectives; and second, we shall from time to time have recourse to other perspectives – historical and philosophical, for example – which clearly lie beyond the scope of social science as we choose to define it. But let us examine each of these points more closely. In looking at classrooms and schools, we are concerned with developing a conceptual weaponry to observe, analyse and think about what goes on in such contexts; with seeking greater understanding of the issues involved; with arriving at explanations for teacher and pupil behaviour; with identifying causes and consequences of actions; with problem-attacking and problem-solving; with the assessment and evaluation of teaching methods and learning outcomes; and with establishing a more secure knowledge base on which to conduct the profession of education, the ultimate aims being facilitation of the teaching – learning process and improvement of the overall functioning of the school. Naturally enough, there are different ways of tackling the kinds of problem embraced by these several objectives: one could, for instance, organize a colloquium in which constructive suggestions put forward by established and successful teachers were freely debated; or one could simply indulge in armchair theorizing about important issues. The utility of such approaches notwithstanding, we believe that the social sciences will take us *closer* to achieving these objectives and solving their implicit problems than rival lines of attack; and that the social sciences are able to do this because they hold particular assumptions about the world, they ask particular questions about it, they have particular methods for finding out about it, and they gather particular kinds of data to answer the questions asked. What these assumptions, questions, methods and solutions are we hope will become clear in our opening chapters.

Of those disciplines making up the social sciences, psychology, social psychology and sociology are of prime interest to us in our study of classrooms and schools.[1] Although these approaches to the study and understanding of human behaviour share for the most part the same scientific basis, the rationale of which we shall consider shortly, many differences exist both within and between these disciplines. Limiting ourselves for the moment to the more obvious differences *between* them, we may say that psychology, for instance, has as its chief object of study the individual organism, shaped by combinations of heredity and environment, the behaviour of which is determined primarily by personal rather than by situational factors. Social psychology, on the other hand, is concerned with the social nature of the individual and the influences other people have on his beliefs, attitudes and behaviour. The social psychologist thus focuses primarily on two factors – the behaviour of the individual as a participant in a social situation, and under-standing the social processes underlying this behaviour. In contrast to both psychology and social psychology, sociology examines the effects of social structure on human behaviour as it is manifested through social controls, social stratification and social institutions.

With these brief descriptions in mind, the appropriateness of psychological, social psychological and sociological studies of classrooms and schools becomes readily apparent. Lest, however, our accounts become congealed and unrealistic by too exclusive a reliance on the social sciences, we shall turn periodically to other perspectives for background, illumination and insight. It would be difficult, for example, to appreciate fully the significance of open education without considering it in historical apparel, just as it would be limiting to discuss mixed ability teaching without regard to its social and philosophical origins.

A characteristic of education in the western world has been its fitful and uneven progress. This has been attributed in the main to too great a dependence on authority and experience as means of advancement and a corresponding reluctance to apply the principles of social science to educational issues. Borg has succinctly highlighted the difficulty:[2]

'Perhaps a major reason for the slow and unsure progress in education has been the inefficient and unscientific methods used by educators in acquiring knowledge and solving their problems. An uncritical acceptance of authority opinion that is not supported by objective evidence and an overdependence upon personal experience have been characteristic of the educator's problem-solving techniques.'

This rather gloomy but nonetheless accurate assessment of the position as it obtained generally for many years and which still characterizes some areas of education has now, fortunately, to be tempered by the knowledge that in the past few years modest advances have been made as a result of the application of the methods of social science to the study of education and its problems. Interestingly, this development has itself resulted in controversy and debate for, in adopting a social scientific orientation, educational research has at the same time absorbed two competing views of the social sciences – the established, traditional view and a more recently emerging radical view. The former holds that the social sciences are essentially the same as the natural sciences and are therefore concerned with discovering natural and universal laws regulating and determining individual and social behaviour; the latter view, however, while sharing the rigour of the natural sciences and the same concern of traditional social science to describe and explain human behaviour emphasizes how people differ from inanimate natural phenomena and, indeed, from each other. These contending views – and also their corresponding reflections in educational research – stem in the first instance from different conceptions of social reality and of individual and social behaviour. It will help our understanding of the issues to be developed subsequently if we examine these in a little more detail.

TWO CONCEPTIONS OF SOCIAL REALITY

The two views of social science that we have just identified represent strikingly different ways of looking at social reality and are constructed on correspondingly different ways of interpreting it. We can perhaps most profitably approach these two conceptions of the social world by examining the explicit and implicit assumptions underpinning them. Our analysis is based on the work of Burrell and Morgan[3] who identified four sets of such assumptions.

First, there are assumptions of an *ontological* kind – assumptions which concern the very nature or essence of the social phenomena being investigated. Thus, the authors ask, is social reality *external* to the individual – imposing itself on his consciousness from without – or is it the product of individual consciousness? Is reality of an objective nature, or the result of individual cognition? Is it a given 'out there' in the world, or is it created by one's own mind?[3] These questions spring directly from what is known in philosophy as the nominalist – realist debate. The former view holds that objects of thought are merely words and that there is no independently accessible thing constituting the meaning of a word. The realist position, however, contends that objects have an independent existence and are not dependent for it on the knower.

The second set of assumptions identified by Burrell and Morgan are of an *epistemological* kind. These concern the very bases of *knowledge* – its nature and forms, how it can be acquired, and how communicated to other human beings. The authors ask whether 'it is possible to identify and communicate the nature of knowledge as being hard, real and capable of being transmitted in tangible form, or whether "knowledge" is of a softer, more subjective, spiritual or even transcendental kind, based on experience and insight of a unique and essentially personal nature. The epistemological assumptions in these instances determine extreme positions on the issues of whether knowledge is something which can be acquired on the one hand, or is something which has to be personally experienced on the other.'[3] How one aligns oneself in this particular debate profoundly affects how one will go about uncovering knowledge of social behaviour. The view that knowledge is hard, objective and tangible will demand of the researcher an *observer* role, together with an allegiance to the methods of natural science; to see knowledge as personal, subjective and unique, however, imposes on the researcher an *involvement* with his subjects and a rejection of the ways of the natural scientist. To subscribe to the former is to be positivist; to the latter, anti-positivist.

The third set of assumptions concern *human nature* and, in particular, *the relationship between human beings and their environment*. Since the human being is both its subject and object of study, the consequences for social science of assumptions of this kind are indeed far-reaching. Two images of the human being emerge from such assumptions – the one portrays him as responding mechanically to his environment; the other, as the initiator of his own actions. Burrell and Morgan write lucidly on the distinction:[3]

'Thus, we can identify perspectives in social science which entail a view of human beings responding in a mechanistic or even deterministic fashion to the situations encountered in their external world. This view tends to be one in which human beings and their experiences are regarded as products of the environment; one in which humans are conditioned by their external circumstances. This extreme perspective can be contrasted with one which attributes to human beings a much more creative role: with a perspective where "free will" occupies the centre of the stage; where man is regarded as the creator of his environment, the controller as opposed to the controlled, the master rather than the marionette. In these two extreme views of the relationship between human beings and their environment, we are identifying a great philosophical debate between the advocates of *determinism* on the one hand and *voluntarism* on the other. Whilst there are social theories which adhere to each of these extremes, the assumptions of many social scientists are pitched somewhere in the range between.'

It would follow from what we have said so far that the three sets of assumptions identified above have direct implications for the *methodological* concerns of the researcher since the contrasting ontologies, epistemologies and models of man will in turn demand different research methods. Investigators adopting an objectivist (or positivist) approach to the social world and who treat it like the world of natural phenomena as being hard, real and external to the individual will choose from a range of traditional options – surveys, experiments, and the like. Others favouring the more subjectivist (or anti-positivist) approach and who view the social world as being of a much softer, personal and man-created kind will select from a comparable range of recent and emerging techniques[3] – accounts, participant observation and personal constructs, for example. We reserve further discussion of what these methods entail until Chapter 2.

Where one subscribes to the view which treats the social world like the natural world – as if it were a hard, external and objective reality – then scientific investigation will be directed at analysing the relationships and regularities between selected factors in that world. It will be predominantly *quantitative*. 'The concern,' say Burrell and Morgan, 'is with the identification and definition of these elements and with the discovery of ways in which these relationships can be expressed. The methodological issues of importance are thus the concepts themselves, their measurement and the identification of underlying themes. This perspective expresses itself most forcefully in a search for universal laws which explain and govern the reality which is being observed.'[3] An approach character-ized by procedures and methods designed to discover general laws may be referred to as *nomothetic*.

However, if one favours the alternative view of social reality which stresses the importance of the subjective experience of individuals in the creation of the social world, then the search for understanding focuses upon different issues and approaches them in different ways. The principal concern is with an understanding of the way in which the individual creates, modifies and interprets the world in which he or she finds himself or herself. The approach now takes on a *qualitative* as well as *quantitative* aspect. As Burrell and Morgan observe, 'The emphasis in extreme cases tends to be placed upon the explanation and understanding of what is unique and particular to the individual rather than of what is general and universal. This approach questions whether there exists an external reality worthy of study. In methodological terms it is an approach which emphasizes the relativistic nature of the social world . . .'[3] In its emphasis on the particular and individual, this approach to understanding individual behaviour may be termed *idiographic*.

In this review of Burrell and Morgan's analysis of the ontological, epistemological, human and methodological assumptions underlying two ways of conceiving social reality, we have laid the foundations for a more extended study of the two contrasting perspectives evident in the practices of researchers investigating human behaviour and, by adoption, educational problems. Box 1.1 summarizes these assumptions in graphic form along a subjective – objective dimension. It identifies the four sets of assumptions by using terms we have adopted in the text and by which they are known in the literature of social philosophy.

Each of the two perspectives on the study of human behaviour outlined above has profound implications for research in classrooms and schools. The choice of problem, the formulation of questions to be answered, the characterization of pupils and teachers, methodological concerns, the kinds of data sought and their mode of treatment – all will be influenced or determined by the viewpoint held. Some idea of the considerable practical implications of the contrasting views can be gained by examining Box 1.2 which compares them with respect to a number of critical issues within a broadly societal and

BOX 1.1

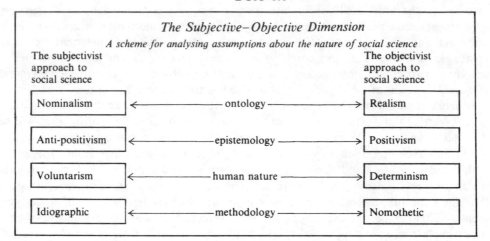

Source: Burrell and Morgan[3]

organizational framework. Implications of the two perspectives for research into classrooms and schools will unfold in the course of the text.

Because of its significance to the epistemological basis of social science and its consequences for educational research, we devote much of the remainder of this chapter to the positivist and anti-positivist debate.

POSITIVISM

Although *positivism* has been a recurrent theme in the history of western thought from the Ancient Greeks to the present day, it is historically associated with the nineteenth century French philosopher, Auguste Comte, who was the first thinker to use the word for a philosophical position.[5] His positivism can be explained in terms of his *Law of Three Stages* according to which the human mind progresses from a theological stage through a metaphysical stage to a final positive stage.[6] At the theological stage, the most primitive, attempts are made to explain behaviour in terms of spiritual or supernatural entities. The metaphysical stage is only a modified version of the earlier stage and sets out to explain behaviour in terms of abstractions, essences or forces which Comte regarded as depersonalized beings of the earlier, theological stage. The final, positive stage dispenses with theological and metaphysical concepts and turns to observation and reason as means of understanding behaviour. More simply, explanation now proceeds by way of scientific description.

Comte's position was to lead to a general doctrine of positivism which held that all genuine knowledge is based on sense experience and can only be advanced by means of observation and experiment. Following in the empiricist tradition, it limited enquiry and belief to what can be firmly established and in thus abandoning metaphysical and

BOX 1.2

Alternative Bases for Interpreting Social Reality
Conceptions of social reality

Dimensions of comparison:	Objectivist	Subjectivist
Philosophical basis	Realism: the world exists and is knowable as it really is. Organizations are real entities with a life of their own.	Idealism: the world exists but different people construe it in very different ways. Organizations are invented social reality.
The role of social science	Discovering the universal laws of society and human conduct within it.	Discovering how different people interpret the world in which they live.
Basic units of social reality	The collectivity: society or organizations.	Individuals acting singly or together.
Methods of understanding	Identifying conditions or relationships which permit the collectivity to exist. Conceiving what these conditions and relationships are.	Interpretation of the subjective meanings which individuals place upon their action. Discovering the subjective rules for such action.
Theory	A rational edifice built by scientists to explain human behaviour.	Sets of meanings which people use to make sense of their world and behaviour within it.
Research	Experimental or quasi-experimental validation of theory.	The search for meaningful relationships and the discovery of their consequences for action.
Methodology	Abstraction of reality, especially through mathematical models and quantitative analysis.	The representation of reality for purposes of comparison. Analysis of language and meaning.
Society	Ordered. Governed by a uniform set of values and made possible only by those values.	Conflicted. Governed by the values of people with access to power.
Organizations	Goal oriented. Independent of people. Instruments of order in society serving both society and the individual.	Dependent upon people and their goals. Instruments of power which some people control and can use to attain ends which seem good to them.
Organizational pathologies	Organizations get out of kilter with social values and individual needs.	Given diverse human ends, there is always conflict among people acting to pursue them.
Prescription for change	Change the structure of the organization to meet social values and individual needs.	Find out what values are embodied in organizational action and whose they are. Change the people or change their values if you can.

Source: adapted from Greenfield[4]

speculative attempts to gain knowledge by reason alone, the movement developed what has been described as a 'tough-minded orientation to facts and natural phenomena.'[5]

Since Comte, the term *positivism* has been used in such different ways by philosophers and social scientists that it is difficult to assign it a precise and consistent meaning. Moreover, the term has also been applied to the doctrine of a school of philosophy known as 'logical positivism'.[7] The central belief of the logical positivists is that the meaning of a statement is, or is given by, the method of its verification.[8] It follows from this that unverifiable statements are held to be meaningless, the utterances of traditional metaphysics and theology being included in this class.

However the term *positivism* is used by philosophers and social scientists, a residual meaning is always present and this derives from an acceptance of natural science as the paradigm of human knowledge.[8] This includes the following connected suppositions which have been identified by Giddens:[9] (1) that the *methodological* procedures of natural science may be directly applied to the social sciences. Positivism here implies a particular stance concerning the social scientist as an *observer* of social reality; and (2) that the end-product of investigations by the social scientist can be formulated in terms parallel to those of natural science. This means that his analysis must be expressed in 'laws' or 'law-like' generalizations of the same kind that have been established in relation to natural phenomena. Positivism here involves a definite view of the social scientist as *analyst* or *interpreter* of his subject matter.[9]

Positivism may be characterized by its claim that science provides man with the clearest possible ideal of knowledge. As one writer has said, 'Positivism gets much of its strength from the contrast between the continuous and agreed progress which has been achieved in the natural sciences since the time of Galileo, and the situation of deadlock and disagreement that has at all times obtained in metaphysical philosophy. This seems to suggest that in the special sciences a fruitful method has been employed, whereas metaphysical philosophers have got lost in an intellectual impasse.'[6] Where positivism is less successful, however, is in its application to the study of human behaviour where the immense complexity of human nature and the elusive and intangible quality of social phenomena contrast strikingly with the order and regularity of the natural world. This point is nowhere more apparent than in the contexts of classroom and school where the problems of teaching, learning and human interaction present the positivistic researcher with a mammoth challenge.

We now look more closely at some of the features of this 'fruitful method', beginning with the assumptions underlying the scientific enterprise.

The Assumptions of Science

You recall that in the introduction we expressed our intention to adopt a social science perspective and to make explicit in the course of this chapter some of the assumptions underlying it. We are concerned in this section, therefore, with looking at five such assumptions underpinning traditional science. Although the assumptions in question are shared by natural and social science, the contrasting nature of their objects of study – inanimate and animate matter respectively[10] – means that the relevance of the assumptions varies quite significantly in relation to the two approaches. How this works out in practice is something we shall consider at the appropriate juncture.

The most important assumption held by the scientist is that of *empiricism*. This key tenet holds that certain kinds of reliable knowledge can only originate in experience. In practice it means that the scientist will only attempt to make statements about the natural or social world that can be verified by empirical testing. The viewpoint has been summed up by Barratt who writes,[11] 'The decision for empiricism as an act of scientific faith signifies that the best way to acquire reliable knowledge is the way of evidence obtained by direct experience.' An approach to understanding the world which claims to be scientific, whether natural or social, must therefore have empirical relevance to the world.[12] As an epithet, empirical is usually contrasted with words such as imaginative, impressionistic, intuitive, rational and speculative.

A second assumption is that of *determinism*. This means that events or occurrences have causes, that they are determined by other events or occurrences; and science proceeds on the belief that these causal links can eventually be discovered and understood, that the events can be explained in terms of their antecedents. Moreover, not only are events determined by other circumstances, but there is regularity about the way they are determined: the universe does not behave capriciously. It is the ultimate aim of science to account for such regularities in terms of laws and relationships. All this is especially relevant to natural science and the world of natural phenomena where causes can be teased out and explanatory laws formulated. The realm of social science, however, requires some qualification. The extremely complex nature of the subject matter of social science makes it often very difficult to arrive at the real cause or causes of an event, especially where they may very well lie in the past; in such circumstances, concomitance rather than causality is sought. In thus seeking events which 'go together', the social scientist is setting his sights on a more modest but at the same time more realistic objective without in any way negating the belief that real causes exist somewhere 'out there'.

A third assumption underlying the work of the scientist is the *principle of parsimony*. The basic idea here is that phenomena should be explained in the most economical way possible. The first historical statement of this principle was by William of Occam when he said that explanatory principles (entities) should not be needlessly multiplied. It may, of course, be expressed in various ways: that it is preferable to account for a phenomenon by two concepts rather than by three or more; that a simple theory is better than a complex one; or as Lloyd Morgan suggested as a guide to the study of animal behaviour – 'In no case may we interpret an action as the outcome of the exercise of a higher psychical faculty, if it can be interpreted as the outcome of the exercise of one which stands lower in the psychological scale.' Inevitably, the precise and more easily quantifiable concepts of the natural scientist will enable him to achieve much more elegant explanations of natural phenomena than will be the case with the social scientist struggling with approximate definitions of social phenomena and generally inadequate means of measuring them.

The fourth assumption we would wish to identify, that of *generality*, played an important part in both the deductive and inductive methods of reasoning. Indeed, historically speaking, it was the problematic relationship between the concrete particular and the abstract general that was to result in two competing theories of knowledge – the rational and the empirical. Beginning with observations of the particular, the scientist sets out to generalize his findings to the world at large. This is so because he is concerned ultimately with explanation and understanding. Of course, the concept of generality presents much less of a problem to the natural scientist working mainly with inanimate matter than to the social scientist who, of necessity having to deal with samples of human populations and the inadequacies of measuring instruments referred to above, has to exercise great caution when generalizing his findings to parent populations.

Scientific theories must, by their very nature, be *provisional*: a theory can never be complete in the sense that it encompasses all that can be known or understood about a given phenomenon. This then expresses our final assumption of science: that its findings provide for immediate needs and hold good only until such times as they are replaced by ones having greater validity, or stronger explanatory power. As Mouly says, 'Invariably, scientific theories are replaced by more sophisticated theories embodying more of the advanced state of the question so that science widens its horizons to include more and more of the facts as they accumulate. No doubt, many of the things about which there is agreement today will be found inadequate by future standards. But we must begin where we are.'[13] Visionaries within the scientific community believe that eventually scientists will arrive at a single theoretical system enabling them to explain the behaviour of molecules, animals and men, at which point the provisional nature of scientific findings will cease. But all this is speculation; let us conclude our review of the assumptions of science by listening to one of the most gifted lay commentators on modern science as he sums up these points for us:[14]

> 'No scientific principles are sacrosanct; no scientific theory is held with religious conviction. Nevertheless, most scientific men believe that there is a final scientific truth about the universe to which successive scientific theories ever more closely approximate. But this is an article of faith. Science is still an adventure, and all its "truths" are provisional.'

Earlier, we were sufficiently bold to claim that a social science perspective would give us a deeper understanding of, and possibly take us nearer to solving, the problems of classroom and school than would other approaches. Our confidence to make such an assertion stems from the empirical nature of social science and also from the tools it employs, in particular the *concept* and the *hypothesis*. So central are these to the thinking and conduct of social research that a more detailed consideration of them is warranted.

The Tools of Science

We said in our introduction that in looking at classrooms and schools we are concerned, among other matters, with developing a conceptual weaponry to observe, analyse and think about the issues involved there. Concepts express generalizations from particulars – *anger, achievement, alienation, man, velocity, intelligence, democracy*. Examining these examples more closely, we see that each is a word representing an idea: more accurately, a concept is the relationship between the word (or symbol) and an idea or conception. Whoever we are and whatever we do, we all make use of concepts. Naturally, some are shared and used by all groups of people within the same culture – *child, love, justice*, for example; others, however, have a restricted currency and are used only by certain groups, specialists, or members of professions – *idioglossia, retroactive inhibition, anticipatory socialization*.

   Concepts enable us to impose some sort of meaning on the world: through them reality is given sense, order and coherence. They are the means by which we are able to come to terms with our experience. How we perceive the world, then, is highly dependent on the repertoire of concepts we can command. The more we have, the more sense data we can pick up and the surer will be our perceptual (and cognitive) grasp of whatever is 'out there'. If our perceptions of the world are determined by the concepts available to us, it follows that people with differing sets of concepts will tend to view the 'same' objective reality differently – a doctor diagnosing an illness will draw upon a vastly different range of concepts from, say, the restricted and simplistic notions of the layman in that context; and a visitor to civilization from a distant primitive culture would be as confused by the frenetic bustle of urban life as would the mythical Martian.

So, you may ask, where is all this leading? Simply to this: that the social scientist has likewise developed, or appropriated by giving precise meaning to, a set of concepts which enable him to shape his perceptions of the world in a particular way, to represent that slice of reality which is his special study. And collectively, these concepts form part of his wider meaning system which permits him to give accounts of that reality, accounts which are rooted and validated in the direct experience of everyday life. These points may be exemplified by the concept of *social class*. Hughes says[15] that it offers 'a rule, a grid, even though vague at times, to use in talking about certain sorts of experience that have to do with economic position, life-style, life-chances, and so on. It serves to identify aspects of experience, and by relating the concept to other concepts we are able to construct theories about experiences in a particular order or sphere.'

There are two important points to stress when considering scientific concepts. The first is that they do not exist independently of man: they are indeed man-made inventions enabling him to acquire some understanding at least of the apparent chaos of nature. The second is that they are limited in number and in this way contrast with the infinite number of phenomena they are required to explain.

A second tool of great importance to the scientist is *the hypothesis*. It is from this that much research proceeds, especially where cause-and-effect or concomitant relationships are being investigated. The hypothesis has been defined by Kerlinger[16] as a conjectural statement of the relations between two or more variables. More simply, it has been termed 'an educated guess', though unlike an educated guess in that it is often the result of considerable study, reflective thinking and observation. Medawar[17] writes incomparably of the hypothesis and its function in the following way:

> 'All advances of scientific understanding, at every level, begin with a speculative adventure, an imaginative preconception *of what might be true* – a preconception which always, and necessarily, goes a little way (sometimes a long way) beyond anything which we have logical or factual authority to believe in. It is the invention of a possible world, or of a tiny fraction of that world. The conjecture is then exposed to criticism to find out whether or not that imagined world is anything like the real one. Scientific reasoning is therefore at all levels an interaction between two episodes of thought – a dialogue between two voices, the one imaginative and the other critical; a dialogue, if you like, between the possible and the actual, between proposal and disposal, conjecture and criticism, between what might be true and what is in fact the case.'

Kerlinger has identified two criteria for 'good' hypotheses.[16] The first is that hypotheses are statements about the relations between variables; and second, that hypotheses carry clear implications for testing the stated relations. To these he adds two ancillary criteria: that hypotheses disclose compatibility with current knowledge; and that they are expressed as economically as possible. Thus if we conjecture that social class background determines academic achievement, we have a relationship between one variable, social class, and another, academic achievement. And since both can be measured, the primary criteria specified by Kerlinger can be met. Neither do they violate the ancillary criteria proposed by Kerlinger.

He further identifies four reasons for the importance of hypotheses as tools of research. First, they organize the efforts of the researcher. The relationship expressed in the hypothesis indicates what he should do. They enable him to understand the problem with greater clarity and provide him with a framework for collecting, analysing and interpreting his data. Second, they are, in Kerlinger's words, the working instruments of theory. They can be deduced from theory or from other hypotheses. Third, they can be tested, empirically or experimentally, thus resulting in confirmation or rejection. And there is always the possibility that a hypothesis, once confirmed and established, may become a law. And fourth, hypotheses are powerful tools for the advancement of knowledge because, as Kerlinger explains, they enable man to get outside himself.

Hypotheses and concepts play a crucial part in the scientific method and it is to this that we now turn our attention.

The Scientific Method

If the most distinctive feature of science is its *empirical* nature, the next most important characteristic is its set of procedures which show not only how findings have been arrived at, but are sufficiently clear for fellow-scientists to repeat them, i.e. to check them out with the same or other materials and thereby test the results. As Cuff and his colleagues say:[12] 'A scientific approach necessarily involves standards and procedures for demonstrating the "empirical warrant" of its findings, showing the match or fit between its statements and what is happening or has happened in the world.' These standards and procedures we will call for convenience *the scientific method*, though this can be somewhat misleading for the following reason: the combination of the definite article, adjective and singular noun conjures up in the minds of some people a single invariant approach to problem-solving, an approach frequently involving atoms or rats, and taking place within the confines of a laboratory peopled with stereotypical scientists wearing white coats and given to eccentric bouts of behaviour. Yet there is much more to it than this. The term in fact cloaks a number of methods which vary in their degree of sophistication depending on their function and the particular stage of development a science has reached. We refer you at this point to Box 1.3 which sets out the sequence of stages through which a science normally passes in its development or, perhaps more realistically, that are constantly present in its progress and on which a scientist may draw depending on the kind of information he seeks or the kind of problem confronting him. This latter point would seem to be particularly relevant in the case of an emerging science, such as the scientific study of educational problems, where many workers in different parts of the world are engaged in studying a wide range of problems in an essentially complicated area. Of particular interest to us in our efforts to elucidate the term *scientific method* are stages 2, 3 and 4. Stage 2 is a relatively uncomplicated point at which the researcher is content to observe and record facts and possibly arrive at some system of classification. Much research in the field of education, especially at classroom and school level, is conducted in this way, e.g. surveys and case studies. Stage 3 introduces a note of added

BOX 1.3

Stages in the Development of a Science

1. Definition of the science and identification of the phenomena that are to be subsumed under it.
2. Observational stage at which the relevant factors, variables or items are identified and labelled; and at which categories and taxonomies are developed.
3. Correlational research in which variables and parameters are related to one another and information is systematically integrated as theories begin to develop.
4. The systematic and controlled manipulation of variables to see if experiments will produce expected results, thus moving from correlation to causality.
5. The firm establishment of a body of theory as the outcomes of the earlier stages are accumulated. Depending on the nature of the phenomena under scrutiny, laws may be formulated and systematized.
6. The use of the established body of theory in the resolution of problems or as a source of further hypotheses.

---

sophistication as attempts are made to establish relationships between variables within a loose framework of inchoate theory. Stage 4 is the most sophisticated stage and often the one that many people equate exclusively with the scientific method. In order to arrive at causality, as distinct from mere measures of association, the researcher here designs an experimental situation in which variables are manipulated to test his chosen hypothesis.

Here is how one noted researcher describes the later stages:[16]

'First, there is a doubt, a barrier, an indeterminate situation crying out, so to speak, to be made determinate. The scientist experiences vague doubts, emotional disturbances, inchoate ideas. He struggles to formulate the problem, even if inadequately. He studies the literature, scans his own experience and the experience of others. Often he simply has to wait for an inventive leap of mind. Maybe it will occur; maybe not. With the problem formulated, with the basic question or questions properly asked, the rest is much easier. Then the hypothesis is constructed, after which its implications are deduced, mainly along experimental lines. In this process the original problem, and of course the original hypothesis, may be changed. It may be broadened or narrowed. It may even be abandoned. Lastly, but not finally, the relation expressed by the hypothesis is tested by observation and experimentation. On the basis of the research evidence, the hypothesis is accepted or rejected. This information is then fed back to the original problem and it is kept or altered as dictated by the evidence. Dewey finally pointed out that one phase of the process may be expanded and be of great importance, another may be skimped, and there may be fewer or more steps involved. These things are not important. What is important is the overall fundamental idea of scientific research as a controlled rational process of reflective enquiry, the interdependent nature of the parts of the process, and the paramount importance of the problem and its statement.'

With stages 3 and 4 of Box 1.3 in mind, we may say that the scientific method begins consciously and deliberately by selecting from the total number of elements in a given situation. The elements the researcher fastens on to will naturally be suitable for scientific formulation; this means simply that they will possess *quantitative* aspects. His principal working tool will be the hypothesis which, as we have seen, is a statement indicating a

BOX 1.4

Does Watching Aggression on TV Cause Kids
to Become Aggressive?

A correlation exists between the amount of time a child spends watching violence on TV and his tendency to choose aggressive solutions to his problems. Does this mean that watching aggression on TV causes kids to become aggressive? Not necessarily. It might. But it might also mean that aggressive kids simply like to watch aggression, and that these kids would be just as aggressive if they watched 'Captain Kangaroo' all day long. But then some experimenters came along and proved that watching violence increases violence. How? By randomly assigning some kids to a situation in which they watched an episode of 'The Untouchables' – a TV series in which people beat, kill, rape, bite, and slug each other for fifty minutes per episode. As a control, they randomly assigned some other kids to a situation in which they watched an athletic event for some length of time. The crucial point: each kid stood an *equal chance* of being selected to watch 'The Untouchables'; therefore, any differences in character structure among the kids were neutralized across the two experimental conditions. Thus, when the investigators found that the kids who watched 'The Untouchables' showed more aggressiveness afterwards than those who watched the athletic event, it does suggest quite strongly that watching violence can lead to violence.

Source: Aronson[18]

relationship (or its absence) between two or more of the chosen elements and stated in such a way as to carry clear implications for testing. The researcher then chooses the most appropriate method and puts his hypothesis to the test. Box 1.4 exemplifies these points. It is a study concerned to answer the question: Does watching aggression on television cause children to become aggressive? The elements selected for investigation were (1) the amount of time a child spends watching violence on television; and (2) his tendency to choose aggressive solutions to this problems. The hypothesis, that there is a relationship between these two factors, was tested in a simple experimental situation using a control group and an experimental group and was found to be upheld. The example is a good illustration of the positivistic approach to the study of social phenomena.

CRITICISMS OF POSITIVISM AND THE SCIENTIFIC METHOD

We have spoken at some length about positivism, the nature of science and the scientific method, yet in spite of the scientific enterprise's proven success – especially in the field of natural science – its ontological and epistemological bases have been the focus of sustained and sometimes vehement criticism from some quarters. Beginning in the second half of last century, the revolt against positivism occurred on a broad front, attracting some of the best intellectuals in Europe – philosophers, scientists, social critics and creative artists; and even today opponents of positivism are made up of a similar cross-section, including some from within the ranks of social scientists themselves. Essentially, it has been a reaction against the world picture projected by science which, it is contended, denigrates life and mind. The precise target of the anti-positivists' attack has been science's mechanistic and reductionist view of nature which, by definition, excludes notions of choice, freedom, individuality, and moral responsibility. One of the earliest and most sustained attacks in the modern age came from Soren Kierkegaard, the Danish philosopher from whose work was to originate the movement that became known as Existentialism. Kierkegaard was concerned with the individual and his need to fulfil himself to the highest level of development. This realization of a person's potential was for him the meaning of existence which he saw as 'concrete and individual, unique and irreducible, not amenable to conceptualization.'[5] Characteristic features of the age in which we live – democracy's trust in the crowd mentality, the ascendancy of reason, scientific and technological progress – all militate against the achievement of this end and contribute to the dehumanization of the individual. In his desire to free people from their illusions, the illusion Kierkegaard was most concerned about was that of *objectivity*. By this he meant the imposition of rules of behaviour and thought, and the making of a person into an observer set on discovering general laws governing human behaviour. The capacity for *subjectivity*, he argued, should be regained. This he regarded as the ability to consider one's own relationship to whatever constitutes the focus of enquiry. The contrast he made between *objectivity* and *subjectivity* is brought out in the following passage:[19]

> 'When the question of truth is raised in an objective manner, reflection is directed objectively to the truth as an object to which the knower is related. Reflection is not focused on the relationship, however, but upon the question of whether it is the truth to which the knower is related. If only the object to which he is related is the truth, the subject is accounted to be in the truth. When the question of truth is raised subjectively, reflection is directed subjectively to the nature of the individual's relationship; if only the mode of this relationship is in the truth, the individual is in the truth, even if he should happen to be thus related to what is not true.'

For Kierkegaard, 'subjectivity and concreteness of truth are together the light. Anyone who is committed to science, or to rule-governed morality, is benighted, and needs to be rescued from his state of darkness.'[20]

Also concerned with the dehumanizing effects of the social sciences is Ions.[21] While acknowledging that they can take much credit for throwing light in dark corners, he expresses serious concern at the way in which quantification and computation, assisted by statistical theory and method, are used. On this point, he writes:

> 'The argument begins when we quantify the process and interpret the human act. In this respect, behavioural science represents a form of collectivism which runs parallel to other developments this century. However high-minded the intention, the result is depersonalization, the effects of which can be felt at the level of the individual human being, not simply at the level of culture.'

His objection is not directed at quantification *per se*, but at quantification when it becomes an end in itself – 'a branch of mathematics rather than a humane study seeking to explore and elucidate the gritty circumstances of the human condition.'

The justification for any intellectual activity lies in the effect it has on increasing our awareness and degree of consciousness. This increase, some claim, has been retarded in our time by the excessive influence the positivist paradigm has been allowed to exert on areas of our intellectual life. Holbrook, for example, affording consciousness a central position in human existence and deeply concerned with what happens to it has written:[22]

> '(O)ur approaches today to the study of man have yielded little, and are essentially dead, because they cling to positivism – that is, to an approach which demands that

nothing must be regarded as real which cannot be found by empirical science and rational methods, by "objectivity". Since the whole problem . . . . belongs to "psychic reality", to man's "inner world", to his moral being, and to the subjective life, there can be no debate unless we are prepared to recognize the bankruptcy of positivism, and the failure of "objectivity" to give an adequate account of existence, and are prepared to find new modes of enquiry.'

Other writers question the perspective adopted by positivist social science because it presents a misleading picture of the human being. Hampden-Turner,[23] for example, concludes that the social science view of man is biased in that it is conservative and must inevitably lead to the social scientist taking an equally conservative view of the human being and having to ignore other important qualities. This restricted image of man, he contends, comes about because the social scientist concentrates on the repetitive, predictable and invariant aspects of the person; on 'visible externalities' to the exclusion of the subjective world; and – at least as far as psychology is concerned – on the parts of the person in his endeavours to understand the whole.

Two other criticisms are commonly levelled at positivistic social science from within its own ranks. The first is that it fails to take account of man's unique ability to interpret his experiences and represent them to himself. Man can, and does, construct theories about himself and his world; moreover, he acts on these theories. In failing to recognize this, positivistic social science is said to ignore the profound differences between itself and the natural sciences. Social science, unlike natural science, 'stands in a subject–subject relation to its field of study, not a subject–object relation; it deals with a pre-interpreted world in which the meanings developed by active subjects actually enter the actual constitution or production of the world.'[24]

Second, the findings of positivistic social science are often said to be so banal and trivial that they are of little consequence to those for whom they are intended, namely, teachers, social workers, counsellors, personnel managers, and the like. The more effort, it seems, that the researcher puts into his scientific experimentation in the laboratory by restricting, simplifying and controlling variables, the more likely he is to end up with a 'pruned, synthetic version of the whole, a constructed play of puppets in a restricted environment.'[25]

These are formidable criticisms; but what alternatives are proposed by the detractors of positivistic social science?

ALTERNATIVES TO POSITIVISTIC SOCIAL SCIENCE

Although the opponents of positivism within social science itself subscribe to a variety of schools of thought each with its own subtly different epistemological viewpoint, they are united by their common rejection of the belief that human behaviour is governed by general laws and characterized by underlying regularities. Moreover, they would agree that the social world can only be understood from the standpoint of the individuals who are part of the ongoing action being investigated; and that their model of man is an autonomous one, not the plastic version favoured by positivist researchers. In rejecting the viewpoint of the detached, objective observer – a mandatory feature of traditional research – anti-positivists would argue that an individual's behaviour can only be understood by the researcher sharing his frame of reference: understanding of the individual's interpretations of the world around him has to come from the inside, not the outside. Social science is thus seen as a subjective rather than an objective undertaking, as a means of dealing with the direct experience of people in specific contexts. The following extract nicely captures the spirit in which the anti-positivist social scientist would work:[4]

'(T)he purpose of social science is to understand social reality as different people see it and to demonstrate how their views shape the action which they take within that reality. Since the social sciences cannot penetrate to what lies behind social reality, they must work directly with man's definitions of reality and with the rules he devises for coping with it. While the social sciences do not reveal ultimate truth, they do help us to make sense of our world. What the social sciences offer is explanation, clarification and demystification of the social forms which man has created around himself.'

The anti-positivist movement has so influenced those constituent areas of social science of most concern to us, namely, psychology, social psychology and sociology, that in each case a movement reflecting its mood has developed collaterally with mainstream trends. Whether this development is seen in competitive or complementary terms depends to some extent on one's personal viewpoint. It cannot be denied, however, that in some quarters proponents of the contrasting viewpoints have been prepared to lock horns on some of the more contentious issues.

In the case of psychology, for instance, a school of humanistic psychology has emerged alongside the co-existing behaviouristic and psychoanalytic schools. Arising as a response to the challenge to combat the growing feelings of dehumanization which characterize much of the social and cultural milieu of the twentieth century, it sets out to study and understand the person *as a whole*.[26] The humanistic psychologist presents a model of man that is positive, active and purposive, and at the same time stresses his own involvement with the life experience itself. He does not stand apart, introspective, hypothesizing. His interest is directed at the *intentional* and *creative* aspects of the human being. The perspective adopted by humanistic psychologists is naturally reflected in their methodology. They are dedicated to studying the individual in preference to the group, and consequently prefer idiographic approaches to nomothetic ones. The implications of the movement's philosophy for the education of the human being have been drawn by Carl Rogers.[27]

Comparable developments within social psychology may be perceived in the emerging 'science of persons' movement. Its proponents contend that because of man's self-awareness and powers of language, he must be seen as a system of a different order of complexity from any other existing system whether natural, like an animal, or artificial – a computer, for instance. Because of this, no other system is capable of providing a sufficiently powerful model to advance our understanding of him. It is argued, therefore, that we must use *ourselves* as a key to our understanding of others and conversely, our understanding of others as a way of finding out about ourselves. What is called for is an *anthropomorphic model of man*. Since anthropomorphism means, literally, the attribution of human form and personality, the implied criticism is that social psychology as traditionally conceived has singularly failed, so far, to model man as he really is. As one wry commentator has pleaded, 'For scientific purposes, treat people as if they were human beings.'[28]

This approach would entail working from a model of man that takes account of the following uniquely human attributes:[28]

'Man is an entity who is capable of monitoring his own performance. Further, because he is aware of this self-monitoring and has the power of speech, man is able to provide commentaries on those performances and to plan ahead of them as well. Such an entity, it is held, is much inclined to using rules, to devising plans, to developing strategies in getting things done the way he wants them doing.'

Social psychology's task is to understand man in the light of this anthropomorphic model. But what specifically would this involve? Proponents of this 'science of persons' approach place great store on the systematic and painstaking analysis of *social episodes*. In Box 1.5 we give an example of such an episode taken from a classroom study. Note how the particular incident would appear on an interaction analysis coding sheet of a researcher employing a positivistic approach. Note, too, how this slice of classroom life can only be understood by knowledge of the specific organizational background in which it is embedded.

BOX 1.5

A Classroom Episode

Walker and Adelman describe an incident in the following manner:

One lesson the teacher was listening to the boys read through short essays that they had written for homework on the subject of 'Prisons'. After one boy, Wilson, had finished reading out his rather obviously skimped piece of work the teacher sighed and said, rather crossly:

T: Wilson, we'll have to put you away if you don't change your ways, and do your homework. Is that all you've done?
P: Strawberries, strawberries. (Laughter)

Now at first glance this is meaningless. An observer coding with Flanders Interaction Analysis Categories (FIAC) would write down:

'7'   (teacher criticizes) followed by a,
'4'   (teacher asks question) followed by a,
'9'   (pupil irritation) and finally a,
'10'   (silence or confusion) to describe the laughter

Such a string of codings, however reliable and valid, would not help anyone to *understand* why such an interruption was funny. Human curiosity makes us want to know *why* everyone laughs – and so, I would argue, the social scientist needs to know too. Walker and Adelman asked subsequently why 'strawberries' was a stimulus to laughter and were told that the teacher frequently said the pupils' work was 'like strawberries – good as far as it goes, but it doesn't last nearly long enough.' Here a casual comment made in the past has become an integral part of the shared meaning system of the class. It can only be comprehended by seeing the relationship as developing over time.

Source: adapted from Delamont[29]

The approach to analysing social episodes which we show in Box 1.6 is known as the *ethogenic method*.[30] Unlike positivistic social psychology which ignores or presumes its subjects' interpretations of situations, ethogenic social psychology concentrates upon the ways in which a person construes his social world. By probing at his accounts of his

BOX 1.6

An Account in Episode Analysis

Observation:

A boy is seen walking down the road and swiftly using his leg to touch another boy's leg.

Boy's account of the episode:

'He called me names so I kicked him.'
'He is not a good friend.'
'No one was watching.'

Observer elicits boy's detailed definitions of 'names', 'friend', and 'no one' to extrapolate from his account the following understanding of the rules governing the particular episode.

When peers who are not good friends call me names and no salient adults are present, I will (ought, should, am entitled to) 'get even' – physical punishment being one behaviour subsumed under that act.

Source: adapted from Levine[31]

actions, it endeavours to come up with an understanding of what that person was doing in the particular episode. The example is purposely simplified and intended only to illustrate the approach rather than the substance in analysing a social episode.

The anti-positivist movement in sociology is represented by three schools of thought – phenomenology, ethnomethodology and symbolic interactionism. A common thread running through the three schools is a concern with *phenomena*, that is, the things we directly apprehend through our senses as we go about our daily lives, together with a consequent emphasis on qualitative as opposed to quantitative methodology. The differences between them and the significant role each plays in contemporary research in classrooms and schools are such as to warrant a more extended consideration of them in the section which follows.

PHENOMENOLOGY, ETHNOMETHODOLOGY AND SYMBOLIC INTERACTIONISM

In its broadest meaning, phenomenology is a theoretical point of view that advocates the study of direct experience taken at face value; and one which sees behaviour as determined by the phenomena of experience rather than by external, objective and physically described reality.[32] Although phenomenologists differ among themselves on particular issues, there is fairly general agreement on the following points identified by Curtis[33] which can be taken as distinguishing features of their philosophical viewpoint:

1. A belief in the importance, and in a sense the primacy, of *subjective consciousness*;
2. An understanding of consciousness as active, as *meaning bestowing*; and
3. A claim that there are certain *essential structures* to consciousness of which we gain direct knowledge by a certain kind of reflection. Exactly what these structures are is a point about which phenomenologists have differed.

Various strands of development may be traced in the phenomenological movement: we shall briefly examine two of them – the *transcendental phenomenology* of Husserl; and *existential phenomenology*, of which Schutz is perhaps the most characteristic representative.

Husserl, regarded by many as the founder of phenomenology, was concerned with investigating the source of the foundation of science and with questioning the commonsense, 'taken-for-granted' assumptions of everyday life.[3] To do this, he set about opening up a new direction in the analysis of consciousness. His catchphrase was 'back to the things!' which for him meant finding out how things appear directly to us rather than through the media of cultural and symbolic structures. In other words, we are asked to look beyond the details of everyday life to the essences underlying them. To do this, Husserl exhorts us to 'put the world in brackets' or free ourselves from our usual ways of perceiving the world. What is left over from this reduction is our consciousness of which there are three elements – the 'I' who thinks, the mental acts of this thinking subject, and the intentional objects of these mental acts.[20] The aim, then, of this method of *epoché*, as Husserl called it, is the dismembering of the constitution of objects in such a way as to free us from all preconceptions about the world.[20]

Schutz was concerned with relating Husserl's ideas to the issues of sociology and to the scientific study of social behaviour. Of central concern to him was the problem of understanding the meaning structure of the world of everyday life. The origins of meaning he thus sought in the 'stream of consciousness' – basically an unbroken stream of lived experiences which have no meaning in themselves. One can only impute meaning to them retrospectively, by the process of turning back on oneself and looking at what has been going on.[3] In other words, meaning can be accounted for in this way by the concept of *reflexivity*. For Schutz, the attribution of meaning reflexively is dependent on the person's identifying the purpose or goal he seeks.[3]

According to Schutz, the way we understand the behaviour of others is dependent on a process of *typification* by means of which the observer makes use of concepts resembling 'ideal types' to make sense of what people do. These concepts are derived from our experience of everyday life and it is through them, claims Schutz, that we classify and organize our everyday world.[3] As Burrell and Morgan observe, 'The typifications are learned through our biographical situation. They are handed to us according to our social context. Knowledge of everyday life is thus socially ordered. The notion of typification is thus . . . an inherent feature of our everyday world.'[3]

The fund of everyday knowledge by means of which we are able to typify other people's behaviour and come to terms with social reality varies from situation to situation. We thus live in a world of *multiple realities* – 'The social actor shifts between these provinces of meaning in the course of his everyday life. As he shifts from the world of work to that of home and leisure or to the world of religious experience, different ground rules are brought into play. While it is within the normal competence of the acting individual to shift from one sphere to another, to do so calls for a "leap of consciousness" to overcome the differences between the different worlds.'[3]

Like phenomenology, ethnomethodology is concerned with the world of everyday life. In the words of its proponent, Harold Garfinkel, it sets out 'to treat practical activities, practical circumstances, and practical sociological reasoning as topics of empirical study, and by paying to the most commonplace activities of daily life the attention usually accorded extraordinary events, seeks to learn about them as phenomena in their own right.'[34] He maintains that students of the social world must doubt the reality of that world; and that in failing to view human behaviour more sceptically, sociologists have created an ordered social reality that bears little relationship to the real thing. He thereby challenges the basic sociological concept of order.

Ethnomethodology, then, is concerned with how people make sense of their everyday world. More especially, it is directed at the mechanisms by which participants achieve and sustain interaction in a social encounter – the assumptions they make, the conventions they utilize, and the practices they adopt. Ethnomethodology thus seeks to understand social accomplishments in their own terms; it is concerned to understand them *from within*.[3]

In identifying the 'taken-for-granted' assumptions characterizing any social situation and the ways in which the people involved make their activities rationally accountable, ethnomethodologists use notions like *indexicality* and *reflexivity*. Indexicality refers to the ways in which actions and statements are related to the social contexts producing them; and to the way their meanings are shared by the participants but not necessarily stated explicitly. Indexical expressions are thus the designations imputed to a particular social occasion by the participants in order to locate the event in the sphere of reality. Reflexivity, on the other hand, refers to the way in which all accounts of social settings – descriptions, analyses, criticisms, etc. – and the social settings occasioning them are mutually interdependent.

It is convenient to distinguish between two types of ethnomethodologists: *linguistic* and *situational*. The linguistic ethnomethodologists focus upon the use of language and the ways in which conversations in everyday life are structured. Their analyses make much use of the unstated 'taken-for-granted' meanings, the use of indexical expressions and the way in which conversations convey much more than is actually said. The situational ethnomethodologists cast their view over a wider range of social activity and seek to understand the ways in which people negotiate the social contexts in which they find themselves. They are concerned to understand how people make sense of and order their environment. As part of their empirical method, ethnomethodologists may consciously and deliberately disrupt or question the ordered, 'taken-for-granted' elements in everyday situations in order to reveal the underlying processes at work. An example of such a disruption of the social order from Garfinkel's own work is given in Box 1.7.

The substance of ethnomethodology thus largely comprises a set of specific techniques and approaches to be used in the study of what Garfinkel has described as the 'awesome indexicality' of everyday life. It is geared to empirical study, and the stress which its practitioners place upon the uniqueness of the situation encountered projects its essentially relativist standpoint. A commitment to the development of methodology and field-work has occupied first place in the interests of its adherents, so that related issues of ontology, epistemology and the nature of man have received less attention than perhaps they deserve.

Essentially, the notion of *symbolic interactionism* derives from the work of G. H. Mead.[35] Although subsequently to be associated with such noted researchers as Blumer, Hughes, Becker and Goffman, the term does not represent a unified perspective in that it does not embrace a common set of assumptions and concepts accepted by all who subscribe to the approach. For our purposes, however, it is possible to identify three basic postulates. These have been set out by Woods as follows:[36] (1) human beings act towards

BOX 1.7

Disrupting Social Order

In order to demonstrate that the 'seen but unnoticed' order of everyday life is an accomplishment, Garfinkel asked some of his students to experiment with disrupting its taken-for-granted routine and familiar nature. The students were asked to see themselves as 'strangers' in their own society, and thereby to suspend their taken-for-granted commonsense understandings. Here is a short extract illustrating the technique:

> S.   Hi, Ray. How is your girl friend feeling?
> E.   What do you mean, 'How is she feeling?' Do you mean physical or mental?
> S.   I mean how is she feeling? What's the matter with you? (He looked peeved).
> E.   Nothing. Just explain a little clearer what do you mean?
> S.   Skip it. How are your Med School applications coming?
> E.   What do you mean? 'How are they?'
> S.   You know what I mean.

Experiments of this nature, Garfinkel suggests, demonstrate that in their everyday lives members expect others to know what they are really talking about. They also show the moral nature of the familiar social world: upsetting the order, not displaying one's competence, can bring moral sanctions from other members who have been 'troubled'.

Source: Garfinkel[34]

things on the basis of the *meanings* they have for them. Man inhabits two different worlds: the 'natural' world wherein he is an organism of drives and instincts and where the external world exists independently of him, and the social world where the existence of symbols, like language, enables him to give meaning to objects. This attribution of meanings, this interpreting, is what makes him distinctively human and social. Interactionists therefore focus on the world of subjective meanings and the symbols by which they are produced and represented. This means not making any prior assumptions about what is going on in an institution, and taking seriously, indeed giving priority to, inmates' own accounts. Thus, if pupils appear preoccupied for too much of the time 'being bored', 'mucking about', 'having a laugh', etc. the interactionist is keen to explore the properties and dimensions of these processes; (2) this attribution of meaning to objects through symbols is a continuous *process*. Action is not simply a consequence of psychological attributes such as drives, attitudes, or personalities, or determined by external social facts such as social structure or roles, but results from a continuous process of meaning attribution which is always emerging in a state of flux and subject to change. The individual constructs, modifies, pieces together, weighs up the pros and cons and bargains; and (3) this process takes place in a *social* context. Each individual aligns his action to that of others. He does this by 'taking the role of the other', by making indications to his 'self' about the 'other's' likely response. He constructs how others wish or might act in certain circumstances, and how he himself might act. He might try to 'manage' the impressions others have of him, put on a 'performance', try to influence the other's 'definition of the situation'.

Instead of focusing on the individual, then, and his or her personality characteristics, or on how the social structure or social situation causes individual behaviour, symbolic interactionists direct their attention at the *nature of interaction*, the dynamic activities taking place between persons. In focusing on the interaction itself as a unit of study, the symbolic interactionist creates a more active image of the human being and rejects the image of the passive, determined organism. Individuals interact; societies are made up of interacting individuals. People are constantly undergoing change in interaction and society is changing through interaction. Interaction implies human beings acting in relation to each other, taking each other into account, acting, perceiving, interpreting, acting again. Hence, a more dynamic and active human being emerges, rather than an actor merely responding to others.

A characteristic common to the phenomenological, ethnomethodological and symbolic interactionist perspectives – and one which makes them singularly attractive to the would-be educational researcher – is the way in which they 'fit' naturally to the kind of concentrated action found in classrooms and schools, an action characterized by 'pupils and teachers . . . continually adjusting, reckoning, evaluating, bargaining, acting and changing.'[36] Yet another shared characteristic is the manner in which they are able to preserve the 'integrity' of the situation where they are employed. This is to say that the influence of the researcher in structuring, analysing and interpreting the situation is present to a much less degree than would be the case with a more traditionally-oriented research approach.

CRITICISMS OF THE NEWER PERSPECTIVES

Critics have wasted little time in pointing out what they regard as weaknesses in these newer qualitative perspectives. They argue that while it is undeniable that our understanding of the actions of our fellow-men necessarily requires knowledge of their intentions, this, surely, cannot be said to comprise *the* purpose of a social science. As Rex has observed:[37]

'Whilst patterns of social relations and institutions may be the product of the actors' definitions of the situations there is also the possibility that those actors might be falsely conscious and that sociologists have an obligation to seek an objective perspective which is not necessarily that of any of the participating actors at all . . . . We need not be confined purely and simply to that . . . social reality which is made available to us by participant actors themselves.'

Giddens[24] similarly argues, 'No specific person can possess detailed knowledge of anything more than the particular sector of society in which he participates, so that there still remains the task of making into an explicit and comprehensive body of knowledge that which is only known in a partial way by lay actors themselves.'

While these more recent perspectives have presented a model of man that is more in keeping with common experience, their methodologies are by no means above reproof. Some argue that advocates of an anti-positivist stance have gone too far in abandoning scientific procedures of verification and in giving up hope of discovering useful generalizations about behaviour.[38] Are there not dangers, it is suggested, in rejecting the approach of physics in favour of methods more akin to literature, biography and journalism? Some specific criticisms of the methodologies used are well directed:[38]

'. . . . If the carefully controlled interviews used in social surveys are inaccurate, how about the uncontrolled interviews favoured by the (newer perspectives)? If sophisticated ethological studies of behaviour are not good enough, are participant observation studies any better?

'. . . . And what of the insistence of interpretive methodologies on the use of verbal accounts to get at the meaning of events, rules and intentions? Are there not dangers? Subjective reports are sometimes incomplete and they are sometimes misleading?'

Bernstein's criticism[39] is directed at the overriding concern of phenomenologists and ethnomethodologists with the *meanings of situations* and the ways in which these meanings are 'negotiated' by the actors involved. What is overlooked about such negotiated meanings, observes Bernstein, is that they 'presuppose a structure *of* meanings (and their history) wider than the area of negotiation. Situated activities presuppose a situation; they presuppose relationships between situations; they presuppose sets of situations.'

Bernstein's point is that the very process whereby one interprets and defines a situation is itself a product of the circumstances in which one is placed. One important factor in such circumstances that must be considered is the *power* of others to impose *their* definitions of situations upon participants. Doctors' consulting rooms and headmasters' studies are locations in which inequalities in power are regularly imposed upon 'unequal' participants. The ability of certain individuals, groups, classes, and authorities to persuade others to accept their definitions of situations demonstrates that while – as ethnomethodologists insist – social structure is a consequence of the ways in which we perceive social relations, it is clearly more than this. Conceiving of social structure as *external* to ourselves helps us take its self-evident effects upon our daily lives into our understanding of the social behaviour going on about us.

The task of social science, it is held, is to develop sets of concepts such as *norms*, *expectations, positions* and *roles* in order to formulate a 'generalizing science of behaviour.' Only in this way is it possible to 'move from the interpretation of one specific action or event . . . to a theoretical explanation of behaviour.'[40]

A PROBLEM OF TERMINOLOGY: THE NORMATIVE AND INTERPRETIVE PARADIGMS

We are drawing to the close of this chapter and so far have introduced and used a variety of terms to describe the numerous branches and schools of thought embraced by the positivist and anti-positivist viewpoints. As a matter of convenience and as an aid to communication, we introduce at this point two generic terms conventionally used to describe these two perspectives and the categories subsumed under each, particularly as they refer to social psychology and sociology. The terms in question are *normative* and *interpretive*. The normative paradigm (or model) contains two major orienting ideas:[41] first, that human behaviour is essentially *rule-governed*; and second, that it should be investigated by the *methods of natural science*. The interpretive paradigm, in contrast to its normative counterpart, is characterized by *a concern for the individual*. Whereas normative studies are positivist, all theories constructed within the context of the interpretive paradigm tend to be anti-positivist.* As we have seen, the central endeavour in the context of the interpretive paradigm is to understand the subjective world of human experience. To retain the integrity of the phenomena being investigated, efforts are made to get inside the person and to understand from within. The imposition of external form and structure is resisted, since this reflects the viewpoint of the observer as opposed to that of the actor directly involved.

Two further differences between the two paradigms may be identified at this stage: the first concerns the concepts of *behaviour* and *action*; the second, the different conceptions of *theory*. A key concept within the normative paradigm, *behaviour* refers to responses either to external environmental stimuli (another person, or the demands of society, for instance) or to internal stimuli (hunger, or the need to achieve, for example). In either case, the cause of the behaviour lies in the past. Interpretive approaches, on the other hand, focus on *action*. This may be thought of as behaviour-with-meaning; it is intentional behaviour and as such, future oriented. Actions are only meaningful to us insofar as we are able to ascertain the intentions of the actor, to share his experience. A great deal of our everyday interactions with one another relies on such shared experiences. A child, for example, raises his arm and keeps it above his head. Should he do this at home while watching television, his parents are likely to find his bodily movements curious ('What's the matter with him?' i.e. what immediate, past event caused him to behave like that?). In the setting of the classroom, however, the action is perfectly understandable to all ('What does Billy want now?' i.e. what does he intend? or, alternatively, Billy is letting me know that he is ready to answer my question when I ask him, i.e. future-oriented intentional behaviour).

As regards *theory*, the normative researcher tries to devise general theories of human behaviour and to validate them through the use of increasingly complex research methodologies which, some believe, push him further and further from the experience and understanding of the everyday world and into a world of abstraction. For him, the basic reality is the collectivity; it is external to the actor and manifest in society, its institutions and its organizations. The role of theory is to say how reality hangs together in these forms or how it might be changed so as to be more effective. The researcher's ultimate aim is to establish a comprehensive 'rational edifice', a universal theory, to account for human and social behaviour.

But what of the interpretive researcher? He begins with *the individual* and sets out to understand *his* interpretations of the world around him. Theory is emergent and must arise from particular situations; it should be 'grounded' on data generated by the research act.[42] Theory should not precede research but follow it. The investigator works directly with experience and understanding to build his theory on them. The data thus yielded will

---

* It may seem paradoxical to some readers that, although we have just described interpretive theories as anti-positivist, they are nevertheless conventionally regarded as 'scientific' (and hence part of 'social science') in that they are concerned ultimately with describing and explaining human behaviour by means of methods that are in their own way every bit as rigorous as the ones used in positivist research (see, for example, Accounts of Episodes in Chapter 2).

be glossed with the meanings and purposes of those people who are their source. Further, the theory so generated must make sense *to those to whom it applies*. The aim of scientific investigation for the interpretive researcher is to understand how this glossing of reality goes on at one time and in one place and compare it with what goes on in different times and places. Thus theory becomes sets of meanings which yield insight and understanding of people's behaviour. These theories are likely to be as diverse as the sets of human meanings and understandings which they are to explain. From an interpretive perspective the hope of a universal theory which characterizes the normative outlook gives way to multifaceted images of human behaviour as varied as the situations and contexts supporting them.

We illustrate the distinction between interpretive and normative approaches with reference to two studies of classrooms. During months of observation in schools and in the course of detailed interviews with teachers, Hargreaves and his co-workers[43] gathered information about 'what was going on' and 'what teachers actually meant' in their interactions with pupils. In actually getting at the realities of the situation, they provide an insightful account of routine deviance in classroom settings – one, incidentally, that will be immediately recognized by experienced teachers. Essentially these researchers were concerned to understand teachers' actions towards their pupils. Their approach was *interpretive*.

Using videotape equipment, Adams and Biddle[44] recorded teachers' interactions with pupils. Aspects of teacher behaviour were then identified by the researchers who used a coding system to quantify and classify such things as 'teacher talk', 'pupil talk' and 'teacher movement about the room'. The purpose of this study was to obtain accurate objective 'facts' about classroom interaction. The approach was *normative*.

The application of interpretive perspectives to more substantive educational matters characterizes the work of Young and his associates.[45] They see the primary purpose of a 'new sociology of education' as being to question much that is taken for granted in the day-to-day life of schools. Why, for example, are certain subjects included in the curriculum and not others? And who says what constitutes a subject? Who defines what its knowledge base should consist of ? In pointing to such issues, Young 'raises questions about relations between the power structure and curricula; the access to knowledge and the opportunities to legitimate is as 'superior' as the relation between knowledge and its function in different kinds of society.' The application of Young's critical perspectives can be illustrated in two recent studies. In the teaching of English, the Rosens[46] have challenged the common emphasis on the study of great literature, arguing that the hidden purpose of this approach is to impose an alien middle class culture upon working class pupils, in effect denying them their sense of identity. A study by Sharp and Green[47] shows how subtle influences of social control intrude upon the child-centred teaching in three infant classrooms to produce similar effects to those readily observable in more formal teacher-centred classes. Studies such as these challenge the assumptions underlying much that takes place in educational practice and they bring new insights into the complexity of the teaching – learning process.

We shall review some other distinctions between the normative and interpretive paradigms at the beginning of the next chapter. For the moment, we refer you to Box 1.8 which summarizes some of the broad differences between the two approaches that we have made so far.

BOX 1.8

Differing Approaches to the Study of Behaviour	
Normative	*Interpretive*
Society and the social system	The individual
Impersonal, anonymous forces regulating behaviour	Human actions continuously recreating social life
'Objectivity'	'Subjectivity'
Generalizing from the specific	Interpreting the specific
Explaining behaviour	Understanding actions
Assuming the taken-for-granted	Investigating the taken-for-granted
Macro-concepts: society, institutions, norms, positions, roles, expectations	Micro-concepts: individual perspective, personal constructs, negotiated meanings, definitions of situations
Structuralists	Phenomenologists, ethnomethodologists, symbolic interactionists

NORMATIVE AND INTERPRETIVE – COMPETING OR COMPLEMENTARY?

In presenting what might appear to be competing paradigms in contemporary social science, we have deliberately avoided showing preference for one over the other, choosing to present each's case impartially (or so we see it). However, to strike strongly partisan attitudes does seem to be the fashionable thing to do in these matters and to waver somewhere between the two viewpoints is to risk being raked by the crossfire. This likelihood notwithstanding, we staunchly support a compromise position which sees the normative and interpretive perspectives as necessary and complementary aspects of a fuller understanding of man's behaviour and experience, believing that some kind of connection or correlation exists between them although this may not at the present time be too apparent. Rather than viewing each approach as separate and self-contained, it is more profitable, as Giddens has suggested, to see all paradigms as mediated by others.[24]

Clearly, the best way forward lies in the judicious use of both approaches with a view ultimately to synthesizing their outcomes into a more comprehensive and unified whole. In writing of the reductionist trend in some areas of the social sciences and of the need to maintain, or to restore, a unified concept of man in the face of scattered data, facts and findings as they are furnished by a compartmentalized science, Frankl[48] writes:

'The pictures we obtain today from the various individual sciences are very disparate. These pictures differ from each other so much that it is becoming more and more difficult to arrive at a unified world-view. But it should be pointed out that such differences, *per se*, need by no means constitute a loss in knowledge. On the contrary, such differences may well make for a gain in knowledge – just consider stereoscopic vision. There is a difference between the right and the left pictures that are offered to you. But it is precisely this difference that mediates the acquisition of a new wholeness, of an additional dimension, the third dimension of space. To be sure, the precondition is that we achieve a fusion between the picture on the right and on the left. And what holds for vision is also true of cognition: unless we obtain a fusion, confusion may be the result.'

Suppose, for example, we wanted to know what young people felt about homework. We could begin by administering a suitably prepared attitude test to a sample of a school population. The data yielded could be processed and interpreted, thus giving us the information we set out to discover, namely, what the sample's opinions on the subject were as mediated by the structure and content of the questionnaire we had designed. Such would be the normative approach. This is not to say, however, that a detailed study of children's conversations on the subject, written accounts, and school biographies over a period of time, along with unobtrusive measures such as the children's own homework records, will not greatly enrich our study of what they think about homework. Whereas the former is primarily concerned with assessing attitudes at a given point in time, what we might call the outcome or *product*, the interpretive researcher is able to study the *process* resulting in the product. Interpretive approaches in this sort of context can hardly be regarded as better, or worse, or even incompatible (though, of course, there may be notable differences – as the quotation from Frankl implies): they must be seen as complementary, as filling a significant gap left by normative research, a gap which is inevitably the result of its chosen method of attack together with the assumptions that this choice implies.

CONCLUSION: THE PURPOSE AND PLAN OF THE BOOK

In the broadest terms the purpose of this book is to take a number of educational issues centring on contemporary classrooms and schools and to show how the social sciences can contribute to our understanding of them in a variety of ways and at a variety of levels. Thus they can provide us with sets of concepts enabling us to perceive, analyse and think about particular situations in particular ways; they enable us to begin to map out and describe hitherto unknown terrains; they enable us to investigate particular issues; they enable us to identify causes and consequences of actions and to establish simple relationships; at a more sophisticated level they enable us to utilize experimental procedures to arrive at more authoritative knowledge; they permit us to understand better the realities of the school situation from contrasting perspectives, normative and interpretive, thereby giving us a more rounded picture; they enable us to take remedial action and sometimes to solve problems; and finally, they enable us to assess and evaluate the procedures used by teachers in their day-to-day endeavours and the impact they have on pupils. In addition, the methodology used by researchers provides them with a problem-attacking and problem-solving approach which when combined with earlier-acquired knowledge, 'will enable them to diagnose problems in educational organizations more accurately and initiate more effective solutions.'[49] We shall be examining these methods more closely in the next chapter.

After a review of the principal methods of research used in the social sciences in Chapter 2, we look in the chapter following this at individual classroom and school factors that influence educational achievement. In Chapter 4 we examine teacher behaviour and teacher perspectives and follow this in Chapter 5 with a complementary review of pupil behaviour and pupil perspectives. Chapter 6 looks at communication in the classroom, both its verbal and non-verbal aspects, and is followed in successive chapters by studies of aspects of group life in classrooms – mixed ability groups, multi-cultural education and open classrooms. Two issues central to the functioning of the school are then discussed – norms and conformity and the school as an organization. The book concludes with Chapter 12, *School and Society*, in which some of the more indirect influences on classrooms and schools emanating from society are reviewed.

SUMMARY

We began the chapter by explaining that the book would be concerned with contemporary educational issues affecting the classroom and school and that these would be examined through a largely social scientific perspective. We then considered two views of the social world which dominate the thinking of social scientists and educational researchers at the present time. Positivism and anti-positivism, the two broad philosophical viewpoints at the centre of each of the two views, were looked at in some detail. The former was discussed and its special character as manifested in science and the scientific method was delineated. After noting criticisms of positivism from a variety of sources, we presented alternatives to positivistic social science. In particular, humanistic psychology, 'a science of persons', phenomenology, ethnomethodology and symbolic interactionism were described in outline. Criticisms of these were likewise examined. Then the problems of terminology were resolved (for the purposes of this book at least) by adopting two generic terms, normative and interpretive, to represent the broadly positivistic and anti-positivistic trends respectively. Selected school studies exemplifying the two paradigms were noted and the chapter closed with a plea that the two paradigms should be seen as complementary rather than as competitive and with a brief outline of the purpose and plan of the book.

ENQUIRY AND DISCUSSION

1. Why have developments in social science lagged behind developments in natural science?

2. What is the relationship of social psychology and the social psychology of education to the other behavioural sciences?

3. What advantages are to be gained by adopting a social science perspective to the study of educational issues and problems?

4. Compare the normative and interpretive paradigms with respect to their assumptions about human nature.

5. Define succinctly *phenomenology*, *ethnomethodology* and *symbolic interactionism*. What have they in common and in what ways do they differ?

6. Why is the interpretive approach to educational research particularly well suited to the study of classrooms?

7. Critically review any one recent interpretive study of classrooms or schools. Try to make explicit the assumptions on which it is based.

8. Choose a school curriculum appropriate to your specialist interests (infant, junior, middle, high, secondary) and question the taken-for-grantedness of it. What deletions and substitutions would you make, and why?

NOTES AND REFERENCES

1. Note: The other disciplines normally included are economics, anthropology and demography.

2. Borg, W. R. (1963) *Educational Research: An Introduction*, New York: Longmans. We are not here recommending, nor would we wish to encourage, exclusive dependence on rationally derived and scientifically provable knowledge for the conduct of education – even if this were possible. There is a rich fund of traditional and cultural wisdom in teaching (as in other spheres of life) which we would ignore to our detriment. What we are suggesting, however, is that total dependence on the latter has tended in the past to lead to an impasse: and that for further development and greater understanding to be achieved education must needs resort to the methods of science.

3. Burrell, G. and Morgan, G. (1979) *Sociological Paradigms and Organizational Analysis*, London: Heinemann Educational Books.

4. Barr Greenfield, T. (1975) Theory about organizations: a new perspective and its implications for schools. In *Administering Education: International Challenge*. (Ed.) Hughes, M. G. London: Athlone Press.

5. Beck, R. N. (1979) *Handbook in Social Philosophy*, New York: Macmillan.

6. Acton, H. B. (1975) Positivism. In *The Concise Encyclopedia of Western Philosophy and Philosophers*. (Ed.) Urmson, J. O. London: Hutchinson, Second Edition.

7. Note: Primarily associated with the *Vienna Circle* of the 1920s whose most famous members include Schlick, Carnap, Neurath and Waisman.

8. Duncan Mitchell, G. (1968) *A Dictionary of Sociology*. London: Routledge and Kegan Paul.

9. Giddens, A. (Ed.) (1975) *Positivism and Sociology*. London: Heinemann Educational Books.

10. Note: This is a somewhat crude distinction: some approaches in the natural sciences are concerned with animate matter – biology, for instance.

11. Barratt, P. E. H. (1971) *Bases of Psychological Methods*. Queensland, Australia: Wiley and Sons Australasia Pty. Ltd.

12. (Eds.) Cuff, E. C. and Payne, G. C. F. (1979) *Perspectives in Sociology*, London: George Allen and Unwin.

13. Mouly, G. J. (1978) *Educational Research: The Art and the Science of Investigation*. Boston: Allyn and Bacon.

14. Sullivan, J. W. N. (1938) *Limitations of Science*. London: Penguin Books.

15. Hughes, J. A. (1978) *Sociological Analysis: Methods of Discovery*. Sunbury-on-Thames: Nelson and Sons Ltd.

16. Kerlinger, F. N. (1965) *Foundations of Behavioural Research*. New York: Holt, Rinehart and Winston.

17. Medawar, P. B. (1972) *The Hope of Progress*. London: Methuen.

18. Aronson, E. (1976) *The Social Animal*. San Francisco: Freeman, Second Edition.

19. Kierkegaard, S. (1974) *Concluding Unscientific Postscript*. Princeton: Princeton University Press.

20. Warnock, M. (1970) *Existentialism*. London: Oxford University Press.

21. Ions, E. (1977) *Against Behaviouralism: A Critique of Behavioural Science*. Oxford: Basil Blackwell.

22. Holbrook, D. (1977) *Education, Nihilism and Survival*. London: Darnton, Longman and Todd.

23. Hampden-Turner, C. (1970) *Radical Man*. Cambridge, Mass.: Schenkman.

24. Giddens, A. (1976) *New Rules of Sociological Method: A Positive Critique of Interpretive Sociologies*. London: Hutchinson.

25. Shipman, M. D. (1972) *The Limitations of Social Research*. London: Longmans.

26. Buhler, C. and Allen, M. (1972) *Introduction to Humanistic Psychology*. Monterey, California: Brooks/Cole.

27. Note: see, for example, Rogers, C. R. (1969) *Freedom to Learn*, Columbus, Ohio: Merrill Pub. Co.; and also Rogers, C. R. and Stevens, B. (1967) *Person to Person: The Problem of Being Human*. London: A Condor Book: Souvenir Press (Educational and Academic) Ltd.

28. Harré, R. and Secord, P. (1972) *The Explanation of Social Behaviour*. Oxford: Basil Blackwell.

29. Delamont, S. (1976) *Interaction in the Classroom*. London: Methuen.

30. Note: Investigating *social episodes* involves analysing the accounts of what is happening from the points of view of the actors and the participant spectator(s)/investigator(s). This is said to yield three main kinds of interlocking material: images of the self and others, definitions of situations, and rules for the proper development of the action. See Harré, R. (1976) The constructive role of models. In *The Use of Models in the Social Sciences*. (Ed.) Collins, L. London: Tavistock Publications.

31. Levine. R. H. (1977) Why the ethogenic method and the dramaturgical perspective are incompatible. *In Journal of the Theory of Social Behaviour*, **7**, 2, 237–247.

32. English, H. B. and English, A. C. (1958) *A Comprehensive Dictionary of Psychological and Psychoanalytic Terms*. London: Longmans.

33. Curtis, B. (1978) Introduction. In *Phenomenology and Education* (Eds.) Curtis, B. and Mays, W. London: Methuen.

34. Garfinkel, H. (1968) *Studies in Ethnomethodology*. Englewood Cliffs, N. J.: Prentice Hall.

35. See Mead, G. H. (1934) *Mind, Self and Society*. (Ed.) Charles Morris. Chicago: University of Chicago Press.

36. Woods, P. (1979) *The Divided School*, London: Routledge and Kegan Paul.

37. (Ed.) Rex, J. (1974) *Approaches to Sociology: An Introduction to Major Trends in British Sociology*. London: Routledge and Kegan Paul.

38. Argyle, M. (1978) Discussion chapter: an appraisal of the new approach to the study of social behaviour. In *The Social Contexts of Method*. (Eds.) Brenner, M., Marsh, P. and Brenner, M. London: Croom Helm.

39. Bernstein, B. (1974) Sociology and the sociology of education: a brief account. In *Approaches to Sociology: An Introduction to Major Trends in British Sociology*. (Ed.) Rex, J. London: Routledge and Kegan Paul.

40. Dixon, K. (1973) *Sociological Theory: Pretence and Possibility*. London: Routledge and Kegan Paul.

41. Douglas, J. D. (1973) *Understanding Everyday Life.* London: Routledge and Kegan Paul.

42. Glaser, B. G. and Strauss, A. L. (1967) *The Discovery of Grounded Theory.* Chicago: Aldine.

43. Hargreaves, D. H., Hester, S. K. and Mellor, F. J. (1975) *Deviance in Classrooms.* London: Routledge and Kegan Paul.

44. Adams, R. S. and Biddle, B. J. (1970) *Realities of Teaching: Explorations with Videotape.* New York: Holt, Rinehart and Winston.

45. (Ed.) Young, M. F. D. (1971) *Knowledge and Control: New Directions for the Sociology of Education.* London: Collier-Macmillan.

46. Rosen, C. and H. (1973) *The Language of Primary School Children.* London: Penguin.

47. Sharp, R. and Green A. (assisted by Lewis, J.) (1975) *Education and Social Control: A Study in Progressive Primary Education.* London: Routledge and Kegan Paul.

48. Frankl, V. (1972) Reductionism and nihilism. In *The Alpbach Symposium: Beyond Reductionism, New Perspectives in the Life Sciences* (Eds) Koestler, A. and Smythies, J. R. London: Hutchinson and Co.

49. Johnson, D. W. (1970) *The Social Psychology of Education.* New York: Holt, Rinehart and Winston.

SELECTED READING

1. Bernbaum, G. (1977) *Knowledge and Ideology in the Sociology of Education.* London: Macmillan and Co. A brief, lucid account of the history of the 'new sociology of education' in Great Britain.

2. Berry, D. (1974) *Central Ideas in Sociology: An Introduction.* London: Constable. A very readable account of major perspectives in social theory.

3. (Eds.) Cosin, B. R., Dale, I. R., Esland, G. M., MacKinnon, D. and Swift, D. (1977) *School and Society: A Sociological Reader.* London: Routledge and Kegan Paul/Open University Press.

4. (Eds.) Cuff, E. C. and Payne, C. G. F. (1979) *Perspectives in Sociology,* London: George Allen and Unwin. An excellent introduction to sociology with especially relevant chapters on the newer perspectives.

5. (Eds.) Filmer, P., Phillipson, M., Silverman, D. and Walsh, D. (1972) *New Directions in Sociological Theory.* London: Collier-Macmillan. A substantial text analysing positivistic sociology and phenomenological alternatives.

6. Outhwaite, W. (1975) *Understanding Social Life: the Method called Verstehen.* London: George Allen and Unwin. This gives an account of pioneers in the development of interpretive approaches in social theory.

2

The Methods of the Social Sciences

You recall that in our consideration of the social sciences in the opening chapter, we contrasted the more traditional approach to the study of social reality with the newer, emergent approach which is gaining recognition among social scientists. The former we referred to as the *normative* approach; and the latter, the *interpretive*. As we saw, the one draws heavily on the scientific method; whereas the other, in eschewing this model, seeks to understand and interpret social phenomena from the inner perspective of man himself. The normative view sees human behaviour in mechanistic terms, largely as a response to antecedent events in the outside world. In its quest for explanation, it uses words like *norm*, *role*, *position*, and *expectation*. The interpretive approach, on the other hand, is concerned with human *action*, behaviour which man as agent knowingly brings about. Elucidation of the 'meanings' of actions are sought with concepts like *intention*, *purpose*, *desire* and *belief*. It is our purpose in this chapter to reflect these two schools of thought in our review of the principal research methods adopted by social scientists with these differing orientations. Some of the methods, like the *experiment*, belong quite unequivocally to the normative tradition; others, like *accounts of episodes*, are emerging techniques of the interpretive school. Still others, like *action research*, may meet the strategic needs of either viewpoint.

Before we begin our review of the methods, let us try to see the difference between the *normative* and *interpretive* perspectives from another point of view – that of the researchers themselves, those who use the methods about to be described. What is their stance as they confront a problem? What is their attitude to the social reality they are trying to explain or understand? What kinds of data[1] will they deem acceptable? Further, what will they do with the data they have gathered? And finally, how do they see the relationship between apparently incompatible sets of data generated by normative and interpretive methods? Imagine two researchers going about their professional tasks: one is committed to the traditional approach with its attendant values and skills derived from the positivistic model; the other, to the more recent interpretive viewpoint. The one, concerned with the outer social world, adopts a detached and neutral role. He is free to stand apart and apply whatever conceptual schema he chooses to the phenomena he has selected for investigation. The other, favouring an inner view of social reality, is much more involved, an involvement which demands participation in the ongoing action as a member of the group he is studying. There is no question of his being neutral: most likely he himself will be changed by the events that he becomes part of. Indeed, this kind of change will provide him with the fresh insights he seeks; with first-hand knowledge of the way the group conceives the world and the 'meanings' its members impute to such conceptions. The traditionalist approaches social reality with preconceptions, manifest in his briefcase crammed with questionnaires, attitude-scales and structured interview schedules. The interpretive researcher, by contrast, will start with the social world *as it is* and, almost in the spirit of an eavesdropper, will tune in to it on *its* terms with unstructured interviews, participant observation, natural conversation, and the like.

To continue our fantasizing a little further, suppose the two researchers have now returned to their respective studies. As educated flies on the wall, we are now in a position to examine the two sets of data. What are we likely to find? How can we designate them? If you thumb through a few texts on research methods in the social sciences, you will probably find a whole string of labels that could be applied to them, rather like this: data from the traditional study would be described variously as *objective, external, quantifiable, explanatory, publicly verifiable* and *replicable*. The interpretive data, however, would be referred to as *subjective, internal, qualitative* (that is, expressed in symbolic forms – language or gesture, see Box 2.1), *interpretative, unique* and *negotiable*. These epithets are fairly exhaustive and would adequately capture the full flavour of the two sets of contrasting data.

BOX 2.1

Quantitative and Qualitative Data

Researchers produce data by translating their observations and inquiries into written notation systems. The difference between qualitative and quantitative research can be stated quite simply in terms of the notation systems used to describe the world. Quantitative researchers assign numbers to qualitative observations. In this sense, they produce data by counting and 'measuring' things. The things measured can be individual persons, groups, whole societies, speech acts, and so on. Qualitative researchers, on the other hand, report observations in the natural language at large. They seldom make counts or assign numbers to these observations. In this sense, qualitative researchers report on the social world much as the daily newspaper does. This simple difference in commitment to notation systems corresponds to vast differences in values, goals, and procedures for doing social research.

Source: adapted from Schwartz and Jacobs[2]

To the extent that both researchers are trying to understand and explain social phenomena, they have a common purpose. It is in their respective attitudes to the data they have gathered that they diverge; and this brings us back to our initial question: what do they do with the data? The normative researcher, committed to the view that there are general and universal laws determining social behaviour, uses his data to check out his hunches about 'objective reality' or 'absolute truth'. In a sense he tries to strait-jacket social reality with his models of man. The interpretive researcher is more flexible in this respect, however, being prepared to seek out modes of explanation *from the data themselves* as expressed in written, spoken or nonverbal form. He would share the view of one observer who wrote:[3]

'Knowledge needed to understand human behaviour is embedded in the complex network of social interaction. To assume what it is without attempting to tap it; to refuse to tap it on the grounds of scientific objectivity; or to define this knowledge with constricting operational definitions, is to do grave injustice to the character and nature of the empirical social world that sociologists seek to know and understand.'

Kaplan has drawn our attention to a particular problem concerning the handling of data in social research.[4] Stemming from the common humanity of the researcher and his subject, it is that behaviour has meaning to the person engaging in it as well as to the observer – the scientist – and that these two meanings do not necessarily coincide. He therefore distinguishes the two kinds as *act meaning* and *action meaning*. The former refers to the meaning an act has for the actor; and the latter, its meaning for the researcher, the observer. The normative researcher, in interpreting an act through the mediation of his chosen theory or hypothesis, does so on the presumption that shared meanings exist between his subject and himself. The validity of his data rests on this presumption. The validity of the interpretive researcher's data, however, and the inferences he draws from them rest on no such presumption, since he is in a position to negotiate and reconstruct meanings from the data with the actor himself.

We come now to our final question: does it follow that sets of data from contrasting studies of the apparently same phenomenon will be compatible? The short answer is: no. Some role-playing studies in the field of social psychology have successfully replicated earlier experimental findings; others have not. Where it is not possible to account for discrepant findings on methodological grounds, social scientists have to accept the likelihood that normative and interpretive approaches, outer and inner perspectives, can and will yield different results. After all, at the level of the individual, psychology recognizes the existence of two distinct personalities – an outer and an inner; the *persona* and the *anima* – which may be, and indeed often are, in opposition.

Earlier we made the point that as authors, we see both the normative and interpretive approaches to the study of social reality as being equally valid; and that for a truer understanding of the complexities of social life, we must acknowledge the interrelationship and interdependence of the two methodologies. Interestingly enough, this point is nowhere better illustrated than in the research undertaken in the field of education. Studies in the social psychology and sociology of education in this country in the 1950s and 1960s tended to reflect the normative paradigm only and partly for this reason had certain weaknesses, chiefly in that they were selective and partial. Since 1970, however, partly through the influence of ongoing research in the United States, studies of classrooms and schools have been initiated which reflect the influence of the interpretive school of thought. Ethnographic techniques such as participant observation began to be used; researchers went into schools without any preconceptions of what went on in them or of what people's views were. For the first time, teachers' and pupils' perspectives on school life were recorded and taken seriously. Thus it was that studies of this kind began to complement – if not supplant in some instances – the more traditional styles of research, thereby enabling a more representative picture of school life in its totality to emerge.

We now review the principal techniques and procedures used in social research. The findings, information and insights described in subsequent chapters derive chiefly from studies employing these methods. They are: *survey methods, case studies, developmental research, experimental and quasi-experimental research, causal research, correlational research, action research, triangulation, accounts of episodes, role-playing, personal constructs, non-directive interviewing* and *content analysis.*

As you will see, we begin with the more traditional methods of research associated with the normative paradigm and proceed to those methods favoured by the interpretive school.

SURVEY METHODS

The range of approaches used in the social sciences specifically to gather information about people has become known collectively as *survey methods.* The principal ones that we shall be concerned with are *observation, questionnaires, interviews* and *documents.* By these means, social research studies samples[5] drawn from large or small populations in order to obtain information on them or, more particularly, 'to discover the relative incidence, distribution and interrelations of sociological and psychological variables.'[6] Survey studies have a *descriptive* purpose and are undertaken to establish the nature of existing conditions, though some are concerned with explanation and hypothesis-testing. It is impossible to catalogue all the areas of investigation in which survey methods are used, so extensive is the coverage; but as a guide, we may detail the four broad types of subject matter that Moser[7] lists: the demographic characteristics of people (family, marital status, age); their social environment (occupation, income, living conditions); their activities (leisure, reading habits, TV viewing habits, for example); and their attitudes and opinions. A survey often begins with a statement of the problem to be investigated, then the following stages are identified: the objective(s) of the survey; the population at which it is directed; the information to be acquired; and the resources necessary and available to undertake the task. Survey methods perform a number of useful functions in the educational sphere. Not only are they of value at a purely descriptive level, they contribute significantly to planning, evaluation, and as preliminaries to more rigorous research.

There are two main types of observation – non-participant observation and participant observation. In the case of the former, the observer stands outside the real life situation he is investigating and systematically records the behaviour of the participants. Accuracy of observation in this context is generally improved by having some degree of selection or control. It is a particularly useful technique for studying small groups and institutions and a notable feature in recent years has been its increasing use in educational settings.

Non-participant observation studies in classrooms and schools generally utilize systematic observation instruments. These are constructed by selecting variables thought to be relevant, describing them in behavioural terms so that they can be readily identified by an observer, and then developing a system for recording them. One of the principal types of recording system is the category kind. A category identifies a specific piece of behaviour ('teacher encourages pupil', or 'teacher ignores pupil', for instance). Category systems deal with a restricted number of variables or aspects of behaviour which are then recorded continuously whenever they occur so as to produce an ongoing record of behaviour. The observer's task using the schedule is to categorize and record behaviour as it occurs. For a review of the numerous instruments available for classroom and school observation, we suggest that you consult Cohen.[8] An example of a structured observation schedule used in recent classroom research may be seen in Box 2.2.

BOX 2.2

A Structured Observation Schedule for the Classroom

1. Number   Late
2. Pencils
3. Uniform
4. Overcoats
5. Chairs
6. Windows
7. Condition   Clean
                Tidy
                Plants
                Posters
                Pictures

    Total

8. Work on walls   0   1   2   3   4
9. Graffiti   0   1   2   3   4

Classroom observation schedule - definitions

This observation schedule was used during the series of classroom observations of the third year and during the administration of the pupil questionnaire.

1. The number of pupils in the class and the number who arrived after the start of the lesson.
2. The number of pencils borrowed from the researchers during the administration of the questionnaire.
3. The number of children not in correct school uniform (as defined by the school).
4. The number of children in outdoor coats or anoraks.
5. The number of broken chairs in the classroom.
6. The number of broken or cracked windows.
7. The decorative condition of the room. One point was given for each of the five items and a total score assigned to each room.
8. The amount of children's work on the walls, coded from 0 to 4. 0 = none, 1 = one quarter of available wall space, 2 = one half of available wall space, 3 = three quarters of available wall space, 4 = all available wall space.
9. The amount of graffiti coded as item 8.

Checklist for beginning and ending of lesson

TO LESSON

33	Start/after break/N.K.		0
	Same room/Double		1
	V. slow		2
34	Lost	0	1
35	Fight	0	1
36	750 yards	0	1

START

37	Outside:	Mill	0
		Enter room	1
		Line up	2
	Inside:	Muddle	0
		Sit	1
		Stand	2
39	Off-task chat to T	0	1
40	Silence	0	1
41	Greeting	0	1
42	Register	0	1
43	Ritual	0	1
44	Seating:	Chosen by children	0
		T directs some	1
		T directs all	2
		N/K	9
45	Re-sources:	Brought by children	0
		On desk	1
		Distrib. by T	2
		Distrib. by monitors	3
		Collected by children	4

| 46-7 | Time to start of work: |
| 48 | No. Late: |

END

49	Timing:	Long		0
		Good		1
		Short		2
		Dismiss before bell		3
50	Stand behind chairs	0	1
51	Silence	0	1
52	Farewell	0	1
53	Line up	0	1
54	Off-task chat to T	0	1
55	Tidy room	0	1
56	Dismiss by row/group/sex	0	1
57	Reports	Individual	0	1
58		Class	0	1
59	Resources:		
	Collected by T		0
	Collected by monitor		1
	Replaced by children		2
	Kept by children		3

CHECKLIST

| 60 | Homework set | 0 | 1 |
| 61 | Homework returned | 0 | 1 |

Outings/trips

Formal punishments:

Formal rewards:

Jobs of e.g. monitors

Source: Rutter et al.[11]

Participant observation describes occasions when the observer interacts in various ways with the situation he is observing, when he engages in the very activities he sets out to observe. It is a method in which the observer 'participates in the daily life of the people under study, either openly in the role of researcher or covertly in some disguised role, observing things happen, listening to what is said, and questioning people, over some length of time.'[9] In the past decade participant observation has played an important part in the methodology of the interpretive approach and has been the basis of a number of distinguished studies in the realm of education, medicine and nursing.[10]

One of the commonest means of gathering information in survey research is the questionnaire. A questionnaire consists of a set of questions designed to elicit information from respondents on chosen topics by means of self-reports. Two kinds of question may be used: the open-ended type which leaves the respondent free to answer in his own words, and the fixed choice type in which the respondent is required to select an answer from those provided. As alternatives to questionnaires, respondents may be given a *check-list* or a *rating scale*. In the former, the respondent is required to select from a list of characteristics what he considers relevant to a given topic; and in the latter, he is asked to rate the strength of his attitude to a particular statement. Given a proposition like 'Teachers are underpaid', for example, the respondent selects from a number of categories ranging from, say, *strongly agree* to *strongly disagree*. Questionnaires, check-lists and rating schedules may deal with a wide variety of subjects, e.g. factual knowledge, attitudes, or opinions.

The *interview* is a face-to-face situation in which the interviewer obtains information relevant to his research problem from the person being interviewed. Broadly, there are three types of interview: the structured or standardized interview; the unstructured or unstandardized interview; and the non-directive interview. As we consider the latter elsewhere in this chapter, we confine our brief comments to the structured and unstructured forms. The structured interview has its content and procedures organized in advance: the sequence and wording of questions are fixed by means of a schedule and the interviewer is left little freedom to modify either. It is this kind of interview which forms the basis of the *field survey*. This sophisticated method of obtaining information makes use of a large field staff of trained interviewers who put their questions to a carefully chosen sample from a large population. The technique is used by organizations like the Gallup Poll which samples people's political views during election campaigns. In contrast to structured interviews, unstructured ones are more flexible, being more like open-ended questionnaires. In the course of an actual unstructured interview, subsequent direction and content may be determined by the interviewee's responses. A prepared schedule may or may not be used. Kerlinger[6] has identified three occasions when the interview may be used: (1) as an exploratory device to help identify variables and relations, and to suggest hypotheses; (2) as a main instrument of research; and (3) to supplement other methods used in research – to follow up unexpected results, to validate other methods, or to go deeper into the motivations of respondents and their reasons for responding as they do.

Finally, we touch on the fourth source of information used in survey research, namely, the *document*. In general terms, there are two kinds of document the researcher may refer to in this context: official documents such as census schedules, case study records, or school reports, for instance; and personal documents like diaries and letters. Sources of this nature often serve to supplement data obtained by other methods in survey research.

CASE STUDIES

Let us now turn to a method which you have no doubt already encountered in your own work – the *case study*. Originating in the practices of law, medicine and social work, the case study method as used in the social sciences is an intensive, detailed analysis and description of a particular social unit – be it an individual, group, institution, community or event – generally within the context of its environment (though there are exceptions to this, as we shall see). The method requires contact with the people studied and involves collection of all available data. It may therefore draw upon social, psychological, behavioural, biographical, environmental or organizational data insofar as these are perceived as relevant to the objectives of the study.

Occasions when the case study may be employed are numerous. It may, for instance, be used as a method of evaluation in an educational programme; or as an ancillary tool in formal evaluative research; or as a follow-up to more rigorous investigations where it can elucidate unexplained or unexpected findings. In educational settings, it is frequently used as an intensive means of gathering information with a view to solving some specific situational problem or to building up a general picture of some area of school life.

Whatever the occasion, however, at the heart of every case study lies a method of observation;[12] and for most purposes this means either non-participant or participant observation. The type of observation used is often dependent on the type of setting in which the research takes place. One could, for example, undertake a study in a 'natural' setting like a school or factory; alternatively, one could conduct an investigation in an 'artificial' setting such as a psychological laboratory or a therapist's clinic. The former may utilize participant observation; the latter, non-participant observation.

The distinctive characteristics of the case study method make it a particularly useful means of complementing more rigorous experimental and other approaches to the same kind of problem. We have already said that being an in-depth study of a single unit, it may provide a complete and structured picture of that unit. More than this, however, it allows us to investigate individual or social processes in natural contexts and for this reason is often closer to real life than many other methods. Another consequence of the natural setting is that the more holistic qualities of the unit are taken into consideration so that its functional properties are not lost sight of.

Other advantages of the method have been identified by Isaac and Michael:[13] because it is intensive, it may bring to light important variables, processes and interactions that deserve more detailed attention; data yielded by the case study method may provide examples to illustrate more generalized findings from other studies; the method is heuristic and is thus rich in discovery potential so it can provide the investigator with insights and hypotheses denied to workers adopting other approaches; if necessary, the researcher using the case study method may reformulate his problem as he goes along – false trails can be abandoned readily and alternatives taken up; and finally, variables which are usually hard to quantify can be handled more easily.

The method does have some disadvantages, however. Case studies are limited in their representativeness and their findings cannot be generalized to other situations, though the findings of a series of related case studies may have wider applicability, assuming there is some measure of agreement in them. In parentheses, we point out that this question of lack of generalizability need not necessarily be a limitation in educational research where unique and often idiosyncratic problems need to be solved. Case studies are scientifically weak in that the degree of control over the multitude of variables operating in the open system which characterizes the method is slight. Finally, the approach is prey to subjective bias of one sort or another, though this can be very considerably minimized with a trained and skilful observer.

A particular kind of case study is that referred to as the *one-shot case study*. This is a type of design in which a single individual or group is observed on a single occasion only. The procedure may be represented diagrammatically thus:

$$\textit{Treatment} \qquad \textit{Post-test}$$
$$z \qquad\qquad t$$

A teacher may attempt to determine whether a new method of teaching reading results in better average scores on a reading test of accuracy and speed taken at a later date. The *scientific* value of such a study is, of course, minimal because there is no control, nor any comparative basis on which the findings may be validated. However, uses of the technique are not infrequent and it may be resorted to if nothing else is possible. Its use would be justified when a unique case presents itself – a young man with remarkable psychic gifts, for instance; or with certain kinds of anthropological studies.

We have already suggested that one of the most fruitful contexts for the application of case study techniques is that of the school where the restriction the method imposes on generalization from the particular need not be too serious. An in-depth study of a child by a student teacher; or a detailed study of a class by its teacher; or an intensive investigation of a whole school by a team of inspectors would be characteristic examples of the case study method in this connection. Fine examples of case studies of this kind are to be found in the comparatively recent past. Wolcott,[14] for example, undertook a participant observation study of the career of an elementary school principal. Lambert et al.[15] used a variety of techniques to investigate boarding schools. And King[16] adopted an interpretive approach in his study of infant classrooms.

DEVELOPMENTAL RESEARCH

We now consider a research method which investigators use far less frequently than either survey methods or the case study approach – *developmental research*. This kind of research investigates patterns of growth and/or change in individuals, groups and institutions and for this reason is a fitting method for measuring the formal and informal processes of education. Unlike most other methods we are considering in this chapter, then, developmental studies are concerned with time trends, that is, with changes that occur over, or as a function of, time.

Within the area of developmental research, a clear distinction is often made between *longitudinal* and *cross-sectional* studies.[12] The longitudinal study gathers data over an extended period of time: a short-term investigation may take several weeks; a long-term study can extend over many years. Where successive measures are taken at different points in time from the *same* respondents, the term *follow-up study* or *cohort study* is used in the British literature, the equivalent term in America being *panel study*. Where different respondents are studied at different points in time, the study is called *cross-sectional*. Where a few selected factors are studied continuously over time, the term *trend study* is employed.

Cohort studies and trend studies are *prospective* longitudinal methods in that they are ongoing in their collection of information about individuals or their monitoring of specific events. *Retrospective* longitudinal studies, on the other hand, focus upon individuals who have reached some defined end-point or state. For example, a group of young people may be the researcher's particular interest (intending social workers, convicted drug offenders or university dropouts, for example) and the questions to which he will address himself are likely to include ones such as: is there anything about the previous experience of these individuals that can account for their present situation?

The longitudinal approach may present difficulties for the researcher, however. This is particularly the case when a problem is studied over a long period – five or ten years, say – in the world at large. Maintaining continuity of staff or providing sufficient financial support may make the enterprise impossible to sustain. Keeping in touch with one's sample can also be problematic. Then there is the possibility of the sample being diminished by people moving away from an area, or death. Attrition of this kind can quite seriously affect sampling procedures. Although problems of a similar nature are still present when a longitudinal study is conducted in an institution like a school or college, they are very much scaled down and present less of a headache for the researcher. Whatever the context, however, other problems can arise from the very nature of the longitudinal design in that it is inflexible and does not allow for modification to the techniques and procedures once the study has got underway.

A cross-sectional study is one that produces a 'snapshot' of a population at a particular point in time. The epitome of the cross-sectional study is a national census in which a representative sample of the population consisting of individuals of different ages, different occupations, different educational and income levels, and residing in different parts of the country, is interviewed on the same day.[17] More typically in education, cross-sectional studies involve indirect measures of the nature and rate of changes in physical and intellectual development of samples of children drawn from representative age levels. The single 'snapshot' of the cross-sectional study provides the researcher with data for either a retrospective or a prospective inquiry.

A cross-sectional study often encompasses more subjects than does the longitudinal approach. It is also more economical and quicker, though the sampling procedures are rather more complicated because the same subjects are not involved and samples from different age-levels have to be carefully matched. There are many occasions when the cross-sectional design is preferable to the longitudinal one simply on practical grounds – there are fewer problems of keeping in touch with one's sample or of sample mortality, for example. One weakness of the cross-sectional study, however, lies in the danger of imputing changes in the subjects to the time process when an alternative explanation exists.

More recent approaches in this field of developmental research have attempted to identify possible causes for measured changes by correlating plausible factors or conditions within the time sequence of a given longitudinal design with the noted patterns of change. An experimental slant may thus be given to procedures when these factors and conditions can be experimentally controlled and manipulated.

BOX 2.3

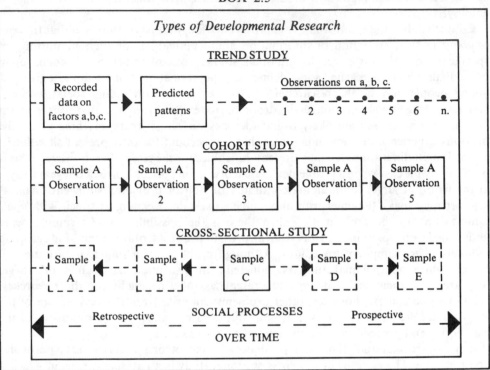

Types of Developmental Research

TREND STUDY

Recorded data on factors a,b,c. → Predicted patterns → Observations on a, b, c.

1 2 3 4 5 6 n.

COHORT STUDY

Sample A Observation 1 → Sample A Observation 2 → Sample A Observation 3 → Sample A Observation 4 → Sample A Observation 5

CROSS-SECTIONAL STUDY

Sample A ← Sample B ← Sample C → Sample D → Sample E

Retrospective   SOCIAL PROCESSES   Prospective

OVER TIME

Source: Cohen and Manion[12]

Box 2.3 summarizes three types of developmental research in graphic form – the trend study, the cohort study, and the cross-sectional study.

EXPERIMENTAL AND QUASI-EXPERIMENTAL RESEARCH

We have already made incidental reference to words like *experimental, control,* and *variable.* The context of these and related terms is that of *the experiment.* This we may define as a situation in which an investigator deliberately varies one or more conditions in order to study the effects of this variation on one or more other features in the situation. The investigator himself would probably be rather more precise in his explanation and say that it was a scientific investigation in which he controls and manipulates at least one variable (which he calls the independent or experimental variable) under pre-determined conditions and observes its effects on at least one other variable (which he refers to as the dependent variable). Taking it a little further, we may say that the independent variable is that variable whose changes are not dependent upon changes in another specified variable; and the dependent variable is that variable whose changes are regarded as being a consequence of changes in the independent variable. There is no such thing, at least from a normative perspective, as an absolutely independent variable. All this sounds rather involved, so let us try to make a little more sense of it with an example.

Imagine a situation in which an instructor in the navy has devised a new way of teaching navigation to trainee navigators (based on programmed learning techniques, for instance) and wants to check its efficiency against the more traditional methods which he normally uses. To do this, he decides to set up an experiment. He begins by taking a random sample of trainees and assigns half of them randomly to Group E. The remainder will make up Group C. Group E constitutes the experimental group which is to be subjected to the new teaching method (the independent variable). The instructor (now taking the role of investigator) begins by giving this group an initial test on navigation (or, more precisely, on that part of the course he is to teach subsequently by the new method). This is known as the pretest stage. The measures are noted and the group is then taught the course (the dependent variable) by the new method. They are then tested a second time with the original test, this stage being referred to as the post-test. If the pretest and post-test are designated T_1 and T_2 respectively, and the new teaching method is symbolized by X, the design of the experiment so far may be expressed thus:

Exp. Group	Pretest	New T.M.	Post-test
E	T_1	X	T_2

It is not sufficient, however, to have the experimental group taught by the new method and to leave it at that – not, at least, in an experimental approach. The investigator requires a criterion or base-line with which to compare the differences between T_1 and T_2 in the diagram above. He therefore takes his second sample of trainees, Group C, which will serve as a control group, thus giving him the point of reference he seeks. After being given the same pretest as Group E, that is, T_1, Group C are taught the same part of the course as Group E, but by traditional methods. Group C are then given the post-test, T_2. The whole design may now be represented as follows:

E	T_1	X	T_2
C	T_1	Y	T_2

The traditional method of teaching is designated by Y. The effectiveness of the new method is indicated by the difference between T_1 and T_2 for Group E (i.e. $T_2 - T_1$); and between T_1 and T_2 for Group C (i.e. $T_2 - T_1$). If there is an improvement in Group E's performance over Group C's, this may be attributed to the independent variable, X, manipulated by the experimenter, i.e. the new teaching method.

The design we have just illustrated, *the pretest – post-test control group design*, is one of the simpler kinds used in experimental research. There are, of course, other, more complicated designs, though most studies in education make use of some form of this classic single variable design, as above.

A well-thought-out experiment provides the most rigorous design for the scientist; and while other designs, like those employed in causal and correlational studies, attempt to uncover possible associations, the purpose of the experiment is to establish true cause-and-effect relationships. A second purpose lies in the testing of predictions derived from theory; and a third, in helping to build up theoretical systems. The experimental method is held in high esteem by researchers – particularly in the natural sciences – for at its most rigorous and successful, it is an excellent means of yielding worthwhile, trustworthy knowledge.

The experimental method differs in various ways from other methods used in social research. These differences arise chiefly from the element of *control* which is introduced into the experimental situation by the researcher. This means that the influence of variables extraneous to the aim of the study is controlled in such a way that the effectiveness of these variables is minimized, nullified, or isolated. There are three main ways of controlling variables. The first, when possible, is the easiest and involves eliminating the variable as a variable. Recall our experiment above. We were investigating the effect of a new teaching method on trainee navigators. If the factor of intelligence had been an extraneous variable which could have distorted the results, we could have minimized the effect of this to a large extent by selecting trainees with the same IQ.

The second means of controlling the effect of extraneous variables is through *randomization*. This means that each subject has an equal chance to be in any condition in the study. Thus, to select a sample *by chance*, and assign them to groups *by chance*, is to randomize both the sample and the group. Randomization thus ensures that the effects of unspecified or unknown variables in the experimental situation which could affect either the independent or dependent variable are evenly distributed throughout each group, so that if they have any effect on the subjects of the experiment, they will affect all groups similarly.

The third means of control involves building the extraneous variable into the design of the experiment as another independent variable. Let us return to our example above. If the trainees had been men *and* women, the sex variable could not have been eliminated and would have to have been built into the design as another independent variable.

It will be helpful at this point if we distinguish three kinds of experiment used in the social sciences. The *laboratory experiment* is a controlled experiment carried out in a laboratory. Most social psychological experiments are performed in college laboratories where maximum control over the relevant variables can be achieved. The *field experiment* is a controlled experiment conducted in a natural, real-life situation such as a school or factory. A *natural experiment* is similar to the controlled field experiment, except that the investigator does not manipulate the independent variable himself but waits for a natural occurrence to manipulate the variable for him (e.g., in testing the hypothesis that comprehensive reorganization increases alienation among teachers, a researcher might compare members of staff in a school undergoing reorganization with a comparable staff in another school *not* experiencing reorganization. He might then examine the degree of alienation before and after the reorganization, using the other school as a control).

There are many occasions, especially in educational research, when it is not possible to control and manipulate the relevant variables, or to randomize samples or groups. The researcher, for example, has no control over *when* his subjects are exposed to a programme, or *which* subjects are exposed to it. These kinds of situation require compromise procedures which are referred to collectively as *quasi-experimental designs*. As Travers[18] says:

'The essential difference between a genuine experiment and a quasi-experiment lies in the fact that, in the genuine experiment, the different conditions to which the different groups are exposed are assigned at random to the groups. In the quasi-experiment the conditions are taken as they are found, in naturally occurring situations. The difference is immense. The genuine experiment necessarily yields more certain knowledge, and should be preferred where possible.'

CAUSAL RESEARCH

At the beginning of this chapter, we said that those researchers holding the normative view see human behaviour largely as a response to antecedent events in the outside world. This means that one of their aims as social scientists is, where possible, to discover causal links between these events and the ensuing behaviour. To this end, various ploys are used by investigators to identify the presumed causes of particular effects. The term *causal research*, however, is generally reserved for those investigations in which possible causes for an existing condition are sought *in the past* by an examination of records or documents, for instance, or by interviewing significant people who were present at the time of the supposed causes. It is the retrospective nature of this kind of *ex post facto* enquiry, as it is sometimes called, which distinguishes it from the experimental method where, as we saw, data are collected under controlled conditions *in the present* and causation is determined by the manipulation and measurement of an independent variable to see what effect it has on a dependent variable. The accounting for a secondary pupil's recurrent attacks of school phobia by examining his records in the primary school would be one example of causal research; studying an attempted suicide's relationship with family and friends to discover reasons for his behaviour would be another example; and attempts to explain the success of a sample of effective teachers by looking into their professional records over a ten-year period would be yet another instance.

The strengths of causal research have been identified by Isaac and Michael.[13] For example, it is appropriate in circumstances where the more powerful experimental method is not possible – when an experimenter is unable to select, control, or manipulate the factors necessary to establish cause-and-effect relationships, as in the three instances quoted in the preceding paragraph; when the control of all variations except a single independent variable may be highly unrealistic; and when laboratory controls for many research purposes would be impracticable, costly, or ethically questionable. The chief weaknesses which the writers identify include: lack of control over independent variables; the problem of distinguishing relevant from spurious causal factors; the possibility that a given consequence may have resulted from the *interaction* of factors instead of a single one; the contingency that a phenomenon may result not only from multiple causes, but from one cause in one instance and another cause in another instance; and the possibility of mistaking covariant factors[19] for clear-cut cause-and-effect ones.

There have been many instances of successful causal research studies in the literature – investigations into the relationship between attitudes and religious or political affiliation; studies of the relationship between school achievement and variables such as social class, race, sex, and intelligence; research on cigarette-smoking and cancer; and studies of teacher characteristics. Box 2.4 summarizes the findings of a causal study investigating factors associated with university failure.

BOX 2.4

Factors Associated with University Failure

Out of 802 students who began their studies at the University of Bradford in 1966, 102 dropped out at the end of their first year. On entry to the university the whole freshman intake had provided academic and personal information about their backgrounds, their interests, their motivations and values.

In a *causal research design*, comparisons were made between dropouts and non-dropouts in an attempt to discover factors associated with university failure.

In line with previous studies, university failure was found to relate: (1) to inferior educational qualifications on entry; (2) to less certainty about choice of career; (3) to a greater degree of worry over abilities to pursue a university course of study; and (4) to feelings of being overwhelmed by the academic work demanded.

Source: adapted from Cohen and Child[20]

CORRELATIONAL RESEARCH

Before we consider correlational studies as such, it might be worthwhile reminding ourselves of the meaning of correlation. Correlation refers to the degree of association between two characteristics or variables, e.g. intelligence and achievement, while the correlation coefficient itself is a statistical value ranging from -1.0 to $+1.0$ expressing the degree of the relationship in quantitative terms. When more than two variables or characteristics are involved, multiple or partial correlation coefficients can be used to indicate how one characteristic is related to a second while the third is held constant. It is important to stress that correlations refer to measures of association and do not necessarily indicate causal relationships between variables.

Correlational research thus investigates the extent to which variations in one factor or variable correspond with variations in one or more other factors or variables, the degree of association being expressed in the correlation coefficient. Correlational studies figure prominently in educational research, though they very often consist of nothing more than two sets of measurements or observations, together with a correlation coefficient. As such they constitute part of what is termed non-experimental research the main characteristic of which is that it is undertaken in the 'real' world as opposed to experimental research, most of which takes place in a laboratory or under laboratory conditions. Correlational research, along with other examples of non-experimental research, may be used as a means of suggesting, clarifying, or refining experimental research findings; and often, a correlational study will suggest hypotheses that can be tested and variables that can be manipulated experimentally later on. The method is particularly suitable when variables are very complex and do not lend themselves to the experimental method and controlled manipulation. It is also useful to the extent that it allows the measurement of several variables and their interactions simultaneously in a realistic setting.

Examples of the use of correlational studies abound in education. They play a significant part, for instance, in the assessment of teacher effectiveness as judged by the learner's performance. Variations are obviously to be found in the conduct of this kind of research, but the most common practice is to associate teacher behaviour with child outcome measures. The independent variables (operationalized aspects of the teacher's behaviour) are usually secured from either a frequency count of specific teacher actions or check marks on a rating scale that calls for an observer making inferences about the teacher. Measures of the independent variables are then compared (or correlated) with measures of the dependent variable such as children's test scores of one kind or another. The correlational approach in this context is used in the absence of experimental studies.

Correlational studies have some limitations, however: as we have said already, they only identify what goes with what, they do not of necessity establish cause-and-effect relationships; they are less rigorous than the experimental approach because they exercise little, or no, control over the independent variables; and they are liable to establish spurious relational patterns.

ACTION RESEARCH

We come now to a very different kind of research procedure – *action research*. The conventional definition of action research identifies it as small-scale intervention in the functioning of the real world and the close examination of the effects of such intervention.[21] Although one of those terms where actual usage more precisely determines definition, the one we offer provides a useful starting point, for action research is basically an on-the-spot procedure designed to deal with a problem that has been located in a specific situation. Whether the latter is a school classroom or a business organization, new skills are developed and new approaches tried in the hope of achieving more successful results. The research is undertaken by the participants in the situation (where this is a classroom, research workers and teachers working on a collaborative basis more often than not) who constantly monitor the procedures adopted. The ensuing feedback is then translated into modifications and adjustments, as necessary, with a view to bringing about improvement to the ongoing process itself rather than to some future occasion, as is the purpose of more traditional kinds of research. That the findings are applied immediately or in the short-term is one of the distinguishing characteristics of action research. In a school setting, a teacher trying out a new idea with his class would be action research at its simplest; whereas a Schools Council project engaging teams of researchers and teachers exemplifies the technique at a more sophisticated level.

The action research movement in education was initiated in the United States in the late 1940s and reached its peak in that country in the early 1960s. At the time, the literature on action research accounted for its inception in the failure of responsible bodies to implement the findings of traditional research endeavours. More than this, however, action research had other attractive qualities. The democratic flavour of its values which were rooted in participation and group planning was found by some of its devotees to be appealing. It offered exchange of ideas and the recognition of group dynamics as well as, in the words of one contemporary observer, 'the opportunity for the creative growth of teachers among bureaucratic rigidities, complexities, conformist traditions and monotonous routines.'[22] To others, action research was a way of stimulating the social and spiritual life of the school, and of creating a social milieu where the participants could co-operate in setting up a better community. 'Group interaction' became the war cry. The claims of the practitioners of action research in education in this country at the present time, while no less instrumental and fervent, are certainly more modest in what they believe can be achieved. They see it chiefly as a means of bringing about changes more expeditiously than would be the case by more conventional means of research; as an approach to problem-solving in school contexts; as a way of implementing innovation and change; as an in-service training device enabling teachers involved in an action research project to improve their teaching skills, gain added insights into complex social situations, and develop self-awareness; and as an opportunity to break down the traditional barriers between academic researchers and practising teachers.

We are now in a position to summarize some of the principal features of action research. It is essentially a practical method and directly relevant to the situation giving rise to it in that the findings may be implemented in the near future to effect lasting improvement: in this sense it is directed at producing *functional knowledge*. We have referred so far to the classroom as a typical setting for action research, yet classic instances of its use are to be found in markedly contrasting settings – village communities, factories, and coal mines, for example. Other characteristics have been noted by Isaac and Michael:[13] action research provides an orderly framework for problem-solving and for new developments, and to this extent is superior to the impressionistic approach that often characterizes developments in education; it is also empirical in that it relies on actual observations and behavioural data; and it is flexible and adaptive, allowing for changes during trial periods and sacrificing control for responsiveness and immediate experimentation and innovation. Another important feature arises from the role of the researcher in the procedure. As a participant observer, his strategy will be quite different from that of the traditional researcher whose stance is much more detached. As Hoyle observes,[23] 'In particular, he will have to relinquish traditional modes of verification in order to manipulate the situation he is studying and in which he himself is involved.' You will readily see the connection between these observations and our earlier remarks on the interpretive researcher's viewpoint.

The chief weakness of action research as a method lies in its lack of scientific rigour. Its purpose is situational, its sample or samples restricted and unrepresentative, and it has little control over independent variables. Hence its findings, while of immediate use in the particular context begetting them and possibly offering some guidance in similar contexts, do not contribute to the general body of scientifically-based knowledge. Of course, these strictures do not apply quite to the same extent in those relatively few instances of action research where an experimental note has been introduced.

Recent years have witnessed a revival of interest in the use of action research in education in Britain, particularly in the field of curriculum development where the techniques and procedures are very well suited to research-based teaching and the introduction of innovatory methods in the classroom. There have been numerous projects initiated by the Schools Council, for example, in which teachers adopt a research stance to their work and collaborate with teams of researchers.

We suggest that if you would like to take this brief account of action research further you have a look at the work of Cooper and Ebbutt[24] and Shipman, Bolam and Jenkins[25] to get some idea of the problems and difficulties arising from the tension generated by the concepts of *action* and *research*, and the implications of these for the researchers and teachers involved.

TRIANGULATION

Picture the following scene: a First Division football ground somewhere in Britain with a fiercely competitive match between two rival teams in progress. From the sea of faces present, four individuals engage our attention – the manager of the home side sitting apprehensively in the stands; an agitated supporter of the visiting team gesticulating wildly behind his team's goal mouth; a photographer from the tabloid press taking worm's-eye-view pictures from the side of the home team's goal; and a policeman on duty along the touchline staring with bland indifference at the action. Now, if we were to ask each of these people to give his account of the match so far, what would be the result? Would there be unanimity of opinion on the match to that point in time? Would they agree wholeheartedly on the merits and otherwise of the respective teams? Hardly, for each account would reflect the individual's prejudices, biases, partisanship, distortion, exaggerations, enthusiasms, dislikes, and so on. Yet each according to his own lights and from his own relative standpoint would be correct. You may now be asking where all this is leading. The answer is that the episode illustrates the *principle of triangulation* in that different accounts of the same event are provided by different observers from different locations or viewpoints. You may be more familiar with the notion of triangulation in other contexts such as surveying, navigation, and military strategy where it means the measuring or pin-pointing of a physical objective from two or more geographical locations.

Although having a clearly figurative connotation in the social sciences, triangulation in this context refers to the use of two or more methodological approaches to a given problem in preference to a single approach. Multiple measures of a concept or multiple observations of a phenomenon will result in a more rounded and accurate view of these aspects of reality than will be the case with conclusions based on a single criterion measure. Imagine two researchers intent on gauging students' attitudes to their course. One may be satisfied with using an appropriate attitude scale and leaving it at that. This would reflect the traditional approach. The other may choose the same attitude scale together with two additional measures – interviewing a sample of students, say, and using some kind of unobtrusive measure like attendance at lectures. The second researcher in adopting the method of triangulation will emerge from his tasks with a fuller view of student attitudes.

The need to develop triangular devices in social research has arisen as researchers have come to realize not only the limitations of established procedures but also the limited use to which these are put. Various writers have identified the more obvious problems in this respect: attitude scales are often selected for their convenience and accessibility rather than for their psychological criteria; many studies are culture-bound, that is, they are limited to one country; the vast majority are also time-bound, that is, are limited to one point in time and do not take into consideration the fact of social change; sociological studies, which by definition imply a macro level of analysis, make excessive use of individuals; and rarely are studies replicated.

One way of meeting some of these criticisms is to make use of more than one method. One commentator expresses it like this:[26] 'Research methods are never atheoretical or neutral in representing the world "out there". They act as filters through which the environment is selectively experienced. By using one's knowledge of how each method may selectively bias or distort the scientist's picture of reality, combinations of methods may be selected which more accurately represent what is "out there".'

Triangulation in social research originally referred to the use of two or more methods in the study of the same objective. This limited view, however, has been extended by Denzin[27] to embrace other kinds of triangulation which we now briefly examine.

We saw earlier that by far the greater percentage of recent studies in sociology were conducted at one point in time only. This single 'snapshot' approach ignores a crucial factor in sociological analysis – the process of social change. *Time triangulation*, though not without its difficulties, goes some way to overcome this problem by combining cross-sectional and longitudinal analyses; and in a similar manner, *space triangulation*, which takes cultural and sub-cultural differences into account, helps to mitigate the parochialism of studies undertaken in the same country or among similar sub-groups within a population.

There are three basic levels of data collection and analysis in sociology. These have been identified by Denzin as (a) the aggregative (or individual) levels; (b) the interactive level (group or relational); and (c) the level of collectivities (organizational, cultural, or societal). Whereas most sociological research is characterized by the use of the aggregative level of analysis as its basic source of data, the more distinctive studies in this field have utilized more than one level of analysis. Such an approach may be termed *combined levels of triangulation*.

Most researchers when planning their studies adhere exclusively to one particular theory; alternative explanations are rarely considered. The purpose of *theoretical triangulation* is to design a research project so that competing theories are borne in mind and put to the test. As one advocate of theory triangulation says: 'Until investigators take theories at odds with their own more seriously in the design of their research there will be little progress made towards unified sociological paradigms.'[26]

In conclusion, we refer briefly to two other types of triangulation. The accounts relating to house-purchase which we quote in the next section illustrate the use of *investigator triangulation*. This involves the use of several as opposed to single observers which will result in more reliable data. *Methodological triangulation* refers to (a) the use of the same method on different occasions (replication); and (b) the use of different methods on the same object of study.

We shall demonstrate the practical applicability of triangulation in the classroom in Chapter 5, *How Pupils See It*.

ACCOUNTS OF EPISODES

One way of analysing and studying the social behaviour of human beings is to make use of episodes. The idea of an episode is a fairly general one and we may define the concept as any coherent part or fragment of social life. Being a natural division of life, it will quite often have a recognizable beginning and end, and the sequence of actions making up its content will have some kind of meaning for the participants. Episodes may thus be of varying duration and reflect many different aspects of life. A child entering a secondary school at eleven and leaving at fifteen would be an extended episode. A half-hour discussion between an interviewer and a TV studio audience on a political issue would be another. And a potential house buyer talking over the purchase of a property with an agent yet another. The content of an episode may include not only perceived behaviour such as gesture and speech, but also the thoughts, feelings and intentions of those taking part.

We shall be considering episodes in further detail later in the book when we examine the ways in which the different kinds contribute to our understanding of school and classroom situations. For the moment, however, we suggest you identify examples of episodes from your own immediate social and professional milieus.

Accounts, which must be seen within the context of episodes as we have just described them, are rich sources of data for ethnographers. They are personal records of the events we experience in our day-to-day lives – our conversations with neighbours, our letters to friends, our entries in diaries. Accounts serve to explain our past, present, and future-oriented actions. By being a commentary upon a particular action, an account deals with 'the problem of how it should be interpreted, speculating on the motives, intentions and characters of those involved, and generally offering some kind of criticism and justification of whatever are taken to be the goings-on.'[28]

Ethnographers insist that, providing accounts are authentic, there is no reason why they should not be used as scientific tools in explaining people's actions. Just how accounts can be authenticated will become clear in the following example of the ways in which ethnographers go about their work. The study is to do with the processes involved in buying a house, an experience many people have at least once in their lives.[29]

From the outset of this particular piece of research, great importance was placed upon the authority of each informant *to account for his own actions*. This means that leading questions and excessive guidance were avoided by the researchers although they established the format of the interview in pilot work before the main research endeavour. Care was taken to select informants who were representative of various house buyer needs (newly weds, divorcees, large families, etc.) and of a range of house styles and prices. The researchers were concerned with the degree to which respondents were actually involved in the house purchase, the recency of the experience, their reasons for participating in the study, and their articulateness and competence in giving information. These early stages of the research, involving selection and collection activities, served as checks on the authenticity of the accounts provided by those from whom it was possible to obtain adequate information. Further ways of establishing authenticity involved (1) checking with respondents through a process of negotiation during the account-gathering stage about their perceptions of the events they described; (2) using secondary evidence such as expert corroboration from solicitors and estate agents, that is comparing 'objective' and 'subjective' realities; and (3) comparing the separate accounts of other participants in the same event, that is, looking at various 'subjective' realities. We illustrate this latter aspect in Box 2.5.

Having gathered accounts from participants, the researchers' task was then to transform them into working documents which could be coded and analysed. Checks on the authenticity of the accounts were again incorporated at this stage of the research as well as standard checks on the inter-coder reliability of those engaged in the transform-

BOX 2.5

Contrasting Subjective Realities

Mrs. Y: 'Agents put us in touch with three people who were interested. Couple X seemed to be the
          absolutely perfect customer. They gave us the offer we wanted, bought some brand new
          carpets over and above the asking price. Some problems followed and things were delayed.
              I don't think the X's were quite aware of the urgency. We got the impression from the
          agents that they were cash buyers. But it turned out they weren't and they had to get a
          mortgage and it was a bit naughty to give us this impression.
              We didn't get on so well with Mr. X and Mrs. X was a bit of a tough cookie. My husband
          had words with her and he got a bit ruffled.'

Mrs. X: 'It started off a very amicable relationship. We came over here and agreed to buy carpets and
          curtains. But the whole situation deteriorated which made the whole thing unpleasant.
          Mr. Y would call every night sometimes he would call twice and harangue and harangue.
          They seemed to think we were cash buyers, the agents having told them so. So I said we are
          cash buyers only in the sense that we don't have anything to sell.
              It all became more and more abusive, finally I got so upset that I refused any more calls
          and anything that had to be said should go via a solicitor. Every time the 'phone goes I would
          just cringe.'

Source: adapted from Brown and Sime[29]

ation of the materials. Depending upon the nature of the research problem and the
objectives of the inquiry, the analyses that then followed could either be qualitative or
quantitative.

The final stage in the research was the production of an *account of the accounts*. Here,
the researchers made explicit the controls that they had applied in eliciting accounts from
participants and in the transformation process itself. Having satisfied the demands of
authenticity in respect of their own account, the final product was ready to be evaluated.
Only when accounts were subjected to these periodic stringent checks for authenticity
were they considered as scientific data.

The report of the housing project above shows the systematic and painstaking way in
which ethnographers gather their data. Probably of more direct interest to student
teachers, however, are the following snippets from the accounts of pupils describing their
ideal teacher together with that teacher's own explanations of how he copes with this very
low ability group (Box 2.6). The reader may wish to look at the researcher's *account of
accounts*[30] in connection with these West Indian pupils' explicit demands for teachers'
discipline and control in a London secondary modern school.

ROLE-PLAYING

Imagine you are a salesman promoting a new Brand X tooth-paste. Your task for the day is
to persuade the owner of a large retail store in your region to switch over to your brand in
preference to an established and rival Brand Y which the owner has purveyed for the past
ten years. Clearly, you have a problem. How would you go about solving it? What would
you do? What would you say? Calling on your past experience, you would rehearse *in*

BOX 2.6

Extracts from Accounts

Question: If you had an ideal teacher, what would she make you do?
Valerie: Learn more, learn a lot more . . . if you had teachers like Mr. Marks, you'd get a good job when you left school with 'O' levels and all that because they make you work.

Two girls tease another, Carol, because she works so hard for Mr. Marks . . .

Diane: At least I'm not a teacher's pet.
Carol: Nor'm I. He just like my work, my work is so good. I'm doing 5th form work (even though she is only in the 4th year).
Valerie: (laughing) Oh, sorry.
Carol: Listen right, if you was doing 5th form work and he keep praising you in class, you'd feel proud. Admit it, come on admit it.
Valerie: (laughing) In a sense yeah.
Carol: Well then I'm proud.
Diane: How many 'excellents' have you got?
Carol: A whole heap you know. My book is 'excellent' everywhere.

Mr. Marks' account is as follows:
The reason is because you have to brainwash them into thinking they're good. I have to continually tell them they can do it, and eventually they do. Now take Carol, she's streaks ahead of all the others and I tell her so. In fact she's ahead of the whole year, comparatively that is . . . Of course the advantage of doing it this way is that there is always something they can have marked, it gives them some incentive. Of course the actual level of their work is pretty low. I shouldn't think any of them will get CSE.

Source: Woods and Hammersley [30]

your mind how you would introduce your new brand, what the owner's reactions might be, how you would counter them if they were unfavourable, and so on, until eventually you had converted him to Brand X. This approach to increasing sales is actually used by salesmen and characterizes the technique known as *role-playing* – imagining or acting out a scenario to see how you would arrive at a pre-specified outcome.

The use of role-playing in psychology and social psychology has a fairly long history. It was first used in the 1930s as a therapeutic technique for alleviating social and emotional problems, a function it still performs in *psychodrama*. In the 1950s and 1960s the technique was applied to studies of attitude and attitude-change. And in *sociodrama* it serves as a means of developing social attitudes and skills among young people. It is only comparatively recently, however, that role-playing has come to be used as a distinctive investigative technique in social psychological experimentation where it is seen by some as a plausible alternative to the ethically questionable techniques of deception that have held sway for so long in that area. It is role-playing in this context, as a method of investigating human actions, that we are particularly interested in. A researcher would justify its use in this sense by saying that since the human actions he wishes to understand are situational and take place within a framework of roles, these roles can be feigned in such a way as to provide a mock-up of 'real life' situations and it is these situations which provide him with the insights into human behaviour that he seeks.

Role-playing in the way we are using the term serves a number of functions – it throws light on people's problem-solving techniques – how they resolve dilemmas, inconsistencies, and contradictions; it allows for the evaluation of decision-making and the way decisions are carried out; it permits the assessment of social skills; it enables researchers to explore people's *beliefs* about the way others behave; it creates new ideas; and it is useful for testing and generating hypotheses about social behaviour. The technique is particularly relevant to the interpretive approach to human behaviour in that it capitalizes on the person as a self-directing agent. In a characteristic role-playing experiment – sometimes referred to as an *as if* experiment – subjects are asked to behave *as if* they were particular persons in a particular situation. The purpose of the experiment is explained to them in advance and they are then asked to behave as they would if the situation were real instead of experimental, or as if they did not know the objective of the research. The method attempts to enlist the subject's aid in actively and conscientiously collaborating with the experimenter. Borg[31] outlines one possible procedure thus:

> 'The subject is usually given material that describes the situation in which he is to
> work and sometimes discusses the nature of the problem he will attempt to solve and
> the identity of other persons who will participate. He studies this material prior to
> the start of the situation, arrives at his solution or method of handling the problem,
> and then attempts to carry out this solution in the role-playing situation.'

Harré and Secord[32] identify *four* types of role-playing. In the first of these, the subject is asked to imagine the outcome of a particular situation which is presented or described to him. In the second, he is put into the situation and asked to enact it. In the third, an imaginary character is specified with distinct traits and the subject is asked to say how the character would behave in the given situation. And finally, the subject may also be put into the situation and asked to perform as a specified character. Types 1 and 3 involve *passive* role-playing; and types 2 and 4, *active* role-playing.

The writers also point out that, in a sense, role-playing studies reverse the usual logic of the formal experiment described earlier in the chapter. As they explain, 'ordinarily, the investigator works from a known set of treatments to an unknown outcome. Although he may have hypotheses about outcomes, he is basically interested in determining what outcomes are produced by the treatment. The role-playing experiment, in contrast, takes as its goal a particular outcome . . . . and sets about producing this desired result.'

Researchers committed to the traditional experiment are sceptical as to the value of the data produced in role-playing experiments. As Freedman has pointed out:[33]

> 'The argument comes down to the simple truth that data from role-playing studies
> consist of what some group of subjects guess would be their reactions to a particular
> stimulus. The subjects are giving their intuitions, their insights or introspections
> about themselves or others. If you are studying the myths and values of a society this
> data would be useful. If you want to know how people behave, it is, at best,
> suggestive. If you are interested in people's intuitions, fine; if you are interested in
> their behaviour . . ., you must ordinarily use the experimental method. Just
> because a significant number of subjects have the same intuition about something
> does not make them correct. We must rely on real data, not on opinion surveys.
> Consensus is not truth.'

An experimenter using role-playing, however, would argue that each method has different objectives and that the role-playing approach may be useful for the study of topics that cannot be tackled by the usual methodology. He would further argue that the role-playing method has great generality, that its findings can be applied to comparable settings, whereas it is often difficult to generalize the findings of traditional laboratory experiments to real-life situations. Since imagination plays an important part in life itself, he would add, there is no reason why make-believe and theatrical procedures should not enter into role-playing studies.

For an example of the use of role-playing in education, we refer you to 'Toreside Comprehensive School' by Ferguson.[34] This is a simulation game for teachers in training that has been run successfully with PGCE students at Liverpool University School of Education. Its objectives are to encourage student teachers to think about the relationships between their specialist subjects in a social setting that is typical of many secondary school senior common rooms. The simulation is structured on realism and conflict and involves four distinct phases:

Phase 1. Volunteer subjects are assigned to subject departments in the imaginary Toreside Comprehensive School (TCS). They are required to act out their roles as teachers of the actual subjects they themselves will eventually teach. They must devise and learn their own scripts. One person in each department is designated Head of Department.

Phase 2. TCS staff under the direction of the headmaster (played by the university tutor) take part in a staffroom discussion the object of which is to reinforce their roles and establish their identities in the minds of other role players.

Phase 3. The headmaster injects a crisis in the staffroom discussion, forcing participants to justify their positions as subject specialists and to explore the overlap and interrelations with other subjects. This is done within an atmosphere charged with those 'irrational' elements that characterize the real situation.

Phase 4. The simulation game is terminated and participants are asked to discuss the exercise in which they have taken part.

The majority of students taking part found the experience to be interesting, enjoyable and instructive.

PERSONAL CONSTRUCTS

We come now to one of the most interesting theories of personality to have emerged this century and one that has particular relevance for the interpretive researcher – *personal construct theory*. It is associated with George Kelly and reflects a clinical approach to understanding personality. It was developed, as were the theories of Freud and Carl Rogers, out of actual contact by its founder with clients who were undergoing therapy. The theory itself is holistic in that Kelly regards the individual person as a totality who must be treated as such. As he expresses it himself, it is the individual person, rather than any part of him, or any group of persons that is the concern of the clinicians. Although Kelly's theory is similar to the theories of Freud and Rogers in that it arose out of clinical practice, it is vastly different in that it is a *cognitive* theory of personality. This means that it stresses the way in which an individual perceives his environment, the way he interprets what he perceives in terms of his existing mental structures, and the way in which, as a consequence, he behaves towards it. The theory is generally regarded as an extremely courageous and imaginative attempt to interpret behaviour in cognitive terms and, more than any other, it is closely related to a technique of personality assessment that is structured, direct and voluntary.

As Kelly is inextricably linked with personal construct theory, it is fitting at this point if we make a slight detour to say a little about the man himself, particularly since his views are compatible to a marked degree with the interpretive perspective on human behaviour. He began his career as a school psychologist in which capacity he dealt with problem children referred to him by teachers. As his experience widened, instead of merely corroborating a teacher's complaint about a pupil, he began to try to understand the complaint in the way the teacher construed it. This change of perspective constituted a significant reformulation of the problem. In practical terms, it resulted in an analysis of the teacher making the complaint as well as the problem pupils. In thus viewing a problem from a wider angle, it was possible to envisage a wider range of solutions. The insights Kelly gained from his clinical work led him to the view that there is no objective, absolute truth and that events are only meaningful in relation to the ways they are construed by the individual. As Pervin notes:[35] 'In Kelly we have a man who dismissed truth in any absolute sense and, therefore, felt free to reconstrue phenomena; a man who challenged the concept of 'objective reality' and felt free to play in the world of make-believe; a man who perceived events as occurring to individuals and, therefore, was interested in the interpretation of these events by individuals; a man who viewed his own theory as only tentative and who consequently was free to challenge views that others accepted as dogma.'

In general terms, Kelly was quite explicit on his views of man's nature. For him, *man is a scientist* in the sense that in his day-to-day life he tries to predict and control phenomena and to anticipate and manipulate events around him. Kelly sees himself in this way, as having theories, putting hypotheses to the test, considering the evidence, and concludes that it is not unreasonable to suppose others are the same. As Pervin says: 'Man experiences events, perceives similarities and differences among these events, formulates concepts or constructs to order phenomena and, on the basis of these constructs, seeks to anticipate events.' To the extent that all men use constructs to organize reality, they are similar. Where they differ, however, is in the constructs they employ.

There are two consequences of this view of man. First, it means that man is essentially oriented to the future; paraphrasing Kelly, we may say that anticipation is carried on so that the future reality may be better represented. And second, it follows that man has the capacity to *represent* the environment rather than merely *respond* to it. And he *represents* it through his own constructs – his personal constructs – by means of which he interprets and re-interprets, construes and re-construes his environment.

Kelly's views on the nature of science are based on the notion of *constructive alternativism*. Adherents of this philosophical position deny the existence of objective reality or absolute truth. Instead, the phenomena of experience may be construed in different ways, each way being equally valid. Kelly went against the mainstream of scientific thinking in a number of ways. He believed, for instance, in the freedom to regard 'make-believe' as an essential feature of science; and that subjective thinking is an important step in the scientific process because it may induce an 'invitational mood' in which one is free to consider as many things as possible. There may be alternative interpretations of an event; or even conflicting hypotheses to explain it. In summary, Kelly rejects what he sees as the restrictive dogma of traditional science in favour of a more creative, open-to-experience stance.

Having outlined Kelly's theory of man and his views of science, we are now in a position to say a little more about his theory of personality. It follows from what we have said that the basic concept in this theory is *the construct*. This is a person's way of construing, or interpreting, events around him in order to determine how he should behave. In Kelly's view, a person *anticipates* events by construing their replications; his thinking is future-oriented. This is in contrast to the traditional view which sees a person as *reacting* to an event. As one writer has said,[36] 'We react not to the stimulus but to what we interpret the stimulus to be.' Thus it is that an individual's personality is his construct system. The constructs he uses enable him to define and interpret his world; it is through them that he can anticipate events.

Kelly went on to develop his own assessment technique which grew out of his personal construct theory. It is known as the *Role Construct Repertory Grid Method* (the Rep. Test) and was designed to be used as a test for eliciting personal constructs. As a test, it is distinctive in being very closely related to a theory of personality. It appears in various forms, though there is a basic procedure common to all. This may be illustrated as follows: a person is asked to name a number of people who are significant to him (these might be *teacher*, *priest*, *mother*, *father*, *friend* and *employer*, for instance). These are known as *elements* in the grid and may on other occasions be objects or concepts. The subject is then asked to arrange the elements into groups of three's in such a manner that two are similar in some way but at the same time different from the third. The ways in which the people may be alike or different are the *constructs* and are usually expressed in bi-polar form (quiet–talkative, mean–generous, warm–cold). The way in which two of the people are similar is called the *similarity* pole of the construct; and the way in which two of the people are different from the third, the *contrast pole* of the construct. A grid can now be constructed by asking the subject to place each person (or element) at either the similarity or contrast pole of each construct (x = one end of the pole, a blank = the other). The result could be as follows:

Constructs	Elements					
	A	B	C	D	E	F
1. quiet – talkative	x	x	x			x
2. mean – generous	x				x	x
3. warm – cold		x			x	

It is now possible to derive different kinds of information from the grid. By studying each row, for example, we can get some idea of how an individual defines each construct in terms of the significant people in his life. From each column, we have a personality profile of each of the significant people in terms of the constructs selected by the subject. At a more sophisticated level, scores derived from the responses can be treated statistically which will result in a *construct universe* for each individual which Kelly claims will define the major personality variables of that individual. There have been a number of instances of the method being used with children and in the context of the school generally.[37]

NON-DIRECTIVE INTERVIEWING

Originating from, and perhaps most readily associated with, psychiatric and therapeutic fields, the *non-directive interview* is characterized by a situation in which the respondent is responsible for directing the course of the interview and for the attitudes he expresses in it (in contrast to the other kinds of interview noted earlier). It has been shown to be a particularly valuable technique because it gets at the deeper attitudes and perceptions of the person being interviewed in such a way as to leave them free from the bias of the interviewer. We shall consider briefly the characteristics of the therapeutic interview and then examine its usefulness as a research technique in the social sciences.

The non-directive, or therapeutic, interview as it is currently understood grew out of the pioneering work of Freud and subsequent modifications to his approach by later analysts. His basic discovery was that if one can arrange a special set of conditions and have his patient talk about his difficulties in a certain way, behaviour changes of many kinds can be accomplished.[38] The techniques developed sought to elicit highly personal data from patients in such a way as to increase the patients' insights and skills in self-analysis, thereby enabling them to help themselves. As Madge[39] observes, it is these techniques which have greatly influenced contemporary interviewing techniques, especially those of a more penetrating and less quantitative kind.

The present-day therapeutic interview has its most persuasive advocate in Carl Rogers who has on different occasions testified to its efficacy. Basing his analysis on his own clinical studies, he has identified a number of characteristic stages in the therapeutic process, beginning with the client's decision to go for help.[40] The counsellor who meets him is friendly and receptive, but not didactic. The next stage is signalled when the client begins to give vent to hostile, critical and destructive feelings. These the counsellor accepts, recognizes, and clarifies. Subsequently, and *invariably*, these antagonistic impulses are used up and give way to the first expressions of positive feeling. The counsellor accepts these also until suddenly and spontaneously 'insight and self-understanding come bubbling through.' With insight comes the realization of possible courses of action and also the power to make decisions. It is in translating these into practical terms that the client frees himself from dependence on the counsellor.

Rogers[41] subsequently identified a number of qualities in the interviewer which he deemed essential: that he bases his work on attitudes of acceptance and permissiveness; that he respects the client's responsibility for his situation; that he permits the client to explain his problem in his own way; and that he does nothing that would in any way arouse the client's defences.

Such then are the principal characteristics of the non-directive interview in a therapeutic setting. But what of its usefulness as a purely *research* technique in the social sciences? There are a number of features of the therapeutic interview which are peculiar to it and may very well be inappropriate in other contexts: for example, the interview is initiated by the respondent; his motivation is to obtain relief from a particular symptom; the interviewer is primarily a source of help, not a procurer of information; the actual interview is part of the therapeutic experience; the purpose of the interview is to change the behaviour and inner life of the person and its success is defined in these terms; and there is no restriction on the topics discussed.

A researcher has a different order of priorities and what appear as advantages in a therapeutic context may be decided limitations when the technique is used for research purposes, even though he may be sympathetic to the spirit of the non-directive interview. As Madge explains, increasingly there are those 'who wish to retain the good qualities of the non-directive technique and at the same time are keen to evolve a method that is economical and precise enough to leave a residue of results rather than merely a posse of cured souls.'[39]

One attempt to meet this need is to be found in a programme reported by Merton and Kendall[42] in which the *focused interview* was developed. While seeking to follow closely the principle of non-direction, the method did introduce rather more interviewer control in the kinds of questions permitted and sought also to limit the discussion to certain parts of the respondent's experience.

The chief value of the non-directive interview and related techniques in education lies in the sounding of attitudes and opinions.

CONTENT ANALYSIS

We conclude our review of research methods in education and the social sciences with a brief examination of the technique known as *content analysis*.

Because the communication process is so vital a part of social interaction from the interpersonal to the international level, the study of the processes and content of communication is a fundamental responsibility of all the social sciences. Consequently, the task has been tackled from a number of contrasting viewpoints and with a variety of tools and conceptual schemata.

Content analysis itself has been described as 'a multipurpose research method developed specifically for investigating a broad spectrum of problems in which the content of communication serves as the basis of inference.'[43] The problems of definition due to changes over time and the nature of the particular problem being studied which we have encountered elsewhere in this chapter beset us again here. If anything, definitions of the term have tended to become less restrictive over the years and for this reason we favour the inclusive definition proposed by Holsti: 'Content analysis is any technique for making inferences by systematically and objectively identifying specified characteristics of messages.'[43] He explains that in a systematic analysis, the inclusion and exclusion of content or categories is done according to consistently applied criteria of selection; and that to have objectivity, an analysis must be carried out on the basis of explicitly formulated rules which will enable two or more persons to obtain the same results from the same documents. Specified characteristics may include readability, for example, or the number of three-syllable words, styles, changes of content, propaganda, and so on.

In his excellent methodological discussion of content analysis, Berelson[44] designates three broad approaches to the analysis of symbolic materials. In the first of these, the researcher is primarily interested in the characteristics of the content itself. In the second, he makes inferences from the nature of the content to features of the sources of the content – either its authors or causes. And in the third, he uses the content to find out something about the recipients or the nature of its effects on the audience for which it is intended. Studies of content analysis may use one or more of these approaches.

With the first approach, the *characteristics of the content*, it is possible to describe trends in communication content; to analyse techniques of persuasion; to compare the various communications of the mass media; to analyse psychological characteristics of individuals; to measure readability of communication materials – particularly relevant in educational contexts; to discover stylistic features; and so on. In studying the *producers or causes of the content*, one can identify the intentions and other characteristics of the communicators; determine the psychological states of persons or groups – no more relevant than in times of international crises or tension; and obtain military or political intelligence. The third approach, the *effects of the content on its recipients*, permits of inferences about the attitudes, interests, abilities, and values of individuals, groups, and populations; their focus of attention; and their attitudinal and behavioural responses to communications.

Understandably, the application of the techniques of content analysis to the field of education has tended to be restricted to examinations of the substantive nature of content. Areas which have been investigated in recent years, while by no means extensive, include: children's compositions; children's conversations; textbooks; readability; curriculum issues; the development of taxonomies; and the measurement of motivation. We recommend that you have a look at Kounin and Gump's study of the influence of punitive and non-punitive teachers on children's concepts of school misconduct[45]; and also Child, Potter, and Levine's[46] examination of children's textbooks and personality development. Both of these studies are reported in Kerlinger.[6] More typically, perhaps, Woods[47] applies the techniques to an analysis of children's reports, a study to which we shall return in Chapter 4.

SUMMARY

We began the chapter by taking up again the theme with which we concluded our opening chapter, namely, the normative and interpretive paradigms. We looked in particular at the researchers involved with the two methods focusing our attention on the kinds of data they would gather and the functions the data would serve in their respective research endeavours. We then went on to outline the characteristics of the principal methods of research used in both normative and interpretive studies. Beginning with those associated with the former, we then considered the kinds of approaches used in interpretive studies.

ENQUIRY AND DISCUSSION

1. What part do data play in normative research? How does this compare with the way they are used in interpretive research?

2. What is the difference between quantitative and qualitative data?

3. What is the relationship between data and theory from a normative researcher's perspective? How does it compare with the stance taken by an interpretive researcher?

4. Discuss Kaplan's notions of *act meaning* and *action meaning*. How far is the normative researcher correct in assuming that shared meanings exist between himself and the subjects he is studying?

5. Distinguish between the roles of the participant observer and the non-participant observer. Compare and contrast any two educational studies in which the techniques of participant and non-participant observation respectively are used.

6. Identify the significant differences between experimental, quasi-experimental and causal research.

7. Devise a small-scale action-research-based project that you could conduct with a class of children over a period of four to six weeks.

8. How would you justify the use of accounts in educational research to a committed normative researcher?

NOTES AND REFERENCES

1. Note: In his *Introduction to Educational Research* (1969) (New York: Macmillan), R. M. W. Travers says that facts collected by scientists are generally referred to as *data* to distinguish them from the day-to-day collection of information in which everyone engages. In this sense, he explains, they represent a special class of information in that they are collected under precisely specified conditions and have meaning only in relation to these conditions.

2. Schwartz, H. and Jacobs, J. (1979) *Qualitative Sociology: A Method to the Madness*. New York: The Free Press.

3. (Ed.) Filstead, W. J. (1970) *Qualitative Methodology: Firsthand Involvement with the Social World*. New York: Markham.

4. Kaplan, A. (1973) *The Conduct of Inquiry*. Aylesbury: Intertext Books.

5. Note: A sample may be defined as a smaller group or a sub-set of a considerably larger population. A range of sampling procedures are available to the researcher.

6. Kerlinger, F. N. (1969) *Foundations of Behavioral Research*. New York: Holt, Rinehart and Winston.

7. Moser, C. A. (1966) *Survey Methods in Social Investigation*. London: Heinemann Educational Books.

8. Cohen, L. (1976) *Educational Research in Classrooms and Schools*. London: Harper and Row.

9. Becker, H. S. and Geer, B. (1970) Participant observation and interviewing. In *Qualitative Methodology: Firsthand Involvement with the Social World*. (Ed.) Filstead, W. J. New York: Markham.

10. For example: Hargreaves, D. H. (1967) *Social Relations in a Secondary School*. London: Routledge and Kegan Paul; Becker, H. S., Geer, B., Hughes, E. C. and Strauss, A. L. (1961) *Boys in White*. Chicago: University of Chicago Press; Olesen, V. L. and Whittaker, E. W. (1968) *The Silent Dialogue: A Study in the Social Psychology of Professional Socialization*. San Francisco: Jossey-Bass.

11. Rutter, M., Maughan, B., Mortimore, P. and Onslow, J. (1979) *Fifteen Thousand Hours*. London: Open Books.

12. Cohen, L. and Manion, L. (1980) *Research Methods in Education*. London: Croom Helm.

13. Isaac, S. and Michael, W. B. (1971) *Handbook of Research and Evaluation*. California: Robert R. Knapp.

14. Wolcott, H. F. (1973) *The Man in the Principal's Office*. New York: Holt, Rinehart and Winston.

15. Lambert, R., Bullock, R. and Millham, S. (1975) *The Chance of a Lifetime?* London: Weidenfeld and Nicolson.

16. King, R. (1979) *All Things Bright and Beautiful?* Chichester: J. Wiley.

17. Bailey, K. D. (1978) *Methods of Social Research*. London: Collier Macmillan.

18. Travers, R. M. W. (1969) *Introduction to Educational Research*. New York: Macmillan and Co.

19. Note: Covariant factors are those factors which change together in such a way as to make it difficult or impossible to know which is the cause and which the effect.

20. Cohen, L. and Child, D. (1969) Some sociological and psychological factors in university failure, *Durham Research Review*, **22,** 365–372.

21. (Ed.) Halsey, A. H. (1972) *Educational Priority, Volume 1: E.P.A. Problems and Policies.* London: HMSO.

22. Columbro, M. N. (1964) Supervision and action research. In *Educational Leadership*, **21**, 297–300.

23. Hoyle, E. (1973) The study of schools as organizations. In *Educational Research in Britain 3.* (Eds.) Butcher, H. J. and Pont, H.B. London: University of London Press.

24. Cooper, D. and Ebbutt, D. (1974) Participation in action research as an in-service experience. *Cambridge Journal of Education*, **42**, 65–71.

25. Shipman, M. D., Bolam, D. and Jenkins, D. (1974) *Inside a Curriculum Project.* London: Methuen and Co.

26. Smith, H. W. (1975) Strategies of social research. *The Methodological Imagination.* New York: Prentice-Hall.

27. Denzin, N. K. (1970) *The Research Act.* Chicago: Aldine Press.

28. Marsh, P., Rosser, E. and Harré, R. (1978) *The Rules of Disorder.* London: Routledge and Kegan Paul.

29. Brown, J. and Sime, J. D. (1977) *Accounts as a General Methodology.* Paper presented to the British Psychological Society, Exeter.

30. Woods, P. and Hammersley, M. (1977) *School Experience.* London: Croom Helm.

31. Borg, W. R. (1963) *Educational Research: An Introduction.* New York: Longmans.

32. Harré, R. and Secord, P. F. (1972) *The Explanation of Social Behaviour.* Oxford: Basil Blackwell.

33. Freedman, J. L. (1969) Role-playing: psychology by consensus. *Journal of Personality and Social Psychology*, **13**, 107–114.

34. Ferguson, S. (1977) Toreside Comprehensive School: a simulation game for teachers in training. In *Aspects of Simulation and Gaming.* (Ed.) Megarry, J. London: Kogan Page.

35. Pervin, L. A. (1970) *Personality: Theory, Assessment and Research.* New York: J. Wiley.

36. Child, D. (1977) *Psychology and the Teacher.* Eastbourne: Holt, Rinehart and Winston, 2nd Edition.

37. See, for example, Chapter 5, *How Pupils See It.*

38. Ford, D. H. and Urban, H. B. (1963) *Systems of Psychotherapy: A Comparative Study.* New York: J. Wiley.

39. Madge, J. (1965) *The Tools of Social Science.* London: Longmans.

40. Rogers, C. R. (1942) *Counseling and Psychotherapy.* Boston: Houghton Mifflin.

41. Rogers, C. R. (1945) The non-directive method as a technique for social research. *American Journal of Sociology*, **50**, 279–282.

42. Merton, R. K. and Kendall, P. L. (1946) The focused interview. *American Journal of Sociology*, **51**, 541–557.

43. Holsti, O. R. (1968) Content analysis. In *The Handbook of Social Psychology, Volume II, Research Methods.* (Eds.) Lindzey, G. and Aronson, E. New York: Addison-Wesley.

44. Berelson, E. (1952) *Content Analysis in Communication Research.* Glencoe, Illinois: The Free Press.

45. Kounin, J. and Gump, P. (1961) The comparative influence of punitive and non-punitive teachers upon children's concepts of school misconduct. *Journal of Educational Psychology*, **52**, 44–49.

46. Child, I., Potter, E. and Levine, E. (1960) Children's textbooks and personality development: an exploration in the social psychology of education. *Psychological Monographs*, **60**, 3.

47. Woods, P. (1979) *The Divided School.* London: Routledge and Kegan Paul.

SELECTED READING

1. Cohen, L. and Manion, L. (1980) *Research Methods in Education.* London: Croom Helm. A review of the principal research methods used in education with recent examples from the literature.

2. (Ed.) Filstead, W. J. (1970) *Qualitative Methodology: Firsthand Involvement with the Social World.* New York: Markham. A selection of articles on aspects of interpretive research.

3. Kerlinger, F. N. (1969) *Foundations of Behavioural Research.* New York: Holt, Rinehart and Winston. A standard work on normative methods of research.

4. King, M. and Ziegler, M. (1975) *Research Projects in Social Psychology*, Monterey, California: Brookes/Cole. An introduction to research methods in social psychology.

5. Millman, J. and Gowin, D. B. (1974) *Appraising Educational Research*, Englewood Cliffs, N. J.: Prentice-Hall. An analysis of eight educational research papers of increasing difficulty.

6. Rosenthal, R. and Rosnow, R. L. (1975) *Primer of Methods for the Behavioural Sciences*, New York: J. Wiley. A brief introduction to research methods and strategies in the behavioural sciences.

3

Educational Attainment

The key word in the title of our book is '*Perspectives*'. We use it to signal our intention to employ several social science approaches in exploring the topics that constitute the separate chapters of our text. The present chapter is no exception. Few topics we have chosen to write about, however, are as complex as *educational attainment*. Indeed, *complex* is somewhat of an understatement when one recalls that in developing their multi-causal model of educational attainment, the Plowden Committee researchers identified no fewer than one hundred and twenty relevant variables!

Our appraisal of the topic is more modest. It arises out of an overall orientation that we described in our introductory chapter as *social scientific*. Pupil, classroom, and school factors in educational attainment are our present concern.

We begin with a brief review of some social factors that are associated with children's achievement in school. This serves as a backcloth to self-contained cameos of *the pupil, the classroom*, and *the school* that then follow. Our separating-out of pupil, classroom and school influences is, of course, purely for purposes of exposition. In reality, these and many other variables interact in complex ways that are as yet only partly understood.

SOCIAL FACTORS IN EDUCATIONAL ATTAINMENT

There is now ample evidence about the relationship between certain social factors and children's attainment. The *National Survey of Health and Development*, a longitudinal study undertaken by Douglas and his co-workers[1] showed that from an early age, differences in pupils' literacy and numeracy are associated with family size and with father's occupation. Such differences moreover, persist throughout secondary schooling to the point of statutory leaving.

A decade after the pioneering research of Douglas, another investigation, *The National Child Development Study*,[2] is currently following a representative sample of British children from birth to adulthood. Preliminary reports from this study show that the factors of social class and family size continue to be associated with substantial differences in children's attainment at the ages of seven[3] and eleven.[4]

The most recently published analyses of the *National Child Development Study* data are concerned with the question of whether the differences between groups of children defined by social class and family size are relatively stable or whether they tend to increase during the period of schooling. These latest findings indicate that the patterns of difference found at the age of eleven, when relatively advantaged children from small, middle-class families show an increasing superiority in their attainment in mathematics and reading, continue to the age of sixteen.

What do these analyses actually say about social class and family size factors as they affect educational attainment? Just how potent are they? As far as social class background is concerned, at sixteen years of age, only 15 % of children from unskilled–manual families can be expected to score above the average mark obtained by middle-class pupils[5] on mathematical and reading attainment tests. The relationship of family size to educational attainment is less straightforward. Much, it seems, depends upon whether other siblings are younger or older than the child being studied. Generally speaking, reading attainment differences are greater than those for mathematics. Moreover the differences associated with the number of older children in the family are greater than those for the number of younger children. It appears that the gap in attainment related to the number of older children in the household is one that develops throughout the years of compulsory schooling.[5]

The National Survey of Health and Development study of Douglas and his associates also revealed differences between the Intelligence Quotients* of children from different social class backgrounds. As in the case of mathematical and reading attainment, these differences were shown to widen as the children grew older. Explanations[6] of the relationship between measured IQ and social factors such as those employed in the longitudinal studies of Douglas[1] and Davie[2] suggest that the concept of measured intelligence should be treated with some circumspection. The account of ability and attainment that now follows is duly cautious.

PUPIL FACTORS IN EDUCATIONAL ATTAINMENT

Ability

We want to avoid a protracted discourse on the nature of intelligence or reference to the nature/nurture controversy in our discussion of the relationship between a pupil's ability

---

* Intelligence Quotient (IQ for short) derives from the concept of *mental age* which is generally expressed in terms of the pupil's *chronological age*. A *mental ratio* is obtained by dividing the child's mental age by his chronological age. This is multiplied by 100 to give his *Intelligence Quotient*.

and his educational attainment. Because there is no way of directly assessing the inborn intellectual potential of a child or of disentangling the countless environmental influences at work, we propose to short cut any discussion of *intelligence per se* and instead, to adopt a definition of *intelligent behaviour* which enables us to take account of the numerous verbal and non-verbal tests that go to make up the armamentarium of the modern psychological investigator. If intelligent behaviour can be thought of as consisting of 'grasping the essentials in a given situation and responding appropriately to them'[7], then the appropriateness of children's responses to intelligence tests is a strong predictor of their future performance on measures of educational attainment, as the work of numerous researchers has shown. We select a recent study by way of example.

Youngman[8] sought to identify the various pupil characteristics that might determine academic performance in secondary school. In addition to *biographical* data (sex and age), his measures included *dispositional* factors (attitudes and personality traits) and *intellectual* factors (ability and prior achievement). Youngman's aim was to assess the nature of the *independent* effects of these pupil characteristics on early secondary school attainment. Put simply, he asked, how strongly does each of these factors *alone* predict pupil performance? In parallel samples of children drawn from rural and urban schools, Youngman* demonstrated the superior power of ability measures to predict performance in contrast to the relative weakness of *attitudinal and personality* assessments. He found that when the biographical and dispositional measures he had chosen were controlled, ability measures were significantly associated with children's attainment on tests of mathematical understanding and reading comprehension. Conversely, neither biographical nor dispositional measures independently determined performance. While Youngman's findings show intellectual measures to be the most important determinants of educational attainment they do *not* thereby rule out non-intellectual variables, for, as we have already noted, social class and family size also relate to educational performance.

Personality

The association between various assessments of personality and educational achievement is by no means as clear as the relationship between ability and attainment that we have just outlined. Two particular dimensions of personality have attracted attention in recent years resulting in a spate of studies using Eysenck's[9] personality inventories in British schools and institutions of higher education. Eysenck proposes that an individual's personality can be expressed along two main dimensions of behaviour. The first, *extraversion*, describes how socially outgoing a person is; the second, *neuroticism*, describes how prone he is to excessive anxiety. Some examples of statements from a short form of Eysenck's inventory together with the direction of their scoring are set out in Box 3.1.

Findings from a number of studies suggest a trend in the relationship between extraversion and attainment. Broadly speaking, extraverts do better when they are younger, but from about fourteen years of age onwards, it is introverts who tend to

---

* Criticisms have been raised in recent years about making direct comparisons between results obtained on intelligence tests and those gained on attainment tests, mainly on statistical grounds but also because intelligence and attainment tests overlap considerably in their content.[10]

BOX 3.1

Extraversion–Introversion (E), Neuroticism–Stability (N) items
from the Junior Eysenck Personality Inventory (JEPI)

Do you nearly always have a quick answer when people talk to you?	(E)
Do you get a thumping in your heart?	(N)
Do you like going out a lot?	(E)
Do you often make up your mind when it is too late?	(N)
Do you like mixing with other children?	(E)
Do you often feel fed-up?	(N)

The scoring key at the right hand side of each question shows whether a 'yes' answer is counted on the E or the N scale.

succeed better in their educational tasks. No such trend has been identified in connection with neuroticism and achievement. Overall, these findings seem a poor pay off for the amount of research effort that has gone into exploring the relationship between personality and attainment. However, the problem is complex, and the paucity of adequate research designs which take account of clouding factors such as different teaching methods and different measures of attainment has hindered progress. That is one side of the coin. The other is to do with the adequacy of Eysenck's approach to personality. Critics[11] have pointed to the oversimplification of his two-dimensional theory and to the fact that he tells us nothing about the unconscious or about long term needs or aspirations. Of more importance to intending teachers is the question of relevance of Eysenck's personality measures in helping teachers in their work with individual children. We have seen that his tests identify broad trends, extraverts, for example do *tend* to do better during the earlier years of schooling than do introverts. But they do not tell us much about individual children; many introverts perform perfectly well in lower school just as many extraverts succeed in higher education. Finally, Eysenck's approach tells us little about the majority of children who bunch toward the centre of the distributions on the dimensions E and N, and who are neither markedly extravert nor introvert, neurotic nor stable.

Less use has been made in Britain of Cattell's[12] Sixteen Personality Factor Questionnaire (16 PF) which, as the name implies, suggests an approach to personality that identifies many more than the two major dimensions of Eysenck. The difference however is more apparent than real since many of Cattell's factors correlate with one another and, when grouped together into broader clusterings which he calls source traits (the two most important of which are identified as *extraversion* and *anxiety*), bear a remarkable similarity to Eysenck's dimensions.

Clearly, personality dimensions are influential in children's educational attainment and in their attitudes towards work. Variations in school achievement are not entirely a question of ability but depend to some extent upon the personal characteristics which can enhance or inhibit the quality of that achievement.

Achievement Motivation

Teachers have long recognized that factors other than, or as well as, ability are related to school achievement. An obvious factor in educational attainment is the desire on the part of pupils to succeed. The topic has been widely investigated by researchers using a variety of motivation measures. Psychologists argue that need for achievement (n'ach for short) is a trait that varies within the population, those with high n'ach being more ready to undertake achievement related tasks and having stronger desires to achieve success than to avoid failure.[13] A related psychological concept to do with motivation and learning is *locus of control*.[14] Briefly, where locus of control is *internal*, a person will attribute success to ability and to necessary effort, while failure will be explained in terms of insufficient application. Conversely, individuals with *external* locus of control are less inclined to see actions as related to outcomes, more readily seeing fate, luck, or a variety of external factors as having played a part. Clearly, n'ach and locus of control have important bearing upon school achievement. There are some broadly similar findings reported in studies that have employed one or other of these two conceptualizations of achievement motivation. In one investigation,[15] scores on an academic motivation inventory were found to relate more closely to pupils' educational attainment than to their reasoning ability. In another,[16] internal locus of control had only a low correlation with intelligence, but was second only to IQ as a predictor of school achievement.

Recalling the discussion in our opening chapter on the application of scientific methods to educational problems, it can be seen that both of these studies are at that stage of sophistication where efforts are made to establish relationships between variables within a tentative framework of psychological theory. One study, however, has tried to go beyond this point to the more difficult task of mapping out the *process of achievement*. It was undertaken in British secondary schools by Banks and Finlayson[17] who sought to tease out factors associated with educational achievement and to say something about their interrelationships over time. The researchers used a technique called hierarchical linkage analysis, a method which groups variables into a series of 'clusters' in such a way that each variable is placed beside those other variables to which it is most highly related. Cluster analysis data can be represented diagrammatically, the variables being linked by lines at different levels: the lower the level at which variables or groups of variables link together, the closer the relationship. We invite the interested reader to conjecture upon the process of achievement as shown in Box 3.2, before reading Banks and Finlayson's explanation in Chapter 6 of their book.

Achievement motivation is learned behaviour, its development beginning in early childhood as a result of the reinforcements of successful activities. The direction and intensity of such reinforcements in producing children with high and low needs for achievement has been shown in a well-known study of parental behaviour towards their sons conducted by Rosen and D'Andrade.[18] Comparing children with high and low n'ach, the researchers characterized the parents of high n'ach children as:

1. Giving more encouragement during a task;
2. Giving more affection on the successful completion of the task;
3. Less likely to show irritation in the event of failure; and
4. Less likely to burden children with over-detailed instructions on how the task should be carried out.

To conclude, our account of achievement motivation research shows that it has been largely psychological in its orientation. We believe that there is a need to redress this imbalance by putting the concept of achievement motivation into a broader theoretical framework of *individual – task – context causation*. This would involve two distinct yet

BOX 3.2

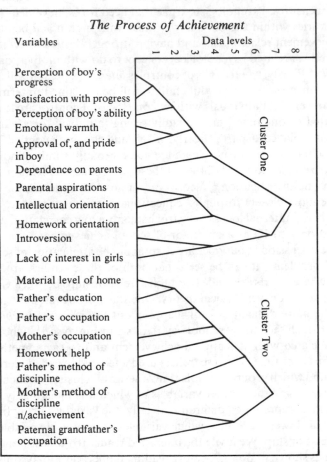

Source: Banks and Finlayson[17]

related orientations on our part. First we should need to ask to what extent particular characteristics of tasks and contexts elicit the need to achieve in certain individuals? Isn't this, after all, what most teachers are about; creating motivation on the spot – in classrooms, in gymnasia, in laboratories – by manipulating tasks in particular contexts for specific pupils? Second, we should need to inquire to what extent need for achievement is related to the location of certain groups within the wider social structure.

Self-Concept

If studies of achievement motivation are numerous, then investigations of pupils' self-concepts and their educational attainment are legion. We touch upon only a fraction of the vast literature[19] on the self-concept.

For present purposes, self-concept can be thought of as the image we have of ourselves as a result of our interactions with important people in our lives. That image consists of all the attitudes, abilities, and assumptions that we hold concerning ourselves. It serves as a guide to our behaviour, affecting the ways in which we approach tasks and the level at which we perform them. One aspect of self-concept that has been widely researched in education is self-esteem. Coopersmith[20] defines self-esteem as the amount of worthiness an individual perceives in himself/herself. We illustrate part of Coopersmith's measure of self-esteem in Box 3.3. The full scale contains 23 items.

BOX 3.3

Coopersmith Self-Esteem Scale Items

I'm not as nice looking as most people.
I often feel upset at school.
I'm a lot of fun to be with.
My parents understand me.
Children pick on me very often.
I never worry about anything.
I'm easy to like.
I don't care what happens to me.

Source: adapted from Coopersmith[20]

Coopersmith's self-esteem scale is typical of many global measures of self that have been used in studies of abilities, attainments, attitudes and values. For example, a recent investigation by Bagley and his associates[21] involving over 400 boys and girls in 18 secondary schools in North-east England reported average correlations between global self-esteem measured on the Coopersmith scale and various intellectual measures as follows:

IQ (.14); Reading Attainment (.01); Critical Thinking Test (.15)

Studies that have used global self-concept measures such as the one illustrated in Box 3.3 have been criticized by Brookover[22] for their lack of specificity, his argument drawing upon the concept of a 'multidimensional self' first proposed some forty years ago by Mead.[23] Brookover's critique is as follows:

'Definitions of self such as "I am noisy", "I am fat", or "I am not talented", may be respectively predictive of how a boy will behave when his teacher leaves the room, the snugness of the clothing he will select, or whether he will take music lessons, *but when added together into a global "real self" may be of little value in predicting his school attendance pattern*.' (our emphasis)

It is more reasonable, he contends, to view the global self-concept as composed of many specific self-concepts, one of which, the *self-concept of ability*, impinges directly upon *academic attainment*.

This is the thrust of Brookover's argument. In a series of longitudinal studies, one of which involved following a cohort of students through the six years of their secondary schooling, Brookover demonstrated the superiority of his specific self-concept measure to predict overall educational attainment when compared with global measures of self-esteem, perhaps an inevitable conclusion when self-concept of ability is assessed by asking questions such as those itemized in Box 3.4 below. Correlations between self-concept of

BOX 3.4

Self-Concept of Ability

How do you rate yourself in school ability compared with those in your class at school?

a. I am the best
b. I am above average
c. I am average
d. I am below average
e. I am the poorest

What kind of grades do you think you are capable of getting?

a. mostly A's
b. mostly B's
c. mostly C's
d. mostly D's
e. mostly E's

In order to become a doctor, lawyer, or university professor, work beyond four years of college is necessary. How likely do you think it is that you could complete such advanced work?

a. very likely
b. somewhat likely
c. not sure either way
d. unlikely
e. most unlikely

Source: adapted from Brookover[22]

ability and grade point average ranged from .43 to .63 over the six years. By contrast, correlations between global self-concept measures and school achievement more typical fall between .20 and .30.

An important finding in Brookover's research was that although a significant proportion of students with high self-concepts of ability achieved at a relatively low level, practically none of the students with lower self-concepts of ability achieved at a high level. From this Brookover concluded that self-concept of ability is a *threshold variable*, that is, a necessary, but *not a sufficient condition for achievement*. The same holds true of the personality and achievement motivation measures that we discussed earlier.

To conclude this short review of self-concept studies we note that unlike the strong association between ability and attainment, the relationships between pupils' self-concepts and their school achievement are only moderately high, but (like those between personality, achievement motivation and attainment) they are sufficiently strong to suggest that teachers have an important part to play in establishing and maintaining positive self-images in their pupils. Specific suggestions as to ways in which pupils can be helped to gain more positive images of themselves as learners include the following:

1. Use teaching techniques which provide each pupil with honest, success experiences. Every pupil is capable of achieving successfully in some area.
2. Demonstrate a continuing faith in each student's ability to achieve. When he has gained confidence in his own abilities, his ability to learn is enhanced.

3. Point out areas of accomplishment rather than focusing on mistakes. Continuing awareness of failure results in lowered expectations, not learning.
4. Make time to talk to pupils, listen to them and support their attempts to express themselves.[24]

CLASSROOM FACTORS IN EDUCATIONAL ATTAINMENT

Explanations of attainment couched solely in terms of pupil attributes ignore other factors that must necessarily feature in an adequate account of school achievement.

The two remaining parts of this chapter are given over to a discussion of the *classroom* and the *school* as environments in which learning occurs. In the section that immediately follows, we identify a number of teacher variables that have been examined in relation to pupil achievement. We deal only briefly with *classroom groups and group processes* since this issue features in our discussions of open classrooms (Chapter 9) and mixed ability teaching (Chapter 7). To conclude the middle section we illustrate a number of recent studies that employ more sophisticated models of the classroom as a place of learning. In the final part of the chapter we look at research which has tried to answer the question, 'Just what is it that makes a school effective?'

Classrooms

The realities of classroom life as revealed in the daily transactions of pupils and teachers in many schools up and down the country stand in stark contrast to what some educational theorists believe is the potential of every classroom to become an exciting and invigorating place of effective learning. But classrooms are very much prisoners of their own history, are they not?

Four assumptions[25] appear to have underpinned the development of the classroom system. First, its prime task was to engender a basic literacy and numeracy and a respect for order in the mass of the population. Second, its model of the learning process drew upon a view of the mind as a muscle which best develops through appropriate exercise. Third, its goals reflected a view that knowledge is conscious and can be translated into words. Correspondingly, words can be translated into knowledge; hence one learns, that is, acquires knowledge, by being told. Finally, the teacher's task was to communicate ordained knowledge to pupils.

It is an open question as to how many contemporary classrooms have managed to escape the constraints of their formative history for in reviews of almost one hundred classroom studies of pupil achievement,[26] it is remarkable how many investigations have (a) employed literacy and numeracy skills as the criterion measures of educational attainment, (b) have been concerned with teacher instructional techniques in one form or another (describing, presenting, clarifying, structuring, questioning etc.) and (c) have used 'taught' materials as measures of educational attainment rather than original and creative work on the part of pupils.

Teacher Instruction

That some teachers are 'better' than others and that experienced practitioners* know a 'good' teacher when they see one is held to be self-evident. A great deal of educational discussion and practice is based upon these two assumptions. Moreover they have generated a considerable amount of educational research. Numerous studies[27] have been concerned to identify what it is that teachers actually *do* that relates to achievement on the part of their pupils. The following aspects of teachers' instructional behaviour by no means exhaust the lines of inquiry that have been reported to date:

1. The teacher's organisation (i.e. systematic, goal directed etc.).
2. The teacher's questioning (factual questions, higher level questions etc.).
3. The teacher's clarity (presentation of information, quality of explanation etc.).
4. The teacher's structuring (beginning, ending lessons, highlighting important parts etc.).
5. The teacher's use of praise.
6. The teacher's use of criticism.
7. The teacher's use of non-verbal approval (smiles, laughs, nods etc.).
8. The teacher's enthusiasm (degree of originality, stimulation of class etc.).
9. The teacher's flexibility and variety (richness and variety of classroom materials and activities).
10. The teacher's personality (warmth, aloofness etc.).
11. The teacher's use of pupils' ideas.

Earlier studies exploring teacher instructional variables used simple associative techniques in which a measure of a teacher variable is correlated with a measure of pupil achievement. Given the simplistic nature of the model of teaching implied in this type of research it is hardly surprising that a hotchpotch of conflicting results has been reported in respect of the great majority of the teacher factors identified above. But it is more than just a naïve model that hinders progress in this area of research. Often as not the variables themselves turn out to be multi-dimensional rather than unitary. Take for example *teacher clarity*. The conflicting results of studies to do with this aspect of the teacher's instructional repertoire arise, in part, from the fact that there is no universally acceptable definition of what teacher clarity is.

Recent studies[28] show teacher clarity to be a multidimensional concept that includes a range of teacher behaviours. In a series of studies, researchers went to over a thousand pupils in American and Australian schools with hundreds of statements about teacher behaviour and asked, 'Which of these behaviours are most often associated with clear teachers?'' Half of the pupils were asked which behaviours described their most clear teacher and the other half, the converse. The researchers identified four groupings of what they termed prime discriminators. Each of these broad groupings could be specifically

---

* During examinations of Final Teaching Practice, a colleague of one of the authors (an ex-headmistress) used to assert that she could *smell* a distinction (as opposed to a mere pass) the minute she put her nose into an Infants classroom!

described by reference to relevant statements of teacher instructional behaviour. We illustrate one such area, '*Providing pupil opportunity*', in Box 3.5 below.

BOX 3.5

Teacher Clarity: Providing Pupil Opportunity

The teacher frequently structures classroom activities to allow time for pupils to think about, respond to and synthesize what they are learning:

(a) gives us a chance to think about what's being taught
(b) explains something and then stops so we can think about it
(c) shows us how to remember things
(d) gives us enough time for practice
(e) teaches at a pace appropriate to the topic and pupils
(f) takes time when explaining
(g) answers pupil's questions
(h) stresses difficult points

Source: adapted from Cruickshank, Kennedy, Bush and Myers[28]

Greater conceptual clarity and the use of more sophisticated models of the teaching–learning process hold out promise of progress in this important area of research.

Teacher Expectations

Many studies have been made of the effects that scientists' expectations of their results have upon the actual findings that they come up with in their laboratories. Teachers, too, have come under the microscope of researchers seeking to understand the effects of teacher expectations upon pupil performance. To date there have been literally hundreds of studies of what have come to be known as *teacher expectation effects*. Two separate lines of inquiry can be identified in the research into teacher expectations. Onc is concerned with the unconscious selectivity and simplifications that teachers resort to in their dealings with children. The other is to do with the deliberate manipulation of teachers' judgements by educational researchers in order to monitor consequent effects upon pupil performance. We illustrate both lines of inquiry.

Rist[29] provides a disturbing account of one teacher's behaviour in a black, urban Infants classroom which was observed from the time of arrival of a new intake of young children. Rist traces the careers of the children from their day of arrival in school to their accomplishments three years later in Grade 2 of the Elementary School. Within a very short time of arrival, and *without any objective evidence of the children's capabilities*, the teacher had allocated each member of her class to one of three tables which then received different work, different amounts of attention, different incentives and different rewards. The teacher had decided upon the seating location of each child on the basis of her perceptions of his/her social class origins and potential ability. What is disturbing is that when Rist returned to the school system some three years later he found that almost the same differentiation existed between these children in their Grade 2 work and performance. The self-fulfilling prophecy had come true!

Self-fulfilling prophecies, it is argued,[30] arise when expectation effects follow a sequence, making a chain of behaviours as follows:

A. The teacher forms differential expectations for pupil performance

B. He then begins to treat children differently in accordance with his differential expectations

C. The children respond differentially to the teacher because they are being treated differently by him

D. In responding to the teacher, each child tends to exhibit behaviour which complements and reinforces the teacher's particular expectations for him

E. As a result, the general academic performance of some children will be enhanced while that of others will be depressed, with changes being in the direction of teacher expectations

F. These effects will show up in the achievement tests given at the end of the year, providing support for the 'self-fulfilling prophecy' notion.

A second study[31] involved the deliberate manipulation of information given to student teachers about pupils' race and social class background.

Intending teachers were given short vignettes describing certain children. For example:

> James Brewster is a ten year old white boy . . .
> His father is a waiter who earns $6000 per year…etc. etc.

The vignettes depicted children in terms of their race and the social class background of their homes. The student teachers were then required to select certain factors which they believed might affect the children's academic attainment over the course of the school year. For example:

1. The amount of effort the child makes;
2. His ability;
3. The difficulty of the work he is asked to do.

Depending on the child's race and social class, the student teachers held significantly different 'explanations' of the child's success at school. Thus recalling our discussion of locus of control earlier in the chapter, they believed that *white children do better than blacks because they are more 'internally responsible' for success or failure than black pupils.*

We give further examples of the effects of teacher expectations in our discussion of *Teacher Behaviour and Teacher Perspectives* in Chapter 4.

Informal Classroom Groups

The teacher's organization and use of various forms of classroom groupings is the subject of discussion in both Chapter 9 (*Open Education*) and Chapter 7 (*Mixed Ability Teaching*).

Here and now, we are concerned with the *informal groups* that arise out of the interactions of the pupil themselves. The structure and functioning of informal classroom groups in primary and secondary schools has been the subject of a great deal of research in Britain, so much so, in fact, that most student teachers know about the work of such familiar names as Hargreaves[32], Lacey[33], Nash[34], and Woods[35]. A common theme running through the findings of these researchers is the power of informal pupil groups to facilitate or to frustrate the teacher's attempts to induce learning. *Inter alia*, their researches have shown:

1. That classroom groups have differing norms, values, and beliefs;
2. That group values are closely allied to the goals that groups pursue;
3. That group norms arise out of the values that group members share;
4. That group norms serve to regulate the conduct of group members;
5. That group norms are enforced by sanctions which reward conformers and punish deviants;
6. That groups are differentiated by a hierarchy of ranks, the hierarchy being an indication of the differences in value placed upon individual members and the differences in power they enjoy;
7. That high ranking group members tend to be those who conform most closely to group norms.

But what has all this to do with pupil achievement? In a perceptive chapter, entitled, '*The Teacher and Group Dynamics*', Hargreaves[36] argues that the teacher is effective in his role as educational leader to the extent that he has extensive and systematic knowledge of the dynamics of the informal groups in his class. It is this knowledge that helps him to avoid making errors of perception, judgement and action. An informed teacher, Hargreaves asserts, would be able to answer the following five basic questions about a class of pupils:

1. What is the composition of the sub-groups or cliques within the class? Which pupils belong to which cliques?
2. What is the culture of each clique? What aspects of conduct are subject to the values and norms of each clique?
3. What is the structure of these cliques? How cohesive are they? Who are the leaders? Who are the most popular? Who are the most influential? Who are the low status members?
4. What is the relationship between cliques? Do they overlap in membership? Do they share a common culture? Is there a hierarchy of cliques? Is there evidence of hostility between cliques?
5. Which pupils do not belong to a clique? Are they aspirants to a clique but for some reason lack the qualifications for acceptance? Are they actively rejected by members? Are they socially isolated because they do not want to belong to a clique? Do they belong to another clique outside the class?

Learning the principles of group dynamics, of course, does not in itself guarantee that the teacher will be effective in promoting learning in his pupils. But it goes a long way to giving him the capacity to see things from their perspectives. We believe that this is such an important insight that we devote a whole chapter to it. (*How Pupils See It*, Chapter 5.)

The Complexity of Classroom Contexts

Global descriptions of classrooms as 'formal' or 'informal', 'traditional' or 'progressive', belie their realities as enormously intricate and continually changing webs of interaction. As researchers have come to grasp the complexity of classroom phenomena, so too their descriptions of classrooms have changed. Nowadays, the features by which classrooms are more commonly characterized are their *multidimensionality, simultaneity, immediacy* and *unpredictability*.[25] Not surprisingly, these new realizations have produced more detailed, sophisticated models of classrooms as guides to educational research. In general, newer models try to take account of the *interactive* nature of the teacher, pupil, and contextual classroom variables that are operative at any one time. We illustrate these more realistic conceptualizations of classrooms by reference to two recent studies.

The research of Madaus and his colleagues[37] was concerned with the effectiveness of secondary schools in the Republic of Ireland. The model guiding the research used 82 variables grouped into five blocks. Thus, variables describing the pupil, such as sex, age, academic self-concept and attitudes were assigned to an *individual* block; variables relating to his socio-economic status and family size were assigned to a *family background* block. In Box 3.6 we reproduce the variables that went to make up the *classroom* block. Notice how, in trying to identify aspects of the classroom that relate to its overall 'climate' or 'press', the researchers make use of *pupils' perceptions* of what teachers expect in regard to achievement, effort, and discipline. This is an issue that we touch upon again in the final section of the chapter.

BOX 3.6

Effectiveness Measures: Classroom Block

1. Percentage of boys in school
2. Size of school (< 150 pupils; 150–350 pupils; > 350 pupils)
3. Mean time spent at homework per day by class
4. Mean number of examination subjects taken by class
5. Number of examination subjects offered by the school
6. Class mean of highest certificate teacher expects pupils to obtain as perceived by the pupils
7. Extent to which pupil reports taking part in games and other non-academic activities
8. Extent to which pupil in class reports interest in art, music, and debate
9. Extent to which pupil reports knowing how to get a job and talks to teacher about his future
10. Class mean of pupils' perception of teachers' expectation regarding conformity to academic press
11. Class mean of pupils' perception of teachers' expectation regarding participation in art, music, and debate
12. Pupils' perception of class discipline (strict or lenient)
13. Teachers' report of the proportion of the class they expect to conform to academic press
14. Percentage of pupils principal feels would be 'better off' attending another type of school
15. Principal's opinion of the optimal school size for best educational practice
16. Availability of counselling service in school (yes/no)

Source: adapted from Madaus, Kellaghan, Rakow, and King[37]

The criterion measures, that is, the measures of educational effectiveness selected by the researchers, were the results obtained in external national examinations that were geared to the curricula of the schools. These were chosen on the basis of their greater sensitivity as indicators of school performance than conventional standardized tests of achievement.

The techniques that the researchers used in the analysis of their data allowed them to associate the variables in each of the five blocks with the various measures of educational achievement in such a way that the separate and the collective contributions of these blocks could be identified. For example, they could ask, 'How well does each block of variables (individual, classroom, family background, etc.), *on its own*, explain educational attainment?' or, 'How well do individual, classroom, and family background variables when *taken together*, explain examination success?'

An important finding in the study was that of the five blocks of variables, the *classroom block* was the most powerful in explaining variations in the results of external exams. Interestingly, the family block was weak as a predictor of school achievement, a finding that contrasts with those reported in other investigations.

A rather different emphasis for classroom research is stressed by Bidwell[38] who argues that so far, we have failed to arrive at an adequate understanding of the *technology of schooling*. Pursuing this theme, Westbury[25] sees teaching as a '*socio-technology of setting and task management*' which is an abstruse way of saying that teachers work within particular classroom constraints which act as important determinants of what children learn, how they learn and how they, the teachers, are able to function. It follows then, that a central concern for research ought to be to understand how classroom contexts affect the nature of the work that children are set and the methods to which teachers have recourse. To illustrate the point simply, and without jargon:

> 'One can attempt to restrict a mathematics curriculum to a sequence of undemanding tasks, done individually in workbooks. This leads to a quiet and orderly classroom, but, we suspect, implies limitations on the mathematical content that will be learned. Part of this phenomenon is unsurprising. As the problems in a workbook are made more challenging, students will need more help from the teacher. This, at the least, will lead to many students wanting to see the teacher for help, which in turn, means a need to wait, with attendant impatience and temptations to disorder. If the subject is genuinely profound, most students may be unable to learn it from independent reading, and class discussion may be necessary – but this means, in many cases, larger group discussion, and a discussion that may be hard to follow, may require careful attention, and may be highly susceptible to disruption by a few individual students.'[39]

Given the need to focus on *classroom contexts*, *task structures* and *teaching methods* and the necessity to include pupil attributes such as *ability*, *motivation* and *prior achievement*, models of classroom learning become extremely complex affairs as we illustrate in Box 3.7.

One final point, suppose it were possible to grasp fully the nature of classroom processes as they relate to pupil achievement, – would we then be able to add classroom effects together, as it were, and determine overall school effectiveness? Westbury suspects that this is an implausible assumption since 'it is the *school as a whole* which frames the classroom which is only one setting amid many in which the processes of education are at work.' Just how researchers have tried to conceptualize school effectiveness is the concern of the fourth and final section of the present chapter.

BOX 3.7

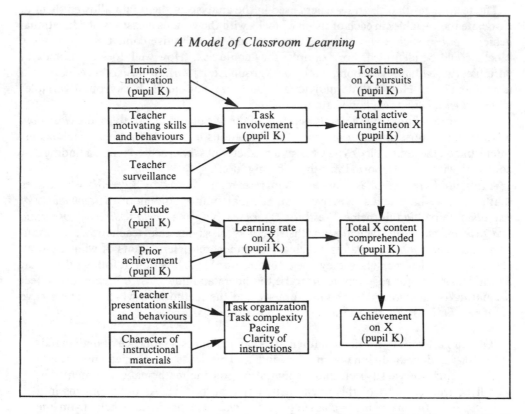

A Model of Classroom Learning

Source: adapted from Harnischfeger and Wiley[40]

SCHOOL FACTORS IN EDUCATIONAL ATTAINMENT

A decade or so ago there was a widespread belief among American educationists that schools make so little difference to children's educational development that it is of small consequence which schools children attend. To a large extent this view arose out of the findings of two highly influential reports, one of which drew its data from four thousand primary and secondary schools spread throughout the United States. The reports of Coleman[41] and Jencks[42] suggested that educational attainment is largely independent of the form of schooling that children experience and therefore efforts to equalize the quality of schools by additional financial and material resources are unlikely to increase achievement to any significant extent. About the same time as these views were making their impact across the Atlantic, similar conclusions were being drawn in Britain as a result of the Plowden Committee's conviction that home influences far outweigh those of the school.

It would be wrong, however, to convey the idea that there was widespread consensus during the early 70s about the impact (or lack of it) that schools have upon children's development. Quite the reverse was and still is true.

'There was immense disagreement on just what *did* have an influence on children's behaviour and attainments. Jensen[43] saw hereditary factors as predominant; Jencks[42] put it down mainly to 'luck'; many people saw family influences as the most important factor[44] [41]; whereas sociologists[45] were more inclined to see the roots of inequality in the economic and political structure of society itself.'[46]

Whatever the outcome of this continuing debate, research into school effects on educational attainment has grown considerably in recent years. Evidence is now accumulating to suggest that schools *do* make a difference in children's educational attainment and in their social behaviour. It is to an examination of this evidence that we now turn, beginning with a brief account of the association between school climate and pupil behaviour.

School Climate and Pupil Behaviour

Even the most casual observer of schools is aware of how much they differ from one another in their 'tone' or 'atmosphere'. Intuitively, the visitor forms impressions from a variety of cues – the way pupils move about corridors, the apparent order or lack of it in classrooms, the way a stranger is received and conducted to the school secretary's office. It is easy enough to defend the 'reality' of such intuitions. It is far more difficult, however, to define and to operationalize the concept to which they refer. '*Tone*', '*atmosphere*', '*school climate*' – what exactly is it and how can it be measured?

Early work in America by Halpin and Croft[47] to do with the organizational climates of elementary schools used questionnaires to elicit teachers' perceptions of the patterns and the quality of their own interactions as members of staff and those obtaining between themselves and their head teachers. In Britain, Finlayson[48] has extended the approach of Halpin and Croft, arguing that the concept of *school climate* (as distinct from *organizational climate*) necessarily includes the assessment of pupils' interpersonal behaviour and their interactions with teachers, as well as the communication that occurs between the school and the community in which it is located. Finlayson's measures of school climate consist of:

1. The perceptions of pupils of the behaviour of other pupils and of their teachers.
2. The perceptions of teachers of some aspects of their colleagues' behaviour.
3. The teachers' perceptions of the behaviour of heads of departments.
4. The teachers' perceptions of the behaviour of the head.

In one important respect Finlayson's approach is similar to that of Madaus and his associates which we discussed earlier in the chapter. Finlayson, too, is concerned with pupils' and teachers' *perceptions* of various aspects of the behaviour of individuals and groups who exercise formal authority over them. While it cannot be assumed that these perceptions accurately map the behaviour to which they refer, they nevertheless represent reality for both pupils and teachers and are the mainspring* of their subsequent behaviour in school.

Box 3.8 illustrates the four major areas that constitute the pupil questionnaire in Finlayson's school climate measures.

BOX 3.8

School Climate: Pupil Perceptions

Pupil behaviour scales

(1)   *Emotional Tone* refers to behaviour which indicates the degree to which pupils perceive their peers deriving social and emotional satisfaction from participation in school activities.
      Example: *Pupils think a lot of this school.*

(2)   *Task Orientation* refers to behaviour which indicates the degree to which pupils perceive their peers to have accepted the tasks set them by the school and to be applying themselves to those tasks.
      Example: *Pupils work here only because they have to.*

(3)   *Concern* refers to behaviour indicative of the degree to which pupils perceive their teachers to be sensitive to the individual needs of pupils. Both task and social/emotional needs are included.
      Example: *Teachers go out of their way to help you.*

(4)   *Social Control* refers to behaviour indicative of the degree to which pupils perceive their teachers to impose their expectations on pupils and to be required to exercise power in an attempt to secure compliance.
      Example: *Teachers soon lose their tempers here.*

Source: adapted from Finlayson[48]

Finlayson used these school climate measures in a study[50] of juvenile delinquency in secondary pupils. Earlier studies by Power[51] and Farrington[52] had proposed different explanations of the wide variations that occur in the proven delinquency rates of secondary schools serving similar urban areas, Power looking to differences within the schools' environments or climates, Farrington on the other hand singling out differential intakes of badly-behaved boys as a more likely explanation. While both studies show the degree to which schools may contribute to delinquent behaviour, they offer little explanation of the social processes involved. By taking an *interactional* rather than a *structural* focus, Finlayson's[50] study of Liverpool secondary modern schools throws light upon the pattern and the quality of pupil – teacher relationships that are associated with high and low incidences of delinquent behaviour. The design of the research involved the use of census data to ensure pairing schools that had similar catchment areas but different delinquency rates. Using data derived from the climate measures, three sets of comparisons were undertaken:

1. Between the perceptions of delinquent and non-delinquent pupils in the same schools;
2. Between the perceptions of upper- and lower-stream pupils in the same school;
3. Between the perceptions of pupils in the high and low delinquency schools.

---

* The importance of *perception* in relation to behaviour has been put succinctly by Heal[49] as follows:

  'Behaviour is linked with perception in a particularly intimate way: a gesture may be neutral in its intention but the response to it depends upon whether it is *seen* as hostile or friendly.'

Finlayson's finding that delinquents were distributed fairly evenly between the streams of high-delinquency schools and that pupils in these schools were generally less orientated towards the work tasks required of them offers stronger support for Farrington's explanation of differentiated school intakes as a likely cause of overall delinquency rates rather than Hargreaves's[32] contention that the internal structure of the school in terms of its streaming precipitates a 'delinquescent' sub-culture in lower stream pupils. Of more immediate importance is Finlayson's finding of differing pupil perceptions of teacher behaviour in high and low delinquency schools. Whether actually the case or not, teacher hostility is what is *perceived* by pupils in high delinquency schools. Pupils see teachers as defensive and authoritarian in their dealings with classes. While such behaviour is perfectly understandable in the circumstances, it could well lead to a cycle of events 'in which the repressive measures which teachers are perceived to adopt could themselves be an important factor in the contribution which the high delinquency schools seem to make to inflating their delinquency problems.'

A rather similar finding to Finlayson's came from a study of primary school characteristics and pupil misbehaviour. Like Finlayson, Heal[53] too, sought out pupils' perceptions of the helpfulness of their teachers, the clarity and fairness of the rules, and the emphasis the school placed on hard work. These perceptions were then related to self-reported misbehaviours in the community. Heal concluded that the most misbehaved children in his study were those attending larger primary schools which employed a more formal system of punishment involving the reporting of classroom incidents to senior staff and the meting out of more serious punishments.

To conclude, Finlayson's research with social climate measures suggests the importance of the school's ethos in relation to children's delinquency but only hints at the specific teacher actions that serve to initiate and maintain particular types of climate. In the study by Rutter and his colleagues that we now turn to, specific features of the social organization of school life which create conditions for teaching and learning are identified and related to school outcomes. Our account to this point has focused upon pupil behavioural correlates of school organization. It is not without significance that of the four major outcomes that are researched by Rutter and his team, three, – attendance, behaviour, and delinquency, have to do with the important question of student behaviour in secondary schools.

Fifteen Thousand Hours (1979)

To date, the most systematic study of school factors associated with educational attainment and pupil behaviour is that reported by Rutter[46] and his associates in the book, '*Fifteen Thousand Hours*'. The title of the book refers to the number of hours children spend in school from the age of five to statutory school leaving at sixteen. The study measures the success of twelve Inner London non-selective schools in terms of pupils' academic achievement, their attendance records, and their behaviour both in and out of school. The research identifies particular features of school life which relate to the four success outcomes, the principal concern of the study being to find out why there are differences between schools in terms of these various measures of pupil behaviour and attainment. Rutter's overall research strategy is diagrammed in Box 3.9.

BOX 3.9

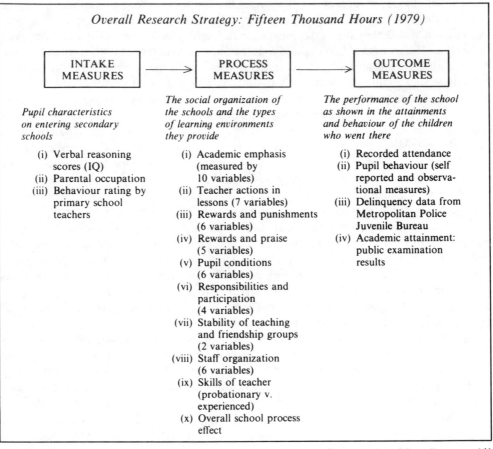

Overall Research Strategy: Fifteen Thousand Hours (1979)

INTAKE MEASURES	PROCESS MEASURES	OUTCOME MEASURES
Pupil characteristics on entering secondary schools	*The social organization of the schools and the types of learning environments they provide*	*The performance of the school as shown in the attainments and behaviour of the children who went there*
(i) Verbal reasoning scores (IQ) (ii) Parental occupation (iii) Behaviour rating by primary school teachers	(i) Academic emphasis (measured by 10 variables) (ii) Teacher actions in lessons (7 variables) (iii) Rewards and punishments (6 variables) (iv) Rewards and praise (5 variables) (v) Pupil conditions (6 variables) (vi) Responsibilities and participation (4 variables) (vii) Stability of teaching and friendship groups (2 variables) (viii) Staff organization (6 variables) (ix) Skills of teacher (probationary v. experienced) (x) Overall school process effect	(i) Recorded attendance (ii) Pupil behaviour (self reported and observational measures) (iii) Delinquency data from Metropolitan Police Juvenile Bureau (iv) Academic attainment: public examination results

Source: adapted from Rutter et al.[46]

As an example of the detailed information collected on school processes, the question of *academic emphasis* was measured by the following ten variables:

1. Homework setting was observed during the first year lessons.
2. Homework reported by third and fourth year maths and English teachers was recorded.
3. Teachers' setting of homework was checked.
4. The percentage of third year pupils expected to gain 'O' level English and mathematics was obtained.
5. Children's work displayed on classroom walls was noted.
6. Total teaching time per week was calculated.
7. Headteacher's reported pastoral emphasis was ascertained.
8. Children's reported use of library was recorded.
9. The degree to which group or supervised course planning occurred was noted.
10. The number of teachers teaching their own subject only was noted.

In accounting for the markedly different academic attainment and behaviour of pupils in the twelve schools the researchers had, of course, to allow for the fact that schools differed somewhat from the outset in the proportions of low-achieving and behaviourally-difficult children entering from primary feeder schools. Making allowance for initial intake differences was done by means of statistical techniques that need not concern us here. What is important is that having made such adjustments, considerable differences still remained between the schools. Even when comparisons were restricted to pupils who were similar in family background and personal characteristics prior to their secondary transfer, the marked variations in attainment and behaviour still remained. The researchers could only conclude that pupils were likely to achieve academically and to behave responsibly if they attended certain schools rather than others. In a word, schools *did* make a difference!

Academic attainment

In looking at pupil attainment in each of the schools, the researchers combined GCE 'O' level and Certificate of Secondary Education grades, weighting the passes according to the grades the children obtained. To grasp fully the meaning of Rutter's findings with respect to academic attainment we need to say a few words about the practice of the Inner London Education Authority at the time of the study of grouping children into three broad bands on the basis of their performance on tests of ability in maths, English and verbal reasoning. The most able 25 % of children came into band 1 (high ability), the middle 50 % into band 2 (medium ability), and the least able 25 % into band 3 (low ability).

Looking at the examination results in the twelve schools as diagrammed in Box 3.10 it can be seen that there are such marked variations between schools that, at the extremes, *the average examination score for low ability children in the most successful school was as good as that for the high ability children in the least successful school!*

School factors associated with academic attainment

Above all else, what characterized the successful school in Rutter's study was the overall 'climate' that had been engendered by staff and pupils working together. The evidence that Rutter brings to support the idea of an overall institutional effect is convincing. Looking at the column of *Process Measures* in the research model outlined in Box 3.9, it can be seen that the last variable (x) is referred to as '*overall school process effect*'. Rutter's statistical analysis shows how the combined effect of the variety of factors that constitute what he calls *School Processes* is more powerful in predicting attainment and behaviour ratings than any individual factor considered on its own. For this and other reasons, Rutter suggests that an overall school 'climate' or 'ethos' might be involved.

It is significant that the factors associated with both attainment and behaviour were to do with school processes rather than with such aspects as the size of the school or its administrative arrangements. It mattered little whether the school was big or small, old or young in terms of its premises, cramped or comfortably-off for space. What did matter and what did relate to academic attainment had to do with:

BOX 3.10

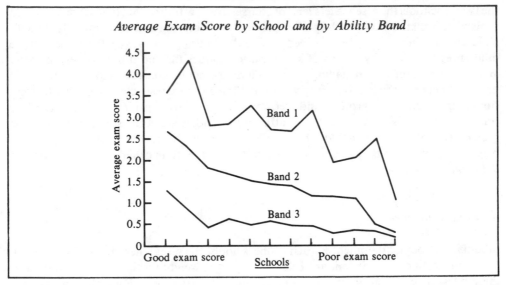

Average Exam Score by School and by Ability Band

Source: adapted from Rutter[46]

1. *The degree of academic emphasis*: pupils perceived that good quality work was expected of them; that homework was regularly set and marked; that teachers expected them to do well in national examinations.
2. *The business-like teaching behaviour of the staff*: lessons were prepared in advance; little time was wasted on extraneous matters; teaching tended to be directed to the class as a whole; feedback on pupils' performance tended to be direct and immediate.
3. *The ready availability of rewards and incentives rather than corporal punishment or unofficial physical sanctions*: discipline was based on the ample use of praise and the teachers' focusing on good behaviour rather than disruptive acts; teachers provided positive models for pupils by being punctual, caring for equipment, abstaining from unofficial physical punishments etc.
4. *The amount of responsibility given to pupils in caring for their own resources or holding positions of trust in school organizations and societies*: schools with better academic and behavioural outcomes were those in which a greater proportion of pupils had had opportunity to exercise leadership and responsibility.
5. *The extent to which pupils felt they could consult with teachers on personal problems*: schools with better academic and behavioural outcomes were those in which teachers were readily available to be consulted by the children about problems and where many children were, in fact, seen by teachers.

But let Rutter* have the last word. What is it that makes good schools *good*? It is:

---

* But not the very last it would seem! Heath and Clifford suggest that Rutter's emphasis on school process variables (46 in number) and his relative neglect of 'out-of-school' factors (only 1 measure of family background) 'stack the cards' in favour of an interpretation showing the importance of the former and the unimportance of the latter. See: Heath, A. and Clifford, P. (1980) The seventy thousand hours that Rutter left out. *Oxford Review of Education*, **6**, 1, 3–119.

'Schools which set good standards, where the teachers provide good models of behaviour, where they (the pupils) are praised and given responsibility, where the general conditions are good and where the lessons are well-conducted.'

Contrast now the findings we have itemized from Rutter's quantitative, measurement-orientated approach with the qualitative, impressionistic account of ten good schools by Her Majesty's Inspectorate. Save only for one or two differences of emphasis, there is a marked similarity in the two reports. We summarize the major points in the Department of Education and Science document[54] in Box 3.11.

BOX 3.11

Ten Good Schools

What specific aspects characterize all ten schools (grammar; comprehensives, secondary moderns, special ESN(M), direct grant, and independent) as good?

1. *Fundamental Objectives*: they seek to achieve their goals by deliberate planning.
2. *Pastoral Care and Oversight of Academic Progress*: pastoral care and academic systems interlock to create an all-round view of the pupil.
3. *Curriculum Design and Academic Organization*: marked by breadth and balance yet experimentation with different kinds of organization to suit different needs.
4. *Staffing and Quality of Work*: purposeful planning, good preparation, variety of approach, regular and constructive feedback to pupils and consistent encouragement to attain.
5. *Use of Premises and Resources*: all schools are at pains to develop close links with parents and to make a contribution to the life of the local community.
6. *Leadership and 'Climate'*: leadership involves above all else the quality of the headteacher's imagination and vision together with his emphasis on consultation, teamwork, and participation in decision-making.

Source: adapted from Department of Education and Science[54]

SUMMARY

We began our appraisal of pupil, classroom, and school factors in educational attainment with a brief account of two longitudinal studies which demonstrate the continuing influence of social class and family size on pupil achievement. For purposes of exposition we separated out pupil, classroom, and school effects, discussing first, research into such pupil factors as ability, personality, achievement motivation, and self-concept in relation to children's academic performance.

We were critical of earlier studies of classroom effects which employed simplistic models of the classroom in which teacher variables such as praise, criticism or quality of questioning are associated with pupil performance outcomes. Classrooms, we decided, are better characterized by their multidimensionality and simultaneity, as environments where teacher expectations, teaching methods, task structures, and pupil attributes interact in complex ways that are only partly understood. We went on to illustrate the complexity of the classroom by reference to two recent studies which have employed more sophisticated models of classroom contexts and processes.

In raising the question, 'What is it that makes a school effective?' we looked first at the concept of school climate as it has been used in studies of pupil behaviour both in and out of school. Rutter's longitudinal study of school factors in educational achievement constituted the major focus of the final part of the chapter. Schools do make a difference, is the conclusion of Rutter and his associates. That is to say, schools which set good standards, where teachers serve as positive models and where pupils are made to feel responsible.

ENQUIRY AND DISCUSSION

1. Using the variables shown in the diagram in Box 3.2, explain how they affect achievement motivation over time. How far are the factors identified by Banks and Finlayson supported by other studies cited in the chapter?

2. Which student in your group do you consider to be the brightest? On what evidence do you base your opinion? How accurate do you think your estimate is? How does your judgment compare with those of others? On what information do they base their assessments?

3. How can teachers best help children to develop realistic, positive self-concepts of ability?

4. Brookover's self-concept of ability measure illustrated in Box 3.4 contains six sub-sections in all. Draw up *six* questions that you would wish to include if you were asked to construct a similar scale suitable for use with British pupils.

5. With the diagram of classroom learning set out in Box 3.7 as an example, construct your own model of classroom learning using all or some of the variables that have been discussed in the chapter.

6. On what criteria do teachers in general assess the effectiveness of their schools? To what do you attribute their choice of factors?

7. Suppose you are a parent visiting a school with a view to transferring your child there. What aspects of school climate might be foremost in your mind as a parent?

8. Use the criteria contained in Box 3.11 to assess just how 'good' the school was in which you did your last teaching practice.

NOTES AND REFERENCES

1. Douglas, J. W. B. (1964) *The Home and the School.* London: McGibbon and Kee.
   Douglas, J. W. B., Ross, M. and Simpson, H. R. (1968) *All Our Future.* London: Peter Davies.

2. Davie, R., Butler, N. R. and Goldstein, H. (1972) *From Birth to Seven.* London: Longman.

3. Fogelman, K. R. (1975) Developmental correlates of family size. *British Journal of Social Work*, **5**, 1.

4. Fogelman, K. R. and Goldstein, H. (1976) Social factors associated with changes in educational attainment between seven and eleven years of age. *Educational Studies*, **2**, 2, 95–109.

5. Fogelman, K. R., Goldstein, H., Essen, J. and Ghodsian, M. (1978) Patterns of attainment. *Educational Studies*, **4**, 2, 121–130.
   The recent studies of Halsey et al., and of Goldthorpe provide unequivocal evidence that social class is still a crucial factor in education, and hence, life chances.
   See
   Halsey, A. H., Heath, A. F. and Ridge, J. M. (1980) *Origins and Destinations: Family, Class and Education in Modern Britain.* Oxford: Oxford University Press.
   Goldthorpe, J. H. (in collaboration with Catriona Llewelyn and Clive Payne) (1980) *Social Mobility and Class Structure in Modern Britain.* Oxford: Oxford University Press.

6. Craft, M. (1970) *Family, Class and Education.* London: Longman.
   Byrne, D., Williamson, B. and Fletcher, B. (1975) *The Poverty of Education.* London: Martin Robertson.
   Swift, D. F. (1968) Social class and educational adaptation. In *Educational Research in Britain.* Butcher, H. J. and Pont, H. B. Vol. 1. London: University of London Press.
   Lawton, D. (1968) *Social Class, Language and Education.* London: Routledge and Kegan Paul.

7. Heim, A. W. (1970) *The Appraisal of Intelligence.* Slough: NFER

8. Youngman, M. B. (1979) Some determinants of early secondary school performance. B.E.R.A. Conference Paper. September 1979.
   Youngman, M. B. and Lunzer, E. A. (1977) *Adjustment to Secondary Schooling.* University of Nottingham: School of Education.

9. Eysenck, H. J. and Eysenck, S. B. (1969) *Personality, Structure and Measurement.* London: Routledge and Kegan Paul.

10. Graham, C. (1970) The relation between ability and attainment tests. *Association of Educational Psychologists Journal and News Letter*, **2**, 5, 53–59.

11. Fontana, D. (1977) *Personality and Education.* London: Open Books.

12. Cattell, R. B. (1965) *The Scientific Analysis of Personality.* Harmondsworth: Pelican.

13. Atkinson, J. W. (1964) *An Introduction to Motivation.* Princeton: Van Nostrand.
    McClelland, D. C., Atkinson, J. W., Clark, R. A. and Lowell, E. L. (1953) *The Achievement Motive.* New York: Appleton Century-Croft.

14. Rotter, J. B. (1966) Generalized expectancies for internal control of reinforcement. *Psychological Monographs,* **80,** 1.
    Lefcourt, H. M. (1966) Internal versus external control of reinforcement: a review. *Psychological Bulletin,* **65,** 206–220.

15. Entwistle, N. J. (1968) Academic motivation and school attainment. *British Journal of Educational Psychology,* **38,** 2, 181–188.

16. Croucher, A. and Reid, I. (1979) Internalized achievement responsibility as a factor in primary school children's achievement. *Educational Studies,* **5,** 2, 179–194.

17. Banks, O. and Finlayson, D. S. (1973) *Success and Failure in the Secondary School.* London: Methuen.

18. Rosen, B. C. (1956) The achievement syndrome: a psychocultural dimension of social stratification. *American Sociological Review,* **20,** 155–161.
    Rosen, B. C. and D'Andrade, R. (1959) The psychosocial origins of achievement motivation. *Sociometry,* **22,** 183–218.

19. Thomas, J. B. (1980) *The Self in Education.* Slough: NFER is an up-to-date survey of the field of self concept studies.
    So too,
    Burns, R. B. (1979) *Self-Concept: Theory, Measurement, Development and Behaviour.* London: Longmans.

20. Coopersmith, S. (1967) *The Antecedents of Self-Esteem.* San Francisco: Freeman.

21. Bagley, C., Verma, G. K., Mallick, K. and Young, L. (1979) *Personality, Self Esteem and Prejudice.* London: Saxon House.

22. Brookover, W. B., Erikson, E. K. and Joiner, L. M. (1967) *Self-Concept of Ability and School Achievement III.* Final Report on Cooperative Research Project No. 2831. East Lansing: Michigan State University.

23. Mead, G. H. (1934) *Mind, Self and Society From the Standpoint of a Social Behaviorist.* Chicago: University of Chicago Press.

24. Purkey, W. W. (1967) *Research Bulletin: The Self and Academic Achievement.* Gainsville, Flo.: Florida Educational Research and Development Council.

25. Westbury, I. (1978) Research into classroom processes: a review of ten year's work. *Journal of Curriculum Studies,* **10,** 4, 283–308.

26. Rosenshine, B. (1976) 'Classroom Instruction'. In *The Psychology of Teaching Methods: 75th Yearbook of the National Society for the Study of Education.* (Ed.) Gage, N. L. Chicago: Chicago University Press. pp 335–371.

27. Rosenshine, B. (1971) *Teaching Behaviours and Student Achievement.* Slough: NFER.

28. Cruickshank, D. R., Kennedy, J. J., Bush, A. and Myers, B. (1979) Clear teaching: what is it? *British Journal of Teacher Education,* **5,** 1, 27–33.

29. Rist, R. G. (1970) Student social class and teacher expectations: the self-fulfilling prophecy in ghetto education. *Harvard Educational Review,* **40,** 411–451.

30. Brophy, J. E. and Good, T. L. (1970) Teachers' communication of differential expectations for children's classroom performance: some behavioural data. *Journal of Educational Psychology,* **61,** 365–374.

31. Cooper, H. M., Baron, R. M. and Lowe, C A. (1975) The importance of race and social class information in the formation of expectancies about academic performance. *Journal of Educational Psychology,* **67,** 2, 312–319.

32. Hargreaves, D. H. (1967) *Social Relations in a Secondary School.* London: Routledge and Kegan Paul.

33. Lacey, C. (1970) *Hightown Grammar.* Manchester: Manchester University Press.

34. Nash, R. (1973) *Classrooms Observed.* London: Routledge and Kegan Paul.

35. Woods, P. (1979) *The Divided School.* London: Routledge and Kegan Paul.

36. Hargreaves, D. H. (1975) *Interpersonal Relations in Education.* London: Routledge and Kegan Paul.

37. Madaus, G. F., Kellaghan, T., Rakow, E. A. and King, D. J. (1979) The sensitivity of measures of school effectiveness. *Harvard Educational Review,* **49,** 2, 207–230.

38. Bidwell, C. E. (1977) Discussion, in *Alternative Research Perspectives on the Effects of School Organization and Social Contexts.* John Hopkins University, Centre for Social Organization of Schools. Report No. 232, cited in I. Westbury (Reference No. 25).

39. Davis, R. B. and McKnight, C. (1976) Classroom social setting as a limiting factor in curriculum content. *Journal of Children's Mathematical Behaviour.* Supplement No. 1, 216–217.

40. Harnischfeger, A. and Wiley, D. E. (1978) Conceptual issues in models of school learning. *Journal of Curriculum Studies,* **10,** 3.

41. Coleman, J. S., Coser, L. A. and Powell, W. W. (1966) *Equality of Educational Opportunity.* Washington: U.S. Government Printing Office.

42. Jencks, C., Smith, M., Acland, H., Bane, M. J., Cohen, D., Gintis, H., Heyns, B. and Michelson, S. (1972) *Inequality: A Reassessment of the Effect of Family and Schooling in America.* New York: Basic Books.
    While Jencks noted the comparative importance of schooling to change people's life chances, he neglected to emphasize its powerful *status-confirming* function, that is to say, the great majority come out as they went in relative to others!

43. Jensen, A. R. (1969) How much can we boost IQ and scholastic achievement? *Harvard Educational Review,* **39,** 1–123.

44. Plowden Report (1967) *Children and their Primary Schools*. London: HMSO.

45. Bowles, S. and Gintis, H. (1976) *Schooling in Capitalist America: Educational Reform and the Contradictions of Economic Life*. New York: Basic Books.

46. Rutter, M., Maughan, B., Mortimore, P. and Onslow, J. (1979) *Fifteen Thousand Hours*. London: Open Books.

47. Halpin, A. W. and Croft, D. B. (1963) *Organisational Climate of Schools*. Chicago: Midwest Administrative Centre, University of Chicago.

48. Finlayson, D. S. (1973) Measuring school climate. *Trends in Education*, **30**, 19–27.

49. Heal, K. H., Sinclair, I. A. C. and Troop, J. (1973) Development of a social climate questionnaire for use in approved schools and community homes. *British Journal of Sociology*, **1**, 222–235.

50. Finlayson, D. S. and Loughran, J. L. (1975) Pupils' perceptions in low and high delinquency schools. *Educational Research*, **18**, 2, 138–145.

51. Power, M. J., Alderson, M. R., Phillipson, C. M., Schoenberg, E. and Morris, J. M. (1967) Delinquent schools? *New Society*. 19th October.

52. Farrington, D. (1972) Delinquency begins at home. *New Society*. 14th September.

53. Heal, K. (1978) Misbehaviour among school children: the role of the school in strategies for prevention. *Policy and Politics*, **6**, 321–332.

54. Department of Education and Science (1977) *Ten Good Schools: A Secondary School Enquiry*. HMI Series. Matters for Discussion 1. London: HMSO

SELECTED READING

1. See Bennett, N. (1976) *Teaching Styles and Pupil Progress*. London: Open Books for an account of teachers' styles of classroom organization and practice as they relate to pupil achievement in the 3Rs. Bennett uses questionnaire methods to identify '*formal*' '*informal*' and '*mixed*' styles.

2. Compare Bennett's approach with that reported in Galton, M., Simon, B. and Croll, P. (1980) *Inside the Primary Classroom*. London: Routledge and Kegan Paul. Galton and his associates employ observation and recording techniques to identify certain styles of teaching ('*individual monitors*', '*class enquirers*', '*group instructors*', and '*style changers*') and to relate these to types of pupil behaviour ('*quiet collaborators*', '*solitary workers*', '*attention seekers*', '*intermittent workers*').

3. Read Heath, A. and Clifford, P. (1980) The seventy thousand hours that Rutter left out. *Oxford Review of Education*, **6**, 1, 3–19 for a strong critique of M. Rutter et al. (1979) *Fifteen Thousand Hours*. London: Open Books.

4. Rather than there being one 'best' method of teaching, certain methods are probably more effective in achieving particular objectives with certain types of pupils. For some recent evidence see:–
   Eggleston, J. F., Galton, M. and Jones, M. E. (1976) *Processes and Products of Science Teaching.* London: Schools Council Research Studies, Macmillan Education.

5. Corrigan, P. (1979) *Schooling the Smash Street Kids.* London: Macmillan, is a very readable account of working class male youth culture as seen through the eyes of boys in Sunderland. It tries to answer such questions as, 'Why do kids play truant from school?' and 'Why do they muck about in classrooms?'

6. Woods, P. (1979) *The Divided School.* London: Routledge and Kegan Paul. Woods is concerned with processes, structures and products of secondary education and the relations of these to 'wider levels' of social structure. He focuses upon the divisions that are reproduced within institutional structures in modern society and shows how conflicts between pupils and teachers are intimately related to these wider, social divisions.

4

Teacher Behaviour and Teacher Perspectives

This chapter is about teacher behaviour and teacher perspectives – their roles as teachers, the ways they perceive and write about the pupils they teach, and the strategies they employ in the classroom to achieve control over pupils. Hammersley[1] has observed that much of the literature on teaching is either speculative or normative in flavour, the latter having resulted chiefly from the use of traditional research methods such as surveys of attitudes and behaviour. The greater part of this literature, moreover, focuses on a comparatively small number of topics having immediate practical relevance. He instances the following in this category: identifying 'good' teaching and correlating it with certain assumed conditions and consequences; discussing whether teaching is or is not a profession; and assessing the degree and nature of role conflict in teaching. This concern with relevance, Hammersley suggests, has led to inadequate theoretical development and to empirical investigations of a rather limited kind.

What is required is a more rounded and comprehensive approach to the study of teaching which will include research of an interpretive kind also; yet comparatively little interpretive research has so far been undertaken. In thus defending the need for the interpretive viewpoint, Hammersley points out that careful ethnographic description of social phenomena is essential if our explanations of them are not to be simply speculative, plausible stories that suit our preferences but bear scant relation to the social world we face; and that the experiences, thoughts and decisions of actors are an important set of social phenomena that require description and explanation. As he says:[1]

> 'The starting point for any analysis should be the perspectives of the actors involved, since embedded in those perspectives are initial clues to the immediate motives for action. This is not to say that these motives are explicitly proclaimed in a participant's accounts of his world or that the full explanation of his actions can be derived from his accounts and actions alone; but actions, accounts and perspectives are points at which description and explanation of social phenomena must begin.'

In our study of teacher behaviour and teacher perspectives, therefore, we shall be drawing upon recent interpretive studies in this area, or utilizing material which was initially derived from this standpoint.

In our opening chapter, we established that the assumptions, beliefs and values underpinning one's perspectives invariably have a cultural basis; that the culture which is our heritage affects the way we structure our thoughts, perceptions and beliefs about the world. This is no less true of the sub-cultures we inhabit: indeed, it is through our immediate sub-cultures that the wider structures of society have their impact.[2] A consequence of this for us is the relationship between teachers' perspectives and their social context. Box 4.1 contains a summary of the possible relationships between teacher perspectives and their social context as identified by Hammersley.[2]

BOX 4.1

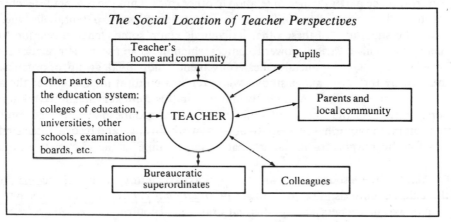

Source: Hammersley[2]

He subsequently establishes a number of points about the external factors making up this social context which he sees as helping to shape and form a teacher's perspectives. First, the factors in question both constrain and facilitate action on the part of the teacher – 'the social context and its interpretation by actors both make certain actions possible and block or make difficult other lines of action which in a different setting or society might be possible.' Second, if teachers are to teach they have to accept some features of their situation as given and beyond their control, and adopt various strategies and techniques which enable them to achieve their goals and meet the requirements of others to some degree in that framework. This means, Hammersley argues, that while we must recognize that teachers are constrained in their activities, the latter cannot be treated as simply the product of external forces. Rather, these activities represent attempts, more or less successful in various ways, to deal with the matrix of forces the teacher has to face. Third, the dimension of time has to be considered: the nature of teacher perspectives, Hammersley explains, is determined both by factors operating at a particular point in time and by factors which have shaped the teacher's perspectives in the past. We can thus expect that different career paths may have important consequences for teacher perspectives. And finally, there are two broad mechanisms by which social forces operate on an actor: the first, *situational control*, refers to the fact that at any point in time an actor will be faced by a particular opportunity structure making certain lines of action possible and others impossible; and second, *cultural influence*, a notion which refers to the structuring of thought and perceptions by one's environment, a structuring that is shared by other members of that society.

Hammersley further explains that the operation of *situational control* and *cultural influence* has been formulated in sociology in terms of the concepts of *role* and *reference group* respectively. The concept of role was initially conceived as a location in a social structure which existed independently of, and constrained, the actions of actors rather than as a set of typifications[3] used by actors to make sense of and act in the world.[2] However, it came to be realized, Hammersley explains, that far from there being agreement over what he terms role definitions, disagreement prevailed: roles are in sets, any one role being partly defined in relation to other roles. Thus the role of the teacher can be formulated in terms of the following *role set*: teacher, pupil, parent, colleague, and bureaucratic superior. All these other individuals claim some rights in relation to the teacher and also have various power resources which they can use in their relationships.[2]

By *reference group*, Hammersley means any agent – individual, group, or organization oriented to by the actor under study – who exercises cultural influence over the actor whether knowingly or unknowingly. By influence in this context is meant the taking over of perspectives. As the impact of different reference groups may often be mutually contradictory, the actor has to adapt to or try to work through and resolve these conflicts if only for the purpose of deciding what action to take in the circumstances facing him.

The value of these four notions and concepts as explanatory tools will become evident as the chapter unfolds. The mechanism of *situational control*, for example, plays an important part in teachers' perceptions and strategies of control; that of *cultural influence*, in teachers' perceptions of children; the concept of *role*, in aspects of teaching; and the concept of *reference group*, in pupil typifications through school reports.

By way of introduction, we shall begin our examination of teacher perspectives by looking at the way in which particular aspects of teaching are viewed by teachers. Our analysis here is based on the work of Hammersley[1] whose principal aim was to describe and critically analyse recent ethnographic work on teachers and pupils. Though we are here only concerned with a particular section of his work, his broad focus was the process of schooling: the rules by which actors make sense of and construct classroom interaction; the means by which they cope with and adapt to their everyday experience in school; the way intelligence, morality, learning and knowledge come to be constructed in schools; the worlds into which pupils are socialized; and the ways pupils are differentiated and selected into and within schools.

Hammersley considers that teaching is often seen as a universal and easily recognized phenomenon involving certain essential qualities; and that the diversity in conceptions of teaching is often overlooked in order to establish one form of teaching as the only real or true one. Even where diversity in teaching is explicitly recognized, he argues, the most common response is to formulate it in terms of a contrast between two types. Thus we have *traditional* versus *progressive*, *formal* versus *informal*, *child-centred* versus *subject-centred*, and *open* versus *closed*. However, the diversity of teaching forms is more complex than is represented by such dichotomies. Researchers investigating variations in teaching have tended to specify the dimensions and interpret the data in too simplistic terms[4]. What is required, Hammersley suggests, is a more adequate description of teacher perspectives. To achieve this, he specifies a number of dimensions on which teaching can vary independently. It is important to stress, however, that although he was to use these dimensions in an examination of examples of ethnographic work in schooling, they were not simply research tools, but were also research products.

The dimensions are organized into five groups: the first is concerned with the *teacher's role*; the second with the way in which *pupil action is conceptualized*; the third and fourth relate to *conceptions of knowledge and learning embedded in different versions of teaching*; and the last deals with *preferred techniques of teaching and organization*.

We shall follow this section by examining in turn teachers' perceptions of children; a case study approach to pupil assessment and typification; teachers' perceptions and strategies of control, using a recent ethnographic study; and typifications of pupils through the official medium of the school report.

ASPECTS OF TEACHING – DIMENSIONS SUGGESTED BY HAMMERSLEY

In proposing six dimensions associated with the *teacher role*, Hammersley identified the varied interpretations imputed to the role by teachers themselves. Briefly, the dimensions in question are: (a) a specialized, authoritative teacher role contrasting with its opposite, an absence of a distinctive teacher role; (b) a teacher role defined and legitimated in terms of *curriculum* in contrast to one defined and legitimated in terms of *method*; (c) a widely defined teacher role contrasting with a narrowly defined one; (d) a role exerting a high degree of control over pupil action in contrast to one exerting a low degree of such control; (e) what Hammersley refers to as a *universalism – particularism* dimension in dealing with pupils, i.e. the evaluation of pupil behaviour and achievement in terms of agreed norms and standards as compared with the evaluation of such factors in terms of *individual* pupil characteristics and circumstances; and (f) the *process – product* orientation in relation to pupil action and learning, i.e. the evaluation of pupil behaviour in terms of *how* an answer is reached, for example, in contrast to whether it is the *right* answer that is reached.

Now these dimensions may look a little overpowering at first sight, so let us look at them more closely. The first dimension has at one pole a view of the teacher as one who possesses specialist knowledge and skills, and whose expertise enables him or her to speak with authority on educational matters – especially to parents and children. It is almost as if he or she has privileged access to educational truths that is denied to others. The contrasting pole, however, sees teaching as an undertaking requiring knowledge and skills that are within most people's grasp, and in which what is to be taught is commonly known and agreed upon. At its most extreme it would perhaps imply that 'everyone's a teacher'. The former view is illustrated in this extract by Kohl:[5]

'Anyone who reads with a certain degree of competency can help others who read less well. This is the case regardless of age or previous educational training.

However, most people in this culture are not accustomed to thinking of themselves as teachers. This is especially true of students in school who undervalue each other's capacity to share knowledge and skills and look to the adult teacher as the source of all learning. Teaching is supposed to be a professional activity requiring long and complicated training as well as official certification. The act of teaching is looked upon as a flow of knowledge from a higher source to an empty vessel. The student's role is one of receiving information: the teacher's role is one of sending it. There is a clear distinction assumed between one who is supposed to know (and therefore not capable of being wrong) and another, usually younger, person who is supposed not to know.'

Hammersley points out, however, that even though there may be agreement among professional teachers on the authoritative teacher role, there is not necessarily agreement on the form that this authority takes; and this leads on to the second dimension. The expertise claimed for the teacher role can be of two main kinds: that which is securely anchored in the knowledge to be taught, the curriculum; or that which is rooted in the methods used to encourage learning.[1] With the former in mind, Hammersley says:

'Where teacher expertise is grounded in the curriculum, the claim is simply that the teacher knows more about history, geography, etc. than do pupils and parents, rather than that he knows more about how to get children to learn. The 'how' is seen as relatively unproblematic. It is not a major focus of attention: a limited number of standard, traditional methods, such as the lecture, the recitation, and individual work are used. Conceptions of teaching which stress the curriculum are probably still dominant in the English state educational system.'[1]

What is implied in the latter, however, where teaching method is stressed, is an awareness not necessarily of subject matter but of the developing human organism, of its biological career, and of the well-rehearsed utterances on the stages of its cognitive and affective development. Such understanding underpins the pedagogical claims made from this perspective.

There may also be differences in the *breadth* of the teacher role embodied in different versions of teaching. In thus identifying this third dimension, Hammersley explains that a teacher may be concerned with teaching specific skills, such as reading or writing, or with teaching a particular subject. On the other hand, he may define his task as the education of the 'whole child', the developing of 'character', or the 'civilizing of pupils'.[1] Hammersley points out, however, that for some whether or not a broad definition of teaching is in operation, the impact of the undertaking is always relatively broad; that the learning of skills cannot be separated from the child's whole identity, from values, or from the world in which learning takes place. This he illustrates with a quotation from Freire:[6]

'Teaching adults to read and write must be seen, analysed and understood in this way. The critical analyst will discover in the methods and texts used by educators and students practical value options which betray a philosophy of man, well or poorly outlined, coherent or incoherent. Only someone with a mechanistic mentality, which Marx would call "grossly materialistic", could reduce literacy training to a purely technical action. Such a naive approach would be incapable of perceiving that technique itself, as an instrument of men in their orientation in the world, is not neutral . . . .

'We begin with the fact, inherent in the idea and the use of the primer, that it is the teacher who chooses the words and proposes them to the learner. Insofar as the primer is the mediating object between the teacher and students, and the students are to be "filled" with words the teachers have chosen, one can easily detect a first important dimension of the image of man which here begins to emerge. It is the profile of a man whose consciousness is "spatialized", and must be "filled" or "fed" in order to know.'

The next dimension along which definition of the teacher role may vary is in the degree of control over pupils and their learning which the teacher claims. Hammersley considers that rules regarding behaviour may cover physical posture and movement, pupil activities, their structure and timing, what is talked about, how, when, by whom and to whom, etc. Teaching may also vary in the degree of control the teacher is required to exercise over what is to be learned, how, when and at what pace. He is careful to point out, however, that the polar opposite of teacher control, that is, absence of teacher control, does not mean chaos, but rather a corresponding increase in *pupil* control.

The fifth dimension extends from universalism to particularism. By the former is meant the interpretation and evaluation of pupils in terms of nothing more or less than the rules governing behaviour, what is to be learned and how, the amount of work required, the standard of work expected, etc. by which the teacher defines the pupil role.[1] Particularism, on the other hand, refers to individual pupil evaluation in terms of his individual characteristics – ability, age, home background, features of his recent biography, and so on – without too close a reference to the normative rules and requirements.[1] An instance of the particularist view is to be found in Box 4.2. Hammersley notes that it is unlikely that teachers conform to either of the two polar positions; most will probably operate under some kind of tension between the two.

BOX 4.2

A Particularistic Approach to Pupil Learning

In an ideal situation, I would *really* start with the child, I would ask, What does he need to know, and what does he want to know? What is he prepared to know? What will help further his growth? What stage of what period of growth is he ready for? Is it important that he watch a caterpillar crawl along a branch? Mostly my job has to do with knowledge, with the acquisition of knowledge. I think this should be my primary responsibility as a teacher: to provide them with knowledge they need. Supposing, for example, a child comes in, in a first grade, who is really very much interested in space and atomic development. Well, this kid's probably ready for it, and so he goes on with it. On the other hand, there are other kids, like one youngster this year, who said, 'What's a carrot?' Obviously he needs a lot of learning about vegetables, soil, seeds, and experiences with those things. In an ideal situation, for me, I would gauge the kinds of knowledge the children are ready for, determine this for each child, and work with him on this basis.

Source: Gracey[7]

To conclude our review of the dimensions associated with the definition of the teacher role, we refer to the distinction drawn by Hammersley between *process* and *product* orientations on the part of the teacher. Process orientation relates to the thinking underlying the production of a product rather than the actual end-product itself, an end-product which is invariably required to conform to certain predetermined criteria. As Hammersley says:[1]

> 'With process orientation, the curriculum is defined as a set of principles which may or may not be entirely specifiable, such as "thinking historically" or even "thinking critically" . . . In the behavioural realm, process orientation refers to a concern with the intentions, motives or causes underlying action as much as to their mere "correctness" in relation to rules. The "right thing" can be done for the "wrong" reasons or be the result of pathological causes and vice versa.'

Product orientation, by contrast, is the evaluation of end-products or actions by or on the part of pupils by reference to certain specified standards laid down by the teacher.[1] In cognitive terms, for instance, this may take the form of evaluation of a pupil's work in the light of the 'right' answers in the teacher's possession. Unlike the process orientation, *how* the answer is reached is regarded as relatively unimportant.

There are three dimensions in the group designated by Hammersley as *the conceptualization of pupil action*. They are: (a) the extent to which pupils are treated as 'licensed adults', as 'apprentice adults', or as 'adults'; (b) the extent to which an individual identifies or explains his own or others' actions in terms of either causal factors (invariably residing outside the actor in question) or free will and individual choice: Hammersley refers to this dimension as *deterministic – individualistic vocabulary of motive*; and (c) the extent to which human nature is assessed in either *pessimistic* or *optimistic* terms.

The first dimension, Hammersley explains, concerns the degree to which pupil action is treated in terms of rights, obligations and capacities normally accorded to adults, or in terms of a modified set of rights, obligations and capacities seen as more appropriate to childhood. The latter position he refers to as the licensed child because while it may involve the attribution of restricted rights and limited capacities, it may also prove a licence to break rules which if broken by adults would constitute a serious offence. What underlies such a licence is a conception of the capabilities of children in relation to those of adults. This notion of the limited or different capacities of children also has implications for what are worthwhile or necessary school activities.

The term 'vocabulary of motive' which Hammersley uses in his description of the second dimension is associated with Wright Mills and refers to the terms in which an individual describes his or other people's actions. By a 'deterministic vocabulary of motive' is meant one which explains a person's actions in causal terms. Thus teachers adopting this position tend to explain children's actions in terms of their mental characteristics. These may in turn be associated with other social causes such as poor home background, one-parent families, lack of suitable stimulus, and so on. In contrast Hammersley explains that by an 'individualistic vocabulary of motive' is meant an explanatory framework in which pupil action is seen in terms of individual responsibility or free will. From this point of view, the onus of 'behaving' and 'learning' rests with the pupil. Failure to meet teacher expectations in these respects may be regarded as an act of moral deviance on his part. As Hammersley explains, 'With a deterministic vocabulary of motives, corrective action, to be successful, has to gear into an existing causal chain whose path has to be determined beforehand. With individualistic explanations, on the other hand, correction is to be achieved by drawing the attention of the offender to the relevant rule and, if necessary, applying sanctions.'[1]

The third and final dimension relating to the conceptualization of pupil action concerns the making of optimistic or pessimistic assumptions about human nature. The contrasting assumptions have been spelt out by Paisey[8] in relation to management theory though their relevance to the willing or unwilling pupil is clearly evident. The pessimistic position involves the following propositions:

1. The average human being has an inherent dislike of work and will avoid it if he can;
2. Thus, most people must be coerced, controlled, directed or threatened with punishment to get them to put forth adequate effort towards the achievement of organizational objectives; and
3. The average human being prefers to be directed, wishes to avoid responsibility, has little ambition and wants security above all.

The optimistic position adopts the following contrasting assumptions:[1]

1. The expenditure of physical and mental effort in work is as natural as play or rest. The average human being does not inherently dislike work. Depending upon controllable conditions, work will be a source of satisfaction (and will be voluntarily performed), or a source of punishment (and will be avoided if possible);
2. External control and the threat of punishment are not the only means of bringing about effort towards organizational objectives. Man will exercise self-direction and self-control in the services of objectives to which he is committed;
3. Commitment to objectives is a function of the rewards associated with their achievement. The most significant of such rewards, for example the satisfaction of ego and self-actualization needs, can be direct products of effort directed towards organizational objectives;
4. The average human being learns under proper conditions not only to accept but seek responsibility. Avoidance of responsibility, lack of ambition and emphasis on security are generally consequences of experience, not inherent human characteristics;
5. The capacity to exercise a relatively high degree of imagination, ingenuity and creativity in the solution of organizational problems is widely, not narrowly, distributed in the population; and
6. Under the conditions of modern industrial life, the intellectual potentialities of the average human being are only partially utilized.

The third group of dimensions refers to the conceptualization of knowledge. They are: (a) required curriculum – no required curriculum; (b) knowledge as objective and universally valid – knowledge as personal and relative; (c) knowledge hierarchically structured in terms of difficulty and status – all knowledge seen as equally available and of equal status; and (d) knowledge as naturally embodied in distinct disciplines or forms – knowledge as general in nature.

In elaborating on these, Hammersley says that most teaching seems to involve the assumption that there is a curriculum, a body of knowledge and skills, that every child in our culture should acquire and develop. However, the opposing assumption, that there is no required curriculum and that the aim is for pupils to enjoy themselves and express their individuality, can also be found among teachers.[9] What is involved here, Hammersley explains, is a dimension not a dichotomy. As he says, 'What is at issue is the clarity of the distinction between school knowledge on the one hand and pupils' knowledge, capacities and personal experiences deriving from outside school on the other. Involved here is the degree to which the latter are ruled out as irrelevant, or putting it positively, the terms on which they are deemed admissible in lessons.' The brief extract in Box 4.3 illustrates this point.

BOX 4.3

	Pupils' 'Outside' Knowledge as Irrelevant
Teacher	You get the white . . . what we call casein . . . that's . . . er . . . protein . . . which is good for you. It'll help to build bones . . . and the white is mainly the casein and so it's not actually a solution . . . it's a suspension of very fine particles together with water and various other things which are dissolved in water . . .
Pupil 1	Sir, at my old school I shook my bottle of milk up and when I looked at it again all the side was covered with . . . er . . . like particles and . . . er . . . could they be the white in the milk?
Pupil 2	Yes, and gradually they would sediment out, wouldn't they, to the bottom . . .?
Pupil 3	When milk goes very sour though it smells like cheese, doesn't it?
Pupil 4	Well, it is cheese, isn't it, if you leave it long enough?
Teacher	Anyway can we get on? . . . We'll leave a few questions for later.

Source: Barnes[10]

At one extreme of the second dimension, knowledge may be conceived as objective and universally valid, that is, as existing independently of the individual and as being applicable to all cases. Scientific knowledge would be the exemplar here. Alternatively, knowledge may be seen as relevant to an individual, a particular culture, or to a specific purpose or occasion.[11] In terms of this latter extreme, then, everyone makes his own personal sense of the world, constructs his own reality; or, alternatively, knowledge is regarded as adequate for a particular purpose, or justified in terms of the criteria of a given culture, and as such loses its validity when no longer identified with that purpose or culture.

The third dimension relating to knowledge concerns the extent to which the conception of it is hierarchically structured in terms of its difficulty and status. Hammersley elaborates thus, 'One pole here stands for a conception of knowledge as ranked in such a way that certain knowledge can only be learned after other knowledge at a lower level has already been mastered and must be learned before it is possible to learn knowledge at the next higher level . . . . This idea of hierarchically structured knowledge is heavily institutionalized in the English education system.'[1]

Finally, there is the question of whether knowledge is contained in distinct disciplines or whether it takes on a more general cast. Where the former extreme is favoured a school curriculum will be neatly divided into the traditional subjects: where the latter extreme holds sway, that is, where boundary lines are not so easily discerned, integrated and inter-disciplinary approaches will be evident.

The fourth set of dimensions concerns assumptions about *the nature of learning*. They are that (a) learning is essentially a collective or an individual, competitive activity; (b) learning is production or reproduction; (c) learning as necessarily intrinsically or extrinsically motivated; (d) the learning path as biologically given or culturally imposed; (e) teacher diagnosis contrasting with pupil intuition; and (f) learning by doing as opposed to learning by hearing about.

With regard to the first of these, learning may be perceived as being an individual undertaking in which a pupil works largely in isolation from other pupils, listening to the teacher, doing written work, or performing practical tasks. In this sense, the learner is dependent upon his own abilities and personal qualities. In this context both self-competition and competition with others may assist in the promotion of learning. In contrast to this, learning may be seen as something which can best occur in a social setting – 'where ideas are exchanged in a co-operative, supportive setting, one person testing out his ideas against those of others, where there is an interaction between one learner's existing knowledge, the knowledge of others and the evidence available.'[1]

As far as the second dimension is concerned, learning can be defined as an act resulting in the production of new knowledge, of new facts and skills. Alternatively, it may be seen merely as the reproduction of knowledge established at a previous stage. Hammersley illustrates a position approaching the former alternative with the following extract:[12]

> 'The alternative involves a radical move away from the traditional "transmission of knowledge" model of teaching and learning . . . (in which) the essential nature of the method by which such knowledge was acquired is neglected . . . I would argue that the ideal situation might include the establishment of a pupil – teacher interaction which recognizes that in itself it is capable of producing both knowledge and the acquisition of knowledge (learning) . . . There can be no doubt that such a process would mean a significant reduction in the amount of factual material "transmitted" and that this along with all the curricular limitations imposed by syllabuses, exams and the like, means that such a change could only come if it was recognized as desirable by a great many people. It is not a change that could be imposed like just another teaching scheme.'

With respect to the third dimension, learning may be seen as only occurring when pupils are intrinsically motivated. This is to say that children will learn when inherently interested in a subject, problem or skill, and for no other reason beyond this. In contrast to this extreme, learning may be seen as something which only comes about when there is extrinsic motivation, that is, when some kind of incentive external to and independent of the specific task is provided. In an educational context such incentives may take a number of forms – verbal approval, grades, or punishment, for example. Hammersley identifies a position midway between these two poles where a teacher might generate intrinsic motivation in his pupils by providing the learning environment with stimulating objects. The former position is illustrated in this quotation from John Holt:[13]

> 'What teachers and learners need to know is what we have known for some time: first, that vivid, vital pleasurable experiences are the easiest to remember, and secondly, that memory works best when unforced, that it is not a mule that can be made to walk by beating it.'

The fourth dimension relating to the nature of learning views the course of learning a child undergoes as being, at one pole, biologically determined and, at the other, culturally imposed. For teachers holding the former view, it is necessary to provide learning experiences, or the circumstances in which they may take place, that are appropriate to the developmental stage a child has reached: the cardinal sin here would be to confront a child with a learning experience before he is ready for it. Teachers subscribing to the latter view, however, will be less sympathetic to this processual standpoint: for them, knowledge will be seen as external to the child and largely independent of a child's particular stage of development. In one way or another, knowledge will have to be imposed on the child.

The next dimension may be seen as a corollary to the preceding one and is concerned with whether the child or the teacher is in the better position to determine the educational needs of the child. If it is the child, then he will sense intuitively what his needs are in this respect; if it is the teacher, then a diagnosis on his part will determine the pupil's needs. Hammersley comments thus:[1]

> 'It may be argued, of course, that a child knows intuitively what he needs and, if allowed to, engages in activities that satisfy his needs and enable him to "develop". The crucial issue here is whether learning is seen as dependent on direct teaching or whether it is something that occurs indirectly. If the former position is taken and the child's needs are seen as open to diagnosis, it is possible and necessary to distinguish between work and play, "productive" and "unproductive" activities, etc. If the latter view is adopted then no such distinctions are possible or required. The allocation of pupils into classes on the basis of age and "ability" and the pitching of lessons so that they are "appropriate" to children of particular ages and abilities can be seen as one position midway between the diagnostic and non-diagnostic poles.'

The final dimension contrasts learning by doing with learning by hearing about. What is involved here is the distinction between direct experience in one form or another and its symbolic representation. Should a child visit the local zoo to see the animals there, or should he sit quietly in class and be told about them by his teacher? Hammersley expresses it thus:[1]

> 'Learning may be seen as the result of "doing", for instance, manipulating physical objects in maths to learn about sets; or of direct experience, for instance, going on a trip to see exotic animals at first hand. Alternatively, this may be seen as unnecessary, learning being defined as hearing about things one didn't know before from the teacher and/or working them out by the manipulation of symbols . . . Here great stress may be placed on the "working up" of knowledge rather than on immediate experience. The first position argues that, to achieve understanding, young children, at least, "cannot go straight to abstractions – they need to handle things".'

The final set of dimensions relates to preferred or predominant techniques of teaching. They thus include: (a) formal versus informal classroom organization; (b) supervision and intervention versus participation and non-intervention; (c) the use of the imperative mode of control plus positional appeals versus reliance on personal appeals; (d) the use of class tests, assessments etc. in relation to the individual child's past performance, or no formal assessment at all; (e) the grouping of pupils and allocation of groups to time/space/knowledge co-ordinates versus no grouping; and lastly (f) the grouping of pupils by age and ability in contrast to random, friendship, or pupil choice grouping.

In the first dimension, formal versus informal classroom organization, the formal organization of a class as a single group with one teacher as its focal point implies the traditional teacher-centred style of teaching which relies on such techniques as teacher exposition, question-and-answer approaches, and individual pupil written work. By informal organization on the other hand is meant smaller groups of pupils working together or sometimes individual pupils working alone. With these kinds of arrangement the teacher resorts to a variety of roles – asking and answering questions, stimulating, and giving advice, for example.

With the second dimension the contrast is between the teacher who supervises pupils and who intervenes whenever the pupil deviates from the rules and the teacher who is a participant in the social situation, not interfering in pupil activity.

By 'imperative mode of control' Hammersley means the use of orders and commands on the part of the teacher perhaps supported by coercive tactics. 'This is often associated,' he explains, 'with the use of positional appeals; appeals to the rights and obligations embedded in particular roles, here those of teacher and pupil.' Personal appeals, in contrast, are appeals to the rights and obligations of one person in his dealings with another.

The fourth dimension relates to assessment. At one end, there is the widespread use of techniques of assessment to test the performance of one pupil in comparison with another. The contrasting pole, however, is characterized by an absence of formal assessment though, as Hammersley points out, it would be unlikely if the teacher were to make no informal assessment of pupil behaviour and of pupils themselves. Between these two extremes, he goes on to explain, comes informal summary comments on pupil performance noted down and filed and tests used to compare an individual pupil's performance now with his performance at some previous time.

The final dimension contrasts the grouping of pupils by age and ability with groupings based on more informal criteria. Hammersley explains it like this:[1]

> 'The grouping of pupils, whether into classes or within classes, may be used as a device to simplify the problem of knowing at what "level" to pitch lessons and/or separate out those prepared to "try" and "work" and those not so prepared. Grouping may on the other hand be rudimentary, a particular teacher being "tutor" for some of the pupils interacting together in an open plan area, or it may be non-existent. Where grouping occurs this may be on the basis of age, "ability" or "trouble" or it may be random or based on pupils' criteria, for instance their friendship choices.'

We turn now to the ways in which teachers perceive the children they teach.

TEACHERS' PERCEPTIONS OF CHILDREN

Every teacher has a clear idea in his own mind of the kinds of children he enjoys teaching and of the ones that cause him anguish, yet it is only comparatively recently that the way teachers perceive and typify the children in their classrooms has been investigated by researchers. In his critical review of the process of typification and person perception in teacher – pupil relationships, Hargreaves[14] identifies three models used by investigators to account for the process of typification. These are *the ideal-matching model, the characteristics model*, and *the dynamic interactionist model*.

The *ideal-matching model* is associated with a relatively early and influential study of teacher – pupil relationships by Becker.[15] He argued that teachers, like members of any service organization, have an image of the ideal client against which actual clients are matched and evaluated as either good or bad. In the classroom, the good pupil is one who approximates closely to the teacher's ideal image, so presenting him with few problems. A bad pupil, by contrast, deviates markedly from the ideal, so reducing the teacher's experience of reward and success in the exercise of his profession. Becker postulates three elements in this model: the problems of teaching, discipline, and moral acceptability. Good pupils conform closely to the ideal in displaying ability and successful learning, in conforming to classroom rules and regulations, and in not offending the teacher's moral standards. As one would expect from an interactionist sociologist, Becker uses interview methods and his analysis concentrates on the way in which pupils from different social classes are judged against this ideal and differentially typified.[15] The basic model is clear: for Becker, typification is a matter of *ideal-matching*.

Hargreaves then refers to comparatively early studies of pupil perception and expectations conducted in Britain. In particular he instances those by Musgrove and Taylor[16], Taylor[17] and Hallworth[18] in which teachers and pupils typify one another in terms of sets of characteristics. As Hargreaves says, 'Actual teachers and pupils are typified as a unique configuration of such characteristics and these typifications are constructed in the form of an identi-kit.' This he refers to as the *characteristics model*.

Ten years later, the impact of symbolic interactionism and phenomenology was being felt by social psychologists in Britain. The basic tenets of interactionism indicated certain preferences and models. With regard to models, interactionists emphasize dynamic or process models which take account of changes in perception and typification over time and reflect contextual or situational variables. With regard to method, interactionists are committed to the interview and participant observation. Nash[19], for example, was committed to observation, but supported his observations of how teachers typify pupils with data derived from Kelly's repertory grid test. Here was a technique which met interactionist canons in that it elicited the member's own constructs rather than imposing them as happens in most attitude and personality tests, yet it also had the advantage of objectivity and quantifiability. Since this is a key study illustrating the characteristics model, we will examine it in more detail.

Inspired by the earlier work on classrooms and classroom life by Holt[13] and Henry[20], Nash's investigations of teachers' perceptions of pupils were but part of a wider scheme attempting to answer what he perceived as the central problem of classroom research: do a teacher's attitudes to her pupils influence their performance in school? Is it that, as he later concludes, children who have the bad luck to be unfavourably perceived by their teachers have a tough time in the classroom? Intriguing as these questions are, we, for our part, will limit ourselves to a brief look at his work on teachers' perceptions of their children and touch only tangentially on the main purpose of the study.

Nash points out that earlier researches had concerned themselves with the overall effects, on large groups of children, of teachers' attitudes to styles of teaching such as streaming or 'permissiveness'. None, he explains, had up to that point attempted to measure directly the attitudes of individual teachers to individual pupils. In order to discover, therefore, whether the school performance of individual children was influenced by their teachers' attitudes towards them, Nash decided that some measure of the teacher's attitudes to each child in her class was needed. To accomplish this he used the approach we have already outlined in Chapter 2 – Kelly's repertory grid technique. This would enable him to find out what constructs were held by teachers towards the children in their classes. In all, eight junior school teachers of classes totalling 236 pupils agreed to go through the procedure independently. Although the constructs the teachers used varied somewhat in detail, there was a surprising agreement among them about what Nash refers to as 'core constructs'. These comprised three distinct constructs found in most teachers' responses and are shown in Box 4.4.

BOX 4.4

The Three Most Frequently Used Constructs with the Ranking Allotted Them by Eight Primary School Teachers

Construct	Teacher								
	A	B	C	D	E	F	G	H	Mode
Hard-working – Lazy	2	2	7	4	1	2	7	4	2
Mature – Immature	5	1	3	1	6	7	5	5	5
Well behaved – Poorly behaved	6	8	4	5	4	4	5	6	6

Source: Nash[19]

From this evidence, Nash concludes that the junior school teachers perceived their pupils primarily in terms of their work habits, their maturity, and their classroom behaviour. All the constructs related to aspects of the child's personality and, interestingly, none deals specifically with the child's abilities (as we shall see, these findings are in marked contrast to those of Taylor[21] whose work we shall consider shortly). As Nash points out, the *hardworking – lazy* construct describes the effort the child puts into his work, not his ability to do it. Only occasionally did Nash elicit constructs to do with ability.

The school was considered locally as 'progressive' and the investigation of the teachers' constructs by means of the repertory grid technique seems to have supported the claims on which this reputation was based. As Nash observes, the teachers appeared to think of, and to judge, their pupils not mainly in terms of their academic ability but by the personality attributes they regarded as important to good progress in school – a perspective we may associate with progressive education.

Still keeping the *characteristics model* in mind, it is interesting to compare the aspects of Nash's work just reviewed with the study by Taylor to which we referred above.[21] Concerning himself with primary children, he set out to achieve two objectives: first, to map out the attributes which teachers use to explain and predict the activities and performance of the children in their classrooms; and second, to ascertain whether the teacher characteristics of *sex* and *formality* contribute in any way to a teacher's perceptual framework.

The subjects in the study comprised 24 men and 24 women primary school teachers from 18 urban and rural schools. Using Kelly's repertory grid technique, as did Nash, Taylor requested the teachers to consider the important ways in which children are alike.

The procedure adopted ensured that in depicting the children each teacher exhausted her repertoire of constructs. In addition, a measure of the degree of formality characterizing each teacher's relationship with her pupils was computed using the Minnesota Teacher Attitude Inventory.

The initial task of the researcher was to identify those constructs which corresponded to each other in meaning, though being described slightly differently. Thus from a total of 446 constructs elicited from the teachers, 81 distinctive attributes were identified. Box 4.5 below lists in rank order the most frequently produced individual constructs by the male and female teachers. The construct occurring most frequently was the one describing the pupils' behaviour in class. This one accounted for approximately 9 % of all those produced. Next in rank order were two constructs concerned with pupils' specific academic achievements in the two principal curriculum areas in the primary school: reading and maths. Equally ranked were constructs describing general ability level and pupils' home background. As Taylor points out, these first five constructs accounted for 37 % of all those used. They clearly indicate to the teacher the importance of *academic performance* and at the same time reflect the salience of *behaviour* and *home background of pupils*.

Box 4.5 also discloses two other features concerning teachers' perceptions: first, there were only a small number of personality dimensions. Only two of the constructs out of the first twelve described pupils' personality characteristics, and the two produced – extraversion and sociability – are conceptually very close to each other; and these also have a low rank order compared with the academic constructs elicited. Second, with two exceptions, there is a broad measure of agreement between both male and female teachers

BOX 4.5

Rank	Construct	Total		Male		Female	
		Rank Order of the Most Frequently Produced Individual Constructs by Male and Female Teachers (n = 48)					
		n	%	n	%	n	%
1	Well behaved	40	8.97	17	6.91	23	11.50
2	Good readers	36	8.07	18	7.31	18	9.00
3	Good at maths	33	7.40	18	7.31	15	7.50
4.5	Intelligent	28	6.28	15	6.10	13	6.50
4.5	Good home background	28	6.28	13	5.28	15	7.50
6	Helpful to teacher	24	5.38	7	2.84	17	8.50*
7.5	Good/interested in sport	22	4.93	14	5.69	8	4.00
7.5	Artistic	22	4.93	14	5.69	8	4.00
9	Hard-working	21	4.71	12	4.87	9	4.50
10.5	Extravert	19	4.26	10	4.06	9	4.50
10.5	Sociable	19	4.26	14	5.69	5	2.50*
12	Neat and tidy work	10	2.24	6	2.44	4	2.00
	Others	144	32.29	88	35.81	56	28.00
	*p = 0.05						

Source: Taylor[21]

in the frequency of individual dimensions produced. As regards the two exceptions, women teachers employ the construct '*helpful to teacher – unhelpful to teacher*' significantly more frequently than do male teachers. Taylor suggests that this might indicate that female teachers are generally more sensitive to the relationship between teacher and individual pupils in class, yet less sensitive than male teachers to peer group relationships within their classrooms.

A more inclusive analysis followed this preliminary stage. This resulted in the 446 constructs being grouped into seven superordinate categories as listed in Box 4.6.

BOX 4.6

Frequency and Percentage of Constructs Employed in Each Category by Forty-Eight Primary School Teachers		
Construct category	n	%
1. Academic achievement	195	43.72
2. Personality characteristics	88	19.73
3. Behaviour and relationship with teacher	69	15.47
4. Home background	38	8.52
5. Interests and hobbies	30	6.73
6. Physical	15	3.36
7. Miscellaneous	11	2.47
Total	446	100.00

Source: Taylor[21]

Inspection of these groupings shows how dominant are the teachers' academic constructs in the perception of children in class. This is a finding quite contrary to that put forward by Nash, who found that teachers perceive their pupils not only, nor even mainly, in terms of their academic ability but more generally in terms of their personality. In fact, the fine discriminations which teachers were able to make regarding their pupils' academic characteristics, with 4.06 academic constructs per teacher, contrasted sharply with the relatively undifferentiated manner in which pupils' personalities were viewed, with an average of 1.82 personality contructs per teacher; and of those personality constructs the most popular were the most concrete and socially visible. Taylor suggests that the relatively small number of agreed personality dimensions indicated that as explainers and predictors of behaviour children's personality attributes do not feature very prominently in the teachers' perceptions. Furthermore, socially less visible personality attributes such as anxiety, sensitivity, kindness and shrewdness were hardly used at all.

As regards the second objective of the study – to ascertain whether the teacher characteristics of *sex* and *formality* contribute in any way to a teacher's perceptual framework – Taylor found that male teachers were more academically oriented in the classroom and that the children's academic characteristics were more salient to them, whereas female teachers regarded other characteristics as of equal importance. The reverse held, however, with respect to 'relationships with teachers' and 'behavioural' constructs, with female teachers using significantly more than the males. This cluster of constructs, Taylor suggests, is particularly relevant to the pattern of authority exercised by the teacher over the pupils, and women teachers do seem to be especially aware of 'pupils I get along with' and those who are 'helpful and polite to me'. It may be as Taylor concludes that dependency reveals itself in the classroom in women teachers' greater sensitivity to the pupils' dependency on her, while men teachers regard this as relatively unimportant.

Perhaps the most interesting finding of this study is that – contrary to Nash – 50 % of the teachers' cognitive space is made up of attributes which cover the academic aptitudes of children. Indeed, teachers' implicit personality theories contain relatively few personality dimensions, and those which are used seem to be those which are rendered most 'visible' in the teaching situation.

As we hinted earlier, the differences between the Nash and Taylor studies might be due to the fact that Nash was working in progressive environments and Taylor in more traditional ones. The contrasting constructs elicited could very well be the result of contrasting perceptions of both teacher and pupil roles.

We have so far considered two of the models identified by Hargreaves – the *ideal-matching model* and the *characteristics model*. We come now to the third one – the *dynamic interactionist model*. As indicated earlier, this model takes into account changes in perception and typification over time and endeavours to reflect situational or contextual variations. One of the earliest attempts to utilize this model, at least in part, was Gannaway's[22] (whose study we shall be examining in more detail in the chapter following). On the basis of interview and observation, he constructed a dynamic model by proposing that teachers are progressively typified by pupils in a given sequence. The teachers are, in effect, subjected to a systematic series of tests by pupils, the first of which is the extent to which the teacher keeps order, followed by the 'can we have a laugh?' and the 'does he understand pupils?' tests. As Hargreaves has pointed out,[14] this is the first British study to specify a dynamic model of pupil typification and has considerable potential, for it can be developed to take account of both situational variations and the longer term career of the pupils' typifications.

More pertinent to our present topic, however, is the more recent work of Hargreaves and his colleagues[23] on teacher typifications of deviant pupils. The model they adopt suggests that the typification process passes through three analytically distinct phases. First, there is a stage of speculation in which the teacher hypothesizes that the pupil is a certain kind of person. Second, there is a stage of elaboration in which the early hypothesis is put to the test and then extended and elaborated. And third, there is a stage of stabilization in which the teacher develops a highly complex but stable typification which is then resistant to change. A fourth stage, that of type transformation, is posited but not developed. Of this model, Hargreaves himself writes that it . . .

'. . . captures the dynamic career of the typification process, but it has two major deficiencies. Its principal application is to the "deviant" pupil and it remains an open question whether it can profitably be applied to the "normal pupil" and it fails to take account of situational variations in any adequate way.'

Box 4.7 contains a short extract from the case study material collated by Hargreaves and his co-workers which illustrates the processes of typification according to this model.

BOX 4.7

An Example of Pupil Typification

Teacher. The other one that stands out, of course, is Steve Roberts. Now with his brother I've had trouble in the past – he's a nice lad, but he can be awkward sometimes, he'll try it on. Steve does not seem to do this very much, not yet anyway. I think he is still feeling his way. Nice lad. He does some of the same tricks as his brother, things like everybody else will be listening and he appears to be listening and then he will come out afterwards and say, 'Now what do I do?' you know. And he also tends to be very tired . . . He falls asleep. I've had to wake him up several times as you've noticed in lessons, because I've had a word with (another teacher) and other people have mentioned the same thing, and he's just not getting to bed on time . . . I think Steve's a stronger character than his brother. He tends to be a leader within his own little group. You notice that the other boys tend to look to Steve very often, whereas (the elder brother) has always been a follower. He has been a loudmouth and a class idiot, whereas I don't think Steve is. He does daft things, but he's not the class idiot. I think in a way Steve has more leadership than (the elder brother) has.

Source: Hargreaves et al.[23]

We continue our study of teachers' perceptions of pupils with a more detailed examination of a case study of teacher typification in an infant school. Allied to the dynamic model proposed by Hargreaves, it too sees the process in ongoing terms.

TEACHER TYPIFICATION AND ASSESSMENT IN INFANT SCHOOLS – A CASE STUDY

The study we draw on at this point is King's sociological investigation of infant classrooms, a case study based on his work in three schools.[24] The theory he used in this undertaking was derived from Weber's action theory[25] which defines social action as 'all human behaviour when and insofar as the acting individual attaches subjective meaning to it.' From this Weberian viewpoint, therefore, the task of the researcher is to *understand* the subjective meanings people assign to their actions. From this perspective, King set out to understand the meanings imputed by teachers to their work in infant classrooms. To achieve this, he made use of three research methods – observation, interview and content analysis of samples of children's work, text books, and school records. By these means he was able to show how teachers' actions and classroom practices relate to their definitions of the nature of young children and their education. We are particularly interested in one aspect of this process – the way teachers typify children.

King found that the processes of typification were inseparable from those of assessing work and behaviour in individual children – 'typification, assessment, teaching, learning, controlling, and being controlled were all aspects of the same flow of action and interaction in the classroom, and were consonant with the teacher's recipe ideologies, particularly those of development and individuality.'[24]

After studying the interaction between teachers and individual children, King found that there were three important points about the way teachers assessed and typified pupils. First, the teachers drew mainly upon their own experience of the child in the classroom situation: other teachers' reports were rarely consulted. Second, three aspects of the individual child's classroom behaviour were noted and built into the typification: compliance with the teacher's rules of behaviour, relationships with other children, and his learning progress. Third, the typifications were not absolute, but varied over time. King analyses the process of typification from the teacher's point of view thus:

> 'Each child possesses a unique, developing personality, which is expressed in his or her compliance with classroom rules, relationships with other children, and learning progress, each of which may influence the others. Children change naturally as they develop, but changes may also be due to changes in home or family circumstances, or illness.'

Box 4.8 contains King's summary of this. It also shows how some knowledge of the various elements and of the teacher's assessments was known publicly by the children in the class, but much was kept private by the teacher, including the typifications of individual children she used the knowledge to construct.

BOX 4.8

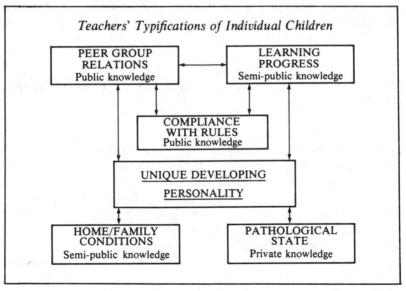

Source: King[24]

Let us look more closely at each of these three aspects of classroom behaviour and the way they affect assessment and typification.

Rules were established in the classrooms studied to structure behaviour. King thus notes that the exercise of social control in relation to those rules involved making assessments of children's behaviour. Teachers' assessments in this respect were public, individual pupils being typified as well or badly behaved.

In one school studied, teachers rated the conduct of their children on a 3-point scale – A good, B satisfactory, C poor. Additionally, they wrote a short description of each child so that the researcher was able to infer what counted as 'good' or 'poor' behaviour and how well- and poorly-behaved children were typified. King found that the teachers' *written* reports used words and expressions similar to the ones used in controlling the children in the classroom. The silly/sensible distinction was used in 11 % of the notes, for example, and quiet/noisy in 21 %. Written assessments similarly took into account the child's presumed maturation: the big/little verbal distinction of classroom encounters became the mature/immature distinction and was used in 10 % of cases. Thus, the A, or well-behaved child, was quiet, sensible, and mature; and C, or badly-behaved child, was noisy, silly, and immature. King himself says:

> 'In the classrooms, teachers expressed more approval of behaviour than disapproval, and generally felt secure in their control. At the Langley school 12 of the 16 teachers gave more As for conduct than either Bs or Cs, and no one gave more Cs than As and Bs. The overall distribution was A 49.6 %, B 32.8 %, and C 17.6 % (total no. 415). In each class about half the children were typified as well behaved, and only a handful were 'naughty' in their behaviour, but in their immaturity they were not usually naughty in intent.'

King points out that the assessment of conduct sometimes included remarks on how a child got on with other members of the class. Although the children were clearly aware of who was friendly with whom, they did not know that these relationships contributed to the teacher's assessment of them: the knowledge was public, the assessment private. Thus, being popular and being able to make friends was viewed favourably. However, concern was felt about those children who preferred their own company, the teachers inferring that they were not happy and settled in school:

> Happy, mixes well.

> Worrying, tends to be an isolate.

A child's peer-group relations were regarded by the teachers as an expression of his or her unique personality:

> Quiet and shy, no special friends.

> Silly, excitable, a bit spiteful to others.

Further, peer-group relationships were sometimes thought to have consequences for compliance with classroom rules:

> Pleasant, reliable child but can be influenced by others to her detriment.

> Easily led. Sometimes influenced by other boys' behaviour.

The third aspect of classroom behaviour is to do with assessing of learning progress. The model of children's ability implied by teachers, King observed, was a *developmental* one. This was particularly apparent in reading sessions where children were moved from one group to another 'frequently', 'at the time', 'any time', 'from day to day'. The criteria that were used for the formation and reformation of reading groups were reading 'level', 'progress', or 'ability', a clear indication being the book or card a child had reached. Typical teacher comments in this connection recorded by King were:

> I change them if they progress or fall back.

Some move as they develop.

If the children progress at different rates then the groups are naturally changed.

Groups have roughly the same level of maturity.

Because the teachers espoused the developmental rather than psychometric model, they rarely spoke of intelligence or intelligent children, preferring to describe their disposition – slow, interested, bright.

As was the case with the other two aspects, a child's *learning progress* was another expression of his or her unique developing personality:

> Immature, easily distracted, lacks concentration.

> Withdrawn, reluctant to try new work.

> Immature, silly, loses interest.

Sometimes a child's progress was related to his general behaviour in terms of compliance with classroom rules:

> He has made very little progress and seeks to be the cause of much trouble and small disturbances amongst other children because of immaturity.

Peer-group relations were also judged to be associated with progress:

> Lacks concentration in a group but works well on own.

> She has learnt to trust her own abilities more and has become more relaxed with other children.

Teachers frequently modified the picture they had of children – 'they observed changes in behaviour, in relations with others and in rates of progress, and consequently changed their typifications.' Again, King relates these acts of redrawing to the underlying developmental model of the child held by the teacher in question:

> He is going through a silly phase at the moment.

> More mature and sensible, behaviour much improved, was rather a lone child but now mixes well.

> Tracy was a very quiet girl when she started school, she would only speak when spoken to and needed directing in everything she did. She has become more integrated with the class, has many friends and enjoys being 'busy' in the Wendy house.

> Conscientious work, gradually gaining confidence in herself.

King observes that changes judged favourable were defined as natural and developmental. Those judged unfavourable were explained in terms of factors which could not be blamed on the innocent child: illness or disability, and home and family circumstances:

> Reliable but lacks confidence probably as a result of the appearance of her skin complaint.

> A quiet child who gets on well with other children but doesn't like big groups. Unsure of himself because of speech difficulties. Attends speech therapy at school.

> He has been in hospital recently for tests for a suspected duodenal ulcer. He can be very aggressive with little provocation.

Similarly with home events:

> Felt left out and needed a lot of attention following birth of new baby.

> Rather confused during period of mother's divorce.

As King explains:

> 'Changes in home circumstances were not thought to have inevitable consequences at school, but when changes in school were not acceptably explicable in terms of development or illness in the child, the teacher actively sought knowledge of the home . . .'

> 'As long as the home and school events occurred at roughly the same time they were assumed to be causally connected in the direction from home to school. This kind of explanation was posed even in the absence of any evidence.'

King asks the question: what were the consequences of teachers typifying or defining individual children in particular ways? This he found was difficult to answer for the following reasons: it was difficult to come to grips with all the possible typifications, since each teacher typified each child in her class; the typifications were not fixed but were modified over time; the typifications were kept largely private. King goes on the ask if then the definitions were only real to the teacher, to whom were the consequences real?

The consequences, he explains, were real for the teachers themselves and they were real in terms of classroom arrangement, the ways they dealt with individual children's work, their interactions with pupils, and the methods used to control their behaviour.

Similarly, the teacher's definitions of individual children were only real for the teacher, but the consequences were real for both teacher and pupil. The teacher arranged for and allowed a child to do things in accord with her typification of the child. This was most obvious in the control of classroom behaviour. Thus:

> 'Mr. Fish has "one naughty boy". "Not bad really – every class has one. He can't sit still, he's always interfering with others." His explanation: the boy's parents run a newsagents, they are up early and close late, and have little time for him. He is left alone, unsupervised, and so has no self-control. "A pleasant boy – quite like him really, but I have to keep on at him all the time."'

King concludes by suggesting that teachers' typifications may have had real consequences for individual children. As he says:

> 'Children defined as ready to read were set to reading. However, this specific event in time cannot be regarded as determining who subsequently was defined as a poor or good reader. Even if an investigation showed that poor readers were those who were started later than good readers, a causal connection would not be established.

Typification, assessment, teaching, learning, controlling, and being controlled were constantly modified in the flow of classroom interaction. Older children assessed and typified as good readers or "over the hill" received less attention from the teacher than those defined as "slow" readers, to be helped up the hill.'

We turn our attention now to another case study[26] which, among other things, investigates secondary teachers' strategies for survival consequent on their perceptions of conflict situations and the need to gain control.

CONTROL IN THE CLASSROOM – STRATEGIES FOR SURVIVAL

The most important part of a teacher's work in school is control. Control has been defined by Woods[26] in the context of school and classroom as successfully dealing with incidents which fracture the teacher's peace, or establishing one's power in a situation which pre-empts such occurrences. He further points out that the traditional, normative means of control utilized by teachers are often inadequate: they were devised for normative children who, he explains, may very well be in a minority. Teachers therefore have to support and bolster up traditional means by others, often individual and improvised, and in some cases frowned on by the establishment. These Woods refers to as *survival strategies*; and it is through the developing and usage of them that teachers are able to accommodate to the fairly raw circumstances that frequently face them. In calling this section 'Control in the classroom – strategies for survival', we aim to look at the various approaches to survival in the secondary school which were identified by Woods in his ethnographic study at Lowfield School.[26]

Socialization

Woods begins by reminding us that the ideal circumstances for teaching will be those where both pupils and teachers share common standards, values and beliefs; where pupils have been socialized into forms of behaviour acceptable to the teachers prior to their arrival at school. Since such conditions are only likely to exist in a minority of schools, such as private institutions, the remaining ones are likely to spend a great deal of time and effort endeavouring to socialize their pupils into tolerable forms of behaviour. The problem facing most teachers is the cultural gap between their attitudes, values and beliefs and those of their pupils. The latter, Woods suggests, might value such qualities as initiative, single-mindedness, activity and individualism; the former, on the other hand, will in all probability prefer receptivity, malleability, docility and conformity. Most schools have a range of procedures to smooth over this gap and achieve some sort of working relationship and in this connection Woods instances some of what he calls 'mortifying techniques' adopted, the aim of which is to 'strip pupils of certain parts of their "selves".' Thus, certain pupil roles are prescribed, others proscribed; patterns of deferent behaviour are encouraged – how to address members of staff, for instance; great emphasis is placed on pupil appearance – clothing, hairstyles, cosmetics and jewellery are carefully vetted so that individual expression is limited. As regards actual social processes Woods says, 'Pupils are given drill in how to move about the school, sit in desks, raise hands, speak to teachers, eat their dinners, treat their fellows; and the puritan ethic of hard work, sober living and good manners is continuously urged upon them.' However, many socialization programmes fail to achieve their purpose and for this reason most teachers have recourse to other methods which we will now consider.

Domination

Where normative means of control do not work, the teacher has to resort to other means. One particularly effective in this connection is *domination* – getting on top of deviant pupils and staying on top. As Woods points out, generally speaking teachers are bigger, stronger and wiser than the children they teach and these qualities can be used to achieve a more coercive form of control over pupils, corporal punishment being the one that comes most readily to mind. Even where this is illegal – and there are a growing number of authorities banning it – there are other means at a teacher's disposal. As Woods observes, 'there is a great deal of punching, knuckling, tweaking, clouting, slapping, slippering, hair-pulling, twisting, rulering and kicking.'

Even more widespread are verbal assaults of a humiliating and nasty kind. Physical confrontation is often accompanied by verbal threats. As Woods notes, the threat is often accompanied 'by "transfixation" whereby the victim is held in a vice-like grip and subjected to a wide and wild-eyed nose-to-nose confrontation. Often, of course, anger is simulated – it is part of the teacher's "presentation of front".'

These features, physical and verbal attacks, diminishing of pupils' selves, are perhaps best illustrated in the gymnasium, Woods suggests, where the PE teacher serves as an exemplar:

> 'It is no coincidence that many PE teachers progress to senior positions with special responsibility for discipline. For many of these, "survival" and "teaching" are synonymous. The survival techniques of games teachers are built into the structure of their teaching, and are based on relentless efficiency, continuous structured physical activity (which pre-empts any countering), strong strident voices (backed up by whistles, hooters, megaphones, etc.) used to prevent the activity from flagging, and a display of potential physical aggression (in shorts, singlets, track-suits, muscles, and the smell of sweat and embrocation, etc.). This is fused into the normative order, so that, barked commands like "stand up straight!", "don't move!", "pull, boy, pull!" appear as part of the manifest curriculum.'

As Woods further points out, mortification techniques are used freely by games staff – there are showers and various stages of undress. Stripping people of their clothes strips them of part of their 'selves'.

Verbal aggression also forms part of school routines and rituals. Woods instances morning assembly in this respect:

'Some moral message is usually offered and enshrined in prayers and a hymn. These are often enunciated with frightening force, as if validated by holy authority. The function is both to alarm and to rally, but the aim is singlefold – conformity.'

Negotiation

Another strategy adopted when normative methods fail is that of *negotiation*: this is based on the principle of exchange. Woods found that techniques used in this connection include appeals, apologies, cajolery, flattery, promises, bribes, exchanges and threats:

'I'm sorry I'm talking a lot this morning but bear with me, please. I do want to get this finished.'

'I thought in the second period we'd have a film, then I thought next week we'd do the nature trail in Aspley Forest, but first I want us to make up those notes.'

Woods explains that in exchange for reasonable behaviour and a representation of 'work' the teacher for his part offers a relaxing of the official demands of the school this in most cases meant some form of absolution from 'work'. This may take the form of watching a film, for example, or listening to records, visits, outings, or an 'easy' time. Alternatively, it may appear in the form of 'community service' – gardening, shopping or making tea for older residents in the neighbourhood. Projects, too, perform a similar function – a break from the grindstone routine and an opportunity to find preferable alternatives to work. In this connection, Woods draws attention to the CSE and the way in which since its introduction it has met *teacher* needs:

'The CSE, in fact, is the biggest aid to teacher survival introduced into schools since the war. It draws many more pupils into the mainstream culture of the school, and still allows pupils their secondary adjustments. Thus if you fall behind in your essays in English, you can always copy somebody else's, merely changing a few words; or you can submit your brother's or a friend's specimen in woodwork – and so on. The CSE has been a success because it has allowed for this – unlike many other innovations.'

In addition, the teacher can back up the principle of exchange with a range of appeals: teacher styles in this respect will vary greatly within a school. As such, appeals can be directed to civilization or society in general and the need for the individual to fit into it; or they can be aimed at the way pupil behaviours can dislocate peer-group norms or the relationship between teacher and class. Of particular interest is the development of a sense of 'togetherness' that can come about particularly between a teacher and his class of 'failures':

'These constitute the biggest potential menace to the school, and hence require a special security arrangement.'

Such is the bond that develops between teacher and class in this situation that the ensuing unit tends to separate itself from the rest of the school:

'Strong identification is made within this unit, with feelings of loyalty, comradeship and regard, so that it acts as its own survival agent. Appeals, if made by their own teacher, rarely fail. Other teachers, however, are invariably driven to other techniques with these forms.'

Another important feature of this strategy is the way that rules and compromises over rules are worked out between teacher and pupils. Personal involvement in this way ensures compliance. Thus, with regard to work teachers often feel obliged to abandon their absolute standards and settle for what they can get from a class or an individual.

Fraternization

Yet another survival technique identified by Woods is that of *fraternization*, the meaning of which is encapsuled in his quotation, 'If you can't beat them, join them.' The aim here then is to strive for good relations with one's pupils with a view to minimizing potential conflict and developing a sense of obligation in them. Although an approach normally associated with the progressive movement in education, Woods found it existing within a traditional framework.

Fraternization, he discovered, took many forms. Young teachers, for example, because of their nearness to pupils chronologically have a natural advantage which can be used to the benefit of all:

'Young teachers, especially, by their appearance, style of dress, manner, speech and interests frequently identify strongly with the pupils. They are often very popular. Implicit alliances can form against the main structure of the school, but, as with teachers of "backward" classes, it can ultimately work in the school's interests, since much bad feeling is defused through this bond with members of staff.'

Some teachers capitalize on themes and interests common to both younger and older generations. Woods instances earthy humour, television and sport in this respect:

'Some lessons I observed abounded in references to popular television programmes, advertisements included. While this might have a pedagogical value, it also has important survival repercussions for the pupils' perceptions of the teacher's identity. Sport also can form a bridge. For example, gangs of adolescent boys follow a football cult. Their discourse consists of jocular abuse directed at others' chosen teams and vigorous championing of one's own at all costs. This aggressive banter is typical of their life style and is indulged in as a form of play. On these terms it is open to teachers, and sometimes they take advantage of it.'

Finally, fraternization can be built into one's teaching through forms of entertainment. One way this may be reflected is through styles of speech having contemporary currency. One teacher observed by Woods, for example, used a local, chatty, pubby style of speech in his teaching which appeared to help him in controlling his pupils. Another, observes Woods, had a cosmopolitan, youthful 'with-it' style which strengthened his identification with his pupils. Another succeeded in connecting almost everything he said to television programmes. Other forms of entertainment include the teacher's own wit and humour directed both at his pupils and himself.

Absence or Removal

A further strategy is absence (or removal). For Woods this is a broad term and includes absolute physical absence at one extreme to physical presence but abnegation of duty or responsibility at another, with a whole range of comparable techniques designed to achieve more or less the same end located linearly and spatially between these two points. And the aim is simple: ensuring survival by absenting oneself from the scene of possible conflict.

As very few achieve what Woods terms 'absolute absence', most have to be satisfied with partial absence, either official or unofficial. As a technique for survival it is perhaps the one that causes most bitterness among staff because more often than not it has to be achieved at the expense of colleagues.

A critical feature in the application of this technique is the time-table. As Woods notes:

'"Survival" features prominently in its construction. "Weak" teachers have to be protected, "good" ones rewarded. "Weak" ones can be given fewer lessons, none of the hard classes and most of the favourable rooms. . . . Whence then come the rewards? Fortunately for the hierarchy there are some "in-between" teachers consisting of a faceless group of those who have not yet "arrived" at the school, a "disloyal" group consisting of those who are leaving or applying for other jobs, and a "rebellious" group who for some reason have got in bad favour with the hierarchy. These take up the slack of "bad" forms, poor rooms and overloaded timetables.'

Thus, Woods concludes, the time-table is manipulated to protect the weak, reward the good and penalize the unknown and unworthy. A prize always in demand is the 'free period' – 'losing one's free periods can be quite traumatic, for survival becomes a bit harder; it can be very much harder if, in exchange for an idyllic "free", one is confronted by somebody else's extreme survival problem – a "bad" form in "bad" circumstances.'

Woods identifies other means resorted to by teachers for achieving 'absence' – unloading problem children onto others (especially where some teachers act as counsellors); taking a day off; prolonging one's break; using delaying tactics in one's lessons or teaching; and taking advantage of new courses and styles of teaching – 'Link courses, work-based courses, Community Service, field work, individual and group projects, all aid teacher survival by virtue of separating the combatants for much of the time.' Another favourite device is that of throwing the onus of work on to the children themselves. Thus, getting pupils to take assemblies or initiate their own work 'cleverly turns the opposition back on itself and neatly fits the fashionable educational philosophy.'

Ritual and Routine

Rituals and routines are invaluable to the teacher for, in imposing a structure on the life of the school, they offer him a basis for establishing control, thereby prolonging his survival chances day by day, year by year. Woods identifies registration, form periods, assemblies, time-tables, lesson structures as the more obvious examples in this connection. And within this structure, individual teachers establish their own personal, sometimes idiosyncratic, formalities. Elaborating on this point, Woods observes:

'Teachers become addicted to routine and ritual. Once instituted, they are extremely difficult to get rid of. Rituals become associated with "tradition" and "ethos" and to change them means discontinuity and disjuncture. Routine is a narcotic, taken to soothe the nerves and mellow the situation. Once established, to do without it would involve the teacher in severe withdrawal symptoms.'

So pervasive is routine in the act of teaching itself that its survival value in that context is often overlooked. Woods identifies, for example, the following procedures in this respect: externally paced pupil activities create fewer management problems than self-paced activities; recitations and textbook teaching can fairly be seen as coping mechanisms; dictating notes has great survival value for it leads pupils to believe 'they are being spared doing their own "work"', and thus secures their cooperation, involving quiet application, for considerable periods of time'; and even the newer teaching techniques have a marked routine element – work cards, structured exercises, group activities, programmed learning, audio-visual techniques, for instance.

The difficulties created by an absence of routine have been predicted by Musgrove,[27] a prediction which Woods considers is now ancient history for all too many teachers:

'The computer will take much of the routine out of teaching in schools, and will make possible far more learning which is not school-based. Although most people complain about the routine in their jobs, they would probably go mad without it. Without routine we are constantly dealing with unique, unprecedented, non-recurrent and non-standard events. This may be exhilarating; it is also exhausting. We can expect teachers to be in a state of constant exhaustion.'

Occupational Therapy

As a further means of survival Woods found that teachers resort to *therapy*. This he defines as a variety of bodily movements accompanied frequently by dulling of the senses. It may be indulged in by both teachers and pupils, though it is usually the teachers who impose it on their pupils. But to what end? Woods explains:

'The aim is to take the edge of boredom or fractiousness, and thus prevent incidents arising.'

He lists the kinds of therapeutic techniques he encountered in his study – drawing maps, pictures, and patterns. 'Play' activities indulged in in the guise of practical work are also useful in this respect:

'The simple experimental kits provided for pupils' tinkering in science lessons allow for this, and for this reason the practical subjects – woodwork, metalwork, cookery, needlework, etc. – have strong therapeutic value. De-inhibiting activities such as free, unstructured swimming are wonderful therapy, and can spread their beneficial effect over several classroom periods before and after.'

Getting pupils to do 'jobs' is another aspect of the therapy. Simple routine jobs are involved here, some useful, others merely time-filling. Thus teachers give instructions to clean the blackboard, tidy the drawers or cupboard, sharpen pencils, and so on. As Woods points out, this can become an 'official' activity for particular individuals or groups in school – those who have rejected the system, pupils in their final year at school. It becomes a preferred alternative to 'mucking about'.

A teacher may engage in time-wasting activities in the course of a lesson as a means of survival. Reviewing one particular teacher's technique in this respect, Woods says, 'It was taken up with arriving late, finishing early, chatting with the pupils before and after, preparation of lesson and materials for it during the lesson itself, interruptions (which seemed to be welcomed and capitalized upon), peripheral story-telling and general nonchalant pace.'

Alternatively, says Woods, a teacher may engage in therapy unilaterally. This he does by keeping himself busy amid the general scene of chaos and indifference. In one science lesson noted, the teacher neutralized the control problem by concentrating exclusively on the stimulus aspect of teaching and totally ignoring the response.

Morale-Boosting

The final aid to survival identified by Woods was that of *morale-boosting*. One of the principal means of achieving this was for the teachers to resort or subscribe to professional rhetoric, either official or personal. *Rhetoric* in this context refers to the use of language, utterances, or phrases that are designed to uplift the user or listener through persuasion. As in other contexts, however, the word carries undertones of insincerity.

We have already instanced the use of rhetoric in passing: pupils organizing their own lessons, for example, or fraternization ('treating the pupils like people'). One of the most fruitful areas for a sustaining rhetoric, however, is the progressive movement in education:

> 'There is now a vast thesaurus of "progressive" vocabulary and idioms, from which
> the teacher might draw to construct his own vocabulary of motives (free expression,
> integrated learning, activity-based learning, project work, free choice . . .).

Woods instances other examples: young teachers are best 'thrown in at the deep end', it is 'good experience' for them. School uniform is championed in the interests of 'equality', preventing the poor being exposed by those children from better homes. Mortification procedures and dominating techniques are represented as socializing devices in the interest of the individual whose naturally savage and uncouth character must be tamed and channelled along the 'right' lines to a civilized society.

Another great morale-booster in the context of the school is what Woods calls the detection and celebration of the enemy's weakness. Thus, teachers' insistence on describing pupils in such ways as 'idle' and 'thick'. From such means, the individual teacher 'might draw renewed strength, after flagging perhaps, towards the end of a double period and allowing the pupils to gain the upper hand. The greatest danger is that teachers should doubt what they are doing. Usually the supportive voice of colleagues available at key points of the day provides sufficient reassurance of his beliefs and reinforcement of status'.

Woods concludes that if teachers want to 'get on' in their careers, they must 'believe' in the rhetoric they create and foster; and the more they 'get on', the more they must believe. 'The firmer the commitment, the greater the accommodation.'

> 'Less committed teachers who have less of an accommodation problem often see through this rhetoric and boost their own morale by merciless teasing and baiting of the upper hierarchy during their absence.'

SCHOOL REPORTS – TYPIFICATIONS ONCE REMOVED

In this section, we look at the ways pupils are described by teachers in school reports, those semi-official documents intended for pupils' parents. Our review is based wholly on the work of Woods[26] who said of reports that 'they constitute the pronouncements of experts, their assessment of the material measured against standard aims and their diagnosis of remedy or improvement. Like doctors' diagnoses, there is something irrefragably incontrovertible about them.' They are the documents periodically completed by teachers, usually at the end of a term, and sent to parents, ostensibly to report on 'progress'. A commonsense view regards them as a kind of objective measure of performance. Grades, usually from A to E or F, increase the appearance of objectivity and the notion of an absolute standard, with comments offering a key to the relationship between the grade and the individual's perceived ability, aptitude and attitude. Of all these factors, the last is usually regarded as the only variable and hence invites most comment, especially if at all deviant. Box 4.9 contains an example of a report quoted by Woods on one pupil's work in the two successive terms (Spring and Summer 1973).

In general terms, Woods notes that reports are not written in relation to an absolute standard for all children, though teachers may want to convey this impression. Rather their comments mask a relativity, that is to say, C satisfactory or B good for a bottom stream pupil has different implications than for similar grades and comments for a pupil in the A stream. As Woods says, 'The two just are not comparable, yet they masquerade, particularly with the classificatory grade, as a universally standardized form of measurement. In fact they measure against different standards and are decided by different criteria.'[26]

Reports contain two indications relating on the one hand to the acquisition of skills and on the other to what kind of social person the pupil is becoming. They involve a notion of 'the ideal' but there are different ideal pupils according to (a) schools aims, and (b) teacher ideology.

In Box 4.10, we enclose the two lists of typical categories, desirable and undesirable, derived by Woods from an examination of comments on reports of two senior groups at Lowfield. As Woods notes, they indicate that teachers rate pupils according to their conformity to their instructional and disciplinary expectations. He quotes Hargreaves on the point:

BOX 4.9

A Typical Report

	Grade	Remarks	Grade	Remarks
English	D	Every effort required	D	Must work harder
Mathematics	D	Great drop lately.	B	Improved
		Seems to lack will-power to improve	C	
Science	–		C	Good progress recently
Woodwork	C	More effort	B	Very good
Practical				
Metalwork	C	Fair	B	Good progress
French	C	Drop this term	C	Improved
History	B	Improved	C	Marginal
Geography	C	Only Just	C	Not enough effort
Art	A	Works well	A	Very good
Craft (pottery)	–		B	Works very well
Music	C	Enthusiastic	B	Works well
RI		Satisfactory		A much better attitude
Games		Works hard		Good

Form teacher: Needs to improve a great deal in his attitude towards work. Behaviour also.

Form teacher: Has improved slightly this term, but still room for more, especially English.

Source: Woods[26]

'The teacher defines the situation in terms of his own roles and goals, especially as they relate to his instructional and disciplinary objectives, and assigns to the pupils roles and goals that are congruent with his own. He selectively perceives and interprets pupil behaviour in the light of his definition of the situation. On the basis of further interaction with the pupils and separated perceptions of them, he develops a conception of individual pupils (and classes) who are evaluated,

BOX 4.10

Report Categories

Desirable	Undesirable
Concentration	Easily distracted, lacks concentration
Quiet	Chatterbox
Industrious (works well)	Lazy
Willing	Unco-operative
Co-operative	
Responsible, mature	Immature
Courteous	Bad-mannered
Cheerful	Sullen
Obedient	Disobedient

Source: Woods[26]

categorized and labelled according to the degree to which they support his definition of the situation. He then responds to pupils in the light of these evaluative labels.'[28]

As long as pupils are normal, conforming, or non-disruptive, their typification is a straightforward and institutionalized matter. Occasionally, however, the process is disturbed by what Woods calls 'special cases', usually because they are of uncommon excellence or an uncommon nuisance; also teachers independently, for idiosyncratic reasons, might form special associations with certain pupils.

We conclude this section and chapter with an example of a teacher typification. Woods asked one teacher to tell him about his class as individuals with a view to opening up the typification world of the teacher acting in his professional capacity. The reply you will find in Box 4.11.

In discussing the teacher's comments on the boys, Woods notes that two polarities are offered: (1) 'introverted', 'not much to offer', against 'alive' and 'quite promising'; (2) 'helpful', 'very nice kid', etc. against other 'illiterates' who are 'behind-your-back merchants'. The teacher talks about them in terms of their disposition to school primarily, and his relationship with them. Within this range of discourse, the teacher emphasizes his ideals which show a commitment to the traditional image. Woods observes:

'Of all the boys, Rudd came closest to it. He was the only one who, in interview, emphasized the ultimate object of gaining as many and as good examination passes . . .'

The example does illustrate the terms in which teachers discuss children in their own confidential arena as one professional to another. It highlights one or two of the clues which teachers look for to identify the pupil (illiteracy, broken home, niceness) and the categories that emerge (struggler, disappointing, promising, good relationships). It also suggests stability – some firm judgments are made, and some predominant typifications that suggest consistency from one context to another (a right lout, isn't he? Very nice. Very difficult to get through to), and a very strong affective area, focusing on his feelings for them. It also illustrates what Woods considers the static, stereotypical mode of teacher typifying which is behind most teachers' judgments of pupils when considering them in the mass, and this includes writing reports.

BOX 4.11

An Example of Teacher Typification

Tony Bowyer – very disappointing. I noticed a decline last year and I spoke to him about it, and he's a right lout, isn't he? Always shuffling around with his hands in his pockets, instead of being a nice young man, as he was, but he's far from . . . This boy, John Cosin, he's got more introverted as time's gone on. He hasn't much to offer, but . . . now this little chap, Falding, he's alive and quite a promising little lad. No comment about Floxton, he's a reasonable lad. Now this one I understand has some problems at home. I don't think he's malicious or anything, but his manners and courtesy are less than you'd expect. Nice chap, Hodges, and this boy (Keele) and this one (Lewis), and him (Lane). I got on well with Moore, though he had a bit of trouble – a bit of petty theft, you know.

Source: Woods[26]

SUMMARY

This chapter has been concerned with aspects of teacher behaviour and teacher perspectives. It began by identifying the need for a more rounded and comprehensive approach to the study of teaching, one that would take in interpretive research also. The starting point for such a task, it was explained, would be the perspectives of teachers themselves. After a brief consideration of related conceptual issues, we went on to consider the varied interpretations imputed to dimensions of the teacher role, our analysis being based on the work of Hammersley. In all, six such dimensions were reviewed. This was followed by an examination of the ways children are perceived by teachers. To this end, three models used by researchers over the years were identified – the ideal-matching model, the characteristics model, and the dynamic interactionist model. Each was illustrated with selections of studies from the research literature. Teachers' perceptions of children were then taken further with reference to a case study of teacher typification and assessment in infant schools. We then went on to consider the matter of control in the classroom and the strategies developed by teachers in this connection. The review of eight strategies which ensued was based on the ethnographic work of Woods. To conclude, we looked at the ways pupils are viewed and described by teachers through the medium of school reports.

ENQUIRY AND DISCUSSION

1. In what ways can a study of teacher perspectives help the beginning teacher?

2. Consider the view that teacher behaviour and teacher perspectives are often regarded in too simplistic a way.

3. Explain the terms *situational control* and *cultural influence* in relation to a teacher's work in the classroom.

4. Take each of the dimensions associated with the teacher role that were referred to in the chapter and identify your own position on each. Remember that they are dimensions and not dichotomies.

5. Briefly distinguish the three models identified by Hargreaves that have been used by researchers in studies of person typification and perception.

6. Why is Kelly's repertory grid technique valued by interpretive researchers? Discuss any research study which uses this method.

7. Discuss Woods' 'strategies for survival' in the light of your own experience of teachers and teaching. What moral arguments would you put forward for or against their use?

8. What can school reports tell us of the ways teachers typify their pupils?

NOTES AND REFERENCES

1. Hammersley, M. (1977) *Teacher Perspectives*. Open University Educational Studies, A Second Level Course, E202, Schooling and Society. Units 9 and 10, Block II. The Process of Schooling. Milton Keynes: Open University Press.

2. Hammersley, M. (1977) *The Social Location of Teacher Perspectives*. Open University Educational Studies, A Second Level Course, E202, Schooling and Society. Units 12 and 13, Block II. The Process of Schooling. Milton Keynes: Open University Press.

3. Note: We have already encountered the term *typification* (Chapter 1, page 20. You will recall that it refers to the means by which an observer makes use of concepts resembling 'ideal types' to make sense of what people do.

4. Note: A notable exception here is Bennett's research on open classrooms (1975) *Teaching Styles and Pupil Progress*. London: Open Books.

5. Kohl, H. (1974) *Reading, How to*. London: Harmondsworth, Penguin Books.

6. Freire, P. (1972) *Cultural Action for Freedom*. London: Harmondsworth, Penguin Books.

7. Gracey, H. (1972) *Curriculum of Craftsmanship: Elementary School Teachers in a Bureaucratic System* . Chicago: University of Chicago Press.

8. Paisey, H. A. G. (1975) *The Behavioural Strategy of Teachers*. Slough: NFER.

9. Note: Compare this with Chapter 9, the status of knowledge, page 290.

10. Barnes, D. (1971) 'Language in the Secondary Classroom', in Barnes, D. et al., *Language, the Learner and the School*. London: Harmondsworth, Penguin Books, revised edition.

11. Note: The connection here with the normative and interpretive paradigms is readily apparent.

12. Porter, J. quoted in Young, M. F. D. (1977) 'School science: innovations or alienation'. In P. Woods and M. Hammersley, *School Experience*. London: Croom Helm.

13. Holt, J. (1970) *How Children Learn*. London: Harmondsworth, Penguin Books.

14. Hargreaves, D. H. (1977) The process of typification in classroom interaction: models and methods. *British Journal of Educational Psychology*, **47**, 274–284.

15. Becker, H. (1952) Social class variations in teacher-pupil relationships. *Journal of Educational Sociology*, **25**, 451–465.

16. Musgrove, F. and Taylor, P. H. (1969) *Society and the Teacher's Role*. London: Routledge and Kegan Paul.

17. Taylor, P. H. (1962) Children's evaluations of the characteristics of the good teacher. *British Journal of Educational Psychology*, **32**, 258–266.

18. Hallworth, H. J. (1962) A teacher's perceptions of his pupils. *Educational Review*, **14**, 124–133.

19. Nash, R. (1973) *Classrooms Observed*. London: Routledge and Kegan Paul.

20. Henry, J. (1963) *Culture against Man*. London: Ransom House.

21. Taylor, M. T. (1976) Teachers' perceptions of their pupils. *Research in Education*, **16**, November, 25–35.

22. Gannaway, H. (1976) Making sense of school. In *Explorations in Classroom Observation* (Eds.) Stubbs, M. and Delamont, S. London: Wiley and Sons.

23. Hargreaves, D. H., Hester, S. K. and Mellor, F. J. (1975) *Deviance in Classrooms*. London: Routledge and Kegan Paul.

24. King, R. (1978) *All Things Bright and Beautiful?* London: Wiley and Sons.

25. See, for example, Weber, M. (1922, 1968) *Economy and Society*. Bedminster; (1948) *Essays in Sociology*. London: Routledge and Kegan Paul; and (1964) *The Theory of Social and Economic Organisation*. Free Press.

26. Woods, P. (1979) *The Divided School*, London: Routledge and Kegan Paul.

27. Musgrove, F. (1960) The decline of the educative family. *Universities Quarterly*, **14**.

28. Hargreaves, D. H. (1972) *Interpersonal Relations and Education*. London: Routledge and Kegan Paul.

SELECTED READING

1. Hargreaves, D. H. (1977) The process of typification in classroom interaction: models and methods. *British Journal of Educational Psychology*, **47**, 274–284. A critical study of the process of typification and person perception in classroom interaction.

2. King, R. (1978) *All Things Bright and Beautiful?* London: Wiley and Sons. A fascinating study of teachers' actions and practices in infant classrooms.

3. Nash, R. (1973) *Classrooms Observed*. London: Routledge and Kegan Paul. A

participant observation study in primary and secondary school classrooms showing how teachers' perceptions of their children influence attainment.

4. Taylor, P. H. (1962) Children's evaluations of the characteristics of the good teacher, *British Journal of Educational Psychology*, **32,** 258–266. A comparatively early study of classroom perception.

5. Woods, P. (1979) *The Divided School*, London: Routledge and Kegan Paul. An important ethnographic study of a secondary school offering a rich account of school life from the viewpoints of teachers, pupils and parents.

6. (Ed.) Woods, P. (1980) *Teacher Strategies*. London: Croom Helm. A collection of interesting and readable articles on aspects of teacher behaviour.

5

How Pupils See It

So much for teacher behaviour and teacher perspectives. But what of the pupils? How do they see their school environment? What sense do they make of it all – the system's efforts to educate them, the teachers at the centre of the task, even work itself? In setting out to look for answers to these questions we are immediately confronted with a dearth of empirical studies in this area, the few that are available to us making up a mere handful of pieces in the total jigsaw. That there should be such a relative neglect of the pupils' viewpoint is due, it has been suggested, to the low status of the pupil role:

> 'Like the position of the child, and the position of the patient, (the pupil's role) lacks status; it commands little respect. Behaviour appropriate to a disvalued position tends to be defined for the occupants of that position by those who occupy related positions of greater status: the role of the child is defined by the adult, the role of the patient by the doctor or nurse, and the role of the pupil by the teacher.'[1]

Calvert argues that in spite of official exhortations claiming a paramount position for pupils' interests, every other group concerned with education – teachers, administrators, planners, parents, employers and society at large – can obtain a better hearing for its own point of view than can the pupil.[1] Recent attempts by pupils to establish their own pressure groups (e.g. the NUSS) have tended to provoke ambiguous and even angered responses from the educational establishment.

Calvert further observes that the writings of educationalists are produced largely for an audience of teachers for whom the problems of teachers are a major preoccupation. She concludes that it is therefore natural to concentrate on the teacher's role and the issues surrounding it: even studies of pupils are produced chiefly with teachers in mind. Greater concern for the teacher role in the literature of education results from another source identified by Calvert: it is that the teacher's position is based on an occupational choice which demands a degree of choice since he is paid to do the work. The pupil, on the other hand, has no such choice: nobody pays him to take on his role and he may choose to remain uncommitted to it.

Thus it is that emphasis tends to be placed on the teacher's role, the role of the pupil is defined by the teacher, and the pupil's own viewpoint neglected:

> 'Because the teacher thus defines the pupil role, he tends to see himself as the more decisive participant in the performance, and thinks of the pupil's role as more receptive than his own. Things are done by the teacher to or for the pupil, just as things are done by the doctor to or for his patient; and the pupil, like the patient, is expected to conform to the expectations thus set up for him.'[1]

If we are to take the pupil's viewpoint seriously, we must ask ourselves which is the better perspective for the researcher to adopt – the normative or the interpretive? The answer clearly will depend on what it is the researcher is attempting to discover and the assumptions associated with his standpoint. Normative studies would make use of attitude-scales, questionnaires and non-participant observation to generate data; pupils would be asked to respond to a predetermined framework, to perceive a slice of reality through a chosen filter implying a particular theory or hunch on the part of the investigator – 'Do you believe that teachers should try to teach pupils to keep the school rules; to know what is right and wrong; to enjoy poetry and plays, art and music?' Interpretive studies, however, are concerned with how individual pupils perceive, interpret or give meaning to an experience. To these ends a researcher would acquire data through natural conversation, open discussion, or from freely composed material on the pupils' part – essays or accounts, for instance.

In seeking pupils' points of view from this perspective, the following are the kinds of question that might be asked:

1. How do pupils interpret their experience of schooling? Are there any differences of opinion among them? How, for example, do 'successful' and 'unsuccessful' pupils respond? Do boys and girls react similarly? And how do pupils in different kinds of school perceive their worlds?
2. How do pupils perceive work? Do they see it more or less in the same way as their teachers? And to what extent are they influenced by the way people outside school perceive it?
3. What do pupils see as the best kind of schooling? To what extent does their actual schooling meet their perceived needs? How do they define the 'good' teacher? In what ways does he differ from the 'bad' teacher?
4. How do pupils see each other? How do younger pupils see older pupils, and vice versa? How do the brighter pupils see the less gifted, and vice versa? And how do pupils from different social backgrounds perceive each other?
5. Finally, just how reliable and valid[2] are pupils' judgements of teachers, their peers, and school experience?

We may legitimately ask ourselves: how useful are the judgements of pupils concerning their schooling? The earliest studies into pupils' perceptions of schooling took place in the United States, the most convincing being those of Veldman and Peck.[3] They concluded that pupil perceptions of teaching performance were sufficiently valid and reliable[2] for teachers to regard them as useful feedback on their performance. Meighan, moreover, found that this general conclusion from the limited research at hand held good for samples of English children, although there appeared to be a few technical aspects of performance, e.g. the effective use of questions and teaching aids, where the perception of pupils was less reliable.[4]

In asking the question whether children's perceptions of teaching subsequently improve performance, Meighan further discovered that the student teachers taking part in the study did modify or attempt to modify their classroom techniques as a result of the things that children drew to their attention. Further uses of pupils' judgements will be touched upon incidentally in the course of the chapter.

Early British studies in this area of pupil perception include Taylor's study of pupil expectations of teachers in which he makes use of content analysis of children's essays;[6] Hargreaves' participant observation study in a secondary school which gathered information, among other matters, on how pupils' interpret some features of school life;[7] and Blishen's study[5] which concentrates entirely on the pupils' view of schooling by providing selections from essays written mostly by secondary school children on the theme, 'The school that I'd like' (see Box 5.1 for a brief extract from this study). Since 1973, there have been a growing number of both normative and interpretive researchers interested in pupils' views of school and schooling and we hope to draw upon their work in the course of the chapter as well as on some of the earlier studies.

BOX 5.1

Children's Perceptions of the Ideal Teacher

'They should be understanding, the children say, and patient: should encourage and praise wherever possible; should listen to their pupils and give their pupils a chance to speak; should be willing to have points made against them, be humble, kind, capable of informality, and simply pleasant; should share more activities with their children than they commonly do, and should not expect all children to be always docile. They should have conscience about the captive nature of their audience; should attempt to establish links with parents; should be punctual for lessons, enthusiastic within reason; should not desert a school lightly; should recognize the importance to a child of being allowed to take the initiative in school work; and, above all, should be warm and personal.'

Source: Blishen[5]

As research into the area of pupil perception is at a comparatively early stage of development, it follows that the few available studies tend to approximate in character to the kinds of research investigations identified at Stage 2 in our model, 'Stages in the development of a science' (Box 1.3), i.e. they are largely exploratory in nature and directed to fact-finding and understanding particular situations. As most are thus 'one-off' case studies, it is naturally too early as yet to generalize their findings to other situations with any great confidence. It is even more difficult, given the information currently available, to integrate the findings from the studies (or the selections that follow in this chapter) so as to present a complete and rounded picture of 'how pupils see it'. Nevertheless, findings from the studies carry sufficient weight for us to begin to trace the outlines and identify significant features of a hitherto unfamiliar area and to open up a potentially rich and fruitful source of insights into how pupils see and make sense of school. Eventually, such studies will enable researchers to build up a corpus of data that will be of value both to the practising teacher and the teacher in training. Although both normative and interpretive studies play an important part in this area, the latter are of particular value to us for the frequently disturbing way in which they force us to question, and sometimes reject, our commonly accepted assumptions about what we imagine pupils think of their schools, schooling and fellow inmates.

We shall begin by looking at pupils' views of school and schooling and then examine in turn their perceptions of work, teachers, and student teachers. The girls' viewpoint will then be considered and we shall close the chapter with an example of the way in which different perceptions of the same situation can be turned to advantage by the researcher.

PUPILS' VIEWS OF SCHOOL AND SCHOOLING

We saw in our introduction to this chapter how only limited research has been undertaken into the pupils' point of view and that it is only in the past twelve years or so that investigators have started to probe this important and promising area. In spite of this comparative neglect, however, a degree of consensus has emerged from the available findings – at least as far as perceptions of school and schooling are concerned – and it is this that we examine now. Our review is based mainly on the work of Meighan[8] who is careful to stress the tentative nature of the conclusions suggested by researchers. Inevitably there are some striking contrasts between findings as well as similarities. One such difference is between the way primary school children perceive their schooling as compared with secondary children. Primary school children, it appears, seem to be more satisfied with their schooling than secondary pupils. The latter become increasingly dissatisfied with school and even the 'successful' pupils are frequently as critical of their secondary experiences as the 'unsuccessful' ones.[8] Indeed, the contrast between the two sectors is sufficiently interesting to justify closer inspection.

In an analysis of descriptive portraits of their teachers provided by seven to eleven-year-old children, Makins[9] noted how observant they were with respect to variations in their teachers' behaviour and mood, even to the point of noticing those teachers who while on duty talked to lonely children in the playground and the occasions when teachers were angry with children because they were angry with themselves. Those teachers who resorted neither to sanctions nor to shouting appeared to achieve most popularity among the children. They allowed children to talk, explained the work clearly, and encouraged the pupils. There was also evidence from the essays that how children are taught is of more importance to them than what they are taught; and that teachers with a particular skill or talent, such as art or sport, were appreciated by their pupils. Makins concludes that in general the pupils involved in the study enjoyed their primary school.

Pupils' opinions of their secondary schooling are often in stark contrast to these views. In Blishen's study[5] referred to earlier, for example, pupils were required to write an essay on 'The school that I'd like'. Blishen notes that the contributions added up to a passionate, earnest and intelligent plea for a new order in our schools. Many pupils drew on their experiences in primary school and used these as a basis by which to compare their secondary schooling. The following comment by one thirteen-year-old summed up their feelings, 'At present the main difference between secondary school and primary school is that primary education is enjoyable and secondary education is absolutely dreary and boring.'

As Meighan comments, the pupils' assessment of their experience of schooling was wide ranging and included the unimaginative building design and the dreary furniture, the examination system and the effect that it had on curricula and learning, the use of prefects as peer group controls, the constraining effect of time-tables and bells, the pettiness of many school rules, and the insistence on compulsory worship and religious education. As he read many of the essays, Blishen was reminded of the image of prison. And for Meighan, the children's responses recalled Goffman's theory of total institutions[10] where he analyses in detail the coercive, non-negotiable and non-consultative nature of many contemporary institutions such as armies, asylums, monasteries, hospitals and prisons.

In another study, Maizels[11] got 330 'unsuccessful' pupils who had just left school or who were on the point of leaving to rate their schools and teachers. In general, both schools and teachers were rated poorly. Few felt that their teachers had encouraged them, had been prepared to listen to their viewpoint, had praised them when they deserved praise, had been pleasant and kind, or had kept their promises. Only 34 % of the sample considered that their teachers had treated them like human beings.

Meighan refers also to a study, this time by Moody,[12] which revealed that pupils were frequently humiliated by teachers. Moody concludes that the primary purpose of this kind of behaviour on the part of the teachers was to make the pupils aware of their insignificance as individuals and their lowly status in the social hierarchy as compared to teachers. Distress and resentment on the part of the pupils was the result of this treatment by the teachers.

There are other studies on pupils' views of their school and schooling, some of which we shall be considering in the course of this chapter. For the moment, we refer you to Box 5.2 which contains Meighan's summary of the general findings in this area. The dissatisfaction with school expressed there immediately prompts

BOX 5.2

The Pupils' Point of View

Although the research on the point of view of the pupils is limited, there emerges a degree of consensus in the general findings:

1. Primary schoolchildren tend to enjoy school, whereas secondary schoolchildren tend to be less happy with their school experiences.
2. Both 'successful' and 'unsuccessful', pupils in secondary schools record dissatisfaction. It is not just a reaction of the 'failures'.
3. The dissatisfaction appears to be marked, and not a minor feature. Only the minority of secondary schools appear to achieve even a pass mark in the eyes of the pupils.
4. The views of the pupils are not merely negative. They are able to offer a wide range of constructive, and mostly, feasible, alternatives.
5. The perceptions of pupils appear to be valid enough and reliable enough to consider seriously as feedback. On more technical aspects of schooling, e.g. use of teaching aids, there appears to be some doubt about the validity of pupils' comments.
6. The pupils' views about preferred teachers show a high degree of consensus as do their views of 'bad' teachers.
7. Pupils are able to recognize some aspects of the hidden curriculum, some of the labelling processes and record their feelings of alienation that result.

And finally, teachers appear to have little to fear from consulting pupils. In the vast majority of cases, the comments of pupils are constructive and sympathetic.

Source: Meighan[8]

the question, why should this be so? As with so many other problematic aspects of contemporary education there is no clear-cut answer. Indeed, how could there be when there are so many shifting factors contributing to the cause. Responsibility for the disaffection must in some cases rest with those teachers who are unable to cope in any professional sense with the children committed to their charge. On the other hand, there are many occasions where the causes for expressed discontent lie well outside a teacher's control. By way of example, let us look at two possible factors contributing to pupils' negative responses – the content of the curriculum and the institutional nature of the school. First the curriculum: even allowing for the changes and development that have taken place in this respect, does it meet the pupils' own perceived needs? Could there be a growing awareness on the part of children of the kinds of things they expect from their schooling? Could it be that the school itself is less aware of them? In other words could the inappropriateness or limitations of the contemporary curriculum contribute to pupil disaffection? Weston and her colleagues[13] suggest that pupils' understanding of what school is for is an important factor to be borne in mind by educationalists. As a result of an attitude questionnaire given to a sample of pupils at two case study schools, the investigators found that while pupils readily concede the importance of the vocational benefits offered by school, they also value highly goals of personal and social development, an area that tends to be neglected by schools in favour of vocational aspirations. The researchers conclude, '. . . as a result of their experiences in and out of school, pupils develop their own views of the qualities and competencies which they value, and which are important to them in the present. Can schools make a positive contribution to this learning process? According to the majority of these pupils the answer is *yes*; teachers could do more than merely hold the ring in this area while vocational goals are pursued.'[13]

Then there is the second factor possibly contributing to pupil dissatisfaction: the institutional nature of the school. As a result of an intense study of two forms in a secondary modern school, Woods[14] found that hostility to the institutional aspects of school was common to both the two forms, one an examination form and the other a non-examination form. He discovered, for example, much evidence of depersonalizing, bureaucratic and instrumental pressure. School was compared to 'the army' or 'prison' and its influence was found to be pervasive:

> 'It's homework mainly. I don't think you ought to do it. When you get home you want to forget school. You want to go out and do something instead of being stuck in working. It's like having continuous school almost.'[15]

If pupils have definite views on what they do not like, can it be said that they have a clear picture of what they do like? The answer again is most decidedly *yes*. We have already listed qualities children wish to see in their teachers in Box 5.1. Blishen[5] also reports on other aspects of schooling. Most pupils, for instance, wanted mixed and comprehensive schools and were critical of the school buildings, particularly the square rooms, unimaginative decoration, desks and the shortage of common rooms for pupils. Examinations were seen as the cause of 'constipated' teaching and alternative forms of assessment were considered to be needed. Children were scornful of prefects, homework, school bells, and religious education. Blishen notes that the comments of the pupils were remarkably sober and well considered. But how do they perceive the activity for which schools exist in the first place – work?

PUPILS' PERCEPTIONS OF WORK

In spite of its centrality in the life of a school and its repercussions in adulthood, how pupils perceive work has received little attention from researchers. One significant contribution in this connection, however, is a study by Woods[16] who, in one secondary school, set out to discover what affected pupils' attitudes to schoolwork from their own perspective. Although he found the notion of *work* difficult to define, referring to it as a 'patchwork of diverse values and purposes, displaying many contradictions and inconsistencies', school in effect served as an interface for two discrepant conceptions of it. On the one hand, there was the model presented to the pupils by the school. This was the official version, although the teachers who were required to represent it felt ambivalent about it *as private individuals*. The model itself is based on traditional protestant ethic notions of work, implying the need for ambition, self-improvement, particular moral values, and a view of work as a worthy end in itself: it holds good for the relatively conservative institution of the school notwithstanding the fact that it is an out-dated conception of work lacking correspondence with society at large where the concept has undergone and, indeed, continues to undergo profound changes.

According to Woods, however, the pupils bring to school another model. His view is that attitudes to work are learned and that this learning takes place partly outside school 'through cultural permeation'. As he explains, 'These pupils' interpretations arise generally from shifting definitions and loci of self mediated to them through mass communication, changing patterns of child-rearing, career opportunities, and so forth.' The effects of growing unemployment among the younger generation and the displace-ment of people by developing technology have yet to be assessed. Features of earlier conceptions of work – its intrinsic worth, the virtues of industry, personal benefits – find no place in the newer conceptions. Woods found that what happens in school under the label *work* is largely an accommodation of these two oppositional tendencies – 'Teachers seek to bridge the gulf by various 'motivating' devices. The whole school day rings to the sound of inducements to work.'

Naturally enough, Woods found that motivation for the pupils in the school did not come from the discredited model which the school attempted to keep alive, but from two other features – *the school's own valuation of work* and, particularly, *the pupils' relationships with the teachers*. In connection with the former, the hierarchy of work dis-tinguishes on the one hand 'O' level, CSE, and non-examination work; and on the other, within these varieties, work that is meaningful, work that is productive, work that is play, and work that is useless. Pupils accept the status of work according to the school's own evaluation of it. Box 5.3 contains an extract of an exchange between the interviewer and examination pupils on the subject of their non-examination classmates.

As regards the second feature identified above, *the pupils' relationships with the teachers*, Woods learned from his interviews and discussions with pupils that work could be both odious and burdensome, *and* pleasant and enjoyable, and that what makes the difference is not so much the content of the work as the relations with the teacher concerned. It is the teacher who can transform the experience. As Woods concludes:

'The simple moral is to make the work count, and for teachers to be human. Fake products, however, or exhortations without structural support, are quickly spotted,

BOX 5.3

> *Comments by Examination Pupils about*
> *their Non-Examination Classmates*
>
> | | |
> |---|---|
> | Int. | Is it as worthwhile as the programme you've been on? |
> | Diane | I think they do more social work – learning about the community more than actual education like maths and English an' that. |
> | Vera | They've been going out a lot, and been doing work around the school, going out for Community Service. |
> | Int. | Is it as worthwhile as the programme you've been on? |
> | Diane | I think it's worthwhile in their own way because a lot of them aren't intelligent enough to take exams, some of them are, but not all of them . . . and they spend their time doing a worthwhile programme really. They can't learn much in maths and English, that sort of thing, but they can learn about the community. |

Source: Woods[16]

and only compound the problem of "how to get pupils to work", an issue itself embedded in antiquated pedagogy.'

We have just seen how in the particular school studied work was mediated through relationships between pupils and teachers; how it became, in Woods' phrase, a 'negotiated activity'. But of course there are in addition other, wider cultural or sub-cultural influences affecting a child's perception of schoolwork and we here touch upon two of them – *social class background* and *parental involvement*. With respect to the former, Willis[17] suggests that counter-school culture is part of the wider working-class culture of a region and ultimately of the nation, and, in particular, runs parallel to what he refers to as 'shop-floor culture'. Both, he argues, share broadly the same determinants: a common impulse to develop strategies for dealing with boredom, blocked opportunities, alienation and lack of control; and both are characterized by chauvinism, toughness, machismo, and independence. In an ethnographic study of a group of working-class boys, Willis set out to find out why working-class children apparently choose working-class jobs where the choice is based on an affirmation of working-class culture.[18] Having used interviewing, group discussion and participant observation, he presents an in-depth study of a group of anti-school working-class lads who reject the world offered them by their teachers.

Opposition to the school is principally manifested in the struggle to win symbolic and physical space from the institution and its rules and to defeat its main perceived purpose – to make you 'work'. Both the winning and the prize – a form of self-direction – profoundly develop informal cultural meanings and practices. By the time a counter-school culture is fully developed, its members have become adept at managing the formal system, and at limiting its demands to the absolute minimum. Exploiting the complexity of modern regimes of mixed ability grouping, blocked time-tabling and multiple ROSLA options, in many cases this minimum is simply the act of registration.

Some of the lads develop the ability of moving about the school at will to a remarkable degree. They construct virtually their own day from what is offered by the school. Truancy is only one relatively unimportant and crude variant of *self-direction* which ranges across vast areas of the syllabus and covers many diverse activities: being free out of class, being in class and not working, being in the wrong class, roaming the corridors looking for excitement, and being asleep in private. The basic skill which articulates these possibilities is being able to get out of any given lesson: the preservation of personal mobility. Box 5.4 contains an extract of a group discussion by members of the school counter-culture on the school curriculum.

BOX 5.4

Attitudes to School and Work as Manifested in a Discussion with Members of a School Counter-culture

Joey	(. . .) of a Monday afternoon, we'd have nothing right? Nothing hardly relating to school work. Tuesday afternoon we have swimming and they stick you in a classroom for the rest of the afternoon. Wednesday afternoon you have games and there's only Thursday and Friday afternoon that you work, if you call that work. The last lesson Friday afternoon we used to go and doss, half of us wagged out o' lessons and the other half go into the classroom, sit down and just go to sleep (. . .)
Spanksy	(. . .) Skive this lesson, go up on the bank, have a smoke, and the next lesson go to teacher who, you know, 'll call the register (. . .)
Bill	It's easy to go home as well, like him (Eddie) . . . last Wednesday afternoon, he got his mark and went home (. . .)
Eddie	I ain't supposed to be in school this afternoon, I'm supposed to be at college (on a link course where students spend one day a week at college for vocational instruction)
Int.	What's the last time you've done some writing?
Will	When we done some writing?
Fuzz	On are, last time was in careers, 'cos I writ 'yes' on a piece of paper, that broke me heart.
Int.	Why did it break your heart?
Fuzz	I mean to write, 'cos I was going to try and go through the term without writing anything. 'Cos since we've cum back, I ain't dun nothing (it was half way through term).

Source: Willis[18]

The connection between family background, parental involvement and educational achievement has been exhaustively researched in some respects. Very well known is the consistent relationship between father's occupation and school achievement, and the influence of factors like material circumstances, family size, level of parental education, and warm and affectionate relationships. However, inter-class differences in perspectives, represented by members' accounts and constructions as revealed by interactionist studies, are less well researched. Too frequently they have been illustrated by researchers who are influenced themselves by the dominant culture, so that accounts of working-class culture have been coloured by evaluations of 'deficiency'. In a study by Woods, however, an interesting relationship was established between pupil and parent perspectives, the latter being distributed across the working and middle classes.[19] The investigation was an exploratory case study and this needs to be borne in mind when its findings are examined. Woods identified five types of parental influence. These were: (1) compulsion; (2) strong guidance; (3) mutual resolution; (4) reassurance; and (5) little or no influence. Table 5.1 shows how these were spread among the twenty seven homes visited by the researcher.

Though numbers were small, the trend towards stronger counselling for the middle class child, rather than simply 'high achieving child', is clearly visible. Woods notes, too, that where working class parents give strong guidance, it tends to be less well informed about school processes and subjects and their linkage with future careers.

Table 5.1 *Distribution of Types of Parental Influence*

Type of influence	Middle Class			Total	Working Class			Total
	3A	3B	3C		3A	3B	3C	
Compulsion	0	2	0	2	0	0	0	0
Strong guidance	1	3	0	4	1	0	1	2
Mutual resolution	2	1	0	3	1	4	1	6
Reassurance	3	0	0	3	0	1	2	3
Little/Nil	0	0	0	0	0	1	3	4
Total	6	6	0	12	2	6	7	15

Source: Woods[19]

In conclusion, Woods says that there are different kinds and amounts of parental advice and influence operating on different groups of pupils. These show a connection with social class. Middle class parents are more likely to be more involved with school processes, show more complex reasoning in accordance with school criteria in advising their children, and to be more persuaded by 'school' factors. Working class parents display less involvement, are less instrumentally oriented, possibly entertain suspicions of school and teachers, have fewer consultations with teachers and their own children, and are more likely to be persuaded by 'personal' factors. Middle class parents, on the other hand, tend to give strong guidance, and to be well informed, critical and coercive, instrumentally oriented and status conscious. Working class parents tend to give less guidance and to be uninformed.

We noted above how work was a 'negotiated activity'. We now look at what research has to tell us of the ways pupils perceive the other party in this act of bargaining – the teachers themselves.

PUPILS' PERCEPTIONS OF TEACHERS

Although investigations into the opinions and perceptions of teachers hold a prominent place in educational research, how pupils perceive their teachers and the opinions they hold of them have tended to be ignored by research. It has been suggested that this may be so because there is a general belief that what pupils think and feel can be manipulated by teachers, the implication being that how they perceive the teacher is largely under his control.[6]

This belief is only partly true, however; and there are at least two possible reasons why pupils' perceptions and opinions should be regarded as important and accorded a central place in educational research. First, if we recognize, as Nash has suggested, that teachers' expectations for their pupils have an effect on their pupils' behaviour, then we should similarly recognize the reciprocal hypothesis that pupils' expectations for their teachers might equally have an effect on their teachers' behaviour. Second, Thompson[20] notes that concern is continuously being voiced about the increasing alienation of pupils from their schools, and that a search is being made for the sorts of changes to the education system which will make schools more relevant and satisfying to the needs of the current generation of school children. Such changes, it is argued, would lead to a population more sympathetic towards the educational system and more successful within it. It is therefore relevant, Thompson concludes, to examine how pupils feel about school and teachers in an attempt to discover the appropriate directions of change.

One of the earliest studies in this area was that of Hollis[21] who, in a normative approach to the issue, asked just over 8000 children to rank seven statements describing a teacher's behaviour. He found that the quality of 'explaining difficulties patiently' was conclusively the most popular, 'being friendly and sympathetic' was ranked second, with 'just and fair' third. Fourth and fifth were 'humour' and 'allowing pupils to ask plenty of questions'. The teacher 'having wide interests' was ranked sixth, while 'discipline' was rated as of least importance. A study by Allen[22] of attitudes to school among secondary modern children found that both boys and girls valued most highly the general competence of the teacher. This finding was corroborated later by Taylor[6] who found that children in general evaluated most highly the 'good' teacher's teaching; and least highly, the 'good' teacher's personal qualities.

Taylor developed rating scales to measure children's views of the 'good' teacher on four categories of behaviour: teaching, discipline, personal qualities, and organization. The scales were developed from an analysis of children's essays and were administered to nearly 900 pupils from several junior, modern, and grammar schools. In general, children were concerned that the 'good' teachers should be firm and be able to keep order. In unstreamed junior schools children rated most highly the teacher's personal qualities, her patience, sympathy and understanding. Among secondary school children it seemed that in the fourth year, boys in particular rated most highly personal qualities such as cheerfulness, good temper, and a sense of humour. Most children rated the 'good' teacher as being firm and fair in her discipline, having a good knowledge of her subject, able to explain difficult points and as being helpful and encouraging.

Findings from the earlier research in this area up to the early 1960s have been summarized by Evans as follows:[23]

> 'Children like teachers who are kind, friendly, cheerful, patient, helpful, fair, have a sense of humour, show an understanding of children's problems, allow plenty of pupil activity and at the same time maintain order. They dislike teachers who use sarcasm, are domineering and have favourites, who punish to secure discipline, fail to provide for the needs of individual pupils and have disagreeable personality peculiarities.'

Nash notes[24] that these findings may be thought unremarkable, but goes on to explain that they become more interesting when they are looked upon as not merely a description of children's likes and dislikes about teachers, *but are a formulation of the rules of conduct which they lay down for them.* He observes that Morrison and MacIntyre were the first to realize that these attitudes and expectations become norms, quoting from them thus:[25]

> 'One expectation of teachers which appears to be shared by many British pupils is that among their primary functions are those of policeman and judge in the classroom . . . . A teacher entering this sort of situation who behaves as if these were not important functions, but as if his task were simply to instruct or as if he will

be accepted as a friend, counsellor and stimulator of ideas, is not likely to be perceived as he perceives himself. He will rather be categorized by pupils as 'soft' and incompetent, and will be given little respect.'

Nash further notes that this idea has been a commonplace of interaction psychology. For example, the way in which children's expectations for their teachers become normative has been specifically discussed by Geer.[26] She argues that the class transforms what the teacher says and does into rules for him to follow: rules which he must not change and which he must apply to all pupils.

This interactionist model enables us to go beyond the mere collection of children's views on the behaviour of their teachers and begin to analyse their status as determinants of teacher action. We need, Nash suggests, to study the 'taken-for-granted' rules that children formulate for their teachers. Taking his own advice, Nash himself investigated how pupils' attitudes to their teachers actually set up expectations which affect the teacher's behaviour.[27] As he explains, the study involved only one class of 12 to 13 year-olds. The children were interviewed individually so that much more probing questions could be asked than would have been possible by using a questionnaire. Each pupil was presented with three cards each bearing the name of one of his teachers. He was then asked to sort the cards into two sets: (1) teachers he 'got on with'; and (2) teachers he did not 'get on with'. The children were not asked to force their answers into a formal set of constructs rather they were encouraged to discuss and compare the teachers as they liked. Analysis of the conversations revealed six constructs which seemed to be commonly held by all, or almost all, pupils. These were: 1. Keeps order   unable to keep order; 2. Teaches you – does not teach you; 3. Explains – does not explain; 4. Interesting – boring; 5. Fair – unfair; and 6. Friendly – unfriendly.

Everyone agreed that teachers should be able to keep order. Pupils who were well behaved considered that the teacher should keep the noisy ones quiet so that they could get on with their work. Less obviously the noisy children also believed that teachers should keep them in order. Indeed, these children commonly blamed the teacher for not doing just this and for being 'soft'. Pupils also expected teachers to teach specific and well-defined subjects and preferred lessons which left them with a feeling of having learned something. They did not regard discussion periods, for example, as proper teaching. Teachers were expected, furthermore, to help and explain when the children were having difficulties in understanding their work. They particularly disliked teachers who told them to 'work it out for themselves' and to 'think'. They appreciated the teacher who made her lessons flow and who made the main points of the lesson clearly in a way that they could understand. Few children enjoyed periods where the teacher continually punctuated the progress of the lesson with questions that seemed disruptive. Fairness was something all children mentioned. They expected firmness, if not strictness, but the teacher was expected to behave fairly to everyone. She should give a warning or a second chance before punishing. She should not punish all children for the faults of the few: inability to catch the guilty ones was not seen as an excuse to blame the whole class. She was not expected to have favourites or to 'pick on' pupils. The children expected to be treated with a degree of equity and if they were not they would protest. Teachers were also expected to be friendly, to talk conversationally, and not to shout nor domineer the class. Several children, particularly girls, said that they were often made upset and nervous by overbearing or inexperienced teachers.

BOX 5.5

Extracts from Secondary School Children's Views of their Teachers

Does this teacher make the work interesting?
Yes, very. She nearly always has another way of learning a point than that in the book.

What sort of things make you like a teacher?
I like teachers who know how to handle a class and teachers who don't ignore noise and bad behaviour. And also I like teachers if they like you.

What sort of things make you dislike a teacher?
Not enough interest in the pupils and the subject. Doesn't recognize pupils as people. Doesn't allow discussion. Dictates notes all lesson, every lesson. Gives up on the less able.

Is there anything you don't like about this teacher?
Yes, his inability to yield to any opposition.

What's the best thing a teacher has ever said to you?
'Never mind, we all make mistakes.'

Source: Blishen[28]

These attitudes were seen by the children as expectations of the normal standards of behaviour for their teachers. It certainly seemed that the expectations the pupils had for their teachers did have a considerable influence on the behaviour of the teachers. It was clear that the teachers the children did not get on with were those who did not keep these expectations. Particularly interesting are implications of this for trainee and beginning teachers. Nash explains thus:

'It is because the classroom is rarely seen as a setting for social action that many novice teachers have such difficulties. Most of the so-called practical training in discipline offered to teachers has no more scientific status than a tip for the Derby. Trainee teachers are told variously to "project the voice", "make your lessons interesting", "isolate the rowdy ones", "clamp down on the first day", and so on. More to the point would be to teach student teachers to learn the members' rules . . . . A new class is not a clean slate passively waiting for the teacher to inscribe his will on it. It is an ongoing social system with very definite expectations about appropriate teacher behaviour. If these are not confirmed the pupils will protest and the re-negotiated patterns of behaviour may not prove to be just what the teacher intended.'

Of special interest to us in our consideration of pupils' perceptions of teachers are those studies which, among other features, attempt to compare children's perceptions of their teachers with those of other adults, notably parents. One of the earliest studies of this kind was that of Wright[29] with pupils from single-sex secondary modern schools in their last year at school. In thus examining their concepts of parents and teachers, Wright concluded that it was those aspects of the personality of teachers which make them more human that are rated less favourably. He considered that his results indicated a need for the adolescent to meet his teacher in a more individual and human way and come to identify more fully with him as a person outside his primary role.

Thompson's study[20] attempted to replicate in part Wright's findings. It was concerned with pupils in their first and fourth years at comprehensive and secondary modern schools and had the added feature that it compared pupils whom their teachers designated as particularly well-adjusted with those designated as maladjusted. The investigation was specifically concerned to discover:

1. Whether Wright's results concerning the way pupils see their teachers can be replicated, and to what extent these are merely a reflection of their views of adults generally;
2. Whether attitudes to school and teachers deteriorate as pupils progress through the school; and
3. In what way deviant pupils' views of school and teachers differ from the views of those pupils considered well-adjusted.

The results of the study were very similar to those of Wright. Teachers were rated more favourably than adults generally on characteristics which they are expected to display in their primary role as teachers. These include factors such as wisdom, success, and hardness. They were rated *less* favourably than the adults, however, on strictly human qualities such as kindness, fairness, and warmth. It was concluded from these findings that if it were considered important for pupils to develop more positive attitudes to their teachers, the latter would need to play a wider variety of roles, so that they were not merely seen as 'impersonal purveyors of knowledge and administerers of discipline.'

Attitudes to both school and teachers did deteriorate as pupils progressed through the system. However, the differences only reach significance[30] for the well-adjusted pupils, owing to the great variability of ratings by the maladjusted boys and girls. A point of interest was that the overall change was due to less favourable ratings on the scales usually found to be favourable to school and teachers. This means that the older pupils did not rate teachers as even less human than they did when they were younger, but did rate them as less wise and successful.

Pupils whom their teachers designated as deviant had less favourable opinions of school and teachers than those designated well-adjusted. The differences, however, appeared to be spread fairly evenly across scales, as no individual scale comparisons reach significance. The researcher hypothesized that a 'teacher-expectation' factor could have been at work here, in which the 'deviation' was *caused* by the teacher's attitude.

One of the difficulties with most of the studies of pupil perception touched upon in this section is that they present *static* conceptions of teachers and teaching. More *dynamic* analyses would take account of pupils' own interpretive processes, of changes over time, and of pupils' ongoing, dynamic relationships with teachers. One study more in line with this conception is Gannaway's.[31] On the basis of interviews and observation, he constructed a dynamic model by proposing that teachers are progressively typified by pupils in a given sequence. The teachers are, in effect, subjected to a systematic series of tests by pupils, the first of which is *can the teacher keep order*? The next test is *can he 'have a laugh'*? And the final test to which he is subjected, *does he understand pupils*? Gannaway suggests that providing the answer to each of these is *yes*, and provided the teacher can put over something of interest in the lesson, then he 'has it made'. The actual implications of these questions are of special interest to us because they connect up with findings from other studies described elsewhere in this section and chapter. The first test, for instance, *can the teacher keep order*?, implies that the pupils expect him to do just that, to keep order. Of equal importance is the second challenge, *can he 'have a laugh'*? What is implied here is that in expecting the teacher to keep order, they do not expect him to be *too* strict, to impose a regime so harsh that the pupils will ultimately rebel. What is called for is a 'nice strictness' in preference to a 'nasty strictness'.[32] The final test, *does he understand pupils?*, is in some ways the most interesting of the three for it implies an understanding of the class *as a class*, *as a group*, in contrast to understanding *individual* children or an aggregate of children. The difference is significant for it means that understanding a group is of a different order to understanding the individual: a different standpoint is required

BOX 5.6

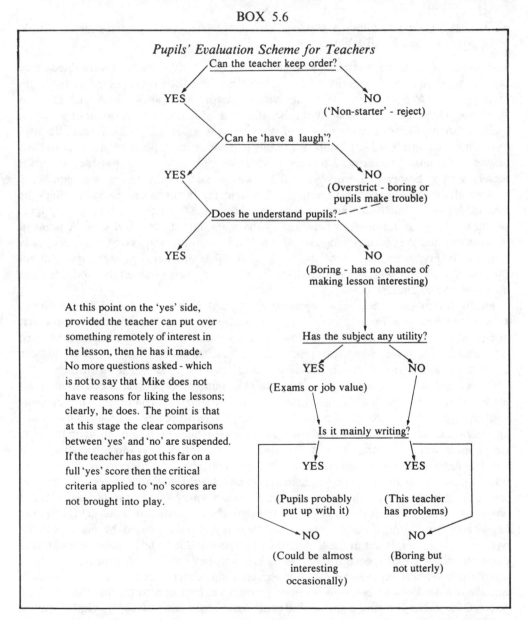

Pupils' Evaluation Scheme for Teachers

Can the teacher keep order?

YES   NO
                                        ('Non-starter' - reject)

Can he 'have a laugh'?

YES   NO
                                        (Overstrict - boring or
                                         pupils make trouble)

Does he understand pupils?

YES   NO
                                        (Boring - has no chance of
                                         making lesson interesting)

At this point on the 'yes' side,
provided the teacher can put over
something remotely of interest in   Has the subject any utility?
the lesson, then he has it made.
No more questions asked - which   YES   NO
is not to say that Mike does not   (Exams or job value)
have reasons for liking the lessons;
clearly, he does. The point is that
at this stage the clear comparisons   Is it mainly writing?
between 'yes' and 'no' are suspended.
If the teacher has got this far on a YES   YES
full 'yes' score then the critical
criteria applied to 'no' scores are
not brought into play.   (Pupils probably   (This teacher
                                      put up with it)   has problems)

                                        NO   NO
                                     (Could be almost   (Boring but
                                      interesting   not utterly)
                                      occasionally)

Source: Gannaway[31]

and different knowledge and skills. We return to this point shortly when we come to consider the girls' viewpoint. Box 5.6 expresses Gannaway's model in diagrammatic form and follows through the consequences of a succession of negative responses to the three inexorable questions just considered. Hargreaves[33] points out that Gannaway's model has considerable potential because it can be readily developed to take account of both situational variations and the longer term career of the pupils' typifications.

A gnawing question which must have been in most readers' minds at some time or other is *how do pupils perceive student teachers*? Are they rated by the same criteria used to assess the experienced professional? Are children's judgments more or less censorious in this respect? Regrettably, little empirical work has been undertaken in this interesting sphere. What has been done, however, is both stimulating and refreshing – as we shall see in the next section.

PUPILS' PERCEPTIONS OF STUDENT TEACHERS

In the 1960s a number of studies were conducted in the United States into pupils' perceptions of the teaching performance of student teachers.[34] The findings from these were sufficiently interesting to stimulate further studies in the 1970s by British researchers and to convince others that how pupils perceive the teaching skills of student teachers is worth taking seriously. Assessment of student teachers is normally undertaken by experienced people in the field of education and teacher education and in the past this was exclusively the case. More recently, however, it has been discovered that although pupils are untrained observers, their perceptions show sufficient consensus and agreement with other assessors to warrant consideration as another source of information against which to check the strengths and weaknesses of students' classroom skills.[35] It is against this background that we here examine the findings of two British studies.

In a study by Cortis and Grayson,[36] children aged between 9 and 11 in several primary schools were taught two lessons by ten student teachers. In each school the two lessons were separated by an interval of two weeks. A total of 270 pupils were taught by the students in the first lessons; and 237 in the second. The student teachers comprised five men and five women. All were taking part in their final teaching practice and all had volunteered to take part in the study. After each of the two lessons, both children and student teachers completed the same questionnaire relating to their performance and attitude. The first of the two lessons was a mandatory 'creative writing' lesson: in the second, the students were allowed to choose their own topic.

After analysing the data from the study, the authors identified the following 'critical incidents' which they define as areas affecting, for good or ill, teaching outcomes. Thus, with respect to the student teachers, the pupils noticed particularly that they: (1) notice/fail to notice hard/poor work; (2) show ability/fail to show ability to organize; (3) answer/fail to answer children's questions; (4) explain/fail to explain things clearly; (5) ask/fail to ask the rest of the class when they cannot themselves answer a child's question; and (6) shout/do not shout at the children. With respect to themselves, the pupils notice that: (1) they are taught new/old subject matter; (2) they enjoy/dislike learning; (3) they have exciting/boring lessons; (4) they have easy/difficult lessons; and (5) they understand/fail to understand the work.

As the authors point out, whether the same pattern of responses would obtain in the case of established teachers (in contrast to student teachers) is a matter for conjecture and further research.

In another study by Meighan[35] 454 pupils in the secondary sector were taught by 17 volunteer student teachers completing a ten-week teaching practice in a variety of subjects. The children were asked to write answers to sixteen questions sampling four areas of teaching performance: *preparation*, *presentation*, *attitudes* and *organization*. The method chosen was to select a class or group of children that a student teacher had worked with at least twice and preferably several times, and to ask each pupil to write down his perceptions of their student teacher's performance in the classroom under two main headings. These were *Things you do well* and *Possible improvements*. Some cue questions were made available on the blackboard or introduced in some way that seemed appropriate to the student teacher. The cue questions were as follows:

1. Preparation	Do I prepare the lessons well?
	Are the lessons interesting?
2. Technique of presentation	Do I speak clearly enough?
	Do I explain things clearly?
	Do I use questions well?
	Do I use sufficient teaching aids?
3. Attitudes to pupils	Am I strict enough or too strict?
	Do I treat you fairly?
4. Class management and discipline	Do I organize lessons well?
	Am I strict enough or too strict?

We give below a selection of children's responses to some of the questions that were asked:

1. Do you think that my lessons are well prepared?
   They usually are, because when we get into the class we've usually got everything set out for us even when you're away.
   Most of the time, but there were odd moments . . . .
   Yes. You can see that a lot of time has been spent on this although a normal teacher would probably not have the time to do this.
   Very well prepared and always ready to change the prepared lesson should other aspects arise.
2. Do the lessons have enough interest for you?
   The lessons I have had have been quite interesting because we have learnt new things.
   I don't think the lessons are explained enough. You should explain why we are doing the lesson.
   I find them boring, but that is the subject.
   No the lessons should be of the children's choice, we should have a choice of lessons.
3. Do I use questions well?
   No. Some questions are not worth asking.
   They are very enquiring and interesting but tend to be just to the front row.
   You word them so that you get the answers you want.
   Questions don't give varying answers, the questions are alike too much.
   Yes, but you should ask individuals not ask for a volunteer.

4. Am I strict enough with the class?

Yes, you are strict enough with us. You know when to have a laugh with us but you also know when to be serious with us.

If you say you'll give detentions, you should.

Isn't very strict, but there's a better atmosphere.

You are not rotten like other teachers. Your strictness is not strict (if you see what I mean). A nice strictness.

The findings of both these studies show that, contrary to received opinion in some quarters, children do have clear and meaningful perceptions of students' teaching performance and consequently have something of value to say. Moreover, given the opportunity to do so, they will not abuse it. Indeed, one of the intriguing consequences of Meighan's study was that after completing their written comments, a 'difficult' class changed its general attitude from one of obstruction to one of co-operation. The author suggests that interesting possibilities are raised concerning the effects on relationships of consulting children about their views on the teaching they receive.

A VIEW FROM THE GIRLS

It would be a comparatively easy task to marshal those well-founded arguments put forward by numerous writers for *not* singling out girls for particular attention in a chapter given over to pupil perspectives. The very act of focusing exclusively on the girls, as one writer explains,[37] presupposes an identifiably different response from the boys which may not necessarily be the case. Such a decision also assumes that generalizations can be made about girls when factors such as age, stream, background, ethnic origin and educational setting may all mean vast differences in response and be more decisive in determining a viewpoint than merely the fact of gender. In addition, by drawing attention to the girls' viewpoint, one is in danger of reinforcing sex-typed labels. Differential treatment of boys and girls in the classroom is well known, as Davies comments, 'Teachers already operate on theories of how the sexes do or should behave in the classroom, and are not only willing to make sex-based generalizations about capabilities and interests, but also appear to give different treatment to the sexes.'[37] By separating out girls' perceptions as a distinct entity, one may be open to the charge of endorsing this behaviour.

Do critics have the last word? Can anything be said to defend the study of a specifically female viewpoint? Hard evidence on this issue is at a premium, but let us look at what is available. As a result of her ethnographic study in a girls' secondary school, Davies concludes[37] that how pupils view features of their school environment depends on the labelling and control aspects of the institution in question and the degree of differentiation between teachers and taught, between 'able' and 'less able', and – of special interest to us – between boys and girls. This latter category seems to suggest that where differentiation between the sexes by teachers is marked, that is, where teachers in general behave in a noticeably different way towards boys and girls, there will be a corresponding difference of viewpoint between the sexes, so that this alone would justify investigating the girls' perspective. But there is also the feminist position. It is self-evident that the secondary years of schooling are crucial in defining a girl's future. Yet there is clear evidence to indicate that at this stage schools exert a complex of influences intentionally or unintentionally harmful to both girls' self-concepts and their life chances. Rosemary Deem, for example,[38] has written *inter alia* of the contrasting cultural expectations of boys and girls and of the curricular discrimination and differentiation prevalent at the secondary stage. Any attempt, therefore, to understand the school-based viewpoint of girls must be seen as one possible line of attack in helping to mitigate these ills.

The few studies undertaken so far on girls' perceptions tend naturally to be exploratory in nature, but the findings are sufficiently significant to warrant considerably more research being pursued in this area. One such study was that of Lomax[39] working in an all-girls secondary modern school. Adopting a normative approach, she used a *school adjustment index* to provide the independent variable against which other school orientation variables were measured. This enabled her to identify a *well-adjusted* and a *badly-adjusted* group of girls. She set out initially to examine the hypothesis that academic school matters were the central concern of the girls at school and that these shaped their feelings about school in general. The findings, however, did not support this and an alternative hypothesis was substituted. This postulated that the *pupil-centred culture* of the classroom was the central concern of the girls in school and that it was this that shaped their orientation to other school matters.

Perhaps the most consequential finding of Lomax's study was that *peer relationships* were the most important feature in the school culture. She says, 'Both well-adjusted and badly-adjusted girls were strongly peer oriented in their view of school. Apparently, school for girls at Rushel was primarily a context for peer group interaction. Learning, teachers and the paraphernalia most often associated with school merely provided the backdrop for these relationships.[39] Similar findings were reported by Davies[37] in her study of both boys' and girls' perceptions of school. She found that in the school studied twice as many girls as boys agreed with the statement, 'Most days I look forward to coming to school.' As Davies observes, school for most of them was a social place, as this comment by a pupil indicates:

'If you couldn't have friends, school wouldn't be anything, would it?'

She also found that the importance of friends at school led inevitably to peer group pressures which tended to discourage open interest in academic work:

'I like maths the best. My mates think I've gone soft cos I like maths. They can't stand maths. I've been top of the class nearly all the time I've been through school.'

Indeed, in a case study conducted among 15 fourth year girls in a London secondary modern school, Furlong[40] found that the defining characteristic of what a school friend should be was someone who could 'join in the fun and make you laugh.'

Researcher: If you had to describe what sort of person you would choose as a school friend, what would she be, someone who makes jokes, or someone who's good at working, or someone who's a mixture or what?

Anne: The mixture is better than just good at work and no jokes, better
                 than working day in and out, writing, writing.

Lomax's findings on aspects of peer group membership for both the well-adjusted and
badly-adjusted girls yield interesting insights on how the two groups view the social
structure. It was found, for instance, that badly-adjusted girls disliked being isolated from
the group more than the others did and expressed a strong dislike for working alone. Both
groups, she found, shared the belief that success and popularity in a group were
dependent on personal characteristics, though badly-adjusted girls saw friendship failure
as being caused by other people rather than themselves. Lomax also points out that
although both groups recognized the importance of peer relationships in school life, the
groups differed in the ways they perceived the basis of such relationships. The well-
adjusted girls emphasized positive qualities like friendship; the badly-adjusted girls saw
the basis in negative terms, the social structure being held together by *not* doing certain
things – by not annoying others, by not fighting, by not breaking rules.

The study also disclosed some interesting findings on the way the girls perceived their
teachers and aspects of teacher behaviour. It was not uncommon, for example, for teachers to establish social distance in order to preserve their authority. This 'distancing' the
girls interpreted as the staff response to their own peer-group relationships and were
naturally critical of it. Lomax explains it like this, 'Social distance was seen by the pupils to
epitomize the teachers' hostility to the important network of peer-group relationships
that girls saw as the centre of school life.' The girls were critical, too, of the teachers'
inability to understand them *as a group*, though they were not perceived as necessarily
unsympathetic to the girls on an individual basis. This view was held by all groups of girls.
The successful teacher, on the other hand, was one who was seen to understand the
problems of young people *as a group*, not as individual problems, and who could bridge
the generation gap.

Girls' perceptions of teachers' expectations of them did not appear to be related to any
particular criticism they had of teachers. Lomax says in this respect:

'Most girls thought that teachers viewed them in a positive or neutral light though
one third of the girls thought that they were assessed negatively by teachers. Girls
who thought that teachers approved of them tended to see this as overall approval
rather than as praise for either their work or behaviour. Girls who perceived
teachers' hostility tended to associate this with condemnation of their behaviour
rather than their work, or as an overall disapproval. Work was the area in which
girls noted least teacher concern.'

In using a *school adjustment index* to measure orientations of well-adjusted and badly-
adjusted girls to other school variables, Lomax found an interesting relationship between
school adjustment and the way the girls perceived many of their problems. The
relationship seemed to be particularly acute where the badly-adjusted girls were
concerned. For instance, those poorly-adjusted girls who had negative attitudes to school
and learning tended to lay the blame for their inability to learn on school rather than on
themselves or on other pupils. Their friendship difficulties they perceived in terms of
incompatibility rather than their own social incompetence, an attitude which again, to
some extent at least, places the blame on other people. Lomax points out too that in their

friendship with teachers, poorly-adjusted girls differed from their classmates by more often seeing teachers as hostile to them and by interpreting the cause of this hostility in behavioural rather than work terms. They were the only girls who had completely negative attitudes to teachers and where these attitudes were justified by explanation, they stressed that teachers were old-fashioned. That the teachers had low expectations of their behaviour was blamed on the belief that teachers were out of touch with the modern world. Overall, as Lomax notes, the badly-adjusted girls 'externalized their dissatisfaction with school life by blaming a constraining world for their own situation within it.'

Notwithstanding the exploratory nature of these studies, they quite clearly indicate that girls' perceptions, as distinct from how boys see their working environment, could become a useful source of information for researchers and practising teachers. Not only do they provide valuable insights into how girls view crucial aspects of school life, they also provide supportive evidence on the nature of a classroom's social structure.

COMBINED PERCEPTIONS: THE USE OF TRIANGULATION IN CLASSROOM RESEARCH

You will recall in Chapter 2 we defined *triangulation* as the use of two or more methods of data collection in the study of some aspect of human behaviour. The approach may be used in both normative and interpretive research where it will normally provide the investigator with sets of quantitative and qualitative data respectively. The classroom based project we are about to review utilized triangulation to help teachers monitor and improve features of their teaching performance by comparing three sets of qualitative data and is a good illustration of how, in some contexts, knowledge of the way a person perceives – or misperceives – a situation can be turned to definite practical advantage. Three perspectives on the teacher's behaviour were examined – the pupils', the participant observer's, and that of the teacher himself. The qualitative data gathered consisted of written, spoken and taped accounts of lessons and incidents in them as well as data from interviews with the actors involved. As it turned out, the teacher's perceptions of his own teaching performance were out of focus with what was really happening. In other words, there was a mismatch between the effect he *thought* he was having on his pupils and the *actual* effect. The particular advantage of triangulation in this context was that it helped to bring about a re-focusing of the teacher's viewpoint and a consequent improvement in his teaching performance.

The idea of the teaching project in which these triangular techniques were used arose from the involvement of one of the research team in the Schools Council Humanities Project. It had been found in the latter that attempts to implement discussion-based inquiry approaches to teaching and learning in the classroom were impeded by teachers' 'habitual and unconscious behaviour patterns.' As the researcher himself explains, 'Pupils' failure to discuss ideas could be explained in terms of teachers' tendencies to "press for consensus", "reinforce some views rather than others", and "promote their own views". It was only by becoming aware of these tendencies that teachers were able to modify their behaviour. Once they became conscious of their salient behaviour patterns they were able to exercise greater control over their classroom performance.'[41]

BOX 5.7

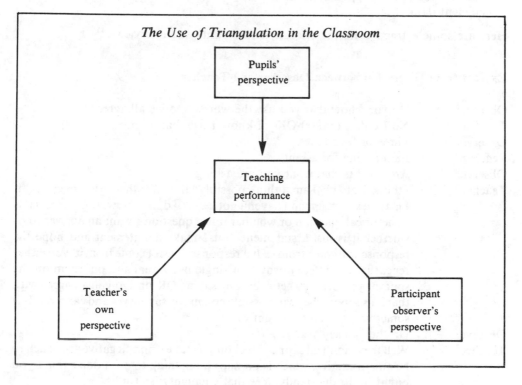

The Use of Triangulation in the Classroom

The organizational framework of the teaching project took in some twelve schools. Across these, a total of 40 teachers worked with two full-time researchers. One of the set tasks was to identify and diagnose in particular situations the problems arising from attempts to implement inquiry – discovery approaches effectively, and to explore the extent to which problems and diagnostic hypotheses could be generalized. A triangular approach was adopted early in the project in order to motivate some of the teachers taking part to monitor their own practices. Triangulation in this context, therefore, involved gathering accounts of a teaching situation from three quite different points of view, viz. the teacher's, his pupils', and the participant observer's. Of the procedure, Walker says:[41]

'Who in the triangle gathers the accounts, how they are elicited, and who compares them, depends largely on the context. The process of gathering accounts from three distinct standpoints has an epistemological justification. Each point of the triangle stands in a unique epistemological position with respect to access to relevant data about a teaching situation. The teacher is in the best position to gain access via introspection to his own intentions and aims in the situation. The students are in the best position to explain how the teacher's actions influence the way they respond in the situation. The participant-observer is in the best position to collect data about the observable features of the interaction between teacher and pupils. By comparing his own account with accounts from the two other standpoints a person at one point of the triangle has an opportunity to test and perhaps revise it on the basis of more sufficient data.'

Here are some extracts from the discussions, accounts and interviews.[41]

Extract from Discussion between Observer and Teacher

Observer	Do you know that you use the words 'Do we all agree?'
Teacher	No I didn't (pause) OK – I know I use that a lot.
Observer	Three or four times.
Teacher	I am asking for assent.
Observer	Are you? Is that what you are asking?
Teacher	I think probably I am. I think possibly I use that when I don't get . . . if I make a statement and haven't got a . . . I don't know sometimes if it is a rhetorical question or whether it is a question I want an answer to or whether it is just a statement, but I make a statement and hope the response will come from it. If a response doesn't come from it, you either repeat it in a different way to a single individual and put them on the spot, or you perhaps get over it by saying OK or 'Do you all agree with that?' I suppose they can possibly con me by saying yes and carry on. It is something I hadn't thought of.
Observer	Do they all say yes?
Teacher	Well they didn't all say no. I reckon you take a non-negative approach to be an affirmative, which is perhaps a big thing to do. I don't think you ought to do that really. Yes that's naughty isn't it?
Observer	Well the thing is I suppose when you say 'Do we all agree?' they can say no.
Teacher	I give them the opportunity to say no.
Observer	They can say no, but how do they see it? If they see it as your seeking agreement . . .
Teacher	I think a lot of the time one must be seeking agreement . . . what I am trying to put forward is what I feel to be a reasonable statement; a true statement. Although I didn't today, I do in fact sometimes put forward daft statements and you do usually find that they disagree if there is something stupid. It was a bit tame today – I mean you were coming in part way through a situation which wanted finishing and therefore I finished it. In terms of them going away and doing things – and I thought you would be more interested in discussion because of the material you had got – your recording technique . . .

Extract from the Observer's Notes (Written during the Lesson)

Look at old tables of results. 'What's happened?' Teacher asks specific pupils questions. When he disagrees raises his voice quizzically as if he disagrees. Question and answer. Hints. When right answer is given it is reinforced by the teacher. 'Right' (guessing game).

Do you all agree with that? Reply by one boy 'Mn'. When boy responds in a way which doesn't fit what the teacher wants it is chopped. People not encouraged to elaborate on ideas. Wants to get them critical of John Innes, compost manufacturer. John Innes made by pupils promotes growth better than commercial product. Asks why paper pots are better than plastic pots. Often makes an interpretation. Asks pupils if it is 'reasonable guess'. Someone murmurs again 'yes'.

Interview with Pupils

Pupil	But he wouldn't ask you what you think your conclusions were, he'll put his own conclusions on the board, and you have to write it. He says do you agree, not always but he don't want to rub it off so you just say yes to keep him quiet.
Observer	You say yes to keep him quiet?
Pupil	Keep him happy . . .
Observer	There was a time when he said he was making a guess and he asked you if you agreed whether it was a reasonable guess. I don't know if you remember that?
Pupil	Yes.
Observer	And one person said yes and everybody else kept quiet. Now what I want to know is whether the person who said yes really did agree with him or just said yes because they thought he wanted them to say yes, and why everybody else kept quiet?
Pupil	Well he would have liked us to say yes, really, 'cause I mean you could see it.
Pupil	If you'd said no you'd waste your time arguing wouldn't you.
Pupil	Yeh, if you ever say no he'll stand there and just keep on and on.
Pupil	He'll keep on till you come to his way of thinking.
Pupil	So it's best to say yes to start with.
Observer	So even if you did disagree when he said 'Do you all agree?' you wouldn't.
Pupil	If you said no he'd keep on to you until you said yes.
Pupil	If you said no he's going to say why not.
Pupil	And if you argued with him he'd come round to the same point where you left off.
Pupil	Back to his way of thinking.

Excerpt from Tape-Recorded Lesson:

Teacher	Yeh, do you all agree with that?
Pupil	Mn.
Teacher	What do you think Derek? I mean are you bothered? . . .Would that be the only thing you want to know about a plant?
Pupil	How to condition it, Sir.
Teacher	Yeh, do you all agree with that?

EXAMINATION OF TRIANGULATION DATA

Examination of the full transcripts will show how a teacher can use the data from the study to clarify, test, and generate his own theories of inquiry – discovery teaching. Even the extracts we have quoted, however, are sufficient to convey the flavour of the research: to illustrate how a teacher can, often unwittingly, impose constraints on pupils' freedom to express themselves. In the first extract, for example, the participant observer in discussion with the teacher draws from him the admission that he achieves consensus by using the phrase, 'Do we all agree?', an acknowledgement corroborated in the taped extract. In the researcher's interview with the pupils, the latter unsolicitedly make the same point: that the teacher brings about acceptance of his ideas by asking for agreement and discouraging argument. As Walker concludes, the normative implications of the teacher's behaviour gradually dawn on him:

Observer Do they all say yes?
Teacher   Well they didn't all say no. I reckon you take a non-negative approach to
          be an affirmative, which is perhaps a big thing to do. I don't think you
          ought to do that really. Yes that's naughty isn't it?

Walker explains that examination of the triangulation data convinced the teacher that in spite of his professed aspirations to implement inquiry – discovery approaches his teaching was in fact formal, structured, and directed, and that using phrases like 'Do you all agree with that?' deliberately fostered his pupils' dependence on his authority position. He goes on to say, 'Having clarified and tested the theory implicit in his practice in this way he later dramatically switched to an unstructured, open-ended approach which he hoped would protect the self-directed learning of his pupils. His conscious switch to a new teaching approach reflected the development of a new theory, the applicability of which would require further self-monitoring. The conscious development of new practical theories from self-monitoring we call *hypotheses*, to highlight the fact that they are open to experiment. If a theory is held unconsciously, as it was initially by the teacher cited, it is not open to experiment. But once it is consciously held by a teacher it is so open.'[41] The researchers subsequently identify a number of general 'hypotheses' that were introduced in the course of the project.

It can be seen from this brief account of the Ford Teaching Project how the use of contrasting perspectives as a means of generating research data in a specifically research-oriented setting may be used to clarify issues and enable teachers to function more effectively.

SUMMARY

We began the chapter by considering why there was a dearth of material on how pupils see aspects of their school environment and then went on to examine the usefulness of pupils' perceptions and judgments of school and schooling. Representative questions a researcher might formulate in connection with pupils' viewpoints were listed. There then followed an examination of pupils' views of school and schooling drawing on recent studies. We then went on to consider pupils' attitudes to school work. This naturally led on to their perceptions of teachers which were seen to have direct practical implications for teachers' own practices. More specifically, pupils' views of the performance of student teachers were then reviewed, using comparatively recent studies by British researchers. The distinctive views of girls were then discussed and the chapter concluded with an illustration of the way contrasting viewpoints of the same incident could help a teacher become more sensitive to his or her own teaching performance and make accommodations as he or she felt necessary.

ENQUIRY AND DISCUSSION

1. What are the distinctive features of ethnographic studies of schools and classrooms?

2. How may the findings of ethnographic studies in classrooms help the practising teacher?

3. Using the evidence noted in the chapter, build up an identikit picture of the kind of teacher children consider desirable. How would you rate yourself against it?

4. Consider the implications of Gannaway's model of pupil perception for the beginning teacher.

5. Critically examine any *one* ethnographic study referred to in the chapter.

6. What are the advantages of knowing something about pupil perspectives?

7. Of what value is it to the teacher to know that girls' viewpoints may differ from boys in some respects?

8. Using more than one technique, ascertain children's views on their school and schooling.

NOTES AND REFERENCES

1. Calvert, B. (1975) *The Role of the Pupil*. London: Routledge and Kegan Paul.

2. Note: *reliability* here refers to the stability or consistency of pupils' viewpoints; *validity*, the degree to which the viewpoint expresses what it claims to express.

3. Veldman, D. J. and Peck, R. F. (1963) Student teacher characteristics from the pupils' viewpoint. *Journal of Educational Psychology*, **54**, 346–355.
   Veldman, D. J. and Peck, R. F. (1964) The influence of teacher and pupil sex on pupil evaluation of student teachers. *Journal of Teacher Education*, **15**, 393–396.

4. Meighan, R. (1974) Children's judgments of the teaching performance of student teachers. *Educational Review*, **27**, November, 52–60.
   Meighan, R. (1977) Pupils' perceptions of the classroom techniques of post-graduate student teachers. *British Journal of Teacher Education*, **3**, 2, 139–148.

5. Blishen, E. (1969) *The School That I'd Like*. London, Harmondsworth: Penguin Books.

6. Taylor, P. H. (1962) Children's evaluations of the characteristics of the good teacher. *British Journal of Educational Psychology*, **32**, 258–266.

7. Hargreaves, D. H. (1967) *Social Relations in a Secondary School*. London: Routledge and Kegan Paul.

8. Meighan, R. (1977) The pupil as client: the learner's experience of schooling. *Educational Review*, **29**, 123–135.

9. Makins, V. (1969) Child's eye view of teachers. *Times Educational Supplement*, 19th September and 26th September.

10. Goffman, E. (1961) *Asylums*. London, Harmondsworth: Penguin.

11. Maizels, J. (1970) How leavers rate teachers. *New Society*, 24th September.

12. Moody, E. (1968) Right in front of everybody. *New Society*, 26th December.

13. Weston, P., Taylor, P. H. and Hurman, A. (1978) Clients' expectations of secondary schooling. *Educational Review*, **30**, 2, 159–166.

14. Woods, P. (1976) Pupils' views of school. *Educational Review*, **28**, 126–137.

15. Note: There were also favourable comments about the institutional nature of the school.

16. Woods, P. (1978) Relating to schoolwork: some pupil perceptions. *Educational Review*, **30**, 2, 167–175.

17. Willis, P. (1976) The class significance of school counter-culture. In *The Process of Schooling: A Sociological Reader*. (Eds.) Hammersley, M., et al. London: Routledge and Kegan Paul/Milton Keynes: Open University Press.

18. Willis, P. (1977) *Learning to Labour*, London: Saxon House.

19. Woods, P. (1977) Parents' influence on pupil experience. In *The Pupil's Experience*, Open University, Educational Studies, A Second Level Course, E202, Schooling and Society, Unit 11: Milton Keynes: Open University Press.

20. Thompson, B. L. (1975) Secondary school pupils' attitudes to school and teachers. *Educational Research*, **18**, 62–66.

21. Hollis, A. W. (1935) *The Personal Relationship in Teaching*. M.A. Thesis, University of Birmingham.

22. Allen, E. A. (1959) *Attitudes to School and Teachers in a Secondary Modern School*. M.A. (Ed.) Thesis, University of London.

23. Evans, K. M. (1962) *Sociometry and Education*. London: Routledge and Kegan Paul.

24. Nash, R. (1974) Pupils' expectations for their teachers. *Research in Education*, November, 46–71.

25. Morrison, A. and MacIntyre, D. (1969) *Teachers and Teaching*. London, Harmondsworth, Penguin Books.

26. Geer, B. (1976) Teaching. In *School and Society*. (Eds.) Cosin, B. R. et al. London: Routledge and Kegan Paul.

27. Nash, R. (1976) *Teacher Expectations and Pupil Learning*. London: Routledge and Kegan Paul.

28. Blishen, E. (1973) Why some secondary teachers are disliked. *Where*, **86**, 330–334.

29. Wright, D. S. (1962) A comparative study of the adolescent's concepts of his parents and teachers. *Educational Review*, **14**, 3.

30. Note: the word *significance* is used here in its statistical sense, i.e. the differences in question have a real cause and have not come about by chance.

31. Gannaway, H. (1976) Making sense of school. In *Explorations in Classroom Observation*, (Eds.) Stubbs, M. and Delamont, S. London: Wiley and Sons.

32. Meighan, R. (1981) *A Sociology of Educating*, Eastbourne: Holt-Saunders.

33. Hargreaves, D. H. (1977) The process of typification in classroom interaction: models and methods. *British Journal of Educational Psychology*, **47**, 274–284.

34. Veldman, D. J. and Peck, R. F. (1969) Influences on pupil evaluations of student teachers. *Journal of Educational Psychology*, **60**, 103–108.
    Veldman, D. J. (1970) Pupil evaluation of student teachers and their supervisors. *Journal of Teacher Education*, **21**, 165–167.

35. Meighan, R. (1977) Pupils' perceptions of the classroom techniques of post-graduate student teachers, *British Journal of Teacher Education*, **3**, 2, 139–148.

36. Cortis, G. and Grayson, A. (1978) Primary school pupils' perceptions of student teachers' performance, *Educational Review*, **30**, 2, 93–101.

37. Davies, L. (1978) The view from the girls. *Educational Review*, **30**, 2, 103–109.

38. Deem, R. (1978) *Women and Schooling*. London: Routledge and Kegan Paul.

39. Lomax, P. (1978) The attitudes of girls with varying degrees of school adjustment to different aspects of their school experience. *Educational Review*, **30**, 2, 117–124.

40. Furlong, V. (1977) Anancy goes to school: a case study of pupils' knowledge of their teachers. In *School Experience*, (Eds.) Woods, P. and Hammersley, M. London: Croom Helm.

41. Walker, R. (1976) *Innovation, the School and the Teacher (I)*, Educational Studies, A Second Level Course, Curriculum Design and Development, E203, Units 27 and 28. Milton Keynes: The Open University Press.

SELECTED READING

1. Blishen, E. (1969) *The School that I'd Like*, London: Harmondsworth, Penguin Books. A most interesting book on pupils' views of school.

2. Davies, L. (1978) The view from the girls. *Educational Review*, **30**, 2, 103–109. A study of the girls' viewpoint with particular reference to control and classroom interaction.

3. Gannaway, H. (1976) Making sense of school. In *Explorations in Classroom Observation*. (Eds.) Stubbs, M. and Delamont, S. London: Wiley. The author proposes a dynamic model to account for the way pupils progressively typify teachers.

4. Meighan, R. (1977) Pupils' perceptions of the classroom techniques of post-graduate student teachers. *British Journal of Teacher Education*, **3**, 2, 139–148. A British study testing the findings of earlier studies in the U.S.A.

5. Willis, P. (1977) *Learning to Labour*, London: Saxon House. An in-depth ethnographic study of a group of anti-school working class boys who reject the world offered them by their teachers.

6. Woods, P. (1978) Relating to schoolwork: some pupil perceptions, *Educational Review*, **30**, 2, 167–175. A study of the way in which work is given significance in a context characterized by conflicting conceptions of the notion.

6

Communication in the Classroom

The process of communication in the classroom is a vastly complicated phenomenon involving the transmission of information from a source and its reception and interpretation by a receiver. More simply, and for much of the time, communication in the classroom may be seen as an *interpersonal* process between the teacher and his pupils – he addresses and questions the pupils, the pupils respond. Included in this interpersonal process are the many incidental exchanges that take place among the pupils themselves. With recent advances in the field of educational technology, the interpersonal mode has been supplemented in some areas by the introduction of *mediated* systems of instruction – programmed learning texts, teaching machines, cassette recorders, language laboratories, and network and closed circuit television, for example. Whether interpersonal or mediated, however, communication in the classroom relies heavily on the written and spoken word: this is to say that communication is *verbal*. At the same time, the substance of communication can be indicated quite independently of words: posture, gesture, and facial expression, for instance, can each in its own way convey information, attitudes, and states of mind. These would be common means of *nonverbal* communication, bodily movements we are barely conscious of that for much of the time serve to reinforce the verbal channel. Thus by contracting his facial muscles in a particular way can a teacher convey unequivocally his displeasure to a wayward pupil; and by the same means (though without necessarily realizing it) will a pupil betray his boredom. That the former instance would be under the conscious control of the person in question and the latter instance, in all probability, not, illustrates just how complicated the problem of communication even at the nonverbal level can become. Recent developments in the areas of language and communication in the classroom and the growing body of research on them point to an increasing awareness of their importance in education and learning.[1]

In reviewing the nature of human communication in the world at large and in the classroom, Hurt and his colleagues[2] identify four features – that it is a *process*; that it is *transactional*; that it is *symbolic*; and that it is *multidimensional*. Let us look at each of these more closely.

In saying that communication is a *process*, the authors mean that it is continuously changing and that accordingly has no tangible beginning, middle or end. They put it like this:

> 'The important thing to remember here, and to be sensitive to, is the fact that as a teacher you initiate communication with (pupils) the moment you enter the classroom, frequently before you say a word. These initial messages to (pupils) are often the most critical in establishing subsequent classroom interaction.'[2]

As part of the continuously changing nature of communication, the person who is communicating has to modify his behaviour in response to what he perceives the other person in turn is communicating (or not communicating) to him. In this sense, communication can be said to be *transactional*. Implied here is a key concept in the communication process – that of *feedback*. In the context we are using the term, it refers to a verbal (or nonverbal) response from a person that has been elicited by another's behaviour towards that person. It is thus in the light of verbal (or nonverbal) feedback from his pupils (or its absence) that the teacher adjusts and adapts to the ongoing process of communication.

In order to communicate his knowledge, his experience, or a specific item of information to his pupils, a teacher has to make use of verbal and nonverbal gestures in order to achieve this. In this way, therefore, communication may be said to be *symbolic* – 'If teachers were unable to abstract and symbolize what they had learned, they would have no tangible means of relating their learning experiences to their (pupils).'[2] Since, however, symbols are arbitrary and flexible, they can result in as many problems as they do advantages as when, for example, the same *verbal* symbol refers to different things, or the same *nonverbal* gesture can be interpreted in a number of ways. The latter case is nicely illustrated in the game of *Charades* where the entertainment value stems from the misunderstandings that ensue.

Finally, in arguing that communication is *multidimensional*, the authors contend that individuals communicate with each other on at least three levels or dimensions – a *cultural* dimension, a *sociological* dimension, and a *psychological* dimension. When people communicate on the cultural dimension, they base their own communication behaviours on characteristics of their own culture or subculture, e.g. beliefs, habits, customs, language. Communication on the sociological level, the authors explain, occurs when we structure our communication behaviour on the basis of a person's reference groups, i.e. the organizations or groups in the wider society that we identify with. To structure our communication behaviours on the expectations we have of such organizations or groups is to communicate on the sociological dimension. As regards the psychological dimension, significant communication only occurs here when we know someone very well, for this involves taking into account his individual characteristics which make him unique as a person. The relevance of these dimensions for the teacher is readily apparent. In thus taking note of the sociological dimension, the teacher is more aware of the kinds of subcultural peer groups individuals in his class identify with (see also Chapter 12) and the way in which they influence – directly or indirectly, for better or worse – his pupils' school work. And the psychological dimension is similarly relevant, for here the teacher has to achieve a suitable balance between communicating with his class *as a class* and at the same time seeing them as an aggregate of individuals each with his own set of unique and idiosyncratic characteristics.

In Box 6.1 we present a model of the communication process in the classroom which will serve as an underlying structure for the remainder of the chapter. Being a model it naturally represents the totality of classroom communication in extremely simplified form; and because we are mainly concerned in this book with broad educational issues as they focus on classrooms and schools, we shall limit ourselves to two facets of communication as an interpersonal process, namely, *verbal* and *nonverbal*. We thereby exclude mediating systems. The model identifies four important features of the communication process together with an optional fifth. They are: (1) the source of the message (the teacher, a pupil, a group of pupils, the whole class); (2) the message itself; (3) the choice of channel (verbal or nonverbal); (4) the receiver of the message (the teacher, a pupil, a group of pupils, the whole class); and (5) the possibility of feedback from both verbal and nonverbal communications, itself expressed verbally or nonverbally.

BOX 6.1

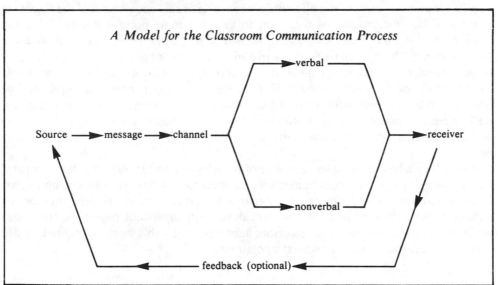

A Model for the Classroom Communication Process

With respect to the first of these features, there are obviously many sources of messages in the communication process in the classroom – books, handouts, the blackboard, tape recorders, and so on. Since, however, we are principally interested in *interpersonal processes*, the people involved in conveying and receiving messages in this context will be our chief concern; people, moreover, whose communication behaviour can, in theory at least, be modified by the operation of feedback from those individuals at whom they direct their messages. This thereby excludes the television screen from our consideration.

Everyday usage of the term *message*, the second feature of the model, tends to limit it to what a person says or to words written on a piece of paper. Yet there is more to the concept of message than merely words. It often happens that *how* a message is delivered in teacher – pupil communication is just as important, indeed sometimes more important, than *what* is said. The *how* of a message is but one facet of the nonverbal elements in classroom communication we shall return to later.

We have already indicated our intention to limit ourselves to the purely human or interpersonal transactions occurring in the classroom. In order to achieve these, the most frequently employed channels of communication are *oral* and *visual* or, using more conventional terms, *verbal* and *nonverbal*. Because we see these two channels as being the most important elements in the model from the particular vantage point we have adopted, we shall concentrate more or less exclusively on them in the pages that follow.

Every person who is a *source* of communication in the classroom is also a *receiver* of information from other sources. Thus teacher and pupils alike can be on the receiving end of a message, the latter receiving it individually, as a group, or as a whole class. Of course, people beyond the classroom, such as the headteacher or the pupils' parents, may also be receivers indirectly, though these are not our concern here.

If learning is to take place in the classroom, the initial communication behaviour of the teacher should affect in some positive and constructive way some aspect or aspects of the pupil's behaviour – cognitively, affectively, or as regards skill acquisition. If the teacher is sensitive and conscientious, he will want to know at some point just what effect his teaching, that is, his communicative acts, has had on his pupils. The essence of *feedback* is that the effect of his teaching is fed back to him either by word of mouth, or in writing, or in action, in such a way that he is able to modify subsequent teaching procedures. Feedback is not necessarily present in the communication process – a pupil may be reluctant to tell his teacher he does not understand, or a teacher may fail to indicate how well or badly a pupil is doing. If, however, feedback is absent for too long, the efforts of the teacher may become, at best, ineffective and, at worst, counter-productive.

We will begin by looking at some aspects of verbal communication in the classroom and then move on to nonverbal communication. As little research has been done on nonverbal communication in the classroom (in comparison, that is, with the growing number of studies in verbal communication), we will draw to a significant degree on the social psychological literature and make judicious inferences where this seems warranted, or else leave the reader to make his own extrapolations.

VERBAL COMMUNICATION

We said in our introduction that the process of communication in the classroom depends to a large extent on spoken and written language: in a word, much of the interpersonal communication there is *verbal*. In considering verbal communication in the classroom, we would subscribe to the view expressed by Wilkinson when he said that the study of language and communication is of value, not to give the teacher a body of information to teach, but to heighten his awareness of the nature of relationships between human beings, and between language, learning and thought.[3] Barnes went further when he said that not only would teachers gain from a more sophisticated insight into the implications of their own use of language, and into the part that language can at best play in their pupils' learning, but also such insights would contribute dramatically to the effectiveness of teaching in schools.[4]

Such views by these and other experts in the field have been endorsed in the Bullock Report, *A Language for Life*,[1] which makes a strong recommendation that 'a substantial course of language in education . . . . should be part of every primary and secondary teacher's initial training, whatever the teacher's subject or the age of the children with whom he or she will be working.'

Educationalists have for long acknowledged the crucial role language plays in the child's education though there is as yet no general agreement on the precise relationship between language and education. Indeed, so Olympian are the peaks of the problem that researchers have to begin modestly in the foothills. There, they investigate a wide range of issues which include language and classroom interaction, the characteristics of talk in the classroom, the most effective ways of studying language and talk in the classroom, the part played by specialist language in the classroom – so called subject – specific language, and the consequences of language disadvantage and deprivation. It is to these that we now turn our attention.

Language and Classroom Interaction

Stubbs has identified a number of important reasons for observing, recording and studying teacher–pupil dialogue in the classroom.[5] The most fundamental reason, he suggests, is that the dialogue that takes place between teachers and pupils *is* the educational process, or the major part of it for most children. No matter how important other factors such as IQ, social class background, parental encouragement, or children's individual language skills appear to be, they nevertheless remain, Stubbs argues, external influences. For all its importance, however, little research has been undertaken on the *interactional aspects* of the teaching process in the classroom. Traditionally, much research on the classroom has been of a normative cast: this is to say that the process of education could best be understood by looking at *input variables* such as intelligence, motivation, social class background, and personality and comparing them with *output variables* – how well a child had done according to an agreed set of criteria. In other words, what happened between the input and output phases was largely ignored: few seemed to be interested in what was actually taking place *inside* the classrooms. Stubbs goes on to suggest that, on common sense grounds alone, it would seem that an understanding of teaching and learning would have to depend, at least in part, on observation of teachers and learners. Although an impressive body of information on learning theory has been built up this century, it has largely been derived from carefully controlled experimental situations. For this reason, it is extremely difficult to extrapolate the findings to 'real-life' contexts: in other words, we still know very little about how children learn in classrooms. Stubbs suggests that the only way to overcome this problem is to observe children in the classroom and, particularly, the way they interact with teachers and other children. Recalling the subject matter of Chapter 1, we may add that the normative and interpretive paradigms appear to be confronting each other in the classroom itself.

In thus pleading for a closer correspondence between what we say about education and detailed empirical investigation of what is actually *said* in the classroom, Stubbs identifies the kinds of specific questions to be asked: given that many messages are conveyed by teachers to pupils, just *how* are they communicated? By *what* 'structure'? What *are* the rules of the verbal game? What specific behaviours? If they are specific, then they can be specified. We might easily continue the list: How are messages received by pupils? How are they assimilated, comprehended, and acted upon? What part does the language of education, or of specialist subjects, play in promoting or hindering communication and learning? And how does a child's background, socially and linguistically, affect the transactions that take place?

Numerous reasons could be advanced no doubt to explain why there has been a shortage of naturalistic studies of classroom interaction. We refer to two of them. First, there is the enormous complexity of communicative behaviour, a complexity which can only be unravelled by on-the-spot observation and analysis. Earlier research methods have functioned more as a deterrent rather than an aid in this respect. The second reason is logically related to the first: because there have been few naturalistic studies, we do not have an appropriate terminology to talk about classroom interaction and the teaching process. As Stubbs says in this regard:

'If one talks to teachers about their classroom experiences, one discovers immediately that there is simply no vocabulary of descriptive concepts for talking about teaching. Despite the vast complexity of second-by-second classroom dialogue, the discussion will be conceptually crude and oversimplified. It is time

BOX 6.2

A Typology of Language Models Illustrating
Some of the Functions Language Can Perform

Instrumental
This is the simplest model, the use of language as 'a means of getting things done', for the satisfaction of personal material needs: serving the 'I want' function.

Regulatory
The use of language as a means of regulating the behaviour of others, serving the function of 'Do as I tell you'.

Interactional
This model refers to the use of language for maintaining and mediating one's relationships with others: serving the 'me and him' (or 'me and mummy') function.

Personal
This is the model which enables the child to express his own individuality: serving the 'here I come' function.

Heuristic
This model refers to language as a means of finding out, questioning: serving the function 'tell me why'.

Imaginative
This model enables the child to project himself into an environment of his own making, to create a world of make-believe: serving the 'let's pretend' function.

Representational
This is the use of language as a means of conveying information and expressing propositions: serving the function of 'I've got something to tell you'.

Source: Halliday[6]

that teachers had an adequate descriptive language for talking about their own professional behaviour.'[5]

The descriptive language and body of concepts referred to by Stubbs together with the theoretical framework to which these will relate can only come from empirical studies of interactional processes at the centre of the action – the classroom itself. In this respect a beginning has been made and it is fitting to close this section with a brief review of some of the more important studies undertaken in this connection in the past ten years or so.[7] Although they need to be seen as exploratory forays, they nevertheless yield interesting insights into the ways in which actors in the classroom situation communicate with each other. Most of them are case studies and are thus based on a detailed description of a group of lessons or even a single lesson.

A pioneering study in the field of classroom language is Barnes' *Language in the Secondary Classroom*.[4] His concern was to record the whole language environment of a first-year class during their first half term in a comprehensive school with a view to investigating the ways in which a teacher's language might impede rather than facilitate learning because of the terminology or style used. He was thus interested in both spoken and written language, and also in the child as a producer and receiver of language. Being readily accessible and having many good examples of classroom exchanges, the book offers a very good introduction to the topic.

In contending that many teachers in talking about their subject use a specialist language of instruction that might be a barrier to children's learning, Barnes identifies three categories: (1) specialist language perceived by the teacher as a potential barrier and therefore carefully 'presented' to them; (2) specialist language not so presented for various reasons; and (3) the language of secondary education which is made up of forms not specific to school subjects, nor likely to be used or heard by pupils in any other situation. We shall return to this theme again shortly when we discuss *subject-specific language*.

In a more recent study,[8] Barnes assumes that language is a major means of learning and that pupils' uses of language for learning are strongly influenced by the teacher's language which, he argues, prescribes them their roles as learners. This assumption thereby involves a shift of emphasis from the more traditional view of language *as a means of teaching*. In operational terms, therefore, this means that we learn, not only by listening passively to the teacher, but by verbalizing, by talking, by discussing and arguing. By studying teacher–pupil interaction, one can begin to see how classroom language offers different possibilities of learning to pupils. Should pupils merely be passive listeners? Or should they be allowed to verbalize at some point? Or should active dialogue with the teacher be encouraged? Just three ways of pupils' participation in learning, but all under the control of the teacher's own speech behaviour.

Like Barnes' earlier study, Mishler's work[9] takes extracts of classroom dialogue and subjects them to perceptive analysis. Unlike Barnes, however, he is more concerned with showing how different cognitive strategies as well as different values and norms are carried in the language used, chiefly in the structure of teachers' statements and in the types of exchange developed between them and the children. By contrasting speech recordings of different first-grade teachers with each other, he sets out to extract different features in the language used and to show how these features reflect both different constructions of reality and different ways of learning about it: this is to say that what teachers say and how they say it creates a particular sort of world for the children.[5]

Mishler's main purpose then is to show how teachers' cognitive strategies are conveyed in the warp and weft of classroom dialogue. To this end, he is concerned with how attention is focused, with how teachers orient themselves and their pupils to the problem under discussion; the procedures for information search and evaluation; and the structure of alternatives, that is, the number of types of alternative answers to a question and their relationship to each other.

Writing of Mishler's work, Stubbs says:[5]

'Mishler's approach is one which could be of direct interest to teachers. By close study of transcribed lessons he shows how quite general teaching strategies are conveyed by the fine grain of a teacher's use of language. Such a study can therefore begin to throw a little light on how children learn what they do in school. Only by close observation of how teachers and pupils actually talk to each other can one discover how concepts are put across, how some lines of inquiry are opened up and others closed off, how pupils' responses are evaluated, and how their attention is directed to the areas of knowledge which the school regards as valuable.'

A similar approach to Mishler's study is that by Gumperz and Herasimchuk.[10] Again, it is based on an analysis of two contrasting tape-recorded lessons: a teacher teaching a group of pupils and an older child, aged six, teaching a younger child, aged five. By a comparative study of the transcripts, the researchers show that the adult and child instructors respectively use different methods of communication. The adult teacher, for instance, relies to a large extent on questioning techniques to elicit answers from his pupils, the variation in his choice of words contrasting with the lack of variation in intonation. The child, on the other hand, draws on a wider range of intonation backed up by frequent repetition.

Commenting on the study, Stubbs notes:[5]

'It would be most useful to teachers if they could be made more aware of the linguistic means by which children may communicate messages, especially where these differ from adult usage. Gumperz and Herasimchuk place useful emphasis on the precise linguistic signals which convey social messages in the classroom, and show that these signs may not only be the words or sentences used, but the way utterances are sequenced, and the paralinguistic signs such as intonation and rhythm.'

In another comparatively recent study, Stubbs himself describes one way in which teachers in relatively traditional lessons control classroom exchanges.[11] A characteristic of much classroom talk is the extent of the teacher's *conversational control* over the topic, over the relevance or correctness of what pupils say, and over when and how much pupils may speak.[5] In traditional lessons, children have few conversational rights. Whereas this has often been pointed out in general, the actual verbal strategies used by teachers to control classroom talk have yet to be systematically studied. What Stubbs shows is that a teacher is constantly monitoring the communication system in the classroom by such utterances as 'You see, we're really getting on to the topic now,' or 'OK, now listen all of you,' or 'Now, we don't want any silly remarks.' The teacher is thus able to check whether pupils are all on the same wavelength and whether at least some of them follow what is being said. Stubbs refers to such language as *meta-communication*. 'It is,' he says, 'communication about communication: messages which refer back to the communication system itself, checking whether it is functioning properly.'[5]

In conclusion, he adds:

> 'Such talk is characteristic of teachers' language: utterances which, as it were, stand outside the discourse and comment on it comprise a large percentage of what teachers say to their pupils, and comprise a major way of controlling classroom dialogue. Use of such language is also highly asymmetrical: one would not expect a pupil to say to a teacher: *That's an interesting point.* Such speech acts, in which the teacher monitors and controls the classroom dialogue are, at one level, the very stuff of teaching. They are basic to the activity of teaching, since they are the acts whereby a teacher *controls the flow of information* in the classroom and defines the relevance of what is said.'[5]

Before moving on to a consideration of talk in the classroom, we refer you to Box 6.2 which illustrates some of the functions that language may perform in the classroom.

Characteristics of Talk

It is only in the past ten years or so that the value of talk in the classroom has attracted the attention it deserves. This has been manifest in the steady flow of articles and books stressing the need for greater emphasis on spoken work in schools,[12] a need that has come about because, some believe, we have tended to devalue talk in the school and classroom. Whether this is true or not, one cannot deny that a considerable amount of talking does take place in schools; and this is so because our own culture depends to a very large extent on the spoken word as a means of transmitting knowledge. In reviewing the main characteristics of classroom talk, particularly that of older children, Edwards and Furlong[13] consider that not only is there so much of it, but that so much of what is said is both public and highly centralized. What they mean by being 'highly centralized' is that for much of the time in classrooms, there is a *single* verbal encounter in that whatever is being said demands the attention of all.

In pursuing the theme of centralized communication further, Edwards and Furlong explain that although it plays a very important part in classroom interaction, its role should not be overstated, for considerable amounts of incidental and unofficial talk take place amid official exchanges. The authors further point out that notwithstanding the occasions when children talk privately to other members of the class, when they offer comments and pose questions when requested to do so, or when they talk 'unofficially', their main communicative role, as far as traditional classrooms are concerned, is *to listen*. This means that the communicative rights of teacher and pupils are very unequal. In effect, the authors point out, teachers usually tell pupils when to talk, what to talk about, when to stop talking, and how well they talked. The normal conversation between two equals stands in marked contrast to classroom exchanges because of this very inequality. In the former, no one has overriding claim to speak first, or more than others, or to decide unilaterally on the subject. The difference between an everyday conversation and a classroom exchange is dramatically realized where each kind is recorded and transcribed. In the case of everyday exchanges, statements are often incomplete, they clash with the statements of others, and they are interrupted. There are also frequent false starts, hesitations, and repetitions.[13] Unless the transcript is edited, it is often difficult to make much sense of. By contrast, exchanges recorded in traditional classrooms are much more orderly and systematic. Indeed, Edwards and Furlong observe that they often look like a play script. As they comment, 'Most utterances are complete, and most speakers seem to know their lines and to recognize their turn to speak. Despite the large numbers, the talk appears more orderly.'[13] Thus it is that whereas in everyday informal conversations there is always the possibility that several speakers will perversely talk against one another or that one individual will eventually appropriate a disproportionate amount of the talking time, in classroom interaction contributors to a discussion must be carefully controlled. The authors point out that this is much more easily achieved if communication rights are *not* equally shared – 'if one participant can speak whenever he chooses to do so, can normally nominate the next speaker, and can resolve any cases of confusion.'[13]

The authors go on to explain that insofar as pupils are ready to be taught, they are likely to acknowledge that an able teacher has the right to talk first, last, and most; to control the content of a lesson; and to organize that content by allocating speaking turns to the pupils. The teacher's right to decide who speaks, when, for how long, and to whom, is mirrored in the small number of interactional possibilities in a typical lesson. Edwards and Furlong refer to such arrangements of speakers and listeners as *participant-structures* which they define as communicative networks linking those who are in contact with one another already, or can be if they choose.[13] Box 6.3 identifies common instances of such participant structures to be found in traditional classrooms. Enlarging on the nature of them, Edwards and Furlong say:

BOX 6.3

Participant-Structures in Traditional Classrooms

In traditional classrooms, the participant-structures in order of decreasing frequency are as follows:

1. The teacher talking to a silent audience, and requiring everyone's attention.
2. The teacher talking to one pupil (asking a question, evaluating an answer, issuing reproof), but assuming that everyone else is taking notice.
3. A pupil talking to the teacher, with the rest of the class as audience.
4. The teacher talking to one or more pupils when the others are *not* expected to listen and may be allowed to talk themselves.
5. Pupils discussing among themselves with the teacher as chairman (neutral or otherwise).
6. Pupils discussing among themselves with the teacher absent.

Source: Edwards and Furlong[13]

'It is not difficult to link these structures intuitively to certain obvious stages in lessons – for example, to the teacher lecturing, checking on the reception of the lecture, inviting queries, sorting out problems, eliciting discussion, and trusting pupils to work on their own . . . What even the simplest list brings out is the limited variety of interactional patterns characteristic of lessons, and how firmly most of them are centred on the teacher. There is usually a formalized allocation of speaking and listening roles. Teachers expect both a 'proper' silence *and* a 'proper' willingness to talk, and they manage the interaction so as to produce orderly and relevant pupil participation.'[13]

The authors go on to consider how this orderliness is achieved. In the well-ordered classroom, they explain, the teacher's turns at speaking are taken as and when he chooses, these being determined by the kinds of pupil he addresses and also the subject matter being taught. Thus teachers appear to talk less to younger pupils, to brighter pupils, and when they are teaching English or social studies, for example, as compared with science or modern languages.[13] However interesting these variations are, they are overshadowed by the difficulty most teachers seem to have in limiting themselves to much less than two thirds of the time available for talking. Because much of the time appropriated by teachers is taken up by giving information and instructions, censuring pupils and evaluating them, Edwards and Furlong consider that most of their talking can described as *telling*.

In seeing teacher talk in this context as *dominant performance*, Edwards and Furlong suggest that the teacher's message is made all the more effective because of his 'front of stage' location. The traditional classroom settings serve as a means of reinforcing the centrally controlled interaction.[14] As they say:

> 'The conventional groupings of desks or tables channel communication to and from the teacher, who is the obvious focus of attention. He can direct his talk to any part of the room, while the natural flow of pupil-talk is either to him or to other pupils through him. It is a setting which makes it difficult for the teacher to avoid talking *at* pupils, or to break up the interaction into more localized encounters. In classrooms which are physically more open, no single focus of attention may be visible at all. Symbolically and practically, there is a switch of emphasis from the teacher to the learner.'[13]

We shall return again to the use of space in classrooms when we consider aspects of nonverbal communication.

But the teacher cannot monopolize the talk totally. There has to be a certain amount of pupil participation; and this presents the teacher with significant managerial problems because of the numbers of children involved. Once a teacher stops talking, Edwards and Furlong ask, how are turns taken? How is the rule of one speaker at a time maintained? Who is to answer a particular question? Normally, it is the teacher's on-the-spot decisions that solve them – 'Turns are allocated, they are not seized, and pupils have to learn to bid appropriately for the right to speak.'[13]

We have been concerned in this section with some characteristics of talk in classrooms and have seen how most participant-structures focus on the teacher who either does the talking or who nominates others to do it. For further consideration of teacher dominance in this context we refer you to the work of Edwards and Furlong[13] who go on to examine further aspects of classroom interaction, including the shaping of meaning – the asking of questions, the management of answers, and the constraints imposed by the social nature of the setting. We now turn our attention to the problems of studying and analysing classroom talk and language and the methods used by investigators to achieve these ends. We concentrate particularly on systematic observation, recent developments in ethnographic approaches, and on the developing science of sociolinguistics.

Analysing Classroom Talk and Language

We saw in the opening chapter of the book how, guided by the suppositions and assumptions of the normative paradigm, the traditional researcher has access to a system of procedures providing him with objective data that enable him either to accept or reject his preferred hunches, hypotheses, or theories about the phenomena engaging his attention at any particular time. Applying this model to the teaching process in the classroom, the researcher employs dispassionate observation to collect his objective data, or he attempts to tease out elements in the situation which 'go together', or he systematically tests cause-and-effect relationships. A possible weakness in this approach, of course, is that the researcher tends only to see what he has, so to speak, programmed himself to see: a purple-coloured filter set before a source of white light (itself a mixture of colours) will only permit him to see purple light, no matter how he holds or angles the filter. Critics of this approach contend that because the choice of method tends to determine, or pre-select, the data, the data are less than 'objective'.

In contrast to this approach is the one modelled on the interpretive paradigm by means of which, as we saw earlier, the researcher sets out to take the phenomena of concern to him *as they are* (that is, without too many preconceptions about their nature, their cause, or their consequences) and to understand them from within. Any theorizing here follows rather than precedes the research act. Explanations are consequent upon the data collected and their interpretation. A difficulty here is that different researchers may very well come up with different interpretations of the same phenomenon.

Of course, these two models may (and probably do) artificially polarize what actually takes place in research: an interpretive researcher, for example, can hardly go into a field situation without some sort of guiding theory, no matter how tentative. However, they are sufficiently useful to us here as broad criteria by which to look at the types of research that have been and are being undertaken in the use of talk and language in the classroom.

The first type of research we consider is that of *systematic observation*. We have already seen that one of the most obvious characteristics of the classroom is the amount of talking that takes place there – official talk between teacher and pupils, sometimes among pupils themselves; and informal talk. For this to be studied by systematic observation, some sort of inventory of what are considered to be the more significant features of the continuous stream of words has to be extracted and recorded. To achieve this, the talk is coded according to a preferred category system (we earlier gave an example of a structured observation schedule in Box 2.2 which illustrates the principle). By this conversion of talk into categories, however, the researcher loses hold of the substantive content of the dialogue. As Furlong and Edwards [15] note, 'Since the observer has to classify everything he hears into whatever number of categories his system provides, the actual words spoken are no longer recoverable. His instant judgments about the interactional significance of those words are what constitute his data.'

As a general rule, the categories chosen by the researcher are imposed on his observations and represent what he has earlier decided are the important features for classroom study. He will operate within a normative perspective and the objective data he collects will be subject to the usual procedures of scientific analysis. Having, therefore, a positivist outlook, the observer will have a determinist slant on human behaviour, that is, he will tend to see the pupil's behaviour as being largely 'caused by' whatever it is the teacher does, so that modification of teacher talk will result in an appropriate change in what the pupil says. Furlong and Edwards put it like this:[15]

'The teacher stimulates, and his pupils respond. Since it is the teacher's behaviour which is seen as explaining whatever patterns of verbal interaction are observed, feeding information back to him about his behaviour at certain critical "decision-points" is intended to enable him to change (and improve) his teaching.'

According to Speier,[16] systematic observation fills a category system with precise, objective and quantifiable data that are derived from its own presuppositions. In so doing it justifies its own existence and so constructs its own reality.

An alternative approach to systematic observation is *ethnographic research*. Unlike the systematic observer who usually studies a number of classrooms, the ethnographer is more likely to investigate one situation only, believing that since different classrooms have certain characteristics in common, scrutiny of one classroom will allow him 'to clarify relationships, pinpoint critical processes and identify common phenomena.'[17] Whereas systematic observers adopt a selective approach to their object of study, the selection having been predetermined by favoured theories, ethnographers go into a situation with a much more open mind, not knowing precisely what they are looking for but at the same time willing to receive whatever is there. Unlike the systematic observer, the ethnographer categorizes his data or formulates his theories *after* the event. Furlong and Edwards lucidly describe the procedures thus:[15]

'Quite deliberately, (ethnographic researchers) adopt a 'catch-what-you-can' approach, making no attempt to control or ignore 'irrelevant' variables. If there is any categorization of the talk, it has to be done retrospectively that is, in forms *derived from* the data. The record must therefore be sufficiently detailed to make possible the reconstruction of what happened. Indeed, the intention may be to present so full a description to the reader that he can "experience a sense of event, presence and action" and also be able to check on the interpretation offered by the researcher.'

We said above that the ethnographer has a 'much more open mind' than the systematic observer. This does not mean he must have a totally open mind, but must have some preconceptions and anticipated problems that will structure his perceptions at least to some extent. In practice, this presents him with a dilemma which has been nicely expressed by Edwards and Furlong thus:[13]

'If the researcher . . . presents the results of his observation as pure description, he is concealing this selectivity. If, on the other hand, he presents his account as being closely guided by theory, then he risks being accused of choosing those events which support his own point of view . . .

Since open-mindedness is impossible, what can be demanded of the researcher is that he should make as clear as he can the basis on which he chose to report what he did (since there was so much else going on that he could have noticed), and from which he interpreted his particular collection of facts.'

The third method of research used in the study of classroom talk is *sociolinguistic investigation*. According to Edwards and Furlong,[13] sociolinguists are concerned with how speech is organized in contexts that are 'typical, recurrent and repeatedly observable',[18] and in 'that part of language behaviour that can be related to social factors and stated in these terms'.[19] In particular, sociolinguists are interested in concepts such as the *form* that speech takes, the *function* it performs in given contexts, and the *competence*, linguistically speaking, of the participants. From a sociolinguistic perspective, investigations are considered easier where there are clear constraints on social situations. For this reason, the traditional classroom with its well defined structure of participant roles and educational objectives offers sociolinguists a potentially fruitful source of basic research data.

One area of potentially great interest to sociolinguists is the specialist language used by individual subjects – especially in secondary education – and it is to this that we now turn.

Subject-Specific Language

An important aspect of language in the classroom is the part it plays in meeting the particular needs of individual subjects. By this we mean the creation or adoption of a specialist terminology and vocabulary to identify and label those features of a discipline that are peculiar to it and which help to distinguish it from other disciplines. Surprisingly, it is only comparatively recently that linguists, educationalists, and researchers have started to look into this vitally important area of *subject-specific language*. Not only is it vitally important for communicative purposes, it is equally important for children's learning. One of the earliest writers to draw attention to the implications for learning of subject-specific language was Rosen. In an unpublished paper entitled 'The Problems of Impersonal Language' he writes:[20]

'Much of the language encountered in school looks at pupils across a chasm. Some fluent children . . . adopt the jargon and parrot whole stretches of lingo. Personal intellectual struggle is made irrelevant and the personal view never asked for. Language and experience are torn asunder. Worse still, many children find impersonal language mere noise. It is alien in its posture, conventions and strategies . . . These are extremes. Many children have areas of confidence and understanding but frequently have to resort to desperate mimicry to see them through.'

Because the topic of subject-specific language, or language register,[21] is such a grossly under-researched area, we can at present only identify the sorts of questions that can be asked in this connection. Thus, we may ask, to what extent are subject-specific languages necessary across the curriculum? Does the use of subject-specific language facilitate learning? Or does it inhibit learning? Does its use affect a teacher's overall discourse? In other words, do the occasions when it is perhaps necessary to use subject-specific language influence those occasions when it is not necessary at all? To what extent do teachers 'colloquialize' a subject-specific language, or colloquialize when the use of a distinctively subject-specific language would be more advantageous? What proportion of a teacher's (or pupil's) spoken language is made up of subject-specific language as compared with normal, everyday language? What has the subject-specific language in one discipline in common with other disciplines? Is there any overlap? Finally, to what extent does a gulf exist between the teacher and pupil when it comes to using subject-specific language in the classroom?

More sophisticated questions have been posed by Edwards.[22] He asks:

'If a subject register *is* apparent, are pupils expected to use it, or just understand it; is a receptive or a productive competence required? Do they learn it by imitation, or by coping with subject-specific tasks in which the form is determined by the function? How does the teacher "mediate" between the language of his pupils, and that which he considers appropriate to his subject? When a teacher says something like this, is it a one-man performance which he does not yet expect his pupils to match, or does he expect an approximation to it, or does he "translate" pupil contributions into the appropriate form while responding to the content of what they say?

Put that into the distillation flask and then distil off, and then we get thermometer recording the correct temperature which is boiling point for acetone. Then we collect the acetone which came over as a distillate'. (Barnes[4])

Answers to questions of this nature must at present be speculative for, as Edwards points out, we know so little about the language that teachers use.

In their interesting analysis of 'subject language', Edwards and Furlong[13] observe that distinctive forms of speech associated with particular social groups may serve two main functions. First, they make it possible to transact business more efficiently by providing a language that is both brief and precise, and second, they symbolize membership of a group and loyalty to it. The special language of school subjects, they suggest, can be seen in this way – as a mixture of intellectual necessity and group solidarity. They go on to explain thus:

'The necessity arises from the development of special terms for objects and ideas of special, perhaps even unique, importance to that discipline. But many more esoteric terms are used than are strictly necessary. This additional usage has been called conventional rather than intellectual, though any implication that they are merely verbal habits would be misleading. Both necessary and conventional usage serve to mark off some special area of interest, and teachers' frequent preoccupation with the right terminology (even when it is hard for an observer to see what the fuss is about) is a way of indicating the separation of academic from everyday knowledge, or of one academic territory from another.'

As pupils are inducted into the use of 'subject languages', not only are they thus in a position to begin to make the fine discriminations denied them by everyday language, their sense of belonging to a particular specialism and specialist group is reinforced.

Because their interests are sufficiently specialist to warrant it, some disciplines have a range of specialist terms so obviously different from their everyday meanings that there is little risk of confusion. One only has to think of subjects like physics or cybernetics. Yet subjects like history or sociology, each of which is concerned in its own way with reflections on human behaviour, draw upon a vocabulary part of which is appropriated from everyday language. It is words which overlap in this way, which have a special significance superimposed on their everyday meaning, which cause problems of communication. In instancing the 'special language' of sociolinguistics, which has its own esoteric terms as well as old words with new meanings, or nuances of meaning, Edwards[22] asks if the special language offers or facilitates new insights, new ways of observing, classifying and relating the phenomena. Or does it, he asks, seem to be a 'translation' which adds nothing to the commonsense knowledge, a new way of *talking* about language which mystifies but does not enlighten?

Tantalizing questions which only more research can answer. We have spoken of the dearth of research in this field, but what has been undertaken so far? One of the pioneering studies in this area is that of Barnes.[4] He investigated language interaction·in twelve lessons in the first term of secondary education. In that part of the study which he called 'The Language of Instruction', Barnes dealt with the topic under three headings – specialist language presented; specialist language not presented; and the language of secondary education. Our principal concern here is with the first of these categories. Under 'specialist language presented', teachers were aware of certain of the technical terms they used and showed this by 'presenting' them, i.e. a term is supplied by the teacher and a definition asked for, or at other times the teacher explicitly gives a name, or asks pupils to give a name, to a concept which has been already established. For example, in one particular chemistry lesson in a grammar school, the words *chromatography, pestle and mortar, suspension, effluent,* and *chlorophyll* were presented to the class. Examples were much less common in the lessons from non-selective schools with the sole exception of a history lesson which presented *city states, patriotic, inquiring mind, language, truce* and *pentathlon.* Neither in science nor maths lessons could a systematic policy be perceived, either in the selection of concepts to be taught or in the order of presentation of the concept and a term to represent it.

Box 6.4 contains an extract from an exchange between a teacher and pupil in a biology lesson. This example underlines an assumption which Barnes found was shared in some degree by six of the twelve teachers observed: that the teaching of terminology is seen as

BOX 6.4

The Use of Terminology in a Biology Lesson

Teacher	Where does it go then?
Pupil	To your lungs, Miss.
Teacher	Where does it go before it reaches your lungs? . . . Paul.
Pupil	Your windpipe, Miss.
Teacher	Down the windpipe . . . Now can anyone remember the other word for windpipe?
Pupil	The trachea.
Teacher	The trachea . . . good . . . After it has gone through the trachea where does it go to then? . . . There are a lot of little pipes going into the lungs . . . what are those called? . . . Ian?
Pupil	The bronchii.
Teacher	The bronchii . . . that's the plural . . . What's the singular? What is one of these tubes called? . . . Ann.
Pupil	Bronchus.
Teacher	Bronchus. . .with 'us' at the end. . .What does 'inspiration' mean. . .?

Source: Barnes[4]

part of the task. As Barnes himself says: 'It is clear from the substitution of "trachea" for "windpipe" that it is not merely the referential function of the word that is valued; the teacher is valuing that of the two synonyms which carries with it (for her, not the pupils, of course) the stronger suggestion of a strictly biological context'.[4]

Side by side with these and similar presentations, some teachers use specialist language without explicitly presenting it. Some of these, Barnes found, were technical terms of the subject which are well enough known to be unlikely to present difficulty: in an English lesson, *stress* and *rhyme*; in physics *diagram* and *pulley*; in mathematics, *point*; and in history, *a major city*.

Others were as much part of the teacher's idiolect as part of the subject register; one mathematics teacher used 'split' repeatedly, whereas another used 'sliced' and 'divided' in similar contexts.

All these examples came from non-selective schools; they were few and trivial enough for their effect upon the children's learning to be ignored. In the grammar schools, however, Barnes found that language of this kind bulked more large. The extract below illustrates the difficulty the teacher in question had in thinking of his subject without using its terminology.

Teacher   If we did it using a different method actually . . . where we heat up the grass
           with acetone actually . . . heating it under, er . . . an enclosed system
           except . . . I'll have to show using a diagram on that . . . well er . . . under
           reflux conditions so that we didn't lose the acetone then we could actually
           finish up with the grass a white colour.

Of this extreme example, Barnes says that 'it can be surmised that this teacher's enthusiasm for his subject and his abundance of knowledge tended to stop him from perceiving his pupils' needs. Talk of this kind would certainly discourage many pupils; it is tempting to make guesses about which pupils would be best able to tolerate such language and to continue to attend to it until such times as they could begin to take part'.[4]

As part of his conclusion to the total study, Barnes says:

' . . . the study so far provides a basis for arguing (a) that some teachers fail to
perceive the pedagogical implications of many of their own uses of language, and (b)
that a descriptive study such as this provides a potential method of helping teachers
to become more aware. Whether they are able to carry over this insight into their
own work has not been shown, however.'[4]

Another study looking at the problem of subject-specific language was undertaken by Richards.[23] It was concerned with identifying existing subject registers and describing their characteristics. Thus the investigation involved the analysis of the language of a selection of school subjects. The three hypotheses formulated at the outset of the study stated that:

1. There is no difference between the language a child encounters in school and his ordinary speech;
2. There is no significant difference in the demands made upon a child's language by the different subjects of the curriculum; and

3. The linguistic features of the language used in the various subject lessons are not sufficiently differentiated as to suggest that they constitute different registers.

The first hypothesis was not upheld, the results indicating that people do encounter language forms which *are* different from their ordinary speech – 'characteristically such language shows increased formality of style, makes use of a specialized vocabulary and contains certain repetitive patterns of syntactic structure which are often more complex than would occur in the language normally employed by the pupil. In some cases the language is peculiar to the subject and appears to have a useful function in that it carries concepts and meanings that cannot be readily expressed in other forms.'

Data collected and analysed in connection with the second hypothesis showed that distinctions with respect to language demands *do* exist among subjects. Examination of the subject histograms in Box 6.5 shows, for example, the proportion of factual to reasoning questions within a subject. Richards herself says, 'Maths makes nearly twice the reasoning demands of any of the arts subjects. Physics and chemistry also show considerably higher proportions of reasoning questions than the remaining subjects. In the same category, biology is slightly ahead of the arts subjects, its reasoning score being identical with its factual score. This factual score is second highest to geography and puts biology farther ahead of the remaining arts subjects in the category than these same arts subjects are ahead of physics and chemistry.'

With regard to the third hypothesis, Richards found that there appears to be grounds for asserting that within schools language varieties exist which can be thought of as rudimentary registers that become increasingly differentiated and in evidence with the pupil's progress through the school. The degree to which a particular variety becomes more or less developed is dependent also on the level of course. When teaching O or A level courses, teachers tend to employ language that is closer to the subject norm depicted in supporting texts than they do when teaching CSE or remedial courses.

We conclude our review of verbal communication in the classroom with a brief examination of a topic which could have far-reaching implications – language deprivation and disadvantage.

Language Deprivation and Disadvantage

In touching upon the issue of language deprivation and disadvantage among children, we immediately find ourselves in the midst of controversy and hedged in by a welter of unresolved difficulties, not the least of which is the lack of unequivocal empirical evidence. The controversy appears to have a number of heads to it. First, there is the terminological debate – is 'disadvantaged' or 'deprived' the more fitting term? Second, there are competing viewpoints – is the problem best viewed psychologically or sociologically? And third, there are important philosophical considerations – what *is* the purpose of education? What is equality? In what sense can 'deprivation' be compensated for?

Further, much of the controversy stems directly from inadequately developed theories and the need for substantial research projects to answer such questions as: What environmental factors influence language performance? Is the language of the disadvantaged child deficient? Does language influence cognitive development? Should

BOX 6.5

Distribution of Individual Categories of Question as a Proportion of All Questions Asked within the Lessons of Each Subject Sample educationalists intervene to help the disadvantaged child develop his language skills? What are the best classroom techniques for dealing with language difficulties? What are the social class differences in language performance? And what can cross-cultural studies tell us in these respects?

The contentious issues of terminology reflect the particular perspectives adopted at different periods of the debate. To begin with, in the early 1960s, children who came from poor families were described as 'culturally deprived'. But this term was later regarded as both misleading and insulting because it ignored the fact that such children had a quite definite culture of their own, though it differed from the dominant one. The term 'culturally deprived' was therefore replaced by 'culturally disadvantaged', which duly recognized a culture, but one which, being different from the dominant one, was regarded as being at a disadvantage. This being the case, the school was seen as an important agent in compensating for this disadvantage.

Any consideration of the concept of social disadvantage must at some point touch upon the issue of *heredity* versus *environment*, whether intelligence is innately determined or whether it can be significantly influenced by the environment. As Moss says,[24] 'If one sees people as falling into different social classes because of differences in innate ability, then it makes little sense to try to change the "laws of nature". However, if one holds the view that a person's class membership (including education and occupational status) is a product of that person's opportunities and experiences, then a democratic society has an obligation to ensure that all its people have an equal access to such opportunities and experiences.'

The concept of intelligence underwent an important change in the late 1950s and early 1960s. Before this period, it was generally felt that intelligence was something a person was endowed with at conception, that the 'amount' was fixed and unchanging, and that members of 'better families' were favoured in this respect. However, with such notions as the reversibility of the effects of deprivation, the role of the environment in promoting this, and the importance of educational challenge, this view of intelligence was greatly modified. With such ideas and this changing conception of intelligence came the idea of *compensatory education* – the development of school programmes designed to remedy the problems of schooling of children from impoverished backgrounds.[24] As Moss explains, 'Such programmes have attempted to assist poor children by compensating for assumed deficits in their early experiences. The experiences in question are those which are thought to be necessary for further learning. These deficits have variously been described and include such things as short attention span, poor language development, deficiences in visual and auditory perception, low levels of motivation towards learning in the school, unfamiliarity with school objects, and so forth.'

Not everyone has welcomed this so-called attempt at compensation. Bernstein, for instance, says that education cannot compensate for society. He attacks the labelling of children and suggests the problem lies in the schools. He criticizes the concept 'compensatory education' which he says 'serves to direct attention away from the internal organization and the educational context of the school' and that it 'implies that something is lacking in the family, and so in the child.' He stresses the need to provide an 'adequate educational environment' in general, and to stop thinking of it in terms of 'compensation'. Like Labov, another critic, he emphasizes the need to consider the child's own existing culture rather than regarding this as a 'deficit system' that needs to be filled out. The implications of these views for language education have yet to be fully drawn.

Most researchers into verbal behaviour in the classroom rely on words alone.[13] As Edwards and Furlong point out, such researchers assume that the verbal behaviour is a sufficient sample of the total behaviour – 'that any nonverbal communication necessary to generate and sustain classroom interaction is either subsumed in, or subordinate to, what is actually said.' In a sense, this assumption is forced on researchers because of the difficulty of obtaining nonverbal data. However, for the remainder of the chapter, we look at some features of nonverbal communication in general in the hope that they will stimulate readers to consider perhaps more seriously than they might otherwise have done their value as means of contact and communication in the classroom.

NONVERBAL COMMUNICATION

In the past few years, the concept of *body language* has become very much part of received usage mainly through the influence of popular articles and books on the subject by writers in both Britain and America. For all the commercial appeal which a not-too-serious look at this topic undoubtedly offers and its novelty as a talking point at cocktail parties where its propositions can be humorously tested, the interest it has attracted does nevertheless reflect but part of a growing awareness of, and serious interest in, that wider area of *nonverbal communication*, the study of which is of increasing concern to both researchers and educators. The earliest studies in the field began to appear as comparatively late as the 1950s and consisted of systematic efforts to transcribe gestures and other nonverbal behaviours, and to understand the culturally prescribed codes that moderate their use and significance in human communication.[25] Since then, a growing number of researchers have begun to investigate those significant areas of nonverbal communication identified by Argyle[26] as follows: facial expression; gaze; gesture and bodily movements; posture; bodily contact; spatial behaviour; clothes, physique and other aspects of appearance; and nonverbal vocalizations. If we still need further justification for studying nonverbal communication, then we might heed the words of Erich Fromm,[27] who writes:

> 'Psychoanalysis teaches one to be sceptical of what a man *says*, because his words usually reveal, at best, only his consciousness; and to read between the lines, to listen with the 'third ear', to read his face, his gestures, and every expression of his body.'

Nonverbal aspects of communication in the classroom are of considerable importance for teachers for at least four reasons. First, the nonverbal messages we transmit are seen as more honest reflections of what we are *really* thinking or feeling at a particular time. The significance of this becomes even more telling when we realize that children have a very fine perception of involuntary nonverbal communication.[28] Second, a child's ability to learn from a teacher depends on the sharing of systems of nonverbal communication – 'without this the child cannot be certain he is following the subtle interconnections in any presentation, he cannot account for certain behaviours such as particular tones of voices, and he cannot feel secure in what he has learned or what the significance of the learning is.'[29] This point may be of special relevance where teachers and pupils come from quite different social backgrounds. Third, human communication is now seen as a complex process involving all modalities and not merely verbal communication.[29] Nonverbal communication thus draws attention to those features of human communication that are non-language and which are often overlooked as part of the total process. The final reason for the importance of nonverbal communication to teachers is that, in line with the broadening focus of the human sciences to take in the 'whole man', new approaches to communication are no longer limited to an analysis of the source, content and reception of messages. Rather, they see communication as a process taking place within a framework of human relationships – 'if we look at the *content* as the end-product of learning, we see people as filing cabinets of information with which to perform certain behaviours. But when we focus instead, on the process, we see people as increasingly competent participants in the human society.'[29] Box 6.6 provides instances of the use of nonverbal language in the classroom setting.

BOX 6.6

Nonverbal Cues in the Classroom

The classroom is a veritable goldmine of nonverbal behaviour, which has been nearly untapped by scientific probes. Acceptance and understanding of ideas and feelings on the part of both teacher and (pupil), encouraging and criticizing, silence, questioning, and the like – all involve nonverbal elements. Consider the following instances as representative of the variety of classroom nonverbal cues: (1) the frantic hand waver who is sure that he or she had the correct answer; (2) the (pupil) who is sure that he or she does not know the answer and tries to avoid any eye contact with the teacher; (3) the effects of (pupil) dress and hair length on teacher–pupil interaction; (4) facial expression – threatening gestures, and tone of voice are frequently used for discipline in elementary schools; (5) the teacher who requests (pupil) questioning and criticism, but whose nonverbal actions make it clear that he or she will not be receptive; (6) a pupil's absence from class communicates; (7) a teacher's trust of (pupils) is sometimes indicated by the arrangements of seating and monitoring behaviour during examinations; (8) the variety of techniques used by (pupils) to make sleeping appear to be studying or listening; (9) the professor who announces that he or she has plenty of time for (pupil) conferences, but whose fidgeting and glancing at a watch suggest otherwise; (10) teachers who try to assess visual feedback to determine (pupil) comprehension; (11) even classroom design (wall colours, space between seats, windows) has an influence on (pupil) participation in the classroom.

Source: adapted from Knapp[30]

Research strategies used in the investigation of nonverbal behaviour may be divided into three interlocking phases. These have been identified by Duncan[25] as follows: (1) that which differentiates and specifies the behaviour in question through a transcription and notation system; (2) that which discovers the extent and nature of internal structure exhibited by the behaviours, i.e. seeing nonverbal behaviour and communication as a tightly organized and social system, like a language, which operates according to a definite set of rules which can be explicated by the researcher; and (3) that which seeks relationships between the nonverbal behaviours and other variables such as personality characteristics, situation, and observer's judgments. These phases can be identified as stages 2 and 3 of our original model of the scientific method outlined in Box 1.3.

We now go on to consider some of the more important nonverbal variables that have been investigated in social psychological and educational research. We begin with a look at the area of *proxemics*, the study of the ways people use space and their immediate environment, for the organization of these factors can have a major impact on communication.

Proxemics – Space and Spatial Behaviour in the Classroom

It has been noted that how we use space along with other variables in a social situation can dramatically affect our ability to achieve certain goals – be they romantic, diplomatic, aggressive, or even educational.[30] This is so because spatial arrangements can give tone to a communication, can stress it, and can even at times take precedence over the spoken word.[31] Thus a teacher addressing a class from behind her desk positioned at the front of the class will achieve an authoritative and less personal quality in what she has to say. If, however, she is conversing with one pupil only about a problem the child has encountered, her manner will be more intimate and informal. More specifically, spatial behaviour involves such notions as *proximity* – the nearness of, or distance between, two people; *orientation* – the angle at which one person faces another; and *movement* – usually determined by the nature of the physical setting.

Hall distinguishes three types of spatial organization:[32] that involving fixed-feature, semifixed-feature, and informal space. Fixed-feature space is determined by fixed, unmoving boundaries, either visible or invisible. Semifixed-feature space is that characterized by the presence of movable objects such as chairs, tables, and desks. And informal space is the distance maintained between two people in conversation. The latter will clearly vary according to such factors as the situation, the nationality, age, status, and relationship of the interactants. These three terms are closely related to two other expressions used in proxemics – *territoriality* and *personal space*.

Territoriality is a term that was developed to describe the behaviour of certain animals in setting up fixed territories which are then strenuously defended against certain types of intruders.[25] The concept thus involves fixed-feature space. Most behavioural scientists agree that territoriality exists among human beings. The presence of fixed or semifixed geographical locations thereby helps to regulate social interaction as well as provoke social conflict – 'Like animals, the more powerful, dominant humans seem to have control over more territory as long as the group or societal structure is stable. Some territorial behaviours around one's home are particularly strong, namely, Dad's chair, Mom's kitchen, Billy's stereo, or Barbara's phone.'[30] In the classroom, a teacher's territorial space, approximating more to Hall's semifixed feature space, is identified by his desk and chair located at the front of the class: a pupil in a traditionally organized classroom likewise has his particular territory – a desk or position at a table. Violations of territory in a classroom can thus result in a certain amount of tension or ill-feeling.

Unlike territorial space, personal space has no fixed or semifixed geographical position,[28] and has much in common with Hall's informal space. Personal space is the area immediately round the individual, an area in which most of his interactions take place. It has been compared to an invisible bubble that moves with the individual and may expand or contract in size depending on the particular situation he finds himself in. It can be measured for an individual by asking another person to approach him from different directions, i.e. head-on, sideways, etc. The points at which he stops the other can be plotted as an envelope: this is his personal space.[26] When only three or four people occupy an average-sized room, each's individual personal space bubble will be quite extensive. As more and more people enter the room, so the existing personal space bubbles naturally contract to accommodate the newcomers each of whom has his own personal space. In extremely crowded conditions such as in underground trains, football crowds and elsewhere, there is great violation of personal space and under these conditions personal space ceases to function in the usual way.[26] With young children, invasion of one's personal space can result in either verbal or physical aggression, or both. This point is borne out in a study by Hutt and Vaizey[33] who examined the effects of varying group density on the behaviour of (1) brain-damaged, (2) normal, and (3) autistic children. Group density varied from fewer than six to greater than twelve. As a function of group density, the researchers found significant changes in three categories of behaviour – (1) aggressive, destructive, (2) social, and (3) boundary (withdrawal to the edges of the room). While all three groups of children showed deterioration of behaviour with increased group density, the brain-damaged children and the autistic children were most affected. Brain-damaged and normal children reacted with increased aggressiveness/destructive behaviour, while the autistic children reacted by withdrawing to the boundary. It has been shown elsewhere, however, that as individuals mature, they increasingly learn to control their responses to invasion of their personal space.

Turning our attention now to the classroom, it is apparent that the average classroom has only a limited amount of space and the way it is used will affect both the kind and the amount of communication that occurs there. The three most common ways of arranging a typical room in terms of teacher and pupils are represented in Boxes 6.7, 6.8, and 6.9. The following discussion is based on the work of Hurt and his colleagues.[2]

BOX 6.7

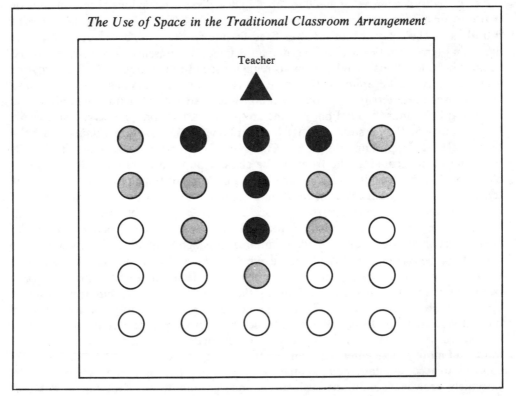

The Use of Space in the Traditional Classroom Arrangement

Teacher

Source: Hurt et al.[2]

Box 6.7 represents the traditional classroom found particularly in the secondary school. In this kind of arrangement, the pupils occupying the dark seats will tend to account for a very large proportion of the total interaction between the teacher and pupils. Those sitting in the grey seats will interact a certain amount, though much less frequently than those in the darkened areas. Pupils in the white seats will tend to participate very infrequently. Several explanations have been suggested for this variation. One reason is that whereas some pupils enjoy communicating with others, a proportion are quite apprehensive – especially when communicating with teachers. The latter will therefore tend to choose the white seats. The former, however, will select the darkened areas and those who are moderately apprehensive will choose the grey areas.

The 'horseshoe' arrangement in Box 6.8 is typically found in colleges and in some of the upper forms of the secondary school. Assuming the pupils have a choice, they will select their seats according to their degree of apprehension. The highly apprehensive pupils will tend to sit to the right and left of the teacher hoping that he or she will have less visual access to them in his or her efforts to maintain contact with the entire group. Some readers may have the opportunity to check out the validity of these claims in their own college seminar work.

BOX 6.8

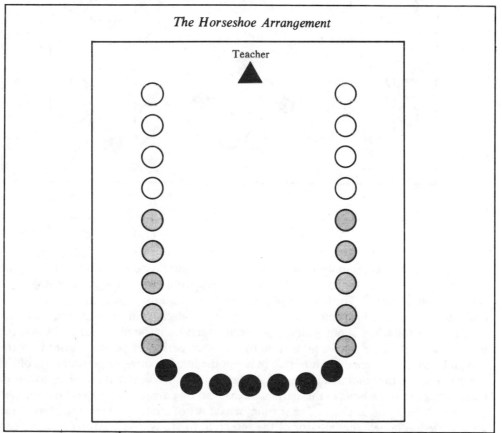

Source: Hurt et al.[2]

The group arrangement depicted in Box 6.9 is very common in primary schools – especially those adopting more progressive practices. It allows for more pupil interaction, but makes interaction with the teacher more difficult, unless he or she moves from group to group. Certain seats within each of the groups will attract those pupils who enjoy talking to the teacher and will be avoided by the more apprehensive children. Again, these are indicated by the degrees of shading. The darker seats represent the areas where the most amount of participation should be expected and the white seats the areas where the more apprehensive pupils will probably choose to sit.

BOX 6.9

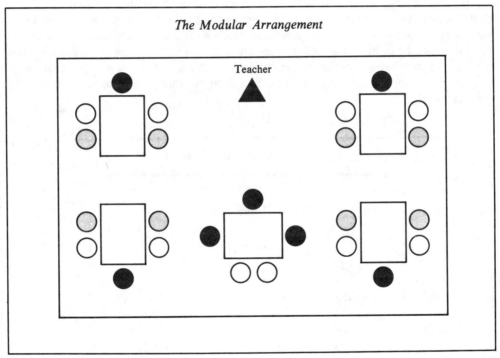

The Modular Arrangement

Teacher

Source: Hurt et al.[2]

These studies on communication in school and college classrooms make up part of the wider body of work on spatial arrangements in small groups, or small-group ecology as it is sometimes termed.[30] The findings of these studies reveal that our seating behaviour is not usually accidental or random. Whether we are conscious of them or not, there are explanations for much of our seating behaviour. It has been found, for instance, that the particular position we choose in relation to the other person or persons varies with the task in hand, the degree of relationship between the interactants, the personalities of the two parties, and the amount and kind of available space.[30] We refer at this point to one of these studies to show how, in this particular case, seating arrangements were determined by the task being undertaken. The seating behaviour of students in their cafeterias and libraries led Sommer, the initiator of the research, to study how students would sit in different task situations.[34] Persons were asked to imagine themselves sitting at a table with a friend of the same sex in each of the following situations:

Conversation: Sitting and chatting for a few minutes before class.
Co-operation: Sitting and studying together for the same exam.
Co-action: Sitting studying for different exams.
Competition: Competing in order to see who will be the first to solve a series of puzzles.

Two types of tables were shown to each subject. One table was rectangular and one was round. Each had six chairs. The results of this study are presented in Box 6.10.

BOX 6.10

Seating Preferences in Four Situations

Seating preferences at rectangular tables

(151 RESPONSES)

Conversation	42%	46%	11%	0%	1%	0%
Cooperation	19	25	51	0	5	0
Co-action	3	32	7	13	43	3
Competition	7	41	8	18	20	5

Seating preferences at round tables

(116 RESPONSES)

Conversation	63%	17%	20%
Cooperation	83	7	10
Co-action	13	36	51
Competition	12	25	63

Source: Sommer[34]

Conversations before class primarily involved corner or 'short' opposite seating at the rectangular tables and side-by-side seating at the round tables. Co-operation seemed to elicit a preponderance of side-by-side choices.

Co-action, studying for different exams, or reading at the same table as another, necessitated plenty of room between the participants and the most distant seating positions were generally selected. Most persons wanted to compete in an opposite seating arrangement. Those who wanted to establish a closer opposite relationship apparently felt that this would afford them an opportunity not only to see how the other person was progressing but would also allow them to use various gestures, body movements, and eye contact to 'upset' their opponents. The more distant opposite position would, on the other hand, prevent 'spying'.

We now go on to consider the communicative value of touch in human interaction.

Touch and Touching Behaviour in Human Communication

The part played by touch in communicating the most basic forms of interpersonal attitude and, to a lesser extent, feelings and emotions is something we perhaps tend to take for granted. Acceptance and friendship, for example, along with hostility, encouragement, tenderness and emotional support can all have their meanings enhanced when accompanied by appropriate touching behaviour. Touch is one of the most primitive forms of communication and precedes other forms of nonverbal communication in the developmental process – 'Newborn infants continue to gain knowledge of themselves and the world around them through tactile explorations. Some of the common touch experiences include the touch of the obstetrician's hands and the hands that change the diapers, feed them, bathe them, rock them and comfort them.'[30] The amount and kind of contact an individual gives and receives from childhood to adulthood varies according to age, sex, situation and relationship, not all of it necessarily eliciting positive reactions.

The important part touch and tactile experiences play in subsequent mental and emotional development is well known. Children having little physical contact during infancy may walk and talk later; some schizophrenic children are reported to have been handled less as infants than normal children; and similar early deprivation has been associated with later difficulties in reading and speech. Montagu[35] cites vast numbers of animal and human studies to support the theory that tactile satisfaction during infancy and childhood is of fundamental importance to subsequent healthy behavioural development of the person. He maintains that we cannot handle a child too much since 'there is every reason to believe that, just as the salamander's brain and nervous system develops more fully in response to peripheral stimulation, so does the brain and nervous system of the human being.'[35] The famous experiments conducted by Harlow with infant monkeys provide conclusive evidence for the importance of touch in the animal world and endorse the points we have just made about the role of touch in human development. Harlow constructed two 'surrogate mother' figures – one was made of wire and provided milk and protection; the other was made out of sponge rubber and terry cloth and did not provide milk. The infant monkeys used by Harlow in his experiments consistently chose the latter, the 'mother' made of sponge and terry cloth. Harlow concluded that the 'mother' perceived as a source of reassuring touch and contact was preferred to the one offering only food and sustenance.

The developmental role of touch to communicate feelings is clearly in evidence in the classroom, though the different effects it has depend on the age and sex of the children. For younger children in the lower primary school, touch can communicate a sense of belonging, security and understanding. Conversely, a child may feel isolated and neglected when a teacher withholds touch and this may lead to negative attitudes to school. Research in orphanages has shown that in a low-touch environment, infants have a higher mortality rate and a higher level of alienation. High-touch environments produce a lower mortality rate among infants and the older children tend to be better socialized. There is also some evidence to indicate that frequent touching facilitates the development of the nervous system of infants, making them more responsive to their environments.

As well as being touched, young children will need also to touch objects in order to learn about their environment. It is not uncommon, for example, for small children to want to touch their teacher's clothing or hair. They will also touch one another a great deal. As children grow older, however, they become more socialized to sexual and social norms and the amount of touching received and given declines.

We noted above that many factors affect the amount and kind of contact in adulthood. One of these is the situation. After investigating the facilitating and inhibiting effect certain situations have on touching behaviour, Henley suggests[36] that people may be more likely to touch when: (1) giving information or advice rather than asking for it; (2) giving an order rather than responding to it; (3) asking a favour rather than agreeing to do one; (4) trying to persuade rather than being persuaded; (5) the conversation is 'deep' rather than casual; (6) at a party rather than at work; (7) communicating excitement rather than receiving it from another; and (8) receiving messages of worry from another rather than sending such messages. Whereas one would perhaps be unwise to draw a general conclusion from these points, there does nevertheless seem to be some evidence to suggest that the initiator of the touching behaviour is often in a more powerful or better informed position than the person being touched.

Although we said in our opening paragraph that touch communicates interpersonal attitudes, feelings and emotions, hard evidence on the meaning of touch is scarce. One who has undertaken work in the field is Argyle.[26] He believes that touch can be decoded as communicating various interpersonal attitudes such as, for instance, sexual interest, nurturance-dependence (cradling or caressing an infant), affiliation (especially friendly relations), and aggression (establishing unfriendly relations). Other touching signals may simply be interpreted as managing the interaction itself. These management touches may guide someone without interrupting verbal conversation. Much of our touching behaviour is accidental and therefore meaningless, as when we bump into someone in a crowded street. The meaning of touching behaviour in school and classroom will fall broadly into the category described by Heslin as *functional-professional* – 'The communicative intent of this impersonal, often "cold" and business-like touching is to accomplish some task – to perform some service.'[37] Examples of this category might be a teacher placing his hand on a pupil's head to indicate his awareness of the pupil's waywardness, or taking the elbow of a new pupil to direct him to an unfamiliar part of the school building.

Differences in touching behaviour may be found between different cultures and between ethnic groups within a culture. Although little empirical research is to be found on this topic, it is clear at the level of everyday observation that such differences exist even in adults, though they are exaggerated even further among children. On the whole, white British children tend to touch less than coloured children and those from Southern Europe. The teacher must recognize that these are set cultural variations and should be viewed in this light.

An interesting point in this connection concerns North American culture. The United States represents a *noncontact* culture (though there is evidence that this may be changing).[30] The establishment of *Encounter Groups* there arose out of the need in part to break down people's inhibitions in this respect. The main purpose of the groups is therapy or training, by means of various individual and interpersonal exercises, many of them involving bodily contact and relationships with other members of the group. Box 6.11 gives some examples of bodily contact exercises used at Esalen where these groups were first conducted.

BOX 6.11

*Examples of the Bodily Contact Exercises used
in Encounter Groups*

(1) *To help people who are withdrawn and have difficulty in making contact with other people*:
    (a) 'Blind milling'. Everyone in the room stands up and wanders round the room with their eyes shut; when they meet someone they explore each other in any way they like.
    (b) 'Break in'. Some of the group form a tight circle with interlocking arms. The person left out tries to break through the circle in any way he can.

(2) *To help people who are unable to express hostility or competition*:
    (a) 'The press'. Two people stand facing each other, place their hands on the other's shoulders and try to press the other to the ground.
    (b) 'Pushing'. Two people stand facing each other, clasping their hands, and try to push each other backwards.

(3) *To help people who have difficulty in giving or receiving affection, who avoid emotional closeness*:
    (a) 'Give and take affection'. One person stands in the centre of a circle with his eyes shut; the others approach him and express their feelings towards him nonverbally however they wish – usually by hugging, stroking, massaging, lifting, etc.
    (b) 'Roll and rock'. One person stands in the centre of a circle, relaxed and with his eyes shut; the group pass him round the group from person to person, taking his weight. The group then picks him up and sways him gently backwards and forwards, very quietly.

Source: Schutz[38]

Body Movement, Posture and Gesture

In most social exchanges, individuals use their hands, arms and head as means of indicating their intentions and responses, as reinforcers to their verbal utterances. Gestural communication of this kind depends for its effectiveness on particular signs having agreed meanings among the participants and these will often be a function of the situation in which they are enacted. And like words, new and additional meanings will arise as situations and people change. In this way bodily movements may serve as a kind of language, their purest and least ambiguous expression being found in the sign language used by deaf people. It will help us here if we look at some of the terms used in connection with bodily movements and gesture and the significance they have in communication language. In particular, we consider *emblems, illustrators, regulators*, and *adaptors*.

Emblems are those conventional gestures having a generally accepted meaning in the culture or group in which they are used. Thus, nodding one's head indicates agreement; shaking a clenched fist represents anger; a deliberate yawn, boredom; shrugging the shoulders, indifference; pointing, giving directions; waving the hand, goodbye, and so on. The meaning of other emblems is less clearcut, however. Indeed, the vocabulary of gesture is one in which, like words, ambiguity is deliberately fostered. After studying the use of emblems in the United States, Johnson, Ekman and Friesen[39] found that they mostly indicate (1) interpersonal directions or commands; (2) the physical or emotional state of the person who is signalling; (3) insults; (4) replies; and (5) the physical appearance of the person. Many of the emblems used by both teachers and pupils in the course of classroom exchanges are to be found in everyday life situations outside school. Can you think of any classroom emblems *not* shared with the world at large?

Illustrators are those nonverbal acts that are intimately linked to spoken discourse. Argyle has identified the different ways in which bodily movements support verbal communication:

In punctuating and displaying the structure of utterances
Emphasizing
Framing, i.e. providing further information about what is said
Illustrating
Providing feedback from listeners
Signalling continued attention
Controlling the timing of one's utterances

As Ekman and Friesen[40] have shown, there are several different ways in which hand movements can illustrate speech. These are: (1) pointing to people (including oneself), or to objects, or turning and facing them; (2) showing a spatial relationship (inside, under); (3) showing spatial movements (through, round); (4) showing tempo and rhythm, beating time, showing slow movements; (5) showing a bodily action; (6) drawing a picture – of a spiral staircase, for instance; (7) showing a direction of thought. As Argyle points out, these illustrations are 'iconic' in that they are examples of, or physically represent, the objects referred to. In some countries there is quite elaborate gesture language and in ordinary conversation some words are replaced by symbolic hand signals. In addition to supplementing the content of communication, gestures accompanying speech help to maintain flow, continuity and synchronization. Normally they are taken for granted but when gestural reinforcement is not possible, then difficulties may arise. A good example is the telephone conversation where the information normally passed through the visual channel has now to be put into the auditory channel. This is achieved by interjections such as 'I see', 'good', or 'go on' which substitute for the gesture. What is interesting in this situation, however, is that people often adapt to it without realizing it.

Regulators are nonverbal acts that maintain and regulate the back and forth nature of speaking and listening between two or more interactants. They also play a prominent role in initiating and terminating conversations. Greetings, for example, perform a regulating function by signalling the beginning of interaction; they also convey information about the relationship between the two communicators and this helps to structure the ensuing dialogue. Nonverbal behaviour involved in greetings includes head movements, eye behaviour, smiling, hand-shaking, and paralinguistic signs ('Ah-hh', or 'Mm-mm'). Similar nonverbal behaviours may be detected in leave-taking situations. Knapp suggests that saying goodbye serves three functions:[30]

1. It signals the end of the interaction.
2. It sometimes summarizes the substance of the discourse.
3. Departure signals indicate supportiveness: they set a positive mood for the next encounter.

Nonverbal gestures play an important part between these two stages, the greeting and the farewell. They help, for example, in determining the frequency, timing and smoothness of turn-taking in the conversation: turn-yielding, turn-maintaining, and turn-denying are given a continuity and coherence.

Adaptors, as the term implies, are those behavioural adaptations we make in response to certain learning situations, e.g. learning to perform some bodily or instrumental action, learning to manage our emotions, learning to satisfy a need, or learning to get along with other people. These behaviours (or some trace of them) seem to appear in situations that the person feels approximate the conditions of the early learning experiences. Generally, we are not aware of performing them, but often feedback from another will make us aware of what we are doing, e.g. scratching one's head when confronted with a problem. Although the research on adaptors is not extensive, there seems to be some consensus that adaptors are generally associated with negative feelings – for oneself or another individual. There are also some useful classifications of different types of adaptors; they include rubbing, scratching, body-touching, picking, and self-grooming. These in turn may be associated with particular mood states.

Body movements, gestures and posture may indicate *attitudes*. The relationship between body movements and attitudes has been studied in the context of liking and disliking towards another person. One aspect of this that has attracted the attention of researchers is that of interpersonal warmth and coldness. Mehrabian,[41] for instance, found that liking is distinguished from disliking by more forward lean, a closer proximity, more eye gaze, more openness of arms and body, more direct body orientation, more touching, more postural relaxation, and more positive facial and vocal expression.

The use of the hands-on-hip position by a standing communicator was also indicative of communicator attitude according to Mehrabian. This position was used with greater frequency while interacting with disliked ones than with liked ones.

Other investigators have explored similar liking/disliking behaviours under the labels of warm/cold. Reece and Whitman identified the body language components that lead to one's being perceived as a 'warm' person.[42] Warmth indicators included a shift of posture towards the other person, a smile, direct eye contact, and hands remaining still. A 'cold' person looked around the room, slumped, drummed fingers, and did not smile. The warmth cues, coupled with the verbal reinforcer 'mm-Hmm', was effective for increasing verbal output from the other person. The verbal reinforcer alone was not sufficient.

Another group of investigators, Clore and his colleagues,[43] collected a large number of verbal statements that described nonverbal liking and disliking. These behaviours were limited to a female's actions towards a male. The large number of behavioural descriptions were narrowed down by asking people to rate the extent to which the behaviour accurately conveyed liking or disliking. Box 6.12 lists in order the behaviours that were rated highest and lowest. An actress then portrayed these behaviours in an interaction with a male, and the interaction was videotaped. To no one's surprise, viewers of the videotape felt that the warm behaviours would elicit greater liking from the male addressee. The interesting aspect of these studies is what happened when the viewers were exposed to a combined tape in which the actress's behaviour was initially cold and then turned warm. The reactions to these videotapes were compared with responses to videotapes that showed totally warm or totally cold portrayals of the actress. People judged that the man on the videotape would be more attracted to the woman who was cold at first and warm later than he would to the woman who was warm for the entire interaction. Further, people felt that the woman whose behaviour turned from warm to cold was less attractive to the man than the woman who was cold during the entire interaction.

BOX 6.12

Behaviours Rated as Warm and Cold

WARM BEHAVIOURS	COLD BEHAVIOURS
Looks into his eyes	Gives a cold stare
Touches his hand	Sneers
Moves toward him	Gives a fake yawn
Smiles frequently	Frowns
Works her eyes from his head to his toes	Moves away from him
Has a happy face	Looks at the ceiling
Smiles with mouth open	Picks her teeth
Grins	Shakes her head negatively
Sits directly facing him	Cleans her fingernails
Nods head affirmatively	Looks away
Puckers her lips	Pouts
Licks her lips	Chain-smokes
Raises her eyebrows	Cracks her fingers
Has eyes wide open	Looks around the room
Uses expressive hand gestures while speaking	Picks her hands
Gives fast glances	Plays with the split ends of her hair
Stretches	Smells her hair

Source: adapted from Clore, Wiggins, and Itkin[43]

Of course, these are relatively isolated studies and one would hesitate to aver that their findings had universal applicability. Nevertheless, they are indicative of some kind of relationship between body movement and attitudes and for this reason alone deserve to be taken with more than a token of seriousness by teachers and intending teachers who should have little difficulty in teasing out the implications for their own classroom performance.

Facial Expression and Eye Movement

The face is generally regarded as the most important area for nonverbal communication. Because of its visibility, we pay a great deal of attention to the messages we receive from other faces, even though facial expressions involve some of the smallest bodily movements. The impact of facial expressions in the classroom may be greater than any other type of nonverbal communication the teacher (and sometimes the pupil) exhibits. As Hurt and his colleagues say:[2] 'The teacher probably communicates more accidentally by his or her facial expression than by any other means. Scientists who study facial expression refer to "micro-momentary movements", changes in expression that constantly occur in all human communicators and are usually so fleeting that it requires highly technical photography to be able to isolate them for study. However, as quickly as they pass across a person's face, they are picked up by other people and produce responses.'

Argyle considers that man's facial expressions may be used in three broadly different ways:[26]

1. *As an indication of personality characteristics.* These may be portrayed by the structural aspects of the face, its typical expression, and perhaps by its characteristic reaction patterns. The control of facial expression, Argyle suggests, is taught by parents as part of cultural socialization. He himself says: 'The reason that impressions of personality are formed from the face is probably that the face is the area which is attended to most; hence people are recognized most readily from their face, and their facial behaviour stands for their personality. This can be controlled to a certain point, so that what is seen is partly the result of self-presentation.'
2. *As an expression of emotions.* These are indicated by slow-moving patterns of expression: *interpersonal attitudes* are expressed similarly. Argyle explains that the expressions of emotional and interpersonal attitudes in man are modified and controlled by cultural rules, and partly directed by cognitive factors.
3. *As interaction signals and signals linked with speech.* These are achieved by appropriate movements of those parts of the face – such as mouth, nose, and eyebrows – which can function more or less independently. When facial expressions of this kind supplement and support speech, they are quite different from emotional expression and involve only parts of the face.

The vital role played by the face's sequence of expressive movements not only in aiding communication but also in establishing and maintaining social relationships has been stressed by various writers. And again we have corroborative evidence from the animal world to support this statement. Argyle[26] refers to an experiment by Izard[44] in which the facial muscles of a young monkey were severed, with the result that the monkey failed to establish a relationship with its mother. In the course of human verbal interaction, the facial movements of both speakers and listeners play a quintessential part. Being largely independent of the emotional state of the speaker or his personality, they are nevertheless an indispensable part of the communication, the interaction, a sort of nonverbal commentary on the dialogue-in-progress. A scheme for classifying these movements has been provided by Birdwhistell.[45] It is based on a detailed study of filmed behaviour and is shown in Box 6.13.

Facial gestures, then, along with other nonverbal signals, are used to enhance the meanings of verbal utterances, to provide the speaker with feed-back from listeners, and to achieve continuing attention. Argyle points out[26] that facial signals can have a peculiar kind of referential meaning in that the signals refer primarily to other signals, either those being sent or those just received. This meaning, he adds, is basically polarized in character – agree/disagree, understand/don't understand. The syntactic structure of these signals may be of several kinds. Thus:

1. During conversation there is a rapid sequence of facial and other signals, which are dependent on the verbal messages for their organization. There is a total system of communication, but the nonverbal is subsidiary to the verbal.
2. These facial signals have definite meanings as reward or punishment, approval or disapproval, and therefore have a direct effect on the behaviour that follows. Thus a signal of puzzlement or incomprehension will lead to attempts to clarify. Signals of

BOX 6.13

A Code for the Face

—○—	Blank faced	○	Out of the side of the mouth (left)
— ⌒	Single raised brow ⌒ indicates brow raised	◐	Out of the side of the mouth (right)
— ⌣	Lowered brow	⌄	Set jaw
∨	Medial brow contraction	⌣	Smile tight — loose o
⋯	Medial brow nods		
⌒⌒	Raised brows	⊢⊣	Mouth in repose lax or tense -
○○	Wide eyed		
—○	Wink	⌒	Droopy mouth
＞ ＜	Lateral squint	⟩	Tongue in cheek
＞＜ ＞＜	Full squint	⌒	Pout
A	Shut eyes with A-closed pause 2 count	+++	Clenched teeth
⋌⋋ or B	Blink ⊣ B-closed pause 5 plus count	⩁	Toothy smile
		⊞	Square smile
◖◗	Sidewise look	©	Open mouth
◗ ◖	Focus on auditor	s◐ʟ	Slow lick — lips
◫ ◫	Stare	ℓ◐ʟ	Quick lick — lips
◎ ◎	Rolled eyes	⌒	Moistening lips
φ φ	Slitted eyes	⌣	Lip biting
◡ ◡	Eyes upwards	⩊	Whistle
—○○—	Shifty eyes	※	Pursed lips
＂○ ○＂	Glare	⟐	Retreating lips
○ ◔	Inferior lateral orbit contraction	※⊣	Peck
△ₛ	Curled nostril	※⌣	Smack
ₛ△ₛ	Flaring nostrils	⊟	Lax mouth
,△,	Pinched nostrils	⩍	Chin protruding
△	Bunny nose	⩊	'Dropped' jaw
△	Nose wrinkle	⊬⊣	Chewing
⌒	Left sneer	⤸ ⤹	Temples tightened
∿	Right sneer	⟨ ⟩	Ear 'wiggle'
		⩬	Total scalp movement

Source: Birdwhistell[45]

dominance may lead to complementary signals of submission/appeasement, or to competing dominance signals. Very often signals of a particular kind elicit similar signals from another, either through sheer imitation or as an exchange of rewards.

3. In particular social settings, there are rules governing the 'rituals' involved – as in greetings, church services, banquets, or sporting occasions. These rules often prescribe what is the correct facial expression at each stage of the ritual – one must look cheerful during greetings, solemn during church services; victors in sport should appear modestly pleased, and so on.

As facial expressions are closely linked to language, they are probably controlled, Argyle suggests, by that part of the brain which controls language.

In responding to children in the classroom, teachers may use facial expressions as reinforcers or as non-reinforcers. Although a teacher has little control over what have been termed 'micro-momentary movements', he does nevertheless have control over more enduring expressions like smiles and frowns. However, it seems that in practice few teachers do actually control these particular signals in order to reinforce or discourage children's responses. More often than not, they respond intuitively without being conscious of whatever their nonverbal behaviour in these respects is communicating. Of course, there are occasions when a teacher does not want to communicate what he is thinking to a pupil: a child whose response to a question is not completely correct but which is on the right lines often needs to be confronted with a dead-pan expression until he gets the answer wholly right. What is called for on the part of the teacher is increased sensitivity to his or her facial expressions and a greater awareness of how they may assist him or her in classroom communication.

We have so far talked about facial expression in general terms without attempting to specify those particular features that go to make up the total impression, though clearly it is the eyes that make up the most important part in terms of communication value. Eye movements are associated with a wide range of human expression: eyes that are wide-open are associated with wonder, frankness, terror, or naivety; downward glances are associated with modesty or self-consciousness; raised upper lids may signal displeasure; a fixed stare is identified with coldness; and eyes rolled upward suggest that another's behaviour is a little 'off-centre'.

Our own society has established a number of eye-related norms. We do not, for example, look too long at strangers in public places. Looking behaviour of this kind is referred to in the literature of social psychology as *gaze* and has only comparatively recently come under the scrutiny of researchers. Kendon[46] has noted four functions of gazing. They are as follows:

1. A cognitive function: to regulate the flow of communication. Visual contact occurs when we want to signal that the communication channel is open. In some instances, eye gaze can almost establish an obligation to interact (e.g. wanting or not wanting to make contact with one's teacher in the classroom).
2. Monitoring – subjects may look at their interactant to indicate the conclusions of thought units and to check their interactant's attentiveness and reactions. When people seek feed-back concerning the reactions of others, they gaze at the other person. If you find that the other person is looking at you, this is usually interpreted as a sign that the other person is attentive to what you are saying.
3. Regulatory – responses may be demanded or suppressed by looking. The importance of this function in the classroom is obvious. Indeed, to be able to stimulate or inhibit a

pupil's response is an important part of the experienced teacher's weaponry.

4. Expressive – the degree of involvement or arousal may be signalled through looking, that is, communicating the nature of the interpersonal relationship.

From his review of studies on gaze and mutual gaze, Knapp made certain predictions as to when there would be more, or less, gazing. These we have summarized in Box 6.14.

BOX 6.14

Occasions for More, or Less, Gazing

Having reviewed a number of factors considered to influence the amount and duration of gaze in human relationships, e.g. distance, physical characteristics, personal and personality characteristics, topics and tasks, and cultural background, Knapp predicted that there would be *more* gazing when:

You are physically distant from your partner
You are discussing easy, impersonal topics
There is nothing else to look at
You are interested in your partner's reactions – interpersonally involved
You are interested in your partner – that is, you like or love the partner
You are of lower status than your partner
You are trying to dominate or influence your partner
You are from a culture that emphasizes visual contact in interaction
You are an extravert
You have high affiliative or inclusion needs
You are dependent on your partner (and the partner has been unresponsive)
You are listening rather than talking
You are female

Knapp predicted *less* gazing when:

You are physically close
You are discussing difficult, intimate topics
You have other relevant objects, people, or background to look at
You are not interested in your partner's reactions
You are talking rather than listening
You are not interested in your partner – that is, you dislike the partner
You perceive yourself as a higher-status person than your partner
You are from a culture that imposes sanctions on visual contact during interaction
You are an introvert
You are low on affiliative or inclusion needs
You have a mental disorder such as autism or schizophrenia
You are embarrassed, ashamed, sorrowful, sad, submissive, or trying to hide something

Source: Knapp[30]

Vocal Cues

Vocal cues, or nonverbal vocalization as it is sometimes called, refer to that wide range of nonverbal sounds made by human beings in the course of speaking to, and interacting with, other human beings. One group characteristic of this kind of behaviour includes laughing, crying, moaning, and hissing. Of more relevance to us in our consideration of communication, however, are those nonverbal vocalizations that accompany speech.

Argyle[26] has identified two types in this regard. First, there are the various aspects of voice quality, unrelated to the contents of speech: these include tone of voice, which communicates emotions and attitudes to other people; and type of voice and accent, which send information about personality and group membership. Secondly, there are vocal features more intimately connected with speech – completing its meaning by means of pitch, stress and timing, providing a commentary on the verbal contents, and governing the synchronization of utterances.

We will now examine the relationship of vocal cues to three aspects of behaviour: (1) the expression of emotions; (2) interpersonal attitudes; and (3) speech.

The expression of emotions

Certain aspects of vocalization have been found to express emotions. These are: speed, loudness, pitch, speech disturbances, and voice quality, e.g. breathing or resonance.

Research on the encoding of emotions has used the method of asking subjects to read verbal materials *as if* they were angry, happy, sad, etc. Other experiments have induced actual emotional states, e.g. anxiety has been brought on by interviewing subjects on topics which are known to be disturbing to them. The vocalizations produced have then been subjected to physical measurement, for loudness, speed, etc. In Box 6.15 we set out a table developed by Davitz[47] as a result of his studies that represents, as well as anything, a composite statement of vocal cues associated with various emotional expressions. The table was compiled to test subjects on their knowledge of vocal characteristics.

This table can be used as a basis for a training programme intended to develop greater sensitivity to the factors associated with emotional expression.

Interpersonal attitudes

There is some overlap here with emotions, since no distinction is made in the voice between anger or love as emotional states, and as attitudes directed towards particular individuals. The Davitz studies, for example,[47] did not distinguish between the two, and included admiration, affection, amusement, anger, boredom, despair, disgust, dislike, fear, and impatience – all of which can be directed towards others. In a series of studies by Argyle and his colleagues,[48] a number of interpersonal styles were created, using tones of voice (while counting numbers), facial expressions, and head orientations. The researchers had no difficulty in creating tones of voice corresponding to friendliness, hostility, superiority, and inferiority, Mehrabian[41] found that tone of voice contributed slightly less than facial expression, but much more than the contents of speech, to impressions of interpersonal attitudes. In another group of studies he and his colleagues studied the voices of people who were trying to be persuasive. They spoke faster, much louder, with a greater range of pitch and loudness, and at a more regular speed. Such speakers were perceived as more persuasive. But did better speakers actually persuade? A number of experiments have varied the number of speech disfluencies and other aspects of speech. More fluent speakers are regarded as more competent, but not as more

BOX 6.15

Characteristics of Vocal Expressions Contained in the Test of Emotional Stability

FEELING	LOUDNESS	PITCH	TIMBRE	RATE	INFLECTION	RHYTHM	ENUNCIATION
Affection	Soft	Low	Resonant	Slow	Steady and slight upward	Regular	Slurred
Anger	Loud	High	Blaring	Fast	Irregular up and down	Irregular	Clipped
Boredom	Moderate to low	Moderate to low	Moderately resonant	Moderately slow	Monotone or gradually falling	—	Somewhat slurred
Cheerfulness	Moderately high	Moderately high	Moderately blaring	Moderately fast	Up and down; overall upward	Regular	
Impatience	Normal	Normal to moderately high	Moderately blaring	Moderately fast	Slight upward	—	Somewhat clipped
Joy	Loud	High	Moderately blaring	Fast	Upward	Regular	
Sadness	Soft	Low	Resonant	Slow	Downward	Irregular pauses	Slurred
Satisfaction	Normal	Normal	Somewhat resonant	Normal	Slight upward	Regular	Somewhat slurred

Source: Davitz[47]

credible or trustworthy, and there is no evidence that they are actually more persuasive.

Vocalizations related to speech

Some nonverbal vocalizations are closely linked to speech. Indeed, some of them are often regarded as part of speech. A wide range of nonverbal signals are related to speech in a number of different ways and can be regarded as part of a total communication system, of which speech is the central part. Timing, pitch and loudness, for example, figure importantly in this respect. Crystal[49] studied three hours' talk by thirty educated speakers of English. He found that there was a high degree of regularity in following many of the rules which he found. Thus, as regards *timing*, utterances vary in speed: a subordinate clause, for example, is spoken faster, and a slower speed is used to give emphasis. Pauses are frequent in speech: ones of under one-fifth second are used to give emphasis; longer ones signal grammatical junctures, such as the ends of sentences and clauses. Other pauses occur in the middle of clauses and may coincide with disfluencies such as repetitions, and changes of sentence.

Similarly, there are standard *pitch* patterns in every language for different kinds of sentence. In English, for example, questions beginning with 'How?', 'What?' etc. are spoken with a falling pitch; but questions with an inversion of subject and verb are accompanied with a rising tone. Pitch patterns can be varied to 'frame' or provide further meaning for an utterance. 'Where are you going?' with a rising pitch on the last word is a friendly inquiry, whereas with a falling pitch it is suspicious and hostile. This expresses more than a paralinguistic attitude to the recipient of the question, additional thoughts on the part of the speaker being implied, and a particular sort of answer being indicated. Pitch patterns can negate the words spoken – when, for example, an utterance is spoken sarcastically, or when the word 'yes' is spoken to indicate such unwillingness that it really means 'no'. Changes of pitch can also be used to accent particular words, though this is done usually by loudness.

The prosodic system of any language includes rules about the patterns of loudness of words in different kinds of sentences. In English the main nouns and verbs are usually stressed. The same sentence may be given different meanings by stressing different words, as in 'they are hunting dogs', or a sentence may retain the same basic meaning but attention can be directed to quite different parts of the message, as in *'Professor Brown's daughter* is *fond* of *modern music'* – each of the italicized words could be stressed, and this could change the significance of the utterance. In stressing *daughter* there is some implicit reference to a *son* – a case where a nonverbal signal refers or helps refer to an absent object. Speakers can make soft contrasts by speaking some words very quietly. In one study,[50] it was found that the amount of stress placed on words in the instructions given to experimental subjects had a marked·effect on their responses. Subjects were asked to rate the 'success' or 'failure' of people shown in photographs. There was a correlation of 0.74 between their ratings and the amount of emphasis placed by the experimenter on the words *success* and *failure* when describing the scale to be used.

In concluding this section on nonverbal communication, we direct the reader's attention to Box 6.16 the contents of which illustrate some of the points we have made by reference to the classroom context.

BOX 6.16

Examples of Nonverbal Communication in a Secondary School

Physical environment A classroom of a former municipal grammar school built in the late twenties or early thirties. One wall contains tall windows. There is a board for notices near the door. Hardboard has been placed along the back wall for display, but is not being used (the room is not a 'subject' or 'specialist' room). Desks of wood with steel frames (purchased in the sixties) are arranged in rows; table at front for teacher's books and papers. There are thirty pupils (14 to 15 years old); even so the room is overcrowded, with little circulation space.

Linguistic The teacher has written on the board and the pupils are copying:
Physiology. Yeast is a saprophyte which can carry out anaerobic respiration, i.e. respiration occurring in the absence of atmospheric oxygen. As in mucor enzymes are involved in digestion, so here numerous complex enzymes are present in yeast and these are collectively termed zymase.

John please sir is that mucor
Teacher yes what did you think it was
John mucus sir
Teacher (*shrugs and raises his eyes heavenwards; slight laugh from one boy*)
    werent you here when we did mucor
John yes sir
Teacher now these enzymes bring about fermentation/you start off with $C_6H_{12}O_6$ on this side (*writes on board*)/what do you end up with/nobody/well its $2CH_5OH + H_5OH + 2CO_2$/(*writes on board*) write that down.

Paralinguistic There is a good deal of silence in this lesson, punctuated by the squeak of the chalk on the blackboard. The teacher is a youngish man, with a quickfire delivery, who pushes his lessons along rapidly, impatient of pauses or digressions. His first question to John is ironic but not unkindly.

Visual Teacher eaglefaced, black hair strictly curtailed at collar. Belted leather jacket. Formal shirt and tie. Pupils, boys and girls, in a variety of dress.

Proxemic The pupils are sitting in tight rows, boys and girls strictly segregated (not from any official policy). Their shoulders are bent most of the time; they glance up at the board to copy. Few look up at John's question. They put their pens down to watch the board for the equation, one or two boys stretching a little.
    The teacher is standing in front. He often walks up and down restlessly.

Kinesic The teacher's eyebrows are expressive, but the class is not responding to him so much as to the work task. When he talks he looks at a point in the air beyond them. A few pupils twist their lips or look puzzled when asked to complete the question; most look impassive. He is not responsive to these looks and, instead of helping them with the answer by, for example, leading them step by step in chemical or layman's terms (alcohol, gas off), he merely supplies the answer.

Tactile There is no tactile communication. People take especial effort to avoid others.

The nature of the communication The physical environment has a slightly unkempt air, and contributes less positively to the learning situation than that of either of the other classrooms. The teacher's stance and behaviour signify pressure and more pressure.

Source: Wilkinson[3]

Developing Nonverbal Skills

Most of the ability we have in sending and receiving nonverbal signals is derived from 'on-the-job' training, the job, in this case, referring to the process of daily living. In short, we learn (not always consciously) nonverbal skills by imitating and modelling ourselves after others and by adapting our responses to the coaching, feedback and advice from others. This feed-back is not necessarily 'about' our behaviour but often takes the form of a response to our behaviour. Feed-back, then, may refer to a person who says 'Well, you don't look happy' . . . Through feed-back we increase our awareness of ourselves and others. We not only learn what behaviours to enact, but how they are performed, with whom, when, where, and with what consequences. Naturally, some of us have more and better 'helpers' than others; some of us seek help more than others. You can practise nonverbal sending and receiving frequently, but without regular, accurate feedback, you may not improve your ability.

Ultimately, the development of nonverbal skills will depend on the following:

1. *Motivation*: The more you desire to learn nonverbal skills, the greater are your chances of doing so. Often this motivation will develop when you feel that such skills will help improve the nature of your career or personal life.
2. *Attitude*: People enter learning situations with productive or unproductive attitudes. You may, for example, be highly motivated, but unproductive attitudes to the learning situation will inevitably lessen the learning outcome.
3. *Knowledge*: The development or reinforcement of any skill is partly dependent on an understanding of the nature of that skill. We seem to obtain a lot of nonverbal knowledge, often unconsciously from watching others as we develop. Some of this knowledge is only known to ourselves when we hear or read about it from another source.
4. *Experience*: Skill cannot be learned in isolation. With the proper guidance and useful feed-back, practice will assist in developing nonverbal skills. The greater the variety of one's experience, the greater are the opportunities for increased learning.

SUMMARY

This chapter has been concerned with some of the issues to do with communication in the classroom. We began in our introduction by identifying some of the characteristics of the topic and by expressing our intention to look in particular at the dominant kinds of communication – verbal and nonverbal. We began with the former by broadly discussing language and classroom interaction. We included in this brief review references to some of the more recent exploratory studies in this area. We then went on to consider some of the characteristics of talk in the classroom and the methods that researchers employ to investigate this subject. This then led on naturally to a look at the issues and problems of subject-specific language, drawing upon studies by way of illustration. We concluded this opening section on verbal communication with a short reference to the problems of language deprivation and disadvantage.

After an introduction to the topic, we began the second section of the chapter on nonverbal communication by looking at proxemics and the use of space in classrooms. This was followed by reviews of touch and touching behaviour; body movement, posture and gesture; facial expression; and vocal cues. Empirical studies from the social psychological literature were cited and implications for education were drawn where this was possible. We concluded by suggesting practical steps for developing nonverbal skills.

ENQUIRY AND DISCUSSION

1. Identify the significant differences between talk in an everyday, social context and talk in the classroom.

2. What do you consider are the advantages and disadvantages of subject-specific language in classroom learning?

3. Outline Bernstein's theory of restricted and elaborated codes.

4. Record a short excerpt of dialogue between teacher and class in any lesson you are able to observe. Transcribe it and use it as a basis for group discussion using ideas and concepts expressed in this chapter.

5. We saw in our introduction how individuals communicate with each other on at least three levels – cultural, sociological, and psychological. How relevant is this analysis to nonverbal communication?

6. Consider some of the ways in which the movable features of a classroom such as chairs, desks and tables can assist or work against a teacher's efforts.

7. Examine the lists of warm and cold behaviours identified by Clore, Wiggins and Itkin in Box 6.12 and draw up what you consider to be corresponding lists of warm and cold teacher behaviours in the classroom.

8. Do a little introspection: consider your own nonverbal skills. Where do your particular strengths lie in this connection and in what respects is there room for improvement?

NOTES AND REFERENCES

1. See, for example, The Report of the Bullock Committee (1975) *A Language for Life*. London: HMSO.

2. Hurt, H. T., Scott, M. D. and McCroskey, J. C. (1978) *Communication in the Classroom*. Reading, Massachusetts: Addison-Wesley.

3. Wilkinson, A. (1975) *Language and Education*. London: Oxford University Press.

4. Barnes, D. (1971) Language in the secondary classroom. In Barnes, D., Britton, J. and Rosen, H., *Language, the Learner and the School*. Revised Edition, London, Harmondsworth: Penguin.

5. Stubbs, M. (1976) *Language, Schools and Classrooms*. London: Methuen.

6. Halliday, M. A. K. (1969) Relevant models of language. In *The State of Language*. University of Birmingham.

7. Note: This review is based on the work of Stubbs, 1976, op. cit.

8. Barnes, D. (1971) Language and learning in the classroom. *Journal of Curriculum Studies*, **3**, 1, 27–38.

9. Mishler, E. G. (1972) Implications of teacher strategies for language and cognition: observations in first-grade classrooms. In *Functions of Language in the Classroom* (Eds.) Cazden, C. B., John, V. P., and Hymes, D. Teachers College, Columbia University, New York: Teachers College Press.

10. Gumperz, J. J. and Herasimchuk, E. (1972) The conversational analysis of social meaning: a study of classroom interaction. In *Sociolinguistics*. (Ed.) Shuy, R. Georgetown Monograph Series on Language and Linguistics, **25.**

11. Stubbs, M. (1976) Keeping in touch: Some functions of teacher-talk. In *Explorations in Classroom Observation*. (Eds.) Stubbs, M., and Delamont, S. London: Wiley.

12. See, for example:
    (Eds.) Jones, A. and Mulford, J. (1971) *Children Using Language*. London: Oxford University Press.
    Rosen, C. and H. (1973) *The Language of Primary School Children*. London: Harmondsworth, Penguin Books.
    Lewis, R. (1973) Speaking in the primary school. *Speech and Drama*, **22,** 2, Summer.

13. Edwards, A. D. and Furlong, V. J. (1978) *The Language of Teaching*. London: Heinemann.

14. Stebbins, R. (1973) Physical context influences on behaviour: the case of classroom disorderliness. *Environment and Behaviour*, **5**, 291–314.

15. Furlong, V. J. and Edwards, A. D. (1977) Language in classroom interaction: theory and data. *Educational Research*, **19**, 2, 122–128.

16. Speier, M. (1973) *How to Observe Face-to-Face Communication: a Sociological Introduction*. Pacific Palisades, California: Goodyear.

17. Hamilton, D. and Delamont, S. (1974) Classroom research: a cautionary tale. *Research in Education*, **11**, 1–16.

18. Firth, J. R. (1957) *Papers in Linguistics*, London: Oxford University Press.

19. Halliday, M. (1973) *Explorations in the Functions of Language*. London: Arnold.

20. Rosen, H. (1971) The problem of impersonal language. Quoted in Barnes, D. Language in the secondary classroom. In Barnes, D., Britton, J. and Rosen, H. *Language, the Learner and the School.* London, Harmondsworth: Penguin.

21. Note: 'Language register' may be defined as a form of speech appropriate to certain circumstances or activities.

22. Edwards, A. D. (1976) *Language in Culture and Class.* London: Heinemann.

23. Richards, J. W. *The Language of Biology Teaching,* unpublished M.Ed. Thesis, University of Newcastle-upon-Tyne. Quoted in Richards, J. W. (1978) *Classroom Language: What Sort?* London: Unwin Educational Books.

24. Moss, M. H. (1973) *Deprivation and Disadvantage?* E202, Block 8: Educational Studies. A Second Level Course, Language and Learning. Milton Keynes: The Open University Press.

25. Duncan, S. (1969) Nonverbal communication. *Psychological Bulletin,* **72,** 2, 118–137.

26. Argyle, A. (1975) *Bodily Communication.* London: Methuen.

27. Fromm, E. (1971) *The Crisis of Psychoanalysis: Essays on Freud, Marx and Social Psychology.* London: Jonathan Cape.

28. Lorenz, K. Innate bases of learning. In Hyden, H. et al. (1969) *On the Biology of Learning,* New York: Harcourt, Brace and World.

29. Byers, P. and Byers, H. (1972) Nonverbal communication and the education of children. In *Functions of Language in the Classroom.* (Eds.) Cazden, C. B., John, V. P. and Hymes, D. Teachers College, Columbia University, New York: Teachers College Press.

30. Knapp, M. L. (1980) *Essentials of Nonverbal Communication.* New York: Holt, Rinehart and Winston.

31. Hall, E. T. (1959) *The Silent Language.* Garden City, New York: Doubleday.

32. Hall, E. T. (1966) *The Hidden Dimension.* Garden City, New York: Doubleday.

33. Hutt, C. and Vaizey, M. J. (1966) Differential effects of group density on social behaviour. *Nature,* **209,** 1371–1372.

34. Sommer, R. (1965) Further studies in small group ecology. *Sociometry,* **28,** 337–348.

35. Montagu, M. F. A. (1971) *Touching: The Human Significance of the Skin.* New York: Columbia University Press.

36. Henley, N. M. (1977) *Body Politics: Power, Sex and Nonverbal Communication.* Englewood Cliffs, New York: Prentice Hall.

37. Heslin, R. (1974) *Steps towards a taxonomy of touching.* Paper presented to the Midwestern Psychological Association, Chicago.

38. Schutz, W. C. (1967) *Joy.* New York: Grove Press.

39. Johnson, H. G., Ekman, P. and Friesen, W. V. (1975) Communicative body movements. *Semiotica*, **15**, 335–353.

40. Ekman, P. and Friesen, W. V. (1969) The repertoire of nonverbal behaviour: categories, origins, usage and coding, *Semiotica*, **1**, 49–98.

41. Mehrabian, A. (1972) *Nonverbal Communication*. Chicago: Aldine-Atherton.

42. Reece, M. and Whitman, R. (1962) Expressive movements, warmth, and verbal reinforcement. *Journal of Abnormal and Social Psychology*, **64**, 234–236.

43. Clore, G. L., Wiggins, N. H. and Itkin, S. (1975) Gain and loss in attraction: attributions from nonverbal behaviour. *Journal of Personality and Social Psychology*, **31**, 706–712.

44. Izard, C. E. (1973) Reported in BBC2 *Horizon* Programme on the Human Face.

45. Birdwhistell, R. L. (1970) *Kinesics and Context*. Philadelphia: University of Pennsylvania Press.

46. Kendon, A. (1967) Some functions of gaze-direction in social interaction. *Acta Psychologica*, **26**, 22–63.

47. Davitz, J. R. (1964) *The Communication of Emotional Feeling*, New York: McGraw Hill.

48. Argyle, M., Salter, V., Nicholson, H., Williams, M. and Burgess, P. (1970) The communication of inferior and superior attitudes by verbal and nonverbal signals. *British Journal of Social and Clinical Psychology*, **9**, 221–231.

49. Crystal, D. (1969) *Prosodic Systems and Intonation in English*. Cambridge: Cambridge University Press.

50. Duncan, S. D. and Rosenthal, R. (1968) Vocal emphasis in experimenter's instruction reading as unintended determinant of subjects' responses. *Language and Speech*, **11**, 20–26.

SELECTED READING

1. Argyle, M. (1975) *Bodily Communication*. London: Methuen. A scholarly and lucidly written introduction intended for the general reader.

2. Barnes, D., Britton, J. and Rosen, H. (1971) *Language, the Learner and the School*. London: Harmondsworth, Penguin Books, Revised Edition. An excellent and readily accessible introduction to the problems and issues of language and learning.

3. Edwards, A. D. and Furlong, V. J. (1978) *The Language of Teaching*. London: Heinemann Educational Books. One of the few books that looks at what actually takes place in the classroom. It is designed to help teachers to think more about the things they normally take for granted.

4. Knapp, M. L. (1980) *Essentials of Nonverbal Communication*, New York: Holt, Rinehart and Winston. A balanced presentation of information necessary for developing a basic understanding of nonverbal behaviour. The book draws on scholarly research of the last thirty years.

5. Marland, M. (1977) *Language across the Curriculum*. London: Heinemann Educational Books. This is concerned with the recommendations of the Bullock Report for Secondary Schools. It embodies a wide range of knowledge and experience.

6. Stubbs, M. (1976) *Language, Schools and Classrooms*. London: Methuen. A short and readable introduction to the basic issues concerning the role of language in education. Highly recommended.

7

Mixed Ability Teaching

Reminiscing on our junior school days and on the pride of parents whose A stream sons gained coveted scholarship places to local grammar schools, the authors recall a rigid system of pupil separation and an emphasis on arithmetic, spelling, punctuation and essay writing that at the time seemed immutable and unquestionable in its classification of children's abilities and its prescriptions for their educational diets.

And yet the grouping of children on the basis of their abilities is a relatively recent practice in Great Britain. The 1898 *Revised Instructions* of the then Education Department addressed to Her Majesty's Inspectorate proposed that 'no difficulty should be put in the way of the honest classification of scholars according to capacity and attainment'. Those *Revised Instructions* were followed in 1917 by the Board of Education's *Suggestions for the Considerations of Teachers* that 'children should be allowed to progress through school at varying rates suited to their individual capacity'.

The increased demand for secondary education at the beginning of the present century was a major impetus towards the classification and separation of pupils by ability. Secondary education, it was widely believed, was the highroad to status and success in a society that was becoming more differentiated and more democratic. By 1927, the *Handbook of Suggestions for Teachers* was able to recommend a three stream system in which backward, ordinary, and quick pupils were identified, separated, and instructed by different and appropriate teaching methods.[1]

The late 1940s and the 1950s marked the heyday of streaming. The 1944 Education Act, it will be recalled, secured 'secondary education for all' according to 'age, ability, and aptitude'. But as Davies[1] observes, the pattern that was adopted to implement the recommendations of the Act was rooted in the Norwood Report's vision of three distinct types of children slotting neatly into existing Grammar, Technical, and Secondary schools. This was the logical synthesis of a demand for secondary education for all and a theory that differing abilities require different educational treatments. For it followed, did it not, that children who had already been streamed by ability during their junior school careers should again be streamed by the type of secondary school they should attend and indeed, by stream *within* that secondary school in order to ensure that their varying aptitudes should be properly catered for? That streaming was 'plain common sense' was widely accepted by most teachers and educationists during the 1950s.

There were signs of unease however. *Primary Education*, issued by the Ministry of Education in 1959 cautioned that 'in the homogeneous class of the streamed school', it had been noted that 'the stimulus to learning is reduced and that the slower children appear slower still, accepting the fact that they are too often called "only B", and making less effort than they might'. In similar vein, the Newsom Report on secondary education drew attention to one consequence of streaming as an increase in the 'feeling of educational inferiority and rejection in the lower forms without corresponding teaching advantages'.

Evidence began to accumulate that cast doubt on the 'plain common sense' of the tripartite division of children into grammar, technical, and secondary modern types. An investigation by the National Foundation For Educational Research into the validity of the screening devices used in allocating children to secondary school places reported that the sorts of tests typically employed by Local Education Authorities were crude and insensitive to the extent that one child in ten was inaccurately placed at 11 +. More was to follow.

Various studies had hinted that summer born children might be at some disadvantage when compared with autumn born in securing A stream places in junior school, their deficit being traced to the early handicap of being streamed after only four terms in school. A National Foundation For Educational Research study carried out by Barker Lunn[2] on a representative sample of 5000 children unequivocally confirmed the distinct disadvantage of the summer born child.

Other studies which pointed to the over-representation of the middle class child in A stream groupings accounted for their findings in terms of the congruence of home – school values and the influence of language in controlling what is learned, the manner in which it is learned, and subsequent possibilities for learning. More recently, a spate of research into teachers' expectations has suggested that judgements about children's abilities and various other attributes can act as self-fulfilling prophecies in pupils' later achievements, while studies such as those by Hargreaves, Lacey, Willis, and Woods on the influence of the school's organization in the creation and maintenance of anti-school subcultures provide evidence of some unintended consequences of streaming by ability.

With the spread of comprehensive schools, mixed ability organization of one form or another increased during the 1970s. Currently, mixed ability teaching is an important feature in a growing number of schools though not as many schools* practise mixed ability teaching as is generally supposed.

But it is time that we defined our terms. What exactly is *mixed ability teaching* and what are the educational principles that underpin this hotly-debated issue?

We begin our discussion by adopting a useful if somewhat arbitrary definition of *mixed ability organization* and then go on to explore the concept of *mixed ability teaching*.

---

* In 65 % of English comprehensive schools most subjects are *not* taught in mixed ability classes. Times Educational Supplement. 28th July 1978.

So many books and articles have been published to do with organizing mixed ability groups in schools and so many definitions of the term 'mixed ability' are now bandied about that it becomes impossible to discuss the topic of mixed ability teaching without adopting some common definition. For present purposes, we propose to follow the lead[3] given in the Department of Education and Science HMI Series: Matters for Discussion 6, *Mixed Ability Work in Comprehensive Schools* and to concentrate on a single definition of mixed ability organization as:

> . . .'one in which, at least up to the end of the third year of the normal secondary course, the curriculum is taught wholly or mainly (i.e. with not more than two subjects excluded) in classes in which the span of ability ranges from significantly below to significantly above the average.'

Adopting such a definition is somewhat restricting. To begin with, it focuses attention exclusively on secondary schools, where, as distinct from their primary counterparts, mixed ability grouping is a comparatively recent innovation which has developed as the comprehensive reorganization of secondary schooling has spread. Moreover, our particular definition rules out of discussion those many schools in which it is the practice to begin secondary education with a diagnostic mixed ability year as a way of sorting pupils into suitable learning contexts for their later school careers. In an increasing number of schools, however, mixed ability teaching occurs up to the end of the third year and involves mixed ability groupings for most subjects apart for setting in such areas as mathematics and foreign languages. One advantage of our definition, particularly when we come to discuss problems of mixed ability teaching, is that it allows us to generalize our comments to a growing number of schools in England and Wales. Another is that it provides opportunity to examine detailed evidence from a recent intensive study[8] of one comprehensive school in which pupils remained unstreamed until the end of the third year.

THE ISSUES

What then of *mixed ability teaching*?

Bailey[4] highlights an important difference between *teaching in mixed ability groups* and *mixed ability teaching*. Mixed ability teaching, he observes, implies a *certain kind of teaching* whereas any kind of teaching can, and does go on in mixed ability groups. This distinction between *mixed ability teaching* and *teaching in mixed ability groups* is extended by Elliott[4] whose discussion of the educational issues involved requires us to differentiate between three principles of equality.

Mixed ability teaching, Elliott argues, takes place when a teacher attempts to regulate his treatment of individual differences by the principle of equality. Thus, in a mixed ability situation, when a teacher adopts a teaching-to-the-whole-class-approach, he fails to regulate his teaching by the idea of equality because his teaching style assumes that the individual differences which make questions about equality of treatment relevant, do not exist. The idea of equality, Elliott goes on to show, is not one single principle; rather, it consists of three distinct yet interrelated principles*. These are:

1. That human beings have a right to equality of respect by virtue of their common humanity.
2. That human beings have an equal right to opportunities for self-development.
3. That human beings have an equal right to opportunities of achieving certain social goals.

The arguments for mixed ability teaching that Elliott advances and the problems of mixed ability that he poses involve clarifying these three principles of equality.

Basic to Elliott's argument is that (a) teachers' attempts to realize one or other of the three principles of equality raise distinctive kinds of problems, and (b), given the circumstances under which most teachers operate, they will experience dilemmas because the three principles of equality can and often do conflict in ways that may not be susceptible to a satisfactory solution. In other words, teachers may find that such dilemmas are only resolvable by the sacrifice of one or more of the principles of equality.

Now all this may sound rather abstract and somewhat removed from the day-to-day problems of the classroom. But Elliott's insights can be illustrated over and over again in the comments of headteachers and teachers on the problems they experience in mixed ability teaching. For example, the DES[3] document, *Mixed Ability Work in Comprehensive Schools*, reports 'a fundamental difficulty (among teachers) to marry concern for individuality with concern for equality'. Her Majesty's Inspectors go on to note that 'sometimes schools, and in particular, individual teachers in the classroom, found it difficult to be sure whether differentiation of work in order to meet the needs of individuals might not re-create inequalities of opportunities which the form of grouping was designed to avoid'. Let us stay with Elliott's exposition a little longer.

One argument for mixed ability teaching derives from the first principle which can be thought of as the *humanistic aspect* of the idea of equality. Simply put, respect for pupils as persons involves the teacher in a professional responsibility to protect and to foster each child's capacity for reflective self-awareness and rational autonomy. The humanistic aspect of equality emphasizes the important respects in which all human beings are alike despite the ways in which allocating individuals to different positions and roles often obscures the common humanity which all share. Social organization, Elliott argues, can increase or decrease our sense of oneness with each other. Does growing awareness of the ways in which streaming imposes constraints on that sense of oneness provide the justification for mixed ability teaching? If the teacher values what all human beings have in common he will want his pupils to come to value each other through a recognition of their common humanity. Mixed ability grouping, Elliott suggests, may therefore be seen as an appropriate means to this end.

Support for mixed ability teaching is often rooted in a second idea of equality. This usage of the concept, stressing the political connotation of equality of opportunity is prescriptive in its assumption that there are respects in which individuals are not equal but ought to be. In its application to educational issues, Elliott distinguishes two uses of the idea of equality of opportunity which we have already identified as principles (2) and (3)

---

* The interested reader may wish to compare this treatment of the idea of equality with the outline of Barth's philosophy of *open education* in Chapter 9.

above. In one use, the equal rights of pupils to satisfy their needs for self-development is asserted and is seen to involve the improvement of their specifically individual talents and capacities. In the second usage, it is the pupil's equal rights to opportunity to scarce social positions of high pay and status that is affirmed. Both principles of equality in education, Elliott argues, are social in the sense that the first prescribes equality of opportunity to achieve the social identity most suited to a person's individual capacities, for example, – artist, teacher, or craftsman. The second prescribes equality of opportunity to achieve those social identities which society invests with high value such as doctor, lawyer and civil servant.

Elliott then goes on to develop a typology of problems that are posed by mixed ability teaching, illustrating the sorts of dilemmas that are raised by teachers' attempts to realize each particular principle of equality. The typology is set out in Box 7.1. It can be seen that each of the principles of equality generates specific problems. Take for example principle (3) *equality of opportunity for social goods*. Here, Elliott raises the question, 'Can mixed ability teaching take place in certain subject areas?' If the development of ability in certain subject areas rather than others is the way to achieving high social status and its accompanying rewards, then giving all pupils equal opportunities for achieving those statuses will create the problem of what to do with the obviously able child in the classroom in which the less able is struggling. Is the able pupil to be denied the achievements he could easily merit in order to eliminate differences between him and the less able?

BOX 7.1

---

*Principles of Equality and Their Concomitant Problems**

1. *Equality of respect for individuals as endowed with the capacity for self-awareness and autonomy*
   Poses problems raised by attempts to wean pupils from dependence on 'authorities'

2. *Equality of opportunity for self-development*
   Poses problems raised by giving individuals opportunities for self-development according to their various talents and capacities.

3. *Equality of opportunity for social goods*
   Poses problems raised by attempts to eliminate individual differences in achievement.

Source: Elliott [4]

The problem we have posed with respect to principle (3) is a real one for many teachers in mixed ability situations. If teachers are fair to the able they run the danger of being unfair to the less able. Conversely, if they are fair to the less able then it is the able who are in danger of being short-changed.* No wonder, Elliott observes, a number of teachers caught in this 'double-bind' situation espouse the belief that some children lack the capacity, regardless of their environment, to develop abilities in certain subject areas. Only in this way can they then support the argument that teaching regulated by the third principle of equality is inapplicable.

The whole of Elliott's article is worthy of close and careful reading.

---

* This charge is made in the DES Series: Matters for Discussion 6, where Her Majesty's Inspectors discuss their visits to a number of comprehensive schools.

THE CLAIMS FOR MIXED ABILITY TEACHING

Assertions that one form of school organization is better than another or that teaching style X is more effective than teaching style Y are often based upon subjective generalizations rather than objective judgement. In the absence of hard facts, some of the benefits that are said to derive from mixed ability teaching also suffer from such generalizations. In this section, we enumerate the advantages that supporters claim for mixed ability teaching. We then go on to evaluate research studies that bear upon these claims.

The kinds of sentiments expressed by many heads and teachers who are committed to mixed ability teaching often seem to arise from their hard won experience and their grasp of the constraints under which most schools operate rather than their burning ideological avowal of principles of equality. Be that as it may, their common concern is frequently a desire to get away from the worst features of streaming and to avoid the production of 'demoralized, demotivated, unteachable middle school groups, bad for themselves, their teachers and other children'.[5]

The arguments put forward for mixed ability teaching can be ordered into two distinct yet interdependent categories,[3] the first relating to pupils' social development, the second having to do with teaching and learning. Arguments concerned with social development include the following:

1. Mixed ability teaching prevents the rejection of the less able that is implied in streaming, setting or banding* thereby demonstrating the equal value of all individuals.
2. Mixed ability teaching avoids a hierarchy of groups with consequent poor morale in the lower groups.
3. Mixed ability teaching disperses pupils who are difficult to handle rather than keeping them together to form anti-social groups.
4. Mixed ability teaching thereby diminishes undesirable feelings of inferiority, superiority or aggression and undesirable attitudes such as competitiveness.
5. Indeed, mixed ability teaching develops cooperative behaviour, maintains good order, encourages self-esteem, security and self-reliance, and fosters good relationships among pupils and between pupils and teacher.
6. Mixed ability teaching helps counteract class differences and works against the continuance of a competitive, elitist, and divided society.

---

* *Streaming* involves the division of children on the basis of their general attainment. Each class is kept together for most subjects. Classes are generally ranked in descending order of academic attainment. Each class may follow a different curriculum.
Setting is a refinement of streaming and involves the block-timetabling together of several forms in order that ability groups can be established in particular subject areas. Thus, setting attempts to distinguish ability and attainment in various subjects.
Banding involves dividing a whole year group into several bands. Within a band, classes are assumed to be roughly similar in ability. It's common practice to establish three or four such bands and to employ different curricula in each of them.

Educational arguments include the following:

1. Mixed ability teaching improves the motivation of lower streams, reduces competitiveness, and encourages cooperative learning.
2. In mixed ability teaching, the expectations that teachers have of their pupils and pupils have of themselves are improved and educational opportunities are kept open longer.
3. Mixed ability teaching tends to show that differences in ability are not as great as is often imagined.
4. Mixed ability teaching helps avoid curricula differentiated by ability and uniformity of pupil treatment accorded to pupils within more homogeneous groups.
5. Mixed ability teaching helps promote access to a common curriculum and to a greater variety of experience for all pupils from the least to the most able.
6. Mixed ability teaching promotes the matching of individual programmes to individual needs.
7. Mixed ability teaching helps avoid the allocation of the ablest teachers to the ablest pupils and discourages teachers from performing traditional, dominant, didactic roles as instructors.
8. Mixed ability teaching encourages new styles of learning such as small group and individual learning techniques.
9. Mixed ability teaching encourages more diverse resources for learning.
10. Mixed ability teaching encourages the assessment of each pupil against his/her own potential and discourages the assessment of pupils in rank order.
11. Mixed ability teaching helps avoid underachievement in less able children and enables all to work at their best pace and level.
12. Mixed ability teaching enables pupils to learn from each other and allows the more able to assist the less able.

So much for the claims. What of the evidence?

THE EVIDENCE

In our evaluation of research into mixed ability teaching, we make use of an important distinction drawn in Chapter 1 between *quantitative* and *qualitative* data. There, you will recall, it was argued that the particular social science perspective that is adopted (i.e. an 'objectivist' or a 'subjectivist' approach) has profound implications for the sorts of questions that researchers ask and the kinds of data they seek. It is fair to say that in general, the *educational* claims that have been made for mixed ability teaching have attracted quantitative approaches to data collection, the evidence consisting of 'hard' facts to do with pupils' academic progress, their exam results, and the extent of their under or over achievement. On the other hand, the *social* claims for mixed ability teaching have tended to generate qualitative evidence in the form of children's accounts of their school experiences and their feelings, as well as data to do with pupils' and teachers' attitudes towards this form of teaching. Apart from the HMI Discussion Document[3] cited earlier and the NFER[9] study which we examine shortly, much of the evidence on mixed ability teaching has been obtained from studies of single schools with all the attendant problems that such data have for the generalizing of research findings. We deal first with the *educational* claims.

There is evidence that mixed ability teaching can provide a larger number of children with a wider range of curriculum experiences than those enjoyed by secondary pupils in schools which practise rigid streaming and that mixed ability teaching can encourage a greater diversity of learning resources and teaching methods. The acid test of mixed ability teaching, however, insofar as its educational claims are concerned is the question of pupil achievement.

Does mixed ability teaching help avoid underachievement in the less able and does it enable all children to work at their best pace and level?

Research findings are contradictory on this vital point. Some studies of single schools offer affirmative evidence, showing (a) a significant growth in the number of less able children staying on for the full five years of schooling in a comprehensive that changed from streaming to mixed ability grouping,[6] and (b), an increasing number of good O level passes among middle ability range pupils, again, in a comprehensive school that introduced mixed ability teaching into its first three years.[7] One particularly well-conducted enquiry undertaken at Banbury School[8] urges caution in attributing pupil achievement to any particular type of grouping. While acknowledging that there may well be some advantages for less able children in mixed ability forms, it is the role of the individual teacher, it is suggested, that is of paramount importance, 'varying teacher – class interactions having a markedly greater initial influence on secondary school progress than the type of grouping practised'.

The report[3] of Her Majesty's Inspectorate into standards of achievement in the eighteen comprehensive schools that formed the basis of its inquiry offers contrary evidence about the effects of mixed ability teaching. In a very small number of schools, it says, pupils were found to be working at an appropriate pace and level in all school subjects and year-groups to which mixed ability organization applied. In most schools however, the Inspectors were concerned about the level, the pace, and the scope of work in a number of subject areas. Their concern was to do with pupils of all abilities; most frequently however, it related to the more able children. Many of the schools' work programmes did not provide for differences of ability, the Inspectors alleged, and while work programmes had been developed with the needs of the average pupil in mind, not even the needs of the average had always been accurately assessed or provided for. Low expectations by teachers and failure to provide appropriate work programmes, the Inspectors reported, resulted in underachievement. Moreover, whereas we cited evidence earlier that mixed ability grouping can provide for a wider range of curriculum experiences, the Inspectors found that mixed ability organization often resulted in the restriction of content in programmes of work, the teachers sometimes choosing to avoid topics or activities they thought too difficult for pupils of average ability or below. It is inevitable that research based on single institutions or drawing on small samples will generate conflicting evidence about the effects of mixed ability teaching. This is why the larger scale study of the NFER[9] into mixed ability teaching is important in the evidence that it can provide. It is to a preliminary report of that study that we now turn.

The NFER Mixed Ability research began in 1975 and extended until the end of 1978. Unlike previous studies of unstreamed groupings by Barker-Lunn[10] and Newbold[8], the NFER project concentrated on classroom processes rather than learning outcomes. Its major concern was to look at ways in which mixed ability groups function in classrooms. From the outset, teachers were involved in the planning and the execution of the study, teachers' experiences being a crucial element in the research programme. Throughout the three years of the project the research team worked with teachers individually and collectively, defining issues of concern and devising strategies by which to explore them.

The working definition of mixed ability teaching adopted by the research team differed from the one we quoted earlier in connection with the investigation undertaken by Her Majesty's Inspectorate. In the NFER project, mixed ability teaching was identified as:

> 'a teaching unit which is not streamed, banded or setted and which is in a non-selective school. The class may or may not contain pupils from a remedial department.'[9]

During the first stage of the study, aspects of mixed ability teaching that were of major concern to schools emerged from discussions with nearly 500 teachers and the 29 headteachers of the institutions involved. These concerns were to do with (1) the organization, preparation and in-service training for mixed ability teaching, (2) classroom organization and teaching methods, (3) ways of providing for the more able and the less able pupil in mixed ability classes, (4) the implications of mixed ability teaching for methods of assessment, and (5) the factors which make for ease or difficulty in mixed ability teaching in specific subject areas.

The second stage of the NFER project was concerned with intensive studies in six comprehensive schools, the research team focusing on one mixed ability class in each first year intake in order to monitor work undertaken in English, mathematics, modern languages and science lessons. A variety of research techniques was used including psychometric measures, interviews, teacher ratings, classroom observations, discussions, questionnaires, an analysis of written materials and an examination of school records. One intriguing question the research team attempted to answer was, 'How do teachers identify more able pupils in their classes and how do they deal with them?'

As one might expect, teachers in general spoke of speed, accuracy and neatness, of the ability to participate in class discussion and to understand new concepts as indicators of the more able child. In certain subjects however, the ability to work on one's own was significantly prized. The commonality of certain criteria in judging the more able pupil and the subject specific nature of others gave the researchers a clearer understanding of what teachers consider mixed ability teaching to entail in their various subject areas. Full details of these analyses are to appear in NFER reports.

An intensive study of five more able and five less able pupils in each classroom was undertaken. Over 500 five continuous minutes of observations were made of these children's activities, their contributions to general classwork and their demands on their teachers. Each interaction between pupil and teacher was classified according to its nature and whether it was initiated by the teacher or the pupil. By way of example, Box 7.2 illustrates the nature and the frequency of pupil-generated interactions classified according to whether the pupils were *more able*, *average*, or *less able*. The data relate to interactions with one teacher during three maths lessons. They show more able pupils as

BOX 7.2

Nature of Pupil-Generated Interactions with One Teacher in Three Maths Lessons						
	Number and Classification of Interactions					
Ability of pupils	'I do not understand'	'I have finished	Task-related questions	Assistance sought with materials	Others	TOTAL
More able Observed Expected	10.00 11.22	9.00 9.18	7.00 4.42	0.00 4.42	8.00 4.76	34
Average Observed Expected	5.00 9.24	8.00 7.56	5.00 3.64	8.00 3.64	2.00 3.92	28
Less able Observed Expected	18.00 12.54	10.00 10.26	1.00 4.94	5.00 4.94	4.00 5.32	38
TOTAL	33.00	27.00	13.00	13.00	14.00	100

Source: adapted from Clunies-Ross and Reid[9]

initiating a significantly greater number of task-related discussions with the teacher and posing a greater number of questions than would normally be expected of a group of this size. By contrast, the less able pupils are seen to request more assistance with materials and with interpreting tasks over which they have difficulty. They also raise fewer task-related questions and have fewer task-related discussions with the teacher than might be expected from this size of group. Analyses such as these helped the researchers build up detailed pictures of what mixed ability teaching actually entailed in various areas of the secondary school curriculum.

What of the claims of mixed ability teaching in relation to pupil's social development?

One of the most interesting studies to throw light on this question, albeit somewhat obliquely, was carried out by Ford[11] who sought to examine the academic and the social arguments in favour of comprehensive education by testing four hypotheses:

1. That comprehensive schools will provide greater equality of opportunity for those of equal talent.
2. That the occupational horizons of children in comprehensive schools will be widened relative to those of children in tripartite schools.
3. That comprehensive school children will show less tendency to mix with children of their own social type than will tripartite children.
4. That comprehensive school children will tend to have views of the class system as a flexible hierarchy while tripartite school children will tend to see this as a rigid dichotomy.

Ford failed to produce support for any of her four hypotheses and went on to account for her results by suggesting that the arguments in favour of comprehensivization are based upon the naive premise that early selection is less likely to occur under a comprehensive system. Early streaming was practised at Cherry Dale, the comprehensive school in Ford's study. Clearly, it was important that Ford's propositions should be retested in a comprehensive school under conditions of non-streaming if the social arguments for the advantages of comprehensivization (which closely parallel those for mixed ability teaching) were to be adequately tested. We report on one study that attempted precisely this and on another, the Banbury project, which provides some pertinent findings on social integration in mixed ability situations.

Cohen and Fisher[12] replicated Ford's study to the letter, using a grammar, a secondary modern, and a comprehensive school drawing from a predominantly working-class catchment area in West Yorkshire. Unlike Cherry Dale however, our comprehensive school of some 1750 children was totally unstreamed until the end of the third year at which time the fourteen year old pupils took an examination to help place them in suitable fourth year courses. Using Ford's original questionnaires, we replicated her study with a sample of 650 children. Like Ford, we also tested the proposition that comprehensive school children will show less tendency to mix with children of their own social type than will tripartite children by employing an Index of Ingroup Preferences as a measure of friendship choices among and between working class and middle class children in our three schools. Ford, it will be recalled, concluded that if any type of schooling diminished the likelihood of class bias in informal classroom relationships it was *not* the comprehensive school but the grammar school. Our findings were quite different.

'In the comprehensive school every group of working class children except the boys in Form 3.2 chose friends from the middle class in roughly the same proportion as they did from the working class . . . In terms of index of ingroup preference calculations, the comprehensive school appeared to be more socially integrated than the tripartite schools at third form level.'[12]

Banbury school provided a 'natural' setting in which to test the claims that mixed ability teaching helps promote the social integration of pupils. The school had a basic federal organization of separate Halls working to a common curriculum. The Halls were matched both socially and academically. At the time of the study however, two of the Halls were streamed in the first year and two Halls employed a mixed ability organization. The inquiry sought to examine the differences that emerged between the two systems of grouping. Phase One of the study reported 'clear evidence of more wide ranging friendship choice in the mixed ability situation' and concluded that 'the analyses support the view that at least in the short term and within the school context, mixed ability grouping at first year level provides more effective integration between pupils of different abilities and backgrounds than does streaming'.

Phase two of the enquiry was concerned with a more long term investigation of the effects brought to light by Phase One as the pupils progressed through the school. All the children incidentally, were in similar teaching and pastoral care systems by the time they reached their fourth year. The report found that by the fourth year the complete friendship patterns 'seemed to be little affected by the grouping system through which the pupils had come'. However, there was more mixing by VRO (intelligence) and socio-economic group within any strong friendship groupings of pupils who had started out in the mixed ability Halls during their first year at Banbury. Newbold concluded that a longer period than one academic year in mixed ability groupings would have resulted in a greater mixing of this kind. Pupils' attitudes were also investigated and it was reported that children from mixed ability groupings had better attitudes towards the school as a social community. The Banbury research findings echo more impressionistic accounts of individual schools which report gains in children's social development resulting from their placement in mixed ability settings.

Part of the preliminary report of the NFER study[9] deals with the social consequences of mixed ability organization. Because Stage I of that study had shown that mixed ability classes were often organized for 'social reasons', the researchers explored the nature and pattern of pupils' friendships in each of the mixed ability classes in the six comprehensive schools that they selected for intensive observation. Pupil questionnaires provided information on working partner choice and friendships. These were supplemented by classroom observations focusing on the five most able and five least able pupils whose

BOX 7.3

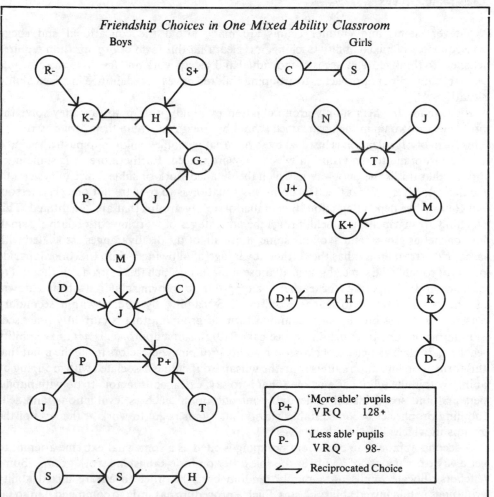

Friendship Choices in One Mixed Ability Classroom

Boys   Girls

P+	'More able' pupils
	V R Q 128+
P-	'Less able' pupils
	V R Q 98-
⟷	Reciprocated Choice

friendship and working partner choices were drawn up in the form of sociograms. By way of example, Box 7.3 shows that in one particular class, a large loosely-knit group of boys contains four of the less able, while the girls in that class demonstrate the reciprocated choices that are a common feature of feminine friendships in this age group.

The data on friendships choices were also plotted in the form of scattergrams and the interpretation of both these and the sociograms was made in light of other relevant factors. *Inter alia*, the NFER study shows that in the first year of secondary schooling friendships may still be strongly influenced by the primary school attended by the pupil. At the same time, subject option choices and/or the organization of remedial provision also affect the formation of new friendship choices at the secondary stage.

CLASSROOM GROUPINGS AND GOAL STRUCTURES

Classroom Groups

Whatever claims and counter claims are made about the educational and social consequences of mixed ability teaching, it is clear that this form of organization requires teachers to think more in terms of individual and group work and less in terms of whole class teaching. Four approaches to grouping children have been identified in mixed ability situations.[13]

First, many teachers simply group children by ability; that is to say, they solve the problems thrown up in the unstreamed school by streaming within their own classrooms. This form of organization is justified by saying that it enables children to push ahead at a pace appropriate to the group in which they are placed. Furthermore, it is sometimes argued that this is the only way in which the detailed work of subject disciplines can be tackled effectively. What teachers do in this situation is to prepare not one class lesson, but four or five depending upon the number of ability groups that are constituted. This teaching arrangement, it is held, brings the advantages of working with relatively small homogeneous groups and avoiding some, if not all, of the disadvantages associated with large scale streaming. It has the further advantage of allowing a child to work alongside pupils of roughly the same ability in all those subjects in which this approach is thought to be relevant. It also permits the teacher to alter groups by moving children 'up' and 'down' as and when their performance requires it. Streaming by ability within secondary classrooms is possibly the most common form of grouping that is currently practised.

In terms of our earlier definition (see page 210) this first approach is *not* mixed ability teaching. In their criticisms of classroom ability grouping, detractors make the point that this form of organization suffers from the selfsame difficulties associated with grouping by ability within the school as a whole. That is to say, extraneous factors to do with pupils' personal and social histories inevitably intrude upon teachers' evaluations, and self-fulfilling prophecies become established so that pupils begin to work at the level of the groups in which they find themselves.

A second approach to classroom grouping is cited as a somewhat extreme attempt to get away from the use of ability as the sole criterion for establishing work groups. Some teachers allocate pupils on a purely random basis in order to ensure mixed ability groupings within mixed ability classes. Such a procedure has little to commend it in so far as it can easily lead to injudicious combinations of pupils. At the same time, it denies the teacher any of the advantages that are to be gained from other forms of classroom groupings.

A third form of classroom grouping which commands the support of many teachers is the practice of allowing children to group themselves on the basis of friendship. Because friendship has an important bearing upon children's behaviour, the judicious use of friendship groups in promoting the ongoing work of the class is something that teachers would do well to consider. We emphasize the word *judicious*, sharing with Kelly the view that allowing children sole responsibility for establishing their own groups can sometimes lead to difficulties. In the last analysis, it is the teacher's responsibility to ensure that the groups that are constituted are appropriate to the task at hand.

A fourth approach to classroom grouping is seen as a compromise between pupil choice and teacher direction; that is, grouping by interest. Clearly, such a method presupposes an interest/enquiry approach to teaching. This being the case, it is logical that pupils should be grouped according to their various interests. Inevitably, grouping by interest overlaps grouping by friendship choice since friendship often plays an important role in the selection of a topic and the subsequent interest that is engendered in it. Again, a judicious degree of teacher direction may be called for in establishing interest groups so as to ensure that the purposes of the activity are best promoted by allowing certain children to work together.

Goal Structures

As well as the specific approaches that teachers adopt when they group children in mixed ability classes there is the further question of the system of goal structures that they initiate. *Goal structure* refers to the ways in which pupils are expected to relate to one another and to teachers in working to accomplish classroom tasks. Three types of goal structure have been identified,[14] – co-operative, competitive, and individualistic. Box 7.4 summarizes the essential features of each type.

Observing secondary school classroom groupings, it is apparent that the type of grouping adopted by the teacher is often associated with one goal structure rather than another. Generally speaking, the use of ability groups in mixed ability classrooms tends to be associated with competitive and/or individualistic goal structures; on the other hand, friendship and interest groupings more commonly relate to co-operative goal structures.

We turn now to review studies which have identified educational and social outcomes in classrooms having co-operative, competitive, and individualistic goal structures. The evidence bears directly upon our earlier outline of the claims that have been made for mixed ability teaching.

Some words of caution however. Our review of the research compiled by Johnson and Johnson[14] in *Learning Together and Alone* is necessarily selective in light of the extensive literature that exists on the effects of differing goal structures. Much of the research, moreover, has been undertaken in social psychological laboratories or, at best, in 'artificial' classrooms in North America so that findings are not directly transferable to British settings and must be treated with some circumspection. That said, a number of

BOX 7.4

Classroom Goal Structures

A *co-operative* goal structure exists when pupils perceive that they can attain their goal if, and only if, the other pupils with whom they are linked can attain their goal. A co-operative goal structure requires the co-ordination of behaviour necessary to achieve the mutual goal. If one pupil achieves the goal, all pupils with whom that pupil is linked achieve the goal. When, for example, pupils are working together to find what factors make a difference in how long a candle burns in a quart jar, they are in a co-operative goal structure.

A *competitive* goal structure exists when pupils perceive that they can attain their goal if, and only if, the other pupils with whom they are linked fail to attain their goal. Competitive interaction is the striving to achieve one's competitive goal in a way that blocks all others from achieving the goal. When, for example, pupils are working to see who can compile the best list of factors influencing how long a candle burns in a quart jar, they are in a competitive goal structure.

When pupils are all working independently to master, say, an arithmetical process, they are in an *individualistic* goal structure. An individualistic goal structure exists when the achievement of the goal by one pupil is unrelated to the achievement of the goal by other pupils; whether or not a pupil achieves his/her goal has no bearing upon whether other pupils achieve their goals. Usually there is no pupil–pupil interaction in an individualistic situation since each pupil seeks the outcome that is best for himself/herself, regardless of whether or not other pupils achieve their goals.

Source: adapted from Johnson and Johnson[14]

general conclusions do emerge which deserve a wide audience. We summarize these below.

Varying Effects of Differing Goal Structures

Anxiety

The relationship between anxiety and learning is complex. Differing degrees of anxiety and different types of task need to be taken into account in any explanation of the relationship between these two variables. Nonetheless, studies suggest that higher levels of anxiety and continued states of anxiety are more likely to occur under competitive goal structures. Co-operative goal structures produce less anxious pupils and provide more congenial learning climates especially for those pupils who are normally rather tense and anxious.

Interpersonal relationships

Friendliness, mutual concern and feelings of obligation are encouraged by co-operative goal structures. Conversely, some studies show that competitive goal structures negatively affect interpersonal relationships in classrooms. Changing from competitive to co-operative group structures has been shown to reduce conflict and hostility and to produce warm and friendly intergroup and interpersonal relationships. Studies in primary school classrooms have shown that co-operative goal structures help children to acquire role-taking or social perspective taking skills, that is, being able to see situations from the point of view of others who are involved.

Intellectual Outcomes

Many studies of *cognitive gains* have had to do with competitive versus co-operative group structures where, typically, research designs compare *interpersonal competition* with various combinations of *intragroup co-operation* and *intergroup competition.*

In general, when tasks have to do with repetitive, drill-like activities or where a high volume of work is required in mechanical-type tasks, then competition often produces better results than either co-operative or individualistic goal structures. Where tasks are more complex and problem-oriented, however, co-operation has been found to produce higher achievement than competition.

Affective Outcomes

By *affective*, we refer to the feelings and the beliefs that are generated in pupils as a result of the ways in which the ongoing work of their classrooms is organized.

The research evidence shows significantly better attitudes towards study among groups working towards co-operative as opposed to competitive goal structures. One area that has received a considerable amount of research has had to do with relationships between different ethnic groups.

Studies of race relations have shown that where (a) the goal is clearly co-operative, (b) the teacher supports inter-ethnic co-operation, (c) the group members are of equal status, and (d) are given a sufficiently long experience of working together, then positive attitude changes towards greater tolerance and mutual respect are produced under co-operative goal structures.

To conclude, despite the rather unfamiliar language in which the research findings to do with competitive, co-operative, and individualistic group structures are reported, there is a familiar ring to the knowledge to be gained from this concentration of research activity. The findings are that the teacher's use of co-operative goal structures in organizing the ongoing work of mixed ability classes promotes the principles of equality that we discussed earlier in the chapter, more readily and more satisfactorily than competitive or individualistic goal structures. The threefold formulation of the principles bears repetition at this point:

(a) That human beings have a right to equality of respect by virtue of their common humanity.
(b) That human beings have an equal right to opportunities for self development.
(c) That human beings have an equal right to opportunities of achieving certain social goals.

TEACHING STRATEGIES: AN OVERVIEW

In this section we have in mind the needs of student teachers and the problems they face in mixed ability teaching situations. We begin with a review of some of the more widely practised teaching strategies and learning styles that student teachers are likely to encounter. Each subsection gives an extended definition where appropriate, outlines important characteristics, highlights strengths and weaknesses, and indicates practical* implications for the student teacher coming into contact with a particular approach perhaps for the first time.

It is important to stress in connection with team teaching, and mixed ability grouping, that we are presenting broad reviews. We do not take account of regional variations with respect to the interpretation (or assumption) of underlying philosophies, organization and administration of attendant practices, or even nomenclature. Nor, for the same reason, do we draw too fine a distinction between what is done with different ages of pupils.

Social Structure and Interaction in Learning Situations

There are a number of forms of interaction between teacher and pupils, and among pupils themselves, which may be found in school learning situations. The particular one operating at any given moment will depend upon the objective of the lesson, the nature of the task in hand, and the implied educational philosophy. We now consider six characteristic learning situations which account for the principal patterns of interaction, both formal and informal, which may be found in the context of the school. Our analysis is based upon the work of Oeser.[15]

Situation 1: the teacher-centred lesson

The principle of interaction underlying the teacher-centred situation may be illustrated as in Example 1. Although only five pupils are represented in the diagram, this figure may vary, with perhaps a notional thirty pupils being a more representative number in this kind of situation.

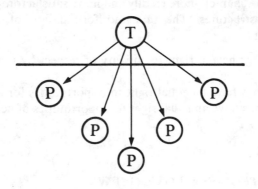

Example 1

---

* Our primary purpose, however, is to provide a range of *perspectives* on classroom organization and practice that can become the focus of discussion. Chapter 9, *Open Classrooms*, complements the practical orientation of the present section in its philosophical treatment of the idea of open education.

The interaction pattern here is one in which the *teacher speaks and the pupils listen*. As Oeser notes, their relationship to him is confined to listening, perceiving, and assimilating; and there is no interaction among the pupils themselves.

A social structure of this kind is found in its pure form in a radio or television broadcast. In a school context, it is found in the *talk* or *lecture* where there is a sharp distinction between the teacher and the class (depicted in the diagram by a continuous horizontal line), and in which the teacher's role is authoritarian, exhortatory, and directive. This kind of interaction style may also form *part* of a class lesson as, for instance, at the outset when the teacher introduces new learning, or in the course of a lesson when he demonstrates a skill, or towards the end of a lesson when he sums up what has gone before. Preparation for a formal examination would present occasions when the teacher-centred approach would be an efficient means of teaching and learning.

Situation 2: the lecture–discussion

The second situation may be seen as a variant of the first, being one in which the pattern of interaction is not wholly dominated by the teacher. It is represented diagramatically in Example 2. Again, the number of pupils may vary, depending upon the circumstances.

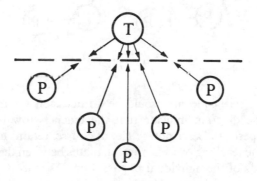

Example 2

Oeser points out that three of the most important aims of the educator are: to turn the latent leadership of a group in the direction of the educational process; to encourage the individual development of leadership; and to encourage co-operative striving towards common goals while discouraging the exercise of authoritarian leadership. The social structures evolving through situations 2, 3, 4, and 5 provide a framework for the achievement of these aims.

The arrow heads in the diagram indicate more or less continuous verbal interaction between teacher and pupils. Although as leader the teacher asks questions, and receives and gives answers, the initiative need not always be his; and competition may develop among the pupils. The sharp distinction between teacher and taught which was an important feature of the first situation and which was represented in Example 1 by means of a continuous horizontal line is now less obvious – hence the broken horizontal line in Example 2.

This kind of learning situation, the pattern of interaction depicted in Example 1, could develop into the pattern illustrated in Example 2.

Situation 3: active learning

Example 3 depicts a social situation in which the teacher allows discussion and mutual help between pupils.

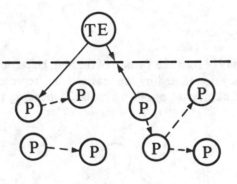

Example 3

Practical work in a science lesson would be an occasion for this kind of situation. The letters TE in the diagram indicate that the teacher now begins to assume the additional role of Expert. As Oeser notes: 'He, of course, retains his other roles as well; but the emphasis in the teaching process now fluctuates between the needs established by the task and the needs of the individual pupils.' For this reason, the situation may be described as *task-* and *pupil-centred* and as one beginning to have a co-operative structure.

Situation 4: active learning; independent planning

Scrutiny of Example 4 shows how this fourth situation evolves logically from the preceding one. The pupils are now active in small groups, and the teacher acts more or less exclusively as an Expert–Consultant (indicated in the diagram by a wavy line).

As Oeser says: 'Groups map out their work, adapt to each other's pace, discuss their difficulties and agree on solutions. There is independent exploration, active learning, and a maximal development of a task-directed leadership in each group.' The social climate is co-operative and the situation may be described as pupil- and task-centred.

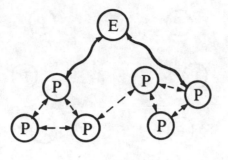

Example 4

Situation 5: group task-centred

A characteristic situation in which a smallish group of individuals is concerned with a particular topic*, project, or problem, is illustrated in Example 5.

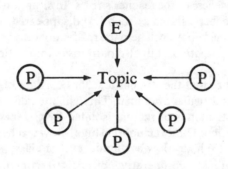

Example 5

A pattern of this kind may thus be found in a seminar or discussion session. The arrow heads indicate that the group as a whole is concerned with the task – its elucidation, clarification, and solution.

The situation is clearly a *task-centred* one in which there is an absence of hierarchical structure. Ideally, the role of the teacher here is simply that of a wise and experienced member of the group (depicted as 'Expert' in the diagram). The more coercive roles traditionally associated with the teacher are out of place in this kind of social structure. The attitudes of members of the group to each other will tend to be co-operative and consultative.

Situation 6: independent working; no interaction

This final situation, illustrated in Example 6, arises when pupils are working quite independently and there is no interaction.

---

* The reader is referred to our discussion of the integrated curriculum in open classrooms, Chapter 9.

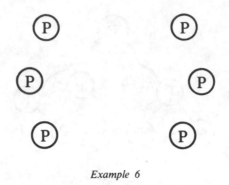

Example 6

This situation will occur when pupils are working at exercises 'on their own', or in a formal examination session.

In summary, Oeser observes that from situations 1 to 4 there is a progressive change from teacher-centred through task-centred to pupil-centred activities, from passive to active learning, and from minimal to maximal participation, with a progressive diminution of the coerciveness of the teacher's roles. In situation 5, the situation is again task-centred, but the teacher's status as such has disappeared.

The six situations outlined above will help the reader not only to understand classroom-based social and learning situations, but also patterns of interaction occurring outside the classroom.

It is of great importance that the student teacher be aware of the sort of situation he wants in a lesson, or at a particular point in it. This will be chiefly determined by his lesson objective together with the kinds of factors isolated by Oeser which will contribute to defining the overall situation. These include: (1) high – low teacher dominance; (2) large – small number of pupils; (3) high – low academic level of class; (4) active – passive pupil participation; (5) individual – co-operative effort; (6) contentious – non-contentious material; (7) strong – weak needs; (8) task and learning oriented – examination oriented; and (9) directing – helping (counselling).

TEACHING STRATEGIES IN MIXED ABILITY GROUPS

Having presented a broad outline of teaching strategies, we turn now to consider the question of mixed ability teaching in more detail.

It is axiomatic that the adoption of mixed ability grouping requires the teacher to employ methods and means of class management that are compatible with it. Using methods that depend for their success upon a more or less homogeneous range of ability invites difficulty and failure.

Much of the time spent teaching mixed ability classes will be devoted to individual and small group work. The advantage of individualized learning in this context is that each child is able to work at a pace best suited to his needs and ability. He is therefore not stretched beyond his capabilities, nor prevented from fully realizing his potential in a particular direction. One of the most efficient means of achieving individualized learning is through preparing individual programmes for the children concerned. This is especially the case in certain basic subjects like mathematics. The implications of this approach for the student teacher are two-fold: (1) a high work load, particularly *before* a lesson; and (2) a considerable amount of record keeping. Using Oeser's notation, we can diagram *individualized* learning in mixed ability groups as in Example 7.

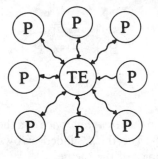

Example 7

The use of *themes* caters for individual and small group needs, especially among older children. A theme in this context may be seen as a central idea (e.g., animals, fire, witches and spells) used as a starting point for learning and one which will engage the children's interests. The main advantage of the theme approach is that it offers a framework within which to operate yet at the same time a considerable degree of freedom to both the children and teacher.

The successful outcome of a theme approach depends very much on the right choice of theme at the outset. It should be neither too narrow in scope nor too general; and sub-topics subsumed under the theme must have coherence arising from their logical interrelationships.

The factors that need to be borne in mind when choosing a theme include the ages, interests, aptitudes, and abilities of the pupils involved in the enterprise. We suggest, too, that the student finds out in advance which children are slow learners, poor readers, or potentially disruptive. Another factor that must not be overlooked is the competence of the student himself. He should not select a theme outside his own limitations, nor one that will demand more time in preparation than he is able or willing to give. Yet another factor concerns the objectives the student has in mind. These must be carefully specified to ensure the successful organization of the undertaking.

Once a theme has been chosen, the next decision concerns whether all the children will work on the same things and engage in the same activities, or whether they will be allowed to choose their own sub-topic from the theme and devote their attention to that. The decision will be influenced by the teacher's objectives, but most likely he will want to make use of one or other of two techniques: the *circus approach* and the *selective approach*. With the former, a pupil will work at each of the sub-topics embraced by the theme in sequence; with the latter, he will select one or two sub-topics and give his attention exclusively to these.

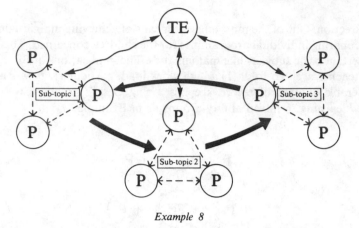

Example 8

Again, using Oeser's notation the *circus approach* to a theme in small group work can be diagrammed as in Example 8. The thick shaded arrows show that each small group engages in each of the sub-topics of the theme.

The *selective approach* to a theme in small group work can be represented as in Example 9.

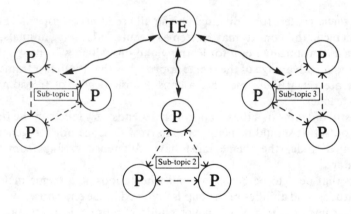

Example 9

A theme can be initiated by means of a lead lesson, for this is one of the more successful ways of arousing interest. A second means of stimulating interest, if pertinent to the chosen theme, is to visit places in the locality having bearing on the work to be explored – a museum or television studio, for example. To make the most of a visit of this kind, the teacher must plan and prepare carefully so he can bring as much as possible to the attention of his pupils. A third means of capturing interest would be to surround the children with examples, materials, and resources relevant to the theme and suggest what they might possibly do with them. This approach has proved especially useful with primary children.

The organization of the theme approach can be particularly daunting for student teachers. No matter how much the children's interest has been aroused, it will be to little avail if the organization is faulty and does not permit the theme's thorough implementation. This can only be achieved by careful preparation and planning.

Once matters are underway, the teacher's main task is to keep a careful watch on the progress of each pupil. This will mean checking that he has adequate materials and resources, striving to maintain the original motivational level, and suggesting ways in which an individual child's efforts may develop. If the work of the class is to be an educational experience, the teacher will find that he has to work just as hard as he would in a more traditional lesson.

One final point arises with subjects which at first glance do not appear to lend themselves to the theme approach. Languages, mathematics, and science, for example, generally require a 'linear' approach, that is, knowledge in these areas has to be developed step by step and cannot easily be approached obliquely from a child's own interests. Where this is the case, provision is usually made in the time-table for either formal teaching or individualized work. However, a change of objectives even with subjects of this nature very often discloses potential for a theme approach.

TEAM TEACHING

Team teaching is an instructional organization implying that two or more teachers share collective responsibility for all or a significant part of the instruction of the same group of children. The notion can only be described in a general way, and Warwick[18] offers the following definition: 'A form of organization in which individual teachers decide to pool resources, interests, and expertise in order to devise and implement a scheme of work suitable to the needs of their pupils and the facilities of their school.'

Example 10 represents one form in which team teaching can occur. Warwick observes that the concept of team teaching enshrines two distinct schools of thought. To some, it is perceived in pragmatic terms – an economic and democratic way of organizing a school. In this case, it offers a convenient administrative framework within which existing structures can survive with some modifications. To others, however, team teaching

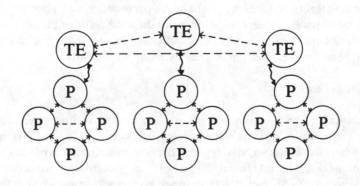

Example 10

represents far more. They perceive it as a re-orientation of the curriculum in such a way that the needs of both teacher and taught are more fully met.

Team teaching, in contrast to the assumptions underlying traditional approaches to education, takes as its starting point the needs of the children and attempts to structure them as fully as possible into the work of the school. It questions the notion that the requirements of either teacher or pupil are best served by an arbitrary division into subject departments, each working in isolation from the others. It does not assume that the only contribution to the classroom situation comes from the teacher directing the children from the front of the class, and seeks new forms of organization in which the individual and the group can play a much greater part.

Advocates of team teaching would argue that as long as traditional academic structures remain, teachers will feel impelled to work in isolation – in their classrooms, departments, and preparation. But as soon as they think and act co-operatively, the possibilities of team teaching can become a reality.

Some Advantages and Disadvantages of Team Teaching

Advantages of team teaching as listed by Stephens[16] include: (1) new organizational patterns may emerge when teachers are prepared to work together; (2) the curriculum becomes less fragmented and less authoritarian by nature; (3) team teaching reasserts the importance of people, and their relationships and reactions to one another within the school context; (4) it facilitates professional growth by providing teachers with opportunities to share ideas, plans, and observations; it also allows for wider use of expertise; (5) it encourages children to develop broader ranges of interests; (6) it permits the organization of a larger group within which a child may find greater compatibility; (7) there are organizational benefits – it cuts down duplication of effort; allows for a freer use of audio-visual equipment; and results in less disruption when a teacher is absent; and (8) new and inexperienced teachers benefit in that they can take on a full teaching load gradually.

Some of the disadvantages may also be noted: (1) some children prefer a close relationship with one class teacher, and this is more difficult to achieve with team teaching; (2) some equally find it difficult to accommodate to a large group; (3) different teachers will have different standards and this may confuse some pupils; (4) there may be differences among teachers themselves – clashes of personality, educational philosophy, or differing attitudes, for example; (5) having more diffused responsibilities may result in a teacher's commitment to particular children suffering; and (6) team teaching increases the power of the head teacher and this is seen by some as a disadvantage.

Aspects of Organisation

The ways in which team teaching is organized are numerous and varied and it is only possible for us to indicate one or two alternatives in this connection. In the primary school, for instance, where team teaching developed in order to meet the needs of vertically grouped classes and of working an integrated day, a team may consist of from two teachers to possibly the whole staff. Allen et al[17], have observed from their studies that the size of the team is often related to the layout of the building and also to the compatibility of the teachers.

Each teacher may then be responsible for a particular aspect of the curriculum – languages or mathematics, for example. In schools where teachers do not want to teach only one subject, they change their activities fairly regularly.

Of the group involved in a team-teaching enterprise, Allen et al[17], say that it 'may consist of all the children in one age group in a school, or it may be vertically grouped as would be the case if the whole school formed one team. Experience has shown that the reception class children benefit from a term on their own to establish themselves securely in school, though where there is a nursery class this is not as necessary.'

Although the children may move freely from one work area to another, they should have a base where they can keep their belongings and a particular teacher of their own.

For team teaching to be effective, there must be co-operation between teachers who should be in frequent contact with each other.

One way of organizing team teaching in the primary school is to have a short meeting of all those involved so that the pupils can be informed of the activities they will be taking part in during the day. Each teacher can then take the opportunity to explain any new activities for which she will be mainly responsible. Allen et al[17], refer to this as a 'catching of interest' time. It is very similar in its intent to the 'lead lesson' approach adopted in some secondary schools (see below). After this the children take up the activity of their choice.

Activities such as physical education, music and movement, story, or television programmes can be accommodated by taking groups out of the team. As Allen et al[17], point out: 'It may be possible for the whole team to lay down tools and go to another activity at the same time. Alternatively it may be necessary for a room to be closed for a period whilst the teacher takes a group for one of these activities.'

The authors also observe that behaviour problems may arise with those children not able to cope with the freedom that team teaching places on them. The solution suggested is for them to be directed to particular activities at set times until the established routine gives them sufficient confidence and security to manage more freedom of choice later.

One approach to team teaching in the secondary school is structured around two basic concepts – the *lead lesson* and *follow-up* work. These may be briefly explained as follows:

The lead lesson

This initiates a sequence of work. It is intended to stimulate interest and capture the imagination. As the work of the period or periods (or however the time allocation is described) following depends on it, it is essential that it has drive, impact, and variety. As Freeman[19] says: 'If (the lead lesson) fails the follow-up work will be difficult because pupil interest will be low and the purpose and direction of the follow-up work unclear.' To ensure success, then, a wide range of techniques and teaching aids needs to be used – possibly film, filmstrips, slides, tape-recorders, television, etc. The lead lesson also serves as a key presentation, bringing together the full group, or a large part of it, ensuring continuity and, where necessary, providing direction.

Although some schools allow an hour or so for a lead lesson, most schools devote twenty to thirty minutes to it. The occasion itself is usually shared among team members according to their particular interests and knowledge. Freeman records that all accounts referring to lead lessons emphasize the importance attached to their *preparation* and *organization*.

Follow-up work

Warwick[18] notes that follow-up work is just as important as the lead lesson and adequate time must be given to it. Maximum benefit will not be derived from the lead lesson unless this is so, and the scheme will be considerably weakened without it. An average of three to five follow-up sessions are necessary each week. The first of these should, ideally, come directly after the lead lesson to enable immediate recapitulation and consolidation of the material and a running through of the work schedule for the week. It is therefore helpful if the lead lesson can be time-tabled for the beginning of a longish session, or a double period. This allows for such immediate follow-up work.

Freeman[19] says that schools tend on the whole to arrange follow-up work either in classes of normal size (20–40 +), or in a system of individuals or small groups (6–15).

The Role of the Teacher

Once the work is underway, the teacher in a team teaching situation acts in an advisory capacity. He knows what material and equipment are available and where various pieces of information can be obtained. His earlier careful planning has ensured this. He also has knowledge of what each group is doing and can thus direct discussion or research if problems are encountered, and possibly merge two or more groups when this would seem desirable. Individuals may be withdrawn from particular groups for various reasons, and from time to time all groups will come together for a formal or semi-formal session.

A further important function concerns the keeping of records of the children's work and achievement. Freeman[19] lists the following characteristics which are used as a basis for assessment in some English schools.

In the classroom. Co-operation with the teacher; co-operation with other children; oral communication; written communication; standard of presenting work; interest; initiative – keenness to work; originality; ability to make decisions; sensitivity; self-understanding; academic potential; consistency; learning attainment – skill, knowledge, recall and understanding.

General. General bearing – speech, poise, confidence, appearance; reliability.

Social habits. Exercises self-control; listens courteously; participates in group activities; demonstrates thoughtfulness for others; cares for materials and property; abides by school rules; and comes into school on time.

Work habits. Has materials and is prepared for work; follows directions; does neat work; works independently and is not easily distracted; uses initiative in thinking; completes work on time; and does independent reading.

Finally, the teacher's task is also one of widening each individual's horizons. Starting with initial achievement, each child can be actively encouraged to take a step outside his specialization and interests.

PROBLEMS IN MIXED ABILITY TEACHING

'The problems of mixed ability teaching centre around slow and fast learners, teacher qualities, and teaching resources.'

BOX 7.5

Social Structures, Interaction, and Learning Situations

Using the situations outlined in the text, attempt some explanation of the following formal and informal occasions for interaction in the context of the school. Bear in mind that some of them may contain more than one of the situations in succession or simultaneously.

1. A schools television programme preceded by a five-minute introduction by the teacher and followed by a ten-minute class discussion led by the teacher.
2. A headmaster addressing the school at morning assembly on the subject of indiscipline.
3. A sports teacher discussing with the school team a recent and important football match against a rival school in which they had been hopelessly outclassed.
4. A teacher giving an illustrated talk to the school's Geographical Society on his recent visit to South America.
5. A needlework lesson in which approximately two thirds of the girls are in their places stitching long hems while the remainder are queuing at the teacher's desk to have the hem started.
6. A member of staff initiating a team teaching project with a twenty-minute 'lead lesson'.
7. A session in which most of the class are working independently with work-card assignments while the teacher is listening to individuals read at the front of the class.
8. A class of thirty-five pupils taking a three-hour 'O' level written examination.
9. A project session in which five groups of six children each are working on different aspects of a theme entitled 'Explorers'.
10. A school choir rehearsing with a teacher for the end-of-term concert.

Source: Cohen and Manion[20]

Such was the consensus of opinion among forty headteachers of Midland comprehensives in a survey[21] of the mixed ability teaching arrangements in their schools. These selfsame problem areas have also been identified in studies of individual schools, in the comments of educationists, and in the reports of Her Majesty's Inspectorate. We say something about each problem in turn.

Slow Learners

'How can one use worksheet assignments when half the class can't read?' This must surely be one of the most frequently voiced comments by teachers in any discussion of mixed ability teaching. Despite the exaggeration of the proportion of non-readers in that rhetorical question, a small but sizeable number of children in the classes of most secondary schools which have a truly comprehensive intake will lack basic skills in reading and in number. What is to be done with these pupils? A number of solutions suggest themselves. First, slow learners (and most poor readers constitute this category), might be winnowed-out at the beginning of their secondary schooling to form a separate group for whom special courses are devised and taught by trained remedial staff. Second, a programme of part-time extraction might be devised in which children needing special help in literacy and numeracy are withdrawn to receive that tuition. Third, teachers might be encouraged to meet the needs of slow learners entirely within the context of mixed ability groups.

The appeal of the first solution, that is, the total extraction of pupils needing remedial help, lies in the benefits that they might enjoy as a result of working in small groups with sympathetic and specialist remedial teachers. The disadvantages however, may well outweigh the advantages. All too frequently such a degree of separation from fellow pupils generates anti-school attitudes and behaviour problems in remedial groups. Part-time group extraction for remedial reading is widely practised in many secondary schools. Davies[1] shows how such a solution can be accomplished:

> 'Pupils needing remedial attention will be scattered across the whole year group when placed initially in forms under the care of a form tutor. These forms will be permanent units which for three, four or five years will be registered together . . . and whose needs will be the concern of the form tutor having responsibility for helping with their problems and keeping their records. These mixed ability units are retained for certain lessons – eg. Art, Handicraft, Housecraft, Music, Physical Education. For all other lessons the year group will be setted into more homogeneous groups. In this way children of all abilities might work together for perhaps a quarter of their time at school.'

While this pattern of remedial help has much to commend it, contributing as it does both to the educational and the social objectives of mixed ability teaching, it has been argued[1] that it serves to minimize rather than to remove the problems of teaching slow learners. Placing children in mixed ability groupings for only twenty-five percent of the school day, Davies suggests, is a guarantee of creating sub-cultures within the student body as a whole, with all the attendant problems that such smaller groupings can generate.

In arguing for the total retention of slower pupils within mixed ability groups, both Kelly[13] and Davies[1] are aware of the enormous demands that such a solution imposes upon most teachers. For Kelly, the social and the emotional advantages to be derived make it unwise and undesirable that non-readers should be excluded from mixed ability work. Kelly's solution is to give these pupils individual assignments in group projects that capitalize upon what strengths they have, such assignments being based upon as many resources that can be used without reading skills as can be obtained or made. It is doubtful that Kelly's solution arouses much enthusiasm among teachers as a whole. Davies' proposal, based as it is on actual practice, is more realistic:

> '. . . at one stage, itinerant remedial help was brought into the mainstream classroom, with a pair of teachers operating in harness, using carefully devised assignments wherein every pupil was guided to tasks with which he or she could cope initially via the use of resources suited to his or her capabilities.'

However desirable Davies' solution, it is contingent upon a relatively small number of pupils needing remedial help and the availability of a large number of remedial staff. In most schools today, this is scarcely a viable proposition. By and large, it is the practice of part-time extraction which is chosen as the way of dealing with slow learners in mixed ability teaching situations.

Fast Learners

What of the fast learner and the gifted child? The following extract from a fourteen year old's essay entitled 'My Dream World' well illustrates the problem of the gifted child who feels underchallenged in a mixed ability teaching situation.

'. . . Ever since I can remember I have enjoyed learning. At H – L – (her primary school) I had every encouragement. I was allowed to work at lunchtimes; there were adequate text-books which we could bring home, and we were 'set' according to ability and speed of working. That meant that those of us with academic ambitions could help and encourage each other. Those less quick to comprehend had lessons geared to their pace.

Since I have been at R – (secondary comprehensive) I have begun to despair of my dream becoming reality (University degree and a Teaching Diploma). It is hard to find satisfaction in working from worksheets. Without textbooks, except for Maths and French, I cannot pursue an idea which interests me, or revise except from my own notes. We have no library at W – E – (her home village) and the public library in L – (nearest town) leaves much to be desired. Why cannot I have textbooks to bring home? Why was it so outrageous for me to ask to take home an atlas to finish some work? Why must I be taught with pupils who have no desire to learn?'

The Report of Her Majesty's Inspectors entitled *Gifted Children in Middle and Comprehensive Schools*[22] highlights the problem of the gifted pupil. Unlike *the handicapped* or *the backward*, groups for which criteria of identification have been established and forms of provision planned, *giftedness* is an ill-defined term. For the vast majority of schools and their teachers, the report concludes, giftedness is neither implicit nor explicit in the day-to-day dialogue of school life. The irony is that whereas gifted children can, and frequently do, work below their potential from lack of challenge or from personal choice, and pass unnoticed, slow learners can less easily disguise their inability to work at the level and pace of their fellows. This latter observation is supported in the findings of a study[23] of able children in mixed ability classes in which Heads of Departments were asked to comment on the problems that mixed ability teaching posed, for bright pupils. They identified the following:

1. Teachers spend too much time with slow learners.
2. Good pupils can get away with not working at an appropriately fast pace.
3. It is hard to cater for the very bright in a mixed situation.
4. Bright pupils fail to cover enough subject content for their needs.
5. Teachers are not doing their best for top pupils – work is aimed at the middle band.
6. The top third of pupils are not stretched.
7. Bright pupils are more diffcult to teach than other pupils.

The research concluded that for bright pupils, the following three needs are paramount:

First, teachers must help bright children to develop appropriate study skills. *Inter alia*, this will involve producing genuinely graded worksheets and instructing able children in methods of self-testing. Second teachers need to encourage bright pupils to develop skills of higher level thinking. This will involve teachers in looking critically at classroom interaction and at their own questioning skills. Third, teachers must come to accept the 'normality' of bright pupils particularly on the emotional level even though they may seem 'old for their age'. The desire not to be different on the part of bright pupils sometimes triggers off underachievement on their part. Bright pupils need to be rewarded for scholastic achievement and at the same time to retain their identities with the class group.

Teacher Qualities

Coping with slow learners, extending gifted pupils, planning and preparing for team teaching all require a high order of professional skills if mixed ability teaching is to be successful. But the adoption of mixed ability teaching is more than simply a matter of pedagogic techniques or organizational expertise; rather, it implies a fundamental rethinking on the part of the school staff of their approach to education. In a word, it requires a shift in teacher *values*.

Over and over again in reports of schools that have successfully changed from a system of streaming to mixed ability teaching there is a key statement to the effect that such radical reorganization would not have been possible without a thorough reappraisal of the purposes of education on the part of the teachers involved. Not that such reappraisals necessarily result in any lessening of the problems and dilemmas that most classteachers are confronted with:

> . . . 'the teacher who commits himself to mixed ability teaching had better be the kind of person who can learn to live with, and tolerate ambivalent feelings about the wisdom of what he does in the classroom situation. In this way, he will continue to search for some way of reconciling the conflicting principles of equality. The teacher who cannot tolerate the discomfort of a certain amount of guilt will tend to succumb to the temptation of oversimplifying the . . . idea of mixed ability teaching.'[1]

'Going mixed ability' requires teachers to make changes that go right to the heart of their professional practice and their thinking in relation to pupils and to knowledge. Stott[24] calls for a new-model teacher, arguing that teachers will have to cease being teachers in the old sense of the word. They must become:

> 'organizers of learning programmes which involves making materials available and seeing that they are properly used; ensuring that the classroom is an orderly place conducive to learning; monitoring the progress of each pupil and re-allocating his role as necessary; making sure that all members of the class get absorbed in some learning process and encouraging them to extend their capabilities; and in general giving the impression that work and attainment are important.
>
> Even if the class are mainly engaged in group-activities the teacher has to be at hand to give an explanation when required, but it will be explaining a problem that the group are facing and to which they want a solution.
>
> Finally, the teacher needs to be there to provide the adult support that most young people need and value. They will appreciate the teacher's interest in them, and consequently will like to produce their work to show what they have done.'

Resources

Mixed ability organization raises a number of practical problems not the least of which is the development and utilization of adequate resources to sustain this system of teaching. Unlike traditional whole-class teaching, a mixed ability regime requires a far greater quantity and variety of learning resources. Most schools that have organized along mixed ability lines have developed some sort of resource centre system either localized within individual subject departments or centralized so as to serve the needs of the whole school.

A resource centre involves six essential elements:

1. Production of home-made resources.
2. Selection and acquisition of other resources.
3. Classification and indexing for retrieval.
4. Storage.
5. Use, including guidance and lending etc.
6. Evaluation and weeding.

The average school resource centre today is likely to contain most or all of the following materials: books, periodicals, maps, models, posters, filmstrips, pictures, records, audio-tapes, slides, and worksheets. Probably the most commonly-used resource is the worksheet or workcard. One inquiry[25] into the use of worksheets revealed that at any one time, there were several basic types in operation in the particular school. For example, there was a *single workcard* used by the whole class, which, because it lacked structure failed to satisfy the extremes of ability. Second, there was a *single structured workcard* which started from concrete problems that were within the grasp of the majority of pupils in the group and proceeded in both depth and breadth to more abstract problems. This type of workcard had the effect of frustrating the least able children who found little success in this arrangement. A third approach involved a *series of shorter workcards* that were designed to complete the whole programme. The cards were graded in difficulty, the earlier ones presenting concrete problems and providing a series of success points for the less able pupils. The later series were designed to extend the more able children and presented them with open-ended, problem-solving tasks. The appeal of this third approach to workcard development is that it allows for a whole range of resource materials to be used as a supplement to the basic programme. Whatever method is adopted, the author (an experienced teacher) identifies certain basic criteria that need consideration. We summarize these in Box 7.6.

BOX 7.6

Preparing Workcards for Mixed Ability Teaching

1. Decisions must be made about the starting point for the programme. This may require a degree of pretesting or a knowledge of pupils' background information from other subjects or from outside the school.
2. The card must start from the pupils' own experience (not what we think is their experience).
3. The programme must move from the concrete and particular to the abstract and general.
4. The card must be developed so that the programme progresses in small manageable steps.
5. Success points must be found for all pupils in the scheme of work i.e. by the use of self-checking systems or discussion with the teacher as a means of offering encouragement or support.
6. The most able pupils must be extended by the use of problem-solving techniques which are not always within their capabilities, therefore demanding the teacher's active involvement.

Source: adapted from Wyatt [25]

Finally the oft-quoted description of mixed ability teaching as 'death by a thousand workcards' points to the injudicious use that some schools make of this key learning resource. The workcard is best seen as one of a number of teaching resources that are appropriate to mixed ability teaching. An unrelieved diet of workcards is a certain recipe for boredom and indiscipline in any classroom.

IMPLICATIONS FOR STUDENT TEACHERS

By now it is abundantly clear that successful teaching in mixed ability classrooms involves a wide range of preparation and a variety of professional skills. Is it possible, one might ask, to identify specific factors that make for effective mixed ability teaching? In proposing a ten point attack on the challenge of mixed ability teaching, Wragg[26] has the particular needs of student teachers in mind. Box 7.7 identifies his proposals which we then present in greater detail.

BOX 7.7

Ten Sets of Skills for Mixed Ability Teaching

Preparatory skills

1. Understanding individual differences amongst children in the class.
2. Understanding the importance of issues to do with language in the classroom.
3. Ability to be a member of a team.
4. Devising and preparing appropriate curricula.

Teaching strategies

5. Using whole class teaching judiciously.
6. Handling small groups.
7. Interacting with individual children.
8. Developing flexibility and adaptability.

Evaluation

9. Monitoring pupils' progress and keeping records.
10. Evaluating one's own teaching and undertaking professional self-development.

Source: Wragg[26]

Individual differences

Mixed ability teaching requires a thorough understanding of individual differences. Teachers need to anticipate difficulties by identifying, for example, those who require more time, those who lack self-confidence, and those who are impulsive.

Language in the classroom

Unless teachers are aware of the crucial importance of language, much of the teaching in mixed ability classes will be misguided. The effective preparation of worksheets, charts and wall displays too, is contingent upon the use of appropriate language.

Team membership

Considerable interpersonal skills are required in mixed ability situations where teachers are frequently required to work in teams in the planning and preparation of course work materials.

Devising and preparing curricula

Because mixed ability teaching poses more planning problems than other forms of classroom grouping, teachers need to acquire the inventiveness, the sensibility and the determination to devise and prepare appropriate curricula.

Using whole class teaching

Contrary to popular belief, mixed ability teaching requires the judicious use of whole class teaching. Stand-up-and-talk skills are therefore very important. Teachers need to be able to command attention, to explain clearly, to speak audibly and distinctly, and to chair proceedings with large groups.

Handling small groups

Teachers need to develop the ability to handle several groups at once. In mixed ability teaching such groups often differ in size, constitution and task in hand. Teaching them requires 'with-it-ness', that is, the ability to work with one group while keeping a vigilant eye on others in the classroom.

Interacting with individuals

Interacting with individual children is a vital skill in mixed ability teaching. Teachers need to be able to secure a high degree of industry from children working on their own. This involves designing appropriate individual assignments and monitoring individual progress.

Developing flexibility and adaptability

Mixed ability teaching requires numerous decisions to be made during the course of any lesson in which, typically, groups and individuals are engaged in several different activities. Success under such conditions demands flexibility and adaptability on the part of the teacher.

Monitoring pupil progress

In mixed ability teaching, regular assessment and recording of children's progress is, if anything, more important than in traditional forms of classroom grouping. Teachers need to learn a wide range of assessment techniques and to develop an awareness of when and why to make evaluative judgments.

Evaluating one's own teaching

More important, perhaps, than evaluating pupils' work is the teacher's assessment of his/her own performance. Ultimately, improvement in teaching only takes place when teachers decide for themselves to change the ways in which they plan, prepare, and initiate learning activities.

SUMMARY

We began the chapter with a brief account of historical events leading up to the emergence of comprehensive schools and the growth of mixed ability organization. Mixed ability teaching was then defined and shown to involve three distinct yet interrelated principles of equality. The social and educational arguments for mixed ability teaching were enumerated and evidence bearing upon the claims for this form of organization was evaluated. Particularly important in this respect is the study of mixed ability teaching undertaken by the NFER, involving some 500 teachers in 29 non-selective schools.

We went on to consider the nature of classroom groups and the effects that varying goal structures have upon both educational and social outcomes. Specifically, we identified research to do with anxiety, interpersonal relationships, and intellectual and affective gains.

A major part of the chapter was given over to an account of teaching strategies in which the advantages and disadvantages of various techniques (in particular, team teaching) were discussed. Four problems in mixed ability teaching – slow learners, fast learners, teacher qualities, and resources – were then identified and suggestions were made for their amelioration.

Finally, under the broad headings of (a) preparatory skills, (b) teaching strategies, and (c) evaluation, we itemized ten areas of expertise which make for effective mixed ability teaching.

ENQUIRY AND DISCUSSION

1. Discuss the view that by providing different work for pupils according to their individual needs, mixed ability teaching inevitably re-creates the inequalities of opportunity that it is designed to avoid.

2. To what age or level of competence do you believe that mixed ability teaching can be effective in your own particular subject area?

3. Does streaming necessarily produce 'demoralized, demotivated, unteachable middle school groups, bad for themselves, their teachers and other children?' In what circumstances can streaming co-exist with other forms of school organization?

4. Can competitive and co-operative goal structures ever co-exist in the day-to-day work of the classroom? Where, and how?

5. Think back to your own experience as a secondary school pupil and to your recent school visits during teaching practice. Do any of the broad teaching strategies set out by Oeser and ourselves tend to predominate in particular areas of the school curriculum?

6. What do you see as the major advantages and disadvantages of team teaching?

NOTES AND REFERENCES

1. Davies, R. P. (1975) *Mixed Ability Grouping*. London: Temple Smith.

2. Barker Lunn, J. C. (1970) *Streaming in the Primary School*. Slough: NFER.

3. Department of Education and Science (1978) *Mixed Ability Work in Comprehensive Schools*. London: HMSO.

4. Bailey, M. Mixed teaching and the defence of subjects. Cited in Elliott, J. (1976) The problems and dilemmas of mixed ability teaching and the issue of teacher accountability. *Cambridge Journal of Education*. **6**, 2, pp 3–14.

5. Davies, B. and Cave, R. G. (1977) *Mixed Ability Teaching in the Secondary School*. London: Ward Lock Educational.

6. Thompson, D. (1974) Non-streaming did make a difference. *Forum*, **16**.

7. Gregson, A. and Quin, W. F. (1978) Mixed ability methods and educational standards. *Comprehensive Education*, **37**.

8. Newbold, D. (1977) *Ability Grouping – The Banbury Enquiry*. Slough: NFER.

9. Clunies-Ross L. and Reid, M. J. (1980) *Mixed Ability Teaching: an exploration of teachers' aims, objectives and classroom strategies.* Slough: NFER (mimeographed). This is a short preliminary report of the NFER's mixed ability project, the only available material at the time of going to press. Fuller details of methodology and findings are to appear in two forthcoming NFER publications. The first will report the views and approaches of the 500 teachers whose evidence provided the data for the first stage of the project. The second is designed to elaborate on the strategies that teachers employ in mixed ability teaching.

10. Barker Lunn, J. C. (1970) *Streaming in the Primary School.* Slough: NFER.

11. Ford, J. (1969) *Social Class and the Comprehensive School.* London: Routledge and Kegan Paul.

12. Cohen, L. and Fisher, D. (1973) Are comprehensive aims being realized? *Journal of Curriculum Studies,* **5,** 2, 166–175.

13. The discussion of four approaches to grouping in schools draws upon Kelly, A. V. (1974) *Teaching Mixed Ability Classes.* London: Harper and Row, pp 45–59.

14. Johnson, D. W. and Johnson, R. T. (1975) *Learning Together and Alone.* Englewood Cliffs, N. J.: Prentice-Hall Inc.

15. Oeser, O. A. (1960) *Teacher, Pupil and Task.* London: Tavistock Publications.

16. Stephens, L. S. (1974) *The Teacher's Guide to Open Education.* New York: Holt, Rinehart and Winston.

17. Allen, I., Douet, K., Gaff, M., Gray, E., Griffiths, C., Ryall, N. and Toone, E. (1975) *Working an Integrated Day.* London: Ward Lock Educational.

18. Warwick, D. (1974) *Team Teaching.* London: ULP.

19. Freeman, J. (1969) *Team Teaching in Britain.* London: Ward Lock Educational.

20. Cohen, L. and Manion, L. (1977) *A Guide to Teaching Practice.* London: Methuen.

21. Dooley, P., Smith, A. and Kerry, T. (1977) *Teaching Mixed Ability Classes. Occasional Paper No.1. Head's reports of procedures and problems.* Nottingham University: School of Education.

22. Department of Education and Science (1977) *Gifted Children in Middle and Comprehensive Schools.* London: HMSO.

23. Kerry, T. (1978) Bright pupils in mixed ability classes. *British Educational Research Journal,* **4,** 2, 103–111.
Bradley, H. W. and Goulding, J. G. (1973) *Handling mixed ability groups in the secondary school.* University of Nottingham: School of Education.
Lydiat, M. (1977) Mixed ability teaching gains ground. *Comprehensive Education,* **35,** 12–19.

24. Stott, D. H. (1979) The challenge of mixed ability. *British Journal of Teacher Education,* **5,** 2, 133–143.

25. Wyatt, H. (1976) Mixed ability teaching in practice. *Forum*, **18**, 2, 45–59.

26. Wragg, E. C. (1978) Training teachers for mixed ability classes: a ten point attack. *Forum*, **20**, 2, 39–42.

SELECTED READING

1. Good, T. L. and Brophy, J. E. (1978) *Looking in Classrooms*. New York: Harper and Row. 2nd edition. Provides a very readable account of life in classrooms. Chapter 9 'Classroom Grouping' considers mixed ability teaching and goal structures.

2. Bradley, H. W. and Goulding, J. G. (1973) *Handling Mixed Ability Groups in the Secondary School*. Nottingham: University of Nottingham, School of Education. Gives useful hints on classroom organization and planning.

3. Boydell, D. (1979) *The Primary Teacher in Action*. London: Open Books. Chapters 3 and 5, 'Classroom Organization' and 'Groups', respectively, contain some insights into the structure and organization of learning groups for younger pupils.

4. Davies, B. and Cave, R. G. (1977) *Mixed Ability Teaching In The Secondary School*. London: Ward Lock Educational. Has specific chapters dealing with problems of mixed ability teaching in various subject areas.
   See also:-Kelly, A. V. (1975) *Case Studies in Mixed Ability Teaching*. London: Harper and Row. and:- (Ed.) Wragg, E. (1976) *Teaching Mixed Ability Groups*. London: David and Charles.

5. Bossert, S. T. (1979) *Tasks and Social Relationships in Classrooms*. London: Cambridge University Press. A very readable empirical study which demonstrates the social consequences of various instructional techniques employed by teachers.

8

Multicultural Education

THE BACKGROUND

Over the past twenty years or so, immigration to Great Britain has brought about fundamental changes in our society. We are now an ethnically-mixed and a culturally-varied nation. One consequence is that our institutions have had to adapt in order to reflect and to cater for the many mixed communities that now exist throughout Great Britain. Schools particularly have had to change to accommodate to the needs of immigrant pupils in many areas.

More than any other institution, education is seen by many to bear a major responsibility for and an influence upon the shape of future society. Thus one of the most pressing problems facing education today is:

> 'What changes, modifications and adaptations of present philosophy, organization and practice are necessary to ensure that the education system of Britain reflects and caters for the needs and aspirations of a multiracial society?'[1]

We begin the chapter with a brief outline of the different educational responses that have been made to the immigration that has taken place during the past twenty years.

Assimilation

The viewpoint that dominated government policy during the early days of immigration in the 1960s was that if newly-arrived immigrants could be supported during their initial period of disorientation following arrival in Great Britain and helped to acquire a working knowledge of the English language then they would quickly be absorbed by the host society and all would be well. Educational responses at this time both nationally and locally reflected a policy of assimilation and led to an emphasis on the teaching of English as a second language, the setting up of reception centres and language centres, and the instituting of school-based language withdrawal groups. It was during this period that the Schools Council project, *English For Immigrant Pupils*, was set in being, producing an abundance of teaching materials and teacher guides.

Quite early in the 1960s, however, a shift of emphasis could be discerned from the wholly linguistic approach of the Schools Council project to a greater concern for concept formation and course content. As Bolton[1] observes, the homelands and cultures of immigrants began to feature more prominently in discussions about the choice of teaching materials and the suitability of teaching approaches. It is not difficult to see why. To teach English you have to teach *about* something and the something that interested and engaged many teachers working with immigrant children was the culture and the lifestyles of these newcomers to British schools. The change in emphasis brought into common parlance the word, *integration*.

Integration

Basically, those who supported the idea of integration rather than assimilation believed that factors other than initial cultural shock and the acquisition of spoken English ought to be taken into account in making educational provision for immigrant groups. They called for more detailed, planned programmes of educational and social support if immigrants were to be able to integrate with the majority society. But as Bolton says, the emphasis was still on integrating minorities with the host society and culture in order to create a culturally homogeneous society. In principle, this meant that it was up to minority groups to adapt and change, few expectations being voiced that the host society itself should modify or alter its attitudes and practices. It was recognized, however, that if integration were to be effected, then the majority society would need to be more aware of the cultural and historical factors associated with various immigrant groups. Implicit here was the view that such knowledge would assist the host society in making allowances for differences in lifestyle, religion and culture that might hinder the integration of some immigrant groups into British society. The educational response to the integrationist view, Bolton observes, was a shift of emphasis from teaching English as a second language to informing teachers about life in the Punjab, life in the Caribbean, and to introducing them to the basic tenets of Islam, Sikhism and Hinduism. 'Life-in-other-lands' type courses for teachers mushroomed, some teachers even going to visit India or the Caribbean on six week tours. The whole response, Bolton notes, was a logical reaction to the fact that the great majority of pupils belonging to ethnic minority groups then in British schools had been born abroad and had spent part of their lives living there.

Cultural Pluralism

The emergence of a second generation of ethnic minority pupils during the late 60s and 70s, together with the realization that neither assimilation nor integration has worked, has led to a growing appreciation on the part of the host society that these earlier ideas of assimilation and integration were both patronizing and dismissive of other cultures and lifestyles. Not just in Great Britain but all over the world, minority groups now actively assert their determination to maintain cultural continuity and to preserve their religious, linguistic, and cultural differences. Increasingly then, the host society is turning its attention to the concept of cultural pluralism. What exactly does this term imply? Simply this, that second generation British-born blacks, Sikhs, Hindus and Moslems, while sharing many of the same interests and aspirations of white pupils are at the same time determined to retain their involvement in the richness of their own minority cultures. Cultural pluralism, then, implies a system that accepts that people's lifestyles and values are different and operates so as to allow equality of opportunity for all to play a full part in society.

The changed awareness of what the objectives of a multiracial society might be has arisen from the fact that to be black or brown or yellow in a predominantly white society is to be different from the majority.[1] Furthermore that awareness has been strengthened by frustrations borne of racial prejudice and discrimination in various sectors of life. The most powerful drive, Bolton believes, has come from the growing knowledge that a person needs to be secure in his own culture and to see that culture respected by others. Only then can he become a confident and competent member in a new society.

What does cultural pluralism involve, in practice? Bolton identifies a variety of complex issues ranging from the problems of adaptation facing Moslem, Hindu and Sikh communities, to the dauntingly difficult task facing young people of Caribbean origin – the creating of a recognizable and homogeneous cultural identity. In educational terms, cultural pluralism involves broadening the content of the curriculum and teaching about race and race relations to all pupils, as well as catering for the educational needs of some minority groups. Above all else, cultural pluralism involves changes on the part of the majority society in its attitudes and practices towards minority groups. Bolton's final comments are directed to teachers:

> 'The complexity of the educational and social issues involved gives teachers a very onerous and difficult task to perform – a task most of them were not prepared for in their teacher training nor in their own experiences of life. It is easy for society to lay the problem down at the door of education and leave it there, but if teachers are to tackle the changes of attitude, practice and approach demanded, they deserve the support and understanding of society.'

ETHNIC MINORITY GROUPS IN BRITAIN

One reason[2] why the Department of Education and Science failed to appreciate fully the difficulties faced by schools with large numbers of pupils from ethnic minority groups was that until 1974 the definition of '*immigrant*' used in making official returns tended to give a distorted picture of the true situation since it did not include children of minority ethnic groups whose families had been resident in Britain for some time but who nonetheless suffered from the same disadvantages as those who fell within the definition of *immigrant*. The results, Hill[2] says, is that the size of the true problem has been underestimated and many children's education has suffered through lack of materials and staff both of which might have been forthcoming had the real picture been more fully appreciated. Like Hill therefore, we use the term *ethnic minority group* in preference to *immigrant* because it enables us to identify a wider group of children whose interests must be considered in any discussion of multicultural education.

But what are the facts?* The three largest ethnic minority groups in Britain are West Indian, Indian and Pakistani. For the most part they are concentrated in urban areas, more than half living in the poorer districts of our ten largest cities. In the section that follows we present brief portrayals of these three (and other) ethnic minority groups. Our account draws on the descriptions in Hill[2] Chapter 2, and de Lobo[3] Chapter 1.

The West Indian

Box 8.1 shows the islands of the Antillean archipelago which together with British Honduras in North America and Guyana in South America, comprise the British Caribbean, commonly referred to as the West Indies.

During the 1950s and 60s when expanding British industry was suffering from serious manpower shortages, many low-paid, physically-arduous jobs whose anti-social hours were unattractive to English workers were filled by immigrant labour from the West Indies. There was a steady influx from the British Caribbean until the 1960s when threats of immigration control caused the flow of West Indians to rise dramatically. In 1971 it was estimated that the number of West Indian people living in Britain was just over 1 % of the total population, a proportion that has remained stable in recent years. At the present time, the number of West Indian-born people leaving Britain exceeds the number of those entering.

Constituting the largest ethnic minority group in Britain, most of the West Indian work force is unskilled or semi-skilled and located in the transport and building trade industries. Many West Indian women are found in service and catering industries and in hospital work. Because of the nature of their employment, West Indians, like other minority ethnic groups, are almost exclusively concentrated in urban areas.

The present West Indian community in the United Kingdom consists of two distinct groups; – those born and educated in the British Caribbean and those who were born or have spent most of their lives here in Britain. This latter group, the bigger of the two, poses some difficulties over nomenclature. What are we to call them? Clearly they are British and not West Indian. For the purposes of our present discussion however, we need to be able to identify them as an ethnic minority group. Various names have been suggested – 'black Britons', 'second-generation West Indians', 'children of West Indian origin' etc.

---

* Precise statistics are difficult to come by. de Lobo (1978) cites a *Sunday Times* (January 1977) breakdown which gave the following information:

The numbers of people who live in Britain who are immigrants is in the region of nearly three million. Of these, about half are white immigrants who have come from Europe, the White Commonwealth and Ireland. The other half have come from the New Commonwealth countries of Asia and Africa, and from countries throughout South East Asia where 'overseas Chinese' have settled. Recent figures show 615 000 Irish; 265 000 Mediterranean Europeans; Asians 618 000; West Indians 236 000; Africans 30 000; Chinese 81 000.

BOX 8.1

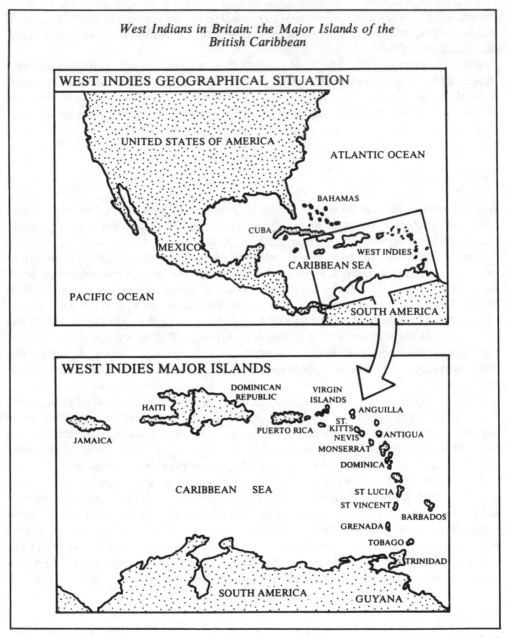

West Indians in Britain: the Major Islands of the British Caribbean

WEST INDIES GEOGRAPHICAL SITUATION

UNITED STATES OF AMERICA

ATLANTIC OCEAN

BAHAMAS

CUBA

MEXICO

WEST INDIES

CARIBBEAN SEA

PACIFIC OCEAN

SOUTH AMERICA

WEST INDIES MAJOR ISLANDS

DOMINICAN REPUBLIC

VIRGIN ISLANDS

HAITI

ANGUILLA

ST. KITTS

PUERTO RICA

NEVIS

ANTIGUA

JAMAICA

MONSERRAT

DOMINICA

CARIBBEAN   SEA

ST LUCIA

ST VINCENT

BARBADOS

GRENADA

TOBAGO

TRINIDAD

SOUTH AMERICA   GUYANA

Source: adapted from Hill[2]

Because many of the cultural and linguistic differences that we shall touch upon are directly attributable to their Caribbean heritage we shall settle for the name 'West Indian', keeping in mind however the inaccuracy that this label represents.

It might be supposed that because West Indians share our language, our faith and our culture they would experience less difficulty in coming to terms with British society than say, Indian or Pakistani immigrants. For a variety of reasons this has not been the case, particularly in respect of West Indian children in our schools. Hill[2] and Bagley[4] provide useful background information on Caribbean life and culture that helps us understand factors connected with West Indian underachievement in school.

Noting the richness and variety in the customs and social organization of the many separate societies that go to make up the British Caribbean, Hill says that it is still possible to identify elements in the Creole* culture that arose out of a common experience of colonialism, slavery, and the plantation system. The strong adherence to European culture and a white ruling class ensured that this European element of Creole culture became the most highly valued. The 'white bias' that characterizes Caribbean society even today accounts to a considerable extent for West Indian immigrants' orientation towards British society and their aspirations to be part of it. Bagley[4] describes a rigid stratification system in Jamaica which motivates many black rural Jamaicans to come to Britain to escape from a society in which white, oriental, and fair people have power and privilege. It is pertinent to consider the background and educational aspirations of this group of immigrants in understanding the problems that their children face in British schools. The power of the European 'model' and European 'ways' still plays such a powerful part in West Indian psychology that often it can lead to a rejection of all that is West Indian. Such self-rejection produces low feelings of self-worth which affect subsequent attitudes and behaviour.

Turning to the West Indian family, the conjugal and marital roles forced upon plantation slaves helps explain why even today, the West Indian family may still retain certain features of their ancestors' life of servitude. A high incidence of illegitimate births, the occurrence of many broken families and children of varied parentage are, according to Hill, part of the legacy of slavery, although he goes on to note recent research that shows West Indian family relationships as much more stabilized than hitherto, largely due to the increasing tendency of West Indian immigrants to arrive in Britain as family units, an event distinctly different from their earlier migration patterns.

The Indian

The Indians, who constitute the second largest ethnic minority group in Britain, can be divided into two separate occupational groupings, professionals such as doctors, teachers, businessmen etc. who originate from all parts of India and are distributed all over the United Kingdom, and semi-skilled or unskilled workers, originating largely from the rural Punjab or from Gujarat (see Box 8.2), and now located in a small number of our major cities. Members of this latter Indian group may speak Punjabi, Gujarati, Tamil, or other Indian languages and practise Hinduism or Sikhism, with a minority following the

---

* *Creoles* are persons of Negro, White, or Negro/White ancestry, born in the Caribbean.[2]

Creole is a separate language in its own right. In Jamaica, Creole has a West African syntax, with mixed African, Spanish, French, Dutch and English vocabulary.[4]

BOX 8.2

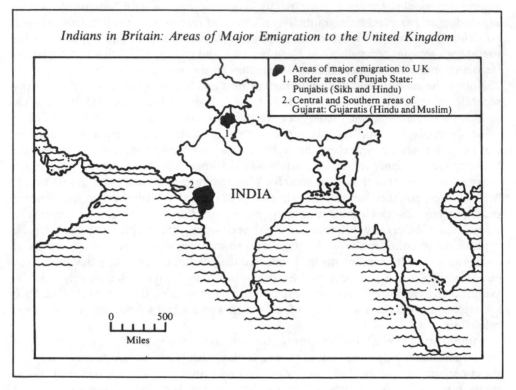

Indians in Britain: Areas of Major Emigration to the United Kingdom

Areas of major emigration to UK
1. Border areas of Punjab State: Punjabis (Sikh and Hindu)
2. Central and Southern areas of Gujarat: Gujaratis (Hindu and Muslim)

INDIA

0   500
Miles

Source: adapted from Hill[2]

teachings of Islam or of Christianity. Social activities among this largest, manual-occupational category of Indian immigrants are almost exclusively restricted to their own ethnic groups; arranged marriages are common and little mixing of the sexes occurs. Indian family structure is of the extended type and is founded on stable conjugal unions. The various members of the family fulfil traditional roles, the father, for example, exercising strong control as authority figure. Compared with the average British family, the Indian family is generally larger and more complex, making greater demands on each of its members but at the same time offering each member greater benefits. In its organization, the Indian family is distinctly different from the English nuclear family. The individual Indian, Hill observes, perceives himself surrounded not by concentric circles containing wives and children, close friends and acquaintances but by his immediate family (which includes all his brothers and sisters as well as his own children), then by kin, including distant relatives, then by members of his village and finally by his linguistic group. Since many Indians are accustomed to living surrounded by their kinsmen, it is understandable that they should try to recreate a similar environment in Britain by setting up small communities in the style of the old country. The head of an Indian family is the eldest male and it is he who makes the major decisions. Thus, the head of many Indian families living in Britain may well be a grandfather domiciled in India. The whole scale of relationships in the Indian joint family, Hill observes, is very different from that in the typical nuclear family in England. Clearly, frustrations and difficulties occur when Indians living in Britain try to copy the nuclear family units of their English neighbours but at the same time retain aspects of the joint family organization that they have been used to. And yet, as economic conditions change, it may well be that the smaller nuclear families that are the norm in contemporary Britain are more able through their size and mobility to take advantage of economic opportunities are they arise.

The Pakistani

Until 1972 Pakistan consisted of two widely-separated parts of the Indian sub-continent known as West and East Pakistan. Nowadays West Pakistan constitutes the Republic of Pakistan and East Pakistan the independent state of Bangladesh. Box 8.3 shows the two countries separated by some thousand miles of Indian territory. Purely for purposes of exposition, we follow Hill and consider Pakistan and Bangladesh together, referring to immigrants from these countries as Pakistani, bearing in mind nonetheless that the distinction between Pakistanis and Bangladeshis cannot be ignored in any real sense.

BOX 8.3

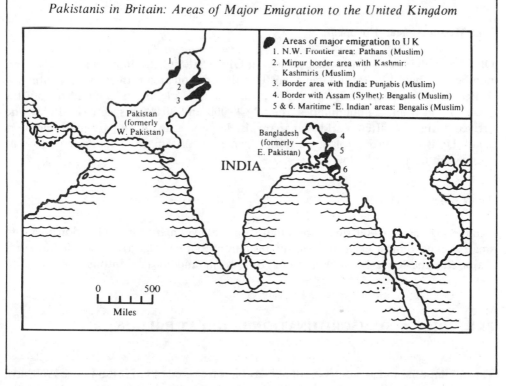

Pakistanis in Britain: Areas of Major Emigration to the United Kingdom

Areas of major emigration to UK
1. N.W. Frontier area: Pathans (Muslim)
2. Mirpur border area with Kashmir: Kashmiris (Muslim)
3. Border area with India: Punjabis (Muslim)
4. Border with Assam (Sylhet): Bengalis (Muslim)
5 & 6. Maritime 'E. Indian' areas: Bengalis (Muslim)

Pakistan (formerly W. Pakistan)

Bangladesh (formerly E. Pakistan)

INDIA

0 500 Miles

Source: adapted from Hill[2]

Most Pakistani immigrants to Britain come from the northern part of Pakistan and Bangladesh, both of these areas being characterized by similar systems of agrarian land tenure and family organization. The great majority of immigrants from such village communities have had little or no formal education. Like the larger Indian immigrant group, the Pakistanis are found in unskilled and semi-skilled occupations in Britain. The Pakistanis, Hill points out, are the closest knit group of immigrants in the United Kingdom. Men wear Western dress but the women retain their traditional costumes. Sexual segregation is strictly enforced, women rarely being allowed out to work. Pakistanis are Moslem by religion and religious observances are rigorously adhered to. Urdu and Bengali are the usual languages spoken at home. Social interaction is almost exclusively limited to their own ethnic group.

With such knowledge of Pakistani immigrants in mind, it is not difficult to see why family and kinship groups serve as the focal point of virtually all areas of social interaction. This extended family, says Hill, crosses over several generations and extends horizontally to take in all male descendants in the father's line in a complex system of reciprocal relationships and obligations. This complicated patterning in the extended family serves specific economic functions for when work is scarce in Pakistan, it is then that fathers and sons may be despatched further afield to find alternative opportunities. In such circumstances, Hill notes, the 'nuclear family' is always dependent on the support of the larger group. In consequence, strong sanctions operate to subject the will of individuals to the collective needs of the group.

The Mediterranean Europeans

Of the mediterranean immigrant groups to Great Britain, the Italians are the largest, numbering about 108 000 and living mostly in the London area with one large contingent in Bedfordshire. Some 75 000 Greek-Cypriots also live mainly in London; so too, the Spanish and Maltese communities, roughly 49 000 and 30 000 respectively. Poles who arrived during and after World War II are also largely settled in and around London. A small Hungarian group of some 16 000 came to Britain in the aftermath of the Hungarian uprising of 1956.

The Chinese

Numbering about 60 000, this ethnic minority group lives mainly in the London area with small groups, almost exclusively in the restaurant and catering trade, located in every major city and town. Most came from Hong Kong and speak Cantonese.

PREJUDICE AND DISCRIMINATION IN GREAT BRITAIN

Various national and local surveys of public opinion carried out in Britain since 1960 have demonstrated the extent of prejudiced attitudes towards ethnic minorities. One of the most substantial surveys was undertaken for the Survey of Race Relations in Britain by Abrams[5] and further analysed by Schaffer[6] and Bagley.[7] Box 8.4 reports Bagley's analysis of data collected from almost 2500 white adults in five areas of high immigration (Lambeth, Ealing, Wolverhampton, Nottingham and Bradford).

BOX 8.4

	ITEM	RESPONSE	Percentage Agreeing
A.	Suppose there are two workers, one coloured and one white, who do exactly the same work. If one, and only one, had to be declared redundant, should it be the coloured or the white worker?	*Sack the coloured worker*	38 %
B.	Suppose there are two workers, one coloured and one white, who do exactly the same work. If one, and only one, had to be promoted, should it be the coloured or the white worker?	*Promote the white worker*	37 %
C.	Do you think the majority of coloured people in Britain are superior, equal or inferior to you?	*Coloured people are inferior*	52 %
D.	Do you think coloured people should be let into Britain to settle on the same basis as other people from abroad, or should there be special regulations for coloured people?	*Discriminatory regulations for entry to Britain*	52 %
E.	Do you feel more or less sympathetic towards coloured immigrants than about white people who live in similar conditions?	*Lack of sympathy for coloured people*	30 %
F.	There are various things that coloured people who have come to Britain could do to improve their own position. What do you think they should do? (Responses were coded for *hostility*)	*Hostile comments about coloured people*	37 %

Proportion of the Population Displaying Different Kinds of Prejudice

Source: adapted from Bagley and Verma[8]

Why should there be such pronounced hostility towards coloured ethnic minorities? What are the origins of such prejudice and discrimination?

Racial Attitudes and the Colonial Tradition[9]

Kiernan[10] argues that the racist values which permeated British colonialism in Africa, Asia, and America are part of a broad European tradition which portrayed Western Christian man as 'the lord of human kind.' Bagley and his associates[11] however, propose that the British tradition in racism has peculiar features not shared with other European powers. As 'offshore islanders', they say, the English had long considered themselves to be a chosen race. The intellectual system which underpinned British colonial racism, Bagley and his colleagues assert, is so massive that it is difficult to know where to begin in documenting it. But begin they do, drawing on sources as varied as the Encyclopaedia Britannica, children's comics, and the historical research of Walvin[12] and Shyllon.[13]

Our attitudes towards coloured people, they say, have remained largely unchanged for the past four hundred years. Furthermore, they assert, our racist assumptions are institutionalized in our language, in policies, and in the practices of government, commerce and education. Racist ideas and assumptions, they conclude, are deeply rooted in British life and thought at all levels.

The Transmission of Racism through the Mass Media and Children's Literature

Pejorative images of ethnic minorities and beliefs in British superiority are transmitted by the mass media at adults and children and are continuously reinforced in newspapers, books, and comics. Hartmann and Husband[14] show how assumptions of British racial superiority are transmitted and strengthened by the media – the press, television, radio, and cinema. And while overtly racist textbooks have disappeared from school classrooms, a newer generation of primers, according to Jeffcoate[15], still present:

> 'demeaning stereotypes of black people in junior school text books in "children of other lands". There are history and geography books published in the last five years (i.e. since 1970) which are disfigured by racial and ethnic bias, and too many publishers have suggested by their practice that the token inclusion of a solitary black in the background of illustrations absolves them from further responsibilities.'

In children's comics and storybooks, Bagley and his associates allege, racist images abound; valiant British heroes still fight and win against enormous odds in battles with treacherous natives in darkest Africa. The extent of such racial stereotyping is well documented by Dummett[16], Laishley[17] and Milner.[18]

Socialization and Racial Attitudes

A burgeoning literature of child development research shows that the ways in which parents rear their children lead to the development of personality and attitudinal characteristics in their offspring. One recent study[11] argues that fathers' authoritarianism and rigid methods of child rearing lead to poor self-esteem in children and, in consequence, to the emergence of attitudinal rigidity and prejudiced views as ways of coping with feelings of low self-worth. Using correlational techniques, Bagley and his associates[11] propose that father's authoritarianism is associated both with son's poor self-esteem and with the amount of racism that the son displays. Their findings are mapped out in Box 8.5.

BOX 8.5

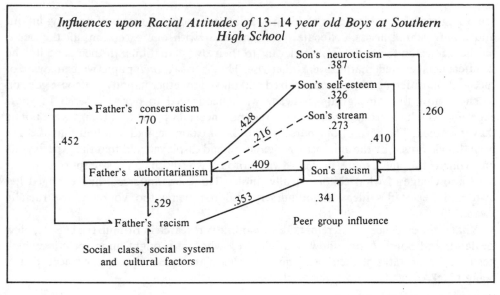

Influences upon Racial Attitudes of 13–14 *year old Boys at Southern High School*

In Box 8.5 the unbroken lines represent hypothetical causal relationships, or patterns of mutual influence. Thus, father's authoritarianism is strongly associated (r = .770) with his conservatism, and with his racism (r = .529). Father's authoritarianism correlates significantly with son's self-esteem. This correlation (r = .428) is stronger than the correlation between father's racism and son's racism (r = .353), suggesting, Bagley argues, that the father's main pattern of influence is via his effect on his son's self-esteem. Clearly other factors, too, influence son's racial attitudes, including peer group influence (r = .341). This latter variable was measured by obtaining the average level of prejudice in the remaining students in the subject's classroom. The path analysis in Box 8.5 also shows that father's authoritarianism correlates with son's stream (r = .216), that is, the academic stream in which the subject is placed at secondary school. This latter finding is in line with those of Miller[19] and Banks and Finlayson[20] on the role of parental authoritarianism in the underachievement of children in secondary schools.

It is important to remember that in correlational studies such as Bagley's direct causal patterns of relationships cannot be deduced. Nevertheless, the technique does permit the researchers to indulge in some fruitful speculation about the possible influences on son's racism. Using a method called multiple regression analysis in which all of the variables are controlled on one another to see which ones have the strongest effect upon the criterion measure (son's racism) the researchers were able to identify *father's authoritarianism*, *son's self-esteem*, and *peer group values* as the ones which remain significant predictors of racial attitudes. They concluded that although father's racist attitudes have a significant connection, probably causal, with his son's attitudes, it is father's authoritarianism that seems to be a major factor to the extent that it influences his son's self-esteem. Boys with poor self-esteem are particularly likely to be prejudiced.

Children's Racial Attitudes

Outlining research evidence on children's racial attitudes to a group of nursery, infant, and junior school heads, Jeffcoate[21] recounts that with one exception, all the head-teachers rejected the findings as irrelevant to their own situations. In their schools, the headteachers insisted, matters were otherwise. That is to say, *their* pupils were unaware of race and the different ethnic groups mixed and played together happily. Jeffcoate goes on to show how the same group of heads was encouraged to devise a series of short experiments which brought home to them in no uncertain terms that things were not as they imagined. The head of one nursery school, for example, had to admit that she had been 'bowled over' by the animosity her children had displayed and that the experiments underlined the fact that, in her own words, 'we teach on assumptions rather than knowledge of what children really think'. This, she confessed, had changed her own and her staff's ideas about nursery children being too young to be racially aware.

What is the evidence? With remarkable unanimity, research in Britain, the U.S.A., New Zealand, and South Africa shows that children who are brought up in societies which bestow inferior status on their racial minorities learn about the relative worth accorded to being black or white from a very early age.

'The dawning of racial awareness at around three is accompanied, or quickly followed, by simple signs of racial preference and rejection, and even five year olds are capable of commenting on the different social and economic roles fulfilled by different racial groups. The net outcome in a country like Britain is that white children will be predisposed to pejorative views of minority races which by the age of eleven or twelve may well have accommodated the familiar array of adult prejudices and stereotypes; and that black and Asian children will be predisposed to ambivalence about their racial selves which may, at worst, degenerate into self-denial, identity conflict, and personality disorder.'[21]

Support for Jeffcoate's assertion of early racial preferences and rejections comes from a large scale survey[22] of pupils' attitudes to multiracial education in Britain involving over 3500 boys and girls from eight to fourteen years of age drawn from British, Indian, Pakistani, West Indian, Kenyan, Asian, Cypriot, and Italian groups. The most striking feature of the survey data was the high incidence of *own group preference* among the older children. Another important finding was the relatively early age (8 +) at which ethnicity featured in friendship choices. In light of the research findings referred to earlier, one suspects that had the NFER researchers included children younger than eight in their sample, then racial preferences and rejections could have been demonstrated at an even earlier age.

Jeffcoate's experimental findings stand in stark contrast to the conclusions reported in the Department of Education and Science Report: *Education Survey 13, The Education of Immigrants*. There, the view is expressed that:

'There seems to be little evidence of prejudice among young children who mix together happily and unselfconsciously despite their evident awareness of differences in colour.'[23]

Box 8.6 identifies some of the comments made by ten and eleven year old white pupils when asked to respond to photographs of the Southall Sikh community in such everyday contexts as the school, the home, the temple, and in shops.

BOX 8.6

Attitudes of White Ten and Eleven Year Olds to Racial Minorities

'I think that it is not right for all them black people to come over and take over shops and things. When I go to town I see more black people taking over stores than white people. I think black people are trying to take over the country.'

'Some day I think that the coloured people are going to take over Britain and the white people will disintegrate.'

'Black people should be sent back because soon the country will be full and there will be no room for us.'

Among all the hostile statements one stood out for its virulence:
'Black people should not be allowed in England because England is meant for whites. England is nearly full of black people. They should be thrown out of England. Black people are funny at weddings. They have to walk round a Koran four times and I think it is very funny. There should only be white people and no more blacks left in England any longer. It is meant for white people only. White people invented more things than blacks so we should have England for whites only . . . Blacks do some of the most queerest things you ever known. They are even putting black people on telly and whites invented it so only whites should go on the telly. It is not right to have black people on the telly even in England.'

Source: adapted from Jeffcoate.[21]

In contrast to Jeffcoate's plea for a planned and systematic attack on racism by the development and implementation of a multiracial curriculum, the DES Document *The Education of Immigrants*[23] argues that:

'There are positive things that schools can do in face of the need to prepare pupils for life in a multi-racial society. This certainly does not call for direct teaching in primary schools and probably not in secondary schools.'

However, Department of Education and Science thinking has changed since *Education Survey 13* was issued in 1971. Implicit in the DES Green Paper *Education in Schools: A Consultative Document* 1977[24] is the view that if we are to avoid racial hostility and promote racial harmony instead, then we must not only meet the special needs of minority groups but also actively influence the attitudes of all teachers, pupils and the host society by encouraging positive attitudes towards cultural and ethnic minorities.

THE EVIDENCE OF UNDERACHIEVEMENT

'Scientific racists', according to Pettigrew[25] assert that differences between black and white in learning ability or intelligence are biological in origin and not, as others would argue, due to social constraints on achievement or differences in motivation. Jensen[26], one of the leading exponents of ethnic differences in intelligence proposes that there are two different types of learning ability which he identifies as Level I and Level II, corresponding roughly to rote learning and conceptual learning respectively. Moreover, while Level I is distributed *similarly* in different populations, Level II is distributed *differently*. According to Jensen, children with white faces have the monopoly of Level II ability. That is to say, blacks are good at rote learning alone, whites are good at both rote and conceptual learning.

Not surprisingly, the ideas of Jensen in America and those of his counterpart, Eysenck,[27] in Britain, have provoked an acrimonious and continuing debate. Both British[28] and American[29] studies have demonstrated that when groups of children are given the opportunity to learn fairly complex concepts from scratch, different ethnic groups achieve similarly. Jensen[30] has returned to the fray recently with a research report directed at those of his many critics who have decried the bias in the design of mental tests which favours the performance of white middle-class children.

His conclusions can be summed up simply:

'If we take bias to mean that the same test for blacks and whites is actually measuring different things, then it is impossible to show that such bias exists. In other words, the differences between blacks and whites in whatever the tests measure are genuine.'[31]

Equally, the responses of Jensen's critics can be simply put: the fact that differences exist between blacks and whites on the same test requires serious study by educationalists because it highlights certain disadvantages among some groups with respect to basic cognitive skills on which the process of education depends. But such differences prove nothing about their genetic origins.

Summarizing the arguments against Jensen's thesis, Bynner[31] identifies three basic objections.

First, there is the biological argument. Jensen defines intelligence in two distinct ways which he then proceeds to equate. The first is biological: the capacity to adapt behaviour. The second is psychological: the capacity for abstract reasoning and problem-solving, involving the use of language and symbols. The biological argument can be used to distinguish between species in terms of their intelligence: thus chimpanzees are more intelligent than rabbits. Clearly these differences in intelligence do have a genetic origin. But to go on from this to say that differences within a species with regard to problem-solving and abstract reasoning must have a genetic base is far more difficult to justify. Can we really talk about 'bright' goldfish and 'dull' goldfish? Language, that distinctive feature of humans that sets them apart from any other species is a remarkably complex skill that is mastered with relative ease by virtually every member of the species. The application of this skill in the development of those activities with which mental tests are concerned need not have any genetic origins at all.

Secondly Jensen's case depends upon amassing evidence for 'isolating' from mental test performances what amounts to a quality of pure reasoning, 'g'. This quality is thought to reside in people independently of any environmental influences to which they are subjected and to correlate only with physical, i.e. genetically-determined attributes. Bynner is critical of Jensen's out-of-date research methods and his attempts to isolate 'g'. Jensen ignores more recent techniques which enable the researcher to test *any* model of the structure of a set of abilities, for example, one ability leading to another rather than them both being caused by something else – 'g'.

Finally, given that differences in test scores between races exist, there are two equally plausible theories to account for them: the *hereditary* and the *environmental* with a range of positions between them. In the absence of total experimental control over human mating, reproduction and development, there is no entirely satisfactory test that can adjudicate between them. Jensen believes in the importance of an inherited component in intellectual capacity. He directs his energies to determining the boundaries it sets on intellectual growth and bases his educational prescriptions on the use of tests to select individuals for appropriate educational environments. In contrast, a psychologist like Hunt, believing in the modifiability of human potential in response to the environment from conception onwards devotes his research to isolating those features in the environment that restrict intellectual growth and devises educational experiences that will enhance it. Nowhere in Jensen's book is there any serious examination of the evidence that fits this alternative perspective which provides just as plausible an explanation of the evidence as he himself presents. Ultimately, says Bynner, it comes down to a distinction between the pessimists and the optimists about human potential.

The evidence for the underachievement of black ethnic minority groups in British schools (in particular, children of West Indian heritage) draws upon two types of study both of which, according to Bagley[4] are marred by lack of adequate controls.

The first type, employing conventional, individually-administered psychometric tests generally fails to control for 'race-of-tester' effect, the second, using group tests or teachers' assessments does not take account of problems inherent in group test situations or of the labelling effect whereby teachers' expectations may be self-confirming. The nub of Bagley's argument is that in respect of both types of research it is *social disadvantage* rather than *race* that is the major factor in West Indian underachievement. What do these studies show?

Work undertaken by Houghton[32] in 1966 which compared the IQ levels of English and West Indian pupils in a disadvantaged urban setting showed that black and white intelligence quotients were similar and both groups' performances were depressed relative to the national norms for the particular test that was used. Significantly lower mean IQ scores for West Indian children in London schools were reported in a study by McFie and Thompson[33] who found an 11-point IQ difference between English and West Indian children and by Yule et al[34] who showed a 14-point difference on a verbal measure of intelligence when comparing English and West Indian pupils.

The first large scale study[35] to demonstrate West Indian underachievement was undertaken by the Research and Statistics Unit of the Inner London Education Authority in 1968. Subsequent research[36] for ILEA which avoided the criticism that teachers' estimates introduced bias into test results nevertheless demonstrated significant under-achievement among West Indian children and showed that even with full education in England, the performance of West Indian pupils was significantly inferior to that of indigenous white children. Early intervention programmes at the pre-school level which introduced a range of cognitive and social activities involving parents and children were among a number of recommended ways of dealing with West Indian under-achievement.[37] However, it was doubted[38] that such programmes in themselves would be able to ameliorate the declining academic achievement of West Indian pupils in London schools within the age range of eight to fifteen years.

Understandably, achievement statistics comparing the performance of so-called immigrant and non-immigrant children in British schools have become a 'hot' political issue, and in consequence, increasingly difficult to come by. That is why the recent research of Driver[39] received so much publicity and comment. Briefly, Driver's study of some 2300 school leavers in five multiracial secondary schools (two in the North, two in the Midlands, and one in the Home Counties) argues that the accepted wisdom of underachievement among West Indian pupils is simply not true. His evidence shows that 'West Inidan girls and boys achieved results that were, for the most part, *better* than those obtained by English boys and girls'. Part of Driver's evidence is summarized in Box 8.7. There, we are given the performance in all subjects averaged for all pupils who were registered as members of the two year course leading to CSE and O-level examinations. What stands out in these results, Driver says, is the drastic difference between the girls from the two ethnic categories. As a quick way of taking in the findings shown in Box 8.7, count the 'firsts' in each row. It will be seen that the rank orders for boys and girls run in different directions for blacks and whites. West Indian girls far excel West Indian boys whereas English boys excel (though not so dramatically) English girls.

BOX 8.7

Rank Order For Overall Achievement in 16 Plus Examinations									
School	A	A	A	B	B	C	C	D	E	E
Leaving year	1	2	3	4	5	6	7	8–10	11	12
	(1975)	(1976)	(1977)	(1976)	(1977)	(1976)	(1977)	(75–77)	(1977)	(1977)
West Indian boys	4	1	3	2	2	3	1	=3	4	2
West Indian girls	1	3	1	1	1	1	4	=3	3	1
English boys	2	2	2	3	3	4	3	1	1	4
English girls	3	4	4	4	4	2	2	2	2	3

Source: Driver[39]

Driver's explanation of these findings runs as follows: the contrapuntal trend in performance for English boys and girls and West Indian boys and girls implies that the opportunities and resources available to young adults in the two ethnic contexts are quite distinct. Driver draws upon studies carried out in the West Indies to argue that West Indians' experience before migration helps shape how they structure their current father/mother/child relationships and how they bring up their children to understand their responsibilities to others. Briefly, economic and social conditions, particularly in rural Jamaica, make for the concentration of power, property and decision-making in the hands of older women whose daughters may depend upon them for shelter and sustenance in raising their own children. On arrival in Britain, Driver notes, it is women rather than their husbands or brothers who are 'the guardians of their family's good name and the providers of its staple income.' Moreover the centrality of the woman's role has been strengthened by the high rate of unemployment particularly among unskilled West Indian men, serving to reinforce the previous patterns of family organization in which adult males are pushed into domestic marginality. Small wonder then, Driver comments, that West Indian girls in school achieve as they do, and conversely, West Indian boys fail to achieve. This contemporary situation in many West Indian families is contrasted with the commonly-held assumption in the majority of working class English homes that daughters do not merit encouragement at school but should be married off before becoming an economic liability to their parents. Lack of encouragement, Driver argues, is reflected in English girls' school achievement. This then, is Driver's basic thesis.

Driver's study has become something of a *cause célèbre* and has been criticized on several grounds: first, one must ask of research proclaiming that West Indian girls do better at school, better than whom? The answer seems to be better than their white schoolfellows in run down city areas. Driver appears to be comparing a broad cross section of black children with a very narrow range of unskilled working class white children. Second, Driver indulges in a chain of speculation about matrifocal family structures in Jamaica and equates these with their urban, black British (not necessarily ex-Jamaican) counterparts without any hard evidence to back up his thesis. Third, the superior achievement of Jamaican girls over boys has been well documented in studies originating in the West Indies.[40]

As one observer[41] writes, it could well be that the generation on whom that work was conducted became the parents to Driver's current school leavers in Britain. Far from being surprised at their daughters success, they might well have expected more than the average level of CSE results that Driver reports.

Finally, as another correspondent[42] observes, West Indian underachievement certainly exists but it may not be due to ethnicity *per se*; rather its origins may lie in institutional racism and in teacher prejudices. We take up the question of teacher expectations and self-fulfilling prophecies later in the chapter.

ETHNIC MINORITY PARENTS AND THE SCHOOL

In a society where racial hostility rather than racial harmony is all too frequently present, the degree of understanding that exists between schools and ethnic minority parents is of crucial importance. It is self-evident that teachers should have accurate knowledge about the expectations that immigrant parents hold for our education system and what it can do for their children. But this raises some difficulties for teachers who are predominantly white, middle-class, and largely inculcated with an ethnocentric view of the world. Although there is an increasing amount of literature available to teachers about the cultures and lifestyles of ethnic minority groups, very little is known about the hopes and expectations that immigrant parents have of the school system in which their children are educated.

A recent study[43] involving interviews with some 700 ethnic minority parents provides timely information that calls into question a number of commonly-held beliefs about immigrant parents' attitudes towards their children's education. Thus, the research found little evidence to support the view that West Indian parents are largely apathetic about visiting their children's schools or that all Asian parents want their sons and daughters to enter professional occupations. Rather, ethnic minority parents, despite the different colonial educational backgrounds from which they come, expect from the English educational system broadly what indigenous parents expect. That is, they expect schools to teach their children in a controlled, orderly, non-racist environment and to equip them with skills and qualifications that will enable them to obtain, at the very least, respectable manual working class jobs and not slip into unemployment and 'disadvantage'.[43] Some, but by no means all, ethnic minority parents hope that their children will be socially mobile into white collar and professional occupations and they expect their children to be given opportunity for mobility and success through the public examinations system. Some of the comparative data from the study are shown in Box 8.8.

Where there were dissatisfactions among ethnic minority parents with their children's schooling, their uneasiness arose both from perceived differences between the English

BOX 8.8

West Indian, Asian, and 'British' Parents and the School

(A) *Parents visit to school in last six months*

	West Indian %	Asian %	'British' %
Have not been	21	31	11
Saw teacher	47	50	48
Saw headteacher	22	15	20
Saw both	9	4	20
Saw careers officer	1	0	1
	100	100	100
	(n = 285)	(n = 202)	(n = 92)

(B) *Reason for school visit (those who had been)*

	West Indian %	Asian %	'British' %
Parent's evening/open day	54	56	53
See child's work	10	13	3
General progress	21	21	29
Academic problem	1	2	3
Discipline problem	6	0	4
Attendance/illness	2	1	2
Can't remember/other	6	6	6
	100	100	100
	(n = 225)	(n = 140)	(n = 92)

(C) *Parental satisfaction with schools*

	West Indian %	Asian %	'British' %
Children doing well/good reports	77	56	64
Good teachers	11	11	22
Regular schooling	5	16	6
Happy at school	4	8	0
Not held back by coloured children	0	0	4
Other	3	9	4
	100	100	100
	(n = 212)	(n = 165)	(n = 63)

Source: adapted from Tomlinson[43]

education system and the overseas education they themselves had received, and from genuine feelings that the English education offered to their children was deficient. The following comments of Asian and West Indian parents show that their concerns were with discipline, curriculum content and teaching methods:[43]

> . . . the teaching here is different. In India children are made to learn, here the teachers are not strict enough. (Indian parent)

> . . . they don't teach him enough about Britain. When I was at school I learned the history and geography of Britain. (West Indian parent)

> . . . my children have only learned to draw pictures. They can't read or write yet. (Pakistani parent)

The research was able to identify what ethnic minority parents meant when they spoke of '*good*' teachers. They had in mind teachers who 'got down to the business of teaching literacy and numeracy in the primary schools, and subjects leading to exam qualifications in the secondary schools'. They preferred teachers who 'pushed' their children but who were at the same time kind and 'non-racist'. Ethnic minority parents, the research reports, were very much aware of the discrimination that their children faced in seeking employment after school and therefore placed great faith in the acquisition of educational qualifications to overcome this disadvantage. And here, it was suggested, ethnic minority parents depended far more on teachers than did 'British' parents for information about which courses were appropriate and which qualifications led to which particular jobs. It is to the employment problems of school leavers from ethnic minority backgrounds that we now turn.

ASPIRATIONS VERSUS OPPORTUNITIES: A CASE STUDY

A growing number of studies[44] show the extent to which young people from ethnic minority groups are disadvantaged in the transition from school to work. It is not our intention here to deal in any depth with the many social and economic issues with which these studies are concerned. Rather, we describe the findings of a recent study to do with Asian youngsters leaving schools in the West Midlands and seeking employment there. This particular project touches upon a number of themes that are relevant to our overall concern with prejudice and discrimination. Brooks and Singh,[45] the researchers, used questionnaire and interview methods with random samples of white and Asian school leavers as well as contacting career teachers and Careers Advisory Services in the area. Four strands of a recurrent theme in immigrant job-opportunity studies run through their report. First, Asian school leavers are more likely to be found in *secondary sector** rather

---

* *Primary sector* and *secondary sector* are terms used in *dual labour market theory*. Briefly, jobs in the *primary sector* enjoy the following characteristics: high wages, good working conditions, employment stability, chances of advancement, equality, and are administered by work rules. Jobs in the *secondary sector*, in contrast, tend to have low wages and fringe benefits, poor working conditions, high labour turnover, little chance of advancement and are often governed by arbitrary and capricious supervision.[46] The concepts of primary and secondary sector jobs are best seen as 'ideal types'.

than *primary sector jobs* and this is particularly the case with Asian girls. Second, Asian school leavers (like other ethnic minority groups) are culturally disadvantaged in both a *racial* and a *class* sense. Recruitment decisions by employers are explicable in terms of 'queue theory' – in short, racial assumptions 'push' Asian (and other black) applicants to the back of the queue. Asian school leavers, particularly girls, are likely to be found in secondary sector jobs for reasons that are to a considerable degree racist. Third, white working class school leavers, according to Brooks and Singh, are socialized into 'realistic' (i.e. attainable) job aspirations within the context of the local labour market. On the other hand, Asian school leavers, despite an English or largely English formal education, have undergone a very different socialization in which their aspirations have been moulded differently. This leads the researchers to their fourth point (and one, incidentally, that is at variance with Tomlinson's findings discussed earlier). Fourth, Asian job aspirations are considerably higher than those of their white working class contemporaries.

Summarizing their research, Brooks and Singh pull these various themes together as follows:

'. . . the job opportunities and actual positions obtained by the small sample of Asian school leavers studied are explicable in terms of dual labour market theory. That is to say, Asian school leavers are 'pushed', as it were, into the secondary job sector by reason of lack of opportunity in the primary area. In this allocation process, racial considerations are powerfully important. On top of this, Asian job aspirations are markedly higher than those of their white working class contemporaries, and all this, it must be remembered, is taking place in the context of a deteriorating job situation for *all* school leavers. In this setting, the Asian applicant is pushed towards the back of the queue.'[45]

LANGUAGE EDUCATION

Derrick[47] observes that 'for native or immigrant children English is the key to their future in this country, thus the teacher has to see that they acquire language for the full range of communication within the school'. Clearly a child can neither learn specific skills nor develop his potential ability until he can learn to speak, understand, read and write the language that is used in school. In this section we concentrate upon some major aspects of language difficulties experienced by children from minority ethnic groups, giving particular attention to the problems facing children of West Indian origin.

The ideas of Bernstein[48] on the ways in which types of language (i.e. the *elaborated code* and the *restricted code*) affect modes of thinking were influential in the early and middle 60s in the setting up of compensatory language programmes for children who were said to be culturally and linguistically deprived. Many of Bernstein's ideas are thought to be applicable to the education of immigrant children who, although born in Britain, do not speak standard English. What in particular are the linguistic limitations of these children said to be? Taylor[49] suggests the following:

1. *Total language deficiency*, where not only is a foreign language spoken, but the written script is alien.
2. *Partial language deficiency*, where some, but very little, English is spoken in the home or where the child has acquired some English from having lived in Britain for a longer period of time. The vernacular script may or may not be based upon the western alphabet.
3. *Dialect impediments*, where some children may speak English fluently, but dialect interposes, or a 'pidgin' English is spoken so that problems of listening, interpreting and later reading and writing are present. This is a particular problem for some West Indian children where Creole dialects are present. We have more to say about this specific difficulty later in the chapter.

The Schools Council Curriculum Development projects[50] for teaching English to immigrant children were a direct response to the urgent need voiced by teachers up and down the country to find ways of helping immigrant children attain linguistic proficiency in English. The specific objectives of the Schools Council Programmes were first, to prepare materials and carefully graded schemes to meet the needs of teachers of non-English speaking children in order to help such pupils achieve an adequate command of English for school and society. Second, the programmes were intended to support the provision of in-service training in order to explain the purposes of the new materials to teachers and to give them opportunity both to use and criticize the materials and to offer positive suggestions for their improvement. In the absence of research evidence showing that there were distinctive problems attached to the teaching of particular ethnic minority groups, the Schools Council Project aimed, initially, to produce a general package of teaching materials for all non-English speaking children. Full details of each of the SCOPE programmes are available in Taylor[49] and Hill[2]. As time went on, specific language kits were developed for use with particular ethnic minority groups. We illustrate two.

BOX 8.9

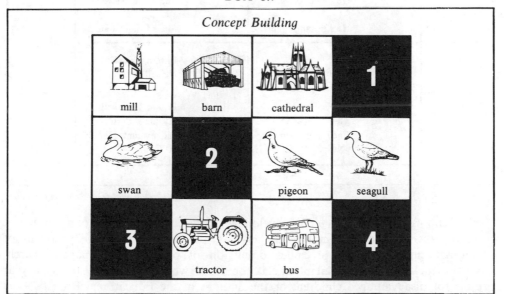

Concept Building

mill barn cathedral 1

swan 2 pigeon seagull

3 tractor bus 4

Source: E. J. Arnold (Publishers)[51]

Box 8.9 shows part of the Activity Book used in Unit 2, *Concept Building*, indicating the type of material specifically developed for use with West Indian children. The intention is to help children develop skills in classifying data. Central to the construction of the unit is the idea of a matrix by means of which children are encouraged to sort objects into sets. Box 8.9 shows that the matrix sheets consist of pictures arranged in rows and columns according to the classes to which they belong. Each matrix is accompanied by a series of workcards which provide children with writing experiences. Unit 2 also includes activity books, matrix cards, matrix builders, missing picture books and magnet cards.

Box 8.10 illustrates the sort of material included in a language kit developed for use with older immigrant children (aged 14 or over) recently arrived from the Indian subcontinent who have little or no command of English. The materials deal with daily activities in a fictitious town, Camley, and are intended to introduce children to simple terms to do with their immediate environment.

BOX 8.10

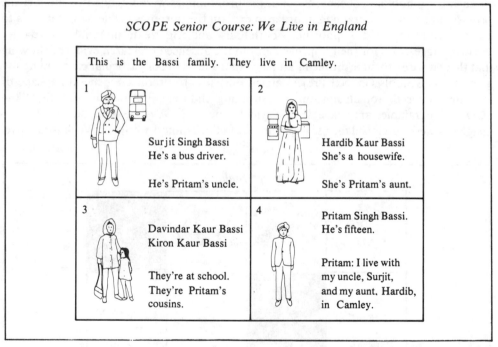

SCOPE Senior Course: We Live in England

This is the Bassi family. They live in Camley.

1 Surjit Singh Bassi
He's a bus driver.

He's Pritam's uncle.

2 Hardib Kaur Bassi
She's a housewife.

She's Pritam's aunt.

3 Davindar Kaur Bassi
Kiron Kaur Bassi

They're at school.
They're Pritam's cousins.

4 Pritam Singh Bassi.
He's fifteen.

Pritam: I live with my uncle, Surjit, and my aunt, Hardib, in Camley.

Source: adapted from Schools Council[50]

The Schools Council Curriculum Development projects were but one of a number of programmes of activity attempting to get to grips with the language problems of immigrant children. Space precludes discussion of pre-school language research, language teaching in multiracial infant classrooms, the work of the NFER in its five year project for disadvantaged children, or the findings of the Educational Priority Area Action Research as they specifically relate to ethnic minority children.

CREOLE INTERFERENCE

In a recent book dealing with the West Indian language issue in British schools, Edwards[52] shows how *Creole interference* plays a crucial role in the underperformance of West Indian children. To understand Edwards' thesis we need to know a little about West Indian Creole. What follows is a summary of the major points set out in Chapters 2 and 3 of Edward's text.

1. The linguistic situation in the West Indies is best seen in terms of a continuum with broad Creole at one end and standard English at the other, the social class and geographical location (rural/urban) of the speaker, together with the particular social situation in which he finds himself, determining which part of the speech continuum will be drawn upon in conversing.
2. Although Creole shares a large part of the vocabulary of English, it is different both in its grammar and its sound system from standard English. Such are the differences that some would argue for Creole being treated as a separate language.
3. West Indians born in Britain are influenced by the Creole spoken by their parents and by older members of the West Indian community. Many use Creole widely in specific social interactions. There is, Edwards observes, great sensitivity as to when and to whom speech from the Creole end of the Creole – standard English continuum is used.
4. Despite the widely-held belief that all forms of non-standard speech are intrinsically inferior, there is nothing to suggest that Creole* or any other non-standard variety of speech is irregular, faulty, or unstructured.
5. The commonly-held view of some teachers that West Indian children are inarticulate and non-verbal is challenged by the evidence that Edwards cites to show the impressive skills of West Indian children in the verbal games that constitute an integral part of their social activities.
6. Given the phonological†, morphological, syntactic and semantic differences of Creole as compared with standard English, we are in a better position to understand why Creole '*interfers*' with the production and comprehension of standard English. Edwards shows in detail how interference operates in speech, in comprehension, in writing, in grammar, and in reading.
7. Edwards concludes that children influenced by Creole are often at a considerable disadvantage when educated through the medium of standard English, experiencing particular difficulties in comprehending and in producing standard English speech.

---

* Edwards[52] shows a section of a higher degree thesis written in Creole to illustrate the point that social acceptability rather than linguistic inadequacy determines the exclusion of non-standard varieties from writing.

† *Phonology* is concerned with sounds in a language; *morphology*, with the form of words and their functional relationships, *syntax*, with sentence construction, and *semantics* with the meaning of words.

ATTITUDES TOWARDS LANGUAGE AND EDUCATIONAL ACHIEVEMENT

As important as the differences that we have noted between Creole and standard English are the attitudes that people hold towards these differences. Teachers in particular should be sensitive to the special problems West Indian pupils face as a result of linguistic interference and should be made aware of the stereotypes that are held about West Indian Creole speech. Box 8.11 reports the results of an experiment[53] into stereotypic attitudes towards speech conducted with student teachers, West Indian children, and their middle-class and working-class 'British' peers.

BOX 8.11

Stereotyped Attitudes to West Indian Speech

The speech of four first year secondary school children was tape recorded. The first was a Barbadian girl, born in Britain and completely bidialectical. She spoke once in the working-class Reading accent that she habitually used in school and later in a West Indian accent characterized by many phonological features of Creole, giving a speech sample that was recognizably West Indian but readily understandable to a speaker of British English. The other speakers were an English boy with a working-class Reading accent, a professor's son who spoke with 'received pronunciation', and a recently-arrived Jamaican girl whose Creole was barely recognizable to a British listener. All spoke fluently for half-a-minute about going to the dentist.

Attitudes towards these speech forms were recorded on questionnaire-type scales together with judgments about each speaker's behaviour, and his/her potential academic ability.

Among the child judges, both British and West Indians viewed West Indian speech negatively. Among the student teachers, no significant differences were found in their attitudes towards the two working class speakers nor towards the West Indian girls. What did emerge, however, were highly significant differences in student teachers' attitudes and evaluations of the middle class boy and the working class speaker, and between the working class children and the West Indian girls. There was an almost unanimous pecking order of preference:

middle class speech, working class speech, West Indian speech.

The same pattern was repeated with respect to judgments about the speakers' behaviour too.

Source: adapted from Edwards[53]

An interesting feature of Edwards' experiment was that it included West Indian children drawn from the same school as the working class children described in Box 8.11. Clearly, West Indians' appraisal of their own speech is of fundamental importance to their linguistic and social behaviour.

Results showed that the West Indian judges tended to agree with both the student teachers and the 'British' child judges that the middle class speech sample had highest status both in terms of speech and behaviour. However, Edwards detected a certain degree of ambivalence in their evaluations of West Indian and working class speech samples. She reports:

'. . . although they showed no marked preferences for either guise in their evaluations of speech, the working class guise was rated favourably on behaviour. West Indian judgments of academic potential and desirability as a member of the school class corresponded most closely to those of the middle class children. That is to say, they too assigned highest status to the middle class boy whom they considered had the greatest academic potential and would be the most interesting member of the class. There was no evidence of any preference for the West Indian speakers, suggesting that feelings of group solidarity do not strongly influence their evaluations.'

Edwards concludes that West Indian children have clearly internalized stereotypes of the dominant white society. Like all minority groups studied to date, she observes, they undervalue the speech and speakers of their own group.

We have here, have we not, all the makings of a self-fulfilling prophecy such as the one that we outline on page 78?

Teachers who do not or are not prepared to recognize the particular problems of Creole-speaking children in their classrooms may conclude that they are educationally backward when they give wrong responses or fail to respond to questions or commands. Features of Creole speech come to be associated with low academic ability and teachers are then led to behave differently towards Creole-speaking children. Low teacher expectations lead to low pupil performance. Looking at this process from the point of view of the child, Edwards notes how especially during the early stages the Creole-speaking pupil may feel threatened by the comprehension difficulties he is experiencing. These and the way in which the teacher behaves towards him produce what she describes as 'a state of linguistic insecurity' such that the child is very likely to appear inarticulate as a result. This, in turn, reinforces the teacher's preconceived ideas and the cycle is thus perpetuated.

A MULTIRACIAL CURRICULUM

Most of the responses of 510 men and women teachers in primary and secondary schools to an NFER questionnaire about multiracial education[22] evoke little surprise. We would expect, would we not, an overwhelming endorsement of the statement that 'schools have a responsibility to promote good race relations amongst pupils'? 94 % of the sample, in fact, concur with this.

The NFER analysis is more revealing of teachers' sentiments when Brittan, the researcher, touches upon questions that appear to threaten the traditional identity of the school and where she searches out the extent to which teachers are prepared to make changes in their curriculum planning and teaching in light of the multiracial composition of contemporary British society. It is all right, it seems, to impart information about the religions and homelands of minority groups. Beyond that, teachers are divided in their opinions, and Brittan detects an overall 'assimilation' viewpoint among her respondents. But given the emphasis on English language teaching during the early years of immigration and the widely-held belief that once English language proficiency had been acquired all other problems would diminish, it is hardly surprising that the majority of teachers in the study should espouse an assimilation objective for Britain as a multiracial society.

The research further revealed that a sizeable proportion of the sample appeared to be unaware of the ways in which school books may reinforce stereotypes and negative, derogatory images of ethnic minorities. Only 43 % of the teachers supported the view that lessons on race relations should be given in school, many feeling that such formal instruction was unnecessary and indeed, likely to be counterproductive. One wonders, Brittan asks, how many teachers are prepared to accept the far-reaching and fundamental curricular changes that are necessary to meet the needs of preparing pupils for life in a multiracial society, changes that cut across most subject divisions and across all age groups?

What would such changes entail? We outline a recent proposal for a multiracial curriculum that, according to its author, is a perfectly natural response to the altered nature of British society and, for many teachers, to the cultural composition of the classes that they now teach.

Jeffcoate[54] defines a multiracial curriculum as one in which choice of content reflects the multiracial nature of British society and the world and draws significantly on the experiences of British racial minorities and cultures overseas. He justifies it on the following grounds:

First, there is what Jeffcoate calls a 'pathological' foundation for developing a multiracial curriculum premised on the assumption that British society suffers from an endemic disease, *racism*. Because the influence of racism is so pernicious and pervasive, schools have a clear duty to make a concerted response by promoting racial self-respect and inter-racial understanding. Second, a multiracial curriculum may be justified on the notion of minority group rights. That is to say, racial minorities are entitled to expect that their cultures will be positively and prominently represented in the school curriculum. Third, there is the traditional view that a fundamental task of the school is to present an accurate picture of society to its pupils; it goes without saying that other races and cultures are important elements in that picture. Fourth, a multiracial curriculum involves pupils in more interesting, stimulating and challenging learning experiences than one which is not.

So much for the justification of a multiracial curriculum. How does one set about selecting learning experiences that might be incorporated within it? Box 8.12 summarizes five criteria of selection.

BOX 8.12

Criteria for Selecting Learning Experiences for a Multiracial Curriculum

1. A curriculum for the final quarter of the twentieth century needs to be international in its choice of content and in its perspective. An insular curriculum focusing on Britain and British values is unjustifiable and inappropriate.
2. Contemporary British society contains a variety of social and ethnic groups; this variety should be made evident in the visuals, stories and information offered to children.
3. Pupils should have access to accurate information about racial and cultural differences and similarities.
4. People from British minority groups and from other cultures overseas should be presented as individuals with every variety of human quality and attribute.
5. Other cultures and nations have their own validity and should be described in their own terms. Wherever possible they should be allowed to speak for themselves and not be judged exclusively against British or European norms.

Source: adapted from Jeffcoate[54]

Having enumerated several criteria for the selection of learning experiences for a multiracial curriculum, Jeffcoate draws on his experiences with the Schools Council to identify some limitations in the organization of materials and methods for multiracial classrooms.

There is little to be said, he warns, for isolating topics on India, Africa or the Caribbean which are not part of a comprehensive multiracial curriculum policy. Where schools have poor relations, such efforts are likely to be counterproductive. In terms of curriculum tactics, a sounder approach is to construct a learning programme around regular themes drawing on a variety of cultures for source materials with which all pupils can identify. That said, the need still remains for some kind of overt, systematic study since themes of themselves cannot provide pupils with an appreciative understanding of the logic and integrity of a way of life different to their own. The humanities curriculum should divide its attention evenly between local and international studies, these serving to complement one another in the process whereby the pupil makes sense of his world. It is particularly important that having decided to incorporate minority cultures into their curricula, schools should avoid defining those cultures solely in terms of patterns of life and experience in countries and continents of origin. It may be far more meaningful for children to look at those minority cultures as they are evolving and taking shape here in Britain. Finally, Jeffcoate has a word or two about development studies, those types of investigation of the Third World that are particularly popular in secondary schools. Too often, it seems, they infringe the fifth criterion we identify in Box 8.12 by making European concepts and categories integral to their operations. The multiracial curriculum involves a change in perspective as well as a change in content, an end, in effect, to ethnocentrism which views other cultures in a disparaging or, at best, condescending light.

To what end, we might ask? What purpose is the multiracial curriculum to serve in the wider tasks of the school?

The Purposes of the Multiracial Curriculum

Jeffcoate identifies two contrasting functions of the school that might be served by the multiracial curriculum, *transmitting culture* or *transforming culture*.

Those who support the view that the primary purpose of the school is to transmit culture would argue that despite the bewildering complexity of knowledge and the variety of beliefs that are available to curriculum planners, it is still possible and desirable to 'winnow out' the best that can be identified by criteria of excellence and pass this on to the next generation. While Jeffcoate supports the view that the curriculum should constitute the school's attempt to 'sift out' all that is excellent, he does not believe that it is the school's primary purpose to transmit a curriculum so constituted since central to that concept is the idea of teaching as instruction and learning as passive reception. Jeffcoate advances the alternative, *transformationist* position, arguing that if a new viable common culture is to emerge, then what has previously served as the 'cultural heritage' must be open to critical revaluation. The prime task of the school in this process is to develop those skills in its pupils which a child-centred philosophy of education regards as indispensable to children becoming autonomous. Besides presenting pupils with its version of excellence, then, the school should also ensure that when its pupils leave, they are equipped with the ability to decide for themselves 'which knowledge is most worth'. But this, Jeffcoate observes, involves the multiracial school in particular difficulties because it serves not one society or culture, but a diversity of cultures whose beliefs and values may not only differ, but at times be in conflict. Consider for a moment the case of Muslim pupils who attend Quran schools in the evening where they are taught the tenets of Islam. There they will certainly not be encouraged to regard what they are told critically whereas during the day they may well find themselves engaged in curriculum studies which require them to form their own opinions and arrive at their own decisions. In other words some children could be placed in the dilemma of attending a daytime school which interprets its function as transformationist and an evening one which sees its purpose as transmissionist. But here, Jeffcoate asserts, so far as maintained schools are concerned, while the cultures of racial minorities should be represented prominently and positively, it is no part of their task to represent those cultures uncritically. The preservation of minority cultures in a fossilized form is not what multiracial schools should be about. Rather, their aim for minority group pupils should be to make them critically aware of their culture and equipped to decide themselves how much to retain. The school's duty is to ensure that its philosophy, its policies and its curricula are such as to enable and accommodate as many choices as are feasible.

SUMMARY

We opened the chapter by noting the responses that have been made to the educational needs of immigrants since their arrival in Britain in the early 1960s. This was followed by a brief account of the homelands, the customs, and the beliefs of the three major ethnic minority groups in this country.

The extent of prejudice and discrimination towards ethnic minorities was discussed in terms of the colonial tradition towards non-English peoples, and the transmission of racial attitudes through socialization, the mass media, and children's literature. Research into children's racial attitudes was examined to show that, contrary to common belief, the dawning of racial awareness occurs at an extremely early age and that by eleven or twelve years of age, many children have acquired the familiar array of adult prejudices and hostilities towards minority groups.

We began our review of the evidence of underachievement in black minority groups by outlining Jensen's proposition that differences in learning ability between blacks and whites are biological in origin. We rehearsed the counter arguments that Jensen's views have elicited before looking particularly at British studies of West Indian pupils' performance in school.

We drew attention to the paucity of information on the views of ethnic minority parents on school and schooling in Britain. What research there is shows that despite the different colonial educational backgrounds from which many of these parents come, they expect of the English educational system broadly what indigenous parents expect, namely that schools should teach their children in a controlled, orderly, non-racist environment and equip them with skills and qualifications to make their way in today's world. We went on, however, to report the results of one recent study which shows the gap that exists between the aspirations of ethnic minority adolescents and the opportunities available to them on leaving school.

Work with ethnic minority children in language education was then reviewed, a whole section being devoted to the particular problems facing West Indian pupils as a result of Creole interference. This was followed by an account of some experimental findings to do with attitudes towards language and educational achievement.

We concluded the chapter by asking what sort of far reaching and fundamental changes are necessary to meet the needs of children preparing for life in a multiracial society. We decided that nothing less than a multiracial curriculum would suffice and went on to identify criteria for selecting learning experiences to be included in such a curriculum.

ENQUIRY AND DISCUSSION

1. What particular problems does a policy of cultural pluralism present to schools in terms of curriculum planning?

2. What are the origins of prejudice and hostility towards certain ethnic minority groups?

3. How might the race-of-the-tester affect the results that children obtain on tests of ability or achievement?

4. What are 'labelling effects' and how might they operate in achievement test situations?

5. Why are school leavers from certain ethnic minority backgrounds more likely to find themselves in secondary sector jobs?

6. What is Creole interference?

7. Discuss the adequacy of the criteria set out in Box 8.12 for a multiracial curriculum.

8. Discuss the role of the school as a *transmitter* and a *transformer* of culture. Which function, in your view, ought to take precedence?

NOTES AND REFERENCES

1. Bolton, E. (1979) Education in a multiracial society. *Trends in Education*, **4**, 3–7. Our introduction draws upon Bolton's excellent summary.

2. Hill, D. (1976) *Teaching in Multiracial schools*. London: Methuen. Our presentation of brief cameos on the backgrounds of Indian, Pakistani and West Indian ethnic minority groups draws on Hill's exposition.

3. de Lobo, E. (1978) *Children of Immigrants To Britain*. London: Hodder and Stoughton.

4. Bagley, C. (1979) A comparative perspective on the education of black children in Britain. *Comparative Education*, **15**, 1, 63–81.

5. Abrams, M. (1968) *National Survey of Race Prejudice*. London: Research Services Document J.4636.

6. Schaffer, R. (1970) *The Extent and Context of Racial Prejudice in Great Britain*. San Francisco: Rand and Associates.

7. Bagley, C. (1970) *Social Structure and Prejudice in Five English Boroughs*. London: Institute of Race Relations.

8. Bagley, C. and Verma, G. K. (1979) *Racial Prejudice, the Individual and Society*. London: Saxon House.

9. Our account summarizes the work of Bagley, C., Verma, G. K., Mallick, K. and Young, L. (1979) *Personality, Self-Esteem and Prejudice*. London: Saxon House, and Bagley, C. and Verma, G. K. (1979) *Racial Prejudice, The Individual and Society*. London: Saxon House.

10. Kiernan, V. (1972) *The Lords of Human Kind: European Attitudes To The Outside World in an Imperial Age*. London: Penguin.

11. Bagley, C., Verma, G. K., Mallick, K. and Young, L. (1979) *Personality, Self-Esteem and Prejudice*. London: Saxon House.

12. Walvin, J. (1971) *The Black Presence*. London: Orbach and Chambers.
    Walvin, J. (1973) *Black and White: The Negro and English Society 1555–1945*. London: Allen Lane.

13. Shyllon, F. (1974) *Black Slaves in Britain*. London: Oxford University Press.

14. Hartmann, P. and Husband, C. (1974) *Racism and the Mass Media*. London: Davis-Paynter.

15. Jeffcoate, R. (1975) Curriculum intervention. *Times Educational Supplement*, December 9th, 24–25.

16. Dummett, A. (1973) *A Portrait of English Racism*. London: Penguin.

17. Laishley, J. (1975) The images of blacks and whites in the children's media. In *White*

Media and Black Britain. (Ed.) Husband, C. London: Arrow Books.

18. Milner, D. (1975) *Children and Race*. London: Pelican.

19. Miller, G. (1971) *Educational Opportunity and the Home*. London: Longman.

20. Banks, O. and Finlayson, D. S. (1973) *Success and Failure in the Secondary School*. London: Methuen.

21. Jeffcoate, R. (1979) *Positive Image: Towards a Multiracial Curriculum*. London: Writers and Readers Publishing Cooperative.

22. Brittan, E. M. (1976) Multiracial education 2. *Educational Research*, **18**, 2, 96–107.

23. Department of Education and Science (1971) *The Education of Immigrants*. Education Survey 13. London: HMSO.

24. Department of Education and Science (1977) *Education in Schools: A Consultative Document*. Cmnd 6869. London: HMSO.

25. Pettigrew, T. (1971) *Racially Separate or Together*. New York: McGraw-Hill.

26. Jensen, A. (1973) *Educational Differences*. London: Methuen.
    Jensen, A. (1973) *Educability and Group Differences*. London: Methuen.

27. Eysenck, H. (1971) *Race, Intelligence and Education*. London: Temple Smith.

28. Stones, E. (1979) The colour of conceptual learning. In *Race, Education and Identity*. (Eds.) Verma, G. and Bagley, C. London: Macmillan.

29. Scrofani, P., Suziedelis, A. and Shore, M. (1973) Conceptual ability in black and white children of different social classes. *American Journal of Orthopsychiatry*, **43**, 541–553.

30. Jensen, A. (1980) *Bias in Mental Testing*. London: Methuen.

31. Bynner, J. (1980) Black and white arguments. *Guardian*, March 18th.

32. Houghton, V. (1966) Intelligence testing of West Indian and English children. *Race*, **8**, 147–156.
    See also:
    Robinson, V. (1980) The achievement of Asian children. *Educational Research*, **22**, 2, 148–150.

33. McFie, J. and Thompson, J. (1970) Intellectual abilities of immigrant children. *British Journal of Educational Psychology*, **40**, 348–351.

34. Yule, W. et al. (1975) Children of West Indian immigrants II: intellectual performance and reading attainments. *Journal of Child Psychology and Psychiatry*, **16**, 1–17.

35. Little, A., Mabey, C. and Whitaker, G. (1968) The education of immigrant pupils in Inner London primary schools. *Race*, **9**, 439–452.

36. Little, A. (1975) The educational achievement of ethnic minority children in London

schools. In *Race and Education Across Cultures*. (Eds.) Verma, G. and Bagley, C. London: Heinemann.

37. Halsey, A. (1972) *Educational Priority: E.P.A. Problems and Policies*. London: HMSO.

38. Mabey, C. (1974) Literacy Survey, Stage 2 – a summary paper on *Immigrant Attainment*. London: Inner London Education Authority. Cited in C. Bagley (1979) Reference 4.

39. Driver, G. (1980) How West Indians do better at school (especially the girls). *New Society*. 27th January, 111–114.

40. Vernon, P. E. (1961) *Selection For Secondary Schools in Jamaica*. Kingston, Jamaica: Ministry of Education.
    Manley, D. R. (1963) Mental ability in Jamaica, *Social and Economic Studies*, **12,** 54–71. Kingston, Jamaica: University of the West Indies.

41. *New Society* (1980) 24th January, Letters.

42. *New Society* (1980) 11th February, Letters.

43. Tomlinson, S. (1980) Ethnic minority parents and education. In *Linking Home and School: A New Review*. (Eds.) Craft, M., Raynor, J. and Cohen, L. London: Harper and Row.
    See also, Ghuman, P. A. S. (1980) Punjabi parents and English education. *Educational Research*, **22,** 2, 121–130.

44. Gupta, Y. P. (1977) The educational and vocational aspirations of Asian immigrants and English school-leavers. *British Journal of Sociology*, **28,** 2, 185–198.
    Fowler, B. Lockwood, B. and Madigan, R. (1977) Immigrant school leavers and the search for work. *Sociology*, **11,** 1, 65–65.
    Department of Employment (1977) *Entering The World of Work: Some Sociological Perspectives*. (Ed.) Brannen, P. London: HMSO.
    Bosanquet, N. (1973) *Race and Employment in Britain*. London: Runnymede Trust.
    Brooks, D. (1975) *Black Employment in the Black Country: A Study of Walsall*. London: Runnymede Trust.

45. Brooks, D. and Singh, K. (1979) *Aspirations Versus Opportunities: Asian and White School Leavers in the Midlands*. Walsall Council For Community Relations/Leicester Community Relations Council.

46. Doeringer, P. B. and Piore, M. J. (1971) *Internal Labour Markets and Manpower Analysis*. Lexington: Mass. D. C. Heath.

47. Derrick, J. (1968) The work of the Schools Council project in English for immigrant children. *Times Educational Supplement*, October 25th.

48. Bernstein, B. (1958) Some sociological determinants of perception. *British Journal of Sociology*, **9,** 154–174.
    Bernstein, B. (1960) Language and social class. *British Journal of Sociology*, **11,** 271–276.

Bernstein, B. (1961) Social class and linguistic development: a theory of social learning. In *Society, Economy and Education* (Eds.) Halsey, A. H., Floud, J. and Anderson, C. A. Glencoe, Ill.: Free Press.

Bernstein, B. (1965) A socio-linguistic approach to social learning. In *Penguin Survey of the Social Sciences.* (Ed.) Gould, J. London: Penguin Books.

49. Taylor, F. (1974) *Race, School and Community: A Study of Research and Literature.* Slough: NFER.

50. Schools Council: *English For Immigrant Children* Curriculum Development Project. Leeds: E. J. Arnold.
    (1969) *Scope 1: An Introductory Course for pupils 8–13 years.*
    (1971) *Scope Handbook 2: Pronunciation for non-English speaking children from India, Pakistan, Cyprus and Italy.*
    (1972) *Scope Senior Course for non-English speaking students 14 years and over.*
    (1972) *Scope 2 for pupils 8–13 years at 2nd stage of English.* (Longmans).
    (1973) *Scope 3 Handbook 3: Language work with infant immigrant children.*
    (1973) Taylor, J. and Ingleby, T. *Scope story book 5–12 years.*
    (1973) Manley, D. *Scope supplementary plays and dialogues.*

51. Schools Council Project on Teaching English to West Indian Children (1972). *Concept 7–9.* Four units for multi-racial classes.
    Unit 1.   Listening with Understanding.
    Unit 2.   Concept Building.
    Unit 3.   Communication.
    Unit 4.   The Dialect Kit.
    Leeds: E. J. Arnold.

52. Edwards, V. K. (1979) *The West Indian Language Issue in British Schools.* London: Routledge and Kegan Paul.

53. Edwards, V. K. (1978) Language attitudes and underperformance in West Indian children. *Educational Review,* **30,** 1, 51–58.

54. Jeffcoate, R. (1979) A multicultural curriculum: beyond the orthodoxy. *Trends in Education,* **4,** 8–12.

SELECTED READING

1. The problems of teaching English as a second language and the question of bilingualism are well covered in:
   Derrick, J. (1968) *Teaching English To Immigrant Children.* London: Longman.
   Derrick, J. (1974) *Language Needs of Minority Group Children: Learners of English as a Second Language.* Slough: NFER

2. The following books contain critiques of racial bias and stereotyping:

Dixon, R. (1977) *Catching Them Young: Sexist, Racist and Class Images in Children's Books*. London: Pluto Press.

Elkin, J. (1976) *Books For The Multiracial Classroom*. London: The Library Association.

Procter, C. (1975) *Racist Textbooks*. London: National Union of Students.

Hill, J. (1976) *Books For Children: The Homelands of Immigrants in Britain*. London: Institute of Race Relations.

(Eds.) Children's Rights Workshop (1970) *Racist and Sexist Images in Children's Books*. London: 233a Kentish Town Road, NW5: Writers and Readers Publishers Cooperative.

3. A short readable account of the experiences of black children in British schools and the attitudes of their teachers is given in:

Giles, R. (1977) *The West Indian Experience in British Schools*. London: Heinemann.

4. A number of bookshops specialize in books which reflect the experiences of ethnic minorities in Britain:

The English Centre	Harriet Tubman Books
Ebury Teachers' Centre	27/29 Grove Lane
Sutherland Street	Handsworth
London SW1	Birmingham-21
New Beacon Books	Bogle l'Ouverture
26 Strand Green Road	5a Chignell Place
London N4 3EN	London W13

5. A number of organizations publish their own journals and educational bulletins to do with multicultural education.

The National Association for Multiracial Education, 19 Margreave Road, Chaddesden, Derby DE2 6JD publishes:

New Approaches to Multiracial Education (three per year)

In addition, two local NAME branches publish:

Change – available from Shenton Primary School, Dunlin Road, Leicester

Issues in Race and Education – available from 58 Collingbourne Road, London W12

The Institute of Race Relations, 249/279 Pentonville Road, London N1 publishes:

Race (quarterly journal)

The Race Today Collective, 74 Shakespeare Road, London SE24 0PT publishes:

Race Today (fortnightly journal)

The Runnymede Trust, Stuart House, 1 Tudor Street, London EC4Y 0AD publishes:

Runnymede Trust Bulletin (monthly bulletin)

The Commission For Racial Equality, Elliot House, 10/12 Allington Street,

London SW1/5EH publishes:
New Community (quarterly journal)
New Equals (bi-monthly bulletin)
Education Journal (bi-monthly bulletin)

9

Open Education

Open education began as an American phenomenon which came into being in the late 1960s and was firmly established in the literature of education by the early 1970s.[1] It is seen by its proponents as a means of implementing a whole set of values relating to the purpose of life, the nature of the individual, and the 'good' society. As open education owes a great deal to European and American progressive theory, however,[1] we begin by sketching the history of progressivism this century, touching upon traditionalism from time to time for points of elucidation and contrast.

Influenced by the philosophy of John Dewey,[2] the progressive movement in education began in a small number of private schools in the United States in the 1920s. Against a background of traditional practices, it spread to other institutions and reached its peak in the 1930s and 1940s, after which it declined and remained at low ebb for some years. As one writer says,[3] 'By the late forties and fifties the term shifted from one of praise to one of opprobrium.' The precise reasons for this decline are not clear. It has been suggested that the movement misunderstood and therefore misrepresented Dewey's principles and, further, that the quality of both teachers and teaching left much to be desired. The movement experienced another setback with the launching of the first Russian satellite, *Sputnik 1*, when critics began to question the effectiveness of American education and its ability to produce scientists of distinction. In demanding more traditional teaching, opponents of progressivism created a climate unfavourable to its further development. Meanwhile, its counterpart in British schools, the *informal movement*, had been out of phase with what had been happening in America. Cradled in the rural schools of England during the Second World War where teachers had had to cope with the influx of evacuees from the towns as best they could, the informal movement took its first tentative steps forward.[4] This initiative was seized upon and developed further by a minority of committed individuals in the early 1960s before the movement was given official impetus by members of the Plowden Committee in 1967. In their Report, they contended that:[5]

'The school sets out deliberately to devise the right environment for children, to allow them to be themselves, and to develop in a way and at a pace appropriate to them . . . It lays special stress on individual discovery, on first hand experience, and on opportunities for creative work. It insists that knowledge does not fall into neatly separate compartments and that work and play are not opposite but complementary.'

It was the apparent success of this informal movement in Britain that was to revive interest in the United States where its own progressive movement was by now in a fairly dormant state. This transatlantic fillip was to lead to the emergence and spread of what became known in that country as *open education*. As one American observer notes,[6] 'As reports of British schools began to reach this country in the late 1960s, many educators found in the British model verification of their beliefs that schools can be "joyous", "humane" places, where children can assume active roles in their own education.'

In this brief review of the fortunes of progressivism, we have used three terms – progressive, informal and open education. It would be easy to assume that they are synonymous since there appears to be a residual core common to all three. They are not synonymous, however, and some clarification at this point will help to avoid confusion later. Open education, as we have seen, emerged from the dying embers of the native progressive movement under the stimulus of the British informal movement. Yet the two American movements, progressive and open, are not the same. Stephens distinguishes between them thus,[6] 'Open education is in no sense a carbon copy of progressive education. Its chief points of departure lie in the more active role of the teacher, greater emphasis on planned environments, clarification of the limits of the child's freedom, and greater concern about the curriculum. Open educators view the teacher's role as decisive. They see no conflict between emphasis on the child's responsibility and direction by the teacher. There is not only room for both, but there is also need for both in open classrooms.' Having revived American interest in an alternative to traditional practices, British informal institutions naturally have more in common with the open schools that were subsequently to appear than with the earlier progressive academies. The more obvious differences existing between British informal and American open philosophies tend rather to reflect societal differences. These resolve into contrasting administrative procedures and emphases rather than educational practices, British schools being characterized by: greater autonomy for teachers and headteachers with respect to curricula and organization; smaller schools; headteachers continuing to teach; less emphasis on formal testing procedures and achievement tests; fewer parent organizations; less grading of children; separate infant schools; and local and national systems of advisory and support services for teachers.[6]

Having identified the more ostensible differences between open education in the United States and the British informal movement, we will from now on use the term *open education* and its derivatives to describe the movement in the United States *and also* its British counterpart.[7] In addition to the convenience from the writers' point of view, there does seem to be ample precedent for this. However, we shall try to avoid masking the more subtle differences between the two movements by making them explicit when the need arises. We continue by looking a little more closely at the meaning of the term, *open education*, and at the kinds of difficulties it gives rise to.

OPEN EDUCATION – AN EXPRESSION IN SEARCH OF A DEFINITION

Critics of open education appear to be at their most vocal when the question of defining the term is raised for however hard they look for a precise, yet all-embracing definition, their quest ends in disappointment. There seem to be a number of factors inhibiting a clear statement of what exactly open education is. We will briefly consider four of them. First, because of the wide variety of practices in different localities and schools, the term is subject to a wide range of definitions and interpretations. Further, being a multidimensional concept, the components making up its practices are in turn each open to different interpretations. The resulting vagueness has been pin-pointed by numerous writers. Crowl, for example, says, 'The term open classroom implies at most a notion of destructuring and perhaps restructuring the classroom, a notion so vague that it is virtually valueless in terms of educational practice.'[8]

Second, open educators themselves rarely make explicit the rationale underlying their practices. There seems to be an almost studied reluctance to define it for fear that, in so doing, it becomes something else; that by expressing open education in the permanency of words, its very virtue, openness, is transformed into its pejorative opposite, closedness.[9] In comparing the term with earlier fashionable notions like 'activity', 'experience', 'self-expression', and 'readiness', Dearden writes, 'It has a more or less definite meaning to the reformers who speak and write in terms of it, but much of what they mean is not conveyed in what they say. It is at their fingertips rather than on the tip of their tongue. Vagueness then enters into communication and before long anything will be called 'open' and the word will have ceased to signify much more than pleasure and approval.'[9]

A third factor obscuring a clear definition of open education stems from the belief by some that it is an ideology, for ideologies, especially emerging ones, tend to be vague.[10] For this reason, it is considered that open education is unlikely to develop a substantially more clear conceptual base. The problem of definition from this perspective is further compounded because open education is, as we have noted earlier, a multidimensional notion embracing such factors as teaching, learning, curriculum, evaluation, and organization.

Finally, there are historical reasons for the lack of precise definition. Various commentators have pointed out that open education arose as a reaction against the philosophy and practices of traditional education and that it can only be defined, therefore, with these in mind. A satisfactory, self-contained definition is unlikely where attributes and characteristics of the traditional movement are implied. On this point, Dearden writes:

'Then in what respects does the open school wish to regard itself as "open"? Each and every one of these respects, I suggest, is defined by reaction against an existing practice, and the term has reasonable precision only for so long as the practices being reacted against are before one's mind. In other words, "openness" is regarded as a virtue of schools in a definite historical context. Abstracted from this context, the term becomes so open in meaning that there is no telling what schools might be thought open to.'[9]

Box 9.1 lists the principal characteristics of traditional education and their reactive counterparts in open education.

BOX 9.1

Characteristics of Traditional and Open Education

	Traditional		Open
1.	Separate subject matter	1.	Integrated subject matter
2.	Teacher as distributor of knowledge	2.	Teacher as guide to educational experience
3.	Passive pupil role	3.	Active pupil role
4.	Pupils have no say in curriculum planning	4.	Pupils participate in curriculum planning
5.	Accent on memory, practice, and rote	5.	Learning predominantly by discovery techniques
6.	External rewards used, e.g. grades, i.e. extrinsic motivation	6.	External rewards and punishments not necessary, i.e. intrinsic motivation
7.	Concerned with academic standards	7.	Not too concerned with conventional academic standards
8.	Regular testing	8.	Little testing
9.	Accent on competition	9.	Accent on co-operative group work
10.	Teaching confined to classroom base	10.	Teaching not confined to classroom base
11.	Little emphasis on creative expression	11.	Accent on creative expression

Source: adapted from Bennett[3]

There is yet another historical reason for the lack of adequate definition of open education and this arises from a characteristic of the English temperament That the English prefer practicalities to theory is well known and is illustrated in the context of education by the inception of the informal movement in the rural schools of World War II that we spoke of earlier. Then, the movement was born out of the immediacy of practical needs. It was something to be done, not talked about; a set of skills to be tested and used, not theorized over. Thus from the outset, English open educators at least have preferred to do rather than explain; to balance their trust in action with a corresponding distrust of theories and systems.[4] It is perhaps not surprising, therefore, that little serious thought has been given to examining the meaning of open education by its proponents.

If defining or conceptualizing open education presents us with a number of problems, perhaps we can turn to its aims and supposed end-products as an alternative way of pinning down this elusive notion. But again we will be thwarted. One writer explains more particularly,[11] 'Typically, there are statements about fulfilling the child's potential; producing people with highly developed thinking skills properly prepared for social participation and exploration of reality; harmoniously developing the whole person; self-actualization. If one searches for an explicit and precise description of the ideal product of open education, one will be disappointed.'

The problems and vagueness surrounding attempts to define open education and identify its end-products can be averted to some extent (though not overcome, of course) by examining what open education *does*. As one writer puts it, 'To define "open education" is to define a program for action.'[12] A close inspection of 'a program for action' will disclose a particular set of characteristics and it is these that we now consider.

THE CHARACTERISTICS OF OPEN EDUCATION

We return at this point to the work of Stephens.[6] In her study of open classrooms in both Britain and the United States, she identified a number of characteristics which may be seen to constitute the basic model of an open classroom. These are: (1) a minimum of lessons to the whole class, most instruction being geared to small groups or individuals; (2) a variety of activities progressing simultaneously; (3) flexible arrangements so that children can engage in different activities for varying periods of time; (4) an environment rich in materials and equipment; (5) freedom for children to move about, converse, work together, and seek help from one another; (6) opportunities for children to make decisions about their work and to develop responsibility for setting and meeting their educational goals; (7) lack of rigid, prescribed curriculum and provision for children to investigate matters of concern to them; (8) some integration of the curriculum, eliminating isolated teaching of each subject; (9) emphasis on experimentation and involvement with materials; (10) flexible learning groups formed around interests, as well as academic needs, and organized by both pupils and teachers; (11) an atmosphere of trust, acceptance of children, and respect for their diversity; (12) attention to individual intellectual, emotional, physical and social needs; (13) creative activities valued as part of the curriculum; (14) a minimum of grading and marking; and (15) honest and open relationships between teacher and pupil and between pupil and pupil. Of course, open environments will vary greatly in the way they select, interpret, and implement these characteristics which, for convenience, may be roughly summarized by the concepts *freedom*, *activity*, and *discovery*. Indeed, it may not be an exaggeration to say that each school will represent a different version of open education.

There are other features underscoring these characteristics and generally pervading the atmosphere of open classrooms. One of these is a sense of optimism. As one commentator expresses it, 'Open education is optimistic, in the traditional sense, in its assessment of human nature, believing that children's curiosity will lead them naturally towards things of educational value, so that if each child's interests are allowed to determine his or her activities in school, they – better than any externally imposed scheme – will lead to the best education for that child.'[11]

A second feature is that of change. Egan observes,[11] 'A further element underlying, and often surfacing in, open education literature is an almost chiliastic* vision of change; a sense that the pace of change is so fast and accelerating, that traditional knowledge and training provide entirely insufficient tools for children to deal with the world in which they are going to be adults.' It is the combination of these two features which accounts for the emphasis in open education on *procedural* and *methodological* matters. The overriding concern in open education is with *process* as opposed to *content*. Indeed, none of the characteristics so far identified tells us anything about the content of the open school curriculum. The assumption is that if the open classroom is functioning adequately and

---

* *Chiliastic* refers to the belief in the Millennium, figuratively a period of great happiness, prosperity and effective government.

squares up to the characterization we have presented so far, each child will acquire knowledge and skills and will thus become educated in the traditional sense. As Egan explains,[11] 'What particular skills and content will be mastered, it is argued, are better determined by the individual child's interests and developing curiosity than by criteria derived from values meaningful to an older generation brought up in a world very different from that which the child will know.'

In conclusion, we refer to another feature of the characterization presented – the extension or opening up of traditional educational concepts. We choose three by way of illustration. The concept of *education* itself, for example, is opened up in the sense that it no longer relates to a specified and often unchanging body of knowledge and skills. Any experience engaging a child's interest is of educational value to him. The concept of *learning*, too, is extended beyond its traditional usage and may embrace *all* experience. And the concept of *responsibility* is yet another undergoing transformation. In the traditional classroom, the notion for the child is equated with obedience; in the open classroom, it implies his participation in decision-making, organizing his day, choosing activities, and exploring his interests. Related concepts undergo similar expansion.

It is precisely these features that have provoked some of the most articulate responses from the critics of open education. We refer you in particular to the articles by Dearden,[9] Myers and Duke,[10] and Egan.[11]

SOME ISSUES

The open education movement has stirred much controversy and debate, especially among philosophers of education,[13] and it is to three issues raised by them that we now turn. We have already seen how open education arose as a reaction against traditional education. One of the difficulties with this 'reactive innovation', as Crowl terms it,[8] is its holistic nature. He explains, 'Everything which immediately preceded the innovation is uncritically rejected. Similarly, the innovation is accepted in its entirety. No attempt is made to distil from the past those things which have proved useful. Thinking is focused not on what the innovation is moving towards, but rather on what it is moving away from.' A related aspect has been highlighted by Peters in his critique of the Plowden Report when he writes, 'What has happened is that *a* method for learning some things has become puffed up into *the* method for learning almost anything.' He detected 'a yearning for some overall recipe for teaching.' His contention is that no such recipe is possible.[14]

A further consequence of 'reactive innovation' is that open education possesses no criteria of its own by which to judge its performance since it defines itself exclusively against the characteristics of traditional education. Egan develops this point when he says, 'Open education lacks or is weak in self-critical referents; it lacks clear means for judging its own success or failure as an educational movement. As the overriding principles are procedural, *whatever* happens when these procedures are operating has to be a success. If the schooling process conforms to the ideals of openness, then *whatever* results is unassailable on educational ground . . . . Proponents of open education have an effective defence against criticism from outside, but must pay a heavy price for such security; they are defenceless against themselves and theoretically helpless when disagreements emerge among them.'[11] A further consequence is that lacking criteria of its own (or not making them explicit) means that open education will continue to be judged by the criteria of traditional education – and found wanting.

Finally, open education is subject to the charge of parochialism because of the limited range of experience offered by it. Egan's indictment exposes a disturbing weakness in the movement, 'They are defenceless against themselves because their facilitating guidance is limited to that range of things that they have themselves found rewarding; they have no grounds on which to appeal beyond these to that wider tradition of what western man has found of persisting value . . . . Lacking the reasons traditional school teachers have for referring constantly . . . to a range of experiences beyond their own, open education teachers must close off educational possibilities for children and tend inevitably towards provincialism.'[11]

Our discussions so far in this section must seem to the reader to be overtly negative and to be doing nothing more than attaching to the concept of open education a constellation of minus signs. Yet in practice the picture is somewhat different for it is manifestly evident from those open schools purposefully and efficiently run by committed teachers that they do provide children with a stimulating and enjoyable environment, bearing out one writer's contention that, so often with educational ideas, to go for the word is to miss the substance.[15] The following extracts relating to the experiences of two American researchers in a sample of open schools are by no means uncommon or unusual in the sentiments they express:[10]

'On average, the children observed were active, happy, verbal, and interested in the activities in which they were engaged . . . .'

'The teachers were active – working with individual children or small groups of children . . . .'

'The quality of instruction and the amount of child learning in the open classrooms visited appeared to exceed that of traditional classrooms . . . .'

Examination of some features of the curriculum, pedagogy, and organization of the open classroom will help us to view the workings of open education in a more practical and no doubt constructive light and will perhaps offset some of the formidable theoretical criticisms aimed at the movement. As a preliminary to this, we shall have a look first at some of the assumptions forming the basis of the open movement's endeavours.

ASSUMPTIONS UNDERLYING THE CURRICULUM OF THE OPEN SCHOOL

Any consideration of the curriculum of open education must be preceded by some reference at least to the assumptions about children's learning and the nature of knowledge which underlie the movement. Rarely are these voiced and it is often the case that open educators themselves are not fully aware of the extent to which they form the basis of their practices. In Box 9.2 we list a set of assumptions concerning children's learning in open classrooms that have been identified by Barth.[16] The classification is

BOX 9.2

Assumptions about Children's Learning

1. Children are innately curious and display exploratory behaviour quite independent of adult intervention.
2. Exploratory behaviour is self-perpetuating.
3. The child will display natural exploratory behaviour if he is not threatened.
4. Confidence in self is highly related to capacity for learning and for making important choices affecting one's learning.
5. Active exploration in a rich environment, offering a wide array of materials facilitates children's learning.
6. Play is not distinguished from work as the predominant mode of learning in early childhood.
7. Children have both the competence and the right to make significant decisions concerning their own learning.
8. Children will be likely to learn if they are given considerable choice in the selection of the materials they wish to work with and in the selection of questions they wish to pursue with respect to those materials.
9. Given the opportunity, children will choose to engage in activities which will be of high interest to them.
10. If the child is fully involved in and having fun with an activity, learning is taking place.
11. When two or more children are interested in exploring the same problem or the same materials they will often choose to collaborate in some way.
12. When a child learns something which is important to him he will wish to share it with others.

Source: Barth[16]

based on his own classroom observations and on discussions with experts on both sides of the Atlantic and though conceding that they will not necessarily be acceptable to every advocate of open education, he does suggest that they reflect the thinking of most. These assumptions need to be studied in conjunction with a further five postulates specified by Barth which relate to children's intellectual development. These claim that: concept formation proceeds very slowly; children learn and develop intellectually not only at their own rate, but in their own style; children pass through similar stages of intellectual development . . . each in his own way, and at his own rate and in his own time; intellectual growth and development take place through a sequence of concrete experiences followed by abstractions; and verbal abstractions should follow direct experience with objects and ideas, not precede them or substitute for them.

Although the influence of various growth theorists may be perceived in the practices of open education, it is the interactionist view of Piaget which most accords with the movement's cognitive position as reflected in the assumptions noted above. Briefly summarizing his views we may say that: there are four consecutive stages of mental development through which all children pass at approximately similar ages – the sensory motor, the pre-operational, the concrete operational, and the stage of formal operations; each child develops intellectual structures, or *schemata*, to represent his world, and as a result of his interaction with his environment, these mental models are continually being modified through the processes of assimilation and accommodation; he has his own conception of reality against which he tests and redefines new experiences and in this sense learning is always personal; and he differentiates between language and thought, so that his language may not adequately represent his thought. Although the implications of Piaget's theories are important for all teachers of young children, they would seem to be a basic requirement for an understanding of the philosophy of open education.

We now assess the status of *knowledge* in open education. What assumptions does open education make about it? Knowledge plays a significant part in the aims and thinking of traditional education where it is seen as a worthy end in itself. Its possession is highly prized in all fields of learning. The philosophy of open education, however, questions the value traditionalists place on it. Barth explains why: 'Implicit in the ideas of open education are assumptions that bring into question not only the importance of knowledge *qua* knowledge, but also its meaning for the learner. Rather than an end in itself, knowledge is seen as a vehicle for the development of processes of thinking such as logic, intuition, analysis and hypothesis formation and as a catalyst that facilitates the individual's development towards the ultimate goals of education – self-esteem, dignity, and control over himself and his world.'[16]

From this perspective, Barth promulgates five assumptions, thus: the quality of being is more important than the quality of knowing: knowledge is a means of education not its end. The final test of an education is what a man is, *not* what he knows. Knowledge is a function of one's personal integration of experience and therefore does not fall into neatly separate categories or disciplines. The structure of knowledge is personal and idiosyncratic, and a function of the synthesis of each individual's experience with the world. There is no minimum body of knowledge which is essential for everyone to know. And it is possible, even likely, that an individual may learn and possess knowledge of a phenomenon and yet be unable to display it publicly. Knowledge resides with the knower, not in its public expression.

In that knowledge is therefore, in Deweyan terms, warranted by virtue of its practical value in answer to practical problems,[17] its function in open education must be largely instrumental.

Critics of open education have been quick to question the movement's attitude to knowledge. Whatever the putative arguments are for bestowing an instrumental role on it, they are interpreted by opponents as rationalizations to cover up the fear of having to specify what children should learn. Egan argues, 'The recent failure of nerve consists in not daring to specify what knowledge is important. The rationale for not daring is the rapid rate of change, but this is a weak excuse except for those who are eager to avoid the hard and persisting questions of education.'[11]

This view of knowledge held by open educators has far-reaching consequences for many aspects of their practices and for this reason tends to invite criticisms of an interrogative kind. Thus, to what extent can open education be said to have aims? Do priorities in learning exist? How far can an adult have control over a child's learning? What is the basis of continuity in learning? And can it have an organizing principle? Is there a logical sequence to knowledge or only a psychological one? How can the outcomes of open education be evaluated in an objective way? And against what criteria can research into open education be pursued? Perhaps most important, however, are the effects of its epistemological base on *the curriculum itself*. Can open educators' assumptions about knowledge admit of the concept? Is there a place for it in open education? What does the word mean to them? Certainly, it does not have the meaning that traditionalists impute to it, that is, a content of information and skills determined by adults and sequenced from the simple to the complex, from where the child is to where the adult would have him.

In contrast, the curriculum of the open classroom has both a teacher *and* a pupil aspect.

It is the interaction between the teacher and pupil which produces what open educators claim is its dynamic and flexible character. As Stephens explains,[6] 'Teachers bring to curriculum development a general knowledge of areas to be included and skills appropriate for certain age groups, plus their own previous experiences and interests. From this background they design the outlines of their curricula. Children in turn help to shape their curricula by their reactions to materials, their changing needs, their blossoming interests. The open curriculum is both planned and unplanned. It is planned in the sense that teachers do not simply drift from day to day, waiting for things to happen. The environment is carefully structured, materials are chosen to provide particular experiences, lessons are planned in response to individual and group needs. Yet the curriculum can also be unplanned in the sense that directions are not always prescribed; there is room for unseen exploration.' That the curriculum is, therefore, a joint responsibility having the quality of both adult and child initiation is its most distinctive characteristic.

SOME CURRICULAR, PEDAGOGICAL, AND ORGANIZATIONAL FEATURES OF OPEN CLASSROOMS

While not necessarily exclusive to the practices of open education, the features we are about to describe generally have a different relationship to the work of an open classroom than is the case with traditional approaches. The features we have selected embrace the integrated day and the integrated curriculum; play; topics and projects; discovery learning; talk; the hidden curriculum; individualization and grouping; and individual attention.

The concepts of the *integrated day* and the *integrated curriculum* are both so subject to wide interpretation and varied practice that we can only refer to each in the broadest way in the limited space available. The *integrated day* is an organizational concept implying that 'set time-tables, or other formalized ways of changing from one activity to another, are abandoned. Instead, the flow of children's learning activities is broken and changed informally and often individually, with a large element of the children's own choice governing the matter.'[15] The approach contrasts with traditional practices whereby the day is divided into set, specified periods for individual subjects. The absence of barriers between subjects in the open classroom is also reflected in the less clear-cut distinction between work and play and between cognitive and affective learning.

Precisely what open educators mean by *integrated curriculum* is not made explicit. Pring suggests[17] that it could be a view about the nature of knowledge – that in some ways knowledge either is all one or is unified within certain broad fields of experience; or that it may be a very loose way of talking about the integrated day, or interdisciplinary inquiry, or the needs of society. In spite of different interpretations, however, they do have in common 'a disapproval of fragmentation of the curriculum, which is said to typify the traditional school; that is, they disapprove of subject barriers, and the compartmentaliz-ing or pigeon-holing of knowledge with its accompanying specialization and frequent irrelevance to real problems.'[17] The work of the class is thus organized around broad, unified themes which embrace a number of subjects. Skills are studied as they are required by the activity and are practised in the course of the significant tasks rather than in isolation.

The educational significance of *play* has been a persistent theme in the writings of theorists from as early as Plato. The prominent role accorded it by initiators of the progressive movement has now assumed one of pre-eminence in the thinking and practices of open educators. Indeed, one writer goes as far as to say that the 'role of play in children's learning is central to an understanding of open education.'[6] We might add, in parentheses, that subtle differences in attitudes to play exist in Britain and the United States. In British schools, for example, play may legitimately merge into bouts of idleness or day-dreaming; in the United States, however, where teachers work in the shadow of concepts like 'productivity' and 'accountability', a more serious view is taken of the notion.

It is not easy to determine from the literature on open education precisely on what the significance of play rests, for empirical evidence of its educational value is difficult to come by and, as Dearden points out, not always favourable.[15] Scrutiny of comparatively recent writings on the subject lead one to infer that play serves a two-fold purpose in the thinking of open educators. First, it seems to cater for a fairly wide range of *children's needs*: these include psychological, personal, social, and educational ones. In this capacity, play will be an important source of knowledge in the sense that open educators imply, that is, the child's 'personal capacity to confront and handle new experiences successfully.'[16] And second, it appears to be an important *integrative factor*, a vital means of breaking down traditional divides. Thus play merges with, or becomes indistinguishable from, work; and the boundaries between other traditional dualisms such as doing and knowing, or intellect and emotions, are similarly blurred by the concept.

Topics and projects are used in the conventional curriculum of the traditional classroom where they supplement the established modes of teaching and learning. In the open classroom, however, they are regarded as a mandatory feature. Indeed, it would be impossible to conceive of the work of an open classroom without them. In general terms, topics and projects have a dual purpose: they serve as means of integrating traditional subjects and at the same time allow children to explore their own interests. The terms may be distinguished from each other in that a topic is a unit of work of limited scope undertaken by an individual child or a small group, whereas a project is a unit of work on a larger scale involving a larger group, a whole class or, occasionally, the entire school. From the standpoint of the open educator, topics and projects have a number of advantages which have been summarized by Stephens as follows,[6] 'They help to integrate the curriculum around unifying themes, thus helping to remove barriers; they permit study of subjects in a manner that has meaning for children, stimulating varied avenues of exploration; they allow pursuit of individual interests; they enhance ability to use varied means of investigating a subject; they help develop social skills connected with working in a group; they encourage child leadership; they foster child initiative; they lead to increased knowledge about many subjects that are not usually part of the curriculum; and they stimulate new interests.'

A concept arising out of the strategies of topic and project work and one generally central to the pedagogy of open education is that of *discovery learning*. Dearden[15] suggests that by its means we may reasonably expect children to learn something new; and to do so through some initiative of their own. He goes on to identify three other points to be borne in mind in any discussion on learning by discovery. First, what is involved primarily is the learning of facts, concepts, and principles rather than skills, techniques, or sensitivities; and that the subjects most relevant to discovery learning are mathematics, science, and environmental studies. Second, discovery learning may be contrasted with the sort of learning usually associated with the traditional classroom, i.e. learning by instruction or demonstration. And third, learning by discovery does not just happen: it comes about as a result of a particular teaching method or strategy. Numerous strategies can be distinguished in this connection; perhaps the commonest one to be found in open classrooms is that of *guided discovery*. By this means, a teacher supports a child's self-chosen activity with questions, commentary, and suggestions.

In Chapter 6 we considered some of the characteristics of *talk* in the traditional classroom. We saw, for example, that it is 'highly centralized', that is, there is a single verbal encounter in that whatever is being said demands the attention of all; and that the communicative rights of teacher and pupils are very unequal, the pupils' role being one mainly of listening. *Talk* in the open classroom, by contrast, occupies a much more strategic position. Indeed, many open educators regard talk as an important index of the degree of openness in a classroom. Adelman and Walker express the point thus,[18] 'What should we look for in classrooms as indicating openness? We consider that the nature of talk is the crucial factor, for talk is the only readily available manifestation of the extent and process by which mutual understandings of what counts as knowledge in any context are transacted.' Openness then by this yardstick is reflected by the quality of action and the significance and nature of the talk taking place in the classroom, and this is best achieved at the individual and small group level. The fundamental problems of openness, as Adelman and Walker point out, revolve therefore around the difficulties of asking and answering questions, and of knowing when to disclose and when to withhold information. To this end, the open classroom, much more than its traditional counterpart, demands of the teacher an awareness of the child's mind and viewpoint and this means that the 'amount of thought sensitivity and empathy that the teacher has to mobilize and accomplish "openness" makes his task more challenging, vulnerable, and exhausting than in a "closed" classroom where the rules for access to knowledge are set rather than negotiated.'[18]

The *hidden curriculum* describes the sum total of relationships, attitudes, values, 'invisible assets', and tacit knowledge existing within a school. It includes the perspectives and assessments both the pupil and the teacher have of each other and their mutual expectations. Although in a sense independent of the official curriculum, the hidden curriculum is related to it in various ways. Soured or hostile attitudes, for example, can have a devastating effect on the work of a school no matter how efficiently organized and seemingly well taught it is. The most potent effects of the hidden curriculum emanate from the points of interaction in the relational structure of the school, where teacher interacts with pupil, pupil with pupil, and teacher with teacher. And it is because teachers and pupils work more closely in informal situations that the hidden curriculum plays such an important part in open schools. One of the most important aspects of it in an open environment may be referred to as the 'pedagogic atmosphere', and this in turn depends upon 'the aggregate of underlying moods that the pupils and the teacher bring to the classroom, for they furnish the medium within which their opening toward each other occurs. It also depends upon the general state of mind that emerges from this aggregate that is created by their being together.'[19] The pedagogic atmosphere of an open environment thus relates to the ambience in which teaching and learning take place. A related concept applicable to all kinds of schools is that of 'organizational climate', a notion equally elusive in terms of both definition and measurement which we examine in more detail in Chapter 11.

Three concepts play a particularly important part in the organization of learning in the open classroom – *individualization, grouping,* and *individual attention. Individualization of instruction* is based on recognition of the fact that not all children can be expected to learn at the same rate. The approach is used in both traditional and open classrooms though its relationship to the content of learning in each case is different. In the traditional classroom, individualization is achieved by varying the pace or duration of learning, by varying the mode of teaching, or by modifying the set curriculum in some way. What these variations have in common, however, is the belief that all children must master a specified curriculum determined by the teacher or the system. A consequence of this is the need for frequent evaluation and testing to check the children's progress. In open classrooms, where individualization is a key concept, children collaborate in formulating their own curricular goals. As Stephens explains,[6] 'The teacher's responsibility is not to decide in advance exactly what each child will study but rather to provide a climate in which individual children can make choices about the curriculum and explore matters of interest to them.' This does not mean that the child does as he likes, or that the teacher abandons all responsibility in this connection, but that the curriculum is freed from the constraint of the traditional approach and now more appropriately meets the unique needs, interests, and abilities of each child.

Individualization is sometimes misinterpreted as meaning that each child works on his own, individually. But this is not the case. It simply means that his individual needs are taken into account. More often than not, these can be most effectively met by *grouping.* As a school's philosophy is reflected in its organization, it is to be expected that the open school will have an 'open' approach to grouping and that therefore different methods of grouping may be used as the circumstances demand. Stephens observes that there are two broad perspectives from which grouping for instruction can be viewed – the intra-school and the intra-class. The former concerns the way children are arranged *within the school* and may include *vertical grouping,* that is, mixed age grouping of children, and *horizontal grouping,* that is, grouping of children according to age. With the latter, intra-class grouping, organization takes place *within a class or teaching unit.* In this category, Stephens identifies three kinds of groups: *instructional* or *interest groups* formed around areas of the curriculum; *organizational groups* related to seating arrangements, administrative details, and so on; and *social groups* formed for the purposes of play or talk. In contrast to groups in traditional classrooms, these tend to be flexible, loosely structured, formed and led by pupils as well as by teachers, and relatively impermanent. Of course, these arrangements do not in any way preclude the occasional need for class teaching, as in story or music.

Individualization involves encounters with the teacher from time to time and we now examine her contribution in the form of *individual attention.* In a classroom environment characterized by high openness, the burden of informal encounters between teacher and child can be very onerous, sometimes totalling as many as 1000 interpersonal contacts a day. For this reason, individual attention can be one of the more problematic concepts in an open environment for it is never far removed from its polar opposite – individual neglect. Let us take this a little further and examine the evidence. Records show that the distribution of teacher help in terms of time spent with each child is unequal. At least two studies conducted in the United States show that in any given period certain children received most of the attention while others were largely ignored.[20] A British study[21] further reveals that two main groups of children received attention – the active hardworkers and the active miscreants. It was concluded that the *average passive* child missed out in this respect, not through any rational policy on the part of the teacher, but because the ongoing classroom pressures limited pupil contact to the two categories identified above. Further, for the neglected child who was also diffident and therefore unlikely to talk even to those other children in his group, the classroom became 'bereft of language, either written or spoken'. Boydell graphically describes the possible consequences of individual neglect:[22]

'Isolation from the teacher, coupled with a fairly high probability that contacts will not be work-oriented when they do occur, is as much a classroom reality for many children as the exhausting never-ending series of individual work conversations are for the teacher. "It's time to pack up", said by a weary teacher at the end of the afternoon, may be all some children have heard her say to them all day!'

Uneven distribution of attention is obviously a serious obstacle to the efficient functioning of the open classroom. Boydell suggests ways of overcoming the problem. One way of increasing children's exposure to adult speech is through the provision of taped materials of various kinds. Another possibility is the introduction of aides and parent volunteers into the classroom under the supervision of the teacher, a way that has been tried with some success in the United States.

THE ROLE OF THE TEACHER IN THE OPEN CLASSROOM

Before examining the role of the teacher in the open classroom, we refer to findings from empirical research which throw some light on teachers' own reactions to open education. First, of those teachers interviewed in one survey study the majority said that they enjoyed working in open schools and would be reluctant to return to conventional settings, in spite of dissatisfaction with some aspects of the approach.[23] Second, higher levels of job satisfaction are achieved by teachers in open classrooms than their counterparts in traditional schools, though whether this is due to the nature of the teaching style or to the possibility that open schools tend to attract teachers having higher levels of job satisfaction anyway is not clear. And third, the more experience teachers have of open education and of the innovations like team-teaching which follow in its wake, the more favourably disposed they become towards it and to the innovations.[6] While these findings do not necessarily meet with universal support from open educators at large, they do provide some evidence that teachers involved in open education are, or become, its strongest supporters though it must be remembered that a self-selecting factor may be operating; that teachers working in open education were in favour of it in the first place and chose it for that reason. We need also to bear in mind that while personal testimony yields interesting insights from an interpretive perspective, it needs to be balanced in this sort of context with rigorous objective inquiry, certainly from the point of view of outcomes.

In Chapter 11 we shall look in a more formal way at the concept of *role* and related concepts within the broader framework of school organization. We are primarily concerned here with the teacher role in the open school and the expectations attached to it. Teachers in primary schools take on a variety of roles in their day-to-day classroom and school activities. In the traditional type of school, for instance, the teacher is first and foremost an instructor or transmitter of knowledge, though the increasingly diffuse nature of her work in recent years demands that she fulfils a number of sub-roles as well. One writer[24] has suggested that these may embrace the roles of parent-substitute, organizer, value-bearer, classifier, and welfare worker.

With the emergence of the progressive movement in the primary sector, however, this traditional conception of the teacher's role has undergone a *fundamental change of focus*. This has arisen as a consequence of the conception of child development underlying the movement and its practices. It is based on the views of those educators and theorists who see education as a process of growth and not something that can be imposed from without, as is the traditional view. For them, education is the realizing of a child's inner potential, something which must come from the child himself. The purpose of the educator in this scheme of thinking is to create an environment favourable to this end. The growth theorist who has had most influence on the thinking of progressive educationalists in Britain is Froebel. His views differ from traditional conceptions chiefly in two ways:

1. Classroom practice should be determined by the need to realize a child's inner potential; and
2. The teacher's role should in consequence be primarily that *of an observer*.

Dearden explains it in this way:[25]

> 'First, practice will be governed by the polarities of inner and outer, or inward and manifest, with the former in each case being praised, preferred and looked to for educational cues and initiatives. This preference for the hidden, inner potentialities of the child is often, indeed, characteristically, expressed in slogans, such as "we teach children, not subjects", or "not into the child but from the child", or "the child must be the agent of his own learning". Everything necessary for the process of education to have direction and drive will be regarded as being present in the child, as a hidden inner potentiality needing only to be stimulated and supplied with the right external conditions for it to unfold and develop. Secondly, in consequence of all this, there will be a conception of the teacher as first and foremost an observer, watching for signs of readiness, looking for spontaneous interests and activities, seeking to read the signs of the inner ripening that will give him his cue. For what he, the teacher, must do will depend very much on the lead which the growing child gives him to follow.'

As well as being primarily an observer, the progressive teacher will assume a related set of sub-roles just as the traditional teacher does. Stephens has suggested a possible range that includes the roles of diagnostician, resource specialist, learning manager, consultant, facilitator and interactor. As she writes,[6] 'All these terms undoubtedly do reflect aspects of the teacher's jobs. As they are interested in individual children, they must diagnose each child's needs. Recognizing the importance of materials and planned environment, they must know about available resources and must manage learning facilities. When teachers encourage children to take an active part in their own learning, they are less likely to lecture than make themselves available as consultants or facilitators. Finally, teachers believe in dialogue with students, and thus they interact with them.'

One writer[26] has likened the role of the teacher in the open classroom to that of the travel agent who 'advises on both individual and group choice of destination and route; who warns that some places are too difficult to reach just yet; and who recommends books and other resources that will enable the traveller to understand new situations he will meet.'

To be effective in an open classroom, a teacher must be able to move from one role to another, almost imperceptively and with great adaptability. How this is done is illustrated in the following extract. It is a description by an observer of an outstanding teacher at work:[27]

'She had excellent eye-contact and vigilance. Some informal teachers operate head down, and fail to see that pupils at one end of the room have lost interest or are disrupting others. (The teacher) has the kindly, beady eye of many a successful practitioner, able to split her attention between the individual or group she is with and the rest of the class. Periodically she scans the class, and is mobile enough to intervene in any problem before it escalates.

'This vigilance is transmitted to the whole class in subtle ways. At intervals she publicly reviews the class's progress. "Now you two are still painting; Ian you're preparing assembly; Neil I think it's time you left that, isn't it?" It represents an alerting of the whole group to the fact that she is publicly aware of what is going on: but it is a light touch.

'Another message regularly transmitted is that of pupil independence. In many informal classrooms, pupils are so dependent on the teacher that she is over-whelmed with crowds of up to 10 or 12 children gathered around her desk, or trailing her around the room. (This teacher) has no more than one or two soliciting her attention at any one time.

"Have more faith in your own judgment", she says to one boy who has crossed out correct solutions to his sums, because he thought that two questions should not have the same answer. "Don't work together if you can do it on your own", she tells another small group; yet co-operative working is also permitted when each participant is making a contribution, and not just riding on the backs of others.

'Setting-up operations are conducted with great clarity. A small group of people is being introduced to some new number work. Explanations are crucial in informal teaching: otherwise children have no proper idea of what the task entails. Both subject matter and the way of handling the task are crystal clear after (the teacher) has explained them, largely by question and answer and a few intriguing mysteries: "I'm not going to say one word about number seven, but you just think carefully about it."

Yet there is even more to the teacher's role in the open classroom than is suggested by this versatility. The very concept, openness, impinges on her function and necessitates a fundamental reorientation to people and features in the working environment. A more sensitive awareness of relationships is demanded; indeed, relationships take on prime importance because some of the defining characteristics of open schooling lie mainly in the nature of the interpersonal transactions taking place there. Being a member of a team, for instance, a teacher has to work much more closely with colleagues than would be the case generally in conventional schools. This may entail all kinds of interactions from *ad hoc* conversations and discussions to meetings of a more formal kind among groups or teams of teachers. It follows that a teacher is more likely to be influenced by those with whom she works and will in turn exert more influence herself on the functioning of the school. Further, relationships with the children will differ quite considerably from those in traditional classrooms. Being characterized by 'openness', they will be based on mutual trust and acceptance rather than on the exercise of, and response to, authority, as is the position in traditional settings. Coop[28] points out that the relationship of the teacher to her materials is also changed. As he says, 'Materials become matters of evidence which pupils and teachers interpret in partnership. The teacher has to be aware of the underlying assumptions of the materials which may affect her work . . . . Materials imply method. Methods imply assumptions that can lie undetected. Therefore the teacher has to develop an awareness of this kind of phenomena, analyse it, and relate it to her own aims and objectives.' The role also invites a new kind of relationship with employing authorities. As Coop again notes, 'There is a need for a two-way communication. In open situations the teachers are users, producers, and demanders of materials. The employers must also become suppliers, counsellors, and supporters of teachers in this situation. This means the development of resource centres and in-service courses.'[28]

Before turning to the problems facing the teacher in the open classroom and the way in which they affect his or her role, we refer you to Box 9.3 which contains a brief extract from a primary school study conducted by the Schools Council. For this particular part of the study, teachers were asked to declare their own personal position with respect to the two broad kinds of teacher role, traditional and progressive. The descriptions listed under traditional roles' and 'progressive roles' are the variables distinguishing the two groups.

The problems facing teachers in open classrooms centre chiefly on two areas – differences of opinion among staff and the way in which the concept of openness affects a

BOX 9.3

The Teacher's Role in the Primary School

Sub-groups of a sample of primary teachers preferring traditional and progressive roles respectively as closest to their own.

Traditional roles	Progressive roles
Older	Younger
More experienced	Less experienced
Longer in present school	Shorter time in present school
Without higher qualifications	With higher qualifications
Married·	Single

Source: Ashton et al.[29]

school's boundary relationships both within and without in the sense that these are now more fluid.[30]

Differences of opinion sometimes arise among practitioners in open education itself and also between open educators and traditionalists impatient of their philosophy. In the first instance, a common cause of disagreement stems from conflicting interpretations of the presumed philosophy underlying the practice. Some, like Kohl for example,[31] take an extreme stand on the teacher's function in the open classroom, advocating that she should keep as much in the background as possible and allow the children to follow their own interests as the will takes them. Opponents of this view take a more moderate line, recommending that the teacher take a more actively responsible part in planning programmes, establishing standards of work and behaviour, and extending children's interests as well as helping to develop them.

More serious because potentially more disruptive are the clashes of values that sometimes arise between teachers of a traditionalist leaning and those holding a progressive viewpoint. The arena for such conflict is more likely to be the secondary school rather than the primary, though ideological differences are not unknown in primary staffrooms. Hargreaves[32] explains how such a clash may reveal itself on the question of interpreting deviancy in the classroom and the consequences of such a confrontation for the school:

> 'Most schools contain a variety of teachers with very different social, political and educational philosophies. We often give them loose labels such as "traditionalists" and "progressives". Accordingly their conceptions of school and classroom rules differ, as do their conceptions of deviant pupils. Certainly some kinds of pupil, such as vandals, are almost universally defined as deviant; but in many other aspects of school life one teacher's deviant is another teacher's darling. Those teachers who wish to maintain their status differential will inevitably define some pupil conduct as cheeky. But the young, progressive teacher who is trying to play down his status differential will define precisely the same pupil conduct as "natural", "open", and even "friendly".
>
> 'Such differences do not make headlines but they are instances of the growing disparities among teachers often within the same school. The effect is to undermine the traditional consensus on which teacher – teacher relations, and much teacher – pupil relations, has rested. The battles are not just between teacher and pupil, which has a long-standing tradition, but between teacher and teacher.'

With the advent of open education has come an increased diffuseness in the teacher's role. This has resulted in the blurring of the boundary between the teacher and the children and this in turn has created thorny problems for the teacher. One observer expresses them in a series of interrogatives:[33] 'What constitutes "guidance"? How far should children be "free" to develop? How much responsibility for their own learning should they take? How much do they want? When does teacher delegation become abdication? Just what concepts are children expected to acquire? The difficulty in answering questions of this nature places considerable role-strain on the teacher.'

Other boundaries in open education become less easy to define also. A teacher is no longer isolated in her own classroom and as she works with individuals and groups, her 'performance' is often 'public'. Whereas this approach may benefit the children greatly, it may at the same time result in adverse consequences for the teacher. Richards explains why:[33] 'This increased visibility could lead to teachers developing less idiosyncratic teaching styles so that, paradoxically, teacher individuality is diminished as child individuality is encouraged.' He further observes that co-operative teaching tends to erode teacher autonomy and this may lead to inter-staff conflict unless carefully managed. As he explains, 'Here the teacher has to *achieve* a role relative to his colleagues. In such teams semi-specialization may develop, possibly partly as a prop to teacher identity threatened by role diffuseness.'

Another boundary issue is that resulting from the *open plan* design to be found in the newer schools. This refers to that distinctive architectural style which frequently characterizes the *mise en scène* for the practice of open education and points up the 'openness' of a room so arranged in a visible and physical sense as compared with the traditional classroom where the teacher's desk at the front of the classroom confronts rows of neatly ordered pupils' desks. As Bennett and Hyland point out,[34] such schools were built to mirror the flexibility perceived in contemporary teaching practice – 'they were to provide a match between the built environment and what educators and architects saw as a significant shift in primary school teaching.' By thus placing greater emphasis on space by replacing traditional architectural arrangements by learning bays and teaching areas, open plan designers assist teachers by implementing concepts like the integrated day, team teaching and vertical grouping. Box 9.4 shows a typical post-war junior classroom that has such amenities for 'learning centred' education.

Open plan design,[36] while greatly assisting the flexibility and informality underlying the open philosophy, can however result in a number of problems for teachers working in such surroundings. These fall into four general categories:[37] (1) There are problems arising from the greater number of distractions compared with conventional classrooms, and to these should be added the problem of noise; (2) there is the problem of work avoidance. Since children in open classrooms usually have more freedom to move about the room it is easier for them to avoid work; (3) there are problems in enforcing even minimum rules of conduct;[38] and (4) there is often the problem of inadequate storage facilities.

Yet another boundary with its fence removed, or at least considerably lowered, is the one between home and school.[39] Consequently, teacher – parent relations tend to be characterized by less isolation and social distance. That the teacher is now frequently a mediator between the child and its parents and sometimes even a social worker represents yet another extension to an already burdensome role which can in some instances bring even further strains, as Richards explains, 'The increased importance attached to the home, plus parents' lack of knowledge and experience of new developments, make a conflict of expectations more likely than in the past, despite attempts at informing parents or involving them in the life of the school.'[33]

It is extremely difficult at this stage in the history of open education to arrive at a fair and balanced assessment of its achievements. What it has done, however, is to polarize educationalsits into two distinct camps – those who see the movement in a favourable light as expressing an enlightened and humane philosophy, and the remainder who view it in more modish terms, as yet another product of an age that has inverted traditional values. The problem of its effectiveness, however, can only be resolved by more fruitful means of evaluation and it is to this issue that we now turn. We begin with the question of

BOX 9.4

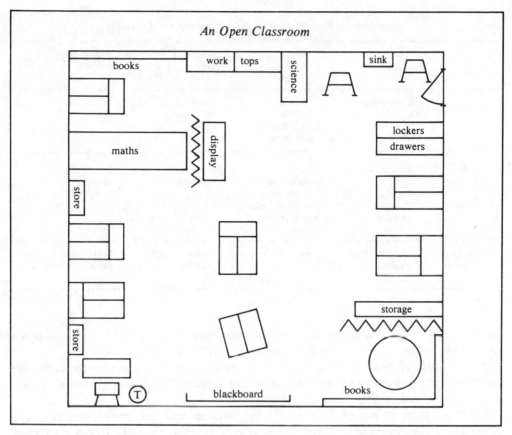

An Open Classroom

Source: Rintoul and Thorne[35]

assessing the degree of openness in a school environment and then examine possible discrepancies between the ideal and the actual in open environments. Finally, we review the kinds of research that have been conducted so far into open education.

ASSESSING OPENNESS IN LEARNING ENVIRONMENTS

Although 'openness' is often used as if it were a unitary concept, it is in effect a multidimensional term, the practical implications of which present a very complicated picture indeed. It is our purpose at this point to show how this complexity may be resolved into more easily understood terms. For analysis and clarification, we use a model designed by Linder and Purdom[40] which we set out in Box 9.5. Although it necessarily over-simplifies the concept of openness when translated into selected activities, it nevertheless

BOX 9.5

Four Dimensions of Openness in Classroom Activities				
	Openness of assignment	*Openness of management* (Teacher's role)	*Openness of process* (Child's role)	*Openness of product*
High Openness	Child plans activities from own interests	Little supervision. No help. Little observation	free exploration or discovery	Not specified
Medium Openness	Teacher and pupil plan together. Child chooses from specified activities	Much supervision. Teacher observes closely and may give suggestions or ask questions	Exploration with guidance	Specified but flexible
Low Openness	Child works on specific assignments	Direct teaching	Follows specific procedures	Specified and predetermined

Source: Linder and Purdom[40]

shows in principle how degrees of openness may apply to different activities and how a working index of openness in relation to these may be arrived at.

As the authors point out, the model enables teachers to analyse and plan their activities intelligently. Each activity can be organized at a level of openness that best fits the situation, the task, and the child.

There are three degrees of openness – high, medium, and low: and (in this particular model) four dimensions of activities – assignments, teacher role, pupil role, and product. The first dimension is concerned with who decides the activity: the teacher, the pupil, or the teacher and pupil in collaboration. The second is concerned with management and the part the teacher plays in supervising the activity. The third relates to the pupil's role and the amount of instrumental control he is subjected to. Finally, the fourth has to do with the extent to which outcomes have been specified in advance.

As you will see from Box 9.5, traditional programmes will be located in the lower categories of the model. The teacher decides on the lesson, gives instructions, has the children follow specific procedures, and expects the answers to be right or wrong. As a teacher moves towards an open classroom, more of the activities will be rated at the higher levels. Of course, a teacher is free to close any of the activities if the need arises. This means that open classrooms have potentially traditional characteristics which may be realized by a teacher if it suits his or her purpose. As the authors themselves say:

'A programme is not always open or closed in every respect. There are degrees of openness in a classroom or an activity. The scale, four dimensions of openness in classroom activities, is a tool for assessing and planning the desired degree of openness.'

The value of Linder and Purdom's model to the teacher in the open classroom is that it can be made increasingly more sophisticated as the situation or need arises. Other dimensions can be introduced quite easily. Take, for instance, the number of activities progressing simultaneously as a possible dimension for assessment; or the system of evaluation employed in a classroom. Is evaluation entirely the responsibility of the teacher (low openness), or of the teacher in conjunction with the pupil (medium openness), or of the pupil with some guidance from the teacher (high openness)? Similarly, factors such as teaching methods, the use of space, and levels of interaction could all be assessed using the same degrees of openness.

DISCREPANCIES BETWEEN THE PARADIGM AND THE PRACTICE

The value to the teacher of the model we have just described resides in the degree of control it enables her to exert over her classroom. It provides her with a point of reference permitting her to open or close selected dimensions to achieve specific ends or meet the needs of particular circumstances. In other words, a teacher with this model in mind can consciously depart from the paradigm of the open classroom in certain ways and for specified periods. It has been shown, however, that there are other instances of the conduct of open education in which the teacher or teachers involved are *not* aware of the extent to which their practices depart from the paradigm. Alternatively, they may be aware of the discrepancy but there is little they can do about it because of the constraints operating on them. Research into this aspect of open education is relatively scant and it is therefore difficult to summarize the findings in a way that is constructive. What we can do, however, is to examine one particular case study where the kind of discrepancy identified above was shown to exist.

In *Education and Social Control*, the study in question, the authors[41] examine the child-centred, progressive approach to education and, as they themselves explain, the application of methods grounded in this approach in three infant classrooms in the infant department of one particular school. Their intention was 'to attempt to study and demonstrate some of the more or less subtle ways in which wider social structural "forces" impinge upon or influence the pedagogy and other social processes at the level of the classroom and the school.' The complex arguments put forward by the authors are summarized in Box 9.6

The progressive teachers in the study are depicted as seeing themselves as in opposition to the assumptions underlying the more formal, traditional approaches to education. In this respect, they do not wish to 'subordinate the child's individuality to some predefined social requirement or impose "high culture" upon the child in an arbitrary fashion because these would frustrate the realization of the child's inner potential.' What the writers show, however, is that the well-intentioned progressive practices of the child-centred teacher produce similar effects to the ones she is reacting against. Examination of Box 9.6 shows that in stressing the freedom of the child, the progressive teacher may find herself unwittingly constrained to act in ways which deny the child the very freedom he

BOX 9.6

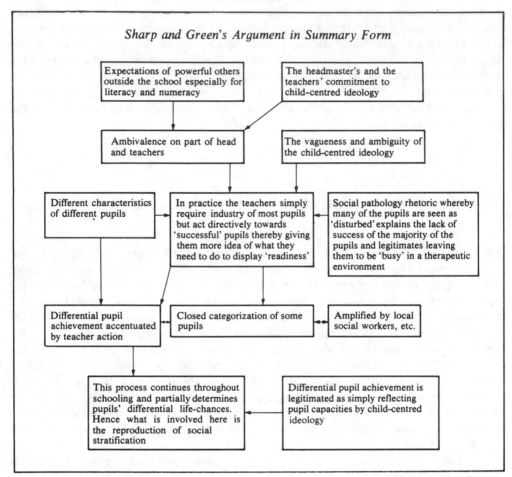

Sharp and Green's Argument in Summary Form

Expectations of powerful others outside the school especially for literacy and numeracy

The headmaster's and the teachers' commitment to child-centred ideology

Ambivalence on part of head and teachers

The vagueness and ambiguity of the child-centred ideology

Different characteristics of different pupils

In practice the teachers simply require industry of most pupils but act directively towards 'successful' pupils thereby giving them more idea of what they need to do to display 'readiness'

Social pathology rhetoric whereby many of the pupils are seen as 'disturbed' explains the lack of success of the majority of the pupils and legitimates leaving them to be 'busy' in a therapeutic environment

Differential pupil achievement accentuated by teacher action

Closed categorization of some pupils

Amplified by local social workers, etc.

This process continues throughout schooling and partially determines pupils' differential life-chances. Hence what is involved here is the reproduction of social stratification

Differential pupil achievement is legitimated as simply reflecting pupil capacities by child-centred ideology

Source: Hammersley[42]

needs to develop from within himself. As a result of their researches, the authors suggest that 'the child-centred educator, with his individualistic, voluntarist, and psychologistic solution to the problem of freedom fails to appreciate the ways in which, even in his own practice, the effects of a complex, stratified industrial society penetrate the school.' They conclude that the radicalism of the progressive educator may well be a modern form of conservatism, and an effective form of social control in the dual sense of achieving classroom discipline and also in preserving a static social order generally.

Instances of the discrepancies between the paradigm of the open classroom and its practices are revealed in the study in the form of two paradoxes. The first paradox is that, according to the philosophy of progressivism, pupils are to be viewed as individuals whose unique needs are constantly to be borne in mind. Teachers are aware of 'the dangers of premature labelling, preferring to retain open minds regarding the potentialities and capabilities of their pupils.' In practice, however, the teachers have stable and hard categorizations of certain pupils. The authors explain, 'Whereas in the teachers' ideology as educationalists, open-mindedness towards all pupils should prevail, in their substantive practice it only seemed to apply to some of them.' The second paradox resides in the fact that the teachers 'claim to be supporters of the egalitarian principle that all pupils are of equal worth, having an equal right to receive an education appropriate to their needs.' Yet the pupils were treated differently in terms of the amounts and kinds of interaction they had with their teachers. The authors go on to say, 'Now the principle of equality does not necessarily commit one to identity of treatment. Nevertheless, it is significant that those pupils whom their teachers regarded as more successful tended to be given far greater attention than the others.'

In fairness to the teachers, however, it must be stressed – as Sharp and Green argue – that these paradoxes are the product of the circumstances in which the teachers have to work. These include the high teacher – pupil ratio and the pressure of significant people outside the school who expect standards of literacy and numeracy to be on a par with those of traditional schools.

RESEARCH INTO OPEN CLASSROOMS

The judicial attitude one invariably adopts to this or that style of teaching is usually based on nothing more substantial than a few spacious generalizations derived from personal inclination, limited experience and hearsay. That this should be so is due to the enduring problems inhibiting the establishment of a coherent and integrated body of hard research evidence enabling us to justify or question the utility of one approach as against another. We need only to remind ourselves of the issues raised so far in this chapter to appreciate the special difficulties associated with open education in this connection – its definition, studied vagueness, lack of criteria, and the like. And then there are problems of greater magnitude above and beyond these that are common to *all* teaching styles and efforts to investigate them: identifying significant variables and selecting the most appropriate method for handling them, for example. Yet these obstacles need not deter us from taking such evidence on open education as is available and using it as a basis for provisional judgment and for indicating directions and issues for the future. It is therefore with these factors in mind that we look at some of the research studies conducted in the past ten years or so.

Research so far undertaken into open education may be broadly classified into two groups – surveys and experimental investigations.[43] The former, usually conducted in a sample of schools, attempt to collect data on a number of factors such as age, sex, intelligence, attitude and academic achievement and subject them to various statistical procedures; the latter, focusing on a particular factor or factors such as 'discovery methods' or selected Piagetian concepts reflecting aspects of the philosophy of open education, are naturally conducted in a more rigorous framework. Evidence from surveys has tended on the whole to reveal open education in a rather unfavourable light. This has become increasingly the case with studies conducted in the 1970s and it is from this period that we select three representative pieces of research to illustrate this trend.

In 1970, Barker Lunn conducted a longitudinal study of children in a sample of streamed and non-streamed junior schools.[44] Although mainly concerned with comparing streaming and non-streaming, she also studied two types of teacher in the non-streamed schools: it is to this part of her work that we refer. Using attitude measures and teaching methods as criteria, she classified the teachers sampled as either 'progressive' or 'traditional'. The former believed in non-streaming, were permissive, favourable to the slow child, tolerant of noise, found corporal punishment distasteful, and preferred 'progressive' teaching methods. The latter were identifiable by opposite characteristics. Data representing pupils' achievement in English tests, problem arithmetic tests, and conceptual arithmetic tests were collected separately for the two types of teacher. Comparisons revealed that whereas the progressive teachers' pupils did fractionally better in the English tests, the traditional teachers' pupils did decidedly better on the two arithmetic tests.

In his research with third and fourth year junior school teachers in the north of England, Bennett[3] identified three general teaching styles: formal, mixed, and informal. Because the mixed style proved difficult to interpret, his principal focus of interest in the study was the contrast between the formal and informal styles. In June 1973, tests of reading, mathematics and English were given to the children whose progress was being studied near the end of their third year. In June the following year, the tests were given again near the end of the children's fourth year so that their progress could be related to the kind of teaching they had experienced. The subsequent interpretation of results was complicated by the fact that some pupils were subjected to an eleven-plus selection procedure while others were not. This notwithstanding, Bennett found that the former made more academic progress than the latter. Further, where there had been an eleven-plus, pupils under informal teaching gained more than those under formal teaching in English and reading, but less than those under formal teaching in mathematics. However, where there was no eleven-plus, pupils under formal teaching gained more than pupils under informal teaching in each of the three subjects.

The findings of another British study by Paisey[45] are in broad agreement with Bennett's in this respect. One of the objectives of Paisey's study was to examine the effects of formal and informal environments on children's achievements. It was hypothesized that children taught by informal methods would be more creative than those taught by formal ones; and that children taught by informal teachers would achieve more highly in class work than those taught by formal teachers. The tests used included Torrance's figural and verbal creativity tests and the British achievement tests in English, mathematics, and study skills. The latter examined the social and scientific aspects of the curriculum in terms of skills and understanding of processes rather than prescribing the form and content of the curriculum. The results were based on a study of sixteen primary schools and revealed that neither of the two hypotheses stated above was supported: informally taught children did not achieve as highly as formally taught ones in basic subjects; nor is the informal teacher more successful in fostering creative thinking than the formal teacher.

If, therefore, we place these representative findings in the context of other survey studies conducted in the 1970s, the burden of the evidence suggests that the value of progressive methods in education has apparently declined over this period. Do the outcomes of experimental studies offer more hope for the movement? We look at two such studies.

In an experiment conducted in two British primary schools, Bowler[46] contrasted a demonstration method in which the teacher performed experiments in elementary magnetism and electricity in front of the class with a guided discovery method in which the children conducted the experiments themselves in groups of four or five. It was found that the demonstration method was more effective than the discovery method in terms of the tests given: written tests of retention, comprehension and application. Another experiment on discovery in a British primary school was reported by Ellis.[47] Using three regular teachers in the infant department, he arranged for each teacher to take one group of children in 'structured' training in Piagetian concepts, one group of children in 'free' training in the same concepts, and one group of children in a control no-training activity. The training occupied nine thirty-minute sessions. In the structured training, the teacher initiated and guided the children's activities very closely as a group. In free training, the teacher attempted to treat each child as an individual, offering guidance as seemed appropriate with the underlying assumptions that the child's intellectual development was primarily a matter for the child himself in his spontaneous activity with the apparatus provided. The teachers expressed the view that the free training was the standard practice. However, tests showed that each teacher obtained better results by using the structured training than by using the free method. Although the difference was not statistically significant, there was a consistent difference unfavourable to the standard practice emphasizing the individual freedom of the child.

In his review of experimental evidence on learning by discovery, Anthony[43] concludes that discovery methods, as contrasted with didactic methods, are disadvantageous in training people to remember and apply the supposedly discovered rules or principles, but that if sufficient guidance is given, discovery methods are advantageous in teaching people how to discover similar principles. Later survey data and experimental data mutually support each other in this respect.

To close this section and the chapter, we examine some of the criticisms voiced in some quarters about research and research procedures in the context of open education and indicate possible avenues of approach for the future. A difficulty with all studies examining the relationship between teaching styles and pupil outcomes is that of accounting for the additional complexities of the world outside the classroom. The effects of parental interest and coaching on school attainment, for example, can never be taken into account in a research design; nor can the incidental learning a child experiences beyond the classroom. Another point to be borne in mind is that the impact of informal schooling may not be immediate, the effects possibly coming to fruition on a 'delayed action' basis long after the researcher has collated and interpreted his data. Perhaps the most obvious point of contention, however, concerns the more or less exclusive reliance on *normative* techniques of investigation in contexts where they are not necessarily the most appropriate. In accordance with the portrayal of the child in the open classroom that we presented incidentally in the course of this chapter, it would often be more fitting if the habitual normative approaches to the study of open environments (surveys, and experiments, for example) were at least to be supplemented with selected interpretive ones, an issue on which some experienced researchers have expressed themselves forcefully thus:[48]

'What little research exists comparing the effects of formal versus informal schools on students has tended to employ indices of traditional academic performance as criterion measures. While such data may eventually prove of interest, an inquiry into the validity of the nonperformance factors supposedly characterizing formal versus informal schools seems more immediately important.'

While survey and experimental research can yield, and have yielded, much needed objective information on aspects of open education, they must by their very nature fail to convey or tap the dynamism, spontaneity and creativity within a truly social setting – hallmarks of the open classroom at its most characteristic and successful. The plea, then, is for a multimethod approach to the study of open education and its practices, the outcomes of which would more adequately represent the wide range of tangible and less tangible features characterizing the movement.

If the researcher in order to capture some of the richness of the open classroom is to be encouraged to adopt a triangular approach to his work, the open educator for his part must make more explicit just what he is trying to do. If, for instance, the assumptions about knowledge suggested by Barth[16] hold for all open classrooms, then it seems on the face of it quite illogical that an open school should perhaps be censured by an external agency for not producing *end-product A* when its whole philosophy and practice was directed to producing *end-product B*; for not developing children's academic skills sufficiently when it was dedicated to fostering personal initiative and self-reliance, say. Even the most extreme of open schools must close at some point where their goals are concerned, a point Dearden trenchantly comments upon:[9]

'If the open school is to continue to be a *school*, its principles must make clear what it regards as worth learning, and it must direct and guide children's learning accordingly. To have no view at all about that, to be quite open about it, is no virtue but educational bankruptcy, and there is then nothing to distinguish the school from say other learning situations in which, for good or ill, children may happen to find themselves.'

Finally, and in some ways most importantly, there is the need to question some of the assumptions on which open education conducts its practices and structures its organization. Some, for example, have questioned the readiness and ability of many beginners and young children to make constructive use of the freedom given them in the informal system, and also the claim that children come to school highly motivated and eager to learn, having appropriate patterns of social behaviour and the skills essential for effective learning. Correspondingly, if a school embodies a progressive philosophy of education, how is it interpreted by its teachers and how do they set about implementing it? This takes us on to the teacher's personal resourcefulness – how she sets about organizing her work, for example, and distributing her time and energy among her pupils. It also involves finding out how patterns of interaction develop, what kinds of exchanges occur, and what the outcomes of these are in terms of academic and non-academic factors. As Corrie says,[49] 'If open schools are to realize their potential we need to know more about the way in which those involved perceive them and the way they organize their everyday actions for educational ends.'

SUMMARY

Having established that open education was initially an American phenomenon, we went on to trace the history of progressivism in education in the United States and Britain, identifying some of the more subtle differences among its manifestations in the two countries and choosing 'open education' as a convenient umbrella term to describe them. Definitional problems relating to open education were discussed and its principal characteristics listed. These were deemed to constitute the basic model for the open classroom. Additional features were described and issues around which controversy and debate frequently centre were located and placed in context. Some of the more crucial assumptions underlying the curriculum of open education were outlined – particularly those to do with children's learning and the nature of knowledge – prior to a discussion of its curricular, pedagogical and organizational features. These comprised the integrated day and the integrated curriculum; play; topics and projects; discovery learning; talk; the hidden curriculum; individualization; groupings; and individual attention. A brief reference to teachers' own perceptions of open education preceded an analysis of the teacher's role and some of its attendant problems. Assessing the degree of openness in classrooms was considered, using a model devised by two American researchers. We then referred to the lack of congruence that sometimes occurs between the philosophy and practice of open education, drawing on case study evidence; and concluded with a selective review of empirical research into open education.

ENQUIRY AND DISCUSSION

1. Much of this chapter leans on what educational commentators think about open education. But what about the teachers who work in open classrooms? If possible, visit a school in your locality claiming to be informal, progressive, or open and ask members of staff how they see open education. You could, for example, compare their assumptions about children's learning and the nature of knowledge with the findings of Barth's own enquiries outlined earlier in the chapter.

2. Using Anthony's chapter[43] as a frame of reference, examine the evidence for or against progressive education.

3. How would you set about introducing the practices of open education to a class that hitherto had been taught in a wholly traditional manner? Linder and Purdom's model[40] will give you a lead in this connection.

4. In reviewing Bennett's research[3] into formal and informal teaching styles, one critic

said,'Given a research design that is so seriously flawed it is doubtful whether any meaningful conclusions can be drawn from the study.'[50] Examine this statement in the light of your knowledge of Bennett's work.

5. A successfully run open school requires, among other ingredients, the active support of parents. Consider ways in which parent participation might be encouraged.

6. Compare and contrast what you perceive as the end-products of learning in an open classroom with those of traditional classrooms.

7. Many researchers into open education use research methods focusing on behaviour for an approach to education which emphasizes experience. How might this paradox be resolved?

8. What do you think Dearden meant[9] when he said that, if schools become too open, they will cease to be schools?

NOTES AND REFERENCES

1. Hyland, J. T. (undated) Open education – a slogan examined. Unpublished paper, Department of Educational Research, Cartmel College, University of Lancaster.

2. For Dewey's forerunners in this connection we suggest you consult the work of Rousseau, Pestalozzi and Froebel.

3. Bennett, N. (1976) *Teaching Styles and Pupil Progress*, London: Open Books.

4. Podeschi, R. and Dennis, L. (1976) The British, Americans and open education: some cultural differences. *Peabody Journal of Education*, **53**, April, 208–215.

5. *Children and their Primary Schools.* (1967) Report of the Central Advisory Council for Education (England), London: HMSO.

6. Stephens, L. S. (1974) *The Teacher's Guide to Open Education.* New York: Holt, Rinehart and Winston.

7. Note: Much of what we say in this chapter applies almost exclusively to the primary school with which the concept of the open classroom is most readily associated. This is not to say, however, that the concept and its implications are inappropriate in secondary education. Indeed, the term, open school, is being applied at the secondary level in this country (see, J. T. Hyland, 'Open education – a slogan

examined.'). What we are saying, however, is that open education is more likely to be found in the primary sector where its philosophical and psychological bases more readily meet pupil needs.

8. Crowl, T. K. (1975) Examination and evaluation of the conceptual basis for open classrooms. *Education (USA)*, **96**, Fall, 54–56.

9. Dearden, R. F. (1974) How open can schools be?, *Education 3–13*, **2**, October, 88–93.

10. Myers, D. A. and Duke, D. L. (1977) Open education as an ideology. *Educational Research*, **19**, 3, 227–235.

11. Egan, K. (1975) Open education: open to what? In *The Philosophy of Open Education* (Ed.) Nyberg, D. London: Routledge and Kegan Paul.

12. Tunnell, D. (1975) Open education: an expression in search of a definition. In *The Philosophy of Open Education* (Ed.) Nyberg, D. London: Routledge and Kegan Paul.

13. See, for example, the collection of papers edited by Nyberg, D. (1975) *The Philosophy of Open Education*. London: Routledge and Kegan Paul.

14. (Ed.) Peters, R. S. (1976) *Perspectives on Plowden*. London: Routledge and Kegan Paul.

15. Dearden, R. F. (1976) *Problems in Primary Education*. London: Routledge and Kegan Paul.

16. Barth, R. S. (1975) Open education: assumptions about children, learning and knowledge. In *Curriculum Design* (Eds.) Golby, M., Greenwald, J., and West, R. London: Croom Helm in association with the Open University Press.

17. Pring, R. (1978) Curriculum integration. In *The Philosophy of Education* (Ed.) Peters, R. S. London: Oxford University Press.

18. Adelman, C. and Walker, R. (1974) Open space – open classrooms. *Education 3–13*, **2**, October, 103–107.

19. Vandenberg, D. (1975) Openness: the pedagogic atmosphere. In *The Philosophy of Open Education* (Ed.) Nyberg, D. London: Routledge and Kegan Paul.

20. Note: The two studies referred to here are: Withal, R. (1956) An objective measurement of a teacher's classroom interaction. *Journal of Educational Psychology*, **47**; and Resnick, L. B. (1972) Teacher behaviour in the informal classroom. *Journal of Curriculum Studies*, November.

21. Garner, J. and Byng, M. (1973) Inequalities of teacher–pupil contact. *British Journal of Educational Psychology*, **43**, 234–243.

22. Boydell, D. (1975) Individual attention: the child's eye view. *Education 3–13*, **3**, April, 9–13. See also the same author's *The Primary Teacher in Action*. London: Open Books, (1979).

23. Meyer, J., Pritchard, D. L. and Moodie, A. G. (1971) *A Survey of Teachers' Opinions regarding Open Plan Areas*, Vancouver Board of School Trustees.

24. Blyth, W. A. L. (1965) *English Primary Education*. Two Volumes, London: Routledge and Kegan Paul.

25. Dearden, R. F. (1972) Education as a process of growth. In *A Critique of Current Educational Aims*, (Eds.) Dearden, R. F., Hirst, P. H. and Peters, R. S. Part I of *Education and the Development of Reason*, London: Routledge and Kegan Paul.

26. Fewkes, D. W. (1978) *The Rationale of Open Education and Personality Characteristics of Open Classroom Teachers*, M. Phil. Thesis, University of Nottingham.

27. Wragg, E. C. (1978) A suitable case for imitation. *Times Educational Supplement*, 15th September.

28. Coop, J. J. (1973) Radix (2): Open education – the changing role of the teacher. *Institute of Education of the Universities of Newcastle-upon-Tyne and Durham Journal*, **25,** 33–37.

29. Ashton, A., Kneen, P., Davies, F. and Holley, B. J. (1975) *The Aims of Primary Education: A Study of Teachers' Opinions*. Schools Council Research Studies, London: Macmillan.

30. Bernstein, B. (1967) Open schools: open society. *New Society*, 14th September.

31. Kohl, H. R. (1970) *The Open Classroom*. London: Methuen.

32. Hargreaves, D. H. (1976) The real battle of the classroom. *New Society*, January 29th.

33. Richards, C. (1974) Changing schools? Changing teachers? *Trends in Education*, **34,** July, 22–26.

34. Bennett, N. and Hyland, T. (1979) Open plan – open education? *British Educational Research Journal*, **5,** 2, 159–166.

35. Rintoul, K. and Thorne, K. (1975) *Open Plan Organization in the Primary School*. London: Ward Lock Educational.

36. Note: It must be pointed out, however, that the presence of an open environment does not guarantee the practice of open education. As Bennett and Hyland in 'Open plan – open education' discovered in their study of open plan schools, design and pedagogy were not necessarily synonymous. Indeed, so unwilling were teachers to forego their territory that walls were replaced by other physical or even psychological barriers – 'in this way the traditional "one teacher one class" system has largely been maintained.'

37. Tanner, L. N. (1978) *Classroom Discipline for Effective Teaching and Learning*. New York: Holt, Rinehart and Winston.

38. Note: For a discussion of some of these problems in the open classroom in the secondary school, see Denscombe, M. (1980) Pupil strategies and the open

classroom. In *Pupil Strategies: Explorations in the Sociology of the School* (Ed.) Woods, P. London: Croom Helm.

39. Note: Writing of this same boundary issue in the open secondary school, Bernstein 'Open schools: open society' observes: '. . . the boundary relation between the home and school has changed, and parents (their beliefs and socializing styles) are incorporated within the school in a way unheard-of in the older schools. The range and number of non-school adults who visit the school and talk to the pupils have increased. The barrier between the informal teenage subcultures and the culture of the school has weakened: often the non-school age-group subculture becomes a content of a syllabus. The outside penetrates the new schools in other fundamental ways. The careful editing, specially for schools, of books, papers, films, is being replaced by a diverse representation of the outside both within the library and through films shown to the pupils.'

40. Linder, R. and Purdom, D. (1975) Four dimensions of openness in classroom activities. *Elementary School Journal*, **16**, 3, 147–150.

41. Sharp, R. and Green, A. (assisted by J. Lewis) (1975) *Education and Social Control.* London: Routledge and Kegan Paul.

42. Hammersley, M. (1977) *Teacher Perspectives*, A Second Level Course, E202, Schooling and Society, Units 9 and 10, Block II, The Process of Schooling. Milton Keynes: The Open University Press.

43. Note: For a balanced and comprehensive review of available evidence on open classrooms, we refer you to the chapter by William Anthony (1979) Progressive learning theories: the evidence. In *Schooling in Decline* (Ed.) Bernbaum, G. London: Macmillan.

44. Barker Lunn, J. C. (1970) *Streaming in the Primary School*, Windsor: NFER.

45. Paisey, G. H. J. (1977) *Pupil achievement as perceived by teachers in formal and informal schools.* M.Phil. thesis, University of Nottingham.

46. Bowler, L. A. (1974) *Discovery and demonstration in junior school physics.* M.Ed. thesis, University of Leicester.

47. Ellis, L. G. (1976) The acquisition of Piagetian conservation by children in school – a training programme. In *Piagetian Research: Compilation and Commentary*, Volume 7 (Eds.) Modgil, S. and Modgil, C. Windsor: NFER.

48. Groobman, D. E., Forward, J. R. and Peterson, C. (1976) Attitudes, self-esteem, and learning in formal and informal schools. *Journal of Educational Psychology*, **68**, 1, 32–35.

49. Corrie, M. (1976) Open plan schools: some research evidence. *Education In The North*, **13**, 33–37.

50. Gray, J. (1976) A chapter of errors: teaching styles and pupil progress in retrospect. *Educational Research*, **19**, 1, 45–56.

SELECTED READING

1. Anthony, W. (1979) Progressive learning theories: the evidence. In *Schooling in Decline* (Ed.) Bernbaum, G. London: Macmillan. An excellent review of a selection of available evidence on progressive classrooms.

2. Dearden, R. F. (1974) How open can schools be? *Education 3–13*, **2**, October, 88–93. A powerful criticism of excessive openness and a plea for the retention of school autonomy.

3. Myers, D. A. and Duke, D. L. (1977) Open education as an ideology. *Educational Research*, **19**, 3, 227–235. A critical and insightful account of open education in the United States based on a study of open classrooms in New York State.

4. (Ed.) Nyberg, D. (1975) *The Philosophy of Open Education*. London: Routledge and Kegan Paul. A collection of scholarly essays by philosophers of education dealing with a range of issues central to open education.

5. Podeschi, R. and Dennis, L. (1977) The British, Americans and open education: some cultural differences. *Peabody Journal of Education*, **53**, April, 208–215. An exploration of significant cultural differences between British open classrooms and their American counterparts.

6. Stephens, L. S. (1974) *The Teacher's Guide to Open Education*. New York: Holt, Rinehart and Winston. A thorough and comprehensive introduction to the study of open classrooms by an author well versed in trends and practices on both sides of the Atlantic.

10

Norms and Conformity

In Chapter 1 we emphasized that normative and interpretive approaches to the study of schools and classrooms should be seen as complementary rather than competing, each adding its own distinctive contribution to our understanding of the complexity of social reality. To that end, the present chapter explores two key concepts, *norms* and *conformity*, first in diverse social settings and then in the particular milieux of schools and classrooms. In these varying contexts, our discussion of the concepts only draws evidence for the most part from positivistic research studies. Our normative orientation redresses the decidedly interpretive stance that we took in two previous chapters where we looked at teacher and pupil perspectives on school and schooling.

The scene is the staffroom of a comprehensive school; the time, half past ten on a Monday morning. During coffee break, Miss Smith, an experienced capable teacher protests to Mr. Jones, Head of Lower School about an unusual occurrence in Class 2A in the period before break. 'I'm absolutely appalled by their conduct,' she complains, 'they've never behaved this way before. For the life of me, I can't think what has come over them.'

Miss Smith's annoyance arises largely as a result of the unexpected. The school has a reputation for good order and discipline, especially in the 'A' streams. This is why Miss Smith is so nonplussed. For some unknown reason, on this Monday morning, 2A did not behave *normally*; they did not conform to the expected. Norms refer to what is generally to be expected. They prescribe the rules of conduct and the procedures that ought to govern the behaviour of members of groups. The rule of good behaviour and quiet application to work has normally been taken for granted by Miss Smith. Now, in future encounters with 2A, she must take steps to re-establish that norm.

Norms and conformity are, of course, inextricably linked. The emergence of even the most basic rules in any group requires agreements among its members, that is, their conformity to some principle which prescribes how they should behave to one another.

Norms lay down the agreed forms of behaviour within a particular culture, society, or group. They set out the rules of conduct upon which members can depend in their interactions with one another. By making possible predictions about how others will behave, norms bring order to the social environment. As well as supervising our overt actions, norms also govern our private beliefs and feelings, and our interpersonal communications. We deal first with norms and behaviour.

A Bedouin Arab is approaching a strange encampment. While still a long way off, he kicks sand high into the air to indicate his whereabouts and thus, his peaceful intentions. On arrival, he touches noses three times with all other males. These norms for establishing contact with unknown fellow Bedouin hold throughout the vast expanse of the Sahara. For its nomadic tribesmen, conformity to these rules serves to establish and to maintain a predictable order in what are potentially dangerous initial encounters. Conformity to norms in this instance is adaptive; it has purpose. The same behaviour between a group of males on the beach at Southend would, to say the least, be misinterpreted!

We said earlier that norms and conformity are closely linked. In everyday usage however, the words themselves evoke quite different reactions. 'Norm' is a neutral word, 'conformity' on the other hand is frequently used in a pejorative sense. Describing someone as a conformist is tantamount to saying that that person is spineless, weak, and lacking in initiative. Yet most of us are conformists in some aspects of our lives because much of our learned behaviour involving conformity to others is both necessary and desirable if we are to live harmoniously together.

In much that we do, we conform without being aware that we are doing so. We conform to the fads and the fashions, to the beliefs and the ways of our particular culture; we are so conditioned to respond to the behaviour of others that we do so unconsciously. This was demonstrated by a researcher and his associates[1] stationed on a busy city pavement playing the well-known prank of staring upwards to see how many people would follow suit. When only one member of the team looked upwards, it was sufficient to cause 4 % of those passing by to respond similarly; when all fifteen of the research staff did so, no less than 40 % of passers-by conformed. A more malicious exhibition of our sensitization to respond to others was the subject matter of a BBC television presentation.[2] Prior to the programme's live transmission and without the knowledge of an innocent member of the studio audience, it had been arranged that on a certain signal everyone should jump to his feet singing 'All things bright and beautiful.' When the signal was given and the whole studio audience responded as one man, a camera recorded the consternation and bewilderment on the face of the naive subject as he too sprang to attention, mouthing meaningless words. His embarrassment was made complete by having to watch a re-run of the episode while the programme presenter explained his behaviour. This was instant, unthinking conformity to a present influence.

It can, of course, be objected that both our examples are somewhat bizarre and that one hardly needs an experiment in order to uncover the nature of unconscious conformity. Yet it is the very taken-for-grantedness of conformity that makes it so difficult for us to become aware of it. Indeed, Garfinkel's[3] interruption of the normal family life of his students by requiring them to live like lodgers in their own homes was designed with the very purpose of causing them (and their families) to remark on the normally unremarkable.

On reflection, it is perhaps not so much the fact of doing what everyone else is doing that is important, rather it is the way in which we subscribe to agreed conventions by fitting our actions appropriately to those of others. Thus, walking along a busy pavement demands very strict adherence to agreed norms if we are to avoid difficulties.

There is one further common basis of our everyday conformity. Often conformity arises as a result of the selective basis on which a group is constituted. Members of a squash club, for example, are likely to be in agreement about the enjoyable nature of their particularly energetic form of recreation just as members of a vegetarian society are likely to share each other's distaste for meat.

WHY CONFORM? CHARACTERISTICS OF THE SITUATION

A traffic warden approaches; we glance at the parking meter. A police car passes; we check our speedometer. In both instances our concern to conform results not from our interactions with readily-identifiable groups; rather, from our knowledge of the costs of non-conformity to specific societal regulations. Often in everyday situations, conformity relates directly to what simply amounts to our estimations of 'reward – cost outcomes.' Costs, of course, are not solely financial. They may be measured in terms of anxiety, discomfort, and indeed, physical coercion as was shown in a classic study[4] in which 'ratebusters' – those exceeding the agreed norms of output, were subjected to painful blows to their arms known as 'binging' – an impressive demonstration of direct group pressure! Another aspect of conformity in such situations is concerned with the degree of surveillance that is present. No doubt in the absence of a traffic warden or police car some of us would behave differently. Surveillance makes for conformity in many situations, not the least in those to do with the classroom behaviour of children. Kounin[5] uses the term 'with-it-ness' to describe the teacher's ability to take in all that is going on within the classroom.

Yet another aspect of the situation that is closely associated with conformity behaviour is often exploited by veteran chairpersons of committees. Watch seasoned headteachers, for example, call for a show of hands in staff-meeting decisions on school policy. They know from experience that public commitment on the part of teachers is more effective in getting things done than their private support for the head's ideas. Research in this area dates back some thirty years to the classic wartime studies of Kurt Lewin. Later studies confirm that conformity increases when people are obliged to take a public stand on issues.[6]

Unlike the findings in the sky-staring experiment reported earlier, there are situations in which being the only person present is a powerful and compelling force to conform to the norms of propriety. In 1964, thirty eight people in New York City passively witnessed a murder without one person going to assist the young victim or even bothering to raise the alarm.[7] This tragedy was influential in initiating a spate of research which has come to be known as 'bystander-effect studies.'[8] Briefly, the evidence suggests that the greater the number of people present, the greater the diffusion of responsibility that occurs. It's almost as though in declining to help, the person in the crowd is asking, 'Well, why me?' On his own, that same individual is forced to face the often unpalatable answer, 'Because you happen to be the only one around who can do something!' The norms governing the situation urge him to conform to what is morally correct. Very often in everyday life conformity and indeed, non-conformity, occur in situations in which we imitate the behaviour of one or more others as the examples in Box 10.1 illustrate.

BOX 10.1

Conformity Behaviour in Natural Settings

In one field study, supermarket shoppers readily conformed to the altruistic behaviour of a model who every minute during the course of the study dropped a coin into a Salvation Army collection box placed at the entrance to the store. When no model was present the takings dropped considerably!

In another study pedestrians persistently went against the traffic signal DO NOT CROSS when they observed a model violate the rule. When no model was there, far fewer disobeyed the regulation.

Source: Bryan and Test[9] and Leftkowtiz et al.[10]

Those of us who have succumbed to the door-to-door salesman and ended up with anything from a brush to a set of encyclopaedias may ruefully have wondered why he is successful despite our initial intentions not to buy. What is it about the way in which he structures the situation that induces our conformity? Often, he employs what is known as the 'foot-in-the-door' technique. It works as follows. We are urged to accept a small token; a gift – absolutely free – no obligation! We take the gift; a plastic soap container, a colour supplement of general knowledge questions, a leather bookmark. Having agreed to this small request and accepted a 'gift', we are now more ready to agree to his real sales pitch. Conformity under these conditions is well supported by research findings.

Last but by no means least in importance, there are aspects of situations in real life and in the social psychological laboratory that strongly urge us to conform. Two examples will suffice. In both hospital waiting rooms and church confessionals procedures are generally so routine, so well-structured, so obviously managed by competent, authoritative experts that conformity is virtually guaranteed. One explanation of the dramatic and disturbing results that Milgram[11] obtained in his electric shock experiments to do with conformity behaviour hinges upon the overpowering press of the experimental situation itself[12], a consideration that we raised in Chapter 1 as a criticism of the positivistic methodology of most experimental studies. Finally, there are occasions in which group members are confronted with danger and stress in extremely adverse environments. One study[13] of a group of undersea explorers who spent ten days in their seabed experimental quarters reported that the hostile environment in which the group was required to work was associated with high group cohesiveness, dependence, and a very close conformity to group norms.

WHY CONFORM? CHARACTERISTICS OF THE GROUP

In a series of classic social psychological experiments Sherif and Asch demonstrated that people rely upon each other in forming their judgments about a variety of social phenomena and conform to others' judgments even when they believe such judgments to be incorrect.

BOX 10.2

Summary of the Sherif and Asch Studies of Conformity

Sherif asked groups of subjects to judge the apparent movement of a tiny light in an otherwise completely dark room. Earlier perception studies had already shown that a stationary light in a dark room appears to move because of the movement of the eyes, but individuals who are alone vary greatly in their perceptions of the distance that this light travels. Sherif found that, as subjects in the presence of others continued to speak in turn, estimates of the light's movement converged. That is, with such a highly ambiguous stimulus, group members used others' judgments to help them make their own. Others defined the array of possible estimates, and the gradual accommodation of group members to each other eventually resulted in the abandonment of minority estimates. A closely arranged cluster of judgments became more and more popular. Sherif concluded that the growing uniformity of judgment, the judgmental norm, was caused by the frame of reference that people in the group provided for each other.

Asch showed lines of varying length to subjects and asked them to choose which one matched the length of a target line. This task would have been easy except for the fact that the subjects heard other members of the group giving incorrect answers. Asch had arranged the procedure so that the subjects had to announce their judgments after they had heard others speak; these other people were actually confederates who had been instructed beforehand to give certain answers, some of which were incorrect. Asch reported that a substantial minority of the subjects gave the same answers as the confederates (even when they knew very well that the other people in the room were wrong). This phenomenon of overt compliance with a group 'norm' was most likely to occur whenever the other people in the group expressed unanimous agreement, i.e. more certainty.

Source: Kiesler [14]

Other studies along the lines of those undertaken by Sherif and Asch show that the size of the group, the unanimity of its members' judgments, and the public or private setting for their responses all relate to the degree to which conformity occurs under experimental conditions. What other factors make for conforming behaviour within the group? In a series of experiments employing electronically-wired booths containing display panels, Crutchfield [15] up-dated the slow and uneconomic methodology of Asch by simulating the judgments of confederates and flashing their responses on the display screens. One important finding he reported was that conformity depends on *who* the other group members are. Their expertise, whether real or imaginary, is strongly related to conformity behaviour. In one experiment, mathematicians were persuaded to yield to false group consensus on questions of simple arithmetical logic because they assumed that other members of the group (whom they could not see of course) were also mathematicians!

The status of group members is also a powerful inducement to conformity as the studies reported in Box 10.3 show.

BOX 10.3

Status and Conformity in Groups

Among aeroplane crews working on a series of problems, there was significantly greater conformity to the judgments of pilots who were high status members than to gunners who were low status, despite the fact that both groups proposed correct answers.

Clues to the solution of problems were given to leaders and to non-leaders, that is, to high and low status members. The clues that the leaders then offered to their fellow group members were generally taken up and the problems were solved. By contrast, when clues were presented by low status members they were more often than not ignored.

Source: Torrance [16] *and Riecken* [17]

One problem social psychologists face in conducting laboratory experiments with groups is that the individuals who compose them rarely share that 'we' feeling which so often occurs in real life groups. Therefore, when studies of behaviour in established groups outside of the laboratory are reported, their findings can be particularly illuminating. One such study was concerned with conformity in urban Boy Scout troops[18]. It was found that the more boys valued their group membership, the greater was their conformity to the norms and the values of the scouting movement. But to what extent, it might be asked, was such conformity a question of reluctance on the part of troop members to appear deviant to their fellow scouts? What are the consequences of deviance?

The extent to which a deviate runs the risk of rejection by group members or possibly ejection from the group depends both upon the degree of deviation and upon certain attributes of the deviant person. A classic study by Schachter[19] demonstrated the punitive reactions of group members towards individuals who persist in their deviancy. Another study by Freedman and Doob[20] showed how deviates are disciplined by being selected for painful, unpleasant tasks rather than rewarding, congenial ones. The deviate in certain classroom groups may be subjected to physical harassment as the extract in Box 10.4 from Hargreaves' study illustrates.

BOX 10.4

Sanctions for Classroom Deviance: an Example

In Forms 4C and 4D the norm was that copying should occur as and when necessary.

'We don't like people who don't copy', said one boy, speaking for the group as a whole, 'I copy off —; he couldn't stop me 'cos I'd smash him'.

Source: Hargreaves[21]

As far as attributes of the deviate are concerned, research suggests that a person's standing in the group is an important determinant of the extent to which that person conforms. Generally, the higher the status, the greater the conformity to group norms. But high standing within a group also means greater security and hence, more opportunity at times, to deviate from group expectations. This was confirmed in an analysis of headteachers' role conceptions reported by Cohen[22] who found that older as compared with younger heads were more ready to take difficult decisions and to risk alienating their teachers. Hollander's concept of 'idiosyncratic credit' offers a persuasive explanation of their behaviour. Because they have held their positions as headteachers for a considerable time, they have had opportunities to 'build up their credit' as leaders with their staffs. Now, when they need to behave idiosyncratically by not conforming to staff expectations, they can do so without too much risk; they are 'well in the black'!

Finally, an interesting occurrence in group situations is the willingness of members to propose more risky solutions to problems than they would countenance as individual decision makers. The phenomenon, called 'risky-shift' has been demonstrated over and over again in a variety of situations.[23]

How can it be explained? Diffusion of responsibility springs to mind as one likely reason. It could be argued that to the extent that each person in a group helps make a decision, then responsibility for it is shared out between those participating and individual accountability is lessened. Another explanation of risky-shift looks at the effects of information sharing in groups. Knowing what other people's decisions are and discovering one's own to be more orthodox and conservative can exert pressure towards greater risk-taking. Yet another attempt to explain the risk-taking phenomenon centres upon the group members themselves. Those favouring high risk, it is argued, are more influential than low riskers. Group discussion allows them to exercise their influence over low risk colleagues. Whatever the explanation of risky-shift, if laboratory experiments of group risk taking have real life analogues, then the implications are important, not the least in children's decision making in school. Careful thought by the teacher about the scope of the decisions she encourages pupils to take and the composition of the decision-making groups she establishes might go a long way to anticipate difficulties in connection with risky-shift in school settings.

WHY CONFORM? CHARACTERISTICS OF THE INDIVIDUAL

In almost all of the experiments we have discussed so far, small numbers of individuals were found who did not conform at all; they were not rebels; rather, independents.

Independents are interesting characters, as often the subject of controversy on the shop floor of the factory as in the classroom of the school. What is it about them that is different? As one would expect, the more self-confident the person, the more often he believes that he has correctly assessed situations, made appropriate responses and thus learned to have faith in his own judgements. Self-confidence, and self-esteem are attributes of the independent person. Before the advent of Women's Liberation Movements, one of the strongest variables associated with conformity behaviour was the sex of the person. Consistently, women were reported to conform more than men. However as we report in Box 10.5, earlier studies of sex and conformity have been criticized for the subtle albeit unintentional biases introduced into their experimental materials and methods.

The relationship between personality and conformity has occupied the attention of researchers for many years. Experimentation in this area is bedevilled by the problem of

BOX 10.5

Sex and Conformity

Research has now shown that men tend to conform more in matters generally associated with female roles, – fashion, child care, and cooking for example, whilst women tend to conform more on questions to do with traditionally male-oriented activities such as sport, motor cars, and politics. On neutral matters, men and women are equally conforming or nonconforming.

Source: Sistrunk and McDavid[24]

adequately defining both personality variables and conforming behaviour to say nothing of the difficulty of accounting for characteristics of the situations in which conformity takes place, not the least important of which are the ways that subjects themselves perceive those situations.[25] Thus while research has pointed to an association between such personality characteristics as dogmatism, authoritarianism, rigidity, and anxiety and conforming behaviour, lack of adequate control for the effects of situational influences urges caution in treating these findings as anything more than suggestive at the present point in time. To expect direct relationships between personality and conformity is, of course, naive. As has been observed, 'Behaviour does not occur in a vacuum; it results from an interaction of behaviour, situation, and task.'[26] Later in the chapter when we look at conformity in school settings, we take up the question of the differing status or prestige that children acquire as a result of their excellence in particular situations or their skills at particular tasks. Differing status bestows different access to power, and this as we shall see, relates directly to conformity behaviour.

For the moment, we turn to look at studies in which individuals are variously made to feel guilty or are given unequal rewards. Each of these situations has been shown to be closely associated with conforming behaviour.[27]

For most of us, the consequence of doing something we know to be wrong is to feel guilty and to wish to make amends. But how? Doing something good to make up for our bad behaviour is one form of retribution; doing something that we find distinctly unpleasant is another way to expiate our guilt. Either way, a guilty person is more likely than a guiltless one to comply to a request to help or to perform some disagreeable task. Research reported in Box 10.6 bears out this conjecture.

BOX 10.6

Guilt and Conformity

Subjects were expressly forbidden to know details of a test they were to be given as part of an experiment. A small number of subjects however, were leaked information about the test by a confederate of the experimenter and thus placed in the invidious position of possibly spoiling the research. The intention was to make them feel guilty and in consequence, to elicit conformity behaviour from them. It was found that nearly twice as many 'guilty' subjects subsequently conformed as did 'innocent' participants.

Source: Freedman et al.[28]

Summarizing the research in this area Freedman[20] notes that 'regardless of the type of transgression – whether lying, scattering valuable notes, delivering electric shocks, or breaking an expensive machine – subjects complied more when they had transgressed than when they had not . . . . Transgression aroused guilt, which, in turn, led to increased compliance.'

Exchange theories with their propositions about 'social justice' have been used to account for conformity behaviour in situations where one party feels over-generously rewarded in comparison with a partner who has expended similar effort in completing a job of work. Exchange theory argues that the person receiving the disproportionately-large reward should feel the injustice of the situation and seek ways of redressing the balance. This is precisely what occurs both in laboratory and in real life situations. Unequally rewarded members of teams readily hand over part of their winnings in order to restore equity.[29]

Finally, simply 'feeling good' can affect the degree to which a person conforms to the norm of being helpful to another. The interested reader may wish to review the evidence presented in an attractively-named experiment, 'Cookies and Kindness',[30] which has application to the classroom. How, for example, can the teacher make opportunities for children to 'feel good' about their day-to-day work in class and what are the resulting changes in the pupils' helpfulness and co-operation one with another?

We begin our discussion of conformity in school by looking at the system of shared rules that represents the formal organization of the school.

NORMS AND THE SCHOOL

All social organizations have rules that govern their procedures. They are what Katz and Kahn call 'system norms'. They serve as an overall framework that regulates behaviour deemed appropriate to the ongoing purposes of an organization.

As a social organization, the school too has norms which specify the behaviour that is expected of pupils and staff. School norms make explicit the rules of conduct and the procedures that ought to direct the day-to-day life of the school community. Notice the word 'ought' and the 'ought-like' character of norms. Norms are not behaviour itself; rather, they refer to desired behaviour; they are evaluative; they stipulate what is considered most appropriate or most to be preferred. In addition, norms specify the amount or the degree of behaviour that is to be expected, that is, they have a qualitative dimension. Norms also vary in their intensity as the study reported in Box 10.7 shows.

BOX 10.7

Headteachers' Beliefs about their Role

On a large number of statements to do with behaviour towards pupils, teachers, and parents, a national sample of headteachers showed a high degree of unanimity over what they considered to be absolutely essential aspects of their professional role. On matters to do with relations with outside institutions and bodies, the picture was different. Here, heads perceived the norms covering these situations as allowing a greater degree of latitude in their behaviour. On many issues to do with the school's external relations, heads indicated that whilst they preferably should or should not comply with certain norms, in actuality, they would decide on their course of action in the light of particular circumstances. Norms then are also marked by a range of tolerable behaviour.

Source: Cohen[22]

Headteachers are important but by no means sole arbiters of school norms. Schools serve local communities which are rich in tradition and often closely linked with their schools in a variety of activities. Together, these same communities constitute the wide society which is regulated by value and belief systems that act as powerful determinants of what is taught in schools. Furthermore, schools are part of a public system of educational provision governed by procedures agreed on at both national and local level. Our immediate concern here however is not so much with outside influences; rather with those that operate within the school itself.

SCHOOLING AND THE LEARNING OF NORMS

One norm that is consistently emphasized in classes as varied as infant reception units and sixth form study rooms is *independence*.

To the question, 'what is learned in school?', Dreeben[31] observes that a central norm that all pupils must learn to acknowledge is that there are tasks that they must do alone. Along with this self-imposed obligation goes the idea that under certain circumstances, others have a legitimate right to expect such independent behaviour. By *independence*, Dreeben refers to characteristics such as self-reliance, personal responsibility and self-sufficiency in handling tasks that, *under different circumstances*, the child could rightfully call upon others for help. It is the phrase *'under different circumstances'* that is significant here. Dreeben's argument is that the circumstances of the school are different from those that obtain either in the home or in occupational employment for which the school is intended as preparation. The norm of independence, he asserts, is learned within a pattern of classroom organizational practices and teacher/pupil actions that are designed to shape the child's experiences. In addition to being removed from family members with whom they have already formed strong dependency relationships, children are confronted with the sheer size of a classroom assemblage which restricts each child's claim to personal contact with the teacher. It is this numerical property of classrooms, Dreeben argues, that reduces pupil opportunity for establishing new dependency relationships with adults and for receiving adult assistance.

Closely related to independent behaviour is the distinction that each pupil must learn to make between *co-operation* and *cheating*. Cheating, Dreeben observes, takes many forms most of which involve collective effort; thus, actions called cheating are closely tied to the instructional objectives of the school and usually involve assisted performance when unaided performance is called for. The irony of cheating *in school* is that in familial and occupational settings, the same kinds of co-operative endeavours are generally considered morally acceptable and even commendable.

Another norm that is strongly stressed in school is achievement. Pupils, Dreeben asserts, come to accept the premise that they should perform their tasks the best they can, and act accordingly. In light of our forthcoming discussion of non-conformity in school we would want to change Dreeben's bold assertion with the qualification *'most* pupils'.

Typically, classrooms are organized along an assignment – performance – evaluation sequence of work ending in the application of achievement criteria to each child's efforts. In this way, pupils learn to deal with the consequences of their successes and failures. For most children schooling provides experiences of winning and losing. But what of failure? Dreeben asks. Is this not a more difficult condition for the pupil to cope with since it involves acknowledgement that the premise of achievement (to which failure is related) is a legitimate principle by which to govern one's actions? Moreover, while the school provides a greater variety of achievement activities than does the family, it has fewer resources for supporting and protecting the child's self-respect in the face of failure. We take up this important issue later in the chapter.

CONFORMITY IN SCHOOL – CHARACTERISTICS OF THE SITUATION

Despite what we said earlier about external pressures impinging upon the school, to a marked degree schools are 'closed' organizations, separated from the wider society, pursuing their purposes with little interaction between themselves and outside agencies. They are miniature societies governed by their own special norms and values. As closed systems, they have been compared with 'total institutions' such as prisons, military units, and mental hospitals. At first sight this might appear a somewhat odd parallel. On reflection however, there are similarities. A pupil is no more able to leave the school which he is legally obliged to attend than a prisoner is at liberty to quit the gaol to which he is confined. Furthermore, in schools as in hospitals, prisons, and military organizations, there are two identifiable sub-systems, one group consisting of those who direct the other.[32] Teachers, observes Brookover, are the 'controllers of the controlled'. In a classic study of teaching, Waller goes even further, describing the teacher – pupil relationship as a 'form of institutionalized dominance and subordination . . . . . (in which) children are defenceless against the machinery with which the adult world is able to enforce its decisions; the result of the battle is foreordained.'[33]

However overdrawn Waller's account may strike today's reader, the conflict model of teaching that lies at its heart provides one view of teaching and learning as social processes which involve conforming behaviour. Geer,[34] using exchange theory propositions, comes to the same conclusion as Waller,

> 'As teacher, A originates interaction for B (pupil) by imparting knowledge or directing him to it. At the same time, A accepts the obligation to see to it that B responds as he (A) wishes. In fulfilling his responsibility, A evaluates the correctness of B's response and controls B's behaviour during the interaction sufficiently to make a correct response possible. Essentially, A's role is that of command and B's of submission.'

Descriptions of traditional schools emphasizing the disciplinary and custodial aspects of the teacher's role provide vivid accounts of coercive teachers and compliant pupils.

An alternative view of the teacher – pupil relationship is based upon a distinction between *membership* and *reference* groups. For some pupils, the school is a membership group, no more, no less. They belong to it because they have to. For others, school is a source of ideals and values. It provides a framework for their developing beliefs and attitudes. For such children, it acts as a reference group. In Box 10.8 we paraphrase Katz and Kahn's[35] discussion of the authority structure of an organization using the school as our example. The school, in Waller's view, is a 'despotism in a state of perilous equilibrium'. But has Waller chosen the right metaphor? The despot has no need to negotiate power; he takes it. Few schools today would continue to function for long under the personal despotism of a

BOX 10.8

The Authority Structure of the School

Only insofar as the majority of members of a school recognize and accept its authority structure as legitimate can staff and pupils get on with the central tasks of teaching and learning. The 'arm' of any authority structure is its system of rewards and punishments, and the legitimate use of that system rests upon the majority's acceptance of the differing degrees of power attached to the various positions of headteacher, staff, prefects and pupils. Illegitimate use of power, whether real or imagined, dissipates majority acceptance and rapidly leads to breakdown. The riot in a Newcastle comprehensive school in 1976 over the use of corporal punishment and the destruction of Hull maximum security prison in the same year over the loss of privileges unequivocally affirm the temporary and negotiated basis upon which authority rests even in total and 'total-like' institutions.

Source: adapted from Katz and Kahn[35]

---

headteacher. 'The power to grant authority', Spady reminds us, 'lies with the pupils. The subordinate party in an authority relationship grants legitimacy to the dominant party by virtue of the latter embodying attributes that the former regards as valuable in promoting his general welfare.'[36] However, as we show later in the chapter (see Box 10.14) teachers' authority rests on more than pupils' willingness to accept subordinate classroom roles.

Implied in our earlier observation on the use of the school as a membership or a reference group is a view of pupils as the active originators of a particular orientation towards school authority. From an interpretive perspective, Cicourel and Kitsuse[37] see it differently. For them, it is the school itself which produces in the course of such activities as streaming and allocating pupils to different curricula, a variety of 'pupil-careers', including the rebel and the delinquent. This view of the school as an active processing agency, the instigator of some children's gradual and increasing non-conformity is central to recent explanations of secondary school deviance. The reader will recall that we touched upon this theme in Chapter 3 in our discussion of school climate and pupil behaviour.

CONFORMITY IN SCHOOL – CHARACTERISTICS OF THE GROUP

'I felt funny . . . . when they said an answer and I didn't think it was right . . . . I felt my heartbeat went down.'

'If you do too much disagreeing people will think you always disagree and get the wrong impression.'

These observations by a seven year old girl and a nine year old boy, respectively, are recorded in a study of conforming behaviour by Berenda[38] in which some eight hundred children between the ages of seven and thirteen were confronted with false consensus judgements in Asch-type situations. Other studies[39] involving ambiguous perceptual judgements like those in Sherif's experiments have also been undertaken with children. Broadly, it seems that conformity is a function of age as the figure in Box 10.9 demonstrates.

BOX 10.9

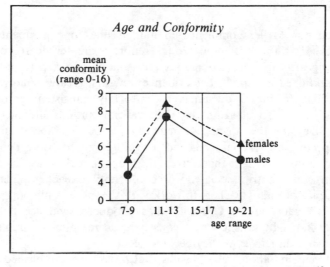

Source: Costanzo and Shaw[40]

Some explanations of the trends shown in Box 10.9 draw upon the psychology of developmental stages. The work of Piaget[41] on children's intellectual and moral development and that of Parten[42] on their developing socializing skills show the very young child as individualistic, largely impervious to the influences of his fellows and thus unaware of any social pressures to conform to their standards. During nursery school and infant school years, the transition from associative to co-operative play marks the child's growing awareness of, and response to, the social influences of his peers. By the age of seven or eight, while most children show a rigid adherence to the rules governing much of their social behaviour, the effect of being out-of-step with the majority view does not yet strike younger children as particularly threatening, notwithstanding the obvious concern expressed by the two young respondents above. The figure in Box 10.9 shows an increasing concession to majority opinion from the age of seven or eight onwards. We must be careful not to read too much into these results. They refer solely to the degree of social influence operating in rather contrived experiments on conformity. Moreover, studies of pupil conformity in differing age ranges which draw upon stage-trait theories such as Piaget's to explain their findings have not shown consistent results when analysed by sex, despite the fact that developmental stages are generally considered as being independent of sex typing. An alternative explanation looks at the differing patterns of social organization that are readily discernible in groups of older pupils and to the differing attitudes of these pupils towards the generality and the flexibility of group norms. This approach has the advantage, too, of helping account for sex differences, quite different clique and coalition formations having been demonstrated in boys' and girls' groups across wide age ranges.[43] More importantly perhaps, laboratory studies of conformity have limited applicability in furthering our understanding of the potency of the peer group in shaping the lives of younger people.

CONFORMITY IN SCHOOL – CHARACTERISTICS OF THE INDIVIDUAL

Notwithstanding our earlier comments on hidden bias in experiments to do with conformity and sex, studies of pupil groups report a greater degree of conforming behaviour among girls in both ambiguous and unambiguous perceptual judgement experiments with mixed groups.[43] The evidence for girls' greater conformity to adult-approved solutions to moral dilemmas is uniformly consistent across American, Canadian, Russian, and British samples.[44] Cultural expectations offer an explanation of these findings. Despite the advances made by Women's Liberation Movements, females are expected, are encouraged, and are taught to be more dependent, more submissive, and more compliant than males in groups, not the least in school groups.

Age too, seems consistently associated with conformity to teacher influence, no doubt reflecting the choice of many teachers to work with the more compliant pre-adolescent rather than with older pupils. Gordon[44] has produced evidence from American, Japanese, and Indian samples showing a consistent decrease in children's eagerness to comply with teacher directives as they become older.

But global statements about relationships that have been established between such factors as age, sex, and personality and classroom conformity tell us nothing of the reality of the classroom situation as it affects and is affected by the ongoing behaviours of its participants. They are rather sterile abstractions about what is essentially a complex and dynamic process of continuous interaction. It is to the structure of classroom groups that we must look in order to identify aspects of ongoing behaviour that are governed by the feelings of attraction existing between pupils (the 'affect' structure) and the varying degrees to which pupils are able to influence one another's behaviour (the 'power' structure).

The Affect Structure

Sociometric techniques provide some indication of the positive and negative feelings that children hold towards one another and the degree to which they seek or avoid each other's company in class or in out-of-school situations. The sociogram in Box 10.10 shows the friendship patterns of children in a racially-mixed second year junior school classroom.

The numbers allocated to individual children are used to compile a sociometric summary chart, recording each child's positive and negative choices (Box 10.10 reports only the positive friendship choices). The vertical line bisecting the circles represents the division between boys and girls. The thick broken line represents the ethnic boundary. Pakistani boys and girls occupy an area in the top segment of the circle approximately proportional to their numbers in the class. Distance from the centre of the circle is approximately proportional to the number of strong choices that a child receives ('strong' choice is defined as any case where an individual chooses the same child three times in response to the following three positive questions: (i) who do you like to sit near in your class?, (ii) who do you like to play with in the playground?, (iii) who would you like to take home to tea?).

BOX 10.10

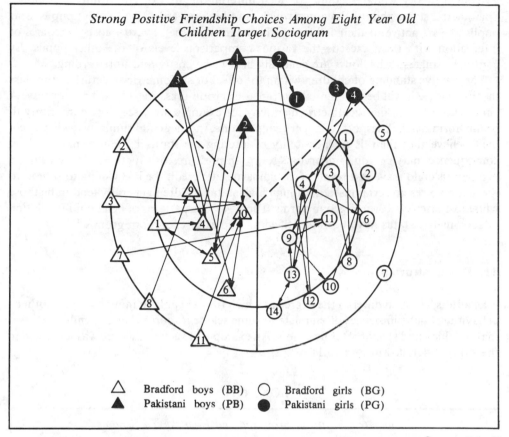

Strong Positive Friendship Choices Among Eight Year Old Children Target Sociogram

△ Bradford boys (BB) ○ Bradford girls (BG)
▲ Pakistani boys (PB) ● Pakistani girls (PG)

Source: Cohen[45]

Children located at or near to the centre of the circle appear to be 'stars'; those located at or near to the perimeter of the circle receive no strong choices and tend to be 'isolates'. Within the inner circle in Box 10.10 are the total number of strong choices received by the whole class. Arrows indicate the direction of choice; reciprocated choices are shown by arrow heads at both ends of the line joining the two pupils.

We can identify the sociometric standing of various children shown in the classroom group in Box 10.10. For example, Bradford boy number 10 and Bradford girl number 9 appear as sociometric stars, while Bradford boy number 2 and Bradford girls 5 and 7 are isolates. There are small friendship cliques within the class too for example, Bradford boys 5 and 10 and Pakistani boy number 2 constitute such a clique. Note that whereas Pakistani boy number 2 both gives and receives positive friendship choices, Pakistani boys number 1 and 3 give friendship choices to Bradford boys but these are not reciprocated.

These illustrations of ongoing relationships in a class of children are important to a teacher's understanding of pupil behaviour for they often relate to the degree of conformity that children exhibit both to their fellow pupils and to their classteacher. Exchange theory would account for such differing degrees of conformity as follows. Sociometric stars exhibit behaviours which have high reward value to other pupils. Star pupils are attractive to their fellows to the extent that the reward – costs outcomes of interaction with them exceeds the various comparison levels of the other pupils. By contrast, isolates' behaviours are generally held to be costly and unrewarding.

The relative standing of children within the affect or sociometric structure of the class means that each will be differentially attuned to group pressures toward conformity. A child who is low in the sociometric hierarchy for example, may see close conformity to group norms as the passport to higher group status. Another child similarly lowly placed, may believe that there is no possibility of altering his status by conforming and, in consequence, may be quite impervious to group pressures or sanctions. There again, a high status child may, as a result of his 'idiosyncratic credit' be less willing to submit to group pressures on certain issues, though high status children generally tend to be those who most often conform to group norms. These varying patterns of behaviour in relation to sociometric status have been identified in studies of classroom groups.[46]

The Power Structure

Like adults, children differ in the degree to which they are able to influence one another's behaviour. Such differences often relate to some scarce resource that one child possesses that is valued and sought after by others. An example of such a resource was identified in the study[47] detailed in Box 10.11.

BOX 10.11

Sociometric Status in Streamed and Unstreamed Schools

In a large scale study of streamed and unstreamed primary schools in Great Britain, it was found that boys of above average ability tended to be sociometric stars in unstreamed classes significantly more often than in streamed classroom groups. One explanation of the finding might be that in the more homogeneous, streamed classes, the occurrence of an above average ability workmate was less rare, given the more restricted ability range in streamed groups. In the unstreamed classes, the relatively greater scarcity of such a person made his contribution to group work tasks more highly valued by his fellow pupils.

Source: Barker Lunn[47]

The extent to which one person is able to influence another's behaviour implies that differing degrees of power exist in their relationship. Within classroom groups such power is manifested in the ability of certain children to meet the needs of their fellow pupils for affection, for help, and for status as the following study by Gold[48] demonstrated. The subjects were children aged between five and twelve years of age. They were required to complete two questionnaires to identify first, what the properties or resources were that children valued most; second, who the particular children were who possessed those resources, and third, which of those children exercised the greatest amount of social influence. Gold showed that those children who were identified as having most social power were also those who possessed more of the valued resources such as helpfulness, fairness, sociability, expertness, fearlessness, and physical strength. Other studies of children's groups in natural settings confirm the relationship between sociometric status and social power[49].

NON-CONFORMITY IN SCHOOL

A great deal has been written about students and pupils whose values and behaviour are antithetical to those of their colleges and schools. For these young people, educational institutions serve as negative reference groups. We confine our discussion to studies of groups in Great Britain.

An early study[50] identified cliques of boys and girls in grammar schools who expressed views in opposition to those of their teachers and who "voted with their feet" by more frequent truancy and by leaving school at the earliest opportunity. Teenage as opposed to school commitment was the subject of a study of secondary school pupils undertaken by Sugarman[51] who found smoking, dating, having long hair, dressing in trendy clothes, and generally achieving well below potential, to be the hallmark of the anti-school group. Like Sugarman, Lacey's[52] study of a Manchester grammar school noted that the attention of the anti-school group was on the bright lights, the coffee bars, and the pop scene beyond the confines of the school. Hargreaves'[21] participant observation study in a secondary modern school traced the emergence of what he described as a 'delinquescent subculture' in the less-academic streams of the school as the pupils progress through their school careers. The classic studies of Lacey and Hargreaves anticipated Willis'[53] in-depth report of a small group of anti-school working 'lads' who reject the norms and values promulgated by their teachers and accepted by their conformist fellow pupils whom they disparagingly identify as 'ear 'oles'. Willis proposes that teacher authority rests upon a system of exchange in which pupil compliance is traded for knowledge and qualifications; – passports to middle class jobs. He goes on to show how teacher authority is effectively undermined by the anti-school group who decide that a working class culture of opposition, linking them to the world of tough, masculine, manual labour, is preferable to conformity to school values.

Thus, the knowledge that the school can offer is no longer seen as a valuable commodity; it can no longer be exchanged for the lads' compliance. Instead, the teachers receive their non-conformity as the extract from Willis' highly-readable account shows. (See Box 10.12.)

As more school-based studies of alienated groups of adolescents are reported, the prime role of the school in initiating and sustaining their disenchantment with school values becomes clearer. The impact of the school is mediated through its system of academic streaming and setting. More academically-able children from middle class homes are over-represented in the 'top' streams or sets; they participate more in the school's social and athletic functions; they stay on longer to reap the rewards of the system. There is some evidence however that in mixed ability schools and in those that delay streaming until the later secondary years the social and academic polarization that results in behavioural problems, truancy, and early leaving can be ameliorated.[54]

BOX 10.12

Non-Conformity in the Hammerton Lads

Joey	You do anything you can here to, you know, go against them. Well, I mean, you vandalise books.
Spike	Yeah, you smash chairs up, take screws out of . . . .
Joey	Really afterwards, you think, 'well, stuff me, our old lady paid for that lot out of tax', but at the time you're doing it, you don't think and you don't really care.
Interviewer	But do you think of it in the same way as smashing bottles or thieving?
Joey	It's opportunity, getting your own back on the teachers . . . . If you think, if you can get your own back on *him* you'll do anything you can (. . . .) revenge, sort of thing, getting revenge.

Source: Willis[53]

COPING WITH NON-CONFORMITY IN SCHOOL AND CLASSROOM

Happily, non-conformity is generally less overt and less disruptive than that emanating from Joey, Fuzz and the rest of the Hammerton 'lads' in Willis' study. In any school, however, there are differences in the needs and the goals of pupils and teachers; there are differences in power; and there is competition for scarce resources such as status and rewards. Such differences give rise to *conflicts of interest. Interest*, according to Johnson[55] refers to benefit, profit, advantage, concern, right or claim. Conflicts of interest, he argues, arise out of:-

1. Difference in needs, values, and goals.
2. Scarcities of certain resources such as power, influence, money, time, space, popularity, and position.
3. Competition or rivalry.

Johnson asserts that there is no way to eradicate conflicts of interest in the school and in the classroom. There are bound to be times when teachers and pupils are in conflict over the imposition of rules, regulations, assignments and responsibilities, over the degree of independence granted to pupils, over the amount of effort committed to academic learning, and over the personal relevance to pupils' immediate concerns of what is being taught. Conflicts of interest are a fact of life and will occur regularly among teachers, between teachers and pupils, and among the pupils themselves no matter what the educational practices and philosophy of the school happen to be.

Given the inevitability of such situations, what is the teacher to do? – avoid conflict or attempt to resolve it? In proposing the latter course of action, Johnson identifies a number of strategies for conflict management in school and classroom.

In the first place, the teacher must try to pinpoint the particular event or events that trigger the expression of conflicts of interest. Triggering events are many and various – a sarcastic remark, a critical comment on a sensitive issue, or simply the fact that two pupils have been required to work in close proximity to one another. Feeling ignored or neglected is frequently a triggering event. Johnson argues that whenever possible, the teacher must chose the right time and place for bringing a particular conflict of interest into the open in order that negotiations can be undertaken towards resolving the issue. A crucial aspect of conflict management is recognizing when either to suppress temporarily the expression of conflict until circumstances are more appropriate or to precipitate it in order to move towards its resolution. It is important to realize that not every conflict of interest *is* negotiable. The mistake that inexperienced teachers sometimes make is to assume that one can *always* openly negotiate the resolution of a conflict. There are times in school when conflicts are better avoided. Nevertheless, Johnson asserts, the vast majority of conflicts of interest in schools and classrooms can be negotiated if only the participants are willing to do so. But what exactly does Johnson mean by *negotiation*?

Negotiation is a process by which individuals who wish to come to an agreement to resolve a conflict, but who disagree about the nature of the agreement, attempt to work out a mutually acceptable settlement. Discussing the process of negotiation of a conflict of interest within a school setting, Johnson identifies two basic goals:

1. Reaching an agreement; and
2. Not damaging (rather, if possible, *improving*) the basic co-operation among the individuals involved.

In any negotiation, he observes, the participants have to be concerned about both the *primary* and the *secondary gains* they achieve for themselves through negotiating. The nature of the particular agreement is the determinant of the *primary gain*; the more favourable the agreement is to an individual's short-term goals, the greater the primary gain for that person. It is the effectiveness of the organization that determines *secondary gain*; the more effective the school (for example), the more the long-term goals of a member will be met and consequently, the greater the long term gain for that person. It follows therefore that in negotiating a resolution to a conflict of interest, a participant must have an eye not only for what is most personally desirable, but also for what is best in improving classroom or school effectiveness.

A strategy for negotiating a constructive settlement of a conflict is set out in Box 10.13.

IMPLICATIONS FOR THE TEACHER IN THE CLASSROOM

'We don't call out, do we, Class 2?' 'Can we all sit down quietly and wait our turns?', 'We only want the very best work for the classroom frieze.'

In the course of any school day, these and countless other exhortations by teachers tell us something about how they interpret their roles as educators of children. Much of the teacher's work in the classroom is concerned with initiating group norms by way of setting standards for pupils' academic attainment, developing appropriate attitudes towards work, and guiding children's social behaviour. In the hands of a skilled and experienced teacher such norms are quickly established and readily demonstrated in the well-ordered, cohesive classroom, alive with a quiet hum of application and industry.

But how does it all come about, the student teacher may ask? How does one begin to establish these basic rules of conduct and procedure that are so essential to successful

BOX 10.13

Negotiating a Settlement of a Conflict of Interest

Step 1: confronting the opposition
A direct expression of one's viewpoint and one's feelings is vital from the outset. Equally important is an invitation to the opposition to be as forthright themselves. Expressing feelings is often difficult but it must be undertaken and should be directed at the issues involved *not* at the persons who are in conflict.

Step 2: jointly defining the conflict
Resolving a conflict necessitates defining it in a way that is acceptable to both sides. Therefore, focus on behaviour, not on individual characteristics; centre discussion on issues not on personalities. Try to define the conflict as a problem to be solved not as a battle to be won at all costs. Coercing pupils into doing what the teacher requires is a short-term strategy with poor long-term payoffs. The smaller and more precise the conflict, the easier it will be to resolve.

Step 3: communicating co-operative intentions
A candid expression of one's intention to co-operate results in: (a) agreements being reached more quickly; (b) a reduction in an opponent's suspicion and defensiveness; (c) a greater comprehension by each protagonist of the other's point of view; and (d) more positive perceptions by both parties to the dispute of each other as understanding and accepting persons.

Step 4: negotiating and perspective taking
Successful negotiation requires sufficient detachment from one's original position to be capable of looking at an issue from alternative perspectives. Perspective-taking involves demonstrating to an opponent that one is capable of accurately perceiving his position and his feelings. This can be achieved by temporarily arguing an opponent's position.
   A central aspect of successful negotiations, therefore, is taking the perspective of one's opponents and influencing them to do the same.

Source: Johnson[55]

teaching? The study[56] of an experienced teacher setting about the task of initiating standards for classroom work and behaviour identified the sequence of procedures illustrated in Box 10.14.

BOX 10.14

Initiating Standards for Classroom Work

First, the teacher established beliefs about his authority by so structuring situations during the first days of his contact with the new class that, in a very natural way, pupils were literally given scores of instructions, both individually and as a group, involving the mechanics of organizing classroom materials, methods, and procedures. The effects of giving so many directives and securing compliance over a wide range of classroom activities was to establish the belief among his pupils that the teacher gave directions and children obeyed them. Second, the teacher's immediate use of sanctions for non-compliance indicated to one and all that disobedience was not to be tolerated. That is, having made a rule about the outcomes of non-compliance and having informed the class of that rule, the teacher was meticulous in carrying out his intentions. Finally, as the children learned the 'ground rules' for their behaviour in class, the teacher gradually transferred the emphasis from his use of personal power to the pupils' responsibility for obedience to rules and regulations.

Source: Smith and Geoffrey[56]

While the account in Box 10.14 sounds somewhat repressive, the teacher in question established these conditions of work and behaviour with a good measure of warmth and humour in his relationships with the children in his charge. Much of his success, no doubt, depended first upon the legitimacy of his claim to be the authority figure in the classroom and second, upon the children's expectations of him as a teacher. Although we have identified these as separate factors they are, of course, closely interrelated.

From the time when their education becomes compulsory, a great deal of pupils' socialization is to do with getting them to accept the authority structure of the school and the legitimacy of the teacher's claim to exert power over them. In this matter most pupils readily acquiesce; indeed they expect teachers to exercise their authority. Hargreaves'[57] summary of research into pupil expectations points unequivocally to children's preferences for teachers who are firm and able to keep control, who use disciplinary methods that are neither too strict nor too lax and who, above all, are impartial.

In initiating class-norms for behaviour and standards most teachers therefore start with a 'bonus' in that children wish them to exercise control. As we have seen, the successful application of that control involves first, establishing rules which, wherever possible, have been formulated with the assistance of the pupils themselves. Second, making those rules quite explicit for each member of the class. And third, giving praise and attention to those who support the rules and invoking agreed-on-punishments for those who break them.

All of this sounds very easy, student teachers may well protest, but it's often much harder to put into practice! The plain answer to such objections is of course that it is not easy to secure class conditions in which all children consistently apply themselves to the tasks in hand with willingness to achieve high standards. There are however insights to be gained from the study of classroom groups which can help the teacher work towards that ideal.

First, children are more likely to work responsibly at what they find interesting and rewarding. It is the teacher's duty, wherever possible, to make classwork as intrinsically satisfying as possible. Second, children are more likely to work independently when the tasks they are set are well-structured and clearly comprehended. Unrest in the classroom, surreptitious chatter, copying from the work of other pupils and the like are often teacher-initiated because of a lack of structure and a failure to clarify the required tasks. Third, with a little thought, the teacher can use group forces to his advantage in the day-to-day work of the class. He might, for example, decide that certain subgroups of children are better separated for particular class activities. There again, he might harness group feelings by initiating healthy competition between groups of children co-operating in some project or extended piece of work. In such situations, the satisfaction of each pupil is dependent upon the maximum contribution that each member makes to the overall group effort. Moreover, knowing the sociometric standing of pupils in such groupings enables the teacher to work through high status members whose behaviour is often modelled by other children. Finally, the teacher would do well to remember that pupils model themselves on his behaviour too. His personal standards, his conscientiousness, and the warmth and patience he shows in his interactions with children provide daily examples for them in their own dealings with their classmates.

In all that we have said so far we have had in mind 'typical' pupils in 'typical' classrooms. But what about those children who regularly present problems in school? What strategies are available to the teacher in coping with these disturbing and worrying children? Leach and Raybould[58] have identified some of the most effective teaching techniques for helping children who present behaviour problems in class. Their discussion centres upon teacher actions that are likely to create what they term a low potential for difficulties in the classroom.

First, they recommend, the teacher should *communicate to all pupils the expectation that she trusts them and has faith in them despite any difficult behaviours that they exhibit.* She should avoid labelling a child as one who characteristically behaves or performs in an unacceptable way. Although she may be tempted to exclude a child with behavioural difficulties from a 'good' group of pupils, there is little experimental evidence for the efficacy of such a strategy. More positively, by her attitude and behaviour, the teacher should communicate to other children in the group that she expects that particular pupil to behave 'normally'. Isolating troublesome children into special groups simply increases their potential for creating classroom difficulties.

Leach and Raybould's second suggestion for dealing with children with behaviour difficulties is reminiscent of the advice given in Box 10.14. *Communicate to the class by your actions that you mean what you say.* Formulate classroom rules, ideally as few as possible, and support them by reasoned argument. For those children who find it difficult to follow such guides, give concrete examples of what behaviours are not acceptable.* In reminding such children about adhering to classroom rules the teacher should again explain why the rules are necessary. Having established rules, see that they are consistently enforced. At all costs avoid any threats or promises which you do not intend to keep. And finally, resist the temptation to make judgements about behaviour which is only *assumed* to have occurred.

The third suggestion of Leach and Raybould reiterates a point we made earlier about how important the teacher's behaviour towards pupils is as a model for their own interactions with one another. *Demonstrate and model the desired behaviours for the classroom groups,* is the advice they give. Children learn by observing what the teacher *does* as much as from what the teacher *says.*

Fourth, *take personal responsibility for maximizing the achievement of all children in the class.* Behavioural difficulties should signal to the teacher that positive action is needed rather than explanations of a child's failure as a result of this, that, or the other factor in his/her home background. Too often such explanations justify a child's exclusion from normal teaching groups and for teacher's neglect of the problem. The central challenge of teaching lies in identifying those children who are most in need of help and in assisting them to learn and to behave in an independent and adaptive way.

A fifth technique for helping children who present behaviour difficulties is to *establish a good standard of classroom management.* On this point, Leach and Raybould suggest that the teacher's energies are best spent in organizing and developing strategies that serve to increase the time children actually spend on the tasks they are given to do. Classroom management then, involves structuring the classroom environment to a greater or to a lesser extent for each pupil in light of the child's demonstrated difficulties.

'In the final analysis, the relative success of any teaching strategy for a child must take into account its effectiveness in enabling him to reach the desired learning outcome in a way that brings him recognition and success and which leads gradually to his taking over responsibility for the planning and evaluation of his own work.'

---

* At the same time however, be ready to examine why the rules present difficulties. Remember *Confucius* – 'when those you rule are unruly, look to your rule.'

SUMMARY

This chapter began by observing that a major purpose of norms is to prescribe agreed forms of behaviour. By agreeing rules of conduct we are able to introduce some degree of predictability into our relationships with our fellow beings, and thus establish order in our social environment.

Characteristics of certain situations, we decided, are directly related to our conformity behaviour. For example, in some situations non-conformity may be simply too costly to contemplate; the degree to which we are under surveillance, the pressures that others direct at us, the punishments that others mete out to us, all of these aspects may compel us to conform. In other situations most of us would find ourselves unable to ignore our social responsibilities urging conformity; in yet others, the powerful effect that models have upon us or the skilful ways others 'set us up', obliges us to conform. Sometimes the situation itself is so well-structured by people we credit with expertise that our conformity is a foregone conclusion. Occasionally the situation is so fraught with danger that we survive only to the extent that we conform.

Characteristics of the groups to which we belong are also closely related to conformity behaviour. The status and expertise of our fellow group members, whether real or imagined is a potent force urging conformity to their point of view, particularly so when we happen to be the only deviant! For most of us, deviance is somewhat disturbing if not unpleasant, since it evokes hostility and punishment from others and can result in expulsion from the group. Groups appear to have an effect upon the riskiness of the decisions that are sometimes taken by their members, the most likely explanation of which has to do with the diffusion of responsibility that occurs in group as opposed to individual situations.

But there are those of us who only conform to situational or to group pressures when we truly believe that conformity is either just or justified. Such individuals, *independents* as they have been called, tend to be more self-confident and higher in self-esteem than their fellows. Beyond these attributes, it is not at the moment clear with what certainty we can talk about conformity in relation to such personality characteristics as dogmatism, authoritarianism, rigidity and so on. Some recent research however suggests that even our varying moods relate to the degree to which we conform. Feeling 'good' and feeling 'guilty', for example, are closely associated with conformity to the norm of helping others.

We began our discussion of norms in school by identifying two central norms, *independence* and *achievement* that are consistently emphasized throughout the pupil's career. In exploring conformity in school, we took a decidedly normative perspective and looked at the school situation, first, in terms of the power of a *total institution* to command the obedience of its subordinate members. The limited applicability of this viewpoint to the school led us to consider an alternative perspective in which the authority system of the school was seen to rest upon the agreement of its members, both children and adults, to abide by a system of values and a set of rules governing the day-to-day life of the school.

We looked next at the relationship between age and conforming behaviour in school and saw how the further differentiation of age groups by sex caused us to question the developmental explanation of conformity behaviour in favour of an approach which examined the differing social organization existing in groups of boys and girls.

Two aspects of the classroom situation, its *sociometric structure* and its *power structure*, were then outlined. The account of the former drew upon exchange theory in describing the differing conformity behaviour of *stars* and *near-isolates*. Exchange theory terms such as *scarce resources* and *social influence* were also used in discussing the second aspect of the classroom situation and the differing degrees of power exercised by children in their relationships with one another.

Finally, we looked at the implications of research into norms and conformity behaviour for the teacher in the day-to-day work of the school and saw how one successful teacher set about initiating desirable standards of work and behaviour in his classroom. We saw too how children's expectations for teacher behaviour can assist the beginning teacher in establishing rules of procedure and regulations for children's conduct in class. We concluded with an outline of a number of effective techniques for handling pupils with behaviour difficulties.

ENQUIRY AND DISCUSSION

1. During school practice or on school visits make a note of the general rules of conduct laid down for children's behaviour in school. Share these with other student-teachers. What particular rules do all schools appear to have in common? Which of these rules are, to your knowledge, frequently disobeyed? Why?

2. Read King, R. (1973) *School Organization and Pupil Involvement: A Study of Secondary Schools*. London: Routledge and Kegan Paul, for an empirical study of the rules and regulations governing a sample of secondary schools in south-west England.

3. On a school visit identify three rules for classroom behaviour that hold for the class in which you are observing. Record (separately for boys and girls) the number of times the rules are broken during any lesson. Compare your findings with those of other student-teachers.

4. Study a small group of children in school, identifying the *sociometric structure* of the group and its *power structure*.

5. Make a detailed study of the ways in which an experienced teacher sets about initiating standards of work and behaviour in the classroom. Compare that teacher's methods with the techniques reported on page 334.

6. Read Hargreaves, D. (1967) *Social Relations in a Secondary School*. London: Rout-

ledge and Kegan Paul, for an account of the differing norms governing the behaviour of boys in 4A, 4B, 4C and 4D.

7. Read Willis, P. E. (1977) *Learning to Labour*. London: Saxon House, for an account of the non-conforming Hammertown 'lads' and the nature of their non-conformity in school.

8. Look at the ways in which a sample of urban secondary schools approached the problems of truancy and disruptive behaviour as reported in: DES (1978) *Truancy and Behavioural Problems in Some Urban Schools*. London: HMSO.

NOTES AND REFERENCES

1. Milgram, S., Bickman, L. and Berkowitz, L. (1969) Note on the drawing power of crowds of different size. *Journal of Personality and Social Psychology*, **13**, 79–82.

2. The Burke Special, 'Learning', BBC 1, April 8th, 1976.

3. Garfinkel, H. (1967) *Studies in Ethnomethodology*. Englewood Cliffs, N. J.: Prentice Hall.

4. Roethlisberger, F. J. and Dickson, W. J. (1939) *Management and the Worker*. Camb. Mass: Harvard University Press.

5. Kounin, J. S. (1970) *Discipline and Group Management in Classrooms*. New York: Holt, Rinehart, and Winston.

6. Lewin, K. (1947) Group decision and social change. In *Readings in Social Psychology*. Newcomb, T. M. and Hartley, E. L. New York: Holt, Rinehart and Winston.
   Argyle, M. (1957) Social pressures in public and private situations. *Journal of Abnormal and Social Psychology*, **54**, 172–175.
   Raven, B. H. (1959) Social influence on opinions and the communication of related content. *Journal of Abnormal and Social Psychology*, **58**, 119–128.

7. Rosenthal, A. M. (1964) *Thirty Eight Witnesses*. New York: McGraw Hill.

8. See particularly, Latane, B. and Darley, J. M. (1970) *The Unresponsive Bystander: Why Doesn't He Help?* New York: Appleton.

9. Bryan, J. H. and Test, M. A. (1967) Models and helping: naturalistic studies in aiding behaviour. *Journal of Personality and Social Psychology*, **6**, 4, 400–407.

10. Leftkowtiz, M., Blake, R. R. and Mouton, J. S. (1955) Status of actors in pedestrian violation of traffic signals. *Journal of Abnormal and Social Psychology*, **51**, 704–706.

11. Milgram, S. (1974) *Obedience to Authority*. New York: Harper and Row.

12. Baumrind, D. (1964) Some thoughts on ethics of research: after reading Milgram, 'Behavioural study of obedience'. *American Psychologist*, **19**, 421–423.

13. Radloff, R. and Helmreich, R. L. (1968) *Groups under Stress: Psychological Research in Sealab II*. New York: Appleton Century Crofts.

14. Kiesler, S. (1978) *Interpersonal Processes in Groups and Organizations*. Illinois: A.H.M. Publishing Corporation.

15. Krech, D., Crutchfield, R. S. and Ballachey, E. L. (1962) *Individual in Society*. New York: McGraw Hill.

16. Torrance, E. P. (1955) Some consequences of power differences on decision making in permanent and temporary three man groups. In *Small Groups: Studies in Social Interaction*. (Eds.) Hare, A. P., Borgatta, E. F. and Bales, R. F. New York: Knopf, pp. 482–491.

17. Riecken, H. W. (1958) The effect of talkativeness on ability to influence group solutions of problems. *Sociometry*, **21**, 309–321.

18. Kelley, H. H. and Volkart, E. H. (1952) The resistance to change of group-anchored attitudes. *American Sociological Review*, **17**, 453–465.

19. Schachter, S. (1951) Deviation, rejection and communication. *Journal of Abnormal and Social Psychology*, **46**, 190–208.

20. Freedman, J. L. and Doob, A. N. (1968) *Deviancy: The Psychology of Being Different*. New York: Academic Press.

21. Hargreaves, D. (1967) *Social Relations in a Secondary School*. London: Routledge and Kegan Paul.

22. Cohen, L. (1971) Age and headteachers' views concerning their role. *Educational Research*, **14**, 1, 35–39.

23. Dion, K. L., Baron, R. S. and Miller, N. (1970) Why do groups make riskier decisions than individuals? In *Advances in Experimental Social Psychology*, (Ed.) Berkowitz, L. Vol. 5. New York: Academic Press, pp. 305–377.
    Zanjonc, R. B., Wolosin, R. J. and Wolosin, M. A. (1972) Group risk-taking under various group decision schemes. *Journal of Experimental Social Psychology*, **8**, 16–30.
    Zanjonc, R. B., Wolosin, R. J., Wolosin, M. A. and Loh, W. D. (1971) Social facilitation and imitation in group risk-taking. *Journal of Personality and Social Psychology*, **20**, 361–378.
    Highbee, K. L. (1971) Expression of 'Walter Mitty-ness' in actual behaviour. *Journal of Personality and Social Psychology*, **20**, 416–422.

24. Sistrunk, F. and McDavid, J. W. (1973) Sex variable in conforming behaviour. *Journal of Personality and Social Psychology*, **17**, 200–283.

25. Mischel, W. (1973) Toward a cognitive social learning reconceptualization of personality. *Psychological Review*, **80**, 252–283.

26. McGrath, J. E. and Altman, J. E. (1966) *Small Group Research.* New York: Holt, Rinehart and Winston, pp. 64–65.

27. Freedman, J. L., Carlsmith, J. M. and Sears, D. O. (1974) *Social Psychology*, 2nd ed. Englewood Cliffs, New Jersey: Prentice Hall, pp. 399–400.

28. Freedman, J. L., Wallington, S. and Bless, E. (1966) Compliance without pressure: the effect of guilt. *Journal of Personality and Social Psychology*, **7**, 117–124.
    See also, Regan, D. T., Williams, M. and Sparling, S. (1972) Voluntary expiation of guilt: a field experiment. *Journal of Personality and Social Psychology.* **24**, 1, 42–45.

29. Berscheid, E. and Walster, E. (1961) When does a harm-doer compensate a victim? *Journal of Personality and Social Psychology*, **6**, 435–441.
    Schmitt, D. R. and Marwell, G. (1972) Withdrawal and reward reallocation as responses to inequity. *Journal of Experimental Social Psychology*, **8**, 207–221.

30. Isen, A. M. and Levin, P. A. (1972) Effect of feeling good on helping: Cookies and Kindness. *Journal of Personality and Social Psychology*, **21**, 384–388.

31. Dreeben, R. (1977) The contribution of schooling to the learning of norms. In *Power and Ideology in Education*, Karabel, J. and Halsey, A. H. New York: Oxford University Press.

32. Brookover, W. and Erikson, E. L. (1969) *Society, Schools and Learning.* Boston: Allyn and Bacon, p. 81.
    Jeremy Bentham's blueprints for both schools and prisons, it will be recalled, aimed to place the schoolmaster and the prison officer in central positions of surveillance at all times!

33. Waller, W. (1932) *The Sociology of Teaching.* New York: Wiley.

34. Geer, B. (1968) Teaching. In *International Encyclopedia of the Social Sciences.* (Ed.) Sills, D. L. New York: Free Press, pp. 560–565.
    Exchange theory can, of course, be applied to adult relationships in school. Gray has developed an 'exchange-conflict' model to describe teacher relationships in school settings. 'Since all members', Gray argues, 'have a range of interests in the organization and they are not all reconcilable, at least at any given moment, a fruitful way of describing what happens in organizations is to view them as areas of conflict'.
    See, Gray, H. L. (1975) Exchange and conflict in the school. In *Management in Education I: The Management of Organizations and Individuals.* Houghton, V., McHugh, R. and Morgan, C. London: Ward Lock Educational, pp. 253–265.

35. Katz, D. and Kahn, R. L. (1966) *The Social Psychology of Organizations.* New York: Wiley.

36. Spady, W. G. (1974) The authority system of the school and student unrest: a theoretical explanation. In *National Society for the Study of Education. 1974 Year Book on Education: Uses of the Sociology of Education.* Chicago: Chicago University Press, pp. 36–37.

37. Cicourel, A. V. and Kitsuse, J. I. (1968) The social organization of the high school and deviant adolescent careers. In *Deviance: The Interactionist Perspective*. (Eds.) Rubbington, E. and Weinberg, M. New York: Macmillan, pp. 124–135.

38. Berenda, R. W. (1950) *The Influence of the Group on the Judgements of Children*. Columbia University, New York: King's Crown Press.

39. Hamm, N. H. and Hoving, K. L. (1969) Conformity of children in an ambiguous perceptual situation. *Child Development*, **40**, 773–784.
    Endler, N. S. and Marino, C. J. (1972) The effects of source and type of prior experience of subsequent conforming behaviour. *The Journal of Social Psychology*, **88**, 21–29.

40. Costanzo, P. R. and Shaw, M. E. (1966) Conformity as a function of age level. *Child Development*, **37**, 967–975.

41. Piaget, J. (1954) *The Moral Judgement of the Child*. New York: Basic Books.

42. Parten, M. L. (1932) Social participation among pre-school children. *Journal of Abnormal and Social Psychology*, **27**, 243–269.

43. Vinacke, W. E. and Gullickson, G. R. (1964) Age and differences in the formation of coalitions. *Child Development*, **35**, 1217–1231.
    Allen, V. L. and Newtson, D. (1972) Development of conformity and independence. *Journal of Personality and Social Psychology*, **22**, 1, 18–30.

44. Gordon, L. V. (1968) Correlates of bureaucratic orientation. *Proceedings of the XVIth International Conference of Applied Psychology*, Amsterdam: Awets and Zeitlinger.
    Gordon, L. V. (1972) *School Environment Preference Schedule*. New York: New York State University at Albany. Mimeographed.

45. Cohen, L. (1976) *Educational Research in Classrooms and Schools: A Manual of Materials and Methods*, London: Harper and Row.

46. McKeachie, W. J., Yi-Gang, L., Milholani, J. R. and Isaacson, R. (1966) Student affiliation motive, teacher warmth, and academic achievement. *Journal of Personality and Social Psychology*, **4**, 4, 457–461.

47. Barker Lunn, J. (1970) *Streaming in the Primary School*, Slough, NFER.

48. Gold, M. (1958) Power in the classroom. *Sociometry*, **21**, 50–60, for a study of dominance in the classroom and the accuracy with which even young children accurately perceive the pecking order of 'toughness' in their classrooms, see, Edelman, M. S. and Omark, D. R. (1973) Dominance hierarchies in young children. *Social Science Information*, **12**, 1, 103–110.

49. Sherif, M. and Sherif, C. W. (1964) *Reference Groups*. New York: Harper and Row.
    Lippitt, R., Polansky, N. and Rosen, S. (1952) The dynamics of power. *Human Relations*. **5**, 37–64.

50. Hallworth, H. J. (1953) Sociometric relations among grammar school boys and girls, *Sociometry*, **16**, 32–45.

51. Sugarman, B. (1967) Involvement in youth culture, academic achievement, and conformity in school. *British Journal of Sociology*, **18,** 151–164.

52. Lacey, C. (1970) *Hightown Grammar*. Manchester: Manchester University Press.

53. Willis, P. E. (1978) *Learning To Labour*. London: Saxon House.

54. Ross, J. M., Bunton, W. J., Evison, P. and Robertson, T. S. (1972) *A Critical Appraisal of Comprehensive Education*. Slough: NFER.
Fisher, D. G. (1973) *Streaming and social class in the comprehensive school*. M.Sc. dissertation, School of Research in Education. Bradford: Bradford University.

55. Johnson, D. W. (1978) Conflict management in the school and classroom. In *Social Psychology of Education: Theory and Research*. (Eds.) Bar-Tal, D. and Saxe, L. New York: John Wiley and Sons, pp. 299–326.

56. Smith, L. M. and Geoffrey, W. (1968) *The Complexities of an Urban Classroom*. New York: Holt, Rinehart and Winston.

57. Hargreaves, D. (1972) *Interpersonal Relations and Education*. London: Routledge and Kegan Paul.

58. Leach, D. and Raybould, E. C. (1977) *Learning and Behaviour Difficulties in School*. London: Open Books.

SELECTED READING

1. (Eds.) White, G. and Mufti, R. (1979) *Understanding Socialisation*. Driffield: Nafferton. Contains two papers on socialization and conformity, one in connection with sex ('Socialisation of Women'), the other to do with ethnicity ('Socialisation and Race').

2. (Eds.) Wrightman, L. S. and Bingham, J. C. (1973) *Contemporary Issues in Social Psychology*. 2nd edition. pp. 173–181, provides a brief account of Milgram's classic experiment in conformity behaviour 'Behavioural study of obedience'.

3. Hargreaves, D. H. (1972). *Interpersonal Relations and Education*. London: Routledge and Kegan Paul. Hargreaves discusses the *mediocrity norm* as it applies both to pupils and to teachers.

4. Good, T. L. and Brophy, J. E. (1978) *Looking in Classrooms*. New York: Harper and Row. 2nd edition. Chapter 6 and 7 deal, respectively with classroom management 'Management I: Preventing Problems', and 'Management II: Coping with Problems Effectively'.

5. Saunders, M. (1979) *Class Control and Behaviour Problems*. London: McGraw Hill. Provides practical answers to problems of establishing and maintaining acceptable behaviour in the classroom.

11

The School as an Organization

In Chapter 1, you will recall, we identified two views of social science that represent strikingly different ways of looking at social reality. We summarized these contrasting perspectives in Box 1.2, setting out various aspects of *objectivist* and *subjectivist* positions as they relate to theory, research, methodology and so on. We begin the present chapter by taking up several of these distinctions again, particularly the ones bearing directly on our interest in the school as an organization.

Let us start by putting the idea of *organization* under our conceptual microscope and looking at two divergent descriptions of organizations as examples. The first is cast very much in the objectivist mould, insisting that organizations (in this case schools) may be likened to organisms, entities that interact with their environments by means of complex input – output relationships. The second, a subjectivist perspective, asks 'do organizations really exist apart from the people that comprise them?'

'The use of social systems theory as a way of understanding school organizations has been increasing, for this concept provides for two types of systems: *open* and *closed*. A closed system is independent of its environment and therefore does not describe schools as organizations. However, a school may be described as an open system when it is characterized by an input – output relationship with its environment. The school exists in a larger environment which is social and physical and interacts with this environment. It responds to inputs of energy and stimuli from its environment and it affects its environment with its output. The organization must be durable and ongoing at the same time. Different organizations are not equally adaptable or durable. In other words, they exhibit different degrees of *organizational health* . . . organizational health includes among other things, the ability of the organization to achieve goals, maintain itself, and adapt to environmental changes.'[1]

'We speak of organizations as if they were real. Organizations "serve functions", "adapt to their environment", "clarify thier goals", or "act to implement policy". What it is that serves, adapts, clarifies or acts seldom comes into question. Underlying widely accepted notions of organizations therefore stands the apparent assumption that organizations are not only real but also distinct from the actions, feelings and purposes of people. It is a mistaken belief in the reality of organizations (that) has diverted our attention from human action and intention as the stuff from which organizations are made.'[2]

In various ways throughout *Perspectives on Classrooms and Schools* we have drawn upon objectivist (normative) and subjectivist (interpretive) perspectives to illuminate specific topics of interest with the distinctive insights that each orientation is able to afford. What of our present concern for the school as an organization? How can we best reconcile the conflicting views of organizations expressed in the quotations above? First, by insisting that both tend to excess in the positions they present; the former by portraying the school as though it were human with a will and intention of its own; the latter by alluding to 'our mistaken belief in the reality of organizations.' Organizations are *not* persons, enjoying varying degrees of health, able to achieve goals or allocate resources but they are nonetheless *real* for all that. A second way of reconciling normative and interpretive views of organizations is to recognize that although we are unable to look down both ends of the telescope simultaneously, it does not follow that we are condemned to look down one end only. Our position in this present chapter is essentially the one we have pursued throughout the text, namely that there is no reason why normative and interpretive approaches should not be seen as complementary rather than competing.

There is good reason to look at schools as they are conceived in various normative theories of organization. The formal organizational chart, for example, much favoured by classical theorists allows us to explore the role structure of the school, the positions occupied by its personnel and the expectations that are attached to those positions. Concepts such as *role, position* and *expectation* help identify those regularities in the organizational framework of the school that persist over time and are common to all schools. Such concepts have heuristic value too. As Hoyle[3] observes, they help us get handholds on the complexity of educational organizations. Equally, there is good reason for us to view schools from phenomenological perspectives, as unique, complex configurations that are continuously being constructed by those involved; where *role-making* rather than *role-taking* better describes the shifting, intricate, here-and-now reality of their day-to-day existence.

We begin our account with an outline of some normative views on the school as an organization which derive from four major approaches to organization theory.[4] Our selection of classical theory, bureaucracy, human relations and systems theory; commits us to an overall perspective that is *management-orientated* rather than sociological, a choice which we believe better meets the needs of the majority of our readers.

NORMATIVE PERSPECTIVES ON SCHOOLS AS ORGANIZATIONS

Classical Theory

At the beginning of the present century efforts to grapple with management problems in industrial organizations led to the emergence of what is often referred to as 'principles of scientific management'. The so-called 'era of scientific management' grew out of the ideas of such people as Taylor, Fayol, Gulick, and Urwick – names that are now commonly associated with *classical theories* of organization.

Classical theory, according to Owens[1], was centred around two basic concerns: the explanation of why people participate in organizations (i.e. *motivation*) and the identification of ways of apportioning out specialized tasks and of differentiating between various levels of authority (i.e. *organization*).

Explanations of *motivation* by classical theorists tend to be couched in crude economic terms. People, so the argument goes, work because they need the money and, in addition, they want to make a profit. Such explanations are more applicable to industrial or commercial ventures than to educational institutions. The views of classical theorists about *organization* however are more relevant to school situations. We summarize their ideas in Box 11.1. Implicit is a belief that organizations should be seen as natural phenomena to be systematically investigated in order to reveal their underlying regularities. A central task, it is said, is to identify those objective factors in the work situation that have profound effects upon behaviour in organizations. 'Get the work situation right,' declare the classical theorists, 'and appropriate human behaviour and organizational performance will follow.'

BOX 11.1

Classical Theorists' Views on Organization

In dealing with organization, classical theorists emphasize division of labour, breaking down the total job into its specialized steps and processes whereby each worker becomes highly skilled in his special task. The organization is structured according to a plan which shapes all the small specialized steps into a pattern, thus assuring that the total task of the organization will be accomplished. In the classical view, not only is the detailed plan vital, but strong central control and careful supervision at every step are essential to keep things co-ordinated. When diagrammed, this type of organization takes on a pyramidal form with a strong executive in control at the top and subordinate executives in successive lower layers of the organization, none of whom has more people under his direct authority than he can personally supervise. The aspects of organization stressed by classical theory – specialization of work, span of control, the pyramid of control, and the clearly segmented divisions – have come to connote what is today known as *formal organization*.

Source: Owens[1]

The application of classical theorists' ideas to the school situation is best illustrated by the *organizational chart*, a map of the formal organizational structure of the school emphasizing the shape of its authority system, its hierarchy of positions, its centralization of control, its clear divisions of function and responsibility and its channels of communication. An example of a school's formal organization is set out in Box 11.2.

BOX 11.2

An Example of School Organization

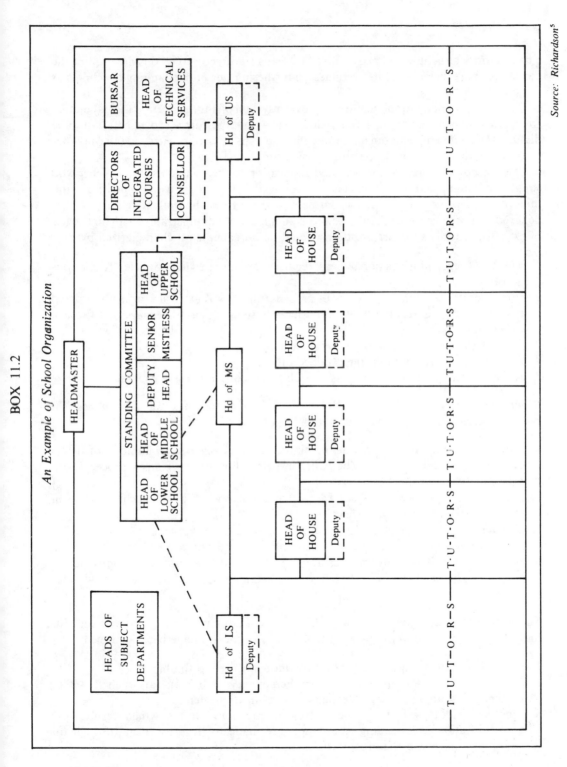

Source: Richardson[5]

Bureaucracy

The authority structure outlined in Box 11.2 leads us directly to a consideration of the concept of bureaucracy and its usefulness in furthering our understanding of schools as organizations.

Contrary to popular opinion, bureaucracy is a system of administration that is adapted to the needs of complex organizations which deal with large numbers of clients, not some diabolical way that officialdom has of surrounding hapless victims with 'red tape' in order to frustrate their attempts to resolve pressing problems!

The concept owes its development and application to the sociologist Max Weber who sought to understand the problems of rapidly developing industrial, political, and military organizations in his native Germany at the turn of the present century. Weber believed that organizations should make maximum use of administrators with high levels of expertise. Ideally such organizations would be bureaucracies, characterized by:

1. Fixed and official jurisdictional areas, regularly ordered by rules, policies, regulations and by-laws.
2. Principles of hierarchy and levels of graded authority that ensure a firmly ordered system of super- and subordination in which those in higher offices supervise those in lower ones.
3. Administration based upon written documents.
4. Administration run by full-time, trained officials.
5. Administration planned according to stable and comprehensive general policies.[6]

When functioning properly, Owens[1] observes, a bureaucracy has four advantages that become increasingly important with the passage of time:

1. *Bureaucracy is efficient.* It provides administrative services to large numbers of clients systematically and uniformly. The staff, consisting of trained specialists, proceeds with little lost time and motion.
2. *Bureaucracy is predictable.* Rules are written and explicit. The hierarchical status of roles, and their authority, is clear.
3. *Bureaucracy is impersonal.* Rules and procedures are applied on the basis of predetermined criteria, and hence, in an unbiased and fair way.
4. *Bureaucracy is fast.* Uniform rules are impartially applied to process thousands of cases quickly. Specialists collaborate on important problems to solve them without delay.

The popularly-held, pejorative view of this system of administration, however, suggests that bureaucracy is not without its critics. Four weaknesses have been identified:

1. Bureaucracy encourages overconformity, inducing 'group think,'
2. In time, bureaucracy modifies the very personality of bureaucrats such that they become the drab, colourless, mechanical 'organization men.'
3. Innovative ideas wilt from the distortion and long delays which result from communications overloading as attempts are made to transmit ideas through the hierarchical layers of the organization.

4. Bureaucracy does not take into account the presence of informal organizations, including the primary groups to which role-incumbents belong.[1]

Can the concept of bureaucracy be applied to an educational system in the way that it is used to describe other organizational conglomerates? Most certainly yes, Warwick[7] asserts, arguing that English education has undergone a complex bureaucratic process arising out of several interrelated, dominant coalitions (the DES, Local Government, the Universities, the Church) backed by the power of the State. The whole enterprise, he insists, is controlled within a legal structure which derives its legitimacy from the 1944 Education Act.

At the level of individual organizations there are bureaucratic characteristics present in schools just as there are in commercial and industrial organizations. We use the phrase 'bureaucratic characteristics' purposely in light of Albrow's[8] observation that the term bureaucracy is best treated as a 'signpost' concept, identifying a whole range of issues to do with the relations of individuals to various features of their organizations. Those bureaucratic characteristics might include, for example, the highly specialized teaching staff in large secondary schools who are recruited on the basis of their expert qualifications. The organizational charts of such schools, moreover, would probably reflect a distinct hierarchical system of authority involving specific lines of command from the headteacher downwards. Later in the chapter we explore some of the conflicts that can arise in schools as a result of their bureaucratic characteristics.

Human Relations

Dismissing the 'economic man' view of motivation propounded by classical theorists as the 'rabble hypothesis', Elton Mayo[9] and his associates undertook a series of studies which came up with some novel findings about the relationship between motivation and organizational productivity. The discoveries were made in experiments carried out at Western Electric's Hawthorne plant in Chicago and led to the enunciation of new concepts of organization to do with *morale, group dynamics, shared decision-making,* and *involvement.* The human relations movement was born. The blatantly mechanistic orientation of classical theorists to the effect that some men were suitable for management while others were only fit to carry out orders was soon to be replaced by a mode of management which emphasized human beings as members of groups, with more intangible motives than the desire for money, such as needs for self-esteem, security and self-expression.

The change of emphasis was brought about by four discoveries made in the Western Electric studies:

1. The 'output' of a worker – hence, the output of the organization – is determined more by his social capacity than his physical capacity.
2. Money is only one motivation for working in an organization; there are other, and perhaps more important rewards that a worker seeks.
3. A highly specialized division of labour is not the most likely way of maximizing the efficiency of an organization.
4. Individual workers react to the organization – its hierarchy, its rules and its reward system – not as individuals, but as members of groups.[1]

Both the 'economic man' view of motivation and the formal organizational chart fell out of favour as explanations of organizational productivity and efficiency. In their place, managers in industry and administrators in public services were urged to look to 'the human side of the enterprise'. Currently, the human relations approach to organizational management is popular and flourishing. It is not difficult to see why. Criticizing concepts such as *democracy*, *participation*, *harmony*, and *conflict resolution* is, according to Perrow, like knocking motherhood and promoting sin!

But the application of concepts like *democracy* to school management is not without difficulty. As Owens observes, it has been a confusing idea both to heads and teachers alike.

> 'At times (headteachers) wishing to do the "right" thing (i.e. be democratic headteachers) would often attempt to decrease the visibility of their power in an honest desire to be democratic not authoritarian. Yet the power was still there, although perhaps momentarily hidden, but it would appear and vanish un-predictably and rapidly. In many situations teachers felt that their positions were not "democratic" at all, but they were being manoeuvred into agreeing to decisions which generally had been arrived at previously. This feeling of being manipulated by a clever administrator who knew clearly where he was heading has probably contributed to a cynicism and suspicion among teachers that are commonly encountered in our schools. The nature of democratic administration has proved to be a difficult one to accept in conjunction with the realities of organizational life in schools.'[1]

Systems Theory

You will recall that at the beginning of the chapter we illustrated the concept of organization by describing a school's relationship with its environment. A school, we said, may be thought of as an open system, inextricably bound to its environment in terms of input – output relationships. The school responds to inputs from its environment and it affects that environment with various outputs. In this section, we explore in greater detail the application of systems theory to our understanding of the school as an organization. We begin with a closer look at open systems.

As well as input-output relationships with their environments open systems have been characterized as described in Box 11.3.

Open systems theory has been widely used as a way of understanding educational organizations at both the macro and micro level. An example of the macro level of organization is the relationship between Local Education Authorities and Central Government in which the LEAs build and maintain schools, staff them, allocate pupils, and through their elected representatives on local councils, see to it that national educational policies are implemented. Central Government finances LEAs by means of block grant procedures and maintains close contact with schools through teams of inspectors whose work is co-ordinated at the Department of Education and Science.

On the micro level of organization the behaviour of individuals in schools has been analysed by Getzels and Guba.[11] They have developed a model of the school as a social

BOX 11.3

Characteristics of Open Systems

1. Open systems tend to maintain themselves in *steady states*. A steady state is characterized by a constant ratio being maintained among the components of the system. By way of example, take a burning candle. When first lit, the flame is small, but it rapidly grows to its normal size and maintains that size as long as the candle and its environment exist.
2. Open systems are *self-regulating*. Pursuing our example from above, a sudden draught will make the flame flicker but when the draught ceases, the flame regains its normal characteristics.
3. Open systems display *equifinality*, that is to say, identical results can be obtained from different initial conditions. Take for example two babies, one born prematurely, the other full-term. While they may look very different at birth and may be at different stages of development, within a matter of months the difference will have disappeared.
4. In part, open systems maintain their steady states through the various parts of the system *functioning without persistent conflicts* that can neither be resolved nor regulated.
5. In part, open systems maintain their steady states through *feedback processes*. Feedback refers to that portion of the output which is fed back to the input and affects succeeding outputs.

Source: adapted from Griffiths[11]

system in which two dimensions, the *personal* and the *organizational* are shown to be significant factors in producing observed behaviour. Some of their concepts like *role-structure* and *expectation* are used in our synthesis of normative perspectives on the school which now follows.

THE SCHOOL AS AN ORGANIZATION: A SYNTHESIS OF NORMATIVE PERSPECTIVES

The Organizational Structure of the School

The organizational chart shown in Box 11.4 was originally intended[12] to illustrate a management structure suitable for small secondary schools. For present purposes it serves to introduce our discussion of the school's organizational structure.

Having identified specific jobs in the school's management structure the authors of the chart indicate some of the responsibilities that might be borne by various senior members of staff.

Headteacher

1. To define and implement the management structure so that the school makes full use of its human and physical resources.
2. To work within the structure, and delegate responsibility and authority at various levels, so as to provide an effective and efficient organization.
3. To keep abreast of current practice and research applicable to the secondary years.
4. To initiate discussion at various levels when the need arises.

BOX 11.4

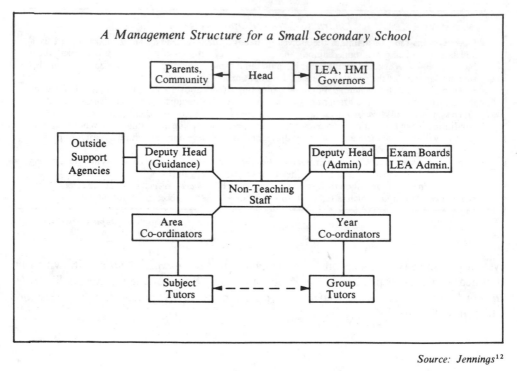

A Management Structure for a Small Secondary School

Source: Jennings[12]

Deputy head (administration)

1. To undertake responsibility, after policy consultation with the head, for all items of requisition.
2. To be responsible for the supervision of the timetabling arrangements and for staff absences and replacements.
3. To be responsible for professional attitudes in the staff-room.
4. To supervise all the aspects of internal administration.

Deputy head (guidance)

1. To be directly responsible to the head for the implementation of curriculum innovation throughout the school.
2. To work closely with the head in order to carry out the school's philosophy in terms of aims, goals and objectives.
3. To be fully conversant with the 'areas of knowledge' approach and its relevance to the common curriculum.
4. To liaise and consult with area and year co-ordinators about pupils' progress in basic skills.

Subject area co-ordinators

1. To ensure that the subject is well-prepared and taught throughout the school, and its significance and purpose understood by all teachers.
2. To prepare a series of area goals based on the stated needs of pupils.
3. To liaise with other area co-ordinators in order to achieve a basis for integrated work and/or disciplinary enquiries.
4. To offer specialist help when requested by year co-ordinators or by the director of studies.

Instead of talking about 'jobs' and 'responsibilities' we shall use the language of role theory.

Traditionally, role theory has developed around two central concepts – *position* and *role*. A *position* is a category of persons who occupy a place in a social relation. Theoretically at least, we should be able to list all of a person's positions and thus locate him in respect of all the social relationships in his society. A *role* is a collection of behaviours that are expected of, or are usually shown by, a person occupying a particular position. The occupier of a position may be referred to as the *role incumbent*. Related social roles can be defined as a *social system*. Within such a system a particular role cannot be considered apart from its relationship with other roles. For example, it is not possible to discuss the role of a teacher without reference to some complementary role such as pupil or parent or headteacher. A collection of complementary roles constitutes the *role-set* for a position.

Armed with these concepts from role theory, let us look at a number of important positions within the organizational structure of the school.

The Headteacher

It is a far cry from the day when Thring of Uppingham summed up the role of the headmaster with the words, 'I am supreme here and I brook no interference.' Nowadays there are schools where major decisions are taken by a majority vote and the headmaster has one vote exactly like everyone else – be it probationary teacher or pupil[13]. More typically, however, as the headteacher job specification suggests, heads exercise wide ranging control over large areas of the day-to-day life of schools. One way of identifying their span of control is set out in Box 11.5. The terms *instrumental* and *expressive* require some comment.

The *instrumental* dimension of the headteacher's role relates to his responsibilities for such matters as the curriculum, the timetable, the organization of school buildings and their equipment etc. The *expressive* dimension refers to those tasks that have to do with maintaining the emotional equilibrium of staff, pupils, and parents. The *administrative – academic* axis of the role model is self-explanatory.

Research suggests that prior to appointment, headteachers may make a name for themselves in the academic – expressive area of the quadrant in Box 11.5. That is to say, it is their skills as classroom practitioners that leads to their promotion to headships. And it is then, as headteachers, that they are required to exhibit very different qualities. Generally speaking, the larger the school, the greater the administrative burden and the more the

BOX 11.5

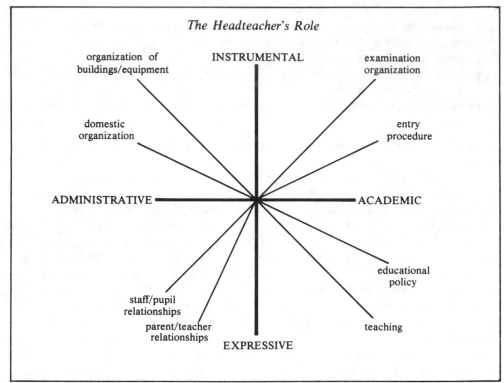

The Headteacher's Role

organization of buildings/equipment

INSTRUMENTAL

examination organization

domestic organization

entry procedure

ADMINISTRATIVE

ACADEMIC

educational policy

staff/pupil relationships

parent/teacher relationships

EXPRESSIVE

teaching

Source: Taylor[14]

likelihood that the head will spend a disproportionate amount of time wrestling with problems in the administrative – instrumental quadrant on tasks for which he has had little or no prior training. This notwithstanding, research[15] shows that those aspects of the headteacher role towards which heads subscribe most strongly are to be found in the academic – expressive and the administrative – expressive quadrants; that is to say, head-teachers are centrally concerned with the welfare of pupils, the quality of teaching, and the relationships between teachers and pupils.

The Deputy Head

We have to draw a distinction between the role of deputy heads in primary and secondary schools. As the management structure in Box 11.4 shows, even in small secondary schools, tasks allocated to deputy heads become focused and specialized, and the trend in the larger comprehensives is towards even greater specialization. In practice then, there is some oversimplification in Burnham's[16] proposal that the sharing of person-centred and task-centred leadership functions between secondary heads and their deputies results in heads becoming the task-centred leaders, leaving their deputies to take on the social – emotional leadership of the staffroom. But there may be some truth in the view that depending on how the headteacher defines his major role orientation (i.e. instrumental or expressive), then the deputy's role serves to complement it in that the latter is ascribed an 'opposite' leadership function by the headteacher.

Research[17] into the deputy headship in primary schools shows that heads and deputies agree that the deputy head should be an effective classroom teacher and that he should play a major role in the administration of the school by mediating head – staff communications and generally facilitating the smooth-running organization of the school. On the other hand, the deputy may be expected to play only a minor part in the supervision of teaching, the formulation of school policies and the taking of major decisions. These task-centred or instrumental aspects of school leadership are generally seen as being the headteacher's sole responsibility.[18]

The Head of Department

The growth of comprehensive schools with their wide-ranging curricula has given rise to organizational and managerial problems that were almost unknown in the smaller schools of the pre-comprehensive era. Particularly in the larger schools, heads of department wrestle with organizational decisions to do with the handling of staff, pupils, and the physical resources of their various subject areas. Some of the more important tasks of the head of department have been identified[19] as follows:

(a) *Staff control.* He must deploy and manage his assistant staff, evaluate their performance and find ways to improve their professional competence; almost certainly, he will be required to assist in the recruitment of new members of staff.
(b) *Pupil control.* He is likely to take some part, probably a major part, in decisions about the deployment and management of large numbers of pupils.
(c) *Resources control.* He has to ensure that all his own and his assistants' courses are properly resourced insofar as this lies within his power; he must ensure that once obtained those resources are used efficiently.
(d) *Communications.* In order to do these things he has to set up an adequate communications procedure within his department and between his department and the rest of the school.

The Teacher

Given the numerous factors that affect what goes on in classrooms (the age and ability of the pupils, the knowledge and experience of the teacher etc.) it seems somewhat futile to formulate broad generalizations about the teacher's role. Nevertheless, there are some observations that can be made from a normative perspective that apply to all classteachers and, incidentally, prepare for our coming discussion of role conflict.

To a large extent, the behaviour of any incumbent of a teacher position is governed by expectations that arise from the various others who constitute the role set. Those others have differing resources of power by which to control a teacher's behaviour. The head, for example, has considerable power resources that he can use in exchange for the obedience and allegiance of his staff including job references, responsibility allowances and the allocation of school equipment. Fellow teachers too exercise control, offering support and co-operation to colleagues who behave as is expected, bringing sanctions to bear when their actions fall outside the range of tolerable behaviour. Parents can also affect a teacher's behaviour, – asking awkward questions privately through the headteacher or publicly at PTA meetings. Her Majesty's Inspectors are particularly powerful role definers at certain points in the career of young teachers. Faced with such a potent array of role definers, how does the teacher cope? Kahn's[20] model set out in Box 11.6 offers an illuminating way of exploring role relationships and the processes of social influence that occur in the day-to-day work of the classteacher.

BOX 11.6

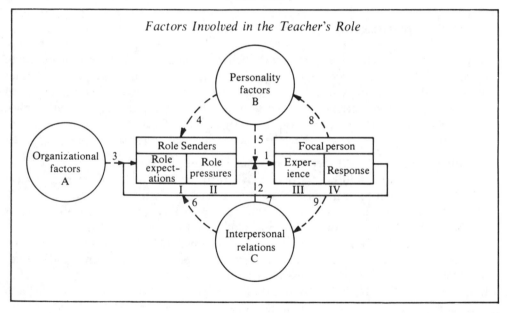

Source: adapted from Kahn[20]

The four boxes in the centre of the model constitute what Kahn and his associates call a *role episode*. Paraphrasing their exposition and applying it to a teaching situation, an episode starts with the existence of a number of *role expectations* held by *role senders* (a head and a head of department perhaps) about a *focal person* (a teacher) and his classroom behaviour. Each role sender behaves towards the focal person in ways determined by his own expectations and his own anticipations of the focal person's responses. The head, for example, demands traditional, formal teaching at all times; the head of department expects creative group work in which pupils are free to try out ideas in their own ways. In Kahn's model, role expectations from role senders lead to role pressures experienced by the focal person.

Arrow 1 indicates that the total set of role pressures affects the focal person whose experience of the situation depends upon the intensity of the pressures and the degree to which they are supportive or nonsupportive, consensual or contradictory in respect of his behaviour. The four boxes represent events at a given moment in time. The direction lines represent a causal sequence. Thus, role expectations (I) result in role pressures (II) which in turn lead to the experience of conflict (III) which results in coping responses (IV) on the part of the focal person. These are perceived and evaluated by the role senders (Arrow 2) and the cycle then resumes. In our example, the teacher's highly formal teaching methods may simultaneously serve to mollify the head teacher and to exasperate the head of department who then sends stronger expectations about the sort of classroom climate he requires in the subject area under his jurisdiction.

The three circles surrounding the boxes represent not momentary events but enduring states of the organization, the person, and the interpersonal relations existing between the focal person and his role senders. Taking account of these factors makes the sequence of events in a role episode more comprehensible. To a large degree, Kahn observes, the role expectations held by members of a role set are determined by the broader organizational context. The organizational structure, its size, degree of specialization and reward system all influence the expectations that are made of specific positions. Organizational circle (A) then, represents a set of variables and Arrow 3 a causal relationship between those variables and the role expectations and pressures that are held about and exerted toward particular positions.

The term personality (Circle B) represents all those factors that describe an individual's predispositions to behave in certain ways – his motives, his values, his sensitivities, his fears, and so on. The model proposes that characteristics of the individual will tend to evoke certain responses from his role senders (Arrow 4). An independently-minded teacher, for example, may elicit strong pressures from the head because only emphatic orders have any effect on him. Arrow 5 suggests that some individuals will experience role pressures differently from others; that is to say, personality factors will intervene between the 'objective' situation as it exists and a focal person's experience of it. Certain reactions to role experiences may lead to modifications in a person's personality organization (Arrow 8), affecting his ability to perform his duties. Continual problems of class management, for example, may have serious consequences for a teacher's mental health.

Circle C is concerned with interpersonal relations. The term refers to more or less stable patterns of interaction between a person and his role senders and to their orientations toward one another. Interpersonal relations, Kahn asserts, fulfil some functions that parallel those identified in Circle B, (personality factors). The model suggests that the kind of pressures exerted by role senders upon a focal person depend to some extent upon the nature of the relations between them (Arrow 6). A head, for example, will often make demands on younger teachers that differ from those that he directs towards more experienced, older members of staff.

Kahn builds a number of feedback cycles into his role model. For example, the extent to which a focal person complies with his role senders' demands is an example of his behaviour that directly affects their future role sending behaviour. (Arrow 2). Another kind of feedback occurs when the focal person tries to initiate a dialogue with his role senders about the problems he experiences in the performance of his duties. This kind of feedback may result in modifications in the demands that are made of him. Two other feedback cycles, Kahn suggests, affect the total process of role sending, the first through the effects of the focal person's responses upon his own personality, the second through the effects of his responses upon his relations with each of his role senders. For example, a teacher's loss of respect for a headteacher is likely to create significant changes in the quality of relations between them (Arrow 9). These changes in interpersonal relations will in turn affect future role sender behaviour on the part of the headteacher (Arrow 6) as well as the teacher's response to it (Arrow 7). Paraphrasing Kahn's analysis, three kinds of reactions seem of particular significance in the process we have exemplified. First, tensions and frustrations on the teacher's part give rise to perfunctory communications with the headteacher. Second, the teacher may attempt to reject or avoid the demands of the head. As with his tensions and frustrations, the teacher's rejection or avoidance may or may not reduce his difficulties, depending on how the headteacher responds in turn. It can be seen that Kahn's model allows for both adjustive and maladjustive cycles. Moreover, it provides for empirical research when the specific variables in each of its panels are delineated and the causal connections between them are specified.

ROLE CONFLICT

Intrarole conflict

Intrarole conflict can be said to occur when, as in our hypothetical example, a teacher experiences incompatible pressures arising out of a headteacher's insistence on traditional formal approaches to learning and a head of department's requirement of child-centred group work. Intrarole conflict exists when the incumbent of a position has incompatible or competing role expectations placed upon him by members of his role set.

Three other types of role conflict have been identified[21]: role ambiguity, personality – role conflict, and inter-role conflict.

Role ambiguity

Role ambiguity refers to the situations where, within a set of complementary positions, there is a wide variation from person to person within each position about the role expectations for one particular position. For example, Cohen's[15] study of a national sample of headteachers in England and Wales revealed that on certain items to do with the headteacher's role, there was wide variation from person to person both among teachers and among parents as to what the headteacher should or should not do.

Personality – role conflict

The 'square peg in a round hole' is often a case of a certain sort of personality becoming a source of role conflict when an individual is unable to meet the requirements of a role because the role demands are incompatible with personal needs or where they violate moral values.

Getzels and Guba's[22] model of personality – role conflict is one that is frequently cited in discussions of the school as an organization. They explain the dilemma of the person who must choose whether he fulfils his individual needs or the requirements attaching to a given role:

'If he chooses to fulfil requirements . . . he is in a sense short-changing himself, and is liable to unsatisfactory personal adjustment; he is frustrated and dissatisfied. If he chooses to fulfil his needs he is short changing his role and is liable to unsatisfactory role performance; he is inefficient and ineffective.'[22]

Inter-role conflict

Inter-role conflict occurs when the same person occupies two competing or incompatible positions simultaneously. In contemporary Britain, for example, many women teachers are also wives and mothers. Kelsall and Kelsall[23] identify their potentiality for role conflict as follows:

'Take, for instance, the case of the mother who wants to return to teaching. She is bound . . . to weigh the loss of the additional benefits which would accrue to her children through the extra care and attention she would be able to give them if she did *not* return to teaching against the gain of other benefits (both material and psychological) that might be expected for her and the family as a whole from her taking such a step.'

Having identified various types of role conflict, we turn now to look at ways of resolving them.

Resolving Role Conflict: Organizational Strategies

There are various ways in which organizations can reduce role conflict among their members. Several so-called *structural arrangements* have been identified by Secord and Backman.[24] For example, participants recognize that certain obligations take precedence over others. One arrangement then, involves ranking role obligations in a hierarchy of priorities. Thus, a headteacher's request for an after-school staff meeting would take precedence over a squash-court booking but not, perhaps, over an inservice lecture scheduled for the same time.

A second structural arrangement for minimizing conflict that is closely related to ranking role obligations has to do with the differing powers of role partners to exert sanctions. Generally, teachers will hasten to fulfil headteachers' requests before dealing with pupils' demands simply because heads have more powerful sanctions at their disposal than pupils. Headteachers themselves, no doubt, exercise similar priorities in their relationships with Chief Education Officers, and as we shall shortly see, even Chief Education Officers (or their counterparts in the United States) bend to the sanctioning powers of their political masters.

A third structural arrangement identified by Secord and Backman concerns the restricting of multiple position occupancy, – an uncouth turn of phrase which can be illustrated by the example of a teacher whose daughter is purposely placed in a parallel class to her own to avoid the embarassment of a potential clash between teacher and mother roles.

The spatial and temporal separation of situations involving conflicting role expectations is yet another way of conflict reduction. During school hours, for example, a teacher is exposed to the expectations associated with his occupational position. But these expectations do not operate at home during the evening hours where they might conflict with expectations associated with such positions as husband and father.

Resolving Role Conflict: Individual Strategies

In a classical study[25] of intrarole conflict resolution, some hundred or more school superintendents were interviewed to find out how they dealt with the incompatible expectations of school board officials, teachers, parents, and other influential groups in their local communities. Some, it seemed, made their decisions about important educational matters on the basis of who among the role senders·'packed the largest punch' in the event of a superintendent's non-compliance. The researchers called these educational leaders, *expedients*. Others discounted the sanctioning powers of role senders and made up their minds solely on the basis of which of the various positions within the role set had the right to expect certain behaviours of them. These superintendents were described as *moralists*. The majority of school leaders, however, were *moral-expedients*, that is to say, they resolved their intrarole conflicts by recourse to balancing both moral and expedient orientations.

What of inter-role conflict? How might this be resolved? The psychological defence mechanisms of rationalization, compartmentalization, repression, and withdrawal, feature in a well-known study of inter-role conflict[26] in which military chaplains were interviewed to find out how they resolved the inherent conflict in the warrior role of an army officer and the pacifist role of a minister of God. All four types of defense mechanism were identified in the explanations proffered by the military chaplains:

rationalization:	'Well someone has to carry the gospel to these boys'
compartmentalization:	'Render unto Caesar the things that are Caesar's. . . . '
repression:	'I don't see any conflict'
withdrawal:	'Look, I'd rather not talk about it'

A study of the resolution of inter-role conflict in school settings which features explanatory concepts such as rationalization and repression has yet to be undertaken. There is, however, a good account of role conflict resolution as practised by British teachers.[27]

Grace interviewed 80 male and female secondary school teachers from an original sample of 150 who had completed questionnaires to do with their perceptions of various role conflicts. Two particular areas of role conflict stood out. One was to do with what Grace described as divergent value orientations, the other with the clash between role commitment and career orientation. The verbatim accounts[27] of the teachers themselves illustrate their concerns:

values
'It is the teacher's business to uphold traditional standards – if the teacher doesn't, who does? A lot of parents aren't worried.'

commitment versus career
'Should one be loyal to one's students and give them continuity, or go glory and cash chasing around the country?'

LEADERSHIP AND DECISION-MAKING IN SCHOOLS

Leadership and decision-making are two closely related issues that take us back to the beginning of the chapter where, you will recall, we discussed various approaches to organization theory. In line with a general consensus among students of organizations, we now intend to simplify our initial treatment and to identify two fundamental models of organization. Following Hoyle[28] we shall refer to them as Model A and Model B. They are, of course, 'ideal' types, serving primarily to illuminate our discussion of leadership and decision-making in schools.

Model A incorporates those characteristics of *bureaucracy* that we outlined on page 348, a hierarchy of positions with their clearly defined responsibilities, where authority is vested in the particular office, etc.

Model B incorporates elements of the *human relations* model that we discussed on page 349, a concern for shared decision-making, for involvement in horizontal rather than vertical patterns of authority, etc.

As Hoyle observes, leadership and decision-making are conceptualized differently in each model. In Model A, leadership is a function of formal position in the hierarchy, the range and scope of decision-making being clearly prescribed. In Model B, leadership is related to the task at hand; it is achieved rather than ascribed, the actual decisions being made collaboratively by those most likely to be affected by them.

Increasingly, Model B has served as the template for training courses in school management, its appeal lying in its democratic ideology, its flexibility and its adaptability in periods of rapid change in educational policy and provision.

One important issue that Hoyle raises in relation to Model B organizations is the problem of *power*. Power, he says, is relatively unproblematic in Model A type organizations since it is legitimated through investing the organizational head with legal authority which he can then partially delegate through the hierarchical structure. But the legitimacy of legal authority becomes more problematic as one moves toward Model B type organizations. Legal authority tends to be underplayed in Model B approaches. There is, however, a growing demand for participation in decision-making in organizations and while legal authority is vested in the head of an organization there are limits to the extent to which other members can exercise ultimate power through the decision-making process. The danger, Hoyle observes, is that unless those limits are spelt out, involvement in decision-making can come to be seen as a mere sham.

The model of organization that best fits most British schools contains elements of both Model A and Model B. That is to say, it is a *professional model*, consisting of, in Litwak's[29] words, 'one part bureaucracy and one part human relations'. In this mixed model, the headteacher remains largely free from external control, enjoying a high degree of authority within the school and usually making the fundamental decisions about the goals and the policies of the school while leaving to his teachers those decisions that relate to their professional practices in the classroom. However, changes are taking place in the nature of the relationship between headteachers' authority and teachers' autonomy. Particularly important are changes in educational practice and the demand from teachers for increased participation in decision-making processes in schools. Hoyle summarizes some of the changes in educational practice in Box 11.7.

BOX 11.7

Changes in Recent Educational Practice		
Dimension	*From*	*To*
CURRICULUM CONTENT	Monodisciplinary	Interdisciplinary
PEDAGOGY	Didactic teaching	Discovery learning
ORGANIZATION OF TEACHING/LEARNING	Rigid timetabling	Flexible timetabling
PUPIL GROUPING	Homogeneous	Heterogeneous
PUPIL CHOICE	Limited	Extensive
ASSESSMENT	Single mode	Multiple modes
BASIS OF PUPIL CONTROL	Positional	Personal
TEACHER ROLES	Independent	Interdependent
ARCHITECTURE	Closed	Open Plan
SCHOOL–COMMUNITY LINKS	Weak	Strong

Source: Hoyle[28]

Against this background of change, Hoyle considers issues relating to authority and professionality. The changes in schools outlined in Box 11.7 illustrate the dilemma of leadership in Model B type organizations. Whereas, it might be argued, the most appropriate pattern of authority in school organizations (staffed as they are by professionals) is '*collegial*', so long as legal authority is vested in the headteacher he is unlikely to relinquish final responsibility to a group of teachers. Thus, *participation* will in all probability turn out to be *consultation*, where in attempting to reconcile expectations for democratic procedures with his legal responsibilities, the head may be tempted to blur the boundaries of his authority in order to appear to satisfy staff demands for greater participation.

Given the size and the organizational complexity of secondary schools to say nothing of the range and variety of their curricula, the dangers of staff participation degenerating into perfunctory consultation, particularly in decisions over teaching schemes, materials and methods, is perhaps more remote than in the primary sector. A glance at the

BOX 11.8

Planning the Curriculum

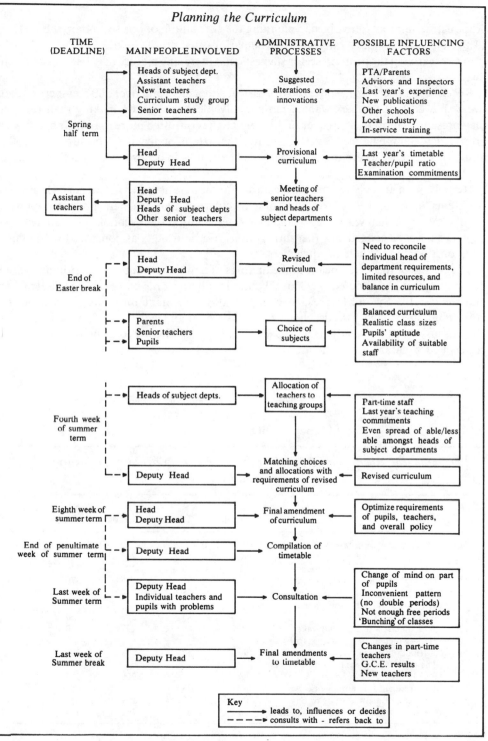

TIME (DEADLINE)	MAIN PEOPLE INVOLVED	ADMINISTRATIVE PROCESSES	POSSIBLE INFLUENCING FACTORS
Spring half term	Heads of subject dept. / Assistant teachers / New teachers / Curriculum study group / Senior teachers	Suggested alterations or innovations	PTA/Parents / Advisors and Inspectors / Last year's experience / New publications / Other schools / Local industry / In-service training
	Head / Deputy Head	Provisional curriculum	Last year's timetable / Teacher/pupil ratio / Examination commitments
Assistant teachers	Head / Deputy Head / Heads of subject depts / Other senior teachers	Meeting of senior teachers and heads of subject departments	
End of Easter break	Head / Deputy Head	Revised curriculum	Need to reconcile individual head of department requirements, limited resources, and balance in curriculum
	Parents / Senior teachers / Pupils	Choice of subjects	Balanced curriculum / Realistic class sizes / Pupils' aptitude / Availability of suitable staff
Fourth week of summer term	Heads of subject depts.	Allocation of teachers to teaching groups	Part-time staff / Last year's teaching commitments / Even spread of able/less able amongst heads of subject departments
	Deputy Head	Matching choices and allocations with requirements of revised curriculum	Revised curriculum
Eighth week of summer term	Head / Deputy Head	Final amendment of curriculum	Optimize requirements of pupils, teachers, and overall policy
End of penultimate week of summer term	Deputy Head	Compilation of timetable	
Last week of Summer term	Deputy Head / Individual teachers and pupils with problems	Consultation	Change of mind on part of pupils / Inconvenient pattern (no double periods) / Not enough free periods / 'Bunching' of classes
Last week of Summer break	Deputy Head	Final amendments to timetable	Changes in part-time teachers / G.C.E. results / New teachers

Key

———▶ leads to, influences or decides

- - - ▶ consults with - refers back to

Source: Bates[30]

administrative process involved in planning the curriculum of one secondary school (Box 11.8) shows the wide range of participation that took place involving all the staff. Research in the primary sector suggests that there, the picture may be somewhat different.

Recent evidence[31] from some 200 primary headteachers and over 500 members of their staffs showed that teachers wanted more involvement in decision-making than they felt they presently enjoyed. Moreover they wanted to be consulted more than their heads were prepared to countenance. Box 11.9 shows the extent of teachers' disaffection. 100 % represents the case where the degree of participation is in accordance with the wishes of the respondent.

It can be seen at once that headteachers are far more satisfied than teachers. On most of the items in Box 11.9 the amount of participation that teachers presently enjoy is significantly less than what they would like to see occur in their schools. Overall, teachers show an average congruence (i.e. satisfaction) of about 60 % as compared with almost 90 % on the part of their headteachers.

The results of this study bear out the findings of a previous inquiry into primary school decision-making conducted by Grover[18] and involving some 300 or more headteachers and their staffs. By and large, Grover reported, heads made more decisions about the curriculum, teaching methods, choice of books etc., than teachers wanted them to make. Our discussion of the headteacher's leadership leads us directly to a consideration of the concept of organizational climate.

BOX 11.9

Percentage of Head Teachers and Teachers whose Preference is Congruent with Perceived Practice

	Item	% Heads	% Teachers	N Heads	N Teachers
1	The aspects of number work to be taught	90	56	218	516
2	The time to be spent on maths	87	60	209	522
3	Having a school scheme in maths	86	51	195	476
4	Class texts to be used in teaching maths	88	55	210	516
5	Ways of grouping pupils in a class for art/craft	87	83	206	520
6	Which class a teacher will take	95	68	227	520
7	Having regular staff meetings to discuss curriculum issues	90	57	209	501
8	The type of progress records to be kept for children	89	56	200	507
9	The frequency of homework	87	73	205	515
10	The type of art materials to buy	90	57	217	514
11	Having a school scheme for art/craft	80	41	162	464

Source: Hoabbs, Kleinberg and Martin[32]

THE ORGANIZATIONAL CLIMATE OF THE SCHOOL

That schools differ one from another is self-evident to anyone who has ever visited a number of schools and sensed the variety in their tone within a few moments of entering their front doors.

What it is that is different is often very difficult to put into words. In consequence, various attempts have been made to operationalize the concept of school climate. One of the most popular and widely used techniques for assessing the organizational climate of schools has been the Organizational Climate Description Questionnaire (OCDQ)[32]. Central to the rationale of the OCDQ is the belief that organizational climate is closely related to the perceived behaviours of teachers and headteachers. The termed *perceived behaviours* is important here. As Owens[1] observes,

'Suppose teachers are asked questions . . . about the school's principal . . . "How considerate is he?", "How approachable and how *genuine* is his manner?" One may object that the principal may actually evidence behaviour quite different than that which the teacher *perceives*. The principal, for instance, may be attempting to emphasize *consideration* in his role behaviour because he associates "consideration" with leader behaviour and he wishes to be a leader. However, if a teacher does not *see* this behaviour as evidencing consideration then to him it is *not* consideration . . . In dealing with the interpersonal relationships which are inextricably bound up in organizational behaviour we are constantly confronted with the truism that much of behaviour is, like beauty, in the eye of the beholder.'

The OCDQ consists of eight subtests, four of which describe aspects of teacher behaviour *as it is perceived by the teachers*, and four have to do with the headteacher's behaviour, again, *as it is perceived by teachers*. For example, one aspect of teacher behaviour is termed *disengagement* – a concept described as the teacher's tendency to be 'not with it', to be merely 'going through the motions' with respect to school duties. One of the headteacher behaviours is described as *aloofness*, that is, a formal and impersonal style in relationships in which the head is seen to 'go by the book' rather than deal with staff in face-to-face situations.

The ways in which schools differ from each other in respect of these four teacher and four headteacher subtests leads directly to their classification in terms of six *school profiles*, identified as *open climate, autonomous climate, controlled climate, familiar climate, paternal climate* and *closed climate*. The constituent elements of two contrasting school profiles are set out in Box 11.10.

Halpin and Croft suggest that OCDQ profiles are most useful when they are seen, not as tests or judgemental measures, but as ways of providing headteachers and staff with feedback for their discussion and analysis of the organizational effectiveness of their particular schools. The OCDQ instrument has had considerably more use in North America than in Great Britain. Its comparative lack of use here is explained by one researcher[33] as follows: '. . . the climate construct bristles with unresolved definitional, ideological, and methodological problems.' But that did not deter him from using the OCDQ as the basis for the development of measures of innovation and change as perceived by headteachers and teachers in opportunity samples of some 120 secondary

BOX 11.10

Characteristics of Open and Closed School Climates	
Open climate	*Closed climate*
High esprit*	Low esprit
Low disengagement	High disengagement
Low hindrance	High hindrance
Average intimacy	Average intimacy
Average aloofness	High aloofness
High consideration	Low consideration
Average thrust	Low thrust
Low production emphasis	High production emphasis

*esprit = staff morale; *hindrance* = the headteacher burdening staff with unnecessary busy-work – routine duties, form filling and the like; *intimacy* = teachers' enjoyment of friendly social relations with one another; *consideration* = the headteacher's attempts to treat staff 'humanly'; *thrust* = the headteacher's efforts to 'move the organisation', to motivate teachers by his personal example; *production emphasis* = the headteacher's close supervision of his staff.

Source: adapted from Halpin and Croft[32]

schools in Northern Ireland. McGeown's[33] Organizational Climate for Change Questionnaire (OCDQ) was found to differentiate significantly between schools in relation to their innovativeness as measured by school level and teacher level measures of adoption and implementation of specific innovations.

In England, Finlayson[34] has developed a School Climate Index (SCI), a measure based on Halpin and Croft's OCDQ, seeking specifically to identify teachers' perceptions of the climates of their particular schools in three extended areas concerned with (1) the head's administrative and decision-making behaviour, (2) the behaviour of heads of department, and (3) the behaviour of colleagues. Together with a pupils' perception of the behaviour of their peers and their teachers, Finlayson suggests that when these four indices are considered together they provide a useful picture of the school as a social system. That, of course, is only a beginning. He goes on to make the important observation that, as yet, we have not *tested* any theories of organizational climate against indices of goal achievement. We give some examples of Finlayson's SCI in Box 3.8.

King's[35] approach to the measurement of school climate is different again. By way of example, he defines the *expressive order* of the school as consisting of the 'modes of approved behaviour it transmits and the activities used in their transmission'. Five methods of organization are seen as constituting the expressive order:

1. The standardization of expressive activities.
2. The standardization of expressive performance.
3. The formalization of expressive activities.
4. The formalization of expressive performance.
5. The ritualization of expressive performance.

Each of these is developed into a questionnaire scale, the first, for example, consists of 55 items. By scrutinizing the official regulations of some 72 secondary schools, King was able to differentiate between them in terms of these five areas of organization and also to identify the generality of certain aspects of climate across all schools. Thus, whereas 90 % of the schools required that *all pupils must attend Sports Day*, only 11 % had a *no eating in the playground* rule.

PASTORAL CARE

Accompanying various innovations in British education over the past twenty or thirty years – the raising of the school leaving age, the introduction of comprehensivisation, the spread of open plan schools with their emphasis on child-centred approaches to learning – there has been a mushrooming in the provision of pastoral care, particularly at secondary school level. In part, at least, the increasing need for pastoral care services has arisen out of changes in the organization of the schools themselves, in the range and scope of their educational and vocational provision and in the diversification of their managerial and leadership structures. In a wider context, the proliferation of pastoral care has been attributed[36] to (1) the growth of an egalitarian political ideology which, in emphasizing the right of each individual to social security, health services, housing, education, and employment has led to a shared belief in the necessity of guiding and supporting individuals through the system; (2) the anxiety-prone nature of advanced industrial societies which creates an acute social need to which pastoral care is a psychotherapeutic response; and (3) the demands for specialization, flexibility and adaptability in a technological society leading to the need for pastoral care structures to guide individuals in making choices and, in the process, to ensure a supply of appropriately qualified labour.

In this section we use the term *pastoral care* in its widest sense to include educational, vocational, and personal services provided by specialist and non-specialist personnel both inside and outside of the school. A typology of pastoral care in Box 11.11 illustrates the scope of our treatment.

BOX 11.11

A Typology of Pastoral Care		
	Status of Provider	
	Specialist (Guidance, Counselling)	*Non-specialist* (Teacher-care)
Educational	Academic counsellor Director of studies	Classteacher Year master Heads of subject departments
Vocational	Careers adviser Youth employment officer	Careers master
Personal	School counsellor Educational psychologist	Form tutor Classteacher Housemaster

Type of Service Rendered

Source: adapted from Best, Jarvis, Ribbins[37]

A Normative Account of Pastoral Care in Schools

Whether undertaken by specialist or non-specialist personnel, pastoral care, according to Hamblin[38], is essentially an intervention in the learning process in order to give pupils support at vulnerable points during their adolescence. Hamblin identifies six dimensions of school counselling that shape the type of performance and the style of counselling adopted by practitioners. These amount, more or less, to job analyses and serve to illuminate the typology of pastoral care set out in Box 11.11.

Field of interest. Personal preferences and the general ethos of the school may cause counsellors to stress either educational, or vocational, or personal counselling as their specific field of interest.

Degree of integration into the school. The counsellor who is not a teacher may see his skills as having little connection with the everyday work of the teaching staff, as more concerned with the abnormal rather than the normal. Conversely, the counsellor who is a teacher may see his task within a developmental, learning theory framework rather than a psychotherapeutic one.

Directiveness versus non-directiveness. Currently, the most powerful model in counselling is the non-directive approach stemming from the client-centred therapy of Carl Rogers. In the context of the school, this approach would stress the central lead that the pupil provides in the counselling process and, as a consequence, the counsellor's stance of unconditional acceptance of the pupil. Directive counselling, by contrast, is behavioural in its orientation, involving the counsellor in teaching certain skills to the pupil by way of remedying particular deficits in the latter's experience.

Pathological versus normal. School counselling should be preventive and concerned with early detection of conditions that distort development. It can, according to Hamblin, become a department of lost causes or prevent pupils reaching treatment agencies if it is defined as being concerned with the severely abnormal.

Focus of attention. The counsellor's attention may be directed towards factors within the pupil or within his environment. Both foci are necessary although the emphasis will differ according to the particular pupil and the specific stage that the counselling programme has reached.

Event versus process. The current emphasis in school counselling is developmental; that is to say, counselling is seen as a process which must be integrated into the day-to-day life of the school. The alternative is termed crisis counselling. This involves the school counsellor expending a great deal of time dealing with unique, pressing, events.

Hamblin develops these six dimensions of school counselling within a systems approach, an input – process – output model that can, he says, be applied either to individual or to group counselling sessions.

In his systems theory approach to school counselling, Hamblin argues that the counsellor must recognize that he is working within a particular social system in which his interventions have an impact upon other activities within that system. These, in turn, impinge upon his counselling work and, in part, determine the effectiveness of his interventions. The model of the counselling process in Box 11.12 shows the need to think about the consequences of intervention. Feedback loops represent the output of

BOX 11.12

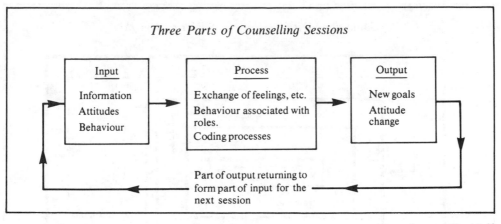

Source: Hamblin[38]

behavioural goals and attitudes as reactions which then become part of the next counselling session. Unless output is related to what is possible and acceptable in the school, Hamblin warns, the pupil may find himself in conflict with teachers and with fellow pupils. The counsellor who is insufficiently alert to this feedback process in equally likely to run into unnecessary difficulties with his colleagues and to create situations in which the pupil is deprived of essential support.

Hamblin next proceeds to place the counselling process into a wider social framework, likening counselling to the smallest member of a set of Chinese boxes. The model, shown in Box 11.13, highlights the importance of transactions across the boundaries of each of the social systems representing the classroom, the school, the home, the neighbourhood etc.

With the model of counselling in the wider social framework in mind (Box 11.13), Hamblin makes the following observations:

1. The social climate of the classroom, the school, the home etc., all influence the counsellor's approach.
2. Outcomes from the counselling interviews interact with what is occurring in these other social systems.
3. Unnecessary conflict is generated when counselling output is grossly at odds with the values and norms of these other systems.
4. The content of each counselling session and the direction it takes partly derive from the social systems in which both counsellor and pupil are located.

An Alternative Explanation of Pastoral Care in Schools

What we have said so far about counselling may be thought of as the manifest part of a school's pastoral role; that is to say guidance personnel are specifically employed to give advice in respect of academic courses, vocational choice, and personal decisions.

BOX 11.13

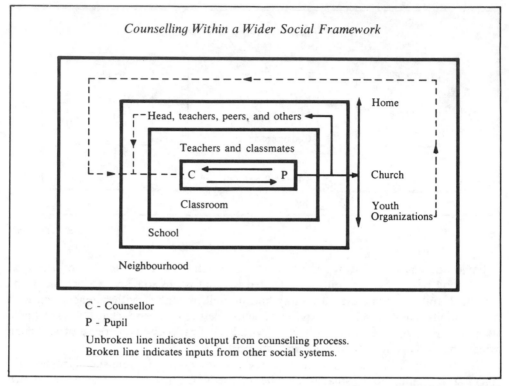

Counselling Within a Wider Social Framework

C - Counsellor

P - Pupil

Unbroken line indicates output from counselling process.
Broken line indicates inputs from other social systems.

Source: adapted from Hamblin[38]

A school's pastoral activities may also have a latent or hidden purpose, namely to promote certain pupils who are categorized as able and to 'cool out' those who are not.

Cicourel and Kitsuse's[39] study of Lakeshore High School showed how students were routinely classified as able or not·so that they could be allocated to the various academic streams thought appropriate to their capabilities. What the counselling system did, however, was to delimit the students' potential development by indicating to them their future educational and occupational chances. Cicourel and Kitsuse found that the school's computerized record system served to establish self-fulfilling prophecies; in a word, students became what it was predicted that they *could* be.

When interviewed, one school counsellor at Lakeshore High admitted that occasionally he had students who did not see the situation realistically. Such students queried why they should work, plan, or strive to better this or that. In the counsellor's opinion, 'They've had misfortunes, with indications of confusion and trouble.' 'Deviant' students like these were more than likely to be seen as potential psychiatric referrals. The same counsellor confessed that at times he had to 'seek' problem students!

Cicourel and Kitsuse's analysis revealed that the *achievement types*, that is, the various groupings of successful or unsuccessful students that counsellors had in mind when carrying out their guidance work bore little relationship to the measures of attainment that these groups actually achieved in school. Achievement types moreover were closely bound up with counsellors' perceptions of the students' social status. One counsellor's perception of the social status hierarchy at Lakeshore High School is set out below.

BOX 11.14

A Counsellor's Categories and Comments on the Question:
'How would you describe each of the student groups?'

1. First there's the main group, the ingroup . . . They're at the forefront of the activities in the school . . . They belong to the Presbyterian Church in Lakeshore . . .
2. Then there's the group just below this. They're trying to attain the (main) group . . .
3. There's the other element. They get into a lot of trouble. Most of the drop-outs are from this group.
4. . . . there's a Negro group here at Lakeshore. They have their own group.
5. Other students are not in a group. They are noteworthy individuals. They're the type that might wear black leotards or carry a guitar.
6. Then there are the rebelling 'loners'. They dress in extreme fashion. They wear their skirts too short. They find it difficult to fit into things at Lakeshore High.

Source: adapted from Cicourel and Kitsuse[39]

In their concluding remarks, Cicourel and Kitsuse refer to the popular characterization of the American school system as one that promotes a *contest* among students whose ability and effort are rewarded by success in terms of social mobility. Cicourel and Kitsuse argue that their data calls such a representation into question.

'Our research supports the view that the student's progress . . . is contingent upon the interpretations, judgements, and action of school personnel vis-à-vis the student's biography, social and personal "adjustment", appearance and demeanour, social class, and "social type", as well as his demonstrated ability and performance.'

That is to say, a *sponsored* rather than a *contest* mobility[40] is seen as a more accurate description of the American school system.

What of an alternative account of guidance and counselling in the context of British secondary schools? Best, Jarvis and Ribbins[37] are critical of the view that pastoral care structures serve to ameliorate the tensions and alleviate the anomic effects of rapid industrialization and urbanization in society at large. Furthermore, they reject normative perspectives of pastoral care structures as the positive, functional, convivial institutions that they are so readily assumed to be. At the micro level of action in specific situations, Best and his associates argue, there exists among teachers an 'unofficial' version of pastoral care that stands in stark contrast to the official version of the conventional wisdom that we outlined earlier. We summarize their alternative account in Box 11.15.

Like Cicourel and Kitsuse, Best and his associates see pastoral care structures as means of facilitating social *control* rather than *order*, where *alienation* rather than *anomie* is the operative concept, and where *deviance* may be seen not as the result of inadequate socialization, but as an understandable response for the individual in terms of the way he defines his situation. Thus,

'Consistent with this would be a reinterpretation of the relationship between the growth of pastoral care and comprehensive reorganization, the increasing size of

BOX 11.15

Pastoral Care: a View from the 'Shop Floor'

Pastoral care is a nuisance, a crashing bore, an impossible impractical, and largely unnecessary diversion from the real job of teaching. So-called pastoral care structures have more to do with providing the school with a workable division into teams for sports and other competitions than they have to do with genuine concern for the welfare of pupils. Similarly, so-called 'pastoral care periods' are actually provided to facilitate petty administrative functions such as marking the register, reading the school notices, and collecting the dinner money. It is unusual, in our experience, for these periods to be used in conscious attempts to 'guide' and 'counsel' pupils: more frequently, the time is passed in idle chatter or glum silence, or in administrative and disciplinary activities. Indeed, 'pastoral care' has on occasion been used as a euphemism for corporal punishment, and the connections in the literature between 'pastoral care structures' and the control of deviance in schools, and the disciplinary-control function of many of those playing 'pastoral care' roles in our experience, suggest that this apparently jaundiced view is not without foundation.

Source: adapted from Best, Jarvis and Ribbins[37]

schools, mixed-ability teaching, ROSLA, and the proliferation of public examinations. Such developments amplify existing problems of organization, administration and control, and create a host of new ones. . . . Pastoral care may well be a mechanism for the imposition of tighter discipline on recalcitrant pupils now that they are perhaps a feature of most secondary schools (not just "modern" schools) and of most teaching groups (not just the "D" stream). "Pastoral care periods" may well become a euphemism for "administration periods" to enable a school of 1500 plus to be run smoothly and efficiently.'[37]

These alternative explanations of the purposes of pastoral care in schools lead us directly to the final section of the chapter in which we consider interpretive perspectives on schools as organizations.

INTERPRETIVE PERSPECTIVES ON SCHOOLS AS ORGANIZATIONS

Remember the story of the blind men trying to describe an elephant? Perrow's[41] comment on organization theorists is that they are all blind men, fumbling about the elephant that they call 'the organization' and dutifully reporting on the warts, the trunk, the knees and the tail, each of them confidently asserting that he has discovered the nature of the beast. But it is worse than that, Perrow says, for they are not even looking for the same animal. The zoological garden of organizational theorists is crowded with a bewildering variety of specimens. Perrow is particularly hard on normative theorists:

'You all sit back . . . and construct theories about these beasts without actually getting into contact with them and asking how they themselves see their different parts and how they function together and move about.'

'In part, your criticism is fair and valid,' normative organizational theorists might reply.

'It *is* important to explore the ongoing social life that constitutes the organization. But is it not the case that the essential things about organizations are their *characteristics as organizations*? Is it not a fact that the central importance of Rutter's study for example (see Chapter 3) is that he identifies the *organizational characteristics* that differentiate between the twelve schools in his sample in terms of their academic and social effectiveness?'

The truth of the matter, of course, is that Perrow's analogy of the blind men is only partly applicable. As he himself observes, normative and interpretive theorists of organizations 'are feeling for quite different things . . . (they) bring different intentions to the study of organizations'. Perrow switches metaphors. 'They are like small children in a sandpit,' he says, 'playing different fantasies, only occasionally acknowledging the other children'.

Perrow's second comment on our efforts to grasp the reality of organizations is less comforting than his first! Be that as it may, this present section of the chapter is given over to an outline of a number of studies of schools as organizations that derive from interpretive perspectives. Interpretive researchers as we shall now show, bring decidedly different intentions to their studies of schools.

In many ways, the school is a particularly appropriate focus of an interpretive perspective. More than most organizations, the school may be consciously seen by those acting within it as a constructed, different, temporary world.[42] Pupils especially may be sensitive to the contrived, imposed nature of the school, for of all those involved, they alone are legally required to participate. An important task of interpretive research is to examine the various constructions that are generated in the world of the school. Pupil perspectives in particular have been the focus of a small but growing number of studies such as we have outlined in Chapter 5. One recent interpretive study[43] conducted in a primary school in north east England is relevant to our present discussion. Robertson's ethnographic research in three classrooms involved interviewing and tape-recording seventy four pupils to elicit their ideas about who were the most powerful adults in the school. The interviews sought children's perceptions of the *importance* and the *power* of various grown-ups in the school community. Depending always on the reaction of the individual child, the interviews proceeded as follows: (1) the child would be encouraged to discuss his/her own family in terms of who was the most important person in the family, who was in charge, who was the boss; (2) the interviewer would then discuss the Friday assembly in school as a way of introducing the idea of the teaching – learning community. Questions would follow such as: Who is the most important person in the school? Who is the next most important? If a child lost track of the people, the interviewer would ask, 'What about Mr X or Mrs Y?' The child would then be asked to place that person on a level above or below the one previously mentioned. This aspect of the interviewing procedure was flexible and often as not the direction came from the child.

What of Robertson's findings? Ten year old pupils' perceptions of power and importance, she reported, more accurately mapped the formal structure of the school than did the views of younger children who placed their own class teachers at the apex of the school's power pyramid (see Box 11.16). That is to say children's perceptions of the headmaster as the source of power became increasingly clear as they grew older. The origins of their perceptions, as we shall see, were of particular interest to the researcher. Some of the children's descriptions of the head are outlined below.

The headmaster

'he smacks people when they're naughty with a big stick.' (5 + child)

'If the big'ns is naughty he gives'm the cane. If the little one's naughty he gives'm the slipper. He does nothing else.' (5 + child)

'He looks after you. Stops fights and people putting on each other . . . runs the school . . . looks after everyone.' (10 + child)

'He owns the school . . . gives you the cane, gives you lines stops you playing football when it's wet, telling you important things, telling you what's right or wrong.' (10 + child)

Several of the children's statements about the headmaster suggested a coercive, disciplinary perspective. This was so much at variance with the views of the school staff (and the researcher) who saw the head as a gentle, tolerant, and totally accessible person, that the question of the origin of those perspectives became the focus of further investigation. *Inter alia*, Robertson established a close association between younger pupils' perceptions of their fathers as 'boss' and their views of the headmaster.

My Dad

he's big, cause he's got big hands. Daddies smack when you're naughty . . . he shouts . . . he has a big voice. (5 + child)

Headmaster

'cos he shouts at yer . . . cos he smacks people.'

To understand the pupils' perceptions of the school secretary as second only to the head in the hierarchy of power and importance, Robertson elicited explanations from the children, the headmaster and the secretary herself.

The pupils

'She's as important as all the teachers who give you sums.'
'She's important . . . helps Mr (Headmaster) with work . . . more important than the teachers.'
'Cos she counts the money, the same as Mr (Headmaster).'
'She helps . . . collects money . . . collects the Lucky Club money.'

BOX 11.16

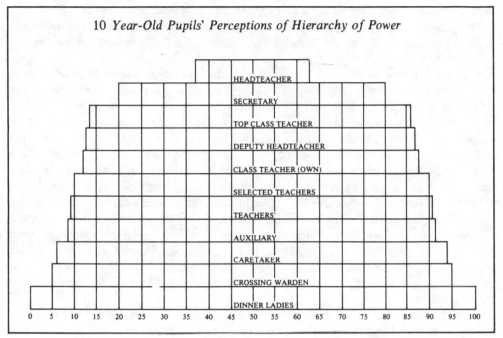

10 *Year-Old Pupils' Perceptions of Hierarchy of Power*

HEADTEACHER

SECRETARY

TOP CLASS TEACHER

DEPUTY HEADTEACHER

CLASS TEACHER (OWN)

SELECTED TEACHERS

TEACHERS

AUXILIARY

CARETAKER

CROSSING WARDEN

DINNER LADIES

0   5   10   15   20   25   30   35   40   45   50   55   60   65   70   75   80   85   90   95   100

Children's percentage ratings of the most important person in the school. Lowest score = highest status; thus dinner ladies who have the lowest status receive 100 % of the ratings.

Source: Robertson[43]

The headmaster

'I would probably think they see Mrs (School Secretary) as important because of her maturity and the fact that she does a tremendous amount. Being in different classes at various times they may well see her as a form teacher. Certainly they see her as someone who will deal with problems, won't stand any nonsense from older ones . . . someone who will ensure that if they have a responsibility, they will carry it out.'

The school secretary

'Well I think they associate me with the Headmaster . . . I won't stand any nonsense from them and if a teacher has not been in the room, sometimes I stand in for the teacher . . . Occasionally I take control, discipline. I think maybe some of the older children might know I am in various activities outside of school, in a position of leadership . . . that may be the reason.'

Robertson's concern for the actors' definitions of the situation follows from W. I. Thomas's[44] famous dictum, 'If men define situations as real they are real in their consequences.' Basically, she argues that in order to understand social interaction within the school we must look to the meanings of situations and the situated meanings within them as they are phenomenologically experienced by the participants themselves.

The advantage of this approach to the educational researcher lies in the distinctive insights that are made available through the analysis of actors' accounts of the ongoing social episodes in which they are involved. Notice that in addition to the accounts of the participants themselves there is the account of the educational researcher who, as an outside observer, recognizes that while explanations must respect the meanings of situations to the actors, they *need not invariably be centred around those meanings*. The ways in which actors define situations are, of course, products of their personal biographies. 'People', Becker and Geer[45] observe, 'carry culture with them, when they leave one group setting for another they do not shed its cultural premises.' An examination of this proposition was undertaken by Kanter[46] in a study of a nursery school. Kanter argued that in contemporary society there is widespread support for the belief that *bureaucracy-like experiences* (getting on with others, adjusting, accommodating and adapting to the demands of specialized roles in organizations etc.) promote health and maturity. The practices of one nursery school, Kanter asserted, translated these bureaucracy-like experiences into concrete form and the behaviour of the children in that school reflected their experience of a phenomenologically bureaucratic world. Educational organizations, she argued, mirror and prepare people for structural conditions in the wider society.

During seven months participant observation, Kanter demonstrated the ways in which the nursery school instituted standardized routines and practices in which 'a rational, mundane, pragmatic world view was presented; in which the exercise of power was disguised and force was not used; in which individual accountability was curtailed severely; in which externally motivating situations were created as incentives to substitute for internal motivation; and in which participants were asked to accept, officially, certain impersonal principles governing and democratizing their relations with others.' The result of such a regime Kanter described as the *organization child*. Like the organization man, the organization child was asked to accept organizational reality as given, adjust to routine, take on a limited rather than a diffuse obligation to the organization, and guide his behaviour by impersonal universalistic principles. Just how these factors entered into the behaviour of the nursery school children was demonstrated in Kanter's accounts of numerous social episodes. She showed how the experiential world of the child as mediated by the school was a rational mundane place in which miraculous things did not occur. To play, the child needed reason for things; play situations had to make sense, they had to match reality as the children knew it. Box 11.17 presents one social episode which Kanter recorded by way of supporting her overall thesis.

The studies of Robertson and Kanter raise substantive questions about the subjective aspects of being a member of a school community. Implicitly, Robertson is asking, 'How do pupils make sense of their experiences in school?' 'How do they come to terms with the routines that are to be obeyed and the conventions that are to be followed?' Kanter's focus, too, is upon the school processes that create the reality that the school has for its pupils. In addition, she asks, 'What is the relationship between that school reality and the overarching experiences in the lives of children beyond the four walls of the school?' These are issues of fundamental importance. Moreover, they are ones that can only be tackled from the vantage point of an interpretive stance.

BOX 11.17

Orientation to Organizational Reality

A girl and two boys are choosing roles for a game on a ship. The girl says she doesn't want to be a dog; one boy asks what she wants to be. She says a human being. The boy says she has to be an animal; she can't decide; rabbit? hamster? guinea pig? 'I couldn't be a squirrel. Yes I could, but I'd have to be trained.' The other boy asks if she wants to be a squirrel. She replies, 'Squirrels run away; they're wild.' He responds, 'You'll be a trained one; you'll obey us.' She says she wants to be something else. The second boy says, 'I like human beings better than animals.' and the first adds, 'Anyway, ships don't have animals.' The girl finally decides she can be an animal however, saying, 'You could be taking them to the zoo.'

Source: adapted from Kanter.[46]

Whereas both Robertson and Kanter are primarily concerned with pupil perspectives, Wolcott's[47] ethnographic study focuses on the headteacher, or more correctly, the principal, since this research is conducted in an elementary school in the United States of America. As we have already seen, the interpretive researcher often adopts the role of a participant observer in the organization in which he is interested, watching and recording the minutiae of happenings and events as they occur or as they are recounted by those involved. Participant observation has been described as a process of waiting to be impressed by recurrent themes that reappear in various contexts.[48] Wolcott's account of the day-to-day life of an elementary school principal well illustrates the 'waiting role' of the participant observer.

Wolcott shadowed Ed Bell, the school principal, for a period of two years, spending several days every week with him in school, at home, at church meetings, accompanying him on school business away from the school building and even going to the local store with him to purchase household requirements. During all of these events, Wolcott maintained a constant written record of the behaviour he saw and the conversations he heard between the school principal and staff, children, family and friends. With the principal's permission, the researcher sifted through his notes, files and personal records. Extensive tape recordings were made of interviews with members of the school staff. The principal himself was persuaded to keep an account of recurring school problems for a period of several weeks. A further observational device used by Wolcott involved noting the activity and the social interaction patterns of the school principal every minute for periods of two hours at a time. This procedure included recording the person with whom the principal interacted, who initiated the interaction, where and when, who was talking, and how many people were involved. Over a period of several weeks Wolcott generated a set of categories for tabulating these interactions. By a careful sampling of the data from these two-hour recordings over ten consecutive school days, the researcher built up a detailed picture of the multifarious demands made upon the school principal in his day-to-day life.

Wolcott's painstaking and detailed observing and recording led to the gradual identification and piecing together of several important strands in the professional life of the school principal. The researcher reveals the complex demands that are made of a school leader and the degree to which Ed Bell succeeds both in his own estimation and in the judgements of those who have to work with him. We illustrate the point with an example.

One particularly difficult task that American school principals face each year is staff evaluation. Because permanence of tenure and financial advancement hang upon a satisfactory evaluation from the principal, the exercise is charged with tension and anxiety on the part of the teachers and principal alike. (The common practice in North America is that the teacher reads what the school principal has to say about her teaching ability and signs the document in his presence.) Wolcott's observation and recording of the evaluation exercise gathered information from the principal and from various teachers. His account shows how the task of teacher evaluation set the principal most clearly apart from his staff and challenged him with difficult decisions which he tackled with an indecisiveness that only added to the stress that everyone involved experienced. Ed Bell is not at all happy with one of his teachers, Mrs Alma Skirmish, and is all set to write a report that will exclude her from his school for the following session. She challenges his evaluation:

'After I read the evaluation, I said to Ed, "So you're going to try to stop me from teaching by saying such things as: I expect that ten years from now you'll be teaching the same way as you're teaching now!' On what grounds can anyone say this? Why, I wasn't teaching the same way as I was a year ago, and certainly not ten years ago . . .'

In the end, however, he has a change of heart following evaluation meetings with her such as the one we report above.

'She really seemed to listen to the things I had to say . . . She runs her classroom like a classroom now, not a Sunday school class . . . She's doing a better job . . . Maybe next year I'll regret it. But right now I feel I'm right.'

Outside of the actual interchanges between principal and teachers, Wolcott is able to look at the staff evaluation exercise and bring to it his own assessment of the principal's leadership:

'I could never escape a personal feeling that Ed made his assessments about new staff quickly (probably on first impression), independent of performance observed in the classroom, and then subsequently accumulated whatever evidence he felt he needed to support those impressions. Although he tended to be cautious when screening candidates for his school or the district, once he decided to accept a candidate for the Taft faculty, the extent of his enthusiasm and optimism took a predictable upward swing.'

Wolcott's study is a very readable and 'real' account of the life of a headteacher. The researcher himself is a strong advocate of the intensive form of participant observation that he describes in his research. At the same time, Wolcott is concerned that would-be researchers are aware of the pitfalls of the ethnographic approach. It is, he says, an excellent method of obtaining certain kinds of data, but it cannot by itself provide the whole picture. In the first place, the ethnographic researcher always faces the problem of the formation of general concepts in pursuing an in-depth study of a single case. Secondly, the participant observation approach is, in Wolcott's words, a high-risk, low-yield venture. It is high risk because unless the fieldwork is eventually translated into a significant readable (and read) monograph, the only possible gain is that made by the researcher in terms of his own research experience. The participant observer approach is low yield because of the considerable investment of time and personal effort that has to be made in order to obtain basic and often commonplace data. Wolcott's somewhat disparaging use of the phrase 'commonplace data' is unnecessary. Arguably, those commonplace data are the very bedrock of what the sociological enterprise is about! Bittner[49] for example, discussing the formal structure of organizations, stresses that the meaning and import (of the formal structure) remains undetermined unless the circumstances and procedures of its *actual use by actors* is fully investigated. A similar point is made by Zimmerman[50] in connection with organizational rules. The issue of what such rules mean to, and how they are used by, personnel on *actual occasions* he says, is ignored as an empirical issue by sociologists who make their own assumptions about what the rules mean and take their own competence to apply them for granted.

The studies of Robertson, Kanter, and Wolcott are included in this section precisely because they *are* concerned with the meanings that school organizational structures have for their participants and they *do* examine the actual uses that actors make of those structures in the ongoing life of their organizations.

SUMMARY

We began the chapter with an outline of four theoretical approaches to the study of schools as organizations, all four conceptions deriving from normative rather than interpretive perspectives. We attempted a synthesis of these approaches when we applied them to our discussion of the organizational structures of schools and to our outline of the duties and obligations attached to the positions of headteacher, deputy-head, head of department, and teacher. We illustrated our account of role conflict with examples of the organizational and individual strategies commonly employed in role conflict resolution. We then went on to talk about the concepts of leadership and decision-making, concluding that a 'professional' model consisting of 'one part bureaucracy and one part human relations' best typified leadership and decision-making in most contemporary British schools. Our analysis of recent studies of school leadership suggested that secondary teachers probably enjoy a greater satisfaction from the degree to which participation in decision-making is encouraged by heads than do primary school staff. Our discussion of the headteacher's leadership led to a consideration of the concept of organizational climate and to the ways in which that construct has been employed in studies of American and British schools.

The purposes and forms of pastoral care provision in secondary schools were then reviewed, first from a normative, 'systems' position, and then from an alternative, interpretive viewpoint. Having introduced an interpretive perspective on schools as organizations, we then devoted the remainder of the chapter to an examination of three empirical studies whose common purpose was to explore the meanings of situations as they were phenomenologically experienced by the pupils, teachers, and headteachers involved.

ENQUIRY AND DISCUSSION

1. What bureaucratic features of school organization have you experienced as a pupil or as a student teacher?

2. Why is 'democracy' difficult to put into practice in schools?

3. As a *teacher* how would you define the major role expectations of the headteacher position? What priorities do you think *parents* would stress generally?

4. Use Kahn's model of a role episode (see Box 11.6) to explain the behaviour of a student teacher faced with incompatible expectations from a classteacher and a college tutor.

5. How might *role ambiguity* serve to lessen rather than heighten role conflict in teaching practice?

6. Discuss the changes in recent educational practice outlined in Box 11.7 as they relate to the teacher's classroom role.

7. Describe any school with which you are familiar in terms of the characteristics detailed in Box 11.10. Compare your description with that of a colleague who knows the same school. Why do you think there are differences in your assessments?

8. In your experience, what truth is there in the description of school pastoral care set out in Box 11.15?

NOTES AND REFERENCES

1. Owens, R. G. (1970) *Organizational Behaviour In Schools*. Englewood Cliffs N. J.: Prentice Hall.

2. Barr Greenfield, T. (1975) Theory about organizations: a new perspective and its implications for schools. In *Administering Education: International Challenge*. (Ed.) Hughes, M. G. London: Athlone Press.

See also Barr Greenfield, T. (1976) Organizational theory: a symposium. *Educational Administration*, **5**, 1, 1–13.
and Barr Greenfield, T. (1978) Where does self belong in the study of organization? *Educational Administration*, **6**, 1, 81–101.

3. Hoyle, E. (1976) Comment, in *Educational Administration*, **5**, 1, 4–6.

4. The Open University (1976) *Schools as Organisations*: A Third Level Course: Management in Education Unit 3 (E321 3). Milton Keynes: Open University Press. See also, Bennett, S. J. (1974) *The School: An Organizational Analysis*. Glasgow: Blackie.
and Dunkerley, D. (1972) *The Study of Organizations*. London: Routledge and Kegan Paul.

5. Richardson, E. (1977) *The Teacher, The School, and The Task of Management*. London: Heinemann.

6. Presthus, R. (1962) *The Organizational Society*. New York: Alfred A. Knopf.

7. Warwick, D. (1974) *Bureaucracy*. London: Longman.

8. Albrow, N. (1974) Is a science of organisations possible? In *Perspectives on Organizations*. Open University, DT352 Units 15 and 16. Milton Keynes: Open University Press.

9. Elton Mayo is perhaps the best known name associated with what has come to be called the *human relations movement*. The famous Western Electric studies are reported in Roethlisberger, F. J. and Dickson, W. J. (1939) *Management and the Worker*. Camb. Mass.: Harvard Univ. Press.

10. Griffiths, D. et al., (1962) *Organizing Schools For Effective Education*. Dansville, Ill., The Interstate Printers and Publisher.

11. Getzels, J. W. and Guba, E. G. (1957) Social behaviour and the administrative process. *School Review*, **65** (Winter) 423–441.
Getzels, H. W. (1958) Administration as a social process. In *Administrative Theory in Education*. Halpin, A. W. Chicago: Midwest Administration Centre, University of Chicago.

12. Gannon, T. and Whalley, A. (1979) The management of a small secondary school. In *Management and Headship in the Secondary School*. Jennings, A. London: Ward Lock Educational.

13. Watts, J. (1976) Sharing it out: the role of the head in participatory government. In *The Role of The Head*. (Ed.) Peters, R. S. London: Routledge and Kegan Paul.

14. Taylor, W. (1964) The training college principal. *Sociological Review*, **12**, 2.

15. Cohen, L. (1970) *Conceptions of headteachers concerning their role*. Unpublished Ph.D. dissertation. University of Keele.
Bull, T. (1978) *A study of some aspects of leadership behaviour of headteachers of primary schools*. Unpublished M.Phil. dissertation. University of Nottingham.

Hughes, M. G. (1972) *The role of the secondary school head.* Unpublished Ph.D. dissertation. University College, Cardiff.

16. Burnham, P. (1968) The deputy head. In *Headship in the 1970s* (Ed.) Allen, B. Oxford: Blackwell.

17. Coulson, A. A. (1976) The attitudes of primary school heads and deputy heads to the deputy headship. *British Journal of Educational Psychology*, **46**, 244–252.
    Coulson, A. A. and Cox, M. V. (1977) Primary school deputy headship: differences in the conceptions of heads and deputy heads associated with age, sex, and length of experience. *Educational Studies*, **3**, 2, 129–136.

18. Grover, A. J. (1972) *Curriculum decision-making in primary schools.* Unpublished M.Sc. dissertation. University of Bradford.

19. Bailey, P. (1973) The functions of heads of departments in comprehensive schools. *Journal of Educational Administration and History*, **5**, 1, 52–58.

20. Kahn, R. L., Wolfe, D. M., Quinn, R. P., Snoek, J. D. and Rosenthal, R. A. (1964) *Organizational Stress: Studies in Role Conflict and Ambiguity.* New York: John Wiley.

21. Johnson, D. W. (1970) *The Social Psychology of Education.* New York: Holt, Rinehart and Winston.

22. Getzels, J. W. and Guba, E. S. (1954) Role, role conflict, and effectiveness. *American Sociological Review*, **19**, 164–175.
    Getzels, G. W. (1963) Conflict and role behaviour in the educational setting. In *Readings in the Social Psychology of Education.* (Eds.) Charters, W. W. and Gage, N. L. Boston: Mass.

23. Kelsall, R. K. and Kelsall, H. M. (1969) *The Schoolteacher in England and the United States.* Oxford: Pergamon Press.

24. Secord, R. F. and Backman, C. W. (1964) *Social Psychology.* New York: McGraw Hill.

25. Gross, N., Mason, W. S. and McEachern, A. W. (1958) *Exploration in Role Analysis.* New York: John Wiley.

26. Burchard, W. (1954) Role conflicts of military chaplains. *American Sociological Review*, **19**, 528–535.

27. Grace, G. R. (1972) *Role Conflict and the Teacher.* London: Routledge and Kegan Paul.

28. Hoyle, E. (1975) Leadership and decision-making in education. In *Administering Education: The International Challenge.* (Ed.) Hughes, M. G. London: Athlone Press. pp. 30–44.

29. Litwak, E. (1961) Models of bureaucracy which permit conflict. *American Journal of Sociology*, **67**, 177–184.

30. Bates, A. W. (1972) The planning of the curriculum. *Headmasters' Association Review*, **70**, No. 215 (July).

31. Hobbs, A., Kleinberg, S. M. and Martin, P. J. (1979) Decision-making in primary schools. *Research in Education*, **21**, 79–92.

32. Halpin, A. W. and Croft, D. B. (1963) *The Organizational Climate of Schools*. Chicago: Midwest Administrative Centre, University of Chicago.

33. McGeown, V. (1979a) School innovativeness as process and product. New University of Ulster (mimeographed).
McGeown, V. (1979b) Organisational climate for change in schools: towards definition and measurement. New University of Ulster (mimeographed).
McGeown, V. (1979c) School principals' decision-making behaviour in the management of innovation. New University of Ulster (mimeographed).
McGeown, V. (1979d) Dimensions of teacher innovativeness. New University of Ulster (mimeographed).

34. Finlayson, D. S. (1975) Organisation climate. *Research Intelligence*, **1**, 22–36.
Finlayson, D. S. (1970) *School Climate Index*. Slough: NFER.
Finlayson, D. S., Banks, O. and Loughran, J. L. (1970) *School Organisation Index*. Slough: NFER.

35. King, R. (1973) *School Organisation and Pupil Involvement: A Study of Secondary Schools*. London: Routledge and Kegan Paul.

36. (Eds) Craft, M. and Lytton, H. (1969) *Guidance and Counselling in British Schools*. London: Arnold & Sons.

37. Best, R. E., Jarvis, C. B. and Ribbins, P. M. (1977) Pastoral care: concept and process. *British Journal of Educational Studies*, **25**, 2, 124–135.

38. Hamblin, D. (1972) Intervening in the Learning Process Unit 17. In *Educational Studies: A Second Level Course, Personality Growth and Learning*. Bletchley, Bucks.: The Open University Press.

39. Cicourel, A. V. and Kitsuse, J. I. (1963) *The Educational Decisionmakers*. Indianapolis: Bobbs-Merill.

40. The concepts *sponsored* and *contest* mobility are found in: Turner, R. H. (1960) Sponsored and contest mobility and the school system. *American Sociological Review*, **25**, 856.

41. Perrow, C. (1974) Zoo story or life in the organisational sandpit. In *Perspectives on Organisations*, DT 352 Units 15 and 16. Milton Keynes: Open University Press.

42. Dale, R. (1973) Phenomenological perspectives and the sociology of the school. *Educational Review*, **25**, 3, 175–189.

43. Robertson, W. (1978) *Language as power: an exploration of perception of power and hierarchy as expressed in the language of children and adults in a primary school*. M.Ed. dissertation: University of Newcastle.

44. Thomas, W. I. (1928) *The Child in America*. New York: Knopf.

45. Becker, H. W. and Geer, B. (1960) Latent culture: a note on the theory of latent social roles. *Administrative Science Quarterly*, **5**, 304–313.

46. Kanter, R. M. (1972) The organization child: experience management in a nursery school. *Sociology of Education*, **45**, 186–212.
    Borman, K. (1978) Social control and schooling: power and process in two Kindergarten settings. *Anthropology and Education Quarterly*, **9**, 1, 38–53.
    King, R. (1978) *All Things Bright and Beautiful? A Sociological Study of Infants' Classrooms*. Chichester: Wiley.

47. Wolcott, H. F. (1973) *The Man in the Principal's Office*. New York: Holt, Rinehart and Winston.

48. Diesing, P. (1971) *Patterns of Discovery in the Social Sciences*. Chicago: Aldine.

49. Bittner, E. (1972) The concept of organisation. In *People and Organisations*. (Eds.) Salaman, G. and Thompson, K. London: Longmans.

50. Zimmerman, D. (1972) The practicalities of rule use. In *People and Organisations*. (Eds.) Salaman, G. and Thompson, K. London: Longmans.

SELECTED READING

1. (Ed.) Sockett, H. (1980) *Accountability in the English Educational System*. London: Hodder and Stoughton. This work contains a number of contributions that touch upon the theme of participation and decision-making in schools.

2. (Ed.) Peters, R. S. (1976) *The Role of the Head*. London: Routledge and Kegan Paul. A useful review of recent research on the role of the headteacher.

3. (Ed.) Jennings, A. (1979) *Management and Headship in the Secondary School*. London: Ward Lock Educational. This contains contributions on the school as an organization, pastoral care, the discipline functions of the headteacher, and problems of management in large and small schools.

4. Burrell, G. and Morgan, G. (1979) *Sociological Paradigms and Organisational Analysis: Elements of the Sociology of Corporate Life*. London: Heinemann. A readable account which relates theories of organization to their wider sociological context.

5. (Ed.) Hammersley, M. and Woods, P. (1976) *The Process of Schooling: A Sociological Reader*. London: Routledge and Kegan Paul. This work provides interpretive perspectives on the organization of teaching and on pupil cultures.

12

School and Society

Our major concern in the previous chapter was to describe the organizational structures and internal arrangements of schools. We saw that the successful accomplishment of activities requires careful and continuous planning together with a recognition on the part of those involved of the rights and obligations attached to the various positions they occupy. The role model that we used to illustrate the school was primarily concerned with internal factors described as 'organizational', 'interpersonal' and 'personality', the model itself depicting the school as a largely self-contained entity. Schools, of course, are not just responsible to themselves nor are they impervious to outside influences. In the first place they serve local communities that are rich in their own traditions and closely linked with their schools in a variety of extra-curricular activities. Those same communities, moreover, are part of a wider society, a society regulated by standards, customs, and beliefs which act as powerful determinants of what is taught in school and how it is taught. Secondly, schools are part of a public system of educational provision governed by politics and procedures agreed on at both national and local level.

In the present chapter our central focus is upon the social environment external to the school. Our intention is to describe certain features of that environment and to look at the ways in which they impinge upon the life and work of schools. The plan of attack is to deal first with what Kogan[1] calls the *decision-making system* of education, that is, those parts of the service with statutory, formal responsibilities and powers for taking decisions. Here we concentrate on local government and its relationship with schools. We then go on to look at what Kogan describes as the *system of influence*, that is to say, those bodies and sources of power that, despite their lack of statutory authority and responsibilities, nevertheless exert pressures upon schools. And here we are necessarily selective in view of the range and diversity of sources that could be included.

Moving outwards from the school as it were in ever widening circles, we turn first to local communities as sources of influence, choosing not urban environments about which so much has already been written, but rural communities and their relationships with schools. We then explore the impact of a potent source of influence that operates at societal level – the mass media. In particular we look at the effects of television violence on children's behaviour and at the role of the media in the amplification of deviance. We conclude Chapter 12 in the manner that we began Chapter 1, by looking at ways in which alternative paradigms of social reality can be brought to bear upon an educational issue. Our task in this final section is to present competing explanations of the purposes that schools serve in society.

LOCAL GOVERNMENT AND THE SCHOOL

At least eight different groups are or may be involved in running a school: the local education authority, other local authorities, the governors or managers, the headteacher, other teachers, the pupils, the parents, and of course, the central government either through its emissaries (Her Majesty's Inspectors, for example) or through the law.[2] For the moment our concern is with the duties and responsibilities of members of the local education authority as they relate to what goes on in schools.

As a result of a major reorganization of local government instituted by the Local Government Act 1972 there are now 104 local education authorities. Their duties are as follows:

1. To contribute towards the spiritual, moral, mental and physical development of the community.
2. To secure the provision of sufficient and efficient schools, and to ensure the provision of adequate facilities for further education for those over compulsory school age.
3. To ensure that all pupils and students take full advantage of the education provided: for example, by financial awards, careers services, health provisions, meal and transport facilities etc.

How are local education authorities constituted so as to discharge their duties?

Elected, unpaid, local authority councillors are organized into a number of standing committees, each committee being responsible to the local council for its business. Under the Local Government Act 1972 the requirement has been continued that councils should establish education committees along the lines approved by the Secretary of State. We need not concern ourselves here with the structure or the representation of local education committees. Rather, our interest is in the local education authority department, first, in its functional divisions carrying centralized responsibilities for various aspects of the authority's work and second, in its professional educational staff, among whom the advisers and local inspectors as the 'eyes and the ears' of the department provide an important point of contact and communication with schools. Box 12.1 illustrates the structure and organization of a typical local education authority department. It shows two distinct* divisions – 'educational', and 'functional', the latter consisting of ad-

---

* Though 'distinct' the educational and functional divisions are, of course, interdependent and interlocking in their day-to-day work.

ministrative officers with responsibilities for such matters as the construction and maintenance of buildings, the requisition and distribution of supplies etc. The function of the chief education officer who, as we see in Box 12.1, heads the hierarchy, is to advise the local education authority on all matters to do with education. This wide brief includes advising on policy, carrying out LEA decisions, and taking decisions for the authority within the policies it has approved. The chief education officer is supported in his work by a number of professional educators. Our particular interest is in one category of this support team, – the local education authority adviser. As his designation suggests, the formal role of the professional adviser is to advise the chief education officer and his deputies. Recent research[3] on the role of the LEA adviser, however, has identified a wider range of expectations and duties which we set out in Box 12.2.

BOX 12.1

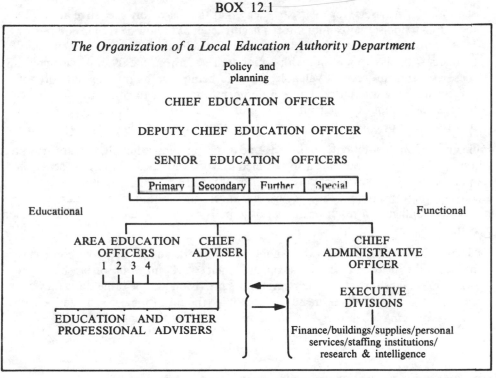

The Organization of a Local Education Authority Department

Policy and
planning

CHIEF EDUCATION OFFICER

DEPUTY CHIEF EDUCATION OFFICER

SENIOR EDUCATION OFFICERS

| Primary | Secondary | Further | Special |

Educational   Functional

AREA EDUCATION OFFICERS   CHIEF ADVISER   CHIEF ADMINISTRATIVE OFFICER
1 2 3 4

EXECUTIVE DIVISIONS

EDUCATION AND OTHER PROFESSIONAL ADVISERS   Finance/buildings/supplies/personal services/staffing institutions/ research & intelligence

Source: adapted from Open University Course E222

Box 12.2 reveals that advisers are highly influential in matters of school policy and planning. The influences that they exert on schools are further illuminated in a recent longitudinal study[4] undertaken in the London boroughs of Hillingdon and Hounslow. Johnson and her associates describe the role of advisers and the ways they are perceived in schools as follows:

'Advisers appear to be better known as individuals in the schools than other staff from the LEA but when teachers mention the relationship they generally see advisers relating to senior staff or the middle management of the

BOX 12.2

The Role of the LEA Adviser

1. Advising governors, managers and headteachers on staff appointments.
2. Giving personal and professional advice to individual teachers.
3. Assessing the teaching ability of probationary teachers and those seeking promotion.
4. Advising individual schools on matters of innovation or reorganization.
5. Inspecting schools/colleges.
6. Making school visits to look at the work of children and teachers.
7. Planning and organizing LEA curriculum projects.
8. Organizing and lecturing on in-service teacher training activities.
9. Advising on the design and equipping of schools/colleges.
10. Advising on organizational changes such as the introduction of middle schools.

Source: adapted from Bolam, Smith and Carter[3]

school . . . . Advisers, for their part, deny that they have any executive authority regarding schools; they cannot direct a headteacher as to how he should conduct or control his school. They can, however, exert considerable influence in their many contacts with classrooms and with senior staff . . . From the schools' viewpoint, these contacts are seen as valuable, advisers being seen as offering support for subject teaching and curriculum development and being there to give advice to headteachers about the general running of the school or staffing problems or to discuss career development or teaching methods with individual teachers.'

Johnson goes on to point out that the LEA advisory function is not all outwards towards schools. Advisers, she notes, are also expected to work with those staff at the department responsible for the needs of schools in respect of resources, finance, buildings etc. Their duality of role means that they occupy an uncertain position in education and may experience conflict as a result of the opposite pulls of *support* and *control*. As Johnson puts it:

'They exist to help teachers do a good job of work and to promote consensus between the field and the department. Their work may, however, highlight limitations and shortfalls in their employer's provision. At the same time, they are employed to help the department grip and shape the educational system and so run the risk of being labelled as "administrative spies" by the schools.'

GOVERNORS, MANAGERS, AND THE SCHOOL

A second group of people belonging to the *decision-making system* of education are school governors and school managers. Recall that the decision-making system refers to those parts of the education service that have statutory, formal responsibilities and powers for taking decisions. Under the terms of the 1944 Education Act* governors and managers of

---

* Historically, managers and governors have connections with schools extending back to the 1870 Education Act and beyond, boards of managers serving the new voluntary elementary schools established under that Act, boards of governors serving grammar schools provided by voluntary bodies and trusts.[5]

schools are statutory bodies with constitutional powers and relationships with local education authorities. Those powers consist of preparing estimates and controlling expenditure, together with appointing staff and exercising 'general oversight' of the conduct and curriculum of schools. In practice, however, local education authorities generally determine estimates and expenditures, and headteachers are largely 'captains of their own ships' over matters to do with the curriculum and the general running of their schools. The most important function of managers and governors is generally that of appointing headteachers. This may well change, however, following the report of a committee of enquiry set up to review the arrangements for the management and government of county primary and secondary schools in England and Wales. The Taylor Committee published its report[6] in 1977 and among its many recommendations were the following:[7]

1. That every school, big or small should have its own governors to look after its interests. (Under the Local Government Act 1972, in the case of secondary schools generally and primary schools situated in metropolitan districts, LEAs may, should they choose, group any two or more schools under a single governing body).
2. That a partnership of the four main interests in the school should guide the composition of the governing body. Thus, one quarter of the governors should represent the local education authority, one quarter the school staff including automatically the headteacher plus elected representatives of the teaching staff and, in larger schools, ancillary helpers. One quarter should be elected by all the parents of children attending the school. Where appropriate, within this grouping, provision should be made for the election of pupil governors, such pupils being elected by their fellows. Finally, one quarter of the governors should consist of community members co-opted by the other three groups.
3. In connection with the powers and responsibilities of the school governors, it is recommended that they should be responsible for ensuring that within the school the head makes adequate and suitable arrangements for consultation both with teaching and non-teaching staff. Governors' minutes should be available in the staffroom unless classified as confidential on any particular issue.
4. In secondary schools, the committee recommended that pupils should be able to set up their own organization for communication among themselves; for the expression of joint views, and for making those views known to the governors.
5. Parents, the committee felt, should be informed, consulted, encouraged to associate and generally recognized as partners in the education process.
6. In connection with the curriculum, the governors should establish the school's objectives, share in the formation of the structure of learning, care and rules necessary to achieve these objectives, and produce regularly more formal appraisals of its performance, having access in its task to the professional guidance of advisers and inspectors.

Clearly the Taylor Report has proposed far-reaching changes in the scope and range of duties presently undertaken by managers and governors of schools, changes that if taken up, would require new legislation. The likelihood, however, is that what has been described[8] as a diminution of the role of the LEA and the headteacher in the event of the

Taylor report recommendations being implemented, reflects a view currently held by many of the interested parties not least by headteachers themselves.

PRESSURE GROUPS AND THE SCHOOL[9]

Up to this point in the chapter our look at the ways in which the social environment outside schools impinges upon their routines and activities has focused entirely on selected aspects of the decision-making system of education, in particular, the part played by the local education authority department and the role of school governors and managers. We turn now to some sources of influence that lack statutory powers or responsibilities yet nevertheless exert pressures upon what takes place in schools. We refer to them all, initially, as *pressure groups*.

A pressure group has been defined[10] as, 'any group . . . which articulates a demand that the authorities in the political system or subsystem should make an authoritative allocation' in its favour. In order to exclude political parties from his definition, the author goes on to add the following qualification that 'such groups do not themselves seek to occupy positions of authority.

Frequently, a distinction is drawn between *sectional* and *promotional* pressure groups. The purpose of a sectional pressure group is to advance and to protect the interests of its own members. In this sense, the National Union of Teachers can be thought of as a sectional pressure group. A promotional pressure group, on the other hand, pursues more altruistic ends. When, for example, the Child Poverty Action Group achieves its goals, individuals other than its own members are the principal beneficiaries.

Whereas the differentiation between sectional and promotional pressure groups relates to aims, the distinction that Kogan[1] draws between *legitimized* and *non-legitimized* pressure groups refers to authority and power.

Legitimized groups, according to Kogan, are those bodies that have an accepted right to be consulted by local authorities, by central government, and by educational organizations such as universities, before policies are authorized. He cites the legitimization granted by the Secretary of State to the National Association of Schoolmasters in their admission to the Burnham negotiations over salary awards. The role of non-legitimized pressure groups, on the other hand, is to challenge accepted authority and institutions until policies are changed. Here Kogan gives the example of STOPP, (the Society of Teachers Opposed to Physical Punishment). In Box 12.3 we identify a number of the major educational pressure groups in Britain today.

Press reports, television interviews, questions in the House of Commons variously attest to the effectiveness or otherwise of educational pressure groups at a national level. But our interest, for the moment, is with the more immediate impact that pressure groups may exert on schools at the local community level. Perhaps the best known example that springs to mind is the affair at William Tyndale Junior School, London. Mr Robin Auld QC who conducted a lengthy inquiry into the teaching, organization and management at that school had a great deal to say about the way that the school system functioned, and he went on to relate the behaviour of those involved in the conflict to the practices and

BOX 12.3

+--+
| *Some Major Educational Pressure Groups in Britain* |
| |
| *Groups*   *Example* |
| Local Authority Associations Association of Municipal Authorities |
| Education Officers   Society of Education Officers |
| Denominational interests   Catholic Education Council |
| Teachers   National Union of Teachers |
| Headteachers   Headmasters Association |
| Higher education   Association of University Teachers |
| Students   National Union of Students |
| Parents   Advisory Centre for Education |
| Institutions   Committee of Directors in Polytechnics |
| Young children   National Campaign for Nursery Education |
| Handicapped children   National Association for Remedial Education |
| Broad policy issues   Child Poverty Action Group |
+--+

Source: adapted from Open University Course E222 Unit 6[9]

attitudes which determine the control of primary schools generally. Much of the concluding chapter of the report[11] is given over to defining the powers and responsibilities of the education authority and of the school managers and to suggesting how these two parties should behave in any conflict over curriculum and teaching matters in a state primary school. Box 12.4 provides a 'blow-by-blow' account of what has come to be

BOX 12.4

+--+
| *The William Tyndale 'Affair'* |
+--+

July 1973:	Mr Head, the headmaster, left.
Sept. 1973:	Brian Haddow joined the staff. Irene Chowles, the deputy head was in charge.
Jan. 1974:	Terry Ellis took up the headship of the school. 217 children on the roll. More than one-third of them in need of remedial help.
April 1974:	Dorothy McColgan joined the staff.
May 1974:	Growing disagreement among the staff about how the school was being run and widespread parental criticism led to complaints being made to the managers: Three managers met Mr Ellis and Mr Haddow.
June 1974:	Parents attacked what was happening at the school at a parents evening.
July 1974:	Mr Haddow and his supporters walked out of a further parents evening. The new District Inspector, Donald Rice, attended the meeting. He had been asked to prepare a report by the ILEA. The latter told the managers to 'cool it'.
Sept. 1974:	Numbers at the school dropped by one quarter. Miss Hart, the Infant School head, complained to the ILEA about behaviour in the Junior School. Two new teachers joined the staff and a child-centred, free-choice, team-teaching approach became the order of the day.
Dec. 1974:	A number of managers again complained to the ILEA. Mr Rice was again asked to report. ILEA decided on 'no action' unless there was evidence of dissatisfaction within the community.
May 1975:	A petition was organized and the managers condemned what was happening in the school. The staff, therefore, decided to ban the managers from the school.
June 1975:	The managers contacted 'The Times'.
July 1975:	ILEA called a meeting of teachers and managers at County Hall. Managers and teachers called for an inspection by the DES but the Authority decided on a local inspection, followed by a formal inquiry.
Sept. 1975:	Teachers went on strike and opened a rival school in a chapel hall.
Oct. 1975:	Formal inspection took place followed by the Auld inquiry.

known as the William Tyndale affair. For our part, it is the role of the various pressure groups in that affair which is of particular interest.

However one may view the outcome of the William Tyndale inquiry, the effectiveness of certain pressure groups was unequivocally demonstrated. Why were they successful? We invite the reader to consider reasons for their success against the following criteria identified by Saran[12].

Political. Education policy makers and pressure groups operate in the educational subsystem which forms part of the wider political system of elections, party, cabinet, government, parliament, courts, the local government system and distribution of powers. Any or all of these may exert constraints on, or offer opportunities for, exerting pressure.

Legitimized pressure groups. These enjoy statutory rights which makes for easier informal, as well as formal contact with policy makers. It also brings the benefit of access to information.

Dependency on pressure group. An authority is more likely to heed pressure group demands if the group's co-operation is important in conducting its affairs. Information and knowledge needed by an authority are, in some cases, obtained from pressure groups. The co-operation of the teaching profession is important to LEAs, especially over policy implementation.

Clear policy line. If an LEA has a decided view on an issue, pressure groups taking an opposing stance are likely to be ignored unless they possess powerful sanctions.

Resources. Legitimized groups are usually more efficiently organized with superior re-sources – staff, money etc. Non-legitimized groups have to rely largely on voluntary efforts; survival for them depends more heavily on the enthusiasm and commitment of members.

Research. Knowledge and information can greatly strengthen the influence of a pressure group especially if the local authority needs the information for policy decisions.

Sanctions. When teachers and parents use sanctions, they are likely to be less effective than in the case of some other pressure groups. Nevertheless, campaigns of disruption can have an impact, and the non-co-operation or low morale of teachers can make policy implementation difficult.

Homogeneity. Single-aim pressure groups are more likely to be united in pursuit of their purpose. Internal consensus is more difficult to achieve on politically-sensitive issues that involve ideological controversy. Lack of such consensus weakens pressure group effectiveness.

Having looked somewhat broadly at relationships between schools and local government, school managers, and a variety of educational pressure groups, it is time that we followed our outline of the William Tyndale affair with some further examples of the ways in which these varying sources of influence affect real schools in real places.

It is common knowledge that significant differences exist in educational provision in the 104 local education authorities in England and Wales. These differences are not due to chance. What has been termed an 'educational split' in our society (roughly North versus South) has been the topic of research[13] aiming to identify non-educational factors in the environment that make for differences in educational opportunity. One factor, *local authority income and provision*, has been the subject of particular attention.[14] Byrne and Williamson[15] argue that educational attainment is a product of the distribution of resources and power in society rather than the distribution of intelligence. Among the factors they identify are the following: (1) social class background; (2) local environmental factors; (3) local authority policy; (4) local authority resources; and (5) local authority provision. These five factors were used in a study of eleven local authorities in north east England in which Byrne and Williamson tried to find out how provision, resources, and local authority policies related to educational attainment.

Two broad trends were identified:

(a) areas with the highest proportion of lower social class members had the smallest resources (measured by penny rate per pupil) but spent proportionally more on education (a reflection of local authority policy decisions). Moreover the spending gave preferential treatment to the primary rather than the secondary area of education.

(b) areas with the highest proportion of higher social class members had the greatest resources but spent proportionally less on education and spent it preferentially on the secondary rather than the primary education sector.

Trend (a) above, Byrne and Williamson termed an *anti-elitist policy*, that is spending more on the sector that benefits the total school population (i.e. the primary area). Trend (b) above, they associated with an *elitist* policy, the spending being directed towards that sector which benefits a minority (i.e. the secondary area). More importantly, Byrne and Williamson noted, these two types of local authority policy were related to educational outcomes. Thus, staying on at school past the statutory leaving age was related to local authority resources and to the proportion of higher social class inhabitants but negatively to the proportion of lower social class inhabitants. Social class factors, the researchers concluded, were most important here, resources and policy decisions playing a mediating role. Social class factors, however, were less importantly associated with staying on into the sixth form and entering further and higher education. Here, it was resources and policy decisions that played the largest part. Thus, 'elitist' authorities had higher rates of staying on, university entrance and 'higher grade' further education while 'anti-elitist' authorities had lower rates of staying on, those students who did stay on, opting for teacher training courses and 'lower grade' further education.

The key role that local authority policy decisions play in the scope and variety of educational provision is demonstrated in Boaden's[16] research. He analysed the spending of local authorities and showed that local expenditure was related both to need (that is, the number of pupils involved) and to the political persuasion of the local council. Labour controlled councils, for example, spent more on education whatever the number of children within the authority.

Having said something about the direct, quantifiable influences that local authorities bring to bear upon schools through their policies over the provision and allocation of resources, we turn now to look at some of the less tangible effects that communities have upon their schools, and, in turn, the part that schools themselves play in the life of their immediate localities.

RURAL COMMUNITIES AND THEIR SCHOOLS

Because *educational disadvantage* is a term that is generally associated with urban areas, government initiatives both in respect of finance and research (Urban Aid Programme, Community Development Projects, Educational Priority Areas) have largely been directed to solving urban problems. But the concept of educational disadvantage is somewhat enigmatic, embracing as it does, a range of factors (poverty, poor housing, family stress, isolation, cultural differences and the like) that variously relate to children's lack of educational progress. Only recently has the question been asked whether these or similar factors also impede the attainment of pupils growing up in rural areas. In this section of the chapter we have specifically chosen to look at schools in rural settings. Our treatment is necessarily brief for whereas there is a burgeoning literature on urban education, research to do with rural communities and their schools is both fragmentary and elusive.[17]

The number of children in primary education in England and Wales is expected to drop from a peak of 5.2 million in 1974 to 3.8 million in 1986.[18] Reorganization programmes necessitated by this trend are likely to be most extensive in areas with a predominantly rural population scattered over a wide area, and it is here that the impact on community life in general is likely to be most felt, for the solution often proposed in the case of small rural primary schools is simply to close them down. Falling rolls and 'educational disadvantage' are closely linked in policy decisions over closures. The arguments[19] put forward to support these policies include:

1. The small rural school implies few staff and hence limitations of professional talent and curriculum change.
2. The small rural school implies small pupil numbers and hence limited interaction possibilities.
3. The small rural school suffers from limited resources, both 'hard' and 'soft'.
4. Small rural schools produce professional isolation which impedes beneficial educational change.
5. Small rural schools are economically inefficient. More effective financial deployment could yield enhanced educational returns.

These 'educational' arguments are reinforced by reference to (a) *individual disadvantage*, in particular, the poor verbal ability of many rural pupils lacking the linguistic stimulus of parents engaged in long hours of physically-exhausting work or of other children situated in remote farms or cottages, (b) *community disadvantage* – in particular, the closing down of bus services and post offices and the increasingly attenuated medical provisions that are available.

What can be said of the advantages of rural schools? Supporters according to Sigsworth,[19] rehearse the following justifications for retaining local village schools:

1. The school has satisfactorily educated generations of villagers and should continue to do so.
2. The village and its school are superior to the community and the school to which children would be transported.
3. The school is a social hub which aids community cohesion.
4. The teacher is a link with the outside world and an essential element in the maintenance of village activities as adviser, organizer, impartial critic and referee.
5. The school represents a force for order and control in the community.
6. If the children's schooling occurs elsewhere they will grow away from family and village and this will produce decline in community life.

As school closures continue in many rural areas, some authorities are experimenting with novel ways of meeting the needs of rural pupils and allaying some of the criticisms of educational disadvantage that we have outlined above. For example, mobile nurseries visit villages twice weekly in one educational authority, schemes of co-operation are developing between rural schools within certain areas involving exchanges between teaching staffs, teachers' centres are taking on wider commitments and initiatives, and plans for positive discrimination towards rural schools involving peripatetic specialist teachers in music, creative drama and football are in hand.

RURAL SCHOOL PUPILS' ATTITUDES: A CASE STUDY

Much that has been written about differences between rural and urban schools is tinged with romantic nostalgia and marked by subjective comments on the 'countryman's scale of values' and by 'affectionate accounts of village schools.'[20] What empirical work has been undertaken has had to do with differences in the attainment, personal and linguistic development, intelligence, and creativity of pupils in rural and urban settings. In his critique of these studies, Twine[21] points to a major weakness in that they tend to make comparisons between extreme examples on a static scale of community types whereas in reality, most communities actually exist somewhere between the ends of a rural – urban continuum. Types of community, moreover, have generally been defined by their size rather than by their nature. What is lacking, Twine asserts, is a study of educational processes within the context of dynamic social development, using a model of community that takes account of the reality of the rural – urban continuum. He goes on to identify four stages along that continuum, designating them as: *traditional rural, – transitional rural, – emergent urban, –* and *wholly urbanized.*

In classifying the catchment areas of 29 junior schools as falling within one or other of these community types, Twine employed the criteria shown in Box 12.5. He then used intelligence tests and attitude scales with some 510 fourth year children, supplementing his pupil data with further information to do with parental occupation, linguistic background (Welsh or English), and length of residence in the particular community. For

BOX 12.5

Factors Used to Determine the Extent of Urbanism Within a Given Area

Factor	Source
Age structure of population	
Density of population	
Percentage of life-residents	
Percentage of immigrants* < 5 yrs.	
Percentage of immigrants < 1 yr.	Census Records (County Reports)
Percentage of population in primary occupations	
Percentage of population in ancillary services	
Percentage of population in 'land-based' occupations	
Extent of 'commuting' to work	
Distance travelled for leisure activities	Questionnaire of
If an immigrant, number of changes of residence in previous 10 yrs.	random sample of
If an immigrant, nature of previous residence	community

* Immigrants in the sense of *newcomers* to the area rather than ethnic minority group members as the term is employed in Chapter 8.

Source: Twine[21]

the more technically-minded reader, a factorial design was employed to analyse the IQ and attitudinal data, each factor having two or more levels. Thus *ability* was classified 'above' or 'below' the mean score, *sex*, male or female, and *social context* as traditional rural, transitional rural, emergent urban, or wholly urbanized. A $2 \times 2 \times 4$ analysis of variance was carried out.

Twine found that the most favourable attitudes held towards school, towards other people, and towards themselves (self-image) belonged to children in traditional rural areas, that is, in communities unaffected by the spread of urbanization. Furthermore, a consistent pattern of attitude levels appeared to follow as the communities progressed through the phases of social change represented by the continuum. During the early stages of increasing urbanism (i.e. the transitional rural period) there seemed to be a marked decline in attitudes, building up again to a new peak during the 'emergent urban' phase although at a significantly lower level than that reached at the traditional rural point on the continuum. In the final stage of becoming wholly urbanized, Twine observes, levels again tended to fall. Box 12.6 presents these results graphically.

Of course, these findings in no way imply that rural/urban differences in school catchment areas *produce* attitudinal changes such as those set out in Box 12.6. Rather, they are suggestive, they are provocative, forcing the researcher to attempt some tentative explanation of the trends he has identified. Twine chose to look at the interpersonal relationships that existed within subgroups in his sample of pupils, arguing that attitudes were contingent upon the extent and the quality of the prevailing peer group relationships. He found that in the schools from the traditional rural and emergent urban areas there was clear evidence of friendship choices being related to the urbanization index, that is, the overall score derived from the criteria set out in Box 12.5. During these two phases there appeared to be a more compact pattern of friendship with many reciprocated choices and connecting links, whereas at schools in the transitional rural and

BOX 12.6

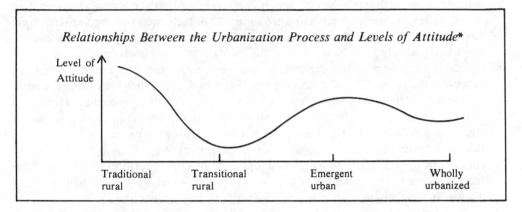

Relationships Between the Urbanization Process and Levels of Attitude*

* The Barker-Lunn[22] scale of attitudes provides eight sets of scores, identifying attitudes towards school, interest in schoolwork, importance of doing well, conformity, relationship with teacher, anxiety in class, social adjustment, and academic self-image.

Source: Twine[21]

wholly urbanized stages Twine reported an absence of identifiable friendship groups, suggesting a lack of cohesion. Again, we must stress the tentative nature of Twine's data and the need for corroborative evidence from other studies.

THE MASS MEDIA: TV VIOLENCE AND ITS EFFECTS ON CHILDREN

Some argue that the mass media (radio, television, cinema, newspapers, magazines, books, records, tapes etc.) are possibly the most important artefacts of our civilization. Certainly they are all-pervasive, prompting one observer[23] to write that 'society can only be understood through a study of the messages and the communication facilities that belong to it.' Others, while holding to the importance of the media in our lives, blame them for what they believe to be a rising crime rate, lowering moral standards, and increasing marital disharmony. It is no part of our brief to discuss the malign influence or otherwise of the mass media on such complex issues. Rather, out intention is to focus on one particular section of the vast literature on mass communication research to ask, 'What are the effects of mass media messages on pupils?' More precisely 'what effects does television in general, and television violence in particular have upon its young viewers?'

Summarizing the findings of a large number of studies, Winston[24] identifies the following general effects of children's television viewing:

1. Contrary to popularly-held views, TV does not adversely affect children's performance at school; 'watchers' are as attentive in class, as good at tests, and as diligent in doing their homework as 'non-watchers'.

2. In certain circumstances television can stimulate children, research with pre-school children showing that television watchers come to school with larger vocabularies than non-watchers. However, such gains are soon lost in the process of regular schooling.
3. Television-watchers read as many books as non-TV watchers. Librarians speak of the stimulating effects that certain TV serials have upon book borrowing.
4. Children do not spend a great deal of time watching adult programmes. There is, however, the possibility of children becoming bewildered when they contrast adult behaviour on the media with the behaviour of adults in their immediate circle.
5. There is evidence that children make short-term modifications in their opinions of adults as a result of their watching adult television programmes.
6. Because children bring to the screen a less complete set of opinions and attitudes, the chances of them being exposed to new opinions or cross pressures or to any of the factors increasing the potentiality of the medium to convert are greater than in adults. This attitude-changing potential increases as children grow older.

The question of the effects of television violence on young people's behaviour arouses such fierce controversy and is of such widespread concern that we propose to review this specific research area in greater detail. Why should the effects of television violence attract such intense interest? Priestland's[25] answer has more than a grain of truth. 'Violence,' he observes, 'is an extremely complex thing. While we profess to dread it and denounce it, each of us also entertains and enjoys it in some form. It is a magnet for hypocrisy.' Studies of television violence can be classified according to the strategies that researchers adopt. We distinguish *content analysis studies*, *experimental studies*, and *survey studies* in the review that follows.

Content Analysis Studies of Television Violence

Numerical counts of the frequency of isolated acts of violence on television tell us nothing about the way in which violence forms part of a dramatic whole nor of the structural meanings of violence in particular situations. We ignore studies involving simplistic content counts and look at the more sophisticated work of Gerbner.[26] Gerbner argues that to understand the television message we need to study four dimensions of it:

1. *Existence*:   What *is* television output, how much of what content and how frequently is it made available to us?
2. *Priorities*:   What is important, how intense or prominent or central are certain factors or elements?
3. *Values*:   What value judgements are implied about which elements in the cultural message system?
4. *Relationships*:   What is related to what, what are the structural meanings of the message?[26]

Applying these four criteria to the study of television violence in the USA, Gerbner and his associates report:-

1. *Existence*:   80% of television drama contained violence. 50% of the leading characters committed violence and 60% were vic-

tims of violence. In an average week there were 400 'casualties' who were either killed or maimed.

2. *Priorities*: The extent of violence in the content of television drama establishes the priority accorded to it. As Fiske and Hartley observe, hardly a play and hardly a character is free from it.

3. *Values*: Gerbner has little to say on the question of values but suggests that cross cultural research is one useful way of studying the values of the mass message system.

4. *Relationships*: Gerbner's detailed study of the structural meanings of violence on television leads him to the conclusion that violence is used in the pursuit of such socially validated ends as power, money, or duty. It is *inter*personal and *im*personal, that is to say, it occurs between strangers. It is not a direct representation of real-life violence; it is never a mere imitation of real behaviour. Rather, it serves to 'externalize' people's motives and status, to make visible their unstated relationships, to personalize social conflicts, for example, between dominant and subordinate groups, between law and anarchy.[26]

Thus, the evidence of content analysis points to a fundamental distinction between real violence and violence in television drama. As Fiske and Hartley[27] see it:

'Television violence is encoded and structured into a governed relationship with the other elements of the drama; this relationship is controlled by rules which are themselves derived from social values, and which are common to all television texts in their particular genre. Our familiarity with the genre *makes us react to violence according to its own internal rules and not as we would to real violence*.'
(our emphasis).

Gerbner's valuable insights shift the emphasis from simplistic content counts of television violence to an examination of the symbolic function of violent content. For him, television violence,* free from the constraints of reality, is *symbolic communication*, – not violence.

Following Gerbner's general approach, the British Broadcasting Corporation[28] undertook an analysis of a representative selection of television programmes. Unlike Gerbner however, whose investigation was confined to entertainment programmes, the BBC looked more broadly at violence on television, and included in its sampling news and current affairs programmes as well as TV drama and fiction. Among other findings the BBC concluded that there was more cartoon violence on American television and more fictional aggression though far fewer 'killings'. The British study is interesting in that it goes beyond simple content analysis in its attempts to get viewers' subjective assessments of violence, that is to say, just what it is that the viewers actually perceive as contrasted with what, in fact, is presented.

---

* But see Fiske and Hartley's[27] perceptive analysis of the ITV drama series, *'The Sweeney'*.

Experimental Studies of Television Violence

Laboratory settings

The most widely-known experimental studies of the effects of filmed aggression on the behaviour of watchers are associated with Bandura[29] and his co-workers. In a series of experiments, children were exposed to films of aggressive adult models attacking dolls. They were then taken to different experimental settings and made 'mildly frustrated' by being denied opportunity to play with attractive toys. Their subsequent behaviour towards dolls was monitored through one-way mirrors by judges who recorded the amount and the type of aggression that the children displayed. Bandura concluded that exposure to filmed aggression produces aggressive reactions in young children. This type of laboratory experiment is typical of many studies that have been conducted both in Britain and the United States which show that violent television content is particularly conducive to observational learning on the part of young children.

Field settings

Laboratory studies, of course, are limited in the type of information that they can provide and different from real life in significant ways. Bandura's studies, for example, demonstrate aggressive acts towards dolls (not towards people) in settings that bear little resemblance to the contexts in which children usually spend their daily lives. Field studies, particularly experimental ones, avoid the restrictions of laboratory-type research. We report on one study[30] which investigated the effects of violent and non-violent television programmes on the naturally occurring aggressive behaviour of pre-school children. Steur and her associates[30] were concerned with a small sample of young children paired on the basis of the amount of time they spent watching TV and for whom a base line observational record of each child's aggressiveness was obtained prior to the experiment. A precise measure of aggressiveness was employed involving hitting or kicking another child or squeezing, choking or holding another down. One child in each pair then watched a single violent programme on eleven different days while the other member of the pair watched a neutral TV programme. Subsequent observations of the children at play were used to record the amount of their physically aggressive behaviour. As the results in Box 12.7 show, children who observed violent television programmes became more aggressive than their matched playmates who had watched neutral film material.

Survey Studies of Television Violence

One of the most sophisticated survey studies of the effects of watching television violence was undertaken by Eron[31] and his co-workers in America. They followed up earlier studies in which a definite relationship between overt aggression and TV violence had been established. Eron and his associates attempted to demonstrate a causal link between the two. They argued that a young adult's subsequent aggressiveness is positively related to

BOX 12.7

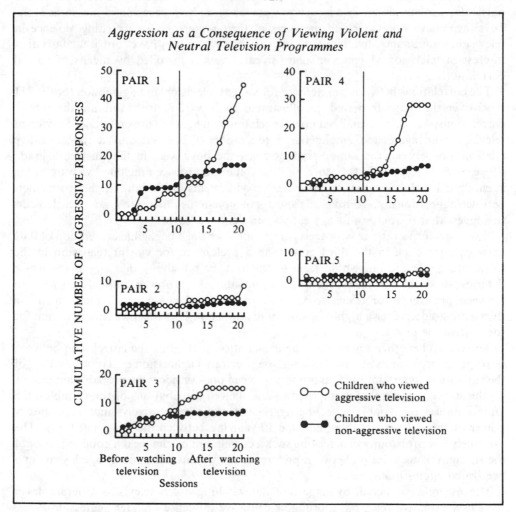

Aggression as a Consequence of Viewing Violent and Neutral Television Programmes

PAIR 1

PAIR 4

PAIR 2

PAIR 5

PAIR 3

CUMULATIVE NUMBER OF AGGRESSIVE RESPONSES

Before watching
television

After watching
television

Sessions

○—○ Children who viewed
aggressive television

●—● Children who viewed
non-aggressive television

Source: adapted from Steur, Applefield and Smith[30]

his preference for violent television when he is eight or nine years old and that his preference for violent television during this critical period is one cause of his aggressiveness.

The approach adopted by the researchers was to examine the correlations across the two variables over a period of time within the framework of a longitudinal design. The cross-lagged analysis which was used in this instance examined the temporal cross correlations of the variables, thus enabling the investigators to eliminate some of the rival hypotheses. Briefly, longitudinal data were collected on 427 teenagers of an original group of 875 children who had taken part in a study of third-grade children (8–9 years old) ten years earlier in 1960. Data on the 427 teenagers were therefore collected in 1970. Of this number, 211 were boys and it is the part of the study involving these that we are particularly interested in. Two measures were taken on both occasions – measures of the boys' aggressive behaviour and measures of their preference for watching violence in television programmes. In addition, other variables which may have contributed to either interest in television violence or aggressiveness were controlled by means of partial correlations.

The correlations between a preference for violent television and aggression for the 211 boys over the ten-year period are illustrated in Box 12.8. In examining the 'outer' correlations, we notice a small but positive relationship between the preference for violent television and aggression among the third graders (0.21), but only a tiny, negative relationship between the same variables when the boys were in the thirteenth grade (19 years old) (-0.05). Further, there is little relationship between the boys' viewing habits in childhood and their television preference as adolescents (0.05), but a higher correlation between aggression in the third grade and aggression in the thirteenth grade, which seems to suggest that the pattern of aggression persists once learnt.

If we now inspect the cross-lagged correlations, we see a negligible correlation of 0.01 between aggression in the third grade and a preference for violent television in the thirteenth grade and this would seem to rule out the possibility that aggression was a determinant of the boys' subsequent television habits. If we now examine the correlation between preference for television violence in the third grade and aggression in the thirteenth grade, we see a highly significant relationship. This effect was not apparent for the girls in the group.

The researchers themselves offer the explanation that while the correlation between third-grade preferences and thirteenth-grade peer-rated aggression explains only 10 % of the variance in aggression, 10 % is impressive when one considers the probable limitations on the size of the correlation imposed by the skewed distributions of the variables, the large numbers of variables affecting aggression, the comparatively small explanatory power of these other variables, and the 10-year lag between measurement times. The extremely low probability of achieving such a correlation by chance is a good indicator of the strength of the relation between preference for violent television at age 8 years and peer-rated aggression at age 19.

The researchers conclude by suggesting that watching violent television programmes in the early formative years has a probable causative influence on later aggression.

The most recent and indeed sophisticated study of the effects of television violence on the behaviour of adolescents was carried out by Belson.[32] It involved some 1650 London boys who were interviewed at home and then at a Survey Research Centre when detailed information was collected during a $3\frac{1}{2}$ hour extended interview. Belson's primary concern was with the effects of *real life* exposure to TV violence and its *real life* consequences in terms of adolescent behaviour. His approach contrasts sharply with laboratory studies which involve experimentation with simulated factors and situations. What of the major findings of Belson's study?

The most noteworthy finding was that high exposure to television violence increases the degree to which boys engage in serious violence. Five types of television violence appear to be the more potent in releasing serious violence by boys. They are:

1. Plays or films in which violence occurs in the context of close personal relations.

BOX 12.8

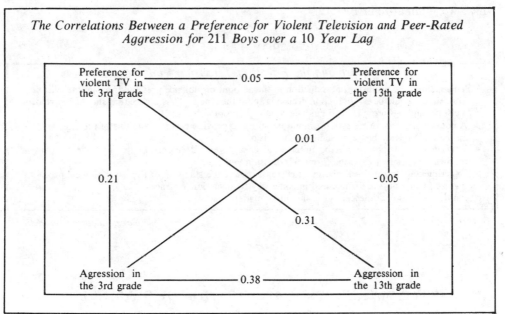

The Correlations Between a Preference for Violent Television and Peer-Rated Aggression for 211 Boys over a 10 Year Lag

Preference for violent TV in the 3rd grade —————— 0.05 —————— Preference for violent TV in the 13th grade

0.01

0.21

- 0.05

0.31

Agression in the 3rd grade —————— 0.38 —————— Aggression in the 13th grade

Source: Eron et al[31]

2. Violent programmes in which violence appears to have been 'just thrown in for its own sake' or is not necessary to the plot.
3. Programmes presenting fictional violence of a realistic kind.
4. Programmes in which the violence is presented as being in a good cause.
5. Westerns of the violent kind.

By contrast, Belson found little or no support for the belief that increases in serious violence occur as a result of watching the following types of programme:

1. Sporting programmes presenting violent behaviour by competitors or spectators. (Excluded here were programmes on boxing and wrestling.)
2. Violent cartoons like Tom and Jerry.
3. Science fiction violence.
4. Slapstick comedy presenting violence or verbal abuse.

Of various explanations of the underlying principles and processes involved in the relationship between TV violence and aggression (imitation, catharsis, triggering and so on) Belson opts for what he terms a *disinhibition process*, that is to say, a process through which those inhibitions against violent behaviour that are ordinarily built up in boys by their parents and by other socializing agencies are progressively eroded by the continuous presentation of violence on television so that eventually, such violent urges as are present in boys are much more likely to 'spill out', as it were, in the form of violent behaviour.[32] Under certain circumstances *imitation* also seems to be involved.

Given the evidence of Belson's research he goes on to make the recommendations which we summarize in Box 12.9.

BOX 12.9

Controlling the Effects of Television Violence
1. There should be a substantial reduction in the amount of violence presented through television.
2. Guidelines should be established in decisions about the type of TV violence that should be avoided. Belson's findings provide such guidelines on a provisional basis.
3. A continuing monitoring system should be set up to provide periodic analysis of the kind and the amount of violence being presented on television.
4. Experimental studies should be initiated of changes and development in boys' mental content following exposure to specific forms of television violence.
5. Experimental studies should be initiated to increase understanding of the psychological processes involved when boys are influenced in some way by television violence.
6. Parallel studies of adolescent girls should be made.

Source: adapted from Belson[32]

THE MASS MEDIA AND THE AMPLIFICATION OF DEVIANCE

Having discussed the impact of television on children's behaviour we turn now to look at the influence of the mass media on the behaviour of certain groups of young people in society. Specifically we ask, 'What part do the media play in creating and sustaining subcultures like Mods, Rockers, Skinheads and Punks?' We find our answer in '*Folk Devils and Moral Panics*', Stanley Cohen's analysis of the rise of the Mods and Rockers in the early 1960s.

Apart from their manifest function of disseminating what is 'newsworthy', the media, according to Stanley Cohen,[33] act as a main source of information about the normative contours of society. Discussing the role of the media in defining and shaping social problems, Cohen introduces his account of the emergence of Mods and Rockers with an outline of the part played by the mass media in *creating* deviance.

> '(They inform) us about right and wrong, about the boundaries beyond which one should not venture and about the shapes that the devil can assume. The gallery of folk-types – heroes and saints as well as fools, villains and devils – is publicised not just in oral-tradition and face-to-face contact, but to much larger audiences and with much greater dramatic resources.'

Much of Cohen's study is devoted to analysing the role of the mass media in creating *moral panics* (e.g. smoking 'pot') and *folk devils* (e.g. Hells Angels). Cohen begins by noting the radical reorientation that has taken place during the last decade in the sociological study of crime, delinquency, drug-taking and other forms of socially deviant behaviour. What he calls the *sceptical* revolution in the study of deviance readers will recognize as broadly synonymous with the interpretive perspective that we have employed throughout this text. The sceptical viewpoint rejects accepted, authoritative, unquestioned assumptions about social phenomena. In the case of *deviance*, for example, it asks, 'deviant to whom?', or 'deviant from what?' The concept of deviance has no taken-for-granted status. On the contrary, it is the focus of close inquiry, – Why does a particular rule, the infraction of which constitutes deviance, exist at all? What are the processes and procedures involved in identifying someone as deviant and applying rules to him? What are the effects and consequences of this application, both for society and the individual?

Cohen's approach is in the best traditions of Becker[34] and Lemert,[35] particularly the latter whose distinction between primary and secondary deviation* is crucial to Cohen's account of the identification, labelling and reactions to Mods and Rocker groups. Briefly, his theme is that every now and then society is subject to periods of moral panic when a condition, an episode, a person or a group of persons emerge to become defined as a threat to societal values. That condition or group is presented in such a stereotyped and stylized way by the mass media that society's moral barricades are quickly manned by right-thinking people. Experts are recruited to find solutions to the condition and ways of coping are agreed on or resorted to. The condition either disappears, soon to be forgotten or becomes more visible, perhaps to the extent that it produces changes in the ways that society perceives itself.

The appearance of various working class youth cultures, Cohen asserts, has been associated with such periods of moral panic. Cohen's explanation of the emergence of Mods and Rockers and of society's reaction to them draws on *deviation amplification theory*, a rather ponderous phrase for what is a relatively easy concept to grasp as we illustrate in Box 12.10. Cohen is at pains to emphasise the limitations of deviation

BOX 12.10

The Process of Deviation Amplification

Initial problem ↓	(stemming from structural and cultural position of working class adolescent)
Initial solution ↓	(deviant action and style)
Societal reaction ↓	(involving elements of misperception, (e.g. in inventory and subsequent distortion in terms of long term values and interests))
Operation of control culture, exploitation and creation of stereotypes ↓	(sensitization, dramatization, escalation)
Increased deviance, Polarization ↓	
Confirmation of stereotypes	(theory proved)

Source: Cohen[33]

---

* *Primary deviation*, in Cohen's usage, refers to behaviour which, although it may be troublesome to the individual, does not produce symbolic reorganization at the level of the self-concept. *Secondary deviation* occurs when the individual employs his deviance or a role based upon it, as a means of defence, attack, or adjustment to the problems created by society's reaction to it.

amplification explanations unless they are set within specific historical and cultural contexts. The context that he elaborates is post-war Britain and the constellation of economic and demographic changes that produced a large unmarried teenage generation whose average wage had increased at twice the rate of the adults'. This relative economic emancipation, Cohen argues, created a group with few responsibilities or social ties and within a short period of time a range of commodities, from clothes to pop music, was being specially designed and presented to this section of society. Cohen then shows how emerging styles and tastes became associated with deviant or publicly disapproved values, citing the Teddy Boys as the first group to be so stigmatized. In exactly the same way, he says, with the Mods and Rockers, such emerging styles became confused with other phenomena, 'the general youth theme', day-to-day delinquency problems and so on. But to return to our particular interest, the role of the mass media in the confrontations that occurred between Mods, Rockers, and police in the mid 1960s. Cohen summarizes the part played by the mass media as follows. In general, they operated to publicize the events leading up to confrontations with the forces of law and order, serving also to gratify the publicity-seeking behaviour of many of their participants. The cumulative effect of the media was to create a triggering-off or contagion effect leading to an amplification of the violence. They also provided the content for deviant role-playing behaviour by transmitting the stereotypical expectations of how persons such as Mods and Rockers ought to act. The general effect of the enormous publicity that the various confrontations received was to magnify the differences between Mods and Rockers and thus to give the groups a greater cohesiveness than they originally possessed. Finally, the media reinforced the polarization between Mods and Rockers on the one hand and the whole of the adult community on the other.

Cohen concluded that more moral panics will be generated and other, as yet nameless, folk devils will be created because as presently structured, our society will continue to generate problems for some of its members – like working-class adolescents – and then condemn whatever solution these groups find.

SCHOOL AND SOCIETY: SOME DIFFERING IDEOLOGIES

In this final section of the chapter we present four explanations of the purposes that schools serve in society. We begin with a *consensual* viewpoint* by R. S. Peters, a philosopher whose influence in teacher education extends over many years. We then explore alternative perspectives deriving from what for the moment can be termed (a) *libertarian philosophy* and (b) *critical sociology*. These latter accounts present differing views of the purposes that schools serve (and ought to serve) yet share common ground in their radical opposition to the arguments of the consensual viewpoint. We close the chapter with (c) a Marxist perspective on the function of schools in capitalist society.

---

* The meaning of the term 'consensual' is made explicit in the outline of Peters' views that follows.

A Consensual Viewpoint

Education, according to R. S. Peters, is 'initiation into worthwhile activities', and schools are the means by which initiation is best achieved. The purpose of the school, the nature of 'initiation' and 'worthwhile activities', the role of the teacher and his relationship with the taught are revealed in Peters' influential book *Education as Initiation*.[36]

Fundamental to Peters' argument is a particular view of the nature of society.[37] According to him, human action is basically purposive, purposes being 'irreducible', that is to say, one cannot go behind them as it were and relate them to yet other values. Because actions and institutions are justified in terms of purpose and since purpose is embodied in actions and institutions, it follows that the rationale of actions and institutions is to be found by inspection. If, for example, one wishes to find out why certain school subjects are included in the curriculum and others are not, then one looks at the existing curriculum and elicits the reasons. Thus, the justification for subjects such as mathematics, science and history is expressed in phrases like 'far ranging cognitive content', 'progressive development', and 'intellectual satisfaction', such qualities being associated with an activity's claim to be *worthwhile*.

A second basic plank in Peters' argument concerns his view of social reality. According to him, social reality resides in the 'impersonal content and procedures which are enshrined in public traditions'. The purpose of education is to initiate pupils into what Peters calls 'the public modes of experience' which encapsulate these traditions. Language and 'forms of knowledge' are the two chief vehicles of the public mode of experience.

Hirst, a colleague of Peters, identifies seven logically distinct forms of knowledge which he says are 'the fundamental achievement of mind'. By being initiated into these seven different forms of knowledge, pupils gain access to that fundamental achievement of mind. According to one critic of Peters,[38] it is quite coincidental that these seven forms of knowledge happen to constitute, more or less, a typical grammar school curriculum! Peters sees the pupil's initiation into these worthwhile activities as a lengthy process, best undertaken in the structural settings of schools. In a revealing turn of phrase, Peters describes the uninitiated as in the 'position of barbarian outside the gates' and elsewhere[39] both he and Hirst ask, 'Who will let the barbarian in? Civilized men do not grow up overnight like mushrooms; they become civilized by being brought up by others who are civilized . . . .' Which brings us directly to the purpose of the school and the role of the teacher.

'Now the teacher, having himself been initiated is on the inside of these activities and modes of thought and conduct.' Peters goes on to speak of teachers as priests, bestowing upon them the role of guardians of the cultural heritage in phrases such as:

> 'If teachers are not thought of as, to varying degrees, authorities on this culture how effective are they likely to be in a society in which most of the pressures on young people are not in the direction of education?'

Notice the view of *social knowledge* implicit in Peters' reasoning. Social knowledge is located outside the individual; it is something into which the pupil has to be initiated in specifically structured settings called schools. Contrast this viewpoint, says Smith[37], with that of Peters' critics who see social knowledge as something that a person begins to share when he is born, a tradition in which he participates, which lives only in so far as the individuals constituting society actively reproduce it. For Peters, knowledge is a *product* rather than a *process*. Such a view of knowledge, Smith observes, is particularly unfortunate in the context of the classroom, for there, if anywhere, the emphasis should be on the active aspect of knowledge, that is, on the ways in which hypotheses are formulated, tried out, discarded or revised.

It is easy to see why critics of Peters' views have described him as the epitome of current educational consensus. One[38] in particular goes further and relates Peters' manner of reasoning to the existing British social structure, arguing that Peters' style of thought is 'an exact replica of the customary mode of response of the English ruling class to a challenge from below.'

Adelstein argues that Peters' method of analysis is 'consensual', or more correctly, it assumes consensus. For example, Peters might analyse a concept such as *curriculum content* first by referring to 'ordinary' language in order to work out what the concept is by focusing on what it might normally be thought to be and then, by refining the meaning of the concept through a series of contrasts with what it is not. 'There is an assumption here', Adelstein notes, 'that all concepts are shared and correct. It does not seem to have occurred (to our analyst) that people might have different, unshared usages and meanings. The vital question of *whose* 'normal usage of a concept is being suggested and whether such usage corresponds to reality is never put.' He concludes, 'the assumption, never validated, of shared usage and experience, of basic consensus, constitutes the core of the ideology . . . and generates its basic power to confuse.'

Strong criticisms indeed, and yet Peters' view of schools as the means of inducting future generations into commonly-accepted knowledge and worthwhile activities through the skills of teachers ('(they) can recognize the elegance of a proof or a paragraph, the cogency of an argument, the clarity of an exposition, the wit of a remark, the neatness of a plot and the justice and wisdom of a decision.'), is one that is widely shared, not least by teachers themselves.

It is a total rejection of such consensus and consensus-thinking that lies at the heart of the alternative critique to which we now turn.

Libertarian Philosophy

A tradition of opposition to officially-provided school systems has existed for a long time, deriving from diverse ideological origins[40] – from nineteenth century working class movements, from socialism and Marxism, from anarchism and libertarianism. We deal first with these latter two ideologies.

The 'problem' of schooling in a libertarian perspective, says Grace,[40] is the problem of human freedom and dignity both of which are denied by oppressive, custodial schools. Contemporary anarchist/libertarian critiques of schooling pose the problem of *liberation* as follows:

'. . . . we live in an unfree society; our schools are unfree; our teachers are unfree; our students are unfree. Somehow we must break into this vicious circle . . . we reject authoritarian concepts of education, however they might be used. The educator who sees himself as the possessor of superior knowledge or skills which he "passes on" to more or less willing disciples . . . is part of an authoritarian or at best paternalistic culture.

The libertarian sees education as a sharing of knowledge, skills and experiences and emphasizes the importance of study aimed at understanding the participants' place in society and the nature of the forces acting upon them – with the object of helping to equip the participants to counter oppressive acts of that society.'[40]

Libertarians have profound objections to the ways in which contemporary society is organized. Above all else, they object to authoritarianism of all kinds, seeking to replace the authoritarian, manipulative society with one based on what one observer[41] describes as 'free, uncoercive intercourse between people, in which individuals and groups each play full and equal part in decisions affecting the nature and quality of their lives.'

In a perceptive review of libertarian ideology, Smith[37] brings out the essential dilemma faced by libertarian teachers, both newly qualified and experienced, in contemporary schools. One long-serving teacher, for example, working with a CSE fourth year group had constructed a course around group discussions on topics suggested by the pupils themselves. When lessons began to disintegrate because of a lack of self-discipline on the students' part, the teacher attempted to solve the problem democratically only to find that the agreed redirection of the work again broke down into disorderly private discussions. At the heart of the problem, of course, was a lack of teacher direction. But this is precisely the objection that libertarians have of the teacher's role – that it is inherently authoritarian. Yet this is the expectation that most pupils themselves hold for the teacher. As one contributor to *Libertarian Education* reports[42]:

'You're the teacher, sir. You should make us sit down. You should tell us what to do and make us do it.'
'I think you should start telling us instead of telling us to do as we please.'
'You should tell us to be quiet.'
'I think that you should be more strict because I for one don't like sitting there just talking for an hour. A lot more people will walk out in future if you don't stop the few people talking and interest the whole class.'

What did the particular teacher do in face of disorder in his CSE class?

'Two students walked towards the door and when I asked why, one said that he didn't agree with what was going on in the room. We discussed the matter and then I said they could do as they thought fit. The spokesman said "Fair enough", and they walked out.'

Now this may appear as a total abnegation of the duties of the teacher in this particular situation; for a libertarian teacher, however, it is in line with his fundamental belief about the quality of the relationship (*the dialogue*) that ought to exist in all learning situations. This is how libertarians express the essence of libertarian educational thought:

'The learner, young or old, is the best judge of what he should learn next. In our struggle to make sense out of life, the things we most need to learn are the things we most want to learn. Curiosity is hardly ever idle. When we learn this way we learn both rapidly and permanently.'[43]

and,

'For me, it is an article of faith that children should and can direct their own lives as soon as they want/need to even if only to direct themselves back to ask for protection or guidance or instruction or to be allowed to join in or watch.'[44]

There is little room, if any, for compromise in these positions, and as Smith[37] observes, the libertarian educational tradition is surprisingly tenacious. To suggest, for example, that libertarians should work within the present structure of educational provision, seeking to influence it in directions in tune with their beliefs invites the reply that since the present structure is built upon coercion it can never work in the true interests of the individual or education. So does the answer for libertarian teachers lie in the growing *free* or *alternative* school movement? Perhaps. Many libertarians however take up posts in the maintained system and face difficulties such as the one we outline in Box 12.11.

BOX 12.11

The Libertarian Teacher and Classroom Discipline

Confronted with a room full of rioting 15 year olds, I tried to be non-authoritarian. 'If you don't want to sit down or do anything then that is fine with me. I'll sit here and read.' Immediately I'm compromising because I have to bawl my head off to make myself heard. I'm also wondering what's going to happen when the teacher next door comes in to complain about the noise. 'I don't like it here any more than you do, but if we have to be here then let's work out what we can do together that will be useful to us.'

Then comes the response from amidst the paper darts, flying chairs, thumping dominoes and twenty different arguments:

'You're the teacher sir. You should make us sit down. You should tell us what to do and make us do it.'

I experienced that situation may times . . . .

Source: adapted from Smith[37]

Looking to the future, one observer[45] forecasts far-reaching changes in the pattern of educational provision, changes that appear to go someway to meeting some of the hopes of libertarian educators. He foresees a re-structuring of current practices and the individualization of learning in which much of the curriculum will take place outside the school in coherent and complementary sets of teaching and learning units organized on the basis of their capacity to contribute to the individual's development of knowledge. Through the use of central storage systems and a network of transmission facilities, the learning units will be readily available to all students according to their needs and regardless of age or time or distance.

Critical Sociology

The publication in 1971 of Michael Young's *Knowledge and Control: New Directions For the Sociology of Education* marked a take-off point for a critical sociology of education which has spread its influence rapidly to thousands of teachers pursuing coursework with the Open University whose Faculty of Education has enthusiastically adopted and disseminated this radical challenge to current orthodoxy.

The intention of a critical sociology of education is to challenge teachers to take a cool, dispassionate look at the assumed characteristics of their pedagogic world, to 'put the world in brackets' in Husserl's famous phrase, to adopt a stance of radical doubt, to be their own theorists – in a word, to *liberate* themselves from official definitions and formulations of 'educational problems'. Young's suggestion that teachers should conceive of societies as 'products of competing definitions and claims to cognitive and moral legitimacy' follows Weber[46] in laying stress on the differential social evaluation of knowledge in terms of a dominant group's ideas of the educated man. The major thrust of Young's argument is summarized in Box 12.12.

BOX 12.12

Critical Sociology: The Arguments of M. D. F. Young[47]

1. *The social distribution of knowledge.* The present structuring of organizational provision serves to preserve the status quo in an unjust society. Schools act as a 'tool of ruling class interests'. Through their system of academic streaming they perpetuate social class divisions. Different curricula are made available to different groups of pupils; there is a divorce between school knowledge and everyday knowledge; there is a stress on competition and examination success.
2. *The stratification of knowledge.* The content of education reflects more than just the 'real' world in an objective way; it reflects middle class values and denies the values of the great mass of people. Knowledge is distributed unequally; there are 'high status' subjects and 'low status' subjects, the latter, especially, being taught to working class children. High status subjects reflect the values of 'high culture' – abstract conceptual thinking, individualistic action, the distancing of academic subjects from everyday life. They are only suited to the values of a dominant class.
3. *Subject knowledge reflects a social construction of reality, not reality itself.* Subject barriers are artificial and arbitrary; they suit the convenience of those in control of education. Subject divisions hinder learning; they separate school knowledge from ordinary experience serving only to increase the sense of ordinary children that school is alien to their lives.
4. *All knowledge is socially constructed.* Knowledge is socially determined; furthermore, the knowledge taught in schools is determined by a narrow middle-class definition of knowledge and reality.
5. *Rationality is a social convention.* The criteria for truth and falsehood are socially constructed and can therefore be altered. Society's version of logical or rational thought is a set of middle-class social conventions.

Adding extra impetus to Young's *Knowledge and Control* was the simultaneous publication in English of the works of Paulo Friere, *Pedagogy of the Oppressed*, *Cultural Action for Freedom*, and *Education for Critical Consciousness*. From the point of view of critical sociology, what exactly is the 'problem' of school in contemporary society? Grace[40] proposes that traditionally, the school's historic function has been the transmission of elements of mainstream culture to a population seen as essentially devoid of its own culture and understandings and viewed as deficient in many ways in its capacity to 'learn' the culture offered to it. In such an enterprise, Grace[40] asserts, the preoccupation of the teacher is with *transmission*, with new strategies (i.e. curriculum development) for the more effective transmission of 'old' knowledge in new pedagogic forms, *none of which challenge the existing status, social determinations or social stratification of existing knowledge forms* (our emphasis).

Critical sociologists of education, according to Grace, wish to change this historic function of the school. Such change would involve a conception of the school as an arena for the realization of a variety of cultural traditions and cognitive styles, an appreciation of the various ways in which people make sense of their world, and a concern with learning as dialogue-participation rather than transmission-reception. Like libertarians, critical sociologists seek the transformation of the role of the school in society. Like libertarians they, too, are centrally concerned with questions of autonomy and control and what passes for 'knowledge' in contemporary society. And like libertarians they, too, wish to see changes come about without necessarily committing themselves to explicit political solutions. In this last respect, libertarians and critical sociologists are to be differentiated from those who espouse a Marxist perspective such as the one that we now illustrate.

A Marxist Perspective

Marxist writers, Grace notes, share a common perspective in that they locate liberation in terms of the overthrow of an oppressive capitalist system of production and social relations by the action of the urban masses. The distinction that Grace draws between the various ideologies we have discussed is set out in Box 12.13.

BOX 12.13

School and Society: Some Differing Ideologies[50]

Ideologies: Anarchism, Libertarian Philosophy, Critical Sociology
Exponents: Goodman, Illich, Freire, Reimer, M. Young
Aims: Liberation from schools as currently conceived and organized in order to achieve
                   states of critical consciousness and personal autonomy without commitment to
                   explicit political solutions.
Ideology: Marxism
Exponents: Bowles and Gintis
Aims: Liberation in terms of the overthrow of an oppressive capitalist system of
                   production and social relations by the action of the proletariat.

These differing ideologies share the following *common perception* of school systems designed for the masses:

1. They provide for *schooling* rather than *education*.
2. They are oppressive and manipulative in character.
3. They are carried out in institutions dominated by bureaucracy, authoritarianism and hierarchy.
4. Their total effect is to control, to domesticate, to make passive and exploitable.
5. In the process, the person is regarded as 'object' rather than as a creatively conscious subject.

Source: adapted from Grace[40]

We take as our example of a Marxist perspective the work of two American economists Bowles and Gintis[48] who argue in their book *Schooling in Capitalist America*, that in capitalist society the function of education is to supply 'appropriately' educated manpower to the economy. Demaine[49], discussing Bowles and Gintis' thesis, notes that there are two modes of appropriateness in the characteristics of manpower supplied to the education system in capitalist society. First, *differentiated manpower* is released to the economy, that is educated manpower or labour at different ages, different lengths of training, with different technical capacities and qualifications. A second mode of appropriateness in the educated manpower supplied to the economy is that it is appropriately *alienated*. Capitalist economies both 'need' and produce an 'alienated' work force. For Bowles and Gintis, the conditions workers are subjected to in capitalist production processes are inimical to the realization of the 'essential' character of human labour. Such inimicality has two consequences. First, workers are alienated or estranged from their essential human character as an effect of capitalist production processes. Second, labour is seen as continually trying to subvert these production processes and an object of capitalist enterprise calculation is to prevent such subversion.[49] Schools, according to Bowles and Gintis, mirror the form of organization of work processes in capitalist societies and thus reflect their 'needs'. Schooling serves to reproduce the forms of consciousness needed by the capitalist class. The education system,[51] they argue, contributes to the reproduction of the class system in society by creating within itself a set of relationships that mirror those in economic life. But because education and the economy have different rates of change – the education system being the less dynamic of the two and tending to operate towards stability, the economic system on the other hand, operating towards rapid change – they are often mismatched with one another. This, Bowles and Gintis assert, is a major cause of educational change. The educational system accommodates to changing economic conditions in two ways. First, by *pluralistic accommodation* in which individuals and groups in pursuing their own interests initiate change and reorientation in the educational system generally along progressive lines. The effect of this is to reinforce an image of an open educational system, an image that is essential if education is to be seen as 'democratic' and thus legitimizing and sustaining the capitalist order in society. Behind that image, Bowles and Gintis assert, there is a framework determined by a small number of capitalists who are outside the political arena of society. Second, educational adjustment to changing economic trends is at certain periods of historic crisis by *concrete political struggle along class lines of interest.* Such struggle typically evokes a twofold response – the raising of wages and the expansion and reform of educational provision.

Thus educational change is used as a substitute for economic reforms. As Reid[51] observes, it shifts the conflict of capitalism from workplace to school and helps remove political force from the contradictions. Bowles and Gintis conclude:

> '. . . the structure and scope of the modern US educational system cannot be explained without reference to both the demands of working people – for literacy, for the possibility of greater occupational mobility, for financial security, for personal growth, for social respect, – and to the imperative of the capitalist class to construct an institution which would both enhance the labour power of working people and help to reproduce the conditions for its exploitation.'

Educational change, Bowles and Gintis assert, can only result from changes in the economy. 'We need, in short,' they say, 'a second American revolution – and a more democratic egalitarian, and participating one at that.'

SUMMARY

This chapter has been concerned with the social environment external to the school. We began by describing the relationships that exist between Local Education Authorities and their schools, looking particularly at the role of advisers in linking Local Education Authority Departments with the schools under their jurisdiction. Within what was described as the *decision-making system* of education, we also examined the changes that are recommended for the work of governors and managers of schools. Next we looked at influences on school policies and programmes that arise out of the activities of educational pressure groups, choosing the William Tyndale affair as an example of the power of particular groups to make changes in a school's organization and curriculum practices. With party political pressure groups in mind, we examined research that shows significant differences in educational provision within the 104 education authorities in England and Wales to be related, *inter alia*, to local authority policies.

Moving outwards from the immediate vicinity of the school we went on to look at the influences of local communities on their schools taking our examples from studies conducted in rural settings. At societal level, we examined in some detail research into the effects of television violence on the behaviour of young children. The role of the mass media in creating and sustaining 'deviant' adolescent subcultures was also explored.

Finally, four explanations of the purposes that schools serve in society were presented – a consensual viewpoint, a libertarian stance, an account from critical sociology and a Marxist perspective on the function of schools in capitalist society.

ENQUIRY AND DISCUSSION

1. In what ways might the roles of the Local Education Authority adviser be conflicting?

2. Identify educational pressure groups *not* listed in Box 12.3 and evaluate the success or otherwise of their recent activities.

3. What advantages do you see in teaching in a rural rather than an urban school?

4. What criticisms can be made of research into the effects of television violence on the behaviour of young people?

5. Apply deviation amplification theory to explain public reactions to groups like Hells Angels.

6. What special difficulties do libertarian teachers face in today's schools?

7. What sympathy do you have for Peters' view of education as initiation?

8. Discuss the validity of each of the five arguments of M. D. F. Young summarized in Box 12.12.

NOTES AND REFERENCES

1. Kogan, M. (1975) *Educational Policy-Making: A Study of Interest Groups and Parliament*. London: George Allen and Unwin.

2. Regan, D. E. (1977) *Local Government and Education*. London: George Allen and Unwin.

3. Bolam, R., Smith, G. and Carter, H. (1976) *LEA Advisers and Education Administration*. Bristol: University of Bristol School of Education.
   For another study of the role of advisers and curriculum development in schools, see Swain, J. R. L. and Fairbrother, R. W. (1977) LEA Advisers: their part in the adoption of the Nuffield Advanced Science Courses, *Educational Studies*, **3**, 3, 235–242.

4. Johnson, D., Ransom, E., Packwood, T., Bowden, K., and Kog, M. (1980) *Secondary Schools and the Welfare Network*. London: George Allen and Unwin.

5. For a full account of the role of managers and governors in schools in England and Wales see:
   Baron, G. and Howell, D. E. (1974) *Government and Management of Schools*. London: Athlone Press.

6. Department of Education and Science (1977) *A New Partnership For Our Schools*. London: HMSO (The Taylor Report)

7. The notes are a summary of an article by Taylor, T. (1977) A new partnership. *Times Educational Supplement*, September 23rd.

8. This is part of the minority report of one member of the Taylor Committee summarized on pages 125–129 of the Taylor Report, see *A New Partnership For Our Schools*. London: HMSO.

9. Our account of pressure groups draws on the outline in, Saran, R. *The Politics of Educational Policy-Making: Pressures on Central and Local Government*. E222 Educational Studies Unit 6. Milton Keynes: Open University Press.

10. (Eds.) Kimber, R. and Richardson, J. J. (1974) *Pressure Groups in Britain*. London: J. M. Dent and Sons.
    For other discussions of pressure groups in education, see:
    Kogan, M. (1975) *Education Policy-Making: A Study of Interests Groups and Parliament*. London: George Allen and Unwin.
    Locke, M. (1974) *Power and Politics in the School System*. London: Routledge and Kegan Paul.
    Rivers, P. (1974) *Politics by Pressure*. London: Harrap.

11. For an abbreviated version of the report on the inquiry into William Tyndale School see *The Times Educational Supplement*, July 23rd 1976.

12. Saran, R. *The Politics of Educational Policy-Making: Pressures on Central and Local Government*. E222 Unit 6. Milton Keynes: Open University Press.

13. Taylor, G. (1971) North and South: The Education Split. *New Society*, **17**, 440, 346–347.

14. See Taylor, G. and Ayres, N. (1969) *Born and Bred Unequal*. London: Longman.

15. Byrne, D. S. and Williamson, W. (1972) Some intra-regional variations in educational provision and their bearing upon educational attainment – the case of the North East. *Sociology*, **6**, 1, 71–87.
    See also: Byrne, D. S., Williamson, W. and Fletcher, B. (1975) *The Poverty of Education*. London: Martin Robertson.

16. Boaden, M. (1971) *Urban Policy-Making: Influences on County Boroughs in England and Wales*. Cambridge: Cambridge University Press.

17. For an up-to-date bibliography see:
    Centre For Information and Advice on Educational Disadvantage (1980) *Educational Disadvantage in Rural Areas*. Manchester.

18. Department of Education and Science (1978) *Report on Education No. 92: School Population in the 1980's*. London: HMSO.

19. We summarize the points made in papers by:
    Lewis, G. (1980) The disadvantages and advantages of small rural schools; and Sigsworth, A. (1980) The Rural School – in, of, or for the community? Three perspectives of educational disadvantage. In *Educational Disadvantage in Rural Areas*. Manchester: Centre for Information and Advice on Educational Disadvantage.

20. Department of Education and Science (1967) *Children and their Primary Schools*. London: HMSO.
    See also: Richmond, W. K. (1953) *The Rural School*. London: Redman.

21. Twine, D. (1975) Some effects of the urbanisation process on rural children. *Educational Studies*, **1**, 3, 209–216.

22. Barker-Lunn, J. (1970) *Streaming in the Primary School*. Slough: NFER.

23. Weiner, N. (1968) *The Human Use of Human Beings*. London: Sphere.

24. Our account draws on Winston, B. (1973) *Dangling Conversations Book 1. The Image of the Media*. Chapter 3. London: Davis-Poynter.

25. Priestland, G. (1974) *The Future of Violence*. London: Hamish Hamilton.

26. Gerbner, G., Holsti, D. R., Krippendorff, K., Paisley, W. J. and Stone, P. J. (1969) *The Analysis of Communication Content*. New York: John Wiley.
    Gerbner, G. (1970) Cultural indicators: the case of violence in television drama. *Annals of the American Association of Political and Social Science,* **338**, 69–81.
    (Eds.) Gerbner, G., Gross, L. and Melody, W. (1973) *Communication Technology and Social Policy*. New York: Wiley-Interscience.

27. Fiske, J. and Hartley, J. (1978) *Reading Television*. London: Methuen.

28. BBC (1972) *Violence on Television*. London: Broadcasting House.

29. Bandura, A., Ross, D. and Ross, A. (1961) Transmission of aggression through imitation. *Journal of Abnormal and Social Psychology*, **63**, 3, 575–582.
    Bandura, A., Ross, D. and Ross, A. (1963a) Imitation of film-mediated aggressive models. *Journal of Abnormal and Social Psychology*, **66**, 1, 3–11.
    Bandura, A., Ross, D. and Ross, A. (1963b) Vicarious reinforcement and imitative learning. *Journal of Abnormal and Social Psychology*, **67**, 6, 601–617.

30. Steur, F. B., Applefield, J. M. and Smith, R. (1971) Televised aggression and the interpersonal aggression of preschool children. *Journal of Experimental Child Psychology*, **11**, 442–447.

31. Eron, L. D., Huesman, L. R., Lefkowitz, M. M. and Walder, L. D. (1972) Does television violence cause aggression? *American Psychologist*, (April), 253–263.

32. Belson, W. A. (1978) *Television Violence and the Adolescent Boy*. London: Saxon House.

33. Cohen, S. (1972) *Folk Devils and Moral Panics*. London: MacGibbon and Kee.

34. Becker, H. S. (1963) *Outsiders: Studies in the Sociology of Deviance*. New York: Free Press.

35. Lemert, E. M. (1951) *Social Pathology: A Systematic Approach to the Study of Sociopathic Behaviour*. New York: McGraw-Hill.
    and Lemert, E. M. (1967) *Human Deviance: Social Problems and Social Control*. Englewood Cliffs, N. J.: Prentice-Hall.

36. Peters, R. S. (1964) *Education as Initiation*. London: Routledge and Kegan Paul.

37. Our account draws on the very readable exposition in Smith, M. (1977) *The Underground Education: A Guide To The Alternative Press*. London: Methuen.

38. Adelstein, D. (Ed.) (undated) *The Wisdom and Wit of R. S. Peters*. Occasional Paper. Students Union of the London Institute of Education.

39. Peters, R. S. and Hirst, P. H. (1970) *The Logic of Education*. London: Routledge and Kegan Paul.

40. Our outline of libertarian philosophy and critical sociology follows a paper by Grace, G. (1977) The 'problem' of the urban school: some Radical and Marxist formulations. In *Urban Education 2. Schooling in the City*. (Eds.) Raynor, J. and Harris, E. London: Ward Lock Educational/Open University Press.

41. *Libertarian Teacher*, No. 9, p. 16. Leicester: Black Flag Bookshops. Now entitled *Libertarian Education*.

42. Cowling, A. Discipline Problems. In *Libertarian Education* cited by Smith, M. (1977) *The Underground Education: A Guide To The Alternative Press*. London: Methuen.

43. A quotation from Keith Paton. 'The Great Brain Robbery' cited in Smith, M. (1977) *The Underground Education: A Guide To The Alternative Press*. London: Methuen.

44. A quotation from John Holt cited by Smith, M. (1977) *The Underground Education: A Guide To The Alternative Press*. London: Methuen.

45. Eggleston, J. S. (1970) *Towards an education for the 21st century: a national perspective*. University of Keele.

46. Weber, M. (1952) *Essays in Sociology*. Translated and edited by C. W. Mills. London: Routledge and Kegan Paul.

47. We are grateful to Peter King, Senior Lecturer in Education, Loughborough University of Technology for the summary contained in Box 12.12.

48. Bowles, S. and Gintis, H. (1976) *Schooling in Capitalist America*. London: Routledge and Kegan Paul.

49. Demaine, J. (1979) IQism as ideology and the political economy of education. *Educational Studies*, **5**, 3, 199–215.

50. Some of the major works of the authors cited in Box 12.13 are as follows:-
    Goodman, P. (1971) *Compulsory Miseducation*. Harmondsworth: Penguin.
    Goodman, P. (1970) *Growing up Absurd*. Harmondsworth: Penguin.
    Illich, I. (1971) *Deschooling Society*. Harmondsworth: Penguin.
    Freire, P. (1972) *Pedagogy of the Oppressed*. Harmondsworth: Penguin.
    Reimer, E. (1971) *School is Dead*. Harmondsworth: Penguin.
    Young, M. (1971) *Knowledge and Control*. London: Collier-Macmillan.

51. Reid, I. (1978) *Sociological Perspectives on School and Education*. London: Open Books.

SELECTED READING

1. Pratt, J., Burgess, T., Allemano, R. and Leck, M. (1973) *Your Local Education*. Harmondsworth, London: Penguin. and Kogan, M. and Eyken, W. van der (1973) *County Hall*. Harmondsworth: Penguin. Both are very readable accounts of most aspects of LEA policies.

2. Dunn, G. (1977) *The Box in The Corner: Television and The Under Fives*. London: Macmillan. A British research report into television and language development in young children.

3. (Eds.) Mungham, G. and Pearson, G. (1976) *Working Class Youth Culture*. London: Routledge and Kegan Paul.

Hebdige, D. (1979) *Subculture: The Meaning of Style.* London: Methuen.
(Eds.) Hall, S. and Jefferson, T. (1977) *Resistance Through Rituals.* London: Hutchinson.
All three books deal with working class youth subcultures in post war Britain.

Bibliography

Abrams, M. (1968) *National Survey of Race Prejudice*. Research Services Document J., 4636, London.

Acton, H. B. (1975) Positivism. In *The Concise Encyclopedia of Western Philosophy and Philosophers* (Ed.) Urmson, J. O. (2nd ed.) London: Hutchinson.

Adams, R. S. and Biddle, B. J. (1970) Realities of Teaching: Explorations with Videotape. New York: Holt, Rinehart and Winston.

Adelman, C. and Walker, R. (1974) Open space – open classrooms. *Education 3–13*, 2 October, 103–107.

Adelstein, D. (no date) *The Wisdom and Wit of R. S. Peters*. Occasional Paper, Students Union of the London Institute of Education.

Albrow, N. (1974) Is a science of organisations possible? In *Perspectives on Organisations DT352* Units 15 and 16, Milton Keynes: Open University Press.

Allen, E. A. (1959) *Attitudes to School and Teachers in a Secondary Modern School*. M. A. Thesis, University of London.

Allen, I., Dovet, K., Gaff, M., Gray, E., Griffiths, C. Ryall, N. and Toone, E. (1975) *Working in an Integrated Day*, London: Ward Lock Educational.

Allen, V. L. and Newtson, D. (1972) Development of conformity and independence. *Journal of Personality and Social Psychology*, **22**, 1, 18–30.

Althusser, L. (1967) *For Marx*. Harmondsworth, London: Penguin.

Althusser, L. (1971) *Lenin and Philosophy and Other Essays*. London: New Left Books.

Anthony, W. (1979) Progressive learning theories: the evidence. In *Schooling in Decline* (Ed.) Bernbaum, G. London: Macmillan.

Argyle, M. (1957) Social pressures in public and private situations. *Journal of Abnormal and Social Psychology*, **54**, 172–175.

Argyle, M., Salter, V., Nicholson, H., Williams, M. and Burgess, P. (1970) The communication of inferior and superior attitudes by verbal and nonverbal signals. *British Journal of Social and Clinical Psychology*, **9**, 221–231.

Argyle, M. (1975) *Bodily Communication*. London: Methuen.

Argyle, M. (1978) Discussion chapter: an appraisal of the new approach to the study of social behaviour. In *The Social Contexts of Method* (Eds.) Brenner, M., Marsh, P. and Brenner, M. London: Croom Helm.

Aronson, E. (1976) *The Social Animal*. (2nd ed.) San Francisco: Freeman.

Ashton, A., Kneen, P., Davies, F. and Holley, B. J. (1975) *The Aims of Primary Education: A Study of Teachers' Opinions*, Schools Council Research Studies. London: Macmillan.

Atkinson, J. W. (1964) *An Introduction to Motivation*. Princeton: Van Nostrand.

Bagley, C. (1970) *Social Structure and Prejudice in Five English Boroughs*. London: Institute of Race Relations.

Bagley, C. (1979) A comparative perspective on the education of black children in Britain. *Comparative Education*, **15**, 1, 63–81.

Bagley, C. and Verma, G. K. (1979) *Racial Prejudice, the Individual and Society*. London: Saxon House.

Bagley, C., Verma, G. K., Mallick, K. and Young, L. (1979) *Personality, Self-Esteem and Prejudice*. London: Saxon House.

Bailey, K. D. (1978) *Methods of Social Research*. London: Collier Macmillan.

Bailey, M. Mixed teaching and the defence of subjects. Cited in Elliott, J. (1976). The problems and dilemmas of mixed ability teaching and the issue of teacher accountability. *Cambridge Journal of Education*, **6**, 2, 3–14.

Bailey, P. (1973) The functions of heads of departments in comprehensive schools. *Journal of Educational Administration and History*, **5**, 1, 52–58.

Bandura, A., Ross, D. and Ross, A. (1961) Transmission of aggression through imitation. *Journal of Abnormal and Social Psychology*, **63**, 3, 575–582.

Bandura, A., Ross, D. and Ross, A. (1963) Imitation of film-mediated aggressive models. *Journal of Abnormal and Social Psychology*, **66**, 1, 3–11.

Bandura, A., Ross, D. and Ross, A. (1963) Vicarious reinforcement and imitative learning. *Journal of Abnormal and Social Psychology*, **67**, 6, 601–617.

Banks, O. and Finlayson, D. S. (1973). *Success and Failure in the Secondary School*. London: Methuen.

Barker Lunn, J. C (1970) *Streaming in the Primary School*. Windsor: NFER.

Barnes, D. Language in the secondary classroom. In Barnes, D., Britton, J. and Rosen, H. (1971) *Language, the Learner and the School*. (Revised ed.) Harmondsworth, London: Penguin.

Barnes, D. (1971) Language and learning in the classroom. *Journal of Curriculum Studies*, **3**, 1, 27–38.

Baron, G. and Howell, D. E. (1974) *Government and Management of Schools*. London: Athlone Press.

Barr Greenfield, T. (1975) Theory about organizations: a new perspective and its implications for schools. In *Administering Education: International Challenge* (Ed.) Hughes, M. G. London: Athlone Press.

Barr Greenfield, T. (1976) Organizational Theory; A Symposium. *Educational Administration*, **5**, 1, 1–13.

Barr Greenfield, T. (1978) Where does self belong in the study of organization? *Educational Administration*, **6**, 1, 81–101.

Barratt, P. F. H. (1971) *Bases of Psychological Methods*. Queensland, Australia: J. Wiley and Sons.

Barth, R. S. (1975) Open education: assumptions about children, learning and knowledge. In *Curriculum Design* (Eds.) Golby, M., Greenwald, J., and West, R. London: Croom Helm in association with Open University Press.

Bates, A. W. (1972) The planning of the curriculum. *Headmasters' Association Review*, **70**, No. 215 (July).

Baumrind, D. (1964) Some thoughts on ethics of research: after reading Milgram 'Behavioural study of obedience'. *American Psychologist*, **19**, 421–423.

Beck, R. N. (1979) *Handbook in Social Philosophy*. New York: Macmillan.

Becker, H. S. (1952) Social class variations in teacher-pupil relationships. *Journal of Educational Sociology*, **25**, 451–465.

Becker, H. S. (1963) *Outsiders: Studies in the Sociology of Deviance*. New York: Free Press.

Becker, H. S. and Geer, B. (1960) Latent culture: a note on the theory of latent social roles. *Administrative Science Quarterly*, **5**, 304–313.

Becker, H. S., Geer, B., Hughes, E. C. and Strauss, A. L. (1961) *Boys in White*, Chicago: University of Chicago Press.

Becker, H. S. and Geer, B. (1970) Participant observation and interviewing. In *Qualitative Methodology: Firsthand Involvement with the Social World*. (Ed.) Filstead, W. J. New York: Markham.

Belson, W. A. (1978) *Television and the Adolescent Boy*. London: Saxon House.

Bennett, N. (1976) *Teaching Styles and Pupil Progress*. London: Open Books.

Bennett, N. and Hyland, T. (1979) Open plan – open education? *British Educational Research Journal*, **5**, 2, 159–166.

Bennett, S. J. (1974) *The School: An Organizational Analysis*. Glasgow: Blackie.

Berelson, B. (1952) *Content Analysis in Communication Research*. Glencoe, Illinois: Free Press.

Berenda, R. W. (1950) *The Influence of the Group on the Judgements of Children*. Columbia University, New York: King's Crown Press.

Bernbaum, G. (1977) *Knowledge and Ideology in the Sociology of Education*. London: Macmillan.

(Ed.) Bernbaum, G. (1979) *Schooling in Decline*. London: Macmillan.

Bernstein, B. (1958) Some sociological determinants of perception. *British Journal of Sociology*, **9**, 154–174.

Bernstein, B. (1960) Language and social class. *British Journal of Sociology*, **11**, 271–276.

Bernstein, B. (1961) Social class and linguistic development: a theory of social learning. In *Society, Economy and Education* (Eds.) Halsey, A. H., Floud, J. and Anderson, C. A. Glencoe, Illinois: Free Press.

Bernstein, B. (1965) A socio-linguistic approach to social learning. In *Penguin Survey of the Social Sciences* (Ed.) Gould, J. Harmondsworth, London: Penguin Books.

Bernstein, B. (1967) Open school: open society. *New Society*, 14th September.

Bernstein, B. (1974) Sociology and the sociology of education: a brief account. In *Approaches to Sociology: An Introduction to Major Trends in British Sociology* (Ed.) Rex, J. London: Routledge and Kegan Paul.

Berry, D. (1974) *Central Ideas in Sociology: An Introduction*, London: Constable.
Berscheid, E. and Walster, E. (1961) When does a harm-doer compensate a victim? *Journal of Personality and Social Psychology*, **6**, 435–441.
Best, R. E., Jarvis, C. B. and Ribbins, P.M. (1977) Pastoral care: concept and process. *British Journal of Educational Studies*, **25**, 2, 124–135.
Bidwell, C. E. (1977) Discussion in, *Alternative research perspectives on the effects of school organization and social contexts*, Report No.232. John Hopkins University: Centre for Social Organization of Schools.
Birdwhistell, R. L. (1970) *Kinesics and Context*. Philadelphia: University of Pennsylvania Press.
Bittner, E. (1972) The concept of organisation. In *People and Organisations*. (Eds.) Salaman G. and Thompson K. London: Longmans.
Blishen E. (1969) *The school that I'd like*. Harmondsworth, London: Penguin Books.
Blishen, E. (1973) Why some secondary teachers are disliked. *Where*, **86**, November, 330–334.
Blyth W. A. L. (1965) *English Primary Education*. Two Volumes, London: Routledge and Kegan Paul.
Boaden, M. (1971) *Urban Policy-Making: Influences on County Boroughs in England and Wales*. Cambridge: Cambridge University Press.
Bolam, R., Smith, G. and Carter, H. (1976) *LEA Advisers and Education Administration*. Bristol: University of Bristol School of Education.
Bolton, E. (1979) Education in a multiracial society. *Trends in Education*, **4**, 3–7.
Borg, W. R. (1963) *Educational Research: An Introduction*. New York: Longmans.
Borman, K. (1978) Social control and schooling: power and process in two kindergarten settings. *Anthropology and Education Quarterly*, **9**, 1, 38–53.
Bosanquet, N. (1973) *Race and Employment in Britain*. London: Runnymede Trust.
Bossert, S. T. (1979) *Tasks and Social Relationships in Classrooms*. London: Cambridge University Press.
Bowler L. A. (1974) *Discovery and demonstration in junior school physics*. M. Ed. Thesis, University of Leicester.
Bowles, S. and Gintis, H. (1976) *Schooling in Capitalist America: Educational Reform and the Contradictions of Economic Life*. New York: Basic Books.
Boydell, D. (1975) Individual attention: the child's eye view. *Education 3–13*, **3**, April, 9–13.
Boydell, D. (1979) *The Primary Teacher in Action*. London: Open Books.
Bradley, H. W. and Goulding, J. G. (1973) *Handling mixed ability groups in the secondary school*. University of Nottingham School of Education.
(Eds.) Brenner, M., Marsh, P. and Brenner, M. (1978) *The Social Contexts of Method*. London: Croom Helm.
British Broadcasting Corporation (1972) *Violence on Television*. London: Broadcasting House.
Brittan, E. M. (1976) Multiracial education 2. *Educational Research*, **18**, 2, 92–107.
Brookover, W. B., Erikson, E. K. and Joiner, L. M. (1967) *Self-Concept of Ability and School Achievement III*, Final Report on Cooperative Research Project No. 2831, East Lansing, Michigan: Michigan State University.
Brookover, W. and Erikson, E. L. (1969) *Society, Schools and Learning*. Boston: Allyn and Bacon.
Brooks, D. (1975) *Black Employment in the Black Country: A Study of Walsall*. London: Runnymede Trust.
Brooks, D. and Singh, K. (1979) *Aspirations Versus Opportunities: Asian and White School Leavers in the Midlands*. Walsall Council For Community Relations/Leicester Community Relations Council.
Brophy, J. E. and Good, T. L. (1970) Teachers' communication of differential expectations for children's classroom performance: some behavioural data. *Journal of Educational Psychology*, **61**, 365–374.
Brown, J. and Sime, J. D. (1977) *Accounts as General Methodology*. Paper presented to the British Psychological Society, Exeter.
Bryan, J. H. and Test, M. A. (1967) Models and helping: naturalistic studies in aiding behaviour. *Journal of Personality and Social Psychology*, **6**, 4, 400–407.
Buhler, C. and Allen, M. (1972) *Introduction to Humanistic Psychology*. California: Brooks/Cole.
Bull, T. (1978) *A study of some aspects of leadership behaviour of headteachers in primary schools*. Unpublished M.Phil. dissertation, University of Nottingham.
Bullock Committee (1975) *A Language for Life*. London: HMSO.
Burchard, W. (1954) Role conflicts of military chaplains. *American Sociological Review*, **19**, 528–535.
Burnham, P. (1968) The deputy head. In *Headship in the 1970s* (Ed.) Allen, B. Oxford: Blackwell.
Burns, R. B. (1979) *Self-Concept: Theory Measurement, Development and Behaviour*. London: Longmans.
Burrell, G. and Morgan, G. (1979) *Sociological Paradigms and Organisational Analysis: Elements of the Sociology of Corporate Life*. London: Heinemann.
Butcher, H. J. and Pont, H. B. (1973) *Educational Research in Britain 3*. London: University of London Press.
Byers, P. and Byers, H. (1972) Nonverbal communication and the education of children. In *Functions of Language in the Classroom*, (Eds.) Cazden, C. B., John, V. P. and Hymes, D. Teachers College, Columbia University, New York: Teachers College Press.
Bynner, J. (1980) Black and white arguments. *Guardian*, March 18th.
Byrne, D. S. and Williamson, W. (1972) Some intra-regional variations in educational provision and their

bearing upon educational attainment – the case of the North East. *Sociology*, **6**, 1, 71–87.

Byrne, D., S. Williamson, W. and Fletcher, B. (1975) *The Poverty of Education*. London: Martin Robertson.

Calvert, B. (1975) *The Role of the Pupil*. London: Routledge and Kegan Paul.

Cattell, R. B. (1965) *The Scientific Analysis of Personality*. Harmondsworth, London: Pelican.

(Eds.) Cazden, C. B., John, V. P. and Hymes, D. (1972) *Functions of Language in the Classroom*. Teachers College, Columbia University, New York: Teachers College Press.

Centre For Information and Advice on Educational Disadvantage (1980) *Educational Disadvantage in Rural Areas*. Manchester.

Child, D. (1977) *Psychology and the Teacher*. (2nd ed.) Eastbourne: Holt, Rinehart and Winston.

Child, I., Potter, E. and Levine, E. (1960) Children's textbooks and personality development: an exploration in the social psychology of education. *Psychological Monographs*, **60**, 3.

(Eds.) Children's Rights Workshop (undated) *Racist and Sexist Images in Children's Books*. London: Writers and Readers Publishing Cooperative.

Cicourel, A. V. and Kitsuse, J. I. (1963) *The Educational Decisionmakers*. Indianapolis: Bobbs-Merrill.

Cicourel, A. V. and Kitsuse, J. I. (1968) The social organization of the high school and deviant adolescent careers. In *Deviance: The Interactionist Perspective* (Eds.) Rubbington, E. and Weinberg, M. pp. 124–135, New York: Macmillan.

Clunies-Ross, L. and Reid, M. J. (1980) *Mixed ability teaching: an exploration of teachers' aims, objectives and classroom strategies*. Windsor: NFER. (mimeograph).

Clure, G. L., Wiggins, N. H. and Itkin, S. (1975) Gain and loss in attraction: attributions from nonverbal behaviour. *Journal of Personality and Social Psychology*, **31**, 706–712.

Cohen, L. (1970) *Conceptions of headteachers concerning their role*. Unpublished Ph.D. dissertation, University of Keele.

Cohen, L. (1971) Age and headteachers' views concerning their role. *Educational Research*, **14**, 1, 35–39.

Cohen, L. (1976) *Educational Research in Classrooms and Schools*. London: Harper and Row.

Cohen, L. and Child, D. (1969) Some sociological and psychological factors in university failure. *Durham Research Review*, **22**, 365–372.

Cohen, L. and Fisher, D. (1973) Are comprehensive aims being realized? *Journal of Curriculum Studies*, **5**, 2, 166–175.

Cohen, L. and Manion, L. (1977) *A Guide to Teaching Practice*. London: Methuen.

Cohen, L. and Manion, L. (1980) *Research Methods in Education*. London: Croom Helm.

Cohen, S. (1972) *Folk Devils and Moral Panics*. London: MacGibbon and Kee.

Coleman, J. S., Coser, L. A. and Powell, W. W. (1966) *Equality of Educational Opportunity*. Washington: US Government Printing Office.

(Ed.) Collins, L. (1976) *The Use of Models in the Social Sciences*. London: Tavistock Publications.

Columbro, M. N. (1964) Supervision and Action Research. *Educational Leadership*, **21**, 297–300.

Coop, J. J. (1973) Radix (2): open education – the changing role of the teacher. *Institute of Education of the Universities of Newcastle-upon-Tyne and Durham Journal*, **25**, 33–37.

Cooper, D. and Ebbutt, D. (1974) Participation in action research as an in-service experience. *Cambridge Journal of Education*, **42**, 65–71.

Cooper, H. M., Baron, R. M. and Lowe, C. A. (1975) The importance of race and social class information in the formation of expectancies about academic performance. *Journal of Educational Psychology*, **67**, 2, 312–319.

Coopersmith, S. (1967) *The Antecedents of Self-Esteem*. San Francisco: Freeman.

Corrie, M. (1976) Open plan schools: some research evidence. *Education in the North*, **13**, 33–37.

Corrigan, P. (1979) *Schooling the Smash Street Kids*. London: Macmillan.

Cortis, G. and Grayson, A. (1978) Primary school pupils' perceptions of student teachers' performance. *Educational Review*, **30**, 2, 93–101.

(Eds.) Cosin, B. R., Dale, I. R., Esland, G. M., Mackinnon, D. and Swift, D. (1977) *School and Society: A Sociological Reader*. London: Routledge and Kegan Paul/Open University Press.

Costanzo, P. R. and Shaw, M. E. (1966) Conformity as a function of age level. *Child Development* **37**, 967–975.

Coulson, A. A. (1976) The attitudes of primary school heads and deputy heads to the deputy headship. *British Journal of Educational Psychology*, **46**, 244–252.

Coulson, A. A. and Cox, M. V. (1977) Primary school deputy headship: differences in the conceptions of heads and deputy heads associated with age, sex and length of experience. *Educational Studies*, **3**, 2, 129–136.

Craft, M. (1970) *Family, Class and Education*. London: Longman.

(Eds.) Craft, M. and Lytton, H. (1969) *Guidance and Counselling in British Schools*. London: Arnold.

(Eds.) Craft, M., Raynor, J. and Cohen, L. (1980) *Linking Home and School: A New Review*. London: Harper and Row.

Croucher, A. and Reid, J. (1979) Internalised achievement responsibility as a factor in primary school children's achievement. *Educational Studies*, **5**, 2, 179–194.

Crowl, T. K. (1975) Examination and evaluation of the conceptual basis for open classrooms. *Education (USA)*, **96**, Fall, 54–56.

Cruikshank, D. R., Kennedy, J. J., Bush, A. and Myers, B. (1979) Clear Teaching: what is it?. *British Journal of Teacher Education*, **5**, 1, 27–33.

Crystal, D. (1969) *Prosodic Systems and Intonation in English*. Cambridge: Cambridge University Press.

(Eds.) Cuff, E. C. and Payne, G. C. F. (1979) *Perspectives in Sociology*. London: George Allen and Unwin.

Curtis, B. (1978) Introduction. (Eds.) Curtis, B. and Mays, W. *Phenomenology and Education*. London: Methuen.

(Eds.) Curtis, B. and Mays, W. (1978) *Phenomenology and Education*. London: Methuen.

Dale, R. (1973) Phenomenological perspectives and the sociology of the school. *Educational Review*, **25**, 3, 175–189.

Davie, R., Butler, N. R. and Goldstein, H. (1972) *From Birth To Seven*. London: Longman.

Davies, B. and Cave, R. G. (1977) *Mixed Ability Teaching in the Secondary School*. London: Ward Lock Educational.

Davies, L. (1978) The view from the girls. *Educational Review*, **30**, 2, 103–109.

Davies, R. P. (1975) *Mixed Ability Grouping*. London: Temple Smith.

Davis, R. B. and McKnight, C. (1976) Classroom social setting as a limiting factor in curriculum content. *Journal of Children's Mathematical Behaviour*, Supplement No. 1, 216–217.

Davitz, J. R. (1964) *The Communication of Emotional Feeling*. New York: McGraw Hill.

Dearden, R. F. (1972) Education as a process of growth. In *A Critique of Current Educational Aims*, Part I of *Education and the Development of Reason* (Eds) Dearden, R. F., Hirst, P. H. and Peters, R. S. London: Routledge and Kegan Paul.

Dearden, R. F. (1974) How open can schools be? *Education 3–13*, **2**, October, 88–93.

Dearden, R. F. (1976) *Problems in Primary Education*. London: Routledge and Kegan Paul.

(Eds) Dearden, R. F., Hirst, P. H. and Peters, R. S. (1972) *A Critique of Current Educational Aims*, Part I of *Education and the Development of Reason*. London: Routledge and Kegan Paul.

Deem, R. (1978) *Women and Schooling*. London: Routledge and Kegan Paul.

Delamont, S. (1976) *Interaction in the Classroom*. London: Methuen.

De Lobo, E. (1978) *Children of Immigrants to Britain*. London: Hodder and Stoughton.

Demaine, J. (1979) IQism as ideology and the political economy of education. *Educational Studies*, **5**, 3, 199–215.

Denzin, N. K. (1970) *The Research Act*. Chicago: Aldine Press.

Department of Education and Science (1967) *Children and Their Primary Schools*. London: HMSO.

Department of Education and Science (1971) Education Survey 13, *The Education of Immigrants*. London: HMSO.

Department of Education and Science (1977) *Gifted Children in Middle and Comprehensive Schools*. London: HMSO.

Department of Education and Science (1977) *Ten Good Schools: A Secondary School Enquiry*. HMI Series, Matters for Discussion I. London: HMSO.

Department of Education and Science (1977) *Education in Schools: A Consultative Document*, Cmnd 6869. London: HMSO.

Department of Education and Science (1978) *Mixed Ability Work in Comprehensive Schools*. London: HMSO.

Department of Education and Science (1978) *Report on Education No. 92, School Population in the 1980s*. London: HMSO.

Department of Education and Science (1976) *A New Partnership For Our Schools*. London: HMSO.

Department of Employment (1977) (Ed.) Brannen, P. *Entering the World of Work: Some Sociological Perspectives*. London: HMSO.

Derrick, J. (1968) *Teaching English To Immigrant Children*. London: Longman.

Derrick, J. (1968) The work of the Schools Council project in English for immigrant children. *Times Educational Supplement*, October 25th.

Derrick, J. (1974) *Language Needs of Minority Group Children: Learners of English as a Second Language*. Windsor: NFER.

Diesing, P. (1971) *Patterns of Discovery in the Social Sciences*. Chicago: Aldine.

Dion, K. L., Baron, R. S. and Miller, N. (1970) Why do groups make riskier decisions than individuals? In *Advances in Experimental Social Psychology* (Ed.) Berkowitz, L. Vol. 5, pp. 305–377. New York: Academic Press.

Dixon, K. (1973) *Sociological Theory: Pretense and Possibility*. London: Routledge and Kegan Paul.

Dixon, R. (1977) *Catching Them Young: Sexist, Racist and Class Images in Children's Books*. London: Pluto Press.

Doeringer, P. B. and Pione, M. J. (1971) *Internal Labour Markets and Manpower Analysis*. Lexington, Mass: D. C. Heath.

Dooley, P., Smith, A. and Kerry, T. (1977) *Teaching Mixed Ability Classes. Occasional Paper No.1 Head's reports of procedures and problems.* School of Education, Nottingham University.

Douglas, J. D. (1973) *Understanding Everyday Life.* London: Routledge and Kegan Paul.

Douglas, J. W. B. (1964) *The Home and the School.* London: McGibbon and Kee.

Douglas, J. W. B., Ross, M. and Simpson, H. R. (1968) *All Our Future.* London: Peter Davies.

Dummett, A. (1973) *A Portrait of English Racism.* London: Penguin.

Duncan, S. (1969) Nonverbal communication. *Psychological Bulletin,* **72,** 3, 118-137.

Duncan, S. D. and Rosenthal, R. (1968) Vocal emphasis in experimenter's instruction reading as unintended determinant of subjects' responses. *Language and Speech,* **11,** 20-26.

Dunkerley, D. (1972) *The Study of Organizations.* London: Routledge and Kegan Paul.

Dunn, G. (1977) *The Box in the Corner: Television and the Under-Fives.* London: Macmillan.

Dreeben, R. (1977) The contribution of schooling to the learning of norms. In Karabel, J. and Halsey, A. H. *Power and Ideology in Education.* New York: Oxford University Press.

Driver, G. (1980) How West Indians do better at school (especially the girls). *New Society,* 27th January, 111-114.

Edwards, A. D. and Furlong, V. J. (1978) *The Language of Teaching.* London: Heinemann.

Edwards, A. D. (1976) *Language in Culture and Class.* London: Heinemann.

Ekman, P. and Friesen, W. V. (1969) The repertoire of nonverbal behaviour: categories, origins, usage and coding. *Semiolica,* **1,** 49-98.

Edelman, M. S. and Omark, D. R. (1973) Dominance hierarchies in young children. *Social Science Information,* **12,** 1, 103-110.

Edwards, V. K. (1978) Language attitudes and underperformance in West Indian children. *Educational Review,* **30,** 1, 51-58.

Edwards, V. K. (1979) *The West Indian Language Issue in British Schools.* London: Routledge and Kegan Paul.

Egan, K. (1975) Open education: open to what?. In *The Philosophy of Open Education,* (Ed.) Nyberg, D. London: Routledge and Kegan Paul.

Eggleston, J. S. (1970) Towards an education for the 21st century: a national perspective. University of Keele.

Eggleston, J. F., Galton, M. and Jones, M. E. (1976) *Processes and Products of Science Teaching.* Schools Council Research Studies, London: Macmillan Education.

Elkin, J. (1976) *Books For The Multiracial Classroom.* London: The Library Association.

Ellis, L. G. (1976) The acquisition of Piagetian conservation by children in school – a training programme. In *Piagetian Research: Compilation and Commentary,* (Eds.) Modgil, S. and Modgil, C. Volume 7, Windsor: NFER.

Endler, N. S. and Marino, C. J. (1972) The effects of source and type of prior experience of subsequent conforming behaviour. *The Journal of Social Psychology,* **88,** 21-29.

English, H. B. and English, A. C. (1958) *A Comprehensive Dictionary of Psychological and Psychoanalytic Terms.* London: Longmans.

Entwistle, N. J. (1968) Academic motivation and school attainment. *British Journal of Educational Psychology,* **38,** 2, 181-188.

Eron, L. D., Huesman, L. R., Lefkowitz, M. M. and Walder, L. D. (1972) Does television violence cause aggression? *American Psychologist,* (April), 253-263.

Evans, K. M. (1962) *Sociometry and Education.* London: Routledge and Kegan Paul.

Eysenck, H. J. (1971) *Race, Intelligence and Education.* London: Temple Smith.

Eysenck, H. J. and Eysenck, S. B. (1969) *Personality, Structure and Measurement.* London: Routledge and Kegan Paul.

Farrington, D. (1972) Delinquency begins at home. *New Society,* 14th September.

Ferguson, S. (1977) Toreside Comprehensive School: a simulation game for teachers in training. In *Aspects of Simulation and Gaming.* (Ed.) Megarry, J. London: Kogan Page.

Fewkes, D. W. (1978) *The rationale of open education and personality characteristics of open classroom teachers.* M.Phil. Thesis, University of Nottingham.

Finlayson, D. S. (1970) *School Climate Index.* Windsor: NFER.

Finlayson, D. S. (1973) Measuring school climate. *Trends in Education,* **30,** 19-27.

Finlayson, D. S. (1975) Organisations Climate. *Research Intelligence,* **1,** 22-36.

Finlayson, D. S., Banks, O. and Houghran, J. L. (1970) *School Organisation Index.* Windsor: NFER.

Finlayson, D. S. and Loughran, S. L. (1975) Pupils' perceptions in low and high delinquency schools. *Educational Research,* **18,** 2, 138-145.

(Eds.) Filmer, P., Phillipson, M., Silverman, D. and Walsh, D. (1972) *New Directions in Sociological Theory.* London: Collier Macmillan.

(Ed.) Filstead, W. J. (1970) *Qualitative Methodology: Firsthand Involvement with the Social World.* New York: Markham.

Firth, J. R. (1957) *Papers in Linguistics.* London: Oxford University Press.

Fisher, D. G. (1973) *Streaming and social class in the comprehensive school*. M.Sc. dissertation, School of Research in Education, Bradford.

Fiske, J. and Hartley, J. (1978) *Reading Television*. London: Methuen.

Fogelman, K. R. (1975) Developmental correlates of family size. *British Journal of Social Work*, **5**, 1, 43–57.

Fogelman, K. R. and Goldstein, H. (1976) Social factors associated with changes in educational attainment between seven and eleven years of age. *Educational Studies*, **2**, 2, 95–109.

Fogelman, K. R., Goldstein, H., Essen, J. and Ghodsian, M. (1978) Patterns of attainment. *Educational Studies*, **4**, 2, 121–130.

Fontana, D. (1977) *Personality and Education*. London: Open Books.

Ford, D. H. and Urban, H. B. (1963) *Systems of Psychotherapy: A comparative study*. New York: J. Wiley.

Ford, J. (1969) *Social Class and the Comprehensive School*. London: Routledge and Kegan Paul.

Fowler, B., Lockwood, B. and Madigan, R. (1977) Immigrant school leavers in search for work. *Sociology*, **11**, 1, 65–65.

Frankl, V. (1972) Reductionism and nihilism. In *The Alpbach Symposium: Beyond Reductionism, New Perspectives in the Life Sciences* (Eds) Koestler, A. and Smythes, J. R. London: Hutchinson.

Freedman, J. L. (1969) Role-playing: psychology of consensus. *Journal of Personality and Social Psychology*, **13**, 107–114.

Freedman, J. L. and Doob, A. N. (1968) *Deviancy: The Psychology of Being Different*. New York: Academic Press.

Freedman, J. L., Wallington, S. and Bless, E. (1966) Compliance without pressure: the effect of guilt. *Journal of Personality and Social Psychology*, **7**, 117–124.

Freeman, J. (1969) *Team Teaching in Britain*. London: Ward Lock Educational.

Freire, P. (1972) *Cultural Action for Freedom*. Harmondsworth, London: Penguin.

Freire, P. (1972) *Pedagogy of the Oppressed*. Harmondsworth, London: Penguin.

Fromm, E. (1971) *The Crisis of Psychoanalysis: Essays on Freud, Marx and Social Psychology*. London: Jonathan Cape.

Furlong, V. (1977) Anancy goes to school: a case study of pupils' knowledge of their teachers. In *School Experience*, (Eds.) Woods, P. and Hammersley, M. London: Croom Helm.

Furlong, V. J. and Edwards, A. D. (1977) Language in classroom interaction: theory and data. *Educational Research*, **19**, 2, 122–128.

Galton, M., Simon, B. and Croll, P. (1980) *Inside the Primary Classroom*. London: Routledge and Kegan Paul.

Gannaway, H. (1976) Making sense of school. In *Explorations in Classroom Observation*. (Eds.) Stubbs, M. and Delamont, S. London: Wiley.

Gannon, T. and Whalley, A. (1979) The management of a small secondary school. In *Management and Headship in the Secondary School*. (Ed.) Jennings, A. London: Ward Lock Educational.

Garfinkel, H. (1968) *Studies in Ethnomethodology*. Englewood Cliffs, New Jersey: Prentice Hall.

Garner, J. and Byng, M. (1973) Inequalities of teacher-pupil contact. *British Journal of Educational Psychology*, **43**, 234–243.

Geer, B. (1968) Teaching. In *International Encyclopedia of the Social Sciences*, (Ed.) Sills, D. L. pp. 560–565, New York: Free Press.

Gerbner, G. (1970) Cultural indicators: the case of violence in television drama. *Annals of The American Association of Political and Social Science*, **338**, 69–81.

Gerbner, G., Holsti, O. R., Krippendorff, K., Paisley, W. J. and Stone, P. J. (1969) *The Analysis of Communication Content*. New York: Wiley.

(Eds.) Gerbner, G., Gross, L. and Melody, W. (1973) *Communication Technology and Social Policy*. New York: Wiley-Interscience.

Getzels, G. W. (1963) Conflict and role behaviour in the educational setting. In *Readings in the Social Psychology of Education* (Eds.) Charters, W. W. and Gage, N. L. Boston, Mass.

Getzels, J. W. and Guba, E. S. (1954) Role, role conflict, and effectiveness. *American Sociological Review*, **19**, 164–175.

Getzels, J. W. and Guba, E. G. (1957) Social behaviour and the administrative process. *School Review*, **65**, (Winter), 423–441.

Ghuman, P. A. S. (1980) Punjabi parents and English education. *Educational Research*, **22**, 2, 121–130.

(Ed.) Giddens, A. (1975) *Positivism and Sociology*. London: Heinemann Educational Books.

Giddens, A. (1976) *New Rules of Sociological Method: A Positive Critique of Interpretive Sociologies*. London: Hutchinson.

Giles, R. (1977) *The West Indian Experience in British Schools*. London: Heinemann.

Glaser, B. G. and Strauss, A. L. (1967) *The Discovery of Grounded Theory*. Chicago: Aldine.

Goffman, E. (1961) *Asylums*. Harmondsworth. London: Penguin.

(Eds.) Golby, M., Greenwald, J. and West, R. (1975) *Curriculum Design*. London: Croom Helm/Open University Press.

Gold, M. (1958) Power in the classroom. *Sociometry*, **21**, 50–60.

Goldthorpe, J. H. (1980) (in collaboration with Llewelyn, C. and Payne, C.), *Social Mobility and Class Structure in Modern Britain*. London: Oxford University Press.

Good, T. L. and Brophy, J. E. (1978) *Looking in Classrooms*. (2nd ed.) New York: Harper and Row.

Goodman, P. (1970) *Growing Up Absurd*. Harmondsworth, London: Penguin.

Goodman, P. (1971) *Compulsory Miseducation*. Harmondsworth, London: Penguin.

Gordon, L. V. (1968) Correlates of bureaucratic orientation, *Proceedings of the XVIth International Conference of Applied Psychology*. Amsterdam: Awets and Zeitlinger.

Gordon, L. V. (1972) *School Environment Preference Schedule*. (Mimeograph) Albany, New York: New York State University.

Grace, G. (1977) The problem of the urban school: some Radical and Marxist formulations. In *Urban Education 2: Schooling in The City*. (Eds.) Raynor, J. and Harris, E. London: Ward Lock Educational/Open University Press.

Grace, G. R. (1972) *Role Conflict and the Teacher*. London: Routledge and Kegan Paul.

Gracey, H. (1972) *Curriculum of Craftsmanship: Elementary School Teachers in a Bureaucratic System*. Chicago: University of Chicago Press.

Graham, C. (1970) The relation between ability and attainment tests. *Association of Educational Psychologists Journal and News Letter*, **2**, 5, 53–59.

Gray, H. L. (1975) Exchange and conflict in the school. In Houghton, V., McHugh, R. and Morgan, C. *Management in Education I: The Management of Organizations and Individuals*, pp. 253–265. London: Ward Lock Educational.

Gray, J. (1976) A chapter of errors: teaching styles and pupil progress in retrospect. *Educational Research*, **19**, 1, 45–56.

Gregson, A. and Quin, W. F. (1978) Mixed ability methods and educational standards. *Comprehensive Education*, **37**, 12–16.

Griffiths, D. (1962) *Organizing Schools for Effective Education*. Dansville, Illinois: Interstate Printers and Publishers.

Groobman, D. E., Forward, J. R. and Peterson, C. (1976) Attitudes, self-esteem and learning in formal and informal schools. *Journal of Educational Psychology*, **68**, 1, 32–35.

Gross, N., Mason, W. S. and McEachern, A. W. (1958) *Explorations in Role Analysis*. New York: John Wiley.

Grover, A. J. (1972) *Curriculum decision-making in primary schools*. Unpublished M.Sc. dissertation, University of Bradford.

Gumperz, J. J. and Herasimchuk, E. (1972) The conversational analysis of social meaning: a study of classroom interaction. In *Sociolinguistics*, (Ed.) Shuy, R. Georgetown Monograph Series on Language and Linguistics, **25**.

Gupta, Y. P. (1977) The educational and vocational aspirations of Asian immigrants and English school-leavers. *British Journal of Sociology*, **28**, 2. 185–198.

Hall, E. T. (1959) *The Silent Language*. Garden City, New York: Doubleday.

Hall, E. T. (1966) *The Hidden Dimension*. Garden City, New York: Doubleday.

(Eds.) Hall, S. and Jefferson, T. (1977) *Resistance Through Rituals*. London: Hutchinson.

Halliday, M. A. K. (1969) Relevant models of language. In *The State of Language*. University of Birmingham.

Halliday, M. A. K. (1973) *Explorations in the Functions of Language*. London: Arnold.

Hallworth, H. J. (1953) Sociometric relations among grammar school boys and girls. *Sociometry*, **16**, 32–45.

Hallworth, H. J. (1962) A teacher's perceptions of his pupils. *Educational Review*, **14**, 124–133.

Halpin, A. W. and Croft, D. B. (1963) *Organizational Climate of Schools*. Chicago: Midwest Administrative Centre, University of Chicago.

(Ed.) Halsey, A. H. (1972) *Educational Priority, Volume 1: E.P.A. Problems and Policies*. London: HMSO.

Halsey, A. H., Heath, A. F. and Ridge, J. M. (1979) *Origins and Destinations: Family, Class and Education in Modern Britain*. Oxford: Oxford University Press.

Hamblin, D. (1972) *Intervening in the Learning Process*. In Educational Studies: A Second Level Course, Personality Growth and Learning, E281, Unit 17. Milton Keynes: Open University Press.

Hamilton, D. and Delamont, S. (1974) Classroom research: a cautionary tale. *Research in Education*, **11**, 1–16.

Hamm, N. H. and Hoving, K. L. (1969) Conformity of children in an ambiguous perceptual situation. *Child Development*, **40**, 773–784.

Hammersley, M. (1977) *Teacher Perspectives*. Open University Educational Studies, A Second Level Course, E202, Schooling and Society. Units 9 and 10, Block II, The Process of Schooling. Milton Keynes: Open University Press.

Hammersley, M. (1977) *The Social Location of Teacher Perspectives*. Open University Educational Studies, A Second Level Course, E202, Schooling and Society. Units 12 and 13, Block II, The Process of Schooling. Milton Keynes: Open University Press.

Hammersley, M. (1976) *The Process of Schooling: A Sociological Reader*. London: Routledge and Kegan Paul/Open University Press.

Hampden-Turner, C. (1970) *Radical Man*. Cambridge, Mass: Schenkman.

Hargreaves, D. H. (1967) *Social Relations in a Secondary School*. London: Routledge and Kegan Paul.

Hargreaves, D. H. (1972) *Interpersonal Relations and Education*. London: Routledge and Kegan Paul.

Hargreaves, D. H. (1976) The real battle of the classroom. *New Society*, January 29th.

Hargreaves, D. H. (1977) The process of typification in classroom interaction: models and methods. *British Journal of Educational Psychology*, **47**, 274–284.

Hargreaves, D. H., Hester, S. K. and Mellor, F. J. (1975) *Deviance in Classrooms*. London: Routledge and Kegan Paul.

Harnischfeger, A. and Wiley, D. E. (1978) Conceptual issues in models of school learning. *Journal of Curriculum Studies*, **10**, 3.

Harré, R. (1976) The constructive role of models. In *The Use of Models in the Social Sciences* (Ed.) Collins, L. London: Tavistock Publications.

Harré, R. and Secord, P. F. (1972) *The Explanation of Social Behaviour*. Oxford: Basil Blackwell.

Hartmann, P. and Husband, C. (1974) *Racism and the Mass Medium*. London: Davis-Poynter.

Heal, K. (1978) Misbehaviour among school children: the role of the school in strategies for prevention. *Policy and Politics*, **6**, 321–332.

Heal, K. H., Sinclair, I. A. C. and Troop, J. (1973) Development of a social climate questionnaire for use in approved schools and community homes. *British Journal of Sociology*, **1**, 222–235.

Heath, A. and Clifford, P. (1980) The seventy thousand hours that Rutter left out. *Oxford Review of Education*, **6**, 1, 3–19.

Hebdige, D. (1979) *Subculture: The Meaning of Style*. London: Methuen.

Heim, A. W. (1970) *The Appraisal of Intelligence*. Windsor: NFER.

Henley, N. M. (1977) *Body Politics: Power, Sex and Non-verbal communication*, Englewood Cliffs, New Jersey: Prentice-Hall.

Henry, J. (1963) *Culture against Man*. London: Ransom House.

Heslin, R. (1974) *Steps towards a taxonomy of touching*. Paper presented to the Midwestern Psychological Association, Chicago.

Hill, D. (1976) *Teaching in Multiracial Schools*. London: Methuen.

Hill, J. (1976) *Books For Children. The Homelands of Immigrants in Britain*. Institute of Race Relations, London.

Highbee, K. L. (1971) Expression of 'Walter Mitty-ness' in actual behaviour. *Journal of Personality and Social Psychology*, **20**, 416–422.

Hobbs, A., Kleinberg, S. M. and Martin, P. J. (1979) Decision-making in primary schools. *Research in Education*, **21**, 79–92.

Holbrook, D. (1977) *Education, Nihilism and Survival*, London: Darnton, Longman and Todd.

Hollis, A. W. (1935) *The Personal Relationship in Teaching*. M. A. Thesis, University of Birmingham.

Holsti, O. R. (1968) Content Analysis. In *The Handbook of Social Psychology* (Eds.) Lindzey, G. and Aronson, E. Volume II, *Research Methods*, New York: Addison-Wesley.

Holt, J. (1970) *How Children Learn*. Harmondsworth, London: Penguin.

Houghton, V. (1966) Intelligence testing of West Indian and English children. *Race*, **8**, 147–156.

Hoyle, E. (1973) The study of schools as organizations. In *Educational Research in Britain 3*. (Eds.) Butcher, H. J. and Pont, H. B. London; University of London Press.

Hoyle, E. (1975) Leadership and decision-making in education. In *Administering Education: The International Challenge* (Ed.) Hughes, M. G. pp. 30–44. London: Athlone Press.

Hoyle, E. (1976) Comment in *Educational Administration*, **5**, 1, 4–6.

Hughes, J. A. (1978) *Sociological Analysis: Methods of Discovery*. Sunbury-on-Thames: Nelson and Sons.

Hughes, M. G. (1972) *The role of the secondary school head*. Unpublished Ph.D. dissertation, University College, Cardiff.

(Ed.) Hughes, M. G. (1975) *Administering Education: International Challenge*. London: Athlone Press.

Hurt, H. T., Scott, M. D. and McCroskey, J. C. (1978) *Communication in the Classroom*. Reading, Mass: Addison-Wesley.

Hutt, C. and Vaizey, M. J. (1966) Differential effects of group density on social behaviour. *Nature*, **209**, 1371–1372.

Hyland, J. *Open Education – A Slogan Examined*. Unpublished paper, Department of Educational Research, Cartmel College, University of Lancester.

Illich, I. (1971) *Deschooling Society*. Harmondsworth, London: Penguin.

Ions, E. (1977) *Against Behaviouralism: A Critique of Behavioural Science*. Oxford: Basil Blackwell.

Isaac, S. and Michael, W. B. (1971) *Handbook of Research and Evaluation*. California: Robert R. Knapp.

Isen, A. M. and Levin, P. A. (1972) Effect of feeling good on helping: cookies and kindness. *Journal of Personality and Social Psychology*, **21**, 384–388.

Jeffcoate, R. (1975) Curriculum intervention. *The Times Educational Supplement*, December 9th, 24–25.

Jeffcoate, R. (1979) A multicultural curriculum: beyond the orthodoxy. *Trends in Education*, **4**, 8–12.

Jeffcoate, R. (1979) *Positive Image: Towards a multiracial Curriculum.* London: Writers and Readers Publishing Cooperative.

(Ed.) Jennings, A. (1979) *Management and Headship in the Secondary School.* London: Ward Lock Educational.

Jencks, C., Smith, M., Acland, H., Bane, M. J., Cohen, D., Gintis, H., Heyns, B., and Michelson, B. (1972) *Inequality: A Reassessment of the Effect of Family and Schooling in America.* New York: Basic Books.

Jensen, A. R. (1969) How much can we boost I.Q. and scholastic achievement? *Harvard Educational Review*, **39**, 1–123.

Jensen, A. (1973) *Educability and Group Differences.* London: Methuen.

Jensen, A. (1973) *Educational Differences.* London: Methuen.

Jensen, A. (1980) *Bias in Mental Testing.* London: Methuen.

Johnson, D., Ranson, E., Packwood, T., Bawden, K. and Kogan, M. (1980) *Secondary Schools and the Welfare Network.* London: George Allen and Unwin.

Johnson, D. W. (1970) *The Social Psychology of Education.* New York: Holt, Rinehart and Winston.

Johnson, D. W. and Johnson, R. T. (1975) *Learning Together and Alone.* Englewood Cliffs, New Jersey: Prentice-Hall.

Johnson, D. W. (1978) Conflict management in the school and classroom. In *Social Psychology of Education: Theory and Research* (Eds) Bar-Tal, D and Saxe, L. pp. 299–326, New York: John Wiley and Sons.

Johnson, H. G., Ekman, P. and Friesen, W. V. (1975) Communicative body movements. *Semiotica*, **15**, 335–353.

(Eds) Jones, A. and Mulford, J. (1971) *Children using Language.* London: Oxford University Press.

Kahn, R. L., Wolfe, D. M., Quinn, R. P., Snoek, J. D. and Rosenthal, R. A. (1964) *Organisational Stress: Studies in Role Conflict and Ambiguity.* New York: Wiley.

Kanter, R. M. (1972) The organization child: experience management in a nursery school. *Sociology of Education*, **45**, 186–212.

Kaplan, A. (1973) *The Conduct of Inquiry.* Aylesbury: Intertext Books.

Katz, D. and Kahn, R. L. (1966) *The Social Psychology of Organizations.* New York: Wiley.

Kelley, H. H. and Volkart, E. H. (1952) The resistance to change of group-anchored attitudes. *American Sociological Review*, **17**, 453–465.

Kelly, A. V. (1974) *Teaching Mixed Ability Classes.* London: Harper and Row.

Kelsall, R. K. and Kelsall, H. M. (1969) *The Schoolteacher in England and the United States.* Oxford: Pergamon Press.

Kendon, A. (1967) Some functions of gaze-direction in social interaction. *Acta Psychologica*, **26**, 22–63.

Kerlinger, F. N. (1969) *Foundations of Behavioural Research.* New York: Holt, Rinehart and Winston.

Kerry, T. (1978) Bright pupils in mixed ability classes. *British Educational Research Journal*, **4**, 2, 103–111.

Kierkegaard, S. (1971) *Concluding Unscientific Postscript.* Princeton: Princeton University Press.

Kiernan, V. (1972) *The Lords of Human Kind: European Attitudes to the Outside World in an Imperial Age.* Harmondsworth, London: Penguin.

Kiesler, S. (1978) *Interpersonal Processes in Groups and Organizations.* Illinois: A.H.M. Publishing Corporation.

Kimber, R. and Richardson, J. J. (1974) *Pressure Groups in Britain.* London: J. M. Dent and Sons.

King, M. and Ziegler, M. (1975) *Research Projects in Social Psychology.* Monterey, California: Brookes/Cole.

King, R. (1973) *School Organisation and Pupil Involvement: A Study of Secondary Schools.* London: Routledge and Kegan Paul.

King, R. (1978) *All Things Bright and Beautiful? A Sociological Study of Infants' Classrooms.* Chichester: Wiley.

Knapp, M. L. (1980) *Essentials of Nonverbal Communication.* New York: Holt, Rinehart and Winston.

(Eds.) Koestler, A. and Smythies, J. R. (1972) *The Alpbach Symposium: Beyond Reductionism, New Perspectives in the Life Sciences.* London: Hutchinson.

Kogan, M. (1975) *Educational Policy Making: A Study of Interest Groups and Parliament.* London: George Allen and Unwin.

Kohl, H. R. (1970) *The Open Classroom.* London: Methuen.

Kohl, H. R. (1974) *Reading, How to.* Harmondsworth, London: Penguin.

Kounin, J. and Gump, P. (1961) The comparative influence of punitive and non-punitive teachers upon children's concepts of school misconduct. *Journal of Educational Psychology*, **52**, 44–49.

Kounin, J. S. (1970) *Discipline and Group Management in Classrooms.* New York: Holt, Rinehart and Winston.

Krech, D., Crutchfield, R. S. and Ballachev, E. L. (1962) *Individual in Society.* New York: McGraw Hill.

Lacey, C. (1970) *Hightown Grammar.* Manchester: Manchester University Press.

Laishley, J. (1975) The images of blacks and whites in the children's media. In *White Media and Black Britain*, (Ed.) Husband, C. London: Arrow Books.

Lambert, R., Bullock, R. and Millham, S. (1975) *The Chance of a Lifetime?* London: Weidenfeld and Nicolson.
Latane, B. and Darley, J. M. (1970) *The Unresponsive Bystander: Why doesn't he help?* New York: Appleton.
Lawton, D. (1968) *Social Class, Language and Education.* London: Routledge and Kegan Paul.
Leach, D. and Raybould, E. C. (1977) *Learning and Behaviour Difficulties in School.* London: Open Books.
Lefcourt, H. M. (1966) Internal versus external control of reinforcement: a review. *Psychological Bulletin,* **65**, 206–220.
Leftkowtiz, M. Blake, R. R. and Mouton, J. S. (1955) Status of actors in pedestrian violation of traffic signals. *Journal of Abnormal and Social Psychology,* **51**, 704–706.
Lemert, E. M. (1951) *Social Pathology: A Systematic Approach To the Study of Sociopathic Behaviour.* New York: McGraw Hill.
Lemert, E. M. (1967) *Human Deviance: Social Problems and Social Control.* Englewood Cliffs, New Jersey. Prentice-Hall.
Levine, R. H. (1977) Why the ethogenic method and the dramaturgical perspective are incompatible. *Journal of the Theory of Social Behaviour,* **7**, 2, 237–247.
Lewin, K. (1947) Group decision and social change. In Newcomb, T. M. and Hartley, E. L. *Readings in Social Psychology.* New York: Holt, Rinehart and Winston.
Lewis, G. (1980) The disadvantages and advantages of small rural schools. In Centre For Information and Advice on Educational Disadvantage, *Educational Disadvantage in Rural Areas.* Manchester.
Lewis, R. (1973) Speaking in the primary school. *Speech and Drama,* **22**, 2, Summer.
Linder, R. and Purdom, D. (1975) Four dimensions of openness in classroom activities. *Elementary School Journal,* **16**, 3, 147–150.
(Eds.) Lindzey, G. and Aronson, E. (1968) *The Handbook of Social Psychology,* Volume II, *Research Methods.* New York: Addison-Wesley.
Lippitt, R., Polansky, N. and Rosen, S. (1952) The dynamics of power. In *Human Relations,* **5**, 37–64.
Little, A. (1975) The educational achievement of ethnic minority children in London schools. In *Race and Education Across Cultures* (Eds.) Verma, G. and Bagley, C. London: Heinemann.
Little, A., Mabey, C. and Whitaker, G. (1968) The education of immigrant pupils in Inner London primary schools. *Race,* **9**, 439–452.
Litwak, E. (1961) Models of bureaucracy which permit conflict. *American Journal of Sociology,* **67**, 177–184.
Locke, M. (1974) *Power and Politics in the School System.* London: Routledge and Kegan Paul.
Lomax, P. (1978) The attitudes of girls with varying degrees of school adjustment to different aspects of their school experience. *Educational Review,* **30**, 2, 117–124.
Lorenz, K. Z. (1969) Innate Bases of Learning. In *On the Biology of Learning* (Ed.) Pribram, K. H. New York: Harcourt, Brace and World.
Lydiat, M. (1977) Mixed ability teaching gains ground. *Comprehensive Education,* **35**, 12–19.
McClelland, D. C., Atkinson, J. W., Clark, R. A. and Lowell, E. L. (1953) *The Achievement Motive.* New York: Appleton Century-Croft.
McFie, J. and Thompson, J. (1970) Intellectual abilities of immigrant children. *British Journal of Educational Psychology,* **40**, 348–351.
McGeown, V. (1979) *School innovativeness as process and product.* (Mimeograph 1979a) New University of Ulster.
McGeown, V. (1979) *Organisational climate for change in schools: towards definition and measurement.* (Mimeograph 1979b) New University of Ulster.
McGeown, V. (1979) *School principals' decision-making behaviour in the management of innovation.* (Mimeograph 1979c) New University of Ulster.
McGeown, V. (1979) *Dimensions of teacher innovativeness.* (Mimeograph 1979d) New University of Ulster.
McGrath, J. E. and Altman, J. E. (1966) *Small Group Research.* New York: Holt, Rinehart and Winston.
McKeachie, W. J., Yi-Gang, L., Milholani, J. and Isaacson, R. (1966) Student affiliation motive, teacher warmth and academic achievement. *Journal of Personality and Social Psychology,* **4**, 4, 457–461.
Mabey, C. (1974) Literacy Survey, Stage 2 – a summary paper on *Immigrant Attainment.* London: Inner London Education Authority.
Madaus, G. F., Kellaghan, T., Rakow, E. A. and King, D. J. (1979) The sensitivity of measures of school effectiveness. *Harvard Educational Review,* **49**, 2, 207–230.
Madge, J. (1965) *The Tools of Social Science.* London: Longmans.
Maizels, J. (1970) How leavers rate teachers. *New Society,* 24th September.
Makins, V. (1969) Child's eye view of teachers. *Times Educational Supplement,* 19th and 26th September.
Manley. D. (1973) *Scope supplementary plays and dialogues.* Schools Council, London: Schools Council: English For Immigrant Children Curriculum Development Project.
Manley, D. R. (1963) Mental ability in Jamaica. *Social and Economic Studies,* **12**, 54–71. Kingston: Jamaica. University of the West Indies.
Marland, M. (1977) *Language across the Curriculum.* London: Heinemann Educational Books.

Marsh, P., Rosser, E. and Harré, R. (1978) *The Rules of Disorder*. London: Routledge and Kegan Paul.
Mayo, E. (1939) Western Electric Studies. In Roethlisberger, F. J. and Dickson, W. J. *Management and the Worker*. Camb., Mass: Harvard University Press.
Mead, G. H. (1934) *Mind, Self and Society From the Standpoint of a Social Behaviourist*. Chicago: University of Chicago Press.
Medawar, P. B. (1972) *The Hope of Progress*. London: Methuen.
(Ed.) Megarry, J. (1977) *Aspects of Simulation and Gaming*. London: Kogan Page.
Mehrabian, A. (1972) *Nonverbal Communication*. Chicago: Aldine-Atherton.
Meighan, R. (1974) Children's judgements of the teaching performance of student teachers. *Educational Review*, **27**, November, 52–60.
Meighan, R. (1977) Pupils' perceptions of the classroom techniques of post-graduate student teachers. *British Journal of Teacher Education*, **3**, 2, 139–148.
Meighan, R. (1977) The pupil as client: the learner's experience of school. *Educational Review*, **29**, 123–133.
Meighan, R. (1981) *A Sociology of Educating*. Eastbourne: Holt-Saunders.
Merton, R. K. and Kendall, P. L. (1946) The focused interview. *American Journal of Sociology*, **51**, 541–557.
Meyenn, R. J. (1980) School girls' peer groups. In *Pupil Strategies*, (Ed.) Woods, P. London: Croom Helm.
Meyer, J., Pritchard, D. L. and Moodie, A. G. (1971) *A Survey of Teachers' Opinions regarding Open Plan Areas*. Vancouver Board of School Trustees.
Milgram, S. (1974) *Obedience to Authority*. New York: Harper and Row.
Milgram, S., Bickman, L. and Berkowitz, L. (1969) Note on the drawing power of crowds of different size. *Journal of Personality and Social Psychology*, **13**, 79–82.
Miller, G. (1971) *Educational Opportunity and the Home*. London: Longman.
Millman, J. and Gowin, D. B. (1974) *Appraising Educational Research*. Englewood Cliffs, New Jersey: Prentice-Hall.
Milner, D. (1975) *Children and Race*. London: Pelican.
Mischel, W. (1973) Towards a cognitive social learning reconceptualization of personality. *Psychological Review*, **80**, 252–283.
Mishler, E. G. (1972) Implications of teacher strategies for language and cognition: observations in first-grade classrooms. In *Functions of Language in the Classroom* (Eds.) Cazden, C. B., John, V. P. and Hymes, D. Teachers College, Columbia University, New York: Teachers College Press.
Mitchell, G. (1968) *A Dictionary of Sociology*. London: Routledge and Kegan Paul.
(Eds.) Modgil, S. and Modgil, C. (1976) *Piagetian Research: Compilation and Commentary*, Vol. 7, Windsor: NFER.
Montagu, M. F. A. (1971) *Touching: The Human Significance of the Skin*. New York: Columbia University Press.
Moody, E. (1968) Right in front of everybody. *New Society*, 26th December.
Morrison, A. and MacIntyre, D. (1969) *Teachers and Teaching*. Harmondsworth, London: Penguin.
Moser, C. A. (1966) *Survey Methods in Social Investigation*. London: Heinemann Educational Books.
Moss, M. H. (1973) *Deprivation and Disadvantage?* Educational Studies, E202, Block 8, A Second Level Course, Language and Learning. Milton Keynes: Open University Press.
Mouly, G. J. (1978) *Educational Research: The Art and the Science of Investigation*. Boston: Allyn and Bacon.
(Eds) Mungham, G. and Pearson, G. (1976) *Working Class Youth Culture*. London: Routledge and Kegan Paul.
Musgrove, F. (1960) The decline of the educative family. *Universities Quarterly*, **14**, 377–385.
Musgrove, F. and Taylor, P. H. (1969) *Society and the Teacher's Role*. London: Routledge and Kegan Paul.
Myers, D. A. and Duke, D. L. (1977) Open education as an ideology. *Educational Research*, **19**, 3, 227–235.
Nash, R. (1973) *Classrooms Observed*. London: Routledge and Kegan Paul.
Nash, R. (1974) Pupils' expectations for their teachers. *Research in Education*, **12**, November, 46–71.
Nash, R. (1976) *Teacher Expectations and Pupil Learning*. London: Routledge and Kegan Paul.
New Society, 24th January, Letters, 1980.
New Society, 11th February, Letters, 1980.
Newbold, D. (1977) *Ability Grouping–The Banbury Enquiry*, Windsor: NFER.
(Ed.) Nyberg, D. (1975) *The Philosophy of Open Education*. London: Routledge and Kegan Paul.
Oeser, O. A. (1960) *Teacher, Pupil and Task*. London: Tavistock Publications.
Olesen, V. L. and Whittaker, E. W. (1968) *The Silent Dialogue: A Study in the Social Psychology of Professional Socialization*. San Francisco: Jossey-Bass.
Open University (1976) *Schools as Organisations: A Third Level Course: Management in Education*. E321 3, Unit 3. Milton Keynes: Open University Press.
Open University (1979) *The Politics of Educational Policy-making: Pressures on Central and Local Government*. E222, Unit 6. Milton Keynes: Open University Press.
Outhwaite, W. (1975) *Understanding Social Life: One Method called Verstehen*. London: George Allen and Unwin.

Owens, R. G. (1970) *Organizational Behaviour in Schools*. Englewood Cliffs, New Jersey: Prentice-Hall.

Paisey, G. H. J. (1977) *Pupil achievement as perceived by teachers in formal and informal schools*. M.Phil. Thesis, University of Nottingham.

Paisey, H. A. G. (1975) *The Behavioural Strategy of Teachers*. Windsor: NFER.

Parten, M. L. (1932) Social participation among pre-school children. *Journal of Abnormal and Social Psychology*, **27**, 243–269.

Perrow, C. (1974) Zoo story or life in the organisational sandpit. In *Perspectives on Organisations*. DT 352 Units 15 and 16. Milton Keynes: Open University Press.

Pervin, L. A. (1970) *Personality: Theory, Assessment and Research*. New York: Wiley.

Peters, R. S. (1964) *Education as Initiation*. London: Routledge and Kegan Paul.

(Ed.) Peters, R. S. (1976) *Perspectives on Plowden*. London: Routledge and Kegan Paul.

(Ed.) Peters, R. S. (1976) *The Role of the Head*. London: Routledge and Kegan Paul.

(Ed.) Peters, R. S. (1978) *The Philosophy of Education*. London: Oxford University Press.

Peters, R. S. and Hirst, P. H. (1970) *The Logic of Education*. London: Routledge and Kegan Paul.

Pettigrew, T. (1971) *Racially Separate or Together*. New York: McGraw-Hill.

Piaget, J. (1954) *The Moral Judgement of the Child*. New York: Basic Books.

Plowden Report (1967) *Children and their Primary Schools*. Report of the Central Advisory Council for Education (England). London: HMSO.

Podeschi, R. and Dennis, L. (1976) The British, Americans and open education: some cultural differences. *Peabody Journal of Education*, **33**, April, 208–215.

Power, M. J., Alderson, M. R., Phillipson, C. M., Schoenberg, E. and Morris, J. M. (1967) Delinquent Schools? *New Society*, 19th October.

Pratt, J., Burgess, T., Allemano, R. and Lock, M. (1973) *Your Local Education*, Harmondsworth, London: Penguin.

Presthus, R. (1962) *The Organizational Society*. New York: Alfred A. Knopf.

(Ed.) Pribram, K. H. (1969) *On the Biology of Learning*. New York: Harcourt, Brace and World.

Priestland, G. (1974) *The Future of Violence*. London: Hamish Hamilton.

Pring, R. (1978) Curriculum Integration. In *The Philosophy of Education* (Ed.) Peters, R. S. London: Oxford University Press.

Proctor, C. (1975) *Racist Textbooks*. London: National Union of Students.

Purkey, W. W (1967) *Research Bulletin: The Self and Academic Achievement*. Gainsville, Florida: Florida Educational Research and Development Council.

Quinton, A. (1975/6) *Social Objects*. Presidential Address, *Proceedings of the Aristotelian Society*.

Radloff, R. and Helmreich, R. L. (1968) *Groups under Stress: Psychological Research in Sealab II*. New York: Appleton Century Crofts.

Raven, B. H. (1959) Social influence on opinions and the communication of related content. *Journal of Abnormal and Social Psychology*, **58**, 119–128.

Reece, M. and Whitman, R. (1962) Expressive movements, warmth, and verbal reinforcement. *Journal of Abnormal and Social Psychology*, **64**, 236–236.

Regan, D. E. (1977) *Local Government and Education*. London: George Allen and Unwin.

Regan, D. T., Williams, M. and Sparling, S. (1972) Voluntary expiation of guilt: a field experiment. *Journal of Personality and Social Psychology*, **24**, 1, 42–45.

Reid, I. (1978) *Sociological Perspectives on School and Education*. London: Open Books.

Reimer, E. (1971) *School Is Dead*. Harmondsworth, London: Penguin.

Resnick, L. B. (1972) Teacher behaviour in the informal classroom. *Journal of Curriculum Studies*, **4** November, 2, 99–109.

(Ed.) Rex, J. (1974) *Approaches to Sociology: An Introduction to Major Trends in British Sociology*. London: Routledge and Kegan Paul.

Richards, C. (1974) Changing schools? Changing teachers? *Trends in Education*, **34**, July, 22–26.

Richards, J. W. (1974) The Language of Biology Teaching. Unpublished M.Ed. Thesis, University of Newcastle-upon-Tyne.

Richards, J. W. (1978) *Classroom Language: What Sort?* London: Unwin Educational Books.

Richardson, E. (1977) *The Teacher, The School and The Task of Management*. London: Heinemann.

Richmond, W. K. (1953) *The Rural School*. London: Redman.

Riecken, H. W. (1958) The effect of talkativeness on ability to influence group solutions of problems. *Sociometry*, **21**, 309–321.

Rintoul, K. and Thorne, K. (1975) *Open Plan Organization in the Primary School*. London: Ward Lock Educational.

Rist, R. G. (1970) Student social class and teacher expectations: the self-fulfilling prophecy in ghetto education. *Harvard Educational Review*, **40**, 411–451.

Rivers, P. (1974) *Politics By Pressure*. London: George G. Harrap.

Robertson, W. (1978) *Language as Power: An exploration of perception of power and hierarchy as expressed in the language of children and adults in a primary school.* M.Ed. dissertation, University of Newcastle.

Robinson, V. (1980) The achievement of Asian children. *Educational Research*, **22**, 2, 148–150.

Roethlisberger, F. J. and Dickson, W. J. (1939) *Management and the Worker.* Camb., Mass: Harvard University Press.

Rogers, C. R. (1942) *Counselling and Psychotherapy.* Boston: Houghton Mifflin.

Rogers, C. R. (1945) The non-directive method as a technique for social research. *American Journal of Sociology*, **50**, 279–282.

Rogers, C. R. (1969) *Freedom to Learn.* Columbus, Ohio: Merrill.

Rogers, C. R. and Stevens, B. (1967) *Person to Person: The Problem of Being Human.* A Condor Book. London: Souvenir Press.

Rosen, B. C. (1956) The achievement syndrome: a psychocultural dimension of social stratification. *American Sociological Review*, **20**, 155–161.

Rosen, B. C. and d'Andrade, R. (1959) The psychosocial origins of achievement motivation. *Sociometry*, **22**, 183–218.

Rosen, C. and Rosen, H. (1973) *The Language of Primary School Children.* London: Penguin.

Rosen, H. (1971) The problem of impersonal language, quoted in Barnes D. Language in the secondary classroom. In Barnes, D., Britton, J. and Rosen, H. *Language, the learner and the school.* (Revised ed.) Harmondsworth, London: Penguin.

Rosenshine, B. (1971) *Teaching Behaviours and Student Achievement.* Windsor: NFER.

Rosenshine, B. (1976) Classroom Instruction. In *The Psychology of Teaching Methods: 75th Yearbook of the National Society for the Study of Education*, (Ed.) Gage, W. L. pp. 335–371, Chicago: Chicago University Press.

Rosenthal, A. M. (1964) *Thirty-eight witnesses.* New York: McGraw-Hill.

Rosenthal, R. and Rosnow, R. L. (1975) *Primer of Methods for the Behavioural Sciences.* New York: Wiley.

Ross, J. M. Bunton, W. J. Evison, P. and Robertson, T. S. (1972) *A Critical Appraisal of Comprehensive Education.*: NFER.

Rotter, J. B. (1966) Generalised expectancies for internal control of reinforcement. *Psychological Monographs*, **80**, 1.

Rutter, M., Maughan, B., Mortimore, P. and Onslaw J. (1979) *Fifteen Thousand Hours.* London, Open Books.

(Eds.) Salaman G. and Thompson, K. *People and Organizations.* London: Longmans.

Saunders, M. (1979) *Class Control and Behaviour Problems.* London: McGraw Hill.

Schachter, S. (1951) Deviation, rejection and communication. *Journal of Abnormal and Social Psychology*, **46**, 190–208.

Schaffer, R. (1970) *The Extent and Context of Racial Prejudice in Great Britain.* San Francisco: Rand and Associates.

Schools Council (1969) *Scope 1: An Introductory Course for pupils 8–13 years.* English for Immigrant Children Curriculum Development Project. London: Schools Council.

Schools Council (1971) *Scope Handbook 2: Pronunciation for non-English speaking children from India, Pakistan, Cyprus and Italy.* English for Immigrant Children Development Project. London: Schools Council.

Schools Council (1972) *Scope 2 for pupils 8–13 years at 2nd stage of English.* English for Immigrant Children Curriculum Development Project. London: Longmans.

Schools Council (1973) *Scope 3 Handbook 3: Language work with infant immigrant children.* English for Immigrant Children Curriculum Development Project. London: Schools Council.

Schools Council (1972) *Concept 7–9*, Four units for multi-racial classes, Unit 1: Listening with Understanding, Unit 2: Concept Building, Unit 3: Communication, Unit 4: The Dialect Kit. Schools Council Project on Teaching to West Indian Children. London: E. J. Arnold.

Schools Council (1972) *Scope Senior Course for non-English speaking students 14 years and over.* English for Immigrant Children Development Project. London: Schools Council.

Schmitt, D. R. and Manvell, G. (1972) Withdrawal and reward reallocation as responses to inequity. *Journal of Experimental Social Psychology*, **8**, 207–221.

Schutz, W. C. (1967) *Joy.* New York: Grove Press.

Schwartz, H. and Jacobs, J. (1979) *Qualitative Sociology: A Method to the Madness.* New York: Free Press.

Scrofani, P., Swziedelis, A. and Shore, M. (1973) Conceptual ability in black and white children of different social classes. *American Journal of Orthopsychiatry*, **43**, 541–553.

Secord, R. F. and Backman, C. W. (1964) *Social Psychology.* New York: McGraw Hill.

Sharp, R. and Green, A. (1975) *Education and Social Control: A Study in Progressive Primary Education.* London: Routledge and Kegan Paul.

Sherif, M. and Sherif, C. W. (1964) *Reference Groups.* New York: Harper and Row.

Shipman, M. D. (1972) *The Limitations of Social Research.* London: Longmans.

Shipman, M. D., Bolam, D. and Jenkins, D. (1974) *Inside a Curriculum Project.* London: Methuen.

(Ed.) Shuy, R. (1972) *Sociolinguistics*. Georgetown Monograph Series on Language and Linguistics **25**.

Shyllon, F. (1974) *Black Slaves in Britain*. London: Oxford University Press.

Sigsworth, A. (1980) The rural school – in, of, or for the community? In Three perspectives of educational disadvantage. *Educational Disadvantage in Rural Areas*. Manchester: Centre For Information and Advice on Educational Disadvantage.

Sistrunk, F. and McDavid, J. W. (1973) Sex variable in conforming behaviour. *Journal of Personality and Social Psychology*, **17**, 200–283.

Smith, H. W. (1975) *Strategies of Social Research: The Methodological Imagination*. New York: Prentice-Hall.

Smith, L. M. and Geoffrey, W. (1968) *The Complexities of an Urban Classroom*. New York: Holt, Rinehart and Winston.

Smith, M. (1977) *The Underground Education: A Guide To The Alternative Press*. London: Methuen.

(Ed.) Sockett, H. (1980) *Accountability in the English Educational System*. London: Hodder and Stoughton.

Sommer, R. (1965) Further studies in small group ecology. *Sociometry*, **28**, 337–348.

Spady, W. G. (1974) The authority system of the school and student unrest: a theoretical explanation. In *National Society for the Study of Education, 1974 Year Book on Education: Uses of the Sociology of Education*. pp. 36–37. Chicago: Chicago University Press.

Speier, M. (1973) *How to observe face-to-face communication: a sociological introduction*. Pacific Palisades, California: Goodyear.

Stebbins, R. (1973) Physical context influences on behaviour: the case of classroom disorderliness. *Environment and Behaviour*, **5**, 291–314.

Stephens, L. S. (1974) *The Teacher's Guide to Open Education*. New York: Holt, Rinehart and Winston.

Steur, F. B., Applefield, J. M. and Smith, R. (1971) Televised aggression and the interpersonal aggression of preschool children. *Journal of Experimental Child Psychology*, **11**, 442–447.

Stones, E. (1979) The colour of conceptual learning. In *Race, Education and Identity* (Eds.) Verma, G. and Bagley, C. London: Macmillan.

Stott, D. H. (1979) The challenge of mixed ability. *British Journal of Teacher Education*, **5**, 2, 133–143.

Stubbs, M. (1976) Keeping in touch: some functions of teacher-talk. In *Explorations in Classroom Observation*. (Eds.) Stubbs, M. and Delamont, S. London: Wiley.

Stubbs, M. (1976) *Language, Schools and Classrooms*, London: Methuen.

(Eds.) Stubbs, M. and Delamont, S. (1976) *Explorations in Classroom Observation*. London: Wiley.

Sugarman, B. (1967) Involvement in youth culture, academic achievement and conformity in school. *British Journal of Sociology*, **18**, 151–164.

Sullivan, J. W. N. (1938) *Limitations of Science*. London: Penguin.

Swain, J. R. L. and Fairbrother, R. W. (1977) LEA advisers: their part in the adoption of the Nuffield Advanced Science courses. *Educational Studies*, **3**, 3, 235–242.

Swift, D. F. (1968) Social class and educational adaptation. In Butcher, H. J. and Pont, J. B. *Educational Research in Britain*. Vol. 1, London: University of London Press.

Tanner, L. N. (1978) *Classroom Discipline for Effective Teaching and Learning*. New York: Holt, Rinehart and Winston.

Taylor, F. (1974) *Race, School and Community: A Study of Research and Literature*. Windsor: NFER.

Taylor, G. (1971) North and South; the education split. *New Society*, **17**, 440, 346–347.

Taylor, J. and Ingleby, T. (1973) *Scope story book 5–12 years*. Schools Council: English For Immigrant Children Curriculum Development Project. London: Schools Council.

Taylor, M. T. (1976) Teachers' perceptions of their pupils. *Research in Education*, **16**, November, 25–35.

Taylor, P. H. (1962) Children's evaluations of the characteristics of the good teacher. *British Journal of Educational Psychology*, **32**, 258–266.

Taylor, W. (1964) The Training College Principal. *Sociological Review*, **12**, 2.

Thomas, J. B. (1980) *The Self in Education*. Windsor: NFER.

Thomas, W. I. (1928) *The Child in America*. New York: Knopf.

Thompson, B. L. (1975) Secondary school pupils' attitudes to school and teachers. *Educational Research*, **18**, November, 62–66.

Thompson, D. (1974) Non-streaming did make a difference. *Forum*, **16**, pp. 45–49.

Tomlinson, S. (1980) Ethnic minority parents and education. In *Linking Home and School: A New Review* (Eds.) Craft, M., Raynor, J. and Cohen, L. London: Harper and Row.

Torrance, E. P. (1955) Some consequences of power differences on decision-making in permanent and temporary three man groups. In *Small Groups: Studies in Social Interaction* (Eds.) Hare, A. P., Borgatta, E. F. and Bales, R. F. pp. 482–491, New York: Knopf.

Travers, R. M. W. (1969) *Introduction to Educational Research*. New York: Macmillan.

Tunnell, D. (1975) Open education: an expression in search of a definition. In *The Philosophy of Open Education* (Ed.) Nyberg, D. London: Routledge and Kegan Paul.

Turner, R. H. (1960) Sponsored and contest mobility and the school system. *American Sociological Review*, **25**, 856.

Twine, D. (1975) Some effects of the urbanisation process on rural children. *Educational Studies*, **1**, 3, 209–216.

(Ed.) Urmson, J. O. (1975) *The Concise Encyclopedia of Western Philosophy and Philosophers*. (2nd ed.) London: Hutchinson.

Vandenberg, D. (1975) Openness: the pedagogic atmosphere. In *The Philosophy of Open Education* (Ed.) Nyberg, D. London: Routledge and Kegan Paul.

Veldman, D. J. (1970) Pupil evaluation of student teachers and their supervisors. *Journal of Teacher Education*, **21**, 165–167.

Veldman, D. J. and Peck, R. F. (1964) The influence of teacher and pupil sex, on pupil evaluation of student teachers. *Journal of Teacher Education*, **15**, 393–396.

Veldman, D. J. and Peck, R. F. (1968) Student teacher characteristics from the pupils' viewpoint. *Journal of Educational Psychology*, **54**, 346–355.

Veldman, D. J. and Peck, R. F. (1969) Influences on pupil evaluations of student teachers. *Journal of Educational Psychology*, **60**, 103–108.

Vernon, P. E. (1961) *Selection For Secondary Schools in Jamaica*. Kingston, Jamaica: Ministry of Education.

Vinacke, W. E. and Gullickson, G. R. (1964) Age and differences in the formation of coalitions. *Child Development*, **35**, 1217–1231.

Wakeford, J. (1969) *The Cloistered Elite: A Sociological Analysis of the English Public Boarding School*. London: Macmillan.

Walker, R. (1976) *Innovation, the School and the Teacher I*. Educational Studies, A Second Level Course, Curriculum Design and Development, E203, Units 27 and 28. Milton Keynes: Open University Press.

Waller, W. (1932) *The Sociology of Teaching*. New York: Wiley.

Walvin, J. (1971) *The Black Presence*. London: Orbach and Chambers.

Walvin, J. (1973) *Black and White: The Negro and English Society 1555–1945*. London: Allen Lane.

Warnock, M. (1970) *Existentialism*. London: Oxford University Press.

Warwick, D. (1974) *Bureaucracy*. London: Longman.

Warwick, D. (1971) *Team Teaching*. London: University of London Press.

Watts, J. (1976) Sharing it out: the role of the head in participatory government. In *The Role of The Head*. (Ed.) Peters, R. S. London: Routledge and Kegan Paul.

Weber, M. (1952) *Essays in Sociology*. Translated and edited by C. W. Mills. London: Routledge and Kegan Paul.

Weiner, N. (1968) *The Human Use of Human Beings*. London: Sphere.

Westbury, I (1978) Research into classroom processes: a review of ten year's work. *Journal of Curriculum Studies*, **10**, 4, 283–308.

(Eds.) White, G. and Mufti, R. (1979) *Understanding Socialisation*. Driffield: Nafferton.

Wilkinson, A. (1975) *Language and Education*. London: Oxford University Press.

Willis, P. (1976) The class significance of school counter-culture. In *The Process of Schooling: A Sociological Reader* (Eds.) Hammersley, M. et al London: Routledge and Kegan Paul/Open University Press.

Willis, P. (1977) *Learning to Labour*. London: Saxon House.

Winston, B. (1973) *Dangling Conversations Book 1. The Image of The Media*. London: Davis–Poynter.

Withal, R. (1956) An objective measurement of a teacher's classroom interaction. *Journal of Educational Psychology*, **47**, 203–212.

Wolcott, H. F. (1973) *The Man in the Principal's Office*. New York: Holt, Rinehart and Winston.

Woods, P. (1977) Parents' influence on pupil experience. In Woods, P. *The Pupils' experience*, Educational Studies, a Second Level Course, E202, Schooling and Society, Unit 11. Milton Keynes: Open University Press.

Woods, P. (1977) *The Pupils' Experience*. Educational Studies, a Second Level Course, E202, Schooling and Society, Unit 11. Milton Keynes: Open University Press.

(Eds.) Woods, P. and Hammersley, M. (1977) *School Experience*. London: Croom Helm.

Woods, P. (1978) Negotiating the demands of schoolwork. *Curriculum Studies*, **10**, 4, 309–327.

Woods, P. (1978) Relating to schoolwork: some pupil perceptions. *Educational Review*, **30**, 2, 167–175.

Woods, P. (1979) *The Divided School*. London: Routledge and Kegan Paul.

(Ed.) Woods, P. (1980) *Pupil Strategies: Explorations in the Sociology of the School*. London: Croom Helm.

(Ed.) Woods, P. (1980) *Teacher Strategies*. London: Croom Helm.

Wragg, E. C. (1978) A suitable case for imitation. *The Times Educational Supplement*, 15th September.

Wragg, E. C. (1978) Training teachers for mixed ability classes: a ten point attack. *Forum*, **20**, 2, 39–42.

Wright, D. S. (1962) A comparative study of the adolescent's concepts of his parents and teachers. *Educational Review*, **14**, 3, 226–232.

(Eds.) Wrightman, L. S. and Bingham, J. C. (1973) *Contemporary Issues in Social Psychology*. (2nd ed.) 173–181.

Wyatt, H. (1976) Mixed ability teaching in practice. *Forum*, **18**, 2, 45–59.

(Eds.) Young, M. D. F. (1971) *Knowledge and Control: New Directions for the Sociology of Education*. London: Collier Macmillan.

Young, M. D. F. (1977) School science: innovations or alienation? In *School Experience*. (Eds.) Woods, P. and Hammersley, M. London: Croom Helm.

Youngman, M. B. (1979) *Some determinants of early secondary school performance*. BERA Conference Paper. September.

Youngman, M. B. and Lunzer, E. A. (1977) *Adjustment to Secondary Schooling*. University of Nottingham: School of Education.

Yule, W. (1975) Children of West Indian immigrants II: intellectual performance and reading attainments. *Journal of Child Psychology and Psychiatry*, **16**, 1–17.

Zanjonc, R. B., Wolosin, R. J., Wolosin, M. A. and Loh, W. D. (1971) Social facilitation and imitation in group risk-taking. *Journal of Personality and Social Psychology*, **20**, 361–378.

Zimmerman, D. (1972) The practicalities of rule use. In *People and Organisations* (Eds.) Salaman, G. and Thompson, K. London: Longmans.

Index

Permissions

The author and publisher would like to thank the following for permission to use copyright material.

Academic Press
Box 12.7 'Aggression as a consequence of viewing violent and neutral television programmes' from F. B. Steur, J. M. Applefield, and R. Smith (1971) Televised aggression and the interpersonal aggression of pre-school children. In *Journal of Experimental Child Psychology*, 11, 442–447.

Addison-Wesley
Box 6.7 'The use of space', Box 6.8 'The horseshoe arrangement' and Box 6.9 'The modular arrangement' from H. T. Hurt, M. D. Scott and J. C. McCroskey (1978) *Communication in the Classroom*.

George Allen and Unwin
Box 6.5 'Distribution of individual categories' from J. W. Richards (1978) *Classroom Language: What Sort?*

American Psychological Association
Box 6.12 'Behaviours rated as warm and cold' from G. L. Clore, N. H. Wiggins and S. Itkin (1975) Gain and loss in attraction. In *Journal of Personality and Social Psychology*, 31, 706–712.
Box 12.8 'The correlations between a preference for violent television and aggression' from L. D. Eron, L. R. Huesman, M. M. Lekowitz, and L. D. Walder (1972) Does television violence cause aggression? In *American Psychologist*, April, pp.253–263.

American Sociological Association
Box 6.10 'Seating preferences in four situations' from R. Sommer (1965) Further studies in small group ecology. In *Sociometry*, 28, 337–348.

E. J. Arnold and Sons
Box 8.9 'Concept building' and Box 8.10 'SCOPE Senior Course' from Schools Council Curriculum Development Projects.

Athlone Press
Box 1.2 'Alternative bases for interpreting social reality' and Box 11.7 'Changes in recent educational practice', from *Administering Education: The International Challenge*. (Ed.) M. Hughes (1975).

Carfax
Box 12.5 'Factors used to determine the extent of urbanization in a given area' and Box 12.6 'Relationships between the urbanization process and levels of attitude' from D. Twine (1975) Some effects of urbanization. In *Educational Studies*, 1, 3, 209–216.

Croom Helm
Extract and Box 2.3 'Types of developmental research' from L. Cohen and L. Manion (1980) *Research Methods in Education.*
Box 2.6 'Extracts from accounts' from P. Woods and M. Hammersley (1977) *School Experience.*
Extracts from *Curriculum Design.* (Eds) M. Golby, J. Greenwald and R. West (1975).

Grove Press (New York)
Extract from W. C. Schutz (1967) *Joy.*

Harper and Row
Box 8.8 'West Indian, Asian, and "British" parents and the school', from S. Tomlinson, Ethnic minority parents in education. In *Linking Home and School: A New Review.* (Eds) M. Craft, J. Raynor and L. Cohen (1980).
Box 10.10 'Strong positive friendship choices among eight-year-old children: target sociogram' from L. Cohen (1977) *Educational Research in Classrooms and Schools: A Manual of Materials and Methods.*

Headmasters' Association
Box 11.8 'Planning the curriculum' from A. W. Bates (1972) The planning of the curriculum. In *Headmasters' Association Review,* **70**, No. 215, July.

Heinemann Educational Books
Extracts from A. D. Edwards and V. J. Furlong (1978) *The Language of Teaching.*
Extracts from G. Burrell and G. Morgan (1979) *Sociological Paradigms and Organizational Analysis.*

Robert R. Knapp (California)
Extracts from S. Isaac and W. B. Michael (1971) *Handbook of Research and Evaluation.*

Kogan Page
Extract from *Aspects of Simulation and Gaming.* (Ed.) J. Megarry (1977).

MacGibbon and Kee
Box 12.10 'The process of deviation amplification' from S. Cohen (1972) *Folk Devils and Moral Panics.*

Manchester University Press
Box 4.5 'Rank order of the most frequently produced individual constructs' and Box 4.6 'Frequency and percentage of constructs' from M. T. Taylor (1976) Teachers' perceptions of their pupils. In *Research in Education,* **16**, 25–35.
Box 11.9 'Percentage of headteachers and teachers whose preference is congruent with perceived practice' from A. Hobbs, S. M. Kleinberg and P. J. Martin (1979) Decision-making in primary schools. In *Research in Education,* **21**, 79–92.

McGraw Hill, (New York)
Box 6.15 'Characteristics of vocal expression contained in the test of emotional stability' from J. R. Davitz (1964) *The Communication of Emotional Feeling.*

Methuen
Box 3.2 'The process of achievement' from O. Banks and D. S. Finlayson (1973) *Success and Failure in the Secondary School.*
Box 7.5 'Social structures, interaction, and learning situations' from L. Cohen and L. Manion (1977) *A Guide To Teaching Practice.*
Boxes 8.1, 8.2 and 8.3 'West Indians, Indians, Pakistanis in Britain' from D. Hill (1976) *Teaching in the Multiracial School.*
Extracts from M. Stubbs (1976) *Language, Schools and Classrooms.*
Extracts from M. Argyle (1975) *Bodily Communication.*

National Foundation For Education Research
Box 7.2 'Nature of pupil generated interactions' and Box 7.3 'Friendship choices in one mixed ability classroom' from L. Clunies-Ross and M. J. Reid (1980) *Mixed Ability Teaching: An Exploration of Teachers' Aims, Objectives and Classroom Strategies.*

Extracts from V. J. Furlong and A. D. Edwards (1977) Language in classroom interaction: theory and data. In *Educational Research*, **19**, 2, 122–128.

New Society
Box 8.7 'Rank order of overall achievement' from G. Driver (1980) How West Indians do better at school (especially girls). In *New Society*, 27 January 1980.

Open Books
Box 2.2 'A structured observation schedule for the classroom', Box 3.9 'Overall research strategy' and Box 3.10 'Average exam score by school and by ability band' from M. Rutter, B. Maughan, P. Mortimore and J. Onslow (1979) *Fifteen Thousand Hours*.
Box 9.1 'Characteristics of traditional and open education' from N. Bennett (1976) *Teaching Styles and Pupil Progress*.

Open University Press
Box 4.1 'The social location of teacher perspectives' from *Schooling and Society*. E202 Units 12 and 13.
Extracts from *Schooling and Society*. E202 Units 9 and 10.
Extracts from *The Pupil's Experience*. E202 Unit 11.
Extracts from *Educational Studies: A Second Level Course*. E203 Units 27 and 28.
Box 9.6 'Sharp and Green's argument in summary form' from *Teacher Perspectives*. E202 Units 9 and 10.
Box 11.12 'Three parts of counselling sessions' and Box 11.13 'Counselling within a wider social framework' from *Educational Studies: A Second Level Course: Personality, Growth and Learning*. Unit 17.
Box 12.1 'The organization of a Local Education Authority Department' from *Educational Studies: The Politics of Educational Policy Making*. E222 Unit 6.

Oxford University Press
Box 6.16 'Examples of nonverbal communication in a secondary school' from A. Wilkinson (1975) *Language and Education*.

Penguin Books
Extracts from D. Barnes, J. Britton and H. Rosen (1971) *Language, the Learner and the School*.

Mrs. W. Robertson, Sunderland Polytechnic
Box 11.16 'Ten-year-old pupils' perceptions of hierarchy of power'.

Routledge and Kegan Paul
Extracts, Box 4.9 'A typical report' and Box 4.10 'Report categories' from P. Woods (1979) *The Divided School*.
Box 4.4 'The three most frequently used constructs with the ranking allotted them by eight primary school teachers', from R. Nash (1973) *Classrooms Observed*.

Saxon House
Box 8.5 'Influences on racial attitudes' from C. Bagley, G. K. Verma, K. Mallick, and L. Young (1979) *Personality, Self-Esteem and Prejudice*.

Tavistock Publications
Six teaching strategy diagrams from O. A. Oeser (1960) *Teacher, Pupil and Task*.

Dr. Taylor
Box 11.5 'The headteacher's role' from W. Taylor (1964) The role of the training college principal. In *Sociological Review*, **12**, 2.

Taylor and Francis
Box 3.7 'A model of classroom learning' from A. Harnischfeger and D. E. Wiley (1978) Conceptual issues in models of school learning. In *Journal of Curriculum Studies*, **10**, 3.

Times Newspapers Ltd
Extract from E. C. Wragg (1978). A suitable case for imitation. In *The Times Educational Supplement*, 15 September 1978.

University of Chicago Press
Box 9.5 'Four dimensions of openness in classroom activities' from R. Linder and D. Purdom (1975) Four dimensions of openness in classroom activities. In *Elementary School Journal*, **16**, 3, 147–150.
Box 10.9 'Age and conformity' from P. R. Costanzo and M. E. Shaw (1966) Conformity as a function of age level. In *Child Development*, **37**, 967–975.

University of Liverpool
Extracts from R. Meighan (1977) Pupils' perceptions of the classroom techniques of postgraduate student teachers. In *British Journal of Teacher Education*, **3**, 2, 139–148.

University of Pennsylvania Press
Box 6.13 'A code for the face' from R. L. Birdwhistell (1970) *Kinesics and Context.*

Ward Lock Educational
Box 9.4 'An open classroom' from K. Rintoul and K. Thorne (1975) *Open Plan Organization in the Primary School.*
Box 11.4 'A management structure for a small secondary school' from *Management and Headship in the Secondary School.* (Ed.) A. Jennings (1977).

John Wiley and Sons
Extracts from L. A. Pervin (1970) *Personality: Theory, Assessment and Research.*
Box 4.8 'Teacher typifications of individual children' from R. King (1978) *All Things Bright and Beautiful?*
Box 5.6 'Pupils' evaluation scheme for teachers' from *Explorations in Classroom Observation.* (Eds) M. Stubbs and S. Delamont (1976).
Box 11.6 'A role episode' from R. L. Kahn, D. M. Wolfe, R. P. Quinn, J. D. Snoek and R. A. Rosenthal (1964) *Organizational Stress: Studies in Role Conflict and Ambiguity.*